# MAPPING
# HACKS™

# Other resources from O'Reilly

**Related titles**

| | |
|---|---|
| Google Hacks | Mac OS X Hacks |
| eBay Hacks | Windows XP Hacks |
| TiVo Hacks | Linux Server Hacks |
| Wireless Hacks | |

**Hacks Series Home**

*hacks.oreilly.com* is a community site for developers and power users of all stripes. Readers learn from each other as they share their favorite tips and tools for Mac OS X, Linux, Google, Windows XP, and more.

**oreilly.com**

*oreilly.com* is more than a complete catalog of O'Reilly books. You'll also find links to news, events, articles, weblogs, sample chapters, and code examples.

*oreillynet.com* is the essential portal for developers interested in open and emerging technologies, including new platforms, programming languages, and operating systems.

**Conferences**

O'Reilly brings diverse innovators together to nurture the ideas that spark revolutionary industries. We specialize in documenting the latest tools and systems, translating the innovator's knowledge into useful skills for those in the trenches. Visit *conferences.oreilly.com* for our upcoming events.

Safari Bookshelf (*safari.oreilly.com*) is the premier online reference library for programmers and IT professionals. Conduct searches across more than 1,000 books. Subscribers can zero in on answers to time-critical questions in a matter of seconds. Read the books on your Bookshelf from cover to cover or simply flip to the page you need. Try it today with a free trial.

# MAPPING
# HACKS™

*Tips & Tools for Electronic Cartography*

*Schuyler Erle, Rich Gibson, and Jo Walsh*

**O'REILLY®**

Beijing · Cambridge · Farnham · Köln · Paris · Sebastopol · Taipei · Tokyo

# Mapping Hacks™

by Schuyler Erle, Rich Gibson, and Jo Walsh

Copyright © 2005 O'Reilly Media, Inc. All rights reserved.
Printed in China.

Published by O'Reilly Media, Inc., 1005 Gravenstein Highway North,
Sebastopol, CA 95472.

O'Reilly books may be purchased for educational, business, or sales promotional use. Online editions are also available for most titles (*safari.oreilly.com*). For more information, contact our corporate/institutional sales department: (800) 998-9938 or *corporate@oreilly.com*.

| | | | |
|---|---|---|---|
| **Editor:** | Simon St.Laurent | **Production Editor:** | Sanders Kleinfeld |
| **Series Editor:** | Rael Dornfest | **Cover Designer:** | Hanna Dyer |
| **Executive Editor:** | Dale Dougherty | **Interior Designer:** | David Futato |

**Printing History:**

| | |
|---|---|
| June 2005: | First Edition. |

 This book uses RepKover™, a durable and flexible lay-flat binding.

ISBN: 0-596-00703-5
[LP]

# Contents

# Foreword

When I first heard that Jo, Rich, and Schuyler were developing an O'Reilly *Mapping Hacks* book, I was thrilled at the extra visibility this could bring to my favorite area of computing. But it wasn't until I started reviewing many of the hacks in this book that I realized just how appropriate mapping was to the Hacks series.

To me, a software hack is something that can be done fairly quickly (in no more than an intense evening), is often a surprising or nontraditional use of technology, and gives a "Wow!" feeling when it works. With the support of many contributors, the authors have done a great job of providing hacks in many different areas of mapping.

I have been working in the geospatial world since 1992. I left a traditional geospatial software vendor in late 1998 to start writing open source software in the same field. My main rationale was that the coolness of mapping should be accessible to a much broader user base than was the case at the time. I felt that releasing the libraries and applications that I wrote as open source would contribute to making that happen. In fact over the last six years, I have seen growth of a strong community of users, developers, and software.

This book demonstrates that my work, and the work of the many people I have collaborated with and admired over the years, has given us a wealth of capabilities. In fact, this book has opened my eyes to the breadth of possibilities now available.

Another aspect of this book that impresses me is the number of hacks that can be implemented by a relatively nontechnical audience. My mother still occasionally shows a vague interest in knowing what I do, but her eyes generally glaze over when I try to describe it. I look forward to buying her a copy of this book and having her apply a few hacks herself. I think this will give her a new appreciation for what I do.

When I started in this industry, my boss regularly explained to me that our pay as programmers might not be high compared to some folks working for banks or insurance companies. But that was because what we did was so much fun, and everyone wanted to do it! While his reasons for providing this explanation, just before salary review time, might have been somewhat disingenuous, his basic point was true. Mapping is fun! I often find myself poring over the fascinating details of a map. When I first implemented "fast roam and zoom" using OpenGL, the president of the company often wandered past and found me sitting in front of my computer just roaming and zooming around huge satellite images like a crazed pilot exploring new terrain.

As we become caught up in the nitty-gritty of the daily use of our technology, we can lose sight of this fun aspect. I think the finest feature of this book is that it really brings back the fun and coolness of mapping!

Enjoy!

*—Frank Warmerdam*
OGR and GDAL developer

# Credits

## About the Authors

Schuyler Erle was born near 39.9° N 75.2° W and later on earned a degree studying linguistics nearby at Temple University. Sometime afterward, he moved west in search of dot-com fame and fortune, but instead ended up near 38.4° N 123° W, writing software for several different departments within O'Reilly & Associates. During his stint at O'Reilly, Schuyler got into wireless networking and, in his spare time, co-wrote the NoCat Authentication System, one of the earliest and still one of the most widely used open source captive portal packages. Not long after, Schuyler's interest in automating the analysis of possible long-distance 802.11 links led to collaboration with Rich Gibson on the NoCat Maps project. Literally moments before giving a talk on this very subject at O'Reilly's Emerging Technology conference in 2003, the two of them met Jo Walsh, who was on hand to give a talk on gonzo collaborative mapping. This meeting proved to be a fateful one, for, a year later, Schuyler and Jo were married near 37.7° N 122.4° W, and the three of them began work on the book you now hold in your hands. Today, Schuyler and Jo spend most of their time around 51.1° N 0.1° W, but tomorrow they may well be found somewhere else entirely. Together with Rich, they have founded Locative Technologies, a California-based consultancy offering design, development, and training in open source GIS and mapping applications.

Rich Gibson believes in the power of personal stories and has unlimited curiosity in the world. He indulges his brilliant, semi-manic children in super-long storytimes, weird science projects, and adventures of many varieties. It is only the steady support of his loving wife that permits him to organize his eccentricity into occasional coherent bursts of creative productivity. Life is very, very good.

Jo Walsh is a freelance hacker and software artist who started out building web systems for the Guardian, the ICA, and state51 in London. Jo is trying to combine her interests in maps, spatial annotation on the semantic web, Wi-Fi geolocation, public transport planning, and bots into something resembling coherence.

## Contributors

- Drew Celley (*http://www.zhrodague.net/~drew*) writes hacks, articles, and software in the South Side of Pittsburgh, PA. He produces videos for *tv.seattlewireless.net*, records music with *bandnight.com*, and develops interesting Internet technologies. Drew is the co creator of *WiFi-Maps.com*, a popular web-based geographic map of Wi-Fi usage. He generally works as a Unix sysadmin and netnanny for startups, dot-coms, established companies, and mega-corporations, while maintaining his sanity and creative drive. In his spare time, he can be found searching for his next contract.

- Dav Coleman is a world-traveling hacker-poet based in San Francisco. He has worked for large corporations (IBM, Verizon Wireless), co-founded a successful software company (Synthematix), and currently does independent consulting. Dav can be found at *AkuAku.org*.

- Rael Dornfest is Chief Technology Officer at O'Reilly Media. He assesses, experiments, programs, fiddles, fidgets, and writes for the O'Reilly Network and various O'Reilly publications. Rael is Series Editor of the O'Reilly Hacks series (*http://hacks.oreilly.com*) and has edited, contributed to, and coauthored various O'Reilly books, including *Mac OS X Panther Hacks*, *Mac OS X Hacks*, the *Google Pocket Guide*, *Google: The Missing Manual*, *Essential Blogging*, and *Peer to Peer: Harnessing the Power of Disruptive Technologies*. He is also Program Chair for the O'Reilly Emerging Technology Conference (*http://conferences. oreilly.com/etech*). In his copious free time, Rael develops bits and bobs of freeware, particularly the Blosxom weblog application (*http://www. blosxom.com*), is Editor in Chief of MobileWhack (*http://www.mobile-whack.com*), and (more often than not) maintains his Raelity Bytes weblog (*http://www.raelity.org*).

- Michael Frumin began his career in original and creative technology-based research while working on advanced networking protocols as an undergraduate at Stanford University. After school, he was a founding member of a team of hackers using their quantitative skills to find proprietary, novel real-time sources of qualitative information for hedge-fund managers. Eager to develop projects in the public domain and for the arts community, Michael accepted the prototype Research Fellowship at Eyebeam where he has been the primary developer of Fundrace. org, the reBlog, ForwardTrack/TomsPetition, Pizza Party, and other works, some still in development. He currently lives in Brooklyn, New York, very close to where he grew up.

- Chris Goad is a computer scientist by training (PhD Stanford, 1980). He worked as a research associate at Stanford from 1980 to 1983 and co-founded two companies: Silma in 1983 and Map Bureau in 1993. His areas of work have included applications of mathematical logic to computation, computer vision, simulation software for 3-D mechanical systems, programming language design, and the semantic web. During the last four years, he has concentrated on applications of semantic web technology to cartography and on the design and implementation of Fabl, a programming language that represents programs as semantic web objects. Chris lives in Astoria, Oregon and works at Map Bureau. See *http://fabl.net/chrisgoad*.

- Thomas Hargrove started the TIGER Map Server (*http://toonarchive. com/tiger_map_server/*), which is a cross-platform server that draws vector-based road maps.

- Chris Heathcote is an interaction designer, with a focus on mobile and wireless experiences. He lives in Helsinki, Finland, and works in Nokia's Insight & Foresight team. He writes about buildings and food at *http://anti-mega.com*, and can be emailed at *c@deaddodo.com*.

- Adam Hill is a humble Amish programmer living in Plano, Texas, where he mostly writes applications for the oil and gas industry, with a few excursions into litigation support for law firms. He has consulted for companies like ARCO Oil and Gas and the law firm of Holland and Hart. Together with some friends, Hill has recently founded a company providing .NET consulting and programming services in the DFW metroplex (*http://www.thregecy.com*). Hill initially became involved with the geographic community through his participation in the NASA World Wind group. He hopes that open source geographic information and apps will enable people to do interesting things and teach them how big the world really is. In his spare time, Hill enjoys cooking exotic meals and exploring the intersection of math and art. He also loves taking care of his beagle and is occasionally heard to play a mean trumpet. You can read about his further adventures at *http://randompixels. typepad.com*, or hang out with him on IRC at *irc.freenode.net/#world-wind*.

- Chris Holmes is lead developer of The GeoServer Project, the open source reference implementation of the Open GIS Consortium's Web Feature Service Specification. He works for The Open Planning Project

(TOPP), a non-profit organization based in New York. TOPP is dedicated to enhancing the ability of all citizens to engage in meaningful dialogue about their environment and funds work on GeoServer to help create a free, distributed, and open geographic information infrastructure. GeoServer is offered to all for free to lower the barriers to make geographic data available, as well as to provide an interoperable basis upon which other locative solutions can be built. Chris is also on the Project Management Committee of GeoTools, the leading Open Source Java GIS toolkit. His interests also include the potential for open source solutions to help implement Spatial Data Infrastructures (SDI) in developing countries. In 2005 he is heading to Zambia on a Fulbright Scholarship to examine in particular the ability of open source to develop capacity by giving users a larger sense of ownership in the software they use, while helping build an SDI using open source GIS software. He graduated from Stanford University with a history major and a computer science minor. And he is into the pudding.

- Anselm Hook is an ex-video-game developer, avid backpacker and mountain climber who seems to always be either arriving or leaving somewhere. Mostly he wants to always have interesting things to see and do when he arrives at the places he arrives at—if you, dear reader, could facilitate that, it would be great thanks! Otherwise he enjoys his family, hanging out with friends, hacking and looking for great new places to explore. His home page is at *http://hook.org*.

- Mike Liebhold is a Senior Researcher for the Institute for the Future (*http://www.iftf.org*), focusing on geospatial infrastructures for proactive, context-aware, and ubiquitous computing, as well as the social implications of a geospatial web for IFTF clients from top-tier companies and public agencies. Most recently, Mike was a producer and program leader at New Geography Conference for the IFTF at the Presidio of San Francisco—a two-day workshop for technologists and strategic planners from top-tier companies and the public to better understand the emerging geospatial information infrastructure. The event included The Fort Scott Locative Experience, a hands-on field exercise for conference attendees exploring a prototype geospatial web combining digital geodata and modern web hypermedia. Previously, Mike was a Visiting Researcher at Intel Labs, working on a pattern language based on semantic web frameworks for ubiquitious computing. He is the co-author of *Proactive Computing through Patterns of Activity and Place* (publication pending). In the 1980s at Apple, Advanced Technology Labs, Mike led the Terraform project, an investigation of cartographic and location-based multimedia. He also led the launch of strategic partnerships with National Geographic, Lucasfilm, Disney, MIT, Bell Labs and others, and then worked as CTO for Times Mirror publishing with TM's aeronautical mapping division, Jeppesen-Sanderson, (now a division of Boeing) and on a "4D" globe project with TM's "Rocket Science" game company. He also worked for two years as a senior consulting architect at Netscape. Most recently Mike has been helping to design and stage collaborative mapping workshops with the Locative Media Lab, a loosely affiliated network of geospatial hackers and artists. Mike publishes his occasional thoughts about microlocal and geospatial computing on his weblog at *http://www.starhill.us/* and can be reached at *mnl@starhill.us*.

- Tom Longson is a programmer who gained an interest in cartography after visiting the Burning Man festival and learning about techno-madics. He has been blogging about cyborgs, robots, GIS, and other futurism since 2002 (*http://igargoyle.com/*). In addition, he co-founded the open source collaborative mapping project called p2pmap (*http://p2pmap.org/*), which uses a pure RDF database and offers blogging-like tools to allow people to share their experiences around the world.

- Mikel Maron is an independent software developer and ecologist. He has built several geographic-oriented projects around the worldKit mapping package, including World as a Blog. Previously, he led development of My Yahoo! in the pre-RSS days. Mikel was awarded a Masters degree from the University of Sussex for building a simulation of the evolution of complexity in food webs. Originally from California, Mikel is presently based mostly in Brighton, UK, with his wife Anna. Links to various things can be found at *http://brainoff.com/*.

- Edward Mac Gillavry is an Internet GIS developer and works for the Dutch National Atlas of Public Health. On his personal web site *webmapper.net*, he writes about the latest trends in location-based services, web cartography, and geo-blogging. He previously worked for an online mapping company in the UK, developing route-planning applications. Edward studied Geoinformatics at the International Institute for Geo-Information Science and Earth Observation (ITC) and received an MA in Geography from Utrecht University in the Netherlands in 2000. He enjoys Indonesian cooking and hopes one day to obtain a black belt in shotokan karate.

- Douwe Osinga was born in Haarlem, The Netherlands. He studied computer science and philosophy in Amsterdam. During the dot-com boom, he founded a number of companies that mostly failed. He now works for Google's European R&D Center in Zurich, Switzerland. You can find more of his hacks, software experiments, and general thoughts at *http://douweosinga.com*.

- Gary Sherman lives and works in Alaska. He has spent much of the last 15 years working with Geographic Information Systems and developing custom applications. His current spare-time activity is Quantum GIS at *http://qgis.org*.

- Raj Singh graduated from Brown University in 1991 with a Bachelor's degree in economics and a minor in computer science. He went to work in environmental consulting, and quickly gravitated towards the GIS side of the business, ending up back in school to learn the technology more formally. He entered the Department of Urban Studies and Planning for a Master's degree and left ten years later with that and a PhD in urban information systems. Don't feel too horrified, though. The actual time he spent in school was much shorter than that, as he also spent almost five years starting a company that developed Internet-based GIS systems. He is currently an information systems architect at a leading engineering firm and a part-time research scientist at MIT.

- Simon St.Laurent (*http://simonstl.com/*) is an editor with O'Reilly Media, Inc. Prior to that, he'd been a web developer, network administrator, computer book author, and XML troublemaker. He lives in Dryden, NY, where he keeps track of what happens at *http://livingindryden.org/*. His books include *XML: A Primer*, *XML Elements of Style*, *Programming Web Services with XML-RPC*, and *Office 2003 XML*.

## Acknowledgments

We would like to thank everyone at O'Reilly Media for making this book possible, and, in particular our editor, Simon St.Laurent, for his efforts and for his enduring patience throughout its composition.

We would also like to thank the following contributors: Frank Warmerdam, Anselm Hook, Chris Heathcote, Tom Longson, Douwe Osinga, Dav Coleman, Ophir Tanz, Adam Hill, Edward MacGillavry, Michael Frumin, Drew from Zhrodague, Mikel Maron, Chris Goad, Simon St.Laurent, Rael Dornfest, Raj Singh, Gary Sherman, Chris Holmes, Thomas Hargrove, and Mike Liebhold.

Thanks to the following Cool People Who Did Something Useful for the Book (or meant to but never really did): Jason Harlan, Drew Woods, Jerritt Collord, Tyler Mitchell, Rob Flickenger, Roger Weeks, Jeff Maggard, Karlis Kalnins, Sonny Parafina, Dan Brickley, Libby Miller, Joshua Schachter, Rolan Yang, Yury Gitman, Earle Martin, Kake Pugh, Ivor Williams, Ben Russell, Saul Albert, Marc Powell, and Wilfried Hou Je Bek.

The following supporters deserve special mention: Rasa Smite and everyone at RIXC in Riga, Latvia; Kristine Briede from K@2 in Liepajas Karosta, Latvia; Laurence Rasel and Nicholas Malevé from Constant VZW in Brussels, Belgium; Marko Peljhan; Marina Gorbis, Stephanie Schacter, and the staff of the Institute for the Future in Palo Alto, California; and Geetha Narayanan and the faculty and staff of the Srishti School of Art, Design, and Technology in Bangalore, India.

Finally, special thanks to Frank Warmerdam, Robert Lipe, and Markus Neteler, among countless others, for their indefatigable contributions to open source GIS.

# Preface

*This ... Geoscope would make it possible for*
*humans to identify the true scale of themselves*
*and their activities on this planet. Humans*
*could thus comprehend much more readily that*
*their personal survival problems related*
*intimately to all humanity's survival.*
—R. Buckminster Fuller, *Critical Path*

Humans are born storytellers. It's part of our chattering simian heritage—as if we taught ourselves language just to be able to spin yarns late at night, around the recently invented campfire. Now, every story, as any school child knows, can be told by answering the five great W questions: *Who? What? Why? When?* and, of course, *Where?* It is this final query that we wish to address in this book.

Indeed, nearly every human story, in one way or another, takes place somewhere! These tales rely on our knowledge of geography, which defines our perceptions of "place" in scientific terms. Geography interests itself in the measurement of locations—their relative positions, dimensions, geometrical relations, and the enumeration of their names and their physical contents. The representation of the story itself is the goal of *cartography*. To tell stories about places, or relay the spatial component of any narrative, we must bring together the science of geography and the art of cartography. Learning to do so in a compelling fashion can be a challenge! The results we cobble together in the process often qualify, in the parlance of our times, as *hacks*.

## Why Mapping Hacks?

The term *hacking* has a bad reputation in the press. They use it to refer to those who break into systems or wreaks havoc with computers as their weapon. Among people who write code, though, the term *hack* refers to a "quick-and-dirty" solution to a problem, or a clever way to get something done. And the term *hacker* is taken very much as a compliment, referring to someone as being *creative*, having the technical chops to get things done. The Hacks series is an attempt to reclaim the word, document the good ways people are hacking, and pass the hacker ethic of creative participation on to the uninitiated. Seeing how others approach systems and problems is often the quickest way to learn about a new technology.

## Maps Tell Stories

Maps are a unique combination of the extremely simple and the extremely complex. Most people are comfortable reading paper maps and perhaps at least drawing sketches of travel directions for friends. Computerized maps are, on the other hand, still a relative novelty, if only because until recently, few people had access to the computing power or storage space needed to do basic cartography or geographic analysis. Historically, this was due to the amount of data and processing typically involved in telling detailed stories about the world. In turn, the complexities of cartography have made it the preserve of a talented and select few. Recently, however, technology has conspired in several ways—portable electronic devices, the Internet, the growing culture of free software—to make it possible to obtain useful, free geographic data instantly and do various interesting things with it on our newly available computing horsepower.

## Location: It's Everywhere

Imagine a world in which we can move about physical places, accessing not only what is stored in our brains but also multiple layers of information that have previously been inaccessible: experiences of friends, colleagues, and complete strangers in the same space; information about who lives and works in the place, their demographic characteristics, and perhaps their political affiliations; crime statistics for the area; the history of community events, from celebrations to calamities; information about businesses in the area and their products; changes that have reshaped the natural environment over time; and much more. This is precisely the physical landscape we will likely inhabit in 10 years.

Wireless location-aware devices, new geospatial software, global location services, and online geodata repositories are all eroding the limitations to human perception, making accessible a rich spectrum of digital information in real time and in real place. The physical landscape we move in will become "deep" with vast amounts of digital information—in text, images, and other sensory forms.

Invisible layers of information that are arguably already implicitly available in the people and objects in a landscape will become visible and explicit. The relationship of physical and virtual objects will become obvious as well. We'll be able to use a variety of devices to tap into geocoded text, images, media, and maps. Tags will link nearby objects to a universe of commentary on their history, value, safety, and meaning. Suddenly, any point in space will be able to be annotated, and those annotations aggregated. Locative annotations might include:

- Environmental or actuarial details
- Historical and cultural information
- Community events and activities
- Micro-local commercial and public service information
- Personal/social stories and preferences
- Qualitative/quantitative psychogeography
- Games and amusements, e.g., geocaching
- Locative spam (!)

Right now, our interfaces to this world are clunky at best, based on heads-down interfaces in which a hiker might miss the beauty and glory of the great outdoors by being over-interested in his interface device. As these interfaces become refined, we will gain a new kind of control over what we see and hear in our environment, selectively filtering and displaying the layers of information linked to the physical environment. We'll click floating graphic objects off and on like "digital Post-It notes." Each individual's physical reality will become increasingly personalized.

The landscape itself will interact with the people who populate it within this emerging geospatial web. Tiny sensors and actuators, gradually embedded in our environment over time, will necessarily operate with some amount of spatial intelligence. The resulting systems will be increasingly aware, able to make complex interactive decisions without human intervention. Not only will they programmatically respond to environmental changes, they will also anticipate our human context and tasks—our focus—to create a safely usable, two-way flow of precisely relevant information.

## Never Be Lost Again (Even if You'd Rather Be)

Much of our newfound ability to tell stories with maps and computers in this context is motivated by the immediate and ongoing knowledge of our exact location with various emerging location-finding technologies. First among these is the satellite-based Global Positioning System, for which one can now find consumer-grade receivers in electronics stores and even outdoor supply shops for less than $100. Originally a military technology—as the Internet itself was—GPS can be used to passively fix a terrestrial location to typically five meters or less, and sometimes to within centimeters. GPS tracklogs and waypoints can make a rich record from which to tell our narratives.

While other devices such as cell phones and PDAs are now also incorporating GPS receivers, satellite reception indoors, or in dense urban or even outdoor settings, can be weak at best. Some commercial wireless networks are carriers that track the locations of users' mobile telephones and digital devices by calculating signal strength and direction from various cell towers. These techniques triangulate location based on calculations from several radio towers.

The United States law called E911 (for emergency 911 services) requires that carrier networks routinely track the location of mobile phones in order to provide emergency services. Since tracking is mandatory, E911 is fundamentally intrusive. Network operators and public agencies always know a user's location. E911 also enables some carriers to offer phone location information, as a paid service to end-user applications.

So far, most carriers are not providing this information to subscribers themselves. Those that do are providing location coordinates, for premium prices, to enable enterprise services such as tracking fleet vehicles, delivery trucks, and freight movement. Vendors of high-end phones are beginning to offer APIs to developers to build new location-aware applications, and some carriers are beginning to offer location-based services to consumers built on these capabilities.

At the University of California San Diego, at Carnegie Mellon, and at dozens of other universities with thousands of Wi-Fi base stations and known locations, engineers have created client-side software to calculate user location via this method. Several commercial vendors are now offering very precise indoor Wi-Fi–based location services for enterprise network applications, such as conditional security access and warehouse management, among others. In addition, Internet-based volunteer groups have already mapped hundreds of thousands of base station locations by "wardriving" with GPS and Wi-Fi enabled laptops. Corporate research labs at companies such as Intel and Microsoft have publicly revealed their work on geolocation software based on Wi-Fi station location. Soon, both open source and proprietary software will make it trivial for users of Wi-Fi devices to know where each other are.

Location sensing will eventually be spectrally independent (that is, not limited to the Wi-Fi spectrum). Software that listens to television and radio signals to calculate location is already beginning to emerge. Radio and television transmission towers have publicly known locations; the new digital television broadcasts also have a digital timestamp. This timestamp allows devices to triangulate location by comparing timestamps, much like the ones GPS satellites provide from orbit, and commercial interests are already using this technique to provide geolocation services. Whatever signals a device is listening to, it will eventually be able to figure out where it is and whether the signals are radio, Wi-Fi, cellular, GPS, or television.

Ultimately, location-sensitive applications might use microsensors and RFID tags that rely on both active client software and passive techniques. These small integrated circuits will be connected to antennas and respond to an interrogating radio signal. They will supply simple identifying information, including location coordinates. When queried, the RFID tag will return such location information as latitude and longitude, effectively serving as a digital survey stake.

All this means that, at least, one might need never be lost in a strange place again—unless one wants to be, by turning off the electronic device. Certainly, it seems that the serendipity of being lost, the freedom to be open to the unknown and unexpected, may itself be lost. What's more, if we ourselves are never lost, then we can also be found by others. The technology to form gleefully Dadaist flashmobs is also potentially the weapon of the unwanted stalker, or of an authoritarian political regime.

## Towards a Semantic (Geo)web

The emerging geospatial web of the future is primarily populated with two sorts of data: traditional cartographic geodata and geocoded hypermedia. Traditional cartographic geodata is already emerging as a commercial growth industry, but geocoded hypermedia may ultimately be the big disruptive innovation of the coming decade.

Part of what's emerging about this technology is actually already decades old. Traditional geodata is the digital map data created and used in geographic information systems (GIS). Such data is sometimes stored in *vector* form, with points used to represent such landscape features as cities and towns, buildings and airports; lines for features such as highways, rivers, and political boundaries; and polygons and irregular shapes that typically describe areas with a common attribute, such as a forest or a nation. Alternately, *raster* data may refer to a map depicting numeric quantities (population, rainfall, etc.), coded concepts (e.g., land use), or Earth imagery (an aerial photograph or a satellite spectrogram).

Because so much geodata is rendered, stored, and displayed in diverse data formats, it's often a challenge to combine different kinds of data to create layered maps. In the United States, an organization called the Open Geospatial Consortium (formerly the Open GIS Consortium) has been leading a concerted effort in government and the GIS industry to create a set of standards to address this problem. However, to use existing GIS data, some conversion will be required. The large volume of legacy GIS data is one of the major challenges to the dynamic use of traditional cartographic data envisioned in the concept of the geoweb.

Beyond traditional geodata, the growth of the Internet and consumer electronics have opened up the locative aspects of digital storytelling. Once geocoded, existing hypermedia becomes potentially searchable by location, and a few web developers have begun to explicitly label web documents and others with location coordinates (latitude and longitude) encoded in HTML in a metadata format, using pre-standard formats, such as GeoURL's "ICBM coordinates." So far there are no widely accepted standards for annotating web hypermedia with geocoordinates. However, several groups in the W3C (World Wide Web Consortium) and IETF (Internet Engineering Task Force) are approaching consensus on some of the necessary standard notations. With these standards, any content on the Web—text, graphics, media, applications—could ultimately be linked to one or more locations by geocoding.

This "tagging" provides a broad palette for innovation and creative expression in the physical-digital landscape. Furthermore, geotagging is a distributed, bottom-up process, and it has the same emergent qualities as the World Wide Web. For these reasons, we expect geocoded hypermedia to be a major disruptive innovation, perhaps on the scale of the World Wide Web—with many unanticipated applications and social consequences.

Just as the success of the World Wide Web required the development of powerful search services such as Yahoo! and Google to provide fast, efficient portals to vast data stores, the geoweb will require a similar capability for geodata searching. The requirements are twofold: the ability to search for traditional GIS data and the ability to geocode hypermedia—and ultimately the ability to link them together.

Currently, there is no comprehensive clearing house on the Web where users might find all of the data they want from all domains of knowledge covering all geographies. Instead, there are hundreds of national, regional, local, academic, private, and individual online gateways to geodatabases or repositories.

The obstacles are obvious: vast amounts of proprietary and domain-specific geodata produced in nonstandard formats or hosted at web sites with nonstandard database search capabilities—including the databases of governments, public agencies, and private companies all over the world. These remain largely unsearched and unsearchable.

While very few geospatial information scientists are working on this challenge, a couple of companies are beginning to provide rudimentary search services for geodata. An example is Iconsoft's AsktheSpider.com search for OpenGIS-conformant spatial web services such as Web Mapping Services (WMS) and Web Feature Services (WFS). Unfortunately, since OpenGIS standard data formats are so new, this is still a minuscule (but growing) resource.

## Locative Media as a Two-Way Street

Like so many other elements of the geo-ecology, early location-based services are using different business models and different standards. A simple classification includes the so-called "walled gardens," or mobile Internet services, and the experimental web landscape.

Telecommunication companies, consumer electronic and automotive companies, and related .net and .com startups are experimenting with new location services, many of which could be described as walled gardens. These are services available only to their subscribers, usually over closed networks.

For example, an owner of a Lexus car in a Verizon network will have access to a set of prepackaged services: canned points of interest, or POIs. Most of these come from one supplier, InfoUSA. This company claims to compile "the world's finest databases" of 14 million U.S. businesses, 200 million U.S. consumers, and 1.2 million Canadian businesses as well as 12 million Canadian consumers. Such services, however, might not be encoded in any of the standard data formats. In many cases, they are fundamentally different from open web-like services using standard data over standard IP networks.

Since most commercial location services operate on IP networks, major industry standards associations are moving toward open standard services. Unlike walled gardens, these services take advantage of a wide range of web-based content and open standards. However, some of the carriers pursuing this strategy are trying to limit access to the services and information by defining the Internet and geodata on it as a mobile application, not as a standard basis for an open marketplace of location-based or open geospatial services. A number of proposals are afoot to limit access to geospatial data and services, to create the basis for proprietary offerings, not unlike AOL or today's cable media.

Meanwhile, based on fairly open mapping protocols like the RDFIG geovocabulary from the W3C, as well as universal HTML, HTTP, and Java platforms, thousands of independent developers worldwide are trying to take advantage of the location-aware applications described previously to build different kinds of location-based services. These academics, researchers, developers, bloggers, artists, cartographers, and GPS hobbyists are experimenting with everything from augmented reality and robotics to psychogeographic and GPS art. The parallels are obvious: while walled gardens and proprietary mobile applications represent the kinds of services offered in the early days by Dialog and Prodigy, the open geoservices look more like the period just before the Web and its web browsers created a game-changing new medium of communication and commerce. If proprietary models don't dominate, some of today's experiments will define the future model for a broad-based platform for location-based services.

## Brother, Can You Spare a Polygon Layer?

Public geodata policies directly or indirectly address geodata access, protection, and use, including such issues as privacy, ownership, and access to public data. These matter, or should matter, to the amateur and professional mapmaker alike, because the basic geographic facts of our world—the locations of places and their shapes—are the very syllables and words and sentences of geographic storytelling, the raw factual substrate from which maps are made.

Government at all levels around the world collects the lion's share of geographic data, much of it in pursuit of the public interest, and their policies about the dissemination of geographic data will ultimately determine how widely accessible geodata will be to the public and the types of applications that will be created using that data. Some of the key policies that will ultimately shape access and use of geodata include data ownership, location privacy, secrecy of sensitive data, and development goals.

Data ownership will ultimately shape not only access to geodata, but also the kinds of developers who get involved in the geoweb. For example, the British government has its Ordinance Survey that creates and manages public geospatial data, including all the roadmaps. Because it is a Trading Fund, though it is a wholly government-owned company, the Ordinance Survey agency is expected to be financially self-sufficient. As a result, it must sell all its data. This policy is obviously frustrating to open source developers. In many countries, access to geodata is even more restricted than in Britain. In the United States, by contrast, the government gives away vast amounts of geospatial data. For example, the digital elevation models collected by the U.S. Geological Survey and the roads data collected by the U.S. Census Bureau are distributed for free on the Web, as are specialty data sets, such as the microclimate models used in precision farming. As a result, geoweb applications are likely to develop much more rapidly in the United States.

Meanwhile, fearing a potential negative impact on location-based mobile commerce, many industry associations are proactively drafting privacy guidelines, while negotiating with regulators over mandatory restrictions. Meanwhile, some carriers are already offering services that allow their customers to track locations of friends and family members. Absent some early regulations, these services appear to be inviting abuse. Fortunately, research labs like Bell Labs and Intel Labs are already crafting privacy application toolkits. Similar to Caller ID, these applications would allow users to selectively reveal their loscation to validated and authentic friends and family members, as well as authorized colleagues.

Security drives another set of policy concerns about geodata. For example, the United States government could fly over the desert with sensors and map high-quality uranium deposits, but it probably would want to keep the results secret. Infrastructure security is another concern. Recently, a graduate student at Columbia University created a map of the Internet and the electrical infrastructure of the United States that was so detailed that the government classified his term paper. And the U.S. Department of Homeland Security is currently soliciting comments on proposals to restrict the otherwise free access to massive amounts of public geodata in America. The California State and National Archaeological Registries also have secret maps of archaeologically sensitive areas because of the problems with artifact hunters. In Utah and Arizona, and even in California, there are still untouched ancient cave art locations and sites where pots still sit on the floor of a cave or dwelling. Archaeological information is an example of information that needs to be protected for the integrity and preservation of the locations.

Governments may invest in mapping resources and infrastructure as part of a deliberate development or financial aid strategy. For example, U.S. farmers are highly productive as a result of U.S. government investment in creating public data repositories. They regularly use sophisticated microclimate and soil information for planting and farm management, yielding higher returns. During its rule of Uganda, the Belgian government invested in mapping Ugandan farms, roads, and political districts. The Uganda government has numerous paper maps; the Minister of Roads has a map of roads, the

Wildlife Minister has a habitat map, and the Minister of Natural Resources has a map of mines. To take advantage of these maps in a broader geospatial web, however, today's Ugandan government would need to make another investment in digitizing these maps, allowing them to be integrated and publicly accessed. Clearly, GIS planners are at a disadvantage in developing countries where spending development money on digital maps versus other pressing needs remains a policy decision for local, regional, and national governments, as well as international development agencies.

—Mike Liebhold

## A Geoscope in Every Home

Regardless of how the geoweb ecology evolves over the next 10 years, one thing is certain: it will demand a new geospatial literacy that today exists only among a small portion of the most highly educated people.

Geospatial, or locative, literacy might be described as the ability to understand, create, and use spatial information and maps in navigating, in describing phenomena, in problem-solving, and in artistic expression—ultimately including the ability to create and utilize information, viewable in place, directly associated with physical reality. There are no programs to help people develop this kind of literacy, and even in the most developed countries, those who have achieved a high level of geospatial literacy have done so largely without a compelling formal curriculum.

Because every map constitutes a representation of a place, some trade-offs or distortions are always involved, in order to emphasize certain aspects of the place at the expense of others. In contradiction to our inherent belief in maps as objective representations of physical reality, largely born of our experiences with road and transport maps, the reality is that the subjective choices made in drawing a map reflect the deliberate or unconscious preferences and biases of the mapmaker, however well intended. True locative literacy, much like literacy in the written word, involves the development of critical map-reading skills, which are attuned to subjectivity and bias in map depictions. The availability of geospatial software and data that are "free as in freedom" stands to offer individuals the opportunity to create their own maps, and thereby to test directly the apparent assumptions of maps made by others.

By the same token, the other half of locative literacy involves the ability to tell one's own story, or that of one's community, through maps and spatial information. The combination of free and open geospatial software and data provides innovators with the chance to tinker and experiment with the art of geographic narrative, without economic or legal obstacles to overcome. For individuals and grassroots organizations, this means nothing less than the ability to explore demographic disparity, political and electoral campaigning, environmental conditions, civil and urban planning, and modeling of telecommunications and transport networks on a useful, practical, and cost-effective basis. We have the highest hopes for this technology to help widen public discourse and encourage effective bottom-up communication about the crucial issues confronting our communities, our society, and our world.

The ultimate goal of this book hearkens back to the vision articulated by R. Buckminster Fuller of the *Geoscope*, an intricately detailed tool for observing the state of the entire world at once:

> ...The new educational technology will probably provide also an invention of mine called the Geoscope—a large two-hundred-foot diameter (or more) lightweight geodesic sphere hung hoveringly at one hundred feet above mid-campus by approximately invisible cables from three remote masts....
>
> The Geoscope may be illuminated to picture the earth and the motion of its complete cloud-cover history for years run off on its surface in minutes so that man may comprehend the cyclic patterning and predict. The complete census-by-census of world population history changes could be run off in minutes, giving a clear picture of the demological patterning and its clear trending. The total history of transportation and of world resource discovery, development, distribution, and redistribution could become comprehendible to the human mind, which would thus be able to forecast and plan in vastly greater magnitude than heretofore. The consequences of various world plans could be computed and projected. All world data would be dynamically viewable and picturable and relayable by radio to all the world, so that common consideration in a most educated manner of all world problems by all world people would become a practical event. (R. Buckminster Fuller, *Education Automation*, 1962)

The Geoscope was to play a central role in a World Game, which Fuller envisioned as:

> ... a scientific means for exploring expeditious ways of employing the World's resources so efficiently and omni-considerately as to be able to provide a higher standard of living for all of humanity—higher than has heretofore been experienced by any humans—and on a continually sustainable basis for all generations to come, while enabling all of humanity to enjoy the whole planet Earth without any individual profiting at the expense of another and without interference with one another, while also rediverting the valuable chemistries known as pollution to effective uses elsewhere, conserving the wild resources and antiquities. (R. Buckminster Fuller, *World Game Packet*, 1969)

Of course, even Fuller in all his brilliance could not have totally comprehended the consequences of the rise of the personal computer and the global data network we call the Internet. Today, it is possible for us to realize Fuller's dream not merely in the form of one enormous Geoscope, but reflected in thousands of little Geoscopes, potentially a Geoscope in every home and on every computing device, all interconnected to each other and to the real world in real time. The ultimate goal is nothing less than the following, in Fuller's own words:

> Think of it. We are blessed with technology that would be indescribable to our forefathers. We have the wherewithal, the know-it-all to feed everybody, clothe everybody, and give every human on Earth a chance. We know now what we could never have known before—that we now have the option for all humanity to make it successfully on this planet in this lifetime. Whether it is to be Utopia or Oblivion will be a touch-and-go relay race right up to the final moment. (Fuller, *Critical Path*, 1980)

With hope for the eventual achievement of the bright outcome of his vision, we respectfully dedicate this work to the memory of R. Buckminster Fuller, and his unflagging commitment to the good of all humanity.

## The Adventure Continues...

Honestly, the field of digital cartography is moving faster today than print media can keep up with! This book, which took unusually long to develop because of the complexity of the subject, witnessed quite a few exciting changes which we and the editorial staff at O'Reilly scrambled to keep up with. In particular, the underlying substrate of spatial projection and database libraries available as open source are rock solid and production ready. The need for development in open source GIS and mapping lies in user interfaces. This is well exemplified by the immediate popularity of Google Maps, which was released as a "beta" just as this book went to press. We dissect Google Maps and explore JavaScript-based knockoffs using Map Server on our weblog at *http://mappinghacks.com/*.

In general, work on user interfaces and on interface design will help lower the technical barriers to personal and community storytelling with maps through the encapsulation of the cartographer's and geographer's expertise in software. Our attempt to actualize this principle takes the form of the Locative Media Toolkit, an open source GUI mapping application. Written in Python with the GTk+ widget set, the Locative Media Toolkit runs on Windows, OS X, and Linux and offers features for aggregating GPS tracks and waypoints, georeferencing base maps by dragging and dropping waypoints, importing and georeferencing digital media based on tracklog timestamps, adding text annotations, and publishing to a variety of formats, including DHTML, SVG, RSS 1.0, worldKit configurations, and UMN MapServer Mapfiles. You can find out more about storytelling with the Locative Media Toolkit at *http://mappinghacks.com/projects/lmt/*.

We've learned a lot in the process of writing this book, and we continue to document the process at *http://mappinghacks.com/*. We thank you, gentle reader, for taking an interest in our work.

## How to Use This Book

> *Books are the compasses and telescopes and*
> *sextants and charts which other men have*
> *prepared to help us navigate the dangerous seas*
> *of human life.*
> —Jesse Lee Bennett, *What Books Can Do For You*

You can read this book from cover to cover if you like, but for the most part, each hack stands on its own, so feel free to browse and jump to the different sections that interest you most. If there's a prerequisite you need to know about, a cross-reference will guide you to the right hack. So, feel free to browse, flipping around to whatever sections interest you most.

## How This Book Is Organized

The book is divided into several chapters, organized by subject:

*Chapter 1, Mapping Your Life*
Find the important places in your life on online road maps and aerial imagery, consider the spatial aspects of your personal digital media collection, and examine geographic data with nongeographic tools.

*Chapter 2, Mapping Your Neighborhood*
The story of your immediate surroundings: politically, demographically, electromagnetically, and in full-color 3-D.

*Chapter 3, Mapping Your World*
From maps of the historical past to maps of other planets, learn why getting a round world to look right on a flat surface is hard, and what to do about it.

*Chapter 4, Mapping (on) the Web*
The World Wide Web offers a fertile environment for dynamic and interactive cartography. Plot your weblog, your photo galleries, major earthquakes, the weather, demographic statistics, and more.

*Chapter 5, Mapping with Gadgets*
Everything you wanted to know about making maps with GPS, building your own car navigation system, getting maps on your cell phone, and other locative fun with cool electronic toys.

*Chapter 6, Mapping on Your Desktop*
How and why "Geographic Information Systems" is far, far more than just a fancy term for making maps on a computer.

*Chapter 7, Names and Places*
> Find the coordinates of things and the things near coordinates.

*Chapter 8, Building a Geospatial Web*
> Learn the fundamental concepts of the emerging geospatial web and how to start building and publishing spatial data repositories.

*Chapter 9, Mapping with Other People*
> Where my story meets your story: Modelling the real, the subjective, and the wholly imaginary.

## Conventions Used in This Book

The following is a list of the typographical conventions used in this book:

**Bold**
> Used to indicate spreadsheet interface elements.

*Italics*
> Used to indicate URLs, Unix commands, filenames, filename extensions, and directory/folder names. For example, a path in the filesystem will appear as */Developer/Applications*.

`Constant width`
> Used to show code examples, the contents of files, console output, as well as the names of variables, commands, and other code excerpts.

**`Constant width bold`**
> Used in examples to show commands and other text that should be typed literally. Also used to highlight portions of code, typically new additions to old code.

`Constant width italic`
> Used in code examples and tables to show sample text to be replaced with your own values.

*Color*
> The second color is used to indicate a cross-reference within the text.

You should pay special attention to notes set apart from the text with the following icons:

> This is a tip, suggestion, or general note. It contains useful supplementary information about the topic at hand.

> This is a warning or note of caution, often indicating that your money or your privacy might be at risk.

The thermometer icons, found next to each hack, indicate the relative complexity of the hack:

beginner          moderate          expert

Whenever possible, the hacks in this book are not *platform-specific*, which means you can use them on Linux, Macintosh, and Windows machines. However, some things are possible only on a particular platform.

## Using Code Examples

This book is here to help you get your job done. In general, you may use the code in this book in your programs and documentation. You do not need to contact us for permission unless you're reproducing a significant portion of the code. For example, writing a program that uses several chunks of code from this book does not require permission. Selling or distributing a CD-ROM of examples from O'Reilly books *does* require permission. Answering a question by citing this book and quoting example code does not require permission. Incorporating a significant amount of example code from this book into your product's documentation *does* require permission.

We appreciate, but do not require, attribution. An attribution usually includes the title, author, publisher, and ISBN. For example: "*Mapping Hacks* by Schuyler Erle, Rich Gibson, and Jo Walsh. Copyright 2004 O'Reilly Media, Inc., 0-596-00703-5."

If you feel your use of code examples falls outside fair use or the permission given above, feel free to contact us at *permissions@oreilly.com*.

## How to Contact Us

We have tested and verified the information in this book to the best of our ability, but you may find that features have changed (or even that we have made mistakes!). As a reader of this book, you can help us to improve future editions by sending us your feedback. Please let us know about any errors, inaccuracies, bugs, misleading or confusing statements, and typos that you find anywhere in this book.

Please also let us know what we can do to make this book more useful to you. We take your comments seriously and will try to incorporate reasonable suggestions into future editions. You can write to us at:

O'Reilly Media, Inc.
1005 Gravenstein Hwy N.
Sebastopol, CA 95472
(800) 998-9938 (in the U.S. or Canada)
(707) 829-0515 (international/local)
(707) 829-0104 (fax)

To ask technical questions or to comment on the book, send email to:

*bookquestions@oreilly.com*

O'Reilly's web site for *Mapping Hacks* lists examples, errata, and plans for future editions. You can find this page at:

*http://www.oreilly.com/catalog/mappinghks/*

The working outline for *Mapping Hacks* ultimately contained almost 200 hacks, half of which had to be discarded in the interests of time and space. You can find some of them on the authors' web site, with free code, data, examples, further hacks, ongoing projects, interesting links, more stuff that didn't fit in the book, and maybe even a dodgy collaborative weblog:

*http://mappinghacks.com/*

For more information about this book and others, see the O'Reilly web site:

*http://www.oreilly.com*

## Got a Hack?

To explore Hacks books online or to contribute a hack for future titles, visit:

*http://hacks.oreilly.com*

# CHAPTER ONE

# Mapping Your Life
## Hacks 1–13

Fiction authors, when first starting out, are often advised to "write what you know." The same rule applies to telling stories with maps. If you are new to creating geographic narrative, we suggest looking to the nearby and the familiar for inspiration and information. As a result, our story begins with "Mapping Your Life."

The spatial rendition of your personal narrative can take many forms. Simply locating the important places in your life on a map, or identifying the highways and byways that lead to those places, can serve as a basis for geographic exploration. But telling your own story to others means being able to make your own maps, however simple and straightforward, of the places you live in or have visited. Going further, we can try to place other elements of our lives on a map, such as photographs of our adventures, in the hopes of bringing new life to the old tradition of vacation photo slideshows.

In this chapter, we've tried to focus on hacks that you can start experimenting with right away. For simplicity's sake, many of them are based on existing software or online services, but, as the book progresses, we'll try to show you how to get your hands dirty building these same basic tools and concepts on your own, with more complexity and expressiveness. Let's get started!

### HACK #1 Put a Map on It: Mapping Arbitrary Locations with Online Services

Your coordinates and their maps: online map services help you to tell your own story.

Plain geographic coordinates tell you where you are, but they don't tell you where you are in relation to your environment. Do you know where 39.5° North, 121.2° West is? Do you know what it is near? Providing this context is one of the basic uses for maps. There is nothing like adding a map to an email or web page to make the point that "wherever you go, there you are on the map." While this book is all about creating maps and doing geographical analysis, it can be hard simply to make a map on your desktop.

Fortunately *http://mapquest.com*, *http://multimap.com*, *http://maps.yahoo.com*, *http://map24.com*, and *http://maporama.com* all provide interfaces that allow you to put links to maps and driving directions on your own web page and in your emails. Map24 and Maporama offer free services, but since they require you to register with their site, this hack focuses on mapping arbitrary locations with MapQuest, Multimap, and Yahoo! using their free linking services, which are described at:

*MapQuest*
> *http://www.mapquest.com/solutions/product.adp?page=linkfree*

*Multimap*
> *http://www.multimap.com/static/freemaps.htm*

*Yahoo!*
> *http://maps.yahoo.com*

Before you start creating hyperlinks to these free mapping services, familiarize yourself with their respective terms of use. If you abide by these terms, you are less likely to find this service taken down the next time you use your web application or when others visit your site and take a look at your work. Generally, the page you are linking to must not be displayed in a frame set. MapQuest also requires that the page you link to not be displayed in a new browser window. As these linking services are free of charge, banner advertising features on the web page you link to cover the cost of providing this service. Also, because of copyright restrictions, you are not permitted to download maps or store them locally.

Free linking services typically work by producing a hyperlink (URI) to a CGI script on a mapping web site. Information about the map you wish to create is passed to the mapping web site through this URI, through any number of parameters and their values, listed in Table 1-1. You then include the URI in your emails or web pages:

```
<a href="http://www.multimap.com/map/browse.cgi?lon=5.08159&lat=52.09022"
title="See where I live!">A map of my house</a>
<a href="http://www.mapquest.com/maps/map.adp?latlongtype=decimal
&longitude=5.08159&latitude=52.09022" title="See where I live!">A map of my
house</a>
```

*Table 1-1. Map services URI parameters*

| URL | MapQuest | Multimap | Required |
|---|---|---|---|
| CGI | *http://www.mapquest. com/maps/map.adp* | *http://www.multimap. com/map/browse.cgi* | Yes |
| Longitude | longitude=5.08159 | lon=5.08159 | Yes |
| Latitude | latitude=52.09022 | lat=52.09022 | Yes |
| Coordinate format | latlongtype=decimal | | Yes (MapQuest) |
| Map size | size=[ big | small ] | mapsize=[ big | small ] | No |
| Zoom level | Zoom=[ 0 - 10 ] | scale=[ 5000 | 10000 | 25000 | 50000 | 100000 | 200000 | 500000 | 1000000 | 2000000 | 4000000 | 10000000 | 20000000 | 40000000 ] | No |

The values for longitude and latitude must be supplied in decimal notation (45.5, −122.25) instead of degrees, minutes, and seconds (45 degrees 30 minutes North, 122 degrees 15 minutes West). MapQuest requires that you specify this by including the `latlongtype=decimal` parameter. The coordinates are supplied using the WGS84 datum. MapQuest and Multimap also allow you to specify the size of the map using the `size` and `mapsize` parameters, respectively.

> The WGS84 datum is a commonly used foundation for spatial systems. Most of the examples in this book use it. You don't need to know much about it, except to know that mixing data that uses WGS84 with data that uses a different datum is likely to give you a lot of mismatches.

You can specify the zoom level, or scale, of a map from the MapQuest web site with the somewhat abstract `zoom` parameter, where a zoom level of 1 generates a map on a national scale and a zoom level of 10 generates a street-level map. Using the Multimap free linking service, you can choose from 13 different scale levels. Note that these scales are not available for all parts of the world; street-level maps are only available in Western Europe, the United States, Canada, and Australia.

## More on the MapQuest LinkFree service

The previous examples focused on using latitude and longitude, but MapQuest LinkFree URLs also accept the address of your target location as a parameter. Here is a sample LinkFree URL that creates the map shown in Figure 1-1:

```
http://www.mapquest.com/maps/map.adp?city=sebastopol&state=CA&address=1005+
gravenstein+hwy+n&zip=95472&country=us&zoom=6
```

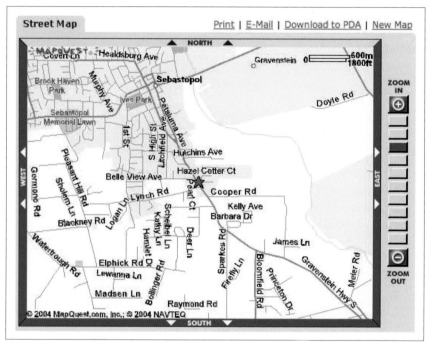

*Figure 1-1. MapQuest LinkFree map of O'Reilly Media, Inc. headquarters*

That long URL can be broken down into the following parts. This is the root of the main MapQuest web site:

```
http://www.mapquest.com
```

They have a directory called Maps that includes a program called *map.adp* that generates the map in response to your parameters:

```
/maps/map.adp
```

When you see a ? in a URL, you know that what follows are parameters (or arguments) for your request. In this case, we are telling the program *map.adp* that we want to see a map for Sebastopol:

```
?city=sebastopol
```

Whenever we have more than one parameter, we need to put a & between parameters so that the web server knows that this is a new parameter (and not just a city called "sebastopolstate"):

```
&state=CA
```

This is the street address. Note how spaces are replaced with + signs. Also note that MapQuest is particular about how streets are named. In this case, it requires you to use the abbreviations "Hwy" and "N". You can't type 1005+gravenstein+highway+north:

```
&address=1005+gravenstein+hwy+n
```

More address parameters:

```
&zip=95472&country=us
```

This parameter sets the zoom level of the map, as described earlier.

```
&zoom=6
```

Using this example as a model, you can assemble your own URLs by substituting in your own data. For more information on LinkFree, see: *http://www. mapquest.com/solutions/product.adp?page=linkfree*.

## Mapping with Yahoo! Maps

Yahoo! Maps provides another commercial option at *http://maps.yahoo.com/*. One nice feature of Yahoo! Maps is that you can navigate to a map, get it just the way you want, and then click on "Link to this Map" above the upper right corner of the map to create an html link to the map shown (see Figure 1-2).

Clicking on "Link to this Map" brings up the screen shown in Figure 1-3.

Opening a map in a new window is nice because it makes it possible for your reader to see both your web site and the applicable map at the same time. The Yahoo! Terms of Service seems slightly less restrictive than MapQuest's in that they do not appear to prohibit opening the Yahoo! map in a new window.

Here is the HTML for the map shown in Figure 1-2:

```
<center>
<img src="http://us.i1.yimg.com/us.yimg.com/i/us/mp/gr/mplogo.gif"
width="99"
height="13" border=0 align=middle alt="[ Yahoo! Maps ]"><br>
<a href="http://us.rd.yahoo.com/maps//maps/extmap/*-http://maps.yahoo.com//
maps_result?csz=Sebastopol%2C+CA+95472-
2811&state=CA&uzip=95472&ds=n&name=&desc=&ed=XoqU8Op_OTr6wxOZ_wJuoU_
JkBnmUzEwp9bv_wQLnUDySVOdOmoR1cXYVOL2deROzT3S.LFdfE3iuDpTymm7_211.Jys.
OUcFKpvvOw_mVLH7a2kwgtg8i6dtg--&zoomin=yes&BFKey=&mag=9">
Map of
1005 Gravenstein Hwy N<br>Sebastopol, CA 95472-2811<br></a></center>
```

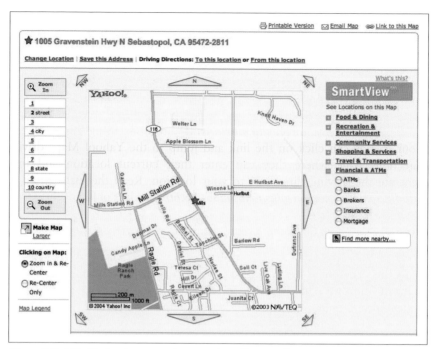

Figure 1-2. O'Reilly headquarters shown on http://maps.yahoo.com

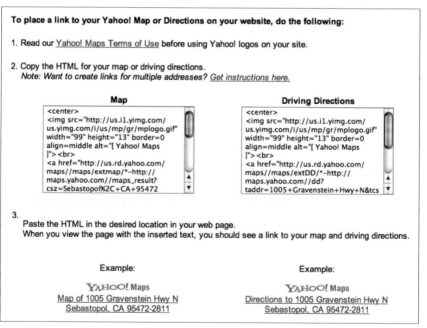

Figure 1-3. Yahoo! "Link to this Map" instructions

To open the map in a new window, add `target ="new"` to the `<a href=…>` tag of the HTML generated by the "Link to this Map" tool.

```
<a href="http://us.rd.yahoo.com/maps//maps/extmap/*-http://maps.yahoo.com//
maps_result?csz=Sebastopol%2C+CA+95472-
2811&state=CA&uzip=95472&ds=n&name=&desc=&ed=XoqU8Op_OTr6wxOZ_wJuoU_
JkBnmUzEwp9bv_wQLnUDySVOdOmoR1cXYVOL2deROzT3S.LFdfE3iuDpTymm7_211.Jys.
OUcFKpvvOw_mVLH7a2kwgtg8i6dtg--&zoomin=yes&BFKey=&mag=9" target="new">
```

You can also create direct links to driving directions using Yahoo! Maps. Your friends can click on the link and jump to the Yahoo! Maps driving directions page where they can enter their current location and then generate the driving directions to your location. Read the instructions at *http://help.yahoo.com/help/us/maps/maps-26.html* for lots of fun.

## See Also

For a source of U.S. maps that allows you more freedom in generating maps, albeit a less polished effect, see "Make Free Maps of the United States Online" **[Hack #14]**. In the Preface, we address the recent release of Google Maps.

*—Edward Mac Gillavry*

### HACK #2 Route Planning Online

Many map services offer a route planner. How do they work and why do they fail?

Maps not only assist you in indicating where you are now, but also help you plan where you want to go next. To help you out, most online mapping services such as Map24, Maporama, MapQuest, and Multimap feature a "driving directions" service on their web sites, which is free, online, and always available. These services provide directions in two different ways: they can give you driving instructions to a location you've just searched for on the site, or they can just help you plan a trip from point A to point B.

A typical route-planning session consists of four stages: address input and validation, address geocoding, route calculation, and route representation. The first two stages revolve around locating a given address in geographic space: translating a human-readable address into a machine-readable pair of coordinates. (You can see these principles in action in "Geocode a U.S. Street Address" **[Hack #79]**.) Instead of worrying about just one address, two addresses must be converted into computer-friendly coordinates. In the third stage, the actual route is calculated. As this stage requires a lot of computer processing, it takes quite a while. In the last stage, the route is represented in a human-readable format as a table of textual instructions and additional information.

## Route Calculation

Road-network data that is used for route calculations is a subset of the data offered by commercial mapping data providers such as AND, GDT, NAVTEQ, and TeleAtlas. These data sets not only include representational information—the road class (to determine line width and line color), the road name, and house number ranges (for labeling)—but also navigational information.

To calculate the shortest or quickest route between two points, routing software borrows from graph theory and relies on (a variation of) the Dijkstra or A* algorithm. These algorithms take into account only the connectivity between navigable features and the difficulty (or impedance) factor of each navigable feature. When calculating the shortest route between two points over a network, the length of the navigable features is used as the impedance factor. When calculating the quickest route, the impedance factor incorporates both feature length and travel speed; the length of the navigable features is combined with their travel speeds to approximate the travel time for each feature.

There are various characteristics of each navigable feature that determine the connectivity between them. The primary attribute is network topology. Most mapping data sets are topological data sets: the geometry of the network consists of nodes and lines. Each intersection of lines is a node. However, in the real world, one cannot always turn onto another road even though the lines that represent these roads intersect in the data model (for example, due to turn restrictions). Also, intersecting lines may represent roads that cross at different levels—e.g., tunnels, overpasses, and bridges. Finally, there may be one-way streets or barriers at the start or end of roads that may prevent you from accessing the road altogether. All these factors affect the real-world connectivity between the elements of the road network.

The impedance factor determines the cost of traveling across a navigable feature. To calculate the shortest or quickest route between two locations, this impedance factor has to be minimized. Calculating the shortest route is the most objective calculation, as it is only the length of the navigable features that determines the route's impedance factor. To calculate the quickest route, the algorithm takes into account both the length of the navigable features and their travel speed to determine the impedance factor. Assigning an accurate travel speed to a navigable feature largely determines the satisfaction of the end user. A basic approximation can be derived from the speed restrictions for various road classes: you can generally travel faster on a major highway or motorway than on a secondary road. However, road class alone still gives a rough approximation. Since it takes longer to drive one mile on a primary road in town than a primary road in the countryside, it's important to determine whether the navigable feature is located in an urban area or not. A third characteristic of a navigable feature that can be easily extracted from the mapping data to provide some further hint for determining the travel speed is the form of way. This is particularly helpful when it comes to slip roads (exits) or roundabouts (traffic circles). Although these traffic situations are part of a particular road class and are situated in the same area as the connecting navigable features, one typically drives slower in these conditions than on other road segments. All these attributes of navigable features are taken into account in assigning travel speeds to navigable features. The more granular this classification of navigable features is, the better the route calculation and the more satisfied the user.

## Driving Instructions

Once the route between the two locations has been calculated, the driving directions are presented on screen. At this stage, the output of the route calculation, a sequential list of navigable features, has to be presented in a human-readable form. Street names and road numbers are the most important information and can be easily extracted from the mapping data sets. You also have to know which turns to take to get from one road into the next. The angles between two connecting features are used to derive the driving instructions for the turn to take:

| Angle between two segments | Standard driving instruction |
| --- | --- |
| 0° | Continue straight ahead onto |
| 45° | Bear right onto |
| 90° | Turn right onto |
| 135° | Make a sharp right onto |
| 180° | Make a U-turn onto |
| 225° | Make a sharp left onto |
| 270° | Turn left onto |
| 315° | Bear left |

Further information can be added by taking into account specific traffic situations such as at traffic circles or exits of highway junctions:

- "At the roundabout take the third exit onto"
- "Leave/Join the highway"

To further enhance the driving instructions, landmarks or points of interest can be added (e.g., "Turn left at the 'Dog and Duck' onto Oxford Street"). This gives the instructions a more conversational tone, so they don't sound like staccato, computer-generated commands.

## Turn Right, Gone Wrong

A company's board meeting had to be postponed, as most of the board members did not arrive in Cardiff on time, because the driving directions did not take into account the Severn Bridge and took them from Bristol around the Severn estuary via Gloucester. A salesman missed out on landing a deal with his blue chip customer as he arrived too late at the meeting to sign the contract. The right turn he had to take according to the directions was not there. On their way to visit their daughter's new house in Kingston, Dorset, her parents found themselves in Kingston, Devon instead.

These ill-advised travelers all followed driving directions from various online mapping services available on the Web today. Although many people successfully rely on these services on a daily basis, things sometimes go wrong. Then, it is neither the person in the passenger seat reading out the instructions that is to blame, nor the online mapping service: their driving directions come with elaborate disclaimers to avoid any liability.

Then what is the source of these problems? Of course, many problems occur at the geocoding stage when entering ambiguous address details that have to be converted to machine-readable coordinates. But focusing on route calculation alone, three groups of problems can be observed in ascending order of severity:

1. Duration of the trip is poorly estimated. Although the route is correct, the calculated duration of the journey is too short or too long.

2. Driving directions take an illogical route. The route deviates strangely from the most direct route.

3. Driving directions take an impossible route or neglect apparent solutions.

The most likely reason for the first problem is the assumption of an average speed for each road class. Most driving direction services do take into account that traffic flow can be severely delayed during rush hours. Furthermore, local knowledge is difficult to incorporate. How would one formalize the driving pattern of a New York City cab driver? When fine-tuning the route calculation, software engineers tend to exaggerate the speeds on major roads while purposely decreasing the average speeds for minor roads. Thus, long distance routes turn out to take much longer than expected, whereas the calculated journey duration for urban routes is generally too short. Although this approach may skew the route calculation towards preferring major roads, the driving directions guide drivers around the town center and instruct them to follow the ring road, although this may not be the shortest route to join the highway on the other side of town.

In addition to the possibility the route calculation is skewed too much toward a preference for major roads, another problem may be that the speed settings of the various road classes may be too similar. In this case, the route calculation generates driving directions that make travelers take many turns, as the resulting differences of the features' impedance factors (interplay of travel speed and feature length) have become almost negligible. Maintaining the distinction between major roads and minor roads, some route-calculation algorithms introduced the concept of a hierarchical network. A hierarchical network typically consists of two or three networks, in which the upper levels are a subset of the lower levels to ensure connectivity. This way, the algorithm can generate driving directions that are more accurately based on the mental hierarchy one has of a road network, instead of relying primarily on travel speeds.

Assuming three hierarchical levels, the route calculation takes into account all navigable features around the start location and the destination. Between the start location and the destination, the route calculation focuses on the major and connecting roads. Thus, the route calculation embeds the mental hierarchy. Furthermore, less navigable features have to be taken into account at higher levels of the hierarchy, so the route can be calculated much faster.

Finally the route calculation may generate routes that are not possible to navigate or may neglect obvious driving routes. These problems point toward issues related to the connectivity in the road network. If the height difference is not modeled in the graph, drivers may be instructed to take a right turn to join a highway from a flyover. Also, recently built roads or new highways may not always be included in the mapping data. First, it takes a while before these changes filter through in the mapping data. Second, once the mapping data has been shipped, it takes a lot of preparation and quality assurance before a new graph can be put into production to calculate routes.

Recently, small-scale mapping data sets covering only the major road network have become available. These data sets have default travel speeds for each navigable feature. This information is typically derived from historical data obtained from GPS-based fleet tracking systems. Also, some route-calculation engines take traffic information feeds to regularly update the speed settings.

## See Also

- *http://www.maporama.com/*
- *http://www.mapquest.com/*
- *http://www.multimap.com/*

*—Edward Mac Gillavry*

## Map the Places You've Visited

Sometimes a simple map showing the places you've been is all you need to start telling the story of your travels.

> I've been everywhere, man
> I've been everywhere, man
> Crossed the deserts bare, man
> I've breathed the mountain air, man
> Travel—I've had my share, man
> I've been everywhere
> —Johnny Cash, "I've Been Everywhere"

In the U.S. and Canada, it's not uncommon to see camping vehicles or RVs sporting a map emblazoned on the side, showing the states and provinces that the vehicle has traveled through. And why not? For many of us, the list of countries we've been to, or the tally of states or provinces we've set foot in, is like a badge of honor, an encapsulation of all the adventures we've had and of all the wonderful places we've come upon in our travels.

Thanks to the miracles of modern technology, it's almost painless to make maps on the Web that highlight the places we've visited and proudly share those maps via web sites or email. A great place to start is World66.com, which describes itself as "the travel guide you write." Among the many cool features of the site is My World66, a page where you can make and export maps of places you've visited, including maps of the U.S., Canada, Europe, and the world. My World66 can be found at *http://world66.com/myworld66/*.

Start by clicking one of the "Visited Places" links, and you'll be taken to a page full of labeled checkboxes, each one corresponding to a place that can be shown on that map. Figure 1-4 shows some of the choices available for the "Visited States" map. Check all the places you've been to in that part of the world, and click "Generate Map." That's all there is to it! Figure 1-5 shows some of the states of the U.S. that Jo has visited.

What's especially hackish about these maps is how they are made: World66 doesn't redraw their maps from scratch each time someone visits their site. Instead, each map is stored in a *GIF image*, a common image format used on the Web. In a GIF image, each pixel is assigned not an individual color, but rather an index of a palette of colors, numbered 0 through 255. World66 takes advantage of this property of GIF images by giving all the pixels for Alabama one index, Alaska another index, Arizona another, and so on up to Wyoming. To render the map, instead of changing the pixels themselves, the web site just changes the color of the palette entry corresponding to each state. Since there are fewer than 256 states in the U.S., provinces in Canada,

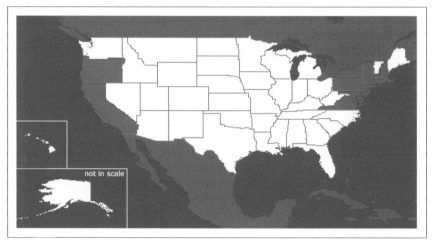

Figure 1-4. Selecting states for the Visited States map

Figure 1-5. Jo hasn't quite been as many places as Johnny Cash, but she's working on it

and countries in the entire world, this trick can be used to make simple maps of places with astonishingly little work.

Now that you've made a map of the places you've visited, what can you do with it? You can save it to disk, for future reference. By viewing the image directly, you'll see that World66 also generates a unique link for each map of a form that is similar to *http://world66.com/myworld66/visitedStates/ statemap?visited=...*, which you can copy and paste into an email to your friends, perhaps. Finally, World66 provides a text box with a bit of HTML that you can paste into a web page to show off your map on your own blog or web site.

Of course, you shouldn't feel limited in your cartographic efforts to recording just the places you have visited. The interface is so simple that a lot of other possibilities immediately spring to mind, like maps of "The Places My Brother Swears He Will Never Visit Again," "Some Countries I Have Collected Stamps from," or the ever-popular "States That Have a Warrant Out for My Arrest." There are countless stories waiting to be told!

## Find Your House on an Aerial Photograph

**HACK #4**

"You Are Here" is a quick piece of wish fulfillment for the amateur cartographer.

The free Terraserver service (*http://www.terraserver-usa.com/*) offered by Microsoft provides a friendly interface for finding things and viewing base maps made from aerial photographs. Once upon a time, Terraserver covered the whole world on a large scale, but now it only republishes USGS maps for the United States The imagery can be as detailed as one-meter resolution—that's one meter per pixel, a pretty good resolution for aerial photography.

### Searching Terraserver

Terraserver provides many different ways to find what you're looking for. Follow the "Advanced Find" link on the left to find the different search options. You can search for an "Address," which Terraserver will attempt to geocode. If the geocoding works, you'll get a list of one or more likely matches from which to choose. It works similarly to the free geocoding service described in "Geocode a U.S. Street Address" [Hack #79].

You can also search for an identified "Place"—any spatial feature noticeable enough to be given a name by the U.S. Geological Survey. Terraserver will do a loose match from the beginning of the name you search for. In "Geocode U.S. Locations with the GNIS" [Hack #85], we describe how to use the freely available GNIS data to build a geocoded index of noticeable places.

If you know the latitude and longitude of your house or other interesting place, select the option "Geographic" from the lefthand menu and ask Terraserver to map the coordinates. You can enter either decimal degrees, which most geo applications prefer for ease of processing, or the older convention of degrees, minutes and seconds.

Figure 1-6 shows a sample Terraserver map: aerial photography from the USGS, showing the location of the O'Reilly Media offices in Sebastopol, California. Many of the free aerial photos are pretty old, though: as this was taken in 1993, it just shows the apple orchard where the O'Reilly campus is now.

*Figure 1-6. Aerial photo of Gravenstein Highway*

## Hacking Terraserver

The Terraserver web site generates URLs for images that look like this:

```
GetImageArea.ashx?t=1&s=10&lon=-122.842232&lat=38.411908&w=600&h=40
```

The t parameter indicates which type of base map you want. t=1 shows you aerial maps, and t=2 shows topographical maps published by the USGS. The s parameter represents a scale—from 10 for small-scale maps at 1-meter resolution, to 19 for large-scale maps at 512-meter resolution.

Back in the day, the good people at ACME Maps provided their own, home-hacked version of a programmatic interface to Terraserver. It allowed you to post coordinates directly and get back map tiles neatly sewn together. It's still available at *http://acme.com/mapper/*.

Now the Terraserver developers have seen the light of making interfaces to programs openly available over the Web, and they provide several web service interfaces, including a Web Map Service, several WSDL interfaces, and an API for the .NET framework. Learn more about what's available at *http://www.terraserver-usa.com/webservices.aspx*. For an example of what can be quickly hacked together with the Terraserver WMS interface, check out *http://hobu.biz/* and type your address into the "geocode" box on the bottom right. This hack uses a smidgen of python to glue *http://geocoder.us/* and Terraserver together.

## Other Good Online Sources of Aerial Photographs

*http://www.terraserver.com* has been around for longer than the better-known Microsoft Terraserver. Its interface is less sophisticated, but the site has a better index of aerial photographs and topo maps from different sources around the Web. It also has false-color Landsat satellite images that cover the whole world, not just the U.S. To see what different sources of aerial photographs and other maps it has for your area, visit *http://terraserver.com/search/coordinates_search.asp*. If you're in the U.S., you can get the coordinates for most addresses from the *http://geocoder.us/* service. One thing to be aware of: if you're using decimal degrees, it's conventional for points west of Greenwich (up to the antipode, 180 degrees away) or below the equator, to be represented as a negative value. But terraserver.com needs you to put in the compass direction instead of a positive or negative value.

## HACK #5 The Road Less Traveled by in MapQuest

**The specified route may get you where you want to be, but what about that other road?**

The interstates are fast and clean, but the Blue Highways are more than a routing choice. The motto of the Blue Line fan is "There is more than one way to get there." One morning I happened to stagger into life at 9:00 A.M., fretting about the coming day. I was in Portland, Oregon, at the O'Reilly Open Source Convention and wanted to get home to Sebastopol, California. The obvious and "simple" route is 656 miles down I-5, past Sebastopol, then a swoop up and around the San Francisco Bay and up 101.

Frankly, it is one of the prettier interstate drives around, but it is still an interstate drive. My car mates were lobbying hard for the purely scenic route along Highway 101. To make things a tad more complicated, we had to pick up yet another passenger in Eugene, Oregon. How much pain and time was that Blue Highway scenery going to cost me? I needed a way to quantify the tedium of the longer journey.

Everyone uses MapQuest to prepare monolithic routes, a single routing that describes the whole trip. I wanted to split that into segments and compare the time and distance of each segment. If you have connectivity, you can create multiple views of the same journey in MapQuest, or use the same techniques in any mapping service that provides directions. As an aside, the connectivity in Lithia Park in Ashland, Oregon, is stellar. The drive from Portland to Ashland is easy, so it is convenient to stop in Ashland to download a bunch of code to play with on the rest of the trip.

## Get the Right Scale

Picking alternative routes requires that we can see them! Since this trip is so long, we can't get enough detail to compare the I-5 and coastal alternatives on one map. The map in Figure 1-7 is useless for alternate route determination! In order to compare alternatives, we need to split our journey into at least two more detailed parts.

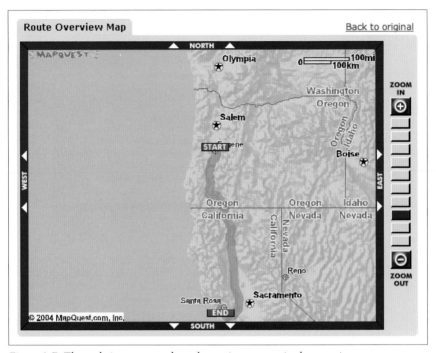

Figure 1-7. The scale is wrong, and no alternatives appear in the overview map

Here we can use the "Open in New Window" trick of most browsers. Navigate through MapQuest to a map that shows your complete trip and then right-click (Ctrl-click on the Mac) on the "+" sign of the Zoom tool that is along the right side of the map. In most browsers, this will open a right-click context menu that includes the option to open the link in a new window.

That's more like it! In Figure 1-8, we can see the coastal route, and we have enough context to know what questions we want to ask next. One key to effective use of electronic maps is to zoom in close enough to see the important details, yet far enough out so as not to get lost in the detail. It is a balancing act for each exploration.

Now zoom in so that you have two identical views of the same map. Next scroll the original, less detailed map down by clicking on the arrows on the

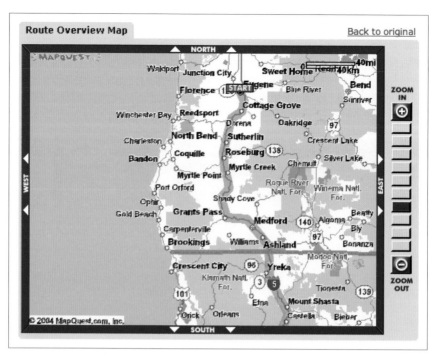

*Figure 1-8. Oregon from Eugene down*

bottom (south) side of the map. The idea is to have windows of each segment of the trip with enough overlap so you can mentally stitch the maps together (see Figure 1-9).

In this case, I need a third map to capture that important area south of Mendocino! So I repeat the process of opening a new window to get three browser windows that, between them, cover the whole trip. In this case, I right-click on the arrows pointing south to open a new window that includes Sebastopol (Figure 1-10).

## There's More Than One Way to Get There!

We want to explore the maps to get ideas about what we want to experience. This is the fun part of the process! First consider your constraints—in our case, we need to pick up Gene in Eugene—and then look at what is possible. Eugene is on I-5, so how would we get to 101? Looking at the Oregon portion of the trip, there are two seemingly reasonable ways to get to Highway 101 on the coast. We can go directly to Florence, or head down Highway 5 to Grant's Pass and then take the little red road to Crescent City in the extreme northwest corner of California.

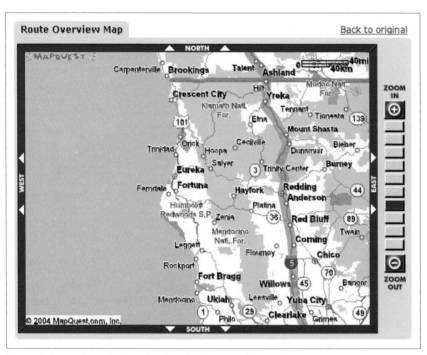

Figure 1-9. Northern California, showing the route down I-5

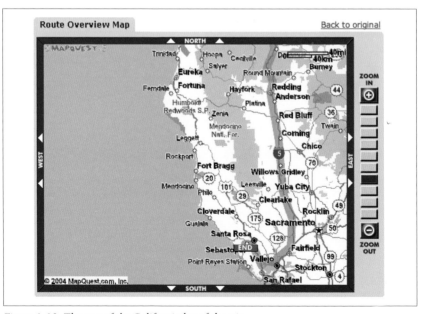

Figure 1-10. The rest of the California leg of the trip

So let's compare these two segments. Open yet another MapQuest window by right-clicking on "New Directions," and let's see what MapQuest has to offer about a trip from Eugene, Oregon, to Crescent City, California (Figure 1-11).

| Maneuvers | Distance | Maps |
| --- | --- | --- |
| **1:** Start out going West on OR-99 N/OR-126 BR W toward E 6TH AVE/OR-99 N/OR-126 BR W. | 0.1 miles | Map |
| **2:** Turn LEFT onto PEARL ST. | <0.1 miles | Map |
| **3:** Turn LEFT onto E 7TH AVE/OR-99 S/OR-126 BR E. Continue to follow OR-99 S/OR-126 BR E. | 1.8 miles | Map |
| **4:** Take the OR-99 S ramp toward I-5 S/ROSEBURG. | 0.5 miles | Map |
| **5:** Merge onto I-5 S. | 136.1 miles | Map |
| **6:** Take the US-199 exit- exit number 55- toward OR-99/GRANTS PASS/CRESCENT CITY. | 0.5 miles | Map |
| **7:** Merge onto GRANTS PASS PKWY. | 2.1 miles | Map |
| **8:** Turn SLIGHT RIGHT onto REDWOOD HWY/US-199 S. | 74.5 miles | Map |
| **9:** Turn LEFT to stay on US-199 S/REDWOOD HWY. | 2.2 miles | Map |
| **10:** Merge onto US-101 S/REDWOOD HWY. | 4.4 miles | Map |
| **11:** Turn RIGHT onto 9TH ST. | 0.1 miles | Map |
| **12:** Turn LEFT onto I ST. | <0.1 miles | Map |
| **13:** End at Crescent City CA | | Map |
| **Total Est. Time:** 3 hours, 59 minutes | **Total Est. Distance:** 223.00 miles | |

*Figure 1-11. Directions from Eugene, OR, to Crescent City, CA*

Interesting! MapQuest picks the interstate for the majority of the trip. The alternative from Eugene → Florence → Crescent City is ignored.

## Using Estimated Time

A note on Estimated Time and using trip segments to get an idea of the heinousness of a route: everyone has a different idea of how long a trip will take, and none of the estimates are "correct." In this case, MapQuest is suggesting an average speed of about 56 mph for the whole leg (223 miles divided by 239 minutes times 60 minutes per hour = 56 miles per hour). Breaking that down, it is 58 mph for the I-5 portion.

I know that I can drive faster on the interstate, but does that mean I'll get there sooner? Who knows! I have a new camera and I'm snap-happy. Maybe we'll stop every 10 miles on either route. Perhaps there is an interesting museum right off the interstate. MapQuest can't tell us what we'll do, but using their idea of travel time and average speed will help us out. See "Will the Kids Barf?" [Hack #7] to get another trick to use with MapQuest.

## Tricking MapQuest with Multiple Routes

MapQuest always gives us the "best" route, where "best" is set by their programmers. If we want to compare different routes, we need to break up our original trip into sections so that MapQuest is forced to give us our preferred route, and then we need to add up the segments.

For example, when we asked for the route from Eugene to Crescent City, MapQuest routed us through Grants Pass. The service won't give us a route from Eugene to Florence, on the coast, and then down to Crescent City. But MapQuest will give us the route from Eugene to Florence, if we ask nicely, and then the route from Florence to Crescent City.

So how do the different options compare? The times and distances for these two options are shown in Figure 1-12.

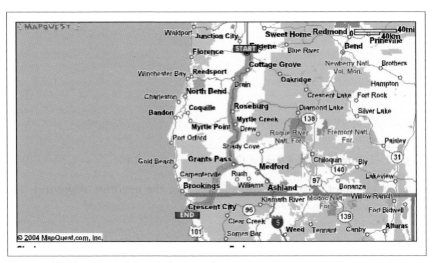

Figure 1-12. Comparing I-5 with the coastal route

The bottom line? The coast route is only 22 miles longer. No problem. It is also nearly an hour and a half longer, and the average speed is 11 mph lower. Ultimately, we elected to go straight down I-5, and we didn't get home until 4:30 A.M., so I'm just as happy that we managed to avoid driving until 6:00 A.M. both going up and coming home.

## Make Route Maps Easier to Read

Trade in complex, hard-to-read maps produced by most online route-finding services for the clean, schematic maps of driving directions made with MSN's LineDrive.

Online route-finding services have, in some ways, revolutionized the task of plotting travel routes. Rather than bothering would-be hosts to tediously—and perhaps inaccurately—describe driving directions to their location by phone or email, the savvy Internet-connected automobile driver can simply say, "I'll just look it up on *[insert your favorite online map service here]*. Forty-five minutes, you say? See you then!" The sheer practical utility of such a tool has been the main driving force behind the development of most online, consumer-oriented mapping services.

The reality, however, is a bit uglier. Often, the maps produced by online route-finding services leave a bit to be desired. Figure 1-13 shows the map generated by MSN Maps & Directions (formerly MapBlast) to depict a driving route between the White House in Washington, DC, and Times Square in New York City. Although this map illustrates the broad sweep of the ideal course across the American landscape, it omits all of the actual details you need in order to avoid getting lost between points A and B. For that, you need to rely on the textual directions printed below the map, but these directions lose the whole sense of spatial illustration embodied by maps in general, and, what's more, the fine print can be awfully hard to read in a bouncing automobile.

Two students from Stanford University, Maneesh Agrawala and Chris Stolte, noticed that hand-drawn route maps focus primarily on the names of roads, turning points, and the general direction of turns, while simplifying, distorting, or simply omitting other details, such as the length and shapes of roads and the exact angles of turns. Indeed, professional cartographers make use of these same techniques, collectively referred to as *cartographic generalization*, to make printed maps clearer and to emphasize their most important aspects. By contrast, online maps preserve every detail of a route, usually at the wrong scale, which means that shorter stretches at the beginning and end of a route often disappear relative to longer stretches in the middle. Furthermore, online map services, following the conventional "road

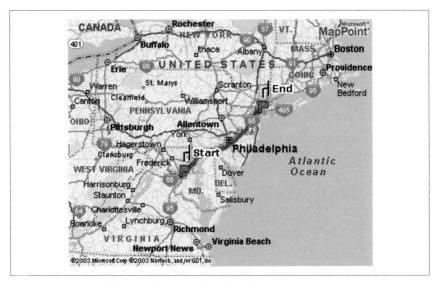

*Figure 1-13. A typical map of the route from the White House to Times Square*

atlas" paradigm, proceed to stuff the map full of all sorts of other details that might be relevant when planning a route, but that only get in the way when simply trying to follow a route. The result is worse than useless, because the driver of an automobile is often the navigator as well, and any map that requires more than a glance to extract crucial information can be a driving hazard.

## Making a LineDrive Map

To that end, Agrawala and Stolte set out to devise a means by which a computer might automatically generate route maps in the style of hand-drawn driving directions, for maximum readability. The result is LineDrive, a service that they developed in conjunction with MapBlast, one of the Web's first consumer-oriented route-finding services. Vicinity, the company that made MapBlast, was subsequently bought by Microsoft and turned into MSN Maps & Directions, but the site still lives at *http://www.mapblast.com/*, and it still offers the LineDrive routing service for both North America and most of Europe.

Creating your own LineDrive driving directions map is simple. Just visit *http://www.mapblast.com/*, and click "Directions" on the navigation bar. Enter an origin and a destination in the form, and be sure to select "LineDrive" as the map style in the radio-button group on the right. Then click "Get Directions," and you're done! Figure 1-14 shows LineDrive's version of the same route from Washington, DC, to New York City.

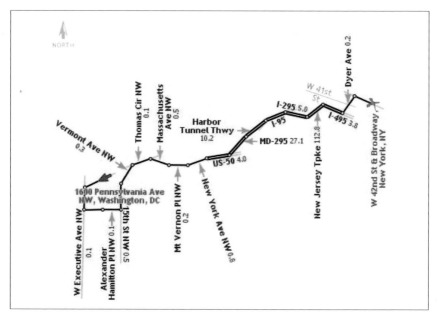

*Figure 1-14. A LineDrive map of the route from the White House to Times Square*

In contrast to the conventional map shown in Figure 1-13, the LineDrive map compresses the 112 miles of the trip spent on the New Jersey Turnpike down to the same length on the map as the 4 miles along US 50 in Maryland or half a mile down 15th St NW in Washington, because all a driver needs to do along each of those road segments is to stay on the road! At the same time, each and every turn required to get from one place to the other is recorded on the LineDrive map, from going round the block with the flow of traffic when leaving the White House, to taking I-295 across the Delaware Memorial Bridge to bypass Philadelphia. The presence of Philadelphia as a thing to bypass is omitted by this map, as are many other irrelevant geographic facts, for the precise reason that you don't actually need to know that Philadelphia exists in order to travel from Washington to New York—you just need to follow the directions on the map. With the elimination of border controls under the Schengen Treaty, European driving maps don't even show national borders—just distances, turns, and route numbers!

## How LineDrive Works

LineDrive uses the same route-finding backend as MSN's standard route maps. However, instead of rendering the usual set of cartographic layers and highlighting the route on top, LineDrive starts by collecting all of the geographic data representing the route and then subjects it to a sequence of generalization techniques, as mentioned earlier. First, it simplifies the shape of each road segment as much as possible, taking care not to add false road intersections, remove actual ones, or distort turn angles too much.

Next, the simplified road segments are laid out on the map, through an iterative search process called *simulated annealing*. At each step, a road segment is randomly selected and its length is scaled by a random amount, or its orientation on the map is adjusted in a random direction, and then the whole route is scaled down to fit within the target viewing window. The new layout is then tested by a scoring function that evaluates the visual acceptability of the layout and assigns a heuristic value representing its "goodness" in terms of several perceptual criteria, such as minimum and relative road lengths, general accuracy of turn directions, and preservation of the original route orientation.

The new layout is then either accepted or rejected based on its relationship to the score of the previous layout and a *temperature* value, which decreases with each iteration. This "temperature" value allows the iterative process to occasionally accept a worse layout early on in the process, which avoids the "local minimum" problem that plagues other kinds of search algorithms, wherein a search settles on a mediocre solution early on and ignores the presence of better overall solutions. As the temperature settles, the search algorithm homes in on progressively better layouts until the final one is selected. The way in which the simulated annealing algorithm slowly "cools off" the map layout parameters is analogous to a metallurgical process called *annealing*, in which internal stresses are removed from a piece of worked metal by heating it and cooling it slowly, to encourage crystalline structures to reform.

A similar process is then used to place the road labels on the map, select additional contextual clues (i.e., cross streets and landmarks) to display, and to adjust the decorations used to identify turning points, road types, and so on. The finished map is then delivered to the user. If you're curious about the specific details of the algorithms used by LineDrive, we strongly encourage you to read Agrawala and Stolte's original paper, entitled "Rendering Effective Route Maps: Improving Usability Through Generalization," which you can find on the Web at *http://graphics.stanford.edu/papers/routemaps/*.

## HACK #7 Will the Kids Barf?

Compare road distance with straight-line distance to create an index of nausea.

As I'm blessed with a sweet but stomach-challenged boy, I'm often looking for routes that are less likely to trigger his "I need to throw up; where's your hat, Daddy?" reflex. The quickest way to trigger that impulse is to go too fast on a curvy road.

I originally developed my own little index of road curviness that I called the "quasi-fractal dimension" of a route. As it turns out, the professionals already have their own measure for this property, and our technical reviewer Edward Mac Gillavry set me straight.

> In spatial analysis, the *network deviousness* is the discrepancy between the lengths of the actual routes in a network and the straight-line distance between the places linked up. For any pair of places on the network it can be measured by the detour index. The detour index is a measure of how directly movement may be made on a network. It is calculated as the ratio of the shortest actual route distance between a given pair of nodes and the direct, straight-line or geodesic distance between the same two points.

> ```
> Detour index = shortest distance on a network between two points /
> direct distance * 100.
> ```

> The minimum value of the index is 100, representing a direct route with no detour. High ratios suggest a weakly connected network but may also reflect the indirectness or deviousness of the individual routes connecting the nodes. The detour index is also referred to as the index of circuity or as the route factor.

So if the straight-line distance between two points is 20 miles, but the road distance is 25 miles, we get a detour index of 25/20 * 100 = 125. The road isn't curvy, honey; it's just devious.

> The Transport Geography web page at *http://www.geog. umontreal.ca/Geotrans/* defines the detour index as direct distance / road distance. According to this definition, the closer it is to 1, the more efficient the route. I prefer Edward's definition on purely esthetic grounds. When I'm calculating something called the "network deviousness" I want *larger* numbers to mean "more devious!"

## Getting the Data

If you know the street address of your starting and ending points, you can use Geocoder.us to get the latitude and longitude, as explained in "Geocode a U.S. Street Address" [Hack #79] Otherwise, try the "How Far Is It" service at *http://www.indo.com/distance*. You can enter two cities, and "How Far Is It" will return the great-circle distance, as shown in Figure 1-15 (the *great-circle* distance is the spherical trigonometry version of straight-line distance).

If you know the latitude and longitude for each end of your trip, this can be plugged into the "How Far Is It" site. "How Far? How Fast? Geo-Enabling Your Spreadsheet" [Hack #11] shows you how to calculate straight-line, "as the crow flies" distance with a "geoenabled" Excel spreadsheet.

## BALI & INDONESIA ON THE NET

Distance between **Sebastopol, California, United States** and **Portland, Oregon, United States**, as the crow flies:

**493 miles (793 km)** (428 nautical miles)

Initial heading from Sebastopol to Portland:
**north (1.0 degrees)**
Initial heading from Portland to Sebastopol:
**south (181.1 degrees)**

See airfares between these two cities in Expedia or Travelocity.
See hotels in these two cities in Expedia or Travelocity.
See driving distance and directions (courtesy MapBlast).

### Sebastopol, California, US

County: **Sonoma County**
Location: **38:23:57N 122:49:33W**
Population (1990): **7004**
Elevation: **78 feet**

### Portland, Oregon, US

County: **Multnomah County**
Location: **45:32:18N 122:39:23W**
Population (1990): **437319**
Elevation: **50 feet**

*Figure 1-15. How far is it?*

Once we have a good direct distance, we can use the techniques described in "The Road Less Traveled by in MapQuest" [Hack #5] to get the estimated time for each segment of the journey, and the "what if the crow has to ride in the back of the van with a hat in his lap" distance. Putting it all together, we get the summary table shown in Figure 1-16.

| Trip Name | Direct Distance | Mapquest Distance (transport Distance) | Detour Index | Mapquest time in minutes | Mapquest MPH estimate |
|---|---|---|---|---|---|
| San Jose to Santa Cruz | 18.4 | 26.92 | 146.30 | 36 | 45 |
| Sacramento to Bakersfield | 260 | 292.45 | 112.48 | 268 | 65 |
| Cloverdale to Little River | 53 | 63.95 | 120.66 | 93 | 41 |
| Willits to Fort Bragg | 24 | 35.35 | 147.29 | 52 | 41 |

*Figure 1-16. Quantifying physical discomfort*

Figure 1-16 shows some trips that are common in my life. The *direct distance* is the straight-line distance between the two points. *Mapquest Distance* is the distance reported by MapQuest. *Detour Index* is calculated as shown earlier. The table also shows the estimated time and the average speed for this trip.

Here we can compare the straight-line distance with the routed distance. Highway 17 over the Santa Cruz Mountains is notoriously curvy. The other numbers yield few surprises. Sacramento to Bakersfield was a ringer! That trip is almost straight down Interstate 5. It has the lowest Detour Index of any of the sample routes.

An awful example of curvy driving is the route from Willits, on highway 101, to Fort Bragg. That section has a 147% distance premium, compared with the straight-line distance.

Assuming these relationships hold true, I can assert that a Detour Index greater than 120 is almost guaranteed to make you sick! I wish to avoid the curvy routes, but some folks like curves, so another use of this technique is to find the curviest possible roads for motorcycle fun. Just remember: for some people, motion sickness is no laughing matter. For the rest of us, it is.

### More Information

"How Far Is It" is the creation of Darrell Kindred. It uses the *geod* program from the PROJ system discussed in much more detail in "Calculate the Distance Between Points on the Earth's Surface" **[Hack #27]**. Darrell also has a Perl program to calculate great-circle distances on the earth. His use of *geod* and his sample code are available at *http://www.indo.com/distance/distance-details.html*. Another useful page is his discussion of using *xearth* to create views of the earth, at *http://www.indo.com/distance/earth-image-info.html*.

### H A C K    Publish Maps of Your Photos on the Web

**#8**    Plotting the photos from your latest trip on a map used to be a chore, until now.

Many of us enjoy sharing experiences and photographs from our travels with our family, friends, and colleagues. A map can provide a better sense of a trip or experience by showing how the images are related both to each other and to the world. Yet it has always been a challenge to share our photographs on an actual map.

93 Photo Street is a novel photo-mapping tool from Transmutable that helps you to tell your story with maps. It makes publishing maps with photographs about as easy as publishing to your blog, by offering a completely menu-driven, drag-and-drop user interface for building and publishing maps

to the Web, as well as a programmer API for those users who want to do more.

As of this writing, it can be downloaded for Windows 2000, XP, or Mac OS X 10.3 or higher for free under a Creative Commons license. You can find it on Transmutable's web site at *http://transmutable.com/93PhotoStreet/*.

The process of using 93 Photo Street is straightforward. The first step is to find a map to use as a backdrop. 93 Photo Street supports two kinds of maps. It supports detailed, although plain, street maps of the United States (using maps provided online by the U.S. Census "Tiger" project), and it supports using images, allowing you to pick any image file and use it as a backdrop.

In this case, I'd like to share my pictures from a vacation in Hawaii. Using a search engine, I can find a number of excellent base maps of Hawaii:

```
http://clusty.com/search?query=hawaii+map&v%3Aproject=clusty-images
http://images.google.com/images?q=hawaii+map
```

By saving one of the maps from these searches to my computer, I can import it into 93 Photo Street using the "Map → Import Map Image" menu item.

Next I open up my collection of photographs and drag my favorite photos from that vacation into 93 Photo Street. The photos then end up in a tray at the bottom of the screen. Although there is a File menu option to load photographs, I prefer to just drag and drop. Figure 1-17 shows a screenshot of this process.

The next step is to set the placement of these photographs. First, you place "pins" on the map indicating where photographs can go, and then you drag each photograph from your tray onto the map. The final result is a collection of photographs pinned to the map at the chosen locations.

The last step is to publish your map. There are two ways to do this. You can just ask 93 Photo Street to build the site locally. Select the menu option "Build → Build with Velocity Templates" to choose from one of the default presentation templates. Figure 1-18 illustrates the process of selecting a presentation template. 93 Photo Street will make an *index.html* file, associate the images and the map together, and put them all on disk under *Documents and Settings\93 Photo Street\Sites*.

Alternatively, you can ask 93 Photo Street to publish the site to your blog automatically. Your blog must support TypePad or MoveableType interfaces, and you will need to have a valid Atom password (often displayed in the personal preferences area of your blog). You may also wish to go to *http://www.typekey.com/* to give yourself a globally valid TypeKey, simply for completeness.

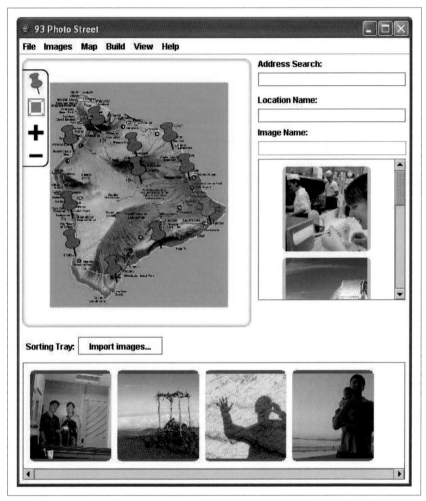

*Figure 1-17. Adding photographs to 93 Photo Street*

As you can see, it would be hard to make an interface that was easier to use than 93 Photo Street—but wait, there's more! There is an open API for developers to extend the service, including:

- A simple XML photo-map file format. Use this to translate from GPS formats into Photo Map files or to translate Photo Map files into one of the emerging RDF vocabularies discussed elsewhere in this book.

- A templating system based on the quite excellent Apache Velocity project. Use this to define new presentation styles and templates to dress up your photo-map presentations.

- An Atom publisher for simple blogging of maps.

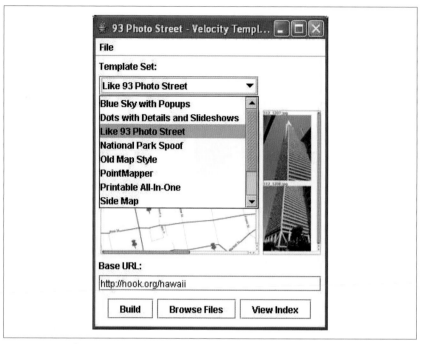

*Figure 1-18. Selecting a presentation template in 93 Photo Street*

- A publisher SDK for doing things like integrating 93 Photo Street with third-party systems.

- A built-in U.S. Census TIGER/Line map download manager and renderer.

- An open source TIGER/Line parser. If you're interested in rendering your own maps of the United States, this is one potential starting point, although there are many others, some of which are covered elsewhere in this book.

- An open source Atom network stack. This could be a starting point for adding publishing support for other blogging services.

The templating system and the publisher SDK are particularly useful together in incorporating map sources that are not freely available for commercial providers. This opens the possibility of merging photo maps with satellite weather images or USGS earthquake maps or any of the other map services on the Web.

Overall the product makes publishing photo maps to the Web "easy enough" that more people may actually do it. Technically an individual could cobble together her own solution, but the ease, convenience, and openness of this tool make it an appealing choice. See "Georeference Digital

Photos" [Hack #10] and "Share Geo-Photos on the Web" [Hack #96] for other methods to add photos to a map.

—*Anselm Hook*

## HACK #9  Track the Friendly Skies with Sherlock

Use the Macintosh OS X search tool or a web browser to track flights.

It always seems to happen: you need to rush to the airport to pick someone up, but you don't even know if the flight is on time. You can go to *http://www.flytecomm.com/cgi-bin/trackflight* to use the "Track a Flight" service and locate flights in progress and show their position on a map. You can also access this service from Sherlock, the Macintosh search tool.

This doesn't supplant the simple act of calling the airline to get the flight status, but it is pretty cool to know that when they say the flight has been delayed two hours, what they really mean is that the flight has yet to leave the ground

Sherlock lives in the *Applications* folder. When the main screen appears, click on the "Flights" icon in the toolbar. You are then offered a search bar, shown in Figure 1-19, where you can search for the flight by airline, flight number, departure, or arrival city.

When flights are "en route," and the data is available, there is a check mark in the chart column.

The interface is seductive, the choices opulent, and the temptation is to spend far too much time exploring the nooks and crannies of the modern air transportation system. Please note this service covers only flights to the United States when they are within U.S. airspace.

### How Does This Work?

This tool searches the flight status information provided by *http://www.flytecomm.com*, which offers "Real-time flight intelligence solutions" that include flight and weather details. An interesting note is that FlyteTrax uses two different map projections: the Lambert Conformal conic projection and the Mercator projection. Both projections are conformal, meaning that lines of constant direction are shown as straight lines (over small areas). This is an important characteristic for flight mapping. The Lambert Conformal conic projection corresponds to the map image of the United States and Canada with which most people are familiar.

Unfortunately, flights do not follow lines of constant direction. The shortest distance between two points is the great circle, which would be depicted as a

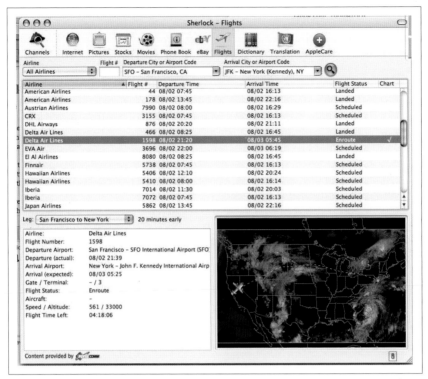

*Figure 1-19. Delta Flight 1598 en route to New York*

curved line on a conformal projection. Because of great-circle routing, an aircraft flying long distances would not be on a straight line for most of the flight. The problem with this representation is that people could be easily misled into thinking that a particular flight they are following has a problem because it is not on the "straight line" between two cities.

*—With projections help from Edward Mac Gillavry*

HACK #10 **Georeference Digital Photos**

Have you ever looked at someone's photo album and wondered where the photos were taken? Using your GPS and digital camera, you can figure out just that, and it's easier than you think.

If your digital camera allows you to set the time, you can use tracklogs from your GPS to add latitude and longitude information to your digital pictures. Since every photo you take with your digital camera contains the time the photo was taken, your computer can use the time a picture was taken to look through the GPS tracklog to find out where you were when you took the photo. As long as the GPS is on and storing tracklogs while you take your photos, you can link the photos to their respective locations.

To start out, just like two robbers about to heist a bank, the digital camera and the GPS need to have their internal watches synced. Since the GPS picks up the current time whenever it locks onto a satellite, it will always be dead-on. The only problem with this method is that if you change time zones, you have to resync your camera's time, since the camera isn't quite as clever. Next, make sure your GPS has a lock on your location, and carry it with you as you photograph. See "Don't Lose Your Tracklogs!" **[Hack #58]** for tricks on saving your tracklogs.

The GPS will record your tracks, giving you a record of your movement that can be later downloaded to your computer. Using the common bit of information, the timestamp, various programs can match up the photos to their respective locations. For the PC, there is Microsoft's free World Wide Media Exchange (WWMX, available at *http://www.wwmx.org/*), RoboPhoto ($35, at *http://robophoto.com*), RoboGeo ($22.95, at *http://robogeo.com*), Quakemap ($10, at *http://www.earthquakemap.com/*), and TopoFusion ($40, at *http://www.topofusion.com/*). You can also use purely web-based services such as GeoSnapper.com or Thingster.com.

Alternatively, and for less than $950 USD, you can get a camera that will do the linking for you. These cameras have built-in GPS receivers or have GPS attachments. As of this writing, you can purchase the older 1.4 mp Kodak DSC 260 series, the costly Nikon DSLR cameras (D1x, D1h, Pro 14n, and Pro SLR/n), or the impressive new Ricoh "Caplio Pro G3" with GPS card. With the cost of GPS chipsets decreasing, more cameras, and even camera phones, are getting into the act. Already the Japanese AU camera phone can take georeferenced images, and other Japanese camera manufacturers are adding GPS to attract new patrons. U.S. camera phones are enabled to find your location in case you call 911, so I hope next year's smart phones will start including this feature.

## How Does This Work?

Digital cameras save extra information about each picture within the image file in an *EXIF header*. This includes the date and time when the image was taken. You can explore this information with the free program Exifer for Windows, available at *http://www.friedemann-schmidt.com/software/exifer/*. RoboPhoto, discussed earlier, also allows you to view EXIF headers. If you are willing to use Perl, you can install the Image::EXIF module from CPAN (from a terminal window in Linux or OS X; typing **sudo perl -MCPAN -e install Image::EXIF<enter>** will probably do it). This bit of Perl will dump the EXIF headers from images that you specify:

```
#!/usr/bin/perl

use Image::EXIF;
use Data::Dumper;

foreach my $file (@ARGV) {
    my $exif = new Image::EXIF($file);
    print "file: $file " . Dumper($exif->get_all_info($file));
}
```

Call it with one or more image names on the command line:

```
$ exifdump.pl DSC_3044.JPG
```

For my images, this returns 60 lines of technical information about the image, including details on the exposure and metering modes. Among this embarrassment of Metadata riches is the Image Generated field. This tells us when the picture was taken:

```
'Image Generated' => '2004:09:01 19:27:35',
```

In database terms, "Time is the universal foreign key." Assuming we are tracking the same thing, we can use the time that things occurred to synchronize information from different devices. So our GPS tracklog has our location timestamped at regular intervals, and our camera timestamps our images. All of the programs that do GPS timestamp image interpolation either pick the closest point, based on time, or they pick the two closest points and return the point where you would have been if you were going a constant velocity between the two points.

The simplest way is to do a straight interpolation. Assume you have these track points (exaggerated in order to make the math easier):

```
38.4        -122.1      2004-09-20 12:20:43
38.5        -122.2      2004-09-20 12:23:53
```

And you have a picture that was taken at 12:21:47 (let's assume your photos are timestamped in UCT to match the GPS tracklog). Where were you when you took that picture? There are two techniques that give reasonable answers for small distances. The easiest way is to calculate the time difference between your two points (190 seconds) and the percentage of that represented by your target time. 12:21:47 is 64 seconds past the start time of 12:20:43, or 64/190 = 34% of the way. Then the (approximate!) point at 12:21:47 is:

```
Lat = 38.4 + .34 * (38.5 - 38.4)
Long = -122.1 + .34 * (-122.2 - (-122.1) )
```

This technique has the advantage of being simple, and for this distance, it is reasonably correct. In "How Far? How Fast? Geo-Enabling Your Spreadsheet" [Hack #11] we explore a sample Geo-enabled Excel spreadsheet. Within that workbook, the sheet titled Georeference provides a simple form that lets you georeference one image at a time. It also demonstrates another approach to interpolating based on time by calculating the bearing between the two reference points and then calculating the lat/long at a given distance from the initial point along that bearing.

## Aim and Composition

Now that you know how to get your photos GPS enabled, what are you going to do? You could use it for scientific purposes like a botanist friend of mine, or take a photo of your storefront to help customers find your business. Real estate, hiking, sailing, driving, and skydiving are all other areas that geo-imagery would apply to. On the other hand, you might want to get personal, with a point-of-view camera mounted on your head. Another aim might be to give "visual" waypoints to a meet-up point for a private party. With the advent of camera phone technology, geo-images may be adopted by protest leaders to organize massive flash mobs. Imagine your cell phone company offering services to show highly rated geo-images near your current location, along with directions to the spot. As any photographer knows, an image can hold a thousand words, and three coordinates: latitude, longitude, and altitude.

## Conclusion

Whatever your purpose, georeferenced images can provide important details to a photo and interesting tidbits to your audience. Sharing said photos could help map the world, as others may have things to say about the places you photograph. My hope is that camera companies like Ricoh will flourish as a result of photographers publishing their results, and wireless providers will start offering this simple service. Once you get the hang of taking geo-images, share your photos for a better view of the world and the people who make it so impressive.

*—Tom Longson*

## HACK #11    How Far? How Fast? Geo-Enabling Your Spreadsheet

How far did I go? How long did it take to get there? Calculating speeds and distances by working with geodata in Excel

Wouldn't it be great if you could ask what-if questions of your geodata? Questions like "How far did I go on that trip?" or "What was my average speed from Tuscan to Tucumcari compared with the leg from Tehachapi to

Tonopah?" A geo-enabled spreadsheet is your willing companion on this journey.

It once happened that I was trapped in a hotel with no connectivity. I had GRASS [Hack #69] on one laptop and lots of tracklogs of our wanderings through Disneyland on another laptop, and no way to get tracklogs from one computer to another. Fortunately, I had a copy of Microsoft Excel on the same computer as the tracklogs. And when all you have is a spreadsheet, then everything looks like rows and columns. As it turns out, tracklogs and waypoints naturally fit into the spreadsheet metaphor. I was able to cobble together an ugly spreadsheet analyzing our trip, but I longed for something more, dare I say, elegant?

I later learned that Jeff Laake of the National Oceanic and Atmospheric Administration faced similar challenges in his work studying marine mammals. He created a set of Visual Basic for Applications macros to add basic geospatial functions to Excel. With Jeff's library, you can turn your spreadsheet into a monster geospatial data processing engine.

I've incorporated Jeff's *geofunc.xla*, with minor extensions, into a sample spreadsheet with examples of the use of most of the functions. Download it at *http://www.mappinghacks.com/data/spreadsheet/geodata_sample.xls*. The original library, and more explanations of the functions, lives at: *http://nmml.afsc.noaa.gov/Software/ExcelGeoFunctions/excelgeofunc.htm*.

The first worksheet, labeled **Function Examples**, demonstrates the use of the library functions. My favorite function is posDist( ), or *position distance*, which is shown in Figure 1-20. This returns the distance in nautical miles between two locations.

| posdist( ) - Calculate the distance between two points, expressed in nautical miles | | |
| --- | --- | --- |
| useage: posdist(lat1, long1, lat2, long2) | | |
| To convert to statute miles: posdist(lat1, long1, lat2, long2) * 1.15 (approximately) | | |
| One degree of longitude on the equator | 60.00 | nautical miles |
| One degree of longitude on the equator | 69.05 | statute miles |
| One degree of latitude on the equator | 69.05 | statute miles |
| One degree of longitude at 45 North | 48.82 | statute miles |
| One degree of latitude at 45 North | 69.05 | statute miles |
| One degree of longitude at 89 North | 1.21 | statute miles |
| One degree of latitude at 89 North | 69.05 | statute miles |

*Figure 1-20. The posDist function in Excel*

One degree of latitude or longitude at the equator should return 60 nautical miles. To convert nautical miles to statute (normal) miles, multiply nautical miles * 1.15. (To be more accurate, multiply by 6076.11549/5280, but 1.15 is less then 0.1% off.) There are about 69 statute miles per degree of latitude or longitude at the equator. The distance between degrees of latitude remain constant as you move east or west. So moving from 89 degrees to 90 degrees

HACK
#11

How Far? How Fast? Geo-Enabling Your Spreadsheet

latitude is 69 miles. But since the lines of longitude converge at the poles, the distance between degrees of longitude decreases as you move toward the poles. The screen capture of the **Function Examples** worksheet shown in Figure 1-20 demonstrates this.

The posDist( ) function suggests possibilities! Excel has useful tools for importing and processing text files, which I use to prepare tracklogs and waypoints for further analysis. In the worksheet titled **small track**, you'll find a sample of a small, cleaned-up tracklog:

| Lat. | Long. | New Seg. Flag | Dist. (yards) | Cum. Distance |
|---|---|---|---|---|
| 33.81252778 | -117.9163028 | [1]; | | |
| 33.81255 | -117.9163444 | [0]; | 15 | 15 |
| 33.81256944 | -117.9161944 | [0]; | 46 | 61 |
| 33.80877222 | -117.9145861 | [1]; | 0 | 61 |
| 33.80862222 | -117.91465 | [0]; | 58 | 119 |

## Importing GPS Waypoints into Your Spreadsheet

GPS waypoints and tracklogs come in a number of common formats. I used the *Garnix* program **[Hack #49]** to load my tracklogs and waypoints from my GPS. Here are the raw waypoints as returned from Garnix for the various Disneyland train stations:

```
33° 48' 35.98" -117° 55'  7.72" 41.0 WGS84 DTRNGATE    "" [wpt_dot N];
33° 48' 39.50" -117° 55' 18.55" 39.0 WGS84 DTRNNEWORL  "" [wpt_dot N];
33° 48' 53.51" -117° 55'  6.29" 54.0 WGS84 DTRNTOONTN  "" [wpt_dot N];
33° 48' 45.45" -117° 54' 56.76" 55.0 WGS84 DTRNTOMORW  "" [wpt_dot N];
```

Each line starts with the latitude in degrees, minutes, and seconds, followed by the longitude, altitude, datum, waypoint name, and some other irrelevant information. When I am on a trip, I like to pick a letter and start all of my waypoints with that letter. This makes it easier later to find and manage my waypoints. For this trip, the letter D seemed appropriate. So these are "Disney TRaiN" waypoints for the Gate, New Orleans Station, Toontown, and Tomorrowland.

Importing the waypoints into Excel is easy. Open the file, which causes the Text Import Wizard to launch. Select "Delimited with Space." The Text Import Wizard interprets the data as fixed width, and the defaults work just fine. However, this is a rather particular use of the word "fine," one in which the data is all present but is nearly completely unusable! The waypoints are in the sheet named **Disney Waypoints** within *geodata_sample.xls*, as shown in Figure 1-21.

Degrees, minutes, and seconds of both latitude and longitude are split into their own cells, and there are degree, minute, and second marks that cause

How Far? How Fast? Geo-Enabling Your Spreadsheet

HACK
#11

| 33° | 48' | 44.88" | -117° | 55' | 19.43" | 33 | WGS84 | DCANOE |
|---|---|---|---|---|---|---|---|---|
| 33° | 48' | 46.32" | -117° | 55' | 8.22" | 35 | WGS84 | DCASTLE |
| 33° | 48' | 47.37" | -117° | 55' | 19.80" | 36 | WGS84 | DGRAVEYARD |
| 33° | 48' | 26.49" | -117° | 55' | 15.47" | 29 | WGS84 | DGRIZZLY |
| 33° | 48' | 41.34" | -117° | 55' | 12.74" | 34 | WGS84 | DJUNGLECRS |
| 33° | 48' | 34.15" | -117° | 55' | 13.11" | 39 | WGS84 | DLUNCHSAT |
| 33° | 48' | 42.39" | -117° | 55' | 19.00" | 34 | WGS84 | DMANSION |
| 33° | 48' | 35.20" | -117° | 55' | 28.55" | 45 | WGS84 | DMONODTOWN |
| 33° | 48' | 40.60" | -117° | 55' | 15.56" | 40 | WGS84 | DPIRATES |
| 33° | 48' | 39.74" | -117° | 55' | 16.80" | 37 | WGS84 | DPIRATEXIT |
| 33° | 48' | 44.87" | -117° | 55' | 21.59" | 39 | WGS84 | DPOOH |
| 33° | 48' | 42.30" | -117° | 55' | 17.63" | 39 | WGS84 | DRAFT |
| 33° | 48' | 42.62" | -117° | 55' | 1.16" | 40 | WGS84 | DROCKBALL |
| 33° | 48' | 44.01" | -117° | 55' | 11.23" | 36 | WGS84 | DSHOOTING |
| 33° | 48' | 44.69" | -117° | 55' | 15.35" | 32 | WGS84 | DSLGHUCKFN |
| 33° | 48' | 34.48" | -117° | 55' | 8.12" | 31 | WGS84 | DSNGATE |
| 33° | 48' | 47.48" | -117° | 55' | 18.61" | 48 | WGS84 | DSPENCTREE |
| 33° | 48' | 43.39" | -117° | 55' | 19.59" | 39 | WGS84 | DSPLASH |
| 33° | 48' | 32.74" | -117° | 55' | 8.28" | 32 | WGS84 | DSTAR |
| 33° | 48' | 43.56" | -117° | 55' | 4.40" | 35 | WGS84 | DSTARTOURS |
| 33° | 48' | 42.52" | -117° | 55' | 10.66" | 37 | WGS84 | DTIKI |
| 33° | 48' | 21.51" | -117° | 55' | 10.84" | 36 | WGS84 | DTORTILLA |
| 33° | 48' | 41.22" | -117° | 55' | 14.26" | 38 | WGS84 | DTREEHOUSE |
| 33° | 48' | 39.71" | -117° | 55' | 18.59" | 46 | WGS84 | DTRNFRONTR |
| 33° | 48' | 35.98" | -117° | 55' | 7.72" | 41 | WGS84 | DTRNGATE |
| 33° | 48' | 39.50" | -117° | 55' | 18.55" | 39 | WGS84 | DTRNNEWORL |
| 33° | 48' | 45.45" | -117° | 54' | 56.76" | 55 | WGS84 | DTRNTOMORW |
| 33° | 48' | 53.51" | -117° | 55' | 6.29" | 54 | WGS84 | DTRNTOONTN |
| 33° | 48' | 25.43" | -117° | 55' | 17.71" | 6 | WGS84 | DZIPLINE |

*Figure 1-21. Raw waypoints, before processing with SplitMinSecToDeg() function*

Excel to treat the numbers as strings. We need to rid ourselves of these vexatious non-numbers and then convert the degree-minute-second (DMS) notation to decimal degree form [Hack #25].

In the absence of Perl, whose technology for manipulating this sort of data is so advanced as to be indistinguishable from magic, we need a bit of Excel function hackery. I've added a copy of the Deg/Min/Sec columns for both latitude and longitude next to the original import and then inserted a set of nested functions to strip the degree, minute, and second marks and cause Excel to treat the values as numbers.

The SplitMinSecToDeg( ) function takes care of stripping off the special character. The minute (') and second (") characters are easy, but I find it easiest to copy the degree symbol and paste it into the formula. Note that I've created named ranges for each column to make this easier to read:

```
=LEFT(lat_deg,FIND("°",lat_deg)-1)+0
=LEFT(lat_min,FIND("'",lat_min)-1)+0
=LEFT(lat_sec,FIND("""",lat_sec)-1)+0
=LEFT(long_deg,FIND("°",long_deg)-1)+0
=LEFT(long_min,FIND("'",long_min)-1)+0
=LEFT(long_sec,FIND("""",long_sec)-1)+0
```

The *geofunc.vba* package includes the function SplitMinSecToDeg( ), which takes degrees, minutes, and seconds that are split into columns and combines them to create decimal degrees. The results are stored in columns A and B:

```
=SplitMinSecToDeg(P11,Q11,R11)
```

HACK
#11

How Far? How Fast? Geo-Enabling Your Spreadsheet

There is a trick to `SplitMinSecToDeg( )` that comes up when you try to do the equivalent function manually. You should be able to convert from DMS to decimal degrees with this formula:

```
=deg_clean+min_clean/60+sec_clean/3600
```

But wait! That shows the original longitude as being −117° 55' 8.44", while the formula then comes up with −116.08099°. What is going on? This is a consequence of using positive and negative numbers to depict latitudes north and south of the equator and longitudes east and west of the prime meridian. The problem is that Disneyland is not at negative 117 degrees of longitude; it is at positive 117 degrees west of the prime meridian. There are many ways to abuse math in Excel, but here is one fix:

```
=SIGN(S11)*(ABS(S11)+T11/60+U11/3600)
```

After this correction, we have the right latitude and longitude! The correction should also be done on latitude, except that because Disneyland is in California, I need not worry about the Southern Hemisphere in this particular example.

I like to develop spreadsheets one step at a time, rather then creating one monstrous, impossible-to-understand formula. Since there is also something to be said for the all-in-one approach, here are the same formulas rolled together at once, which are stored in the sheet labeled **Disney Waypoints-all in one**:

```
=SplitMinSecToDeg(LEFT(D11,FIND("¬Ø",D11)-1)+0,LEFT(E11,FIND("'",E11)-
1)+0,LEFT(F11,FIND("""",F11)-1)+0)
=SplitMinSecToDeg(LEFT(G11,FIND("¬Ø",G11)-1)+0,LEFT(H11,FIND("'",H11)-
1)+0,LEFT(I11,FIND("""",I11)-1)+0)
```

This sheet also uses the `posDist( )` function to calculate the distance between successive waypoints. This sets the stage for "Create a Distance Grid in Excel" **[Hack #12]**.

## Importing GPS Tracklogs into Your Spreadsheet

Importing a GPS tracklog follows the same model as importing the waypoints. A Garnix format tracklog looks like this:

```
33° 48' 30.58" -117° 54' 48.88" 35.0 WGS84 01:21:45-2004/03/14 [1];
33° 48' 30.89" -117° 54' 53.44" 35.0 WGS84 01:23:26-2004/03/14 [1];
33° 48' 30.89" -117° 54' 54.60" 30.0 WGS84 01:23:40-2004/03/14 [0];
33° 48' 30.89" -117° 54' 54.60" 39.0 WGS84 01:23:46-2004/03/14 [0];
```

Each line contains latitude, longitude, altitude (if supported by your GPS unit), datum, timestamp, and new-segment flag. The new-segment flag is set when that track point represents the start of a new segment— either because the GPS was turned off, or too much time has passed. In "Turn Your Tracklogs into ESRI Shapefiles" **[Hack #71]**, we'll see what happens when you treat

How Far? How Fast? Geo-Enabling Your Spreadsheet

HACK
#11

all track points as part of the same line. The center cannot hold, and random straight lines blur the clarity of the trip!

The sheet **Disney Track** shows a sample tracklog that has been imported into Excel and processed to a clean display of lat/long (Figure 1-22).

| | A | B | C | D | E | F | G |
|---|---|---|---|---|---|---|---|
| 1 | Sample Track Log from Disneyland, Showing distance and speed | | | | | | |
| 2 | | | | | | | |
| 3 | Feet in a nautical mile | | | 6076 | | | |
| 4 | Lat Dec | Long Dec | New Segmen | Dist-feet | Cum Dist-ft | elapsed time | speed mph |
| 5 | 33.8125278 | -117.9163 | [1]; | | | | |
| 6 | 33.81255 | -117.91634 | [0]; | 15 | 15 | 23 | 0.44 |
| 7 | 33.8125694 | -117.91619 | [0]; | 46 | 61 | 154 | 0.20 |
| 8 | 33.8087722 | -117.91459 | [1]; | 0 | 61 | 0 | 0.00 |
| 9 | 33.8086222 | -117.91465 | [0]; | 58 | 119 | 5 | 7.91 |
| 10 | 33.8085806 | -117.91474 | [0]; | 30 | 149 | 9 | 2.29 |
| 11 | 33.8086 | -117.91512 | [0]; | 117 | 266 | 27 | 2.96 |
| 12 | 33.8086861 | -117.91519 | [0]; | 37 | 303 | 13 | 1.93 |
| 13 | 33.8086861 | -117.91519 | [0]; | 0 | 303 | 2 | 0.00 |
| 14 | 33.8089222 | -117.91519 | [0]; | 86 | 389 | 18 | 3.26 |
| 15 | 33.8091806 | -117.91521 | [0]; | 94 | 484 | 22 | 2.93 |
| 16 | 33.8092667 | -117.91523 | [0]; | 32 | 516 | 18 | 1.22 |
| 17 | 33.8092028 | -117.91536 | [0]; | 45 | 561 | 99 | 0.31 |
| 18 | 33.8091806 | -117.91572 | [0]; | 111 | 672 | 44 | 1.71 |

geodata_sample2.xls

Figure 1-22. Track log with distance, time, and speed

## Calculating Cumulative Distance and Speed

With latitude, longitude, and the new-segment flag in columns A, B, and C, we can calculate distance. We must first look at the new-segment flag. If this is a new segment, indicated by [1];, then we should skip calculating the distance. Otherwise the distance in feet is given with the posDist( ) function multiplied by the number of feet in a nautical mile.

```
=IF(C6="[0];", posdist(A5,B5,A6,B6)*$D$3,0)
```

And the cumulative trip distance:

```
=SUM($D$5:D6)
```

The Garnix datestamp is well suited for Excel. You can subtract the timestamp of the previous track point from the current timestamp to get the elapsed time. To make it more interesting, you need to check the new-segment flag and ignore the time between segments (unless you are calculating a time stopped). You also need to multiply the elapsed time by the number of seconds in one day in order to get the elapsed time in seconds. Assuming the following timestamps are in cells P5 and P6, then:

```
3/13/2004   5:44:30 AM
3/13/2004   5:44:53 AM
```

```
=IF(C6="[0];", (P6-P5)*86400,0)
```

which equals 23 seconds elapsed time.

In those 23 seconds we went 15 feet. So to calculate the speed in miles per hour, we need to convert 23 seconds to hours, and 15 feet to miles.

This checks that the elapsed time is not zero and then converts feet in D6 to miles, and seconds in cell F6 to hours:

```
=IF(F6<>0,(D6/5280)/(F6/3600),0)
```

So 15 feet in 23 seconds is about 0.44 mph. Way down in row 104, we went 43.43 mph. Quite the thrill park! (Hey, when riding with a five and six year old, 43.43 mph is pretty darn fast!)

## Geo-Enabling Other Spreadsheets

Once you have played with the sample sheet, you'll want to install the macros as a plug-in, so you can use the geospatial functions in your own spreadsheets. You can get a copy of the VBA functions from *http://www.mappinghacks.com/data/spreadsheet/geofunc.xla*.

Download the file and place it in Excel, select Tools → Add-ins, and click Select. Navigate to your download directory, select the file *geofunc.xla*, and click Open. Congratulations, you now have a geo-enabled spreadsheet!

The original version of the *geofunc.xla* library lives at *http://nmml.afsc.noaa.gov/Software/ExcelGeoFunctions/excelgeofunc.htm*. There is also more information about the original functions in the library at that site.

Loading geodata into a spreadsheet extends the great tools we are accustomed to in numerical analysis to the problems of acquisition, management, and presentation of information with a geospatial component.

## HACK #12 Create a Distance Grid in Excel

Create tables showing the distance and bearing between pairs of points, using a simple add-in library for Excel.

Creak out of the car, road blurred eyes, accelerator stiffened joints, then wander dazed to the large grid that shows you at "Forgotten Rest Area #17" and the distance to anywhere you'd want to be. The joy of gas station city-distance grids! Look down the left column for "Where I am" and across to find "The promised end of the trip," and read the measure of your pain. Now all the fun and excitement can be yours again, in the comfort of your very own home!

Start by downloading *http://www.mappinghacks.com/data/spreadsheet/sample.xls*, as described in "How Far? How Fast? Geo-Enabling Your Spreadsheet" [Hack #11]. The sheet labeled **train grid**, shown in Figure 1-23, depicts a sample distance grid for a set of waypoints of train stations at

Disneyland. The grid shows the straight-line distance between any two points in yards. Look down column B and locate the Main Gate in cell B24, then move across to column G and read the distance from the Main Gate to the Tomorrowland train station, which is 445 yards.

| 19 Distance in Yards between selected attractions | | | | | | | |
|---|---|---|---|---|---|---|---|
| 21 | Disney Downtown | Tomorrowland Mono | Main Gate Trn | New Orleans Square Trn | Tomorrowland Trn | Toon Town Trn | Pirates of the Carribean |
| 22 Disney Downtown | 0 | 911 | 583 | 316 | 957 | 878 | 408 |
| 23 Tomorrowland Mono | 911 | 0 | 427 | 596 | 68 | 320 | 504 |
| 24 Main Gate Trn | 583 | 427 | 0 | 325 | 445 | 593 | 268 |
| 25 New Orleans Square Trn | 316 | 596 | 325 | 0 | 644 | 584 | 92 |
| 26 Tomorrowland Trn | 957 | 68 | 445 | 644 | 0 | 383 | 552 |
| 27 Toon Town Trn | 878 | 320 | 593 | 584 | 383 | 0 | 507 |
| 28 Pirates of the Carribean | 408 | 504 | 268 | 92 | 552 | 507 | 0 |

*Figure 1-23. The distance between train stations at Disneyland*

The distance grid represents the "as the crow flies" distance. Calculating road distance requires routing algorithms and databases that are beyond the scope of this hack.

The **train grid** sheet also includes a bearing grid to show your straight-line course from point to point. Remember your mnemonics of direction: Never (North, 0 degrees) Eat (East, 90 degrees) Smelly (South, 180 degrees) Worms (West, 270 degrees) (or "Never Eat Sour Watermelons").

Take a look at the next worksheet, labeled **equator grid**, as shown in Figure 1-24. This is the same basic table, but this one shows the distance and direction within one degree of the equator and the prime meridian: from (0°, 0°) to (1°N, 0°), (1°S, 0°), (0°, 1°W), (0°, 1°E), (1°N, 1°E), and (1°S, 1°W). This sheet displays distances in statute miles, as opposed to yards. The conversion factor is set in the cell labeled **conversion_factor** (C14).

| 19 Distance in Miles | | | | | | | |
|---|---|---|---|---|---|---|---|
| 21 | 0,0 Origin | 1 deg N | 1 deg S | 1 deg W | 1 deg E | 1 deg NW | 1 deg SW |
| 22 0,0 Origin | 0 | 69 | 69 | 69 | 69 | 98 | 98 |
| 23 1 deg N | 69 | 0 | 138 | 98 | 98 | 69 | 154 |
| 24 1 deg S | 69 | 138 | 0 | 98 | 98 | 154 | 69 |
| 25 1 deg W | 69 | 98 | 98 | 0 | 138 | 154 | 69 |
| 26 1 deg NW | 69 | 98 | 98 | 138 | 0 | 69 | 154 |
| 27 1 deg NW | 98 | 69 | 154 | 154 | 69 | 0 | 195 |
| 28 1 deg SW | 98 | 154 | 69 | 69 | 154 | 195 | 0 |
| 29 | | | | | | | |
| 30 | | | | | | | |
| 31 | | | | | | | |
| 32 Bearing/Course from location in Column B to location in row 21 | | | | | | | |
| 33 | 0,0 Origin | 1 deg N | 1 deg S | 1 deg W | 1 deg E | 1 deg NW | 1 deg SW |
| 34 0,0 Origin | n/a | 0 | 180 | 270 | 90 | 45 | 225 |
| 35 1 deg N | 180 | n/a | 180 | 225 | 135 | 90 | 207 |
| 36 1 deg S | 0 | 0 | n/a | 315 | 45 | 27 | 270 |
| 37 1 deg W | 90 | 45 | 135 | n/a | 90 | 63 | 180 |
| 38 1 deg E | 270 | 315 | 225 | 270 | n/a | 0 | 243 |
| 39 1 deg NW | 225 | 270 | 207 | 243 | 180 | n/a | 225 |
| 40 1 deg SW | 45 | 27 | 90 | 0 | 63 | 45 | n/a |

*Figure 1-24. Distance and bearings near the equator and the prime meridian*

The point of this test sheet is to do a simple sanity check on the data. How far is it from (0°, 0°) to (1°N, 0°)? It should be 69 statute miles. And what is the bearing? Due North, or 0 degrees. And from (1°S, 1°W) to (0°, 0°) should be approximately the Pythagorean distance of $\sqrt{(69^2 + 69^2)}$, or 97.58 statute miles.

## Making Your Own Grid

While a distance grid of the train stations of Disneyland may be fascinating to Disneyphiles, you are likely more interested in the stories intrinsic to your own personal landmarks and waypoints. The sheets named **Your_Data_Here**, **Your Distance Grid**, and **Your Bearing Grid** are for you! They start out showing yet more waypoints from Disneyland because, after all, everyone should have the tools to determine that it is about 152 yards from the Enchanted Tiki Room to the entrance to Pirates of the Caribbean, but you can paste up to 96 points into **Your_Data_Here** and automatically get a distance grid in **Your Distance Grid** and a bearing grid in **Your Bearing Grid**.

The limit of 96 points is purely arbitrary. Feel free to examine the structure of the sheets and extend them to infinity and beyond. To use these sheets, paste your own point name, latitude, and longitude into **Your_Data_Here** (Figure 1-25) starting at B5:D5 and going as far as B100:D100.

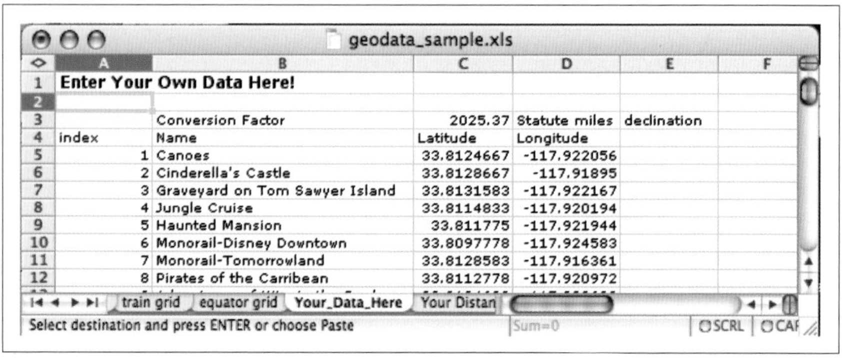

Figure 1-25. Enter your points into this sheet

The posDist( ) function returns distance in nautical miles. To convert these to statute miles, you need to enter the conversion factor of (approximately) 1.15 into cell C3. To convert to yards, enter 2025 (which is the current default), and for feet, 6075. You can also enter a compass declination in cell F3. This number will be added to the values in the Bearing table to correct for the difference between true and magnetic north.

## Let's Go Diving

One potential use of this grid might be to enter the waypoints for underwater diving sites in your area of interest. Chuck Tribolet has a nice page of GPS resources for diving Monterey Bay, California at *http://www.garlic.com/~triblet/swell/gps.html*, including a list of dive locations with latitudes and longitudes. As a diver, I might find it useful to have distance and bearing grids on hand for these locations—that way, after a dive, I can quickly consider distance in my decision of where to dive next. Figure 1-26 shows an example distance grid for this use case. Similarly, Figure 1-27 shows a sample bearing grid.

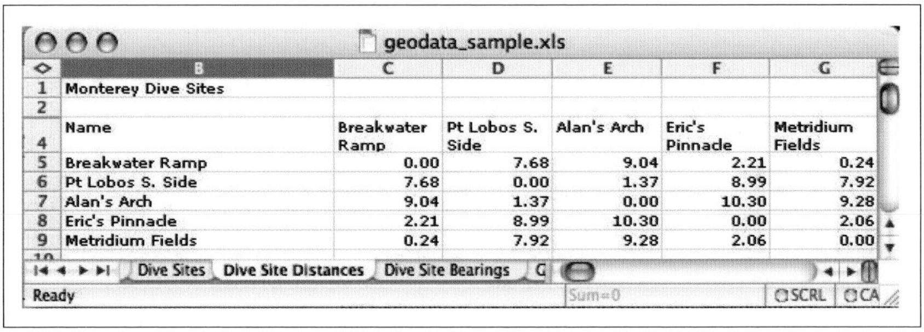


| | B | C | D | E | F | G |
|---|---|---|---|---|---|---|
| 1 | Monterey Dive Sites | | | | | |
| 2 | | | | | | |
| 4 | Name | Breakwater Ramp | Pt Lobos S. Side | Alan's Arch | Eric's Pinnacle | Metridium Fields |
| 5 | Breakwater Ramp | 0.00 | 7.68 | 9.04 | 2.21 | 0.24 |
| 6 | Pt Lobos S. Side | 7.68 | 0.00 | 1.37 | 8.99 | 7.92 |
| 7 | Alan's Arch | 9.04 | 1.37 | 0.00 | 10.30 | 9.28 |
| 8 | Eric's Pinnacle | 2.21 | 8.99 | 10.30 | 0.00 | 2.06 |
| 9 | Metridium Fields | 0.24 | 7.92 | 9.28 | 2.06 | 0.00 |

*Figure 1-26. Distance grid of selected Monterey area dive sites*

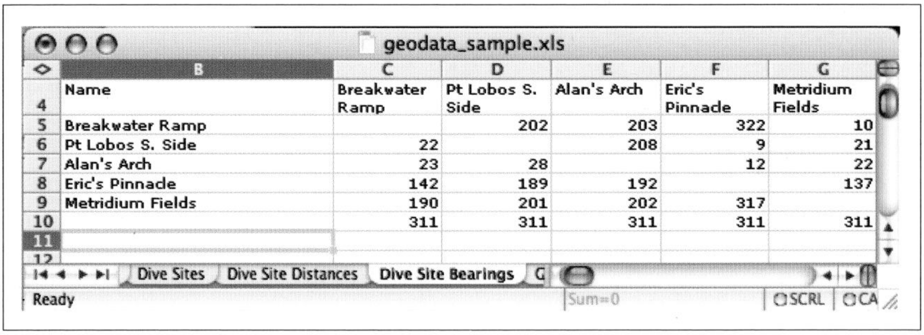


| | B | C | D | E | F | G |
|---|---|---|---|---|---|---|
| 4 | Name | Breakwater Ramp | Pt Lobos S. Side | Alan's Arch | Eric's Pinnacle | Metridium Fields |
| 5 | Breakwater Ramp | | 202 | 203 | 322 | 10 |
| 6 | Pt Lobos S. Side | 22 | | 208 | 9 | 21 |
| 7 | Alan's Arch | 23 | 28 | | 12 | 22 |
| 8 | Eric's Pinnacle | 142 | 189 | 192 | | 137 |
| 9 | Metridium Fields | 190 | 201 | 202 | 317 | |
| 10 | | 311 | 311 | 311 | 311 | 311 |
| 11 | | | | | | |

*Figure 1-27. Bearings between selected Monterey area dive sites*

While these tables do provide the literal distance and bearing between points, they don't consider actual barriers to navigation, such as the absence of roads or the presence of cliffs. You might think that you could get home to the Breakwater Ramp in Monterey Harbor from a dive at the south end of Point Lobos by steering a course of 22 degrees. Unfortunately for you, there are a number of miles of nonaqueous dirt between these points. Happy diving, and watch out for rocky points!

## HACK #13 Add Maps to Excel Spreadsheets with MapPoint

If you have both Microsoft Excel and Microsoft MapPoint, you can add maps to your spreadsheets with a few clicks.

A lot of people manage address lists and other address-based data in Microsoft Excel, but while Excel provides all kinds of graphing capabilities, it doesn't know much about maps. If you add Microsoft MapPoint to your system (another $250, admittedly), you can show your Excel data on a map quite easily.

As the November 2004 election is coming up as I'm writing this, I've been doing a lot of work with voter registration rolls. One of my spreadsheets, actually an export from Access, is a list of street addresses and party affiliations, as shown in Figure 1-28.

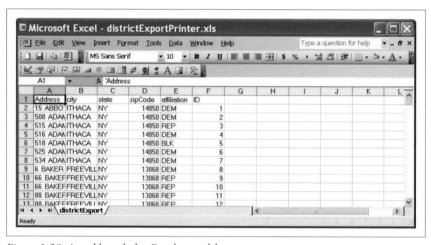

*Figure 1-28. An address-laden Excel spreadsheet*

Because MapPoint 2004 is installed on the same computer, Excel shows an extra toolbar button to the left of the font-choice drop-down box. Clicking on that button inserts a MapPoint object on the spreadsheet and also starts up the Link Data Wizard, shown in Figure 1-29. (If you have more than one area of data on the spreadsheet, select the part you want to map before clicking the button.)

MapPoint will make an educated guess about data types based on headers in the document, and you can use the drop-down boxes to correct it if it's wrong. MapPoint will accept a variety of geographic data types, varying by country. For the United States, it accepts any three of address, city, county, state, country/region, ZIP Code, three-digit ZIP Code, census tract, metropolitan area,

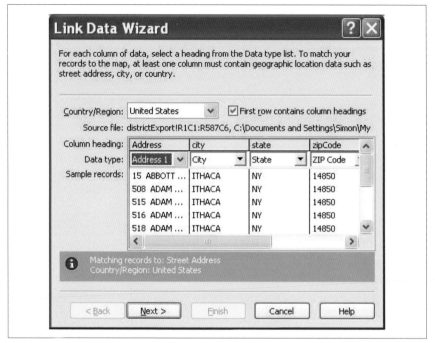

Figure 1-29. The Link Data Wizard's initial interpretation of the address data

latitude, and longitude. Once you've chosen the correct data types, MapPoint will ask to identify a primary key, as shown in Figure 1-30.

If all you plan to plot is the one area currently being examined, you don't really need a primary key. If, however, you're combining multiple sets of data, such as customer addresses and customer spending amounts, you'll want something like a customer ID number to act as your primary key connecting the data.

When you click Finish, you may not be quite done, however. MapPoint will do what it can to interpret your data, but it may not know everything, especially if roads have been built or names changed over time. If that happens, you'll see something like Figure 1-31, asking for help.

In this case, I had to skip a few records, but there were a few times where the problem related to abbreviations that didn't match up, and it was easy to pick a choice that matched. Once you finish this process, you'll be rewarded with a pushpin map like that shown in Figure 1-32.

The pushpins are sort of useful, but they don't reflect all the data that was included, notably party affiliation. Fortunately, MapPoint lets you do more than just add pushpins. The toolbar now shows some additional icons. Just above the zoom adjuster is a button for "Data Mapping Wizard," showing a

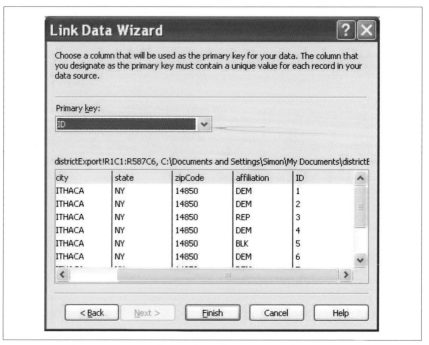

Figure 1-30. Choosing a primary key in the Link Data Wizard

Figure 1-31. Helping MapPoint find an address

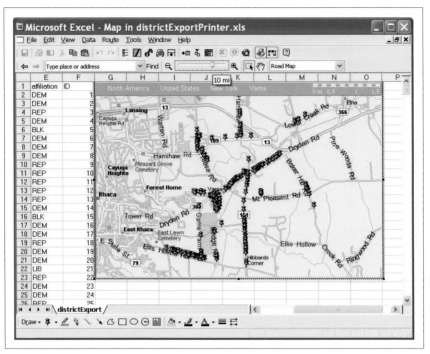

*Figure 1-32. The initial map generated by MapPoint*

set of green fields. Clicking on that brings up many more options, shown in Figure 1-33.

There are lots of different choices here. Shaded areas are great if you're aggregating one kind of data, while pie and column charts can show details for a given area. The pushpin map already in use is an option, but for showing party affiliation, the Multiple Symbol choice is likely the best option. If you click the Multiple Symbol button and choose Next, you'll be asked where to get the data that chooses the symbol, as shown in Figure 1-34.

MapPoint offers lots of choices for getting data. MapPoint itself includes demographic data for the United States down to the Census Tract level, and it will let you import or link data from other sources, such as spreadsheets or databases. In this case, the data needed, party affiliation, is already in the data associated with the map, so just clicking the Next button works fine. The Data Mapping Wizard then asks what data to use and what level to show them at, as shown in Figure 1-35.

In this case, affiliation is the key, and street address is an appropriate level for displaying it. MapPoint can only display up to eight different choices here, and voters in this area have nine different political affiliations, so MapPoint displays the warning shown in Figure 1-36.

*Figure 1-33. MapPoint presentation styles*

*Figure 1-34. Choosing the source for the data behind the symbol*

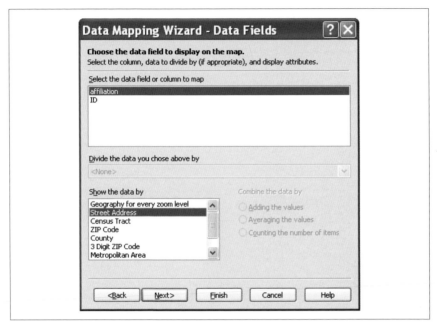

*Figure 1-35. Choosing the particular data behind the symbol*

*Figure 1-36. An error, as MapPoint has a limited number of multiple symbols supported at once*

Unfortunately MapPoint doesn't let me choose to keep the two Working Families voters in the list, but 2 out of 841 voters and 1 of 542 addresses is probably okay for this demonstration. The next screen, shown in Figure 1-37, lets you choose the symbols to use on the map to represent different affiliations.

The drop-down boxes let you choose symbols and colors, and you can also change the labels used. In this case, because many of these houses are right next to each other, I chose the smallest symbol available and used color to distinguish party.

When I'm done, I have a completed map, shown in Figure 1-38.

The house-by-house presentation looks better when you zoom in further, as shown in Figure 1-39.

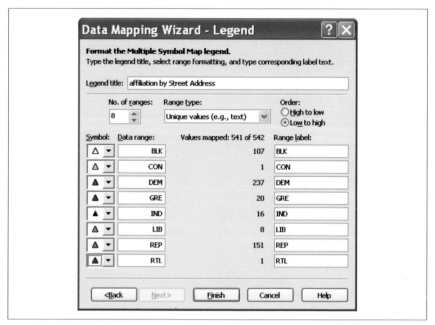

Figure 1-37. Choosing symbols for the data

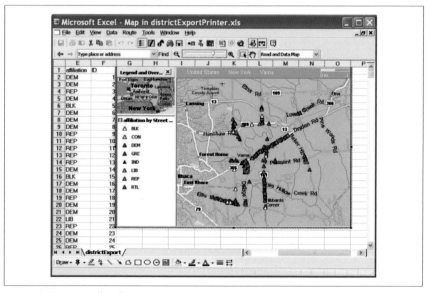

Figure 1-38. A completed map

As long as you open the spreadsheet on a (Windows) computer running MapPoint, you'll be able to zoom around the map, change the icons, link new data, and more. You can also open the map in the full MapPoint pro-

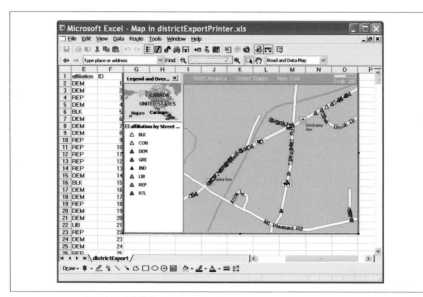

Figure 1-39. A completed map, zoomed in for higher detail

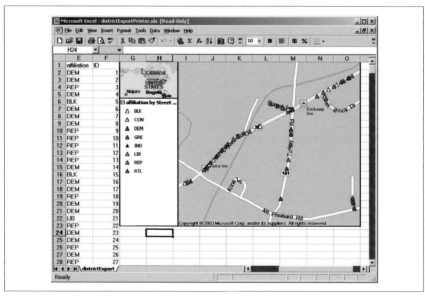

Figure 1-40. Opening the spreadsheet in a copy of Excel on a computer without MapPoint installed

gram if you like and save a copy out for other work. However, if you open the spreadsheet in a copy of Excel without access to MapPoint, you'll still have a picture, as shown in Figure 1-40, but with no interactivity.

—Simon St.Laurent

# CHAPTER TWO

# Mapping Your Neighborhood
## Hacks 14–21

*Stand in the place where you live*
*(Now face north)*
*Think about direction*
*Wonder why you haven't before*
—REM, "Stand"

Beyond the scope of our own lives, we find the past, present, and future of the places we inhabit and the other people that inhabit them. Maps offer the chance to tell new narratives about familiar places. From health code violations to campaign contributions, from demographic models to elevation models, our immediate environment is awash in geographic detail, waiting to be shown on a map and its stories told to the world. In this chapter, we explore the dimensions that "Mapping Your Neighborhood" can take on.

### HACK #14  Make Free Maps of the United States Online

The U.S. Census Bureau's TIGER Map Server isn't fast or fancy, but the maps it makes are free and entirely hackable.

Although the maps made by MapQuest, map24.com, and other commercial mapping services are nice looking, fast, and reasonably effective, their use is severely limited by their licensing terms. What's more, you can't easily map your own data on top of the digital maps these services produce. However, in the United States, we enjoy a remarkable plethora of public-domain geographic data, much of it in the form of the Census Bureau's TIGER/Line data set, which the Bureau uses as the basis for the *TIGER Map Server*, a free web-based mapping service, covering the entire United States. You can browse their maps manually, or programmatically generate unencumbered, public-domain maps through their service for your own purposes. We'll look at both of these uses of the TIGER Map Server.

The TIGER/Line data set, which the Census Bureau updates annually, contains vector data about streets, highways, waterways, political boundaries, parks, metropolitan areas, and more, all collected as part of the Bureau's mission to enumerate the population of the United States to ensure the fair apportionment of federal congressional districts. Blessedly, the Bureau publishes the raw TIGER/Line data for free, all several dozen gigabytes of it, already collected at taxpayer expense, on the Census Bureau web site for anyone to download and make use of. In doing so, they set a shining example to the rest of the world of what it means for government to provide and support a national geographic data infrastructure.

## Browsing the Web Interface

The TIGER Map Server Browser lives at *http://tiger.census.gov/cgi-bin/ mapsurfer*. With no other options supplied to it, the Browser loads a map of Washington, DC, by default. Included are the usual web-based map interface buttons for panning and zooming, and, on the upper right, a set of radio buttons selects the action that's taken when the map is clicked on. While the zoom in, zoom out, and recenter commands are pretty standard for an online map service, that's where the similarity to other such services ends. The next two commands allow you to put a marker of your choice anywhere on the map with a click and then download a GIF image of the map you've created. Further down the right side, you can select precisely which features you want displayed on the map. Let's see you do that, MapQuest! Figure 2-1 shows the basic web interface to the TIGER Map Server.

That's just for starters, though. If you scroll down the page, you'll see form elements that allow you to request a map centered at a particular latitude and longitude, or one based on a search for a particular location or ZIP code. Additionally, there's an interface that allows you to select a particular graphical marker from a list—a ball, pin, or other icon—and place it on the map, either by selecting the appropriate radio button at the top and then clicking on the map, or by entering latitude and longitude coordinates. There's also a form field that allows you to add a label to the marker. Figure 2-2 shows a TIGER Map Server map of downtown Washington, DC, with a blue pin identifying the Lincoln Memorial.

Now, this may not be the finest map you've ever seen, from the standpoint of cartographic design, but it already scores over many other mapping services in two important respects. First, you can do whatever the heck you want with it—these maps are in the public domain. Second, you can plot your own stuff on it. These maps can help tell *your* story.

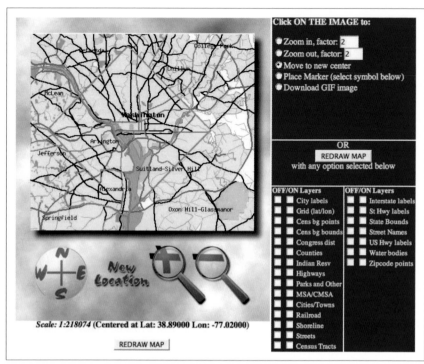

Figure 2-1. The basic web interface to the TIGER Map Server

Figure 2-2. The Lincoln Memorial, as shown by the TIGER Map Server

## Mapping a List of Points

It gets even better. What if you want to display more than one marker on the map at a time? See the text field labeled *Marker URL*? It turns out that if you make a list of waypoints, you can put it on the Web somewhere and use the Marker URL field to tell the TIGER server to fetch it and map it. Here are the first six entries in a list of geysers in Yellowstone National Park, taken from the GNIS [Hack #85] and rendered in the TIGER Map Server's ad hoc Marker URL "format":

```
# Excerpted list of GNIS geyser features from Park County, WY
-110.4347,44.6203:red5:Black Dragons Cauldron
-110.6833,44.7000:red5:Fearless
-110.8167,44.7167:red5:Jet
-110.7528,44.6833:red5:Monument
-110.4333,44.6247:red5:Mud Volcano
-110.7067,44.7056:red5:Porkchop
```

The first line is a comment, as indicated by the hash mark (#) at the beginning of the line. For the remainder of the file, each line is a waypoint, with three colon-separated fields. The first field is *longitude, latitude*, separated by a comma. The next field is the marker type, which we'll get into more detail about in a minute. Finally, the last field is just the name of the waypoint. This particular file contains a total of nine entries. If we post the file at *http://mappinghacks.com/data/geysers.txt*, we can put that URL into the TIGER Map Server web form, set the latitude and longitude to something appropriate, and hit "Redraw Map." The result looks something like Figure 2-3.

 Remember that many, if not most, online mapping applications expect longitudes west of the prime meridian and latitudes south of the equator to be negative values. Also, don't forget that the Marker URL format puts longitude and not latitude first—because longitude is actually the *x*-coordinate.

## Hacking the Hack

The best part about the TIGER mapping service is that you don't have to use their web interface to make maps; you can automatically generate them by crafting a custom TIGER Map Server URL that specifies the details for the map you want. The map image, which is rendered in a simple sinusoidal projection, is then returned in GIF format. The request URL takes the following basic form:

```
http://tiger.census.gov/cgi-bin/mapgen?param=value&param=value&…
```

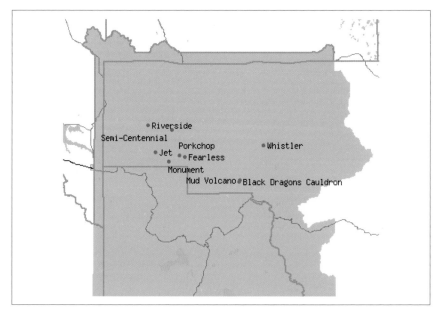

*Figure 2-3. Some Yellowstone geysers, mapped via Marker URL*

The types of parameters available for direct request are in essence the same as those used in the web interface. For example, this URL will generate a nice, simple map of Lower Manhattan in New York City, which is shown in Figure 2-4:

```
http://tiger.census.gov/cgi-bin/mapgen?lat=40.739&lon=-73.99&wid=0.06&ht=0.
08&iwd=480&iht=640
```

The lat and lon parameters specify latitude and longitude, respectively, in decimal degrees. The wid and ht parameters specify the width and height of the maps in decimal degrees, while iwd and iht parameters specify the width and height of the desired map in pixels. So the map in Figure 2-4 should come out 480 pixels wide by 640 pixels high. If the aspect ratio specified by iwd and iht is different from that specified by wid and ht—and remember that, in the continental U.S., a degree of latitude is about 1.5 times longer than a degree of longitude—then the map coverage may come out a little differently than requested, but that shouldn't ordinarily present a problem.

The TIGER Map Service supports a whole lot of other tweakable parameters. Table 2-1 lists some of them. See the TIGER Map Service instructions page at *http://tiger.census.gov/instruct.html* for exact details.

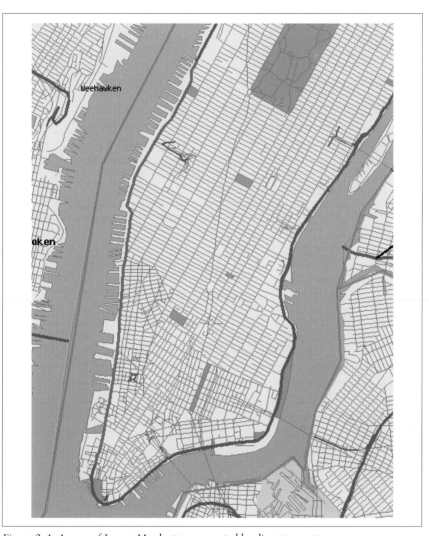

*Figure 2-4. A map of Lower Manhattan generated by direct request*

*Table 2-1. Some useful TIGER Map Server direct request parameters*

| Parameter | Description | Notes |
|---|---|---|
| lat | Latitude of the map center in decimal degrees | Values for the continental U.S. range from around −125 to −67. |
| lon | Longitude of map center in decimal degrees | Values for the continental U.S. range from around 24 to 49 |
| wid | Width of map coverage in decimal degrees | 1° of longitude = ~55 mi at 24° N, ~40 mi at 49° N |

*Table 2-1. Some useful TIGER Map Server direct request parameters (continued)*

| Parameter | Description | Notes |
|---|---|---|
| ht | Height of map coverage in decimal degrees | 1° of latitude = ~60 mi or 100 km |
| iwd | Width of map image in pixels | Defaults to 512 pixels |
| iht | Height of map image in pixels | Defaults to 256 pixels |
| legend | Show map legend instead | If set to on, the map legend is returned in place of the map. |
| mark | Map marker locations, in format *lon,lat,marker;lon,lat,marker;...* | See *http://tiger.census.gov/instruct.html* for a complete list of marker types |
| murl | URL to a list of map markers to display | See the previous section, "Mapping a List of Points," for details about the marker file format |
| on | Explicitly include certain map features | See *http://tiger.census.gov/instruct.html* for a complete list of map features |
| off | Explicitly exclude certain map features | See *http://tiger.census.gov/instruct.html* for a complete list of map features |

## Mapping Census Data

But, wait, there's more! The TIGER Map Service also offers a means for generating simple maps of the Census Bureau's demographic data, in the form of *thematic statistical maps*. From the web interface, you can select a demographic variable, such as median income or population density, and a level of granularity to display that variable at, from statewide all the way down to a few city blocks. For example, Figure 2-5 shows the percentage of renter-occupied housing units in San Francisco at the Census block group level.

These maps were the precursor to the *American FactFinder*, which is a web site hosted by the Census Bureau at *http://factfinder.census.gov/*. The American FactFinder offers an unbelievable wealth of demographic information about the United States, as well as a whole suite of interactive maps based on the TIGER/Line data. We absolutely recommend devoting some spare time to exploring their site, especially if you have a particular interest in mapping demographics. However, we elected to devote an entire hack to the older TIGER Map Service because, for our purposes, the maps it produces are a lot easier to hack than those of its somewhat flashier successor.

## The Pros and Cons of the TIGER Map Service

Before you get excited and start building mission-critical applications based on the TIGER Map Server, there are a few things to consider about these maps. First, they are made from map data dating back to 1997, so the maps

*Figure 2-5. A thematic map of renter-occupied housing units in San Francisco*

may be somewhat outdated. Second, the TIGER Map Server is sometimes inexplicably slow or doesn't respond at all. Third, the service comes with no warranty at all. To quote from their instructions page:

> The Census Bureau has continued to maintain the TIGER Mapping Service because it has proved useful to the general public. It was never intended to be a robust all-purpose mapping system to meet the needs of high-volume government, business or other organizations' applications... *Any application that uses our mapping service does so at the user's risk.* The Census Bureau plans continue to try to maintain the TIGER Mapping Service for at least the near future at its current level, *but we accept no obligation to provide special support (or timely repair) of the system* so that it can meet some other governmental, commercial or organizational mission.

On the other hand, as we've seen, these maps are pretty hackable—and they're free!

## HACK #15 Zoom Right In on Your Neighborhood
### And thereby give new meaning to the term "ICBM coordinates."

I like pretty pictures that move. Sadly, most maps are stable and don't move. Biologists have a special word for systems that are stable and no longer move, and that word is "dead." Let's get the defibrillation paddles out and put some life into our maps. "Put a Map on It: Mapping Arbitrary Locations with Online Services" [Hack #1] describes how to find a location using

MapQuest, and it will get you a map. But where is the place described by that map? My daughter wanted to know where New Orleans is. She went to MapQuest and searched. And MapQuest presented exactly what she asked for. Try it! The city appears on the banks of Lake Ponchartrain. But where the heck is that? Molly zoomed out, and out, and out, until Texas appeared. "Ah, I see now where it is."

To save her from the effort of ever again clicking "zoom out" three times in rapid succession, I wrote a little script called *boomzoom.cgi*. I called it this, because the first person who saw it said that it looked like the earth as viewed from a rapidly approaching ICBM. Now, as it turns out, my friend wasn't all that far off: Cartographers actually have a term for this kind of instant zoom-in orientation, which they call *ballistic navigation*. But somehow "boomzoom" was the name that stuck for me.

You can run it at *http://www.mappinghacks.com/cgi-bin/boomzoom.cgi*. Enter the latitude, longitude, and text to mark your center point, and then select "Make zoomy thing," as shown in Figure 2-6.

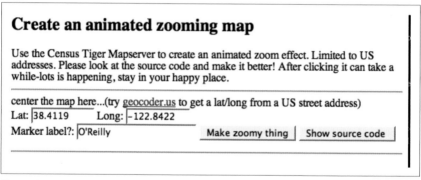

Figure 2-6. Boomzoom's initial screen

The Boomzoom program proceeds to fetch about 10 images from the TIGER Map Server **[Hack #14]**, and then stitches them together to make an animated GIF. Each image is shown for just long enough to give an idea of what it is showing, before giving way to the next. Figure 2-7 shows the first image of a "boomzoom" on the O'Reilly campus in Sebastopol, CA.

## The Code

You can run the same basic code on your desktop, as well. Since the TIGER data allows us to grab map images directly, we can automate the process with this bit of Perl, which we'll just call *zoom.pl*:

```
#!/usr/bin/perl
use LWP::Simple;
```

*Figure 2-7. Can you find O'Reilly?*

```
my $lat = 38.4034; # center on this latitude
my $long = -122.8185; # center on this longitude.

my $mlat = 0;   # put a marker on this latitude
my $mlong = 0; # put a marker on this longitude.
my $mlabel = 'your_label'; # label for your marker. No whitespace!

my $wid = 20; # starting width in degrees
my $minwid = .001; # ending width in degrees
my $cnt = 0;
while ($wid >= $minwid) {
        $wid = $wid * .3;
        my $url = "http://tiger.census.gov/cgi-bin/mapper/map.
gif?lat=$lat&lon=$long&wid=$wid&ht=$wid&iht=359&iwd=422&&on=majroads&mlat=$m
lat&mlon=$mlong&msym=redpin&mlabel=$mlabel&conf=mapnew.con";
        $cnt = sprintf("%03.0f", $cnt);
        open OUT, ">zoom_$cnt.gif";
        print OUT get $url;
        close OUT;
        $cnt++;
}
```

Obviously, most of the hard work in this script is done by the enormous URL that we send to the TIGER Map Service to generate the link. For more information on how to tweak this URL to your satisfaction, check out "Make Free Maps of the United States Online" [Hack #14].

### Running the Code

Enter your own U.S. location in place of the latitude and longitude lines, place the script in an empty directory, and run it with **perl zoom.pl**. The script fetches a series of maps centered on that location, narrowing the scale of the map by 10% each time. The maps will be stored as numbered image files, with the names *file_000.gif* through *file_008.gif* or so.

Next, we'll animate this collection of GIF images using the *convert* tool from ImageMagick. ImageMagick is available for Unix/Linux, Windows, and Mac OS X platforms. Unix/Linux binaries are available via your favorite package manager, or from *http://www.imagemagick.org/*.

Once you've got ImageMagick loaded, creating your animated ballistic navigation is a cinch:

```
convert -adjoin -delay 10 zoom_*.gif oreilly.gif
```

The delay is measured in hundredths of a second, so this creates an animation of 10 frames per second.

### More Ballistic Tomfoolery

This hack uses standard animated GIFs, so there's nothing stopping you from interposing your own images, as you preserve the *zoom_###.gif* naming convention. You could, for example, replace the last image with a picture of your house or even a series of ever-closer views of the blueprints to your home. Another hack would be to change the center (lat, long) of the image request so that you could have an animated pan effect. You could even use Perl's Image::Magick module to automate the whole process. The possibilities, while not literally endless, are legion.

### Install Boomzoom on Your Own Site (Please!)

Consider that the Boomzoom script on *http://mappinghacks.com/* has to fetch around 10 images from the TIGER Map Service and then generate a fairly large animated GIF. This makes it a bit greedy for bandwidth! Fortunately, you can install it on your own system! If you have a web server that supports CGIs, you can probably install *boomzoom.cgi* on your own site. You can download the code from *http://mappinghacks.com/code/*. You will also need to install ImageMagick (*http://www.imagemagick.org/*) and the Image::Magick Perl module from the CPAN.

 Under OS X, you can enable a local copy of the Apache web server by going to System Preferences→Sharing and turning on "Personal Web Sharing." Copy the *boomzoom.cgi* source code to the folder */Library/WebServer/CGI-Executables*.

# Who Are the Neighbors Voting For?

**#16** Fundrace can show you which political candidates and parties have the most
support in your area—and which of your neighbors are supporting them.

The financial machinations of presidential election campaigns are not as distant, highbrow, or incomprehensible as one might think, and the web site
*http://www.fundrace.org/* will show you why. Enter your address and ZIP
Code into its Neighbor Search, as shown in Figure 2-8, and you are immediately provided with a vista of the political landscape of your neighborhood.
By aggregating and geocoding campaign contribution records, Fundrace
allows you to uncover a little more about the pocket depth and political sentiment of your friends, coworkers, relatives, and neighbors.

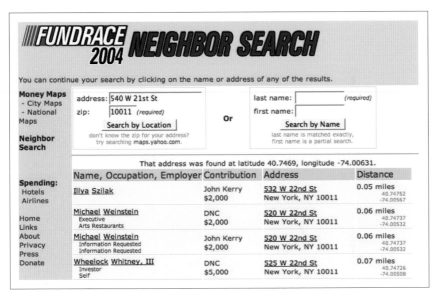

*Figure 2-8. A Fundrace Neighbor Search*

Fundrace is the result of questions asked and hacks committed by researchers working at Eyebeam (*http://eyebeam.org/*), a nonprofit, nonpartisan arts
and technology organization in New York City. Fundrace is built on a database of presidential campaign finance records published by the United States
Federal Election Commission (FEC). These records include the amount and
date of each contribution totaling over $200, along with the name, mailing
address, occupation, and employer of the corresponding contributor. With
individual contributions to campaigns capped at $2,000, and campaigns
raising tens of millions of dollars at a stroke, this amounts to a fair heap of
information for anyone to try to interpret meaningfully.

In the autumn of 2003, the financing of the presidential primary campaigns, especially those using grassroots fundraising over the Web, was a prevalent topic in the national media. The content and presentation style of other existing campaign finance web sites, such as *http://www.opensecrets.org/* and *http://www.fecinfo.com/*, did not seem likely to attract the attention of anyone who wasn't actively seeking out this information already. The first iteration of Fundrace consisted of a number of simple statistical rankings and a handful of national fundraising maps, intended to help people draw some distinctions among the wide field of candidates running at the time.

Despite offering a modicum of satire, Fundrace 1.0 didn't reach much further than other sites of a similar nature. By far, the most popular feature of the initial experiment was the national red-versus-blue Money Map (Figure 2-9), in which each county was shaded either red or blue, depending on whether Republicans or Democrats had raised more money there, respectively.

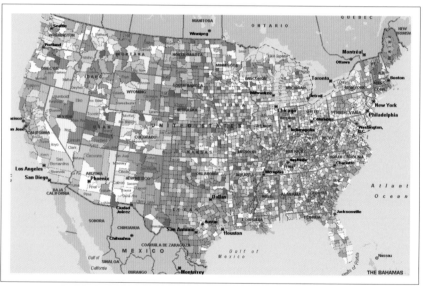

*Figure 2-9. A Money Map of the United States, Democrats versus Republicans, by county*

The next step in the right direction came when a Bostonian monthly magazine of some repute asked to publish one of Fundrace's maps. They liked the national red-versus-blue but were also interested in something a little more localized. Finally, it became time to geocode the data. After cleaning up the messier street addresses [Hack #81], Fundrace used MapPoint to plot contributions onto what is probably the most recognized several-miles-square chunk of land on Earth: Manhattan. Aggregating by individual building, as shown

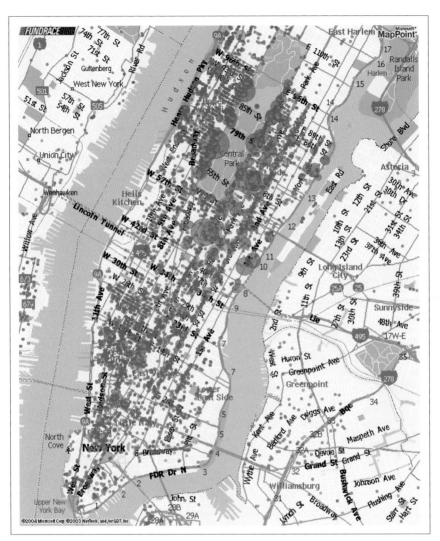

*Figure 2-10. A Fundrace map of Manhattan*

in Figure 2-10, while maintaining the red-versus-blue coloring convention, produced an immediately intuitive and stark picture of sociopolitical geography.

What quickly became clear upon making this map of New York was that this data could serve as a lens not only for viewing the different candidates but for looking at the world in general. It also became clear that the principle of locality was as applicable as ever. People are most interested in the data that is physically nearest to them. Thus was born the Fundrace

Neighbor Search. With contributors' addresses already geocoded, it was a simple matter of geocoding the query address and sorting by Euclidean distance to find the user's closest contributing neighbors.

As they say, the rest is history. The idea, and its results, were so compelling that within only a couple of days of launching the Neighbor Search and city-level Money Maps, Fundrace.org was an extremely hot web site. Web logs couldn't link fast enough, the site was receiving an onslaught of traffic, and the national media was knocking down our door. From all channels, the feedback Fundrace received covered a broad range of opinions. We received many emails thanking us for the valuable public service performed by the site. We also received numerous requests, none honored, to remove records from our database.

Some people were shocked to discover the political leanings of their friends or relatives. Others were embarrassed to know that their whole office could see whose campaign they had contributed to. The occasional amateur watchdog contacted Fundrace about perceived violations of campaign finance law, and a number of academics, hackers, and GIS professionals requested a copy of our database for their own exploration.

Probably the most contentious aspect of Fundrace was the fact that it revealed the home addresses of contributors. Many considered this a serious threat to personal privacy, but there already existed a number of web sites (including the FEC's) where the same information, as part of the public record, could be obtained. Fundrace is of the opinion that the more people who become aware of the public nature of this information, the better. At the very least, if a large enough constituency of voters were to decide that the risks outweigh the benefits, the FEC's policy could be changed.

In the United States of America there exists a tradition of public access to certain kinds of government records. This access is rooted in the principle of government accountability, a necessary feature of any legitimate democracy. The tradition has, of late, been reinforced by so-called Freedom of Information Legislation (FOIL), and by the ease of disseminating such information via the Internet. Despite this trend, the average citizen still seems largely unable make good use of FOIL and the Internet to understand and participate in his own government. Officially published data and documents are often disorganized, poorly documented, or simply too voluminous to handle with limited skills and resources. Fortunately, this leaves plenty of room for hackers like us, and organizations such as Eyebeam, to do lots of interesting and relevant work.

Fundrace is a proof positive example that abstruse government data can excite and engage people, and that all it takes is a few good hacks.

—*Michael Frumin*

## Map Nearby Wi-Fi Hotspots

Create interesting and useful maps of local and international Wi-Fi hotspot coverage.

Ever wonder how you can track the wireless networks in your neighborhood, or near your office—or how you can find free wireless connectivity when you're away from your home and office? I wondered the same thing, and so with the help of Eric Blevins, we created *http://www.WiFiMaps.com* for exactly this purpose.

WiFiMaps.com is a web-based, interactive map of wireless networks, with detailed street-level maps. If you're looking for open Wi-Fi nodes nearby, you can use the web site to browse geographical areas, perform various types of searches, and compare location or user statistics. The wireless node data is kept up to date by users who upload their wardriving data. Figure 2-11 shows a map of some of the Wi-Fi hotspots found in California, made with data contributed to WiFiMaps.com.

### The Art of Wardriving

*Wardriving* is the geek sport of driving about (or walking, or biking, or even flying) while searching for wireless networks. The idea is to connect a GPS and wireless card to your portable computer, hop in the car, fire up your favorite wardriving program, and go out for a drive. As you move, the GPS records your location and some of the parameters of what your wireless card hears. The software on your portable computer takes note of the GPS coordinates and signal strength, and it usually beeps when a new network is found.

> The term *wardriving* hearkens back to the script kiddie practice of *wardialing*, where a computer automatically dials phone numbers sequentially, looking for computer networks to crack into. Don't be misled by the aggressive sound of the term, however. The practice of wardriving can be carried out on an entirely passive—and legitimate—basis.

Mapping wireless networks can reveal patterns that are not always obvious. In the Wi-Fi map of California (Figure 2-11), we see the expected concentration of networks mirroring the populated parts of the state, but we also see the string of networks down the main highways.

Wardriving works because wireless networks broadcast *beacon packets* to identify themselves. Listening for these beacons does not require connecting to a network, and is (probably) legal. A number of people and businesses intentionally leave their networks open for use, and it is legal to connect to these networks. For instance, down the street from me is a network called

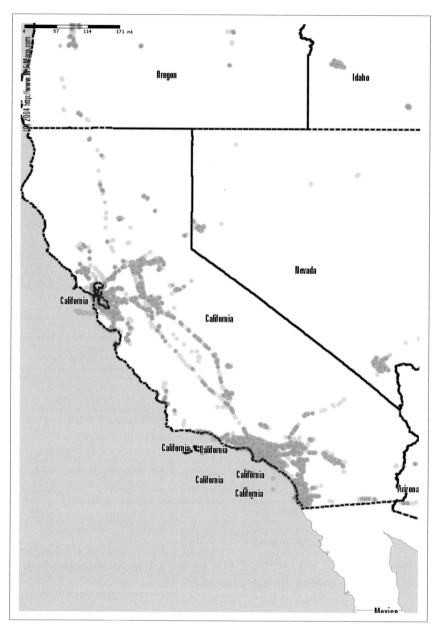

*Figure 2-11. Wi-Fi hotspots in California*

"Beehive," which corresponds to the coffee shop of the same name that has a giant sign reading "Free Wireless Internet." A network named "Go Away" is most likely private. In between these extremes lies a vast gray area, where determining which networks are intended to be open is a policy question beyond the scope of this hack.

## Collecting Data with NetStumbler

The most popular wardriving package for Windows is called NetStumbler, and it's available from *http://www.netstumbler.com/*. This package supports several different wireless cards, GPS logging, and a few extra features, and it's what I use when wardriving. On Linux and BSD, you can use Kismet, available from *http://www.kismetwireless.net/*, which has features similar to NetStumbler's— but you will also need to run *gpsd* [Hack #57]. On the Mac, try MacStumbler (*http://www.macstumbler.com/*) or KisMAC (*http://binaervarianz.de/projekte/ programmieren/kismac/*).

> Unfortunately, getting wardriving software to work with different kinds of wireless hardware can be quite a challenge sometimes, and the details are beyond the scope of this book. For more information on getting your wireless network detection software working, take a look at *Wireless Hacks* (O'Reilly).

WiFiMaps.com parses most of the native wardriving log formats. NetStumbler will export to *WiScan* format, a text-based format, or its own binary *.ns1* format. Regardless of which format you save your scans in, you'll want to upload them to WiFiMaps.com.

## Uploading Your NetStumbler Logs

After your wardrive, take your resulting files and upload them to *http:// WiFiMaps.com/* by selecting the "upload" link at the top of the main page. You can create an account or upload anonymously. The upload parsing script will run once every night and publish the results in the morning. From there, you can determine the number of networks and individual points you have found, and you can browse the maps to see your results.

You can see from the image shown in Figure 2-12 that *warchalking* symbols are used to indicate the existence of security; the )( symbol shows an open network, while the () stands for a closed network. The colors are also used to indicate security: red for closed, blue for open. Experiment with zooming in and out, and panning through your area.

> The best part about WiFiMaps.com is that it's completely built on open source tools. The map-rendering uses MapServer [Hack #91], and the data is stored in a PostGIS database [Hack #87]. Both of these tools are covered in detail later in the book.

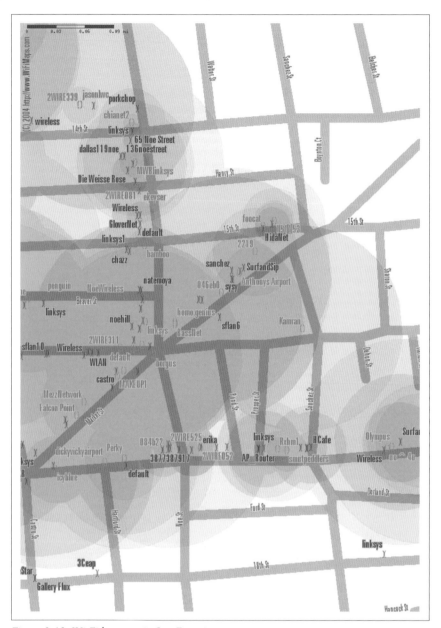

*Figure 2-12. Wi-Fi hotspots in San Francisco*

## Warning, Traffic Ahead!

If you don't have lots of spare time, simply wardriving your commute can show you the networks on your route. You can vary your route sometimes, in order to cover a wider distance. Even covering the same area repeatedly is useful for picking up signals that are missed the first time or are very faint.

Wardriving can become a bit of an obsession. To maximize your coverage, print out the Wi-Fi maps of your areas and take them with you. Mark the roads you travel on, and drive through populated intersections a couple of times—this will improve the quality of your collected data. A good source for other wardriving tips and tricks can be found at *http://wardrive.net/*.

Please pay attention to the road, to pedestrians, and to other types of hazards! Wardriving can be loads of fun, but make sure you enjoy it in a safe and productive way.

*—Drew from Zhrodague*

## HACK #18 Why You Can't Watch Broadcast TV

Find out why radio and TV reception can be poor, even if you're near a broadcast tower.

Do not adjust your set! Fiddling with that dial may do your crackly reception no good at all. Much like Wi-Fi, broadcast television signals need a clear line of sight for transmission and can be blocked by hills or other large obstructions. In this hack, we'll use a free software application for *NIX called *SPLAT!* to explain why you can—or can't—watch your favorite broadcast TV station where you live.

According to its web site, SPLAT! is a "terrestrial RF path analysis application for Linux/Unix." *Radio frequency path analysis* models how radio signals travel over different terrains to figure out how far a radio signal can reach. This technique gives reasonable estimates for the spectrum between 20 MHz and 20 Ghz: from FM radio to satellite-based microwaves. Using SPLAT! we can work out coverage areas for FM radio, television, and even Wi-Fi [Hack #17], but not AM or shortwave radio. (At lower frequencies, these kinds of radio signals bounce off the underside of Earth's ionosphere. This is why lower frequency radio can travel a long way, but it's harder to estimate how far away that may be.)

SPLAT! relies on the 1:250k digital elevation models provided for free by the U.S. Geological Survey, making it only useful for plotting radio and television reception in the United States. Fortunately, GRASS, that Swiss Army chainsaw of free GIS tools, can be persuaded to plot line-of-sight viewsheds using any terrain data [Hack #74].

## Getting Started with SPLAT!

You can download SPLAT! from its homepage at *http://www.qsl.net/kd2bd/splat.html*. Grab the latest tarball, which as of this writing was *splat-1.1.0.tar.gz*, and unpack and build it as follows. The SPLAT! application and utilities will install under */usr/local* by default:

```
# tar zvfx splat-1.1.0.tar.gz
# cd splat-1.1.0
# ./configure
# ./install all
```

 You'll need to make sure you have the *zlib* and *bzip2* development libraries installed on your system in order to build SPLAT! correctly. On Debian Linux, try **apt-get install zlib1g-dev libbz2-dev**. On Red Hat and Fedora, install the RPMs for *bzip2-devel* and *zlib-devel*.

Now you need a model of your terrain: a *digital elevation model*, or DEM. You can get the 1:250k (a.k.a. "1 degree") DEMs from the USGS EROS Data Center at *http://edc.usgs.gov/geodata/*. Click on the "1:250k DEM" link, and then select "FTP via State" or "FTP via Graphics." As of this writing, the "FTP via Graphics" link will show you a map that you can click to zoom in on, but clicking the actual quadrangle to download the model caused a *404 File Not Found* error. Still, you can use this map to figure out which quadrangles you need and then use the "FTP via State" link to actually download them. Be sure to get the compressed, rather than uncompressed, DEM files.

For our example, we'll look at reception for KQED-TV, San Francisco's public television station, in the Bay Area. We need to download the compressed DEMs for both the eastern and western halves of the Santa Rosa, Sacramento, San Francisco, San Jose, and Monterey quadrangles. We also need the eastern half of the Santa Cruz quadrangle (because there isn't a western half). These files range in size from a few dozen kilobytes to about a megabyte and a half.

## Making Terrain Models for SPLAT!

After downloading the DEM data, you should end up with a directory full of files with *.gz* extensions. You can convert these DEMs to SPLAT!'s data format using the *postdownload* utility that ships with SPLAT!. Do this for each of the compressed DEM files you downloaded:

```
$ postdownload san_francisco-e.gz
Uncompressing san_francisco-e.gz...
Adding record delimiters...
2402+1 records in
```

```
17261+1 records out
8837884 bytes transferred in 3.280152 seconds (2694352 bytes/sec)
Reading "delimited_file"... 25%... 50%... 75%... Done!
Writing "37:38:122:123.sdf"... Done!
Removing temp files...
Done!
```

SPLAT! should create a bunch of files in the same directory with filenames like *36:37:120:121.sdf*. The numbers in the filename correspond to the latitude and longitude of the edges of the original DEM file. If these files are going to live in a different directory than the one you're running SPLAT! from, you need to put that directory path on a single line in a file called *.splat_path* in your home directory.

SPLAT! uses the *Longley-Rice Irregular Terrain Model* to estimate how radio frequencies travel. The model needs some parameters to describe atmospheric conditions that affect how radio waves travel. SPLAT! provides sensible defaults in a file called *sample.lrp*. Copy this file from the *splat-1.1.0/* source directory into your current directory, and rename it *splat.lrp*. Here's a snippet from the beginning of the file:

```
15.000   ; Earth Dielectric Constant (Relative permittivity)
0.005    ; Earth Conductivity (Siemens per meter)
301.000  ; Atmospheric Bending Constant (N-units)
300.000  ; Frequency in MHz (20 MHz to 20 GHz)
5        ; Radio Climate (5 = Continental Temperate)
0        ; Polarization (0 = Horizontal, 1 = Vertical)
0.5      ; Fraction of situations (50% of locations)
0.5      ; Fraction of time (50% of the time)
```

These values are fed to the Longley-Rice model to calculate radio propagation properties. Though the defaults work for most purposes, you might want to change them. For example, to model San Francisco, we changed the Radio Climate value to 6 for "maritime temperate," and altered the dielectric constant and conductivity for an urban environment. This is described in detail in the comments that accompany *splat.lrp*, which are recommended reading for serious SPLAT! hackers.

## Finding Your Radio Frequency Transmitter

In the United States, the Federal Communication Commission publishes information about all licensed transmissions on their web site. To make our maps, we need to know the location and height of the antenna, and the radio frequency that the station broadcasts on. You can search for a TV station at *http://www.fcc.gov/mb/video/tvq.html* or search for an FM radio station at *http://www.fcc.gov/mb/audio/fmq.html*. Try entering a call sign, such as KQED or WGBH. If you don't know the call sign, just enter your location and, optionally, the broadcast channel you wish to search on. Select the

"TV Short List" or "FM Short List" output. This should return a list of one or more station facilities, with hyperlinks to view the full details. We found three results for "KQED," two of them ordinary analog television, and one digital TV transmitter. Here's a bit of the query result:

```
KQED            CA  SAN FRANCISCO                  USA

    Licensee: KQED, INC.
    Service Designation: TV  'Full Service' TV Station or Application (analog)

    Channel 9 (186-192 MHz) Licensed
    File No.: BLET  -356           Facility ID No: 35500
    CDBS Application ID No.: 301073

    Antenna Structure Registration Number (ASRN): 1001289

    37 ° 45' 19.00"  Latitude              Zone: 2
    122° 27' 6.000"  Longitude (NAD27)       Frequency Offset: + (plus)
                                Polarization: Horizontally Polarized (H)
    Effective Radiated Power (ERP):         316.  kW ERP
    Ant. Height Above Average Terrain (HAAT):   509.0 meters HAAT
    Ant. Radiation Center Above Mean Sea Level:  541.0 meters RCAMSL
    Ant. Radiation Center Above Ground Level:    530. meters RCAGL
```

All the information we need is right there. SPLAT! expects to find its transmitter and receiver locations in individual text files with a *.qth* extension, which is the Amateur Radio code for "location." Create a file called *kqed.qth* with the following contents:

```
KQED
37 45 19.0
122 27 6.0
530m
```

The *.qth* file has a simple format. The first line is the transmitter label. The second and third lines are latitude north and longitude west, respectively—in degrees, minutes, and seconds (DMS). You can also provide decimal degrees, instead of DMS values. Finally, the last line in the file specifies the antenna height above ground level in meters, which we took from the RACGL value given earlier. If you leave off the "m," SPLAT! assumes you mean height in feet, instead.

Don't forget that SPLAT! expects degrees of longitude west of the prime meridian as positive values instead of the negative values used for west longitude by most mapping tools! (The author got tripped up by this.)

Also, note that KQED-TV transmits on Channel 9, which has a mean transmission frequency of 189 MHz, instead of the 300 MHz value we gave in *splat.lrp*. If you're feeling particular, you can make a copy of *splat.lrp* with the same name as the *.qth* file—in this case, *kqed.lrp*—and update the transmission frequency. SPLAT! will look for this file and use it instead, if it exists.

## Drawing Maps with SPLAT!

Now, let's make some maps! The following command tells SPLAT! to make a coverage, or *viewshed*, map for the transmitter listed in *kqed.qth*, given receivers with antennas 20 feet above ground level, which is probably a reasonable height for a television antenna mounted on the roof of a house. The map will be output in Portable Pixmap (PPM) format to a file called *kqed.ppm*.

```
$ splat -t kqed -c 20.0 -o kqed.ppm
```

SPLAT! should report loading the *.sdf* files we created earlier and then announce that it will compute line-of-site coverage for the given location. Finally, after a great deal of computation, it should spit out the requested map file. Most X11 graphics viewers can read PPM files with no trouble, but the format itself is uncompressed, and the maps that SPLAT! produces can be quite large. In the case of the KQED example, the generated PPM was 3600 pixels on a side and weighed in at over 38 megabytes! We can use the fantastic *netpbm* tools that ship with most Linux distributions to massage this file into something a little more manageable, like a PNG file:

```
$ pnmtopng kqed.ppm > kqed.png
```

 If you don't have *netpbm* installed, you can get it pretty easily. It's available from Debian APT, and binary packages exist for most other *NIX distributions.

Assuming 3600 pixels is a little wide for your viewing preferences, you can use the *netpbm* tools to scale down the image before converting it to another format:

```
$ pnmscale -xsize 1200 kqed.ppm | pnmtojpeg > kqed.jpg
```

After scaling down the file and converting it to a JPEG, our coverage map of KQED-TV is now a mere 118k. If you take a look at the map in a graphics viewer, you'll see something that looks like Figure 2-13.

As you can see, SPLAT! generated a nice grayscale topographic map of the Bay Area using the terrain data, with water features colored blue. The transmitter is shown as a small, labeled red dot near the center of the map (which may be hard to see if you scaled down the image before viewing it, but it's there), and the coverage area is shown in green.

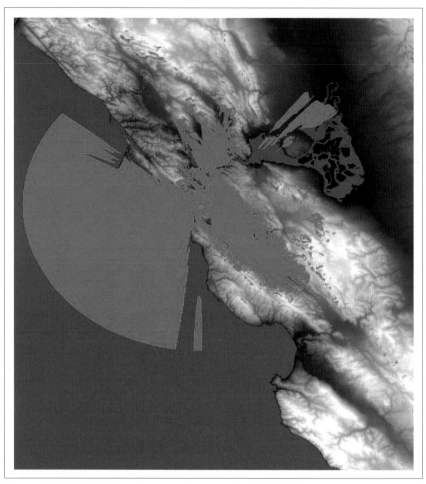

*Figure 2-13. A SPLAT! broadcast coverage map for KQED-TV*

If your map has large blocks of blue where you were expecting to see land, then you may need to obtain and convert more DEMs to cover the missing ground, as described above. If you've converted the additional files, but you're still seeing errant ocean, double-check the filenames of the converted *.sdf* files to make sure that the latitude and longitude values in the filename are correct.

## Adding Context to the Coverage Map

Now, although the coverage map we made for KQED-TV is interesting, and quite cool in its own right, it's lacking personal context. We can see where the reception coverage extends to, but it's hard to tell where exactly that is on your mental map. Fortunately, SPLAT! offers a way of adding city locations and political borders to help orient you and readers of your coverage map.

You can get city location data from the U.S. Census Bureau at *http://www.census.gov/geo/www/cob/*. Download the Incorporated Places data for California in Arc/info Ungenerate format from this site, unzip it, and feed it to the *citydecoder* utility that ships with SPLAT! Use the *sort* command to put the list in alphabetical order, and direct it to a text file:

```
$ unzip pl_d00_ascii.zip
Archive:  pl06_d00_ascii.zip
  inflating: pl06_d00.dat
  inflating: pl06_d00a.dat
$ citydecoder pl06 | sort > cities.txt
```

This program parses the Arc/info data and builds a list of cities like this:

```
Acton, 34.482799, 118.177736
Adelanto, 34.559360, 117.440527
Adelanto, 34.584723, 117.336024
Agoura Hills, 34.149436, 118.764436
Alameda, 37.784305, 122.294460
Alamo, 37.861848, 121.992778
```

The list of cities simply contains a name, a north latitude, and a west longitude, separated by commas. As you can see, there are two entries for the town of Adelanto—this is quite common, and a little bit frustrating! Let's draw the KQED coverage map again, but this time with the city location file we just created:

```
$ splat -t kqed -c 20.0 -s cities.txt -o kqed_with_cities.ppm
```

Figure 2-14 shows our new map, which has a constellation of inhabited places marked with red dots and labels. SPLAT! only displays cities within the current area of interest, and only those cities whose labels do not overlap with each other. If we zoom in a bit, we can see that KQED-TV can not only be picked up throughout San Francisco, but also across the Bay in Oakland and away south toward Santa Clara. But KQED reception is likely to be crackly in Walnut Creek, Sacramento, or Santa Cruz.

The frustrating thing about this map, however, is that, because of the way that SPLAT! shows city data, the one point that it chooses to show for San Jose, out of the five available in *cities.txt*, happens to be an urban-area outlier that extends beyond the coverage region of KQED-TV. In fact, most of the city lies to the north of the plotted point, well within the green area. As a result, this map makes it seem as if KQED cannot be received in downtown San Jose, when in fact it probably can. The only good way around this is to check the *cities.txt* file against another source of data and pare it down by hand to just the cities you're interested in.

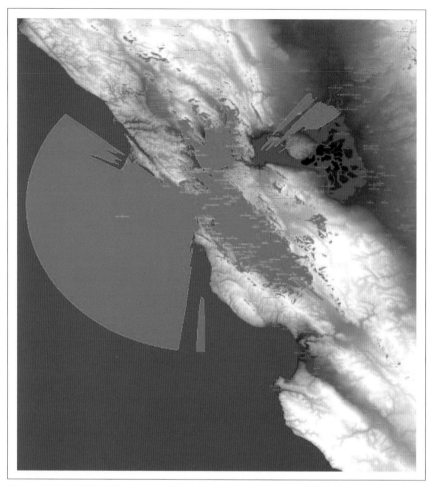

*Figure 2-14. KQED-TV's potential broadcast coverage, including cities*

### Hacking the Hack

The astute reader will have noticed that KQED-TV has not one, but two antennas listed with the FCC. It happens that the second KQED-TV antenna on Sutro Tower, a mere 57 meters above ground level, is the station's backup antenna. In the event that the main antenna at the top of the tower, 500 meters above, malfunctions in an earthquake, the station can switch over to the backup antenna to give us our natural disaster news. By how much is KQED-TV's reception radius reduced when their main antenna is knocked out? SPLAT! can help us visualize the answer to this question.

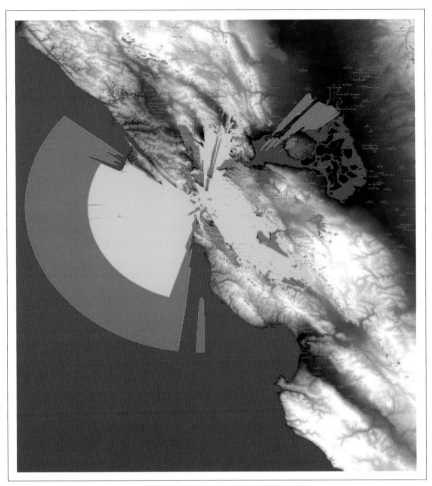

*Figure 2-15. Overlapping broadcast coverage in SPLAT!*

First, we'll make a *kqed_backup.qth* file, containing the same location as *kqed.qth*, but with a different description and antenna height.

```
KQED (Backup)
37 45 19.0
122 27 6.0
57m
```

Then we'll ask SPLAT! to show us the viewsheds of both antennas overlaid.

```
$ splat -t kqed kqed_backup -c 20.0 -s cities.txt -o kqed_overlap.ppm
```

Figure 2-15 shows the coverage of the first antenna listed in green, and the overlap between them in yellow. KQED-TV's two antennas are well placed on Sutro Tower. Even if the main antenna ceases to function, the backup antenna will still reach many of KQED's loyal viewers.

## Caveats

Clearly, SPLAT! is useful software. It does a small set of things—RF propagation and coverage analysis—and it does them fairly well. Still, there are minor caveats to using it. The map size isn't really configurable, there's not much way to control which cities get shown and/or which color they get shown in, and the only supported base map is the digital elevation model used to calculate lines of sight. In "Plot Wireless Network Viewsheds with GRASS" [Hack #74], we'll look at how to circumvent some of the limitations of SPLAT! by replicating its basic functionality in GRASS.

## HACK #19 Analyze Elevation Profiles for Wireless Community Networks

A web application and a few digital elevation models can significantly ease the pain of building wireless community networks in remote areas.

If you're trying to build wireless community networks out in the hills, like the NoCat Network has done in Sonoma County, California, the first thing you discover is that hills eat Wi-Fi signals for lunch. Modern wireless networking technologies, like 802.11b, need a line of sight to establish a connection, and any significant amount of intervening terrain, trees, or buildings between two points will quickly ruin your chances of setting up a long-distance, point-to-point wireless connection. In places where DSL and cable are unavailable, however, point-to-point community wireless links are often the only way that local residents can get high-speed Internet connectivity, so there's often a lot of motivation to find ways to work with the surrounding terrain.

Naturally, the first question a newbie asks when he shows up at a community network meeting is, "Can I get on the network?" The answer is, inevitably, "That depends. Where do you live?" Armed with the GPS coordinates of the newbie's house, you can do a certain amount of terrain analysis using digital elevation models (DEMs) in commercial software like TopoUSA or free software like GRASS. The downside to this is that, if you have 50 would-be participants in a community network, then the total number of possible links to evaluate is, apropos of nothing else, 50 x 49 ÷ 2 = 1225. That's a lot of work to do by hand!

There had to be a better way. Our ambition was to create a tool that would allow a community member to get their house on the NoCat Network with nothing more than a compass and a Wi-Fi card with a high-gain antenna. We demonstrated that, using GRASS, we could extract elevations from 10-meter-resolution USGS DEMs along the line connecting two locations and use them to plot a contour profile with Perl and the GD::Graph module from the CPAN. If the elevation of the straight line in three dimensions between those two points is less than or equal to the elevation at any point along that line, then there's a hill in the way, and a link probably won't be feasible. If the elevation of the line of sight is above ground elevation along the whole distance, then a wireless connection might be possible (but see the caveats mentioned later in this hack).

We took the contour profiler from GRASS and combined it with a web-based network node database, so that any new locations would be automatically tested against all existing locations for link viability. Finally, we added a rudimentary address geocoder based on TIGER/Line for users who didn't know their GPS coordinates already. The result was NoCat Maps, which now lives at *http://maps.nocat.net/*.

Now, when people come to NoCat Network meetings and ask how they can get on the network, they're told to go to the web site and add themselves to the database. If they know their GPS coordinates, they can enter them there; otherwise, their address is looked up in the TIGER/Line database of Sonoma County. The application analyzes the elevation profile along the line of sight to every other possible node and then presents the user with a list of possible connections, as shown in Figure 2-16.

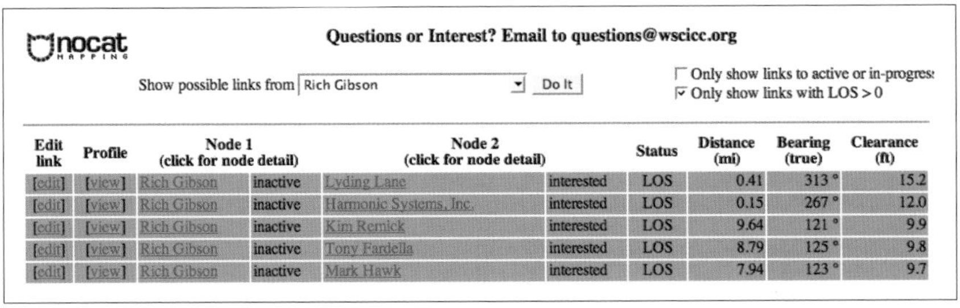

**nocat** — MAPPING

Questions or Interest? Email to questions@wscicc.org

Show possible links from [Rich Gibson ▾] [Do It]

☐ Only show links to active or in-progres:
☑ Only show links with LOS > 0

| Edit link | Profile | Node 1 (click for node detail) | | Node 2 (click for node detail) | | Status | Distance (mi) | Bearing (true) | Clearance (ft) |
|---|---|---|---|---|---|---|---|---|---|
| [edit] | [view] | Rich Gibson | inactive | Lyding Lane | interested | LOS | 0.41 | 313° | 15.2 |
| [edit] | [view] | Rich Gibson | inactive | Harmonic Systems, Inc. | interested | LOS | 0.15 | 267° | 12.0 |
| [edit] | [view] | Rich Gibson | inactive | Kim Remick | interested | LOS | 9.64 | 121° | 9.9 |
| [edit] | [view] | Rich Gibson | inactive | Tony Fardella | interested | LOS | 8.79 | 125° | 9.8 |
| [edit] | [view] | Rich Gibson | inactive | Mark Hawk | interested | LOS | 7.94 | 123° | 9.7 |

*Figure 2-16. View likely point-to-point links at a glance*

The listing of possible links comes sorted by *clearance*, approximately how much room a link has to spare, given the intervening terrain, ignoring Fresnel zones and so on. Antennas are assumed to be at least 5 meters off the ground, so the maximum possible clearance is about 16 feet. A negative clearance indicates the presence of a hill at least that high in the way. Additionally, since we know the latitude and longitude of both points, we can calculate the straight-line distance and true bearing for each possible link. This means that, if you know that there's a live antenna at a given node and NoCat Maps suggests that a link might be possible, you can go outside with a Wi-Fi card, your own high-gain antenna, and a compass and give it a shot, before you ever show up at a meeting.

The original contour profile has been preserved, as well. If you click the "View" link next to any pair of nodes in the node listing, you get a PNG file depicting the line of sight and the elevation profile between them. Figure 2-17 shows a potentially successful link, while Figure 2-18 shows one doomed to failure.

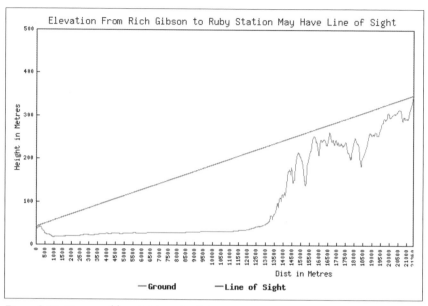

Figure 2-17. One possible point-to-point link

What are the caveats of using such an application? First, the data takes no account whatsoever of *ground clutter*—i.e., buildings, trees, etc. Realistically, it's difficult to do so, because these things change a bit from month to month and year to year. One approach, suggested by Jerritt Collord, might be to integrate the 30-meter-resolution Shuttle Radar Topography Mission (SRTM) data, which could be compared against a matching DEM to infer the presence of ground clutter.

However, even were we to correlate against SRTM data, we'd still run into the other general caveat of NoCat Maps, which is that the resolution of the DEMs isn't perfect for the task. Experience shows that 10 meters in one direction or another can easily be make-or-break for a wireless link, much less 30 meters. As a result, NoCat Maps does rate some proven, working wireless links as being impossible, and it calls some other links possible that later turn out not to be. The practical upshot is that NoCat Maps is intended to provide a rule of thumb, a starting point for planning community networks, rather than a definitive resource. If a link looks marginal, it's often worth trying anyway!

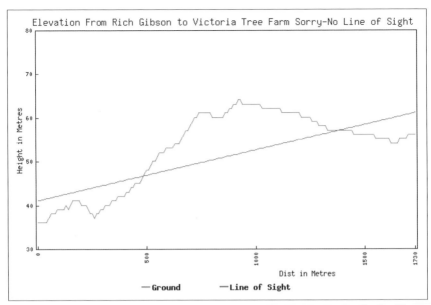

Figure 2-18. *This is not the link you are looking for—move along*

Creating an application like NoCat Maps has become much easier in the last three years. For starters, you no longer need to create your own custom geocoder to get the latitude and longitude of a particular street address; instead, you can use *geocoder.us*, as described in "Geocode a U.S. Street Address" [Hack #79] and "Automatically Geocode U.S. Addresses" [Hack #80]. One can also lighten the load of the application quite a bit by using the Geo::GDAL Perl module from the CPAN to directly access DEM files, instead of having to integrate with GRASS. There are plans afoot to improve NoCat Maps and to publish a new version of the software under the GPL, so that anyone can download and implement a NoCat Map database for her own community network. We recommend checking *http://maps.nocat.net/* for more details.

### HACK
### #20 Make 3-D Raytraced Terrain Models

Convert digital elevation models into exciting scenes of rendered terrain, using the free raytracer POV-Ray.

The free topographical map data from the USGS makes a fine candidate for creating three-dimensional scenes of territory. The POV-Ray 3-D raytracer allows you to easily import any image for use as a *height field* in creating a scene with a ground terrain. POV-Ray is available in source code form, and you can get binaries for Linux, OS X, and Windows from *http://povray.org/*.

POV-Ray has a bit of a reputation for its steep learning curve, but we're not going to do anything terribly complicated with it. We can feed it an image file to use as a height field, with simple parameters that control its display. Once we've done that, we can drape satellite or aerial imagery over the ray-traced terrain model, to give it a realistic look. The only really tricky bits are getting the digital elevation models into an image format that POV-Ray likes and orienting the satellite imagery so that it matches the underlying height field.

## Getting the Terrain Data

We picked Crater Lake, a lake formed in the caldera of an enormous and ancient volcano in Oregon, to render in our example, because it's a very distinctive-looking terrain feature. If you're in the U.S., you can get data from the USGS Seamless Data Distribution System **[Hack #67]** at *http://seamless.usgs. gov/*. We elected to download both the 1" National Elevation Data (NED) as well as the Landsat composite imagery for the area surrounding Crater Lake. Then we drew a box around the lake on the map using the area-download tool, and we were given a pop-up window allowing us to download both files. Make sure that the border of your download selection box stays green!

If you're outside the United States, SRTM data for the whole world at 90m resolution is theoretically available from NASA, as well as ground imagery, including Landsat and MODIS data. The Global Land Cover Facility at *http: //glcf.umiacs.umd.edu/* is a good place to look for this sort of data, as is the GLOBE Project at *http://www.ngdc.noaa.gov/seg/topo/globe.shtml*.

Chances are good that your digital elevation model came in the form of a GeoTIFF or, if you got it from the USGS SDDS, a set of Arc/Info Grid files. You'll want to convert this to a 16-bit PNG file, because POV-Ray doesn't understand 16- or 32-bit TIFF files, and 8-bit data is unsuitable for storing most interesting elevation data sets. We can use the *gdal_translate* utility from GDAL to accomplish this conversion:

```
$ gdal_translate -ot UInt16 -of PNG -scale 68893806 crater_lake_dem.png
Input file size is 1596, 1088
```

For *68893806*, substitute the name of the directory into which you unpacked the file from the USGS SDDS service, or the name of your GeoTIFF. *gdal_translate* is covered in much more detail in "Convert Geospatial Data Between Different Formats" **[Hack #68]**.

> If your elevation model happens to be loaded into a GRASS 5.7 location, you can use the r.out.pov command to generate a height field in Targa format, which POV-Ray will accept:
>
> ```
> $ r.out.pov map=elevation_model tga=dem.tga
> ```

## Modeling Terrain With POV-Ray

POV-Ray, which is essentially a program for describing a three-dimensional scene, takes a *.pov* file as its primary input. The *.pov* file that we're using to generate a simple 3-D map of our terrain is as follows:

```
camera {
    location <0, .25, 0>
    look_at <.01, 0, .5>
}

light_source { <0, 3000, 0> color <1,1,1> }        // sunlight

height_field {
    png "crater_lake_dem.png"
    smooth
     pigment {
         gradient y
         color_map {
             [ 0 color <.25 .25 .25> ]
             [ 1 color <1 1 1> ]
         }
     }
    translate <-0.5, 0, 0>
    scale <1, .1, 1>
}
```

All *.pov* files contain two important elements: a *camera*, and at least one *light source*. The camera describes the location and orientation of the scene's viewing point. By default, the scene is one "unit" wide in any direction, which is why all our numbers are fractional. The location and look_at commands place our camera somewhat above ground level, looking ahead and down toward the ground. We define a light_source to be our "sun," 3,000 units directly overhead—i.e., very far away. Colors are specified as a vector of red, green, and blue, so <1,1,1> gives us a white light.

Finally, we define the height_field as being based on our digital elevation model, smoothed out (so that the elevation changes aren't jagged), centered on the middle of the model, and then scaled so that the peaks stand out relative to the width and breadth of the elevation model. The coordinate system that POV-Ray uses corresponds to <x, z, y>, where $x$ is side to side, $z$ up and down, and $y$ forward and back. Picking a $z$ scale that makes the relative height of the elevation model look correct when rendered appears to be more or less a matter of trial and error.

Finally, the height field in our example is colored with a gradient along the $z$- (i.e., vertical) axis that runs from dark gray at the lowest elevation to white at the highest. We render this *.pov* file with the following POV-Ray command:

```
$ povray +A +W800 +H600 +Icrater_lake.pov +Ocrater_lake.png
```

The +W and +H options specify the image width and height, and +A turns anti-aliasing on, which makes the rendering look nicer but take longer. We get a grayscale model of the terrain, as illustrated in Figure 2-19. Not bad for a first try.

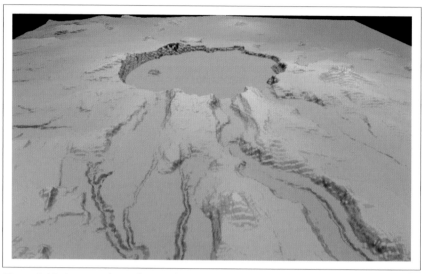

*Figure 2-19. A grayscale rendering of Crater Lake*

> To save time when experimenting with POV-Ray settings, try leaving anti-aliasing turned off. This will speed up rendering time by at least a factor of two—and then, when you've got your *.pov* file tweaked just the way you want it, you can do one more rendering pass with anti-aliasing turned on.

## Color Your Terrain with an Image Map

POV-Ray also offers an `image_map` function in POV-Ray, which allows us to specify an image with which to color each value in the height field represented by your elevation raster layer. You can use the color values in the terrain image itself for a basic grayscale height-shaded effect. With your favorite graphics program, you can adjust the palette in the image to produce a more colorful effect, in a similar fashion as that described in "Hack on Base Maps in Your Favorite Image Editor" **[Hack #32]**.

The excellent *terraform*, available for GNOME on Linux and
Mac OS X, has a selection of color maps that you can apply
over your image and save into a *.png* for POV-Ray's con-
sumption. Visualize your terrain image as a heat map, a
desert, or a strange radioactive alien wasteland. If you
haven't played with *terraform*, start with the pointers in
"Map Imaginary Places" **[Hack #100]**.

Load your scene into *terraform* and select View → Colormap
→ Wasteland, for example. From the View → Type menu,
*terraform* will generate various views, two-dimensional and
pseudo-three-dimensional perspectives of your elevation
model. You can export the results of a view at any time to a
file—in *.png* or VRML form—or export the scene as a 3-D
plane to POV-Ray, or as a 2D bitmap to the GIMP. You can
add the PNGs to your *.pov* file as color maps. *terraform* is a
wonderfully flexible program!

If you have another image containing a map in the same projection with the
same extents as your DEM, you should be able to drape it over the top of
your terrain model. We obtained a composite Landsat image of Crater Lake
in GeoTIFF format from the USGS SDDS at the same time that we downloaded the NED elevation model that we used earlier. Since POV-Ray will
read 24-bit TIFF images, and our Landsat GeoTIFF has the same projection
and extents as our DEM, we can just drop it right into our *.pov* file by
replacing the `pigment` section of the `height_field` entry with the following:

```
pigment {
    image_map {
        tiff "75178917.tif"
        interpolate 2
        once
    }
    rotate <90, 0, 0>
}
```

The `tiff` instruction points to our GeoTIFF file. If our imagery weren't in
24-bit TIFF format, we could have used *gdal_translate* to convert it to PNG
format, and then put a `png` command in our `image_map` instead. The
`interpolate` command improves the look of the rendering, and the `once`
command tells POV-Ray not to tile the image. Finally, because POV-Ray
expects the `image_map` in a different orientation than the one we are providing, we rotate the whole `pigment` by 90 degrees in the *x*-axis to line it up with
the underlying DEM.

To improve the highlights in the Landsat composite, we also add an additional light source to the top of our file, like so:

```
light_source { <100, 500, 10000> color <1,1,1> } // ambient light
```

Also, we want a realistic background for our terrain model, so we render a clear blue sky in the background, by adding the following sky_sphere section to the end of our *.pov* file:

```
sky_sphere {
    pigment {
      gradient y
      color_map {
        [ 0.2  color <.5 .75 1> ]
        [ 1.0  color <0 0 .5> ]
      }
      scale 2
      translate -1
    }
}
```

Finally, we rerun the rendering process as before. This time, it takes about 90 seconds on our machine, but the result, as shown in Figure 2-20, looks pretty fantastic! The important thing is that the elevation model and the image map need to have the same extents and be more or less in the same projection in order to line up. If they don't, you can use *gdalwarp* to trim and/or reproject the elevation model to match the image map, so that they do line up. Again, *gdalwarp* is covered in more detail in "Convert Geospatial Data Between Different Formats" **[Hack #68]**.

## Rendering Hand-Drawn Maps in 3-D

Of course, you don't have to drape satellite imagery over a digital elevation model. In particular, *digital raster graphics* (DRGs) of the USGS's hand-drawn topographic maps make great image maps for 3-D terrain. Figure 2-21 shows an example of a USGS DRG of the 7.5-minute El Capitan quadrangle draped over the matching 10-meter USGS DEM, rendered from just above the valley floor, looking towards El Capitan.

We obtained the DRG from the California Spatial Information Library at *http://gis.ca.gov/* and got the DEM for the same quadrangle from the free download service at *http://gisdatadepot.com/*. Of course, *gdal_translate* works just as well on the SDTS-format DEMs provided by *gisdatadepot.com* as it does on your standard GeoTIFF. We then copied the *.pov* file from our rendering of Crater Lake and changed the camera location and angle so that it looks eastward from the valley bottom. Finally, we set the scale to <1, .2, 1> to emphasize the valley's contours.

*Figure 2-20. A raytraced rendering of Crater Lake, colored with Landsat imagery*

*Figure 2-21. A raytracing of Yosemite Valley, looking towards El Capitan*

In general, tourist maps, and even many online satellite-derived, vector-based maps such as MapQuest's, don't exactly correspond to the real topography of the surface—the area of a park there, the width of a street here, the shape of a mall elsewhere. Older maps may have measuring discrepancies, built up over the years, or bits of the topography may have genuinely changed since they were drawn. The process of taking an old or evocative map and stretching it so that it matches up with a more accurate base model is sometimes referred to as *rubbersheeting*, and it's a technique that David Rumsey uses to overlay nineteenth century maps over scenic terrain [Hack #23]. See "Georeference an Arbitrary Tourist Map" [Hack #33] for more details about augmenting the spatial accuracy of non-GIS maps.

As a final note, POV-Ray can even be used to render terrain found in the Solar System! This very possibility is explored in "Map Other Planets" [Hack #34].

> But wait, there's more! POV-Ray can also generate successive frames of "fly-through" sequences, allowing you to pan and zoom a camera through your rendered terrain. An open source video encoder, such as *mencoder*, can then be used to stitch these frames together into sometimes breathtaking short animated clips. See *http://mappinghacks.com/projects/povray/* for further exploration of this idea.

## HACK #21  Map Health Code Violations with RDFMapper

With this simple web service, you can build interactive Flash maps from arbitrary data sources in RSS or RDF.

RDFMapper is a web service that searches an RDF file for resources with geographic locations and returns a map overlaid with dots representing the located resources. Clicking on a dot displays information about the clicked resource. Arbitrary images can be treated as maps, so the service can be used for any kind of image annotation.

One big advantage of using RDF for spatial annotation is that it allows data of different types to be mingled freely. RDF is built from a series of "vocabularies": for example, there are vocabularies for weblog posts (RSS), for personal descriptions (FOAF), for restaurants (ChefMoz), for time and events (RDFCalendar), for geometry (RDFGeom2d), and for geography (RDFIG Geo). These vocabularies can be mixed together in the same RDF documents. Any kind of RDF content can be annotated with geographical location, simply by dropping in latitude and longitude properties from the simple Geo vocabulary at *http://www.w3.org/2003/01/geo/wgs84_pos#*, which describes latitude and longitude in WGS84. Then, RDFMapper can be used to make instant maps of the content. The RDF approach integrates geodata into any domain where it is relevant, without requiring any changes to schemas or data models.

There are innumerable sources of RDF on the Web. Among them are weblogs whose "feeds" are in RSS 1.0 (the RDF dialect of RSS), and descriptions of people and their relationships encoded using the FOAF ("friend of a friend") namespace. Many other sources exist. (For example, the contents of the DMOZ open directory, *http://dmoz.org/*, are available in RDF.)

But it's easy to roll your own, as Dav Coleman chose to do when making maps of health code violations in San Francisco. On its web site, the city publishes lists of all food service providers, along with enticing details of the violations they've committed: Unsafe Food Source, Vermin, Personal Hygiene, and so on. He used a few Perl scripts to scrape the site, extract the health code details and the street addresses of the restaurants, and locate them using a geocoding service such as *http://geocoder.us/* (see "Geocode a U.S. Street Address" **[Hack #79]** for details on how to do this easily yourself). He published the results as an RDF file (available at *http://mappinghacks. com/data/sfhealth.rdf*), giving the name and location of each restaurant for which a health code violation had been reported.

The following HTML invokes RDFMapper to map the contents of this RDF file. It sends a set of key-value pairs to the web service, which returns a map in *.swf* (Macromedia Flash) format:

```
<form id ="form1" ACTION="http://www.mapbureau.com/rdfmapper/2.0/m.fsp"
enctype="text/plain" METHOD="POST">
<input type="hidden" name="basemap"
value="http://www.mapbureau.com/basemaps/sanfrancisco.0.xml"/>
<input  type="hidden" name="content"
value="http://mappinghacks.com/data/sfhealth.rdf"/>
<input type="hidden" name="extractor" value="extractTopicLocation"/>
<input type="hidden" name="pageGen" value="pageGen0"/>
<input type="hidden" name="itemTitleGen" value="itemTitleGen0"/>
<input type="hidden" name="itemGen" value="itemGen1"/>
<input type="hidden" name="pageTitle" value="SF Health Code Violations"/>
<input type="hidden" name="styleSheet"
value="http://www.mapbureau.com/rdfmapper/2.0/style1.css"/>
</form>
<a href = "javascript:document.forms['form1'].submit( );">Submit</a>
```

When this invisible form is submitted by clicking on the "Submit" link, it performs an HTTP POST to the RDFMapper web service. RDFMapper puts together a map and sends it back to the client.

Figure 2-22 shows the RDFMapper visualization of the RDF file of health code violations. You can view information about individual restaurants by clicking on the appropriate dot on the map. This could be a "how to lie with maps" story: the only level of metadata visually displayed is that there is a violation of some kind there; this could be one relatively innocuous citation for "Holding Temperatures" a degree or two too warm, or a string of violations including Vermin and Contaminated Equipment. On this map, they all look the same qualitatively. However, this is hopefully a good illustration of using RDF as an intermediary format. RDFMapper can also be used to map web data that is not already presented in RDF, with the help of quick conversion scripts.

*Figure 2-22. The RDFMapper map of San Francisco health code violations*

## The RDFMapper Web Service in Depth

The basemap parameter passed to the RDFMapper service specifies the URL of a file in RDFMap format describing the map that is to appear in the background. This RDFMap file specifies the URL of the image and the parameters of the geographic projection that applies to the image. The image is either a JPEG or a *.swf* file. A catalog of maps suitable for use with RDF-Mapper can be found at *http://www.mapbureau.com/viewer*. You can also create your own base maps from existing images by encoding the relevant projection data in RDFMap format.

The content parameter specifies the URL of the RDF file to be mapped.

Most of the remaining parameters denote functions defined in the *Fabl* programming language, an open source language designed specifically for manipulating RDF. (Fabl is implemented within RDF as well; see *http://fabl. net* for more details.) Parameters naming Fabl functions may take the form:

```
<function_name>
```

or

```
<URL-of-Fabl-code-file>#<function_name>
```

In the former case, the function is taken from a library of utility functions for RDFMapper, available at *http://www.mapbureau.com/libsrc/rdfmapper_utils-2.0.fbl*. In the latter case, the function is taken from the specified Fabl code file. See the *rdfmapper_utils-2.0.fbl* file for documentation of the utilities used in the previous example, such as itemGen1, extractTopicLocation, and so on. If, as is often the case, the functions appearing in the library suit the purposes of an application, there is no need to develop new versions.

The extractor parameter denotes a Fabl function that, when given an RDF resource, returns a geom2d:Point representing its location, or nil. RDFMapper maps everything (that is, all resources) in the content file for which extractor returns a non-nil value. Here's a sample extractor:

```
geom2d:Point function extractGeoLatLong(Resource x) {
    var geom2d:Point rs;
    if  ((count(x,geo:lat)>0) && (count(x,geo:long)>0))
        {
        rs = new(geom2d:Point);
        rs . geom2d:x = x.geo:long;
        rs . geom2d:y = x.geo:lat;
        return rs;
        }
    return nil ~  geom2d:Point;
}
```

In English, this code reads: "If geo:lat and geo:long each take on at least one value within some resource *x*, then extract the corresponding values, package them as a geom2d:Point, and return that Point."

Additional details about RDFMapper, including a complete description of all parameters, can be found at *http://www.mapbureau.com/rdfmapper/2.0*.

## Hacking RDFMapper

Although RDFMapper is designed to plot locations from geo-annotated RSS and RDF, there are workarounds in case your hosted online journal service, such as Blogger, doesn't have the facility to let you add new tags and namespaces to your RSS feed.

RDFMapper's extractLocation function gets around this issue by scanning the content of posts for text of the form `<geo:long>124.123</geo:long><geo:lat>46.16</geo:lat>`. Such text can be hidden from the reader of the weblog by embedding it in a span of the form:

```
<span style="display:none" xmlns:geo="http://www.w3.org/2003/01/geo/wgs84_
pos#">
     <geo:long>124.123</geo:long><geo:lat>46.16</geo:lat>
</span>
```

It's not pretty, but it works! The following RDFMapper parameters will map a Blogger weblog:

```
name="basemap" value="http://www.mapbureau.com/basemaps/astoria.0.xml"
name="content" value="http://rdfmapperexample.blogspot.com/rss/
rdfmapperexample.xml"
name="extractor" value="extractLocation"
name="itemGen" value="itemGen0"
```

Using this hack, any weblog with an RSS feed can be mapped with RDF-Mapper. In fact, RDFMapper is a generalization of an earlier service called Blogmapper, which mapped weblogs but not other varieties of RDF. If you just want to map blog posts, then you might have a look at Blogmapper itself, at *http://blogmapper.com/*.

—*Chris Goad*

# CHAPTER THREE

# Mapping Your World

## Hack 22–34

*A map of the world that does not include
Utopia is not worth even glancing at,
for it leaves out the one country at which
Humanity is always landing.*

—Oscar Wilde

Maps help us to find ourselves in the world. Ever wonder where you'd be if you dug a hole through the center of Earth? Aside from the practical problems of having your component atoms rendered into mush by the heat and pressure, you'd probably end up somewhere unexpected! Once you've dug yourself out of that mess, take a look at what happens when you couple an obsession for maps with a vision and a bit of cash [Hack #23]. If you haven't yet tired of the world of maps, then check out NASA's free World Wind software [Hack #24] to view the planet from top to bottom.

If you want to move further into the world of maps, you can learn what different cartographic projections [Hack #28] do for your view of the world and then use Buckminster Fuller's Dymaxion projection [Hack #31] to explore a radical alternative to the "North is Up" school of cartography. There are more hacks to show you how to calculate distances, convert coordinates from one form to another, and even show you how to take a random tourist map and use it as a base map to tell your own stories.

And finally, if Earth isn't what comes to mind when you read "Mapping Your World," or if one world is *not* enough, you can revel in "Map Other Planets" [Hack #34]!

# Digging to China

**#22**   Impale the planet and debunk urban myths with some basic arithmetic.

If you started digging straight down and didn't stop, according to a popular phrase you'd be "digging to China." Is this really true? You might think that calculating this requires some awesome spherical trigonometry, but we can work this out from latitude and longitude values with a simple transformation.

Imagine that the Earth is an orange, and slice it into four quarters, demi-hemispheres. Slice the Earth in half along the equator, and the halves in half along the prime meridian. Looking at the quartered Earth along the prime meridian, with London facing you:

> Top-right quarter is from 0° to 90° N latitude, 0° to 180° E longitude.
> Top-left quarter is from 0° to 90° N latitude, 180° W to 0° longitude.
> Bottom-right quarter is from 90° S to 0° latitude, 0° to 180° E longitude.
> Bottom-left quarter is from 90° S to 0° latitude, 180° W to 0° longitude.

It can help to examine a physical globe of the Earth that shows the lines of latitude and longitude.

A line going through the center of the sphere from one point comes out at another point in the opposite quadrant—its *antipode*. (This is why English people call the Australian continent *the Antipodes*.) So the latitude of the second point is the inverse, the negative mirror image of the first one, which we can obtain by simply flipping north to south, and south to north.

Similarly, longitude is measured 180 degrees around the spheroid in either direction from Greenwich, England, with negative values for westward bearings and positive values for eastward bearings. To figure out the longitude for the antipode, we need to subtract the longitude from 180 *and* flip the direction east to west, or vice versa.

Suppose, for example, we start digging straight down in San Francisco, in the vicinity of 37.7° N latitude and 122.4° W longitude. According to our simple transformation, the antipode from here is at 37.7° S, 58.4° E. Are we really digging to China? Figures 3-1 and 3-2 show how this looks on an orthographic projection of the world.

So we're not actually digging to China. Instead, ignoring the physical impossibilities of boring a hole straight through the planet, we should end up at the bottom of the Indian Ocean somewhere near Madagascar. Somehow that just doesn't have quite the same ring to it, does it?

These maps were made with the *pscoast* utility from the excellent GMT suite of Unix plotting and projection tools, which outputs PostScript, thusly:

```
$ pscoast  -R0/360-/-90/90 -JG58.4/-37.7/5 -B30g30/15g15 -W > map.ps
```

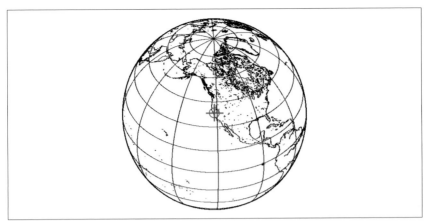

*Figure 3-1. Digging a hole from San Francisco...*

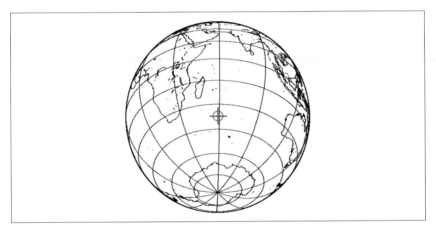

*Figure 3-2. ...and coming out in the Indian Ocean*

"Experiment with Different Cartographic Projections" **[Hack #28]** explores the myriad features of GMT in much more depth.

HACK
#23 ## Explore David Rumsey's Historical Maps

Putting older maps online opens up possibilities that would likely stun the old cartographers.

While most of the hacks in this book focus on how to create and use maps that reflect the world as it is now, there are lots of reasons to look back at older maps. Apart from the remarkable cartography and design of many of the best older maps, these maps can help us see what features of our world mapmakers considered important before the advent of superhighways, or even canals and railroads.

The David Rumsey Map Collection (*http://www.davidrumsey.com*), which began as a physical map collection 20 years ago, offers over 10,000 maps that visitors can explore online. Casual visitors can zoom in to appreciate fine detail, while other users can overlay these maps with more recent ones, using the combination to evaluate change over time.

> These maps are available online, but are *not* free for the taking. Contact Cartography Associates at *carto@luna-img.com* if you have questions about using these maps for particular projects. Cartography Associates also sells framed and unframed reproductions of many of the maps at *http://davidrumsey.com/reproductions.html*.

The site offers several options for browsing, from a simple in-brower viewer, to a separate Java client application, to a set of tools for integrating the maps with GIS data. One of those tools even lets you visit the map in three dimensions. For starters, the insight Browser, as shown in Figure 3-3, is probably the easiest to use, though it requires that pop-up ad blocking be turned off. (I switched browsers rather than tinker with settings.)

*Figure 3-3. Opening the collection with the insight Browser*

You can wander through all 10,000 maps, or you can search using the options on the lefthand side. I chose to search by State/Province, picked New York from the list, and clicked past the first 100 maps before finding the one I was looking for, in the top left corner of the selection shown in Figure 3-4. Double-clicking on the selected map brings up another window displaying the map and navigation details, as shown in Figure 3-5. Zooming in to a portion of the map where my house now stands, as shown in Figure 3-6, I can see the creek, with sawmills marked by Xs and other mills as circles on Xs, along with the beginnings of the local road system.

Figure 3-4. Maps of upstate New York from 1829

Most of what you'll want to do in this mode is zoom in and out. The printer button prints a small version of the map on ordinary paper; it's not going to let you take a full image with all the details in the map.

While you can spend hours looking over old maps, the site has a few wilder features to offer as well, notably its 3-D viewing experience at *http://davidrumsey.com/GIS/3d.htm*. You'll want broadband network access and a reasonably fast computer to use this feature. It crashed my old 600 MHz ThinkPad but ran fine on a 1.8 GHz eMachines with 384 MB of RAM.

The Yosemite Valley map is the most developed of the six currently available maps, as it starts from an 1883 survey map of the valley and also permits an overlay with much more recent U.S. Geological Survey maps. Using the mouse, arrow keys, and spacebar, you can swoop through the valley, enjoying the detail of the maps, and you can also choose how much of the new map you see through the old map. It's hard to demonstrate the feeling

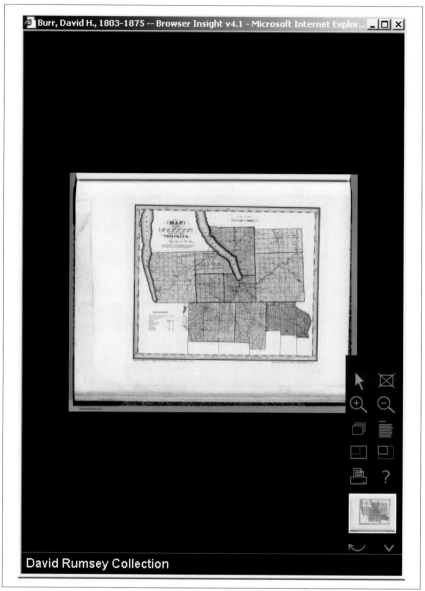

*Figure 3-5. An 1829 map of Tompkins County, New York, with options for exploring it*

the viewer provides in a book, but Figure 3-7 will give you some idea of what to expect as you explore the valley.

You can also change the view from 1883 to the present using the Z, X, C, V, and B keys. Figures 3-8 through 3-10 show a similar part of the map at different settings.

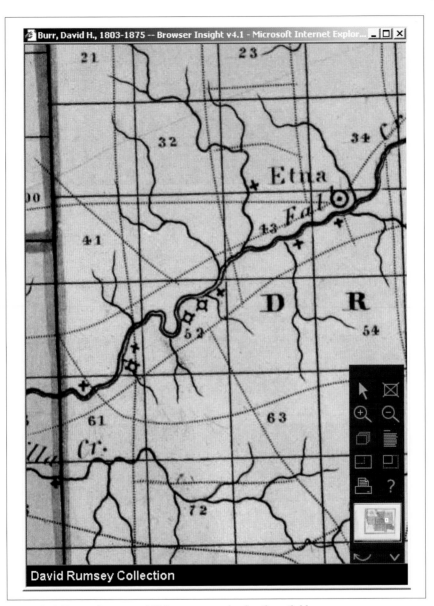

*Figure 3-6. Zoomed in on an 1829 map to see the detail available*

While the 3-D maps are stunning, the collection also offers 2-D maps that combine historical maps with more recent ones through a GIS viewer. Whether you want to explore technical possibilities or stock your wish list with data and tools, the David Rumsey Collection is a fine place to start!

*—Simon St.Laurent*

*Figure 3-7. Looking over the Yosemite Valley, through a 3-D rendering of an 1883 map*

*Figure 3-8. Looking over the Yosemite Valley from Sentinel Dome, using just the 1883 map*

Figure 3-9. Looking over the Yosemite Valley from Sentinel Dome, using both the 1883
map and the USGS map

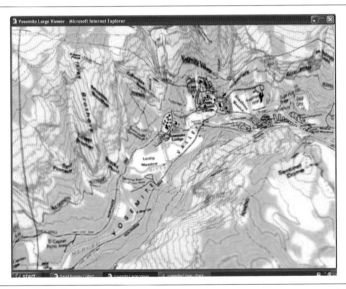

Figure 3-10. Looking over the Yosemite Valley from Sentinel Dome, using just the USGS
map

# HACK #24    Explore a 3-D Model of the Entire World

NASA's World Wind software lets you explore an unbelievable wealth of geospatial imagery, rendered in 3-D in real time.

World Wind is a newcomer to the world of GIS software. Similar in premise to the shiny but ultimately rather expensive Keyhole package (*http://www.keyhole.com/*), NASA's World Wind application allows you to explore a real-time 3-D rendering of planet Earth from orbit all the way down to ground level, using your keyboard and mouse to navigate. The package is available for free—as in both beer and speech—and has access to over 20 terabytes of data, including Landsat and Terraserver imagery, USGS topo maps, and much more. World Wind loads and caches its data sets dynamically as you zoom in, so broadband and a fast graphics card are an absolute must!

## Getting the Software

First off, go to *http://learn.arc.nasa.gov/worldwind/* and grab a copy of the software. At 235 MB, it's a hefty download, but that constitutes the "starter set" of data needed by the application. Double-click on the *.exe* file, and it will install like any other Windows application. Make sure you pick a location on your hard drive that has plenty of space, because as you zoom around on the globe and use various features, you will begin to download and store a *lot* of data on your computer. If the application is installed correctly, you will be greeted with a nice Blue Marble–textured globe, as shown in Figure 3-11.

## Basic Navigation

Navigation is pretty simple. Hold down the left mouse button and move the mouse to rotate the globe. You can use the scroll wheel, or hold down the left and right mouse buttons together to zoom the scene. Holding down the right mouse button alone allows you to use the mouse to tilt the scene, and if there is elevation data for the area, you will be treated to a 3-D view like Figure 3-12. If you just click on the screen, it will center your view to that point. If you click on the "Key Chart" icon in the upper right corner, you can get a list of all the keyboard navigation options as well.

Once you zoom in to a certain altitude, you will see a NASA logo in the upper right corner and a red rectangle on the map. This icon lets you know that World Wind is requesting more data over the network, so be patient.

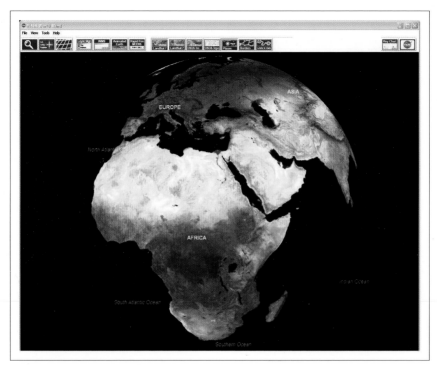

*Figure 3-11. World Wind's startup view*

## Exploring the Available Data Sets

World Wind has many data sets you can play with:

*Blue Marble*
> The textured globe you see when you start the application.

*Landsat 7*
> The default data set when you zoom in. The resolution of Landsat 7 is 15 meters per pixel. There are two varieties, normal and "pseudo," which is a false color map produced using the infrared bands in Landsat imagery.

*Shuttle Radar Topography Mission (SRTM)*
> Digital elevation data for a given area. If you tilt the view by holding down the right mouse button and moving the mouse, you will be able to see mountains and valleys.

*USGS/Terraserver 1 meter*
> The Terraserver images are the highest-detail maps World Wind can use at the moment. With these, you can see cars and swimming pools.

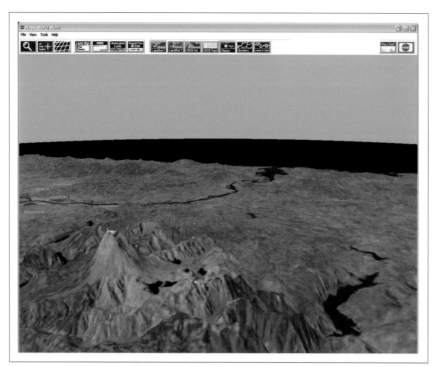

*Figure 3-12. Mt. St. Helens, as rendered in World Wind*

*USGS Topo*

These are the traditional hand-drawn USGS contour maps of a given area.

These data sets are activated by the icons across the top of the application, as shown in Figure 3-11. They can also be manipulated by the Layer Manager, by going to Tools → Layer Manager.

There are three specialty data sets that World Wind can use as well:

*MODIS*

NASA's MODIS satellite data is used to provide markers that point out notable meteorological and geological events happing all over the globe: storms, fires, floods, and even volcanoes. If you click on the markers, you can get high-resolution images of the events at a point in time.

*Living Earth*

These are various animations of phenomena on Earth produced by the Goddard Space Flight Center. Everything from hurricanes in Florida to sandstorms in China to fires in Yellowstone.

*GLOBE*

The GLOBE data set is primarily composed of various statistics gathered from the surface of the earth: rainfall, temperature, humidity, etc.

All these specialty sets can be explored under the Tools menu.

World Wind also features over four million place names and boundary lines for countries and states, which you can view by selecting the "Borders and Places" icon on the toolbar. If you click on the big magnifying glass icon or go to Tools → Place Finder, you will get a dialog box where you can type in a name to be taken directly to that location, as shown in Figure 3-13.

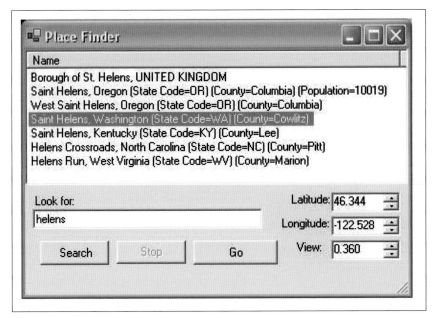

*Figure 3-13. World Wind's Place Finder dialog*

## A Sneak Peek into the Past

Since World Wind is part of a NASA initiative to help educators, they are providing a peek at some future features of the program. If you click on the "Lewis and Clark" icon in the toolbar, World Wind will overlay the route Lewis and Clark took on their journeys, as shown in Figure 3-14. The numbered icons are interactive, and clicking on them will open a journal entry on the Lewis and Clark web site (*http://www.lewis-clark.org/*).

Currently, there are no end-user tools to build the overlay files, but since this is an open source project, hopefully the tools will be forthcoming.

## Final Thoughts

Until now, a desktop-mapping application of this magnitude would have been a pretty ambitious project, but it seems like NASA has pulled it off

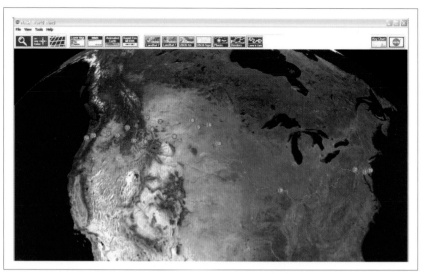

*Figure 3-14. Lewis and Clark's journey, as shown in World Wind*

with World Wind. There is no SourceForge repository for it, but there is an active community in their forums, located at *http://learn.arc.nasa.gov/worldwind/forums/*. Thanks to Moore's Law, we now have the ability to play this data back on the hardware on our desktop. How far we have come from vellum and quill pens!

—Adam Hill

## HACK   Work with Multiple Lat/Long Formats
## #25

While latitude and longitude stay constant, their representations don't. You can still use new data with a traditional map, if you know a few key conversions.

Even the novice cartographic hacker has noticed that there are at least three common ways to represent latitude and longitude, and at least two conventions for direction. Traditionally, mariners use degree-minute-second (DMS) notation. Computer types find decimal degrees easier to process, and, just to make life more interesting, some people write coordinates with integer degrees and minutes in decimal form. Your GPS receiver may use one style by default, and your mapping tools or your waypoint listing may use another, which can lead to inconvenience and confusion. Fortunately, this situation is pretty easy to deal with.

Latitude and longitude, of course, are just *x*- and *y*-coordinates on a great spherical grid that covers the world. Lines of latitude, referred to as *parallels* (because they never intersect), extend 90 degrees north and south of the equator. Lines of longitude are referred to as *meridians* and extend 180 degrees west and east of the *prime meridian*, which passes through the site of the Royal Observatory in Greenwich, England. Southern latitudes and western longitudes are often represented as negative numbers. Minutes are shown with a single quote ('), and seconds are signified with a double quote (").

In traditional notation, one particular spot in the O'Reilly parking lot is at 38° 24' 57.636" north latitude, 122° 50' 27.348" west longitude.

 Each minute of change in latitude or longitude at the equator equals one nautical mile, or 6,076 feet. So one second of latitude or longitude is approximately 100 feet. This means that 57.636 seconds of North latitude implies a precision of about an inch, which is well beyond the precision of the GPS used to take this reading.

## A Couple of Easy Ways to Convert

If you are working with your own waypoints, you can avoid conversion altogether. Set your GPS to display coordinates in the format that matches your map. On some Garmin units, for example, this is found under Menu → Setup → Position → Position Format.

The easiest way to handle conversions is to let an online coordinate converter do the work. The Federal Communications Commission (FCC) runs one such site at *http://www.fcc.gov/mb/audio/bickel/DDDMMSS-decimal.html*. You simply enter your coordinates in the format you have, and the coordinates are returned in the format you're after.

## Converting Lat/Long to Lat/Long on Paper

But if you want to understand what's actually happening, you need to understand some basic formulas. Going back to the O'Reilly parking lot example, you can convert coordinates from DMS format to decimal-degree format by dividing minutes by 60 and seconds by 3600 and adding all three quantities together to get the desired result:

```
38° 24' 57.636" =  38 + 24/60 + 57.636/3600 =   38.4160°
122° 50' 27.348" = 122 + 50/60 + 17.348/3600 = -122.8381°
```

Since this is west of Greenwich, we mark the longitude as negative.

The converse, converting decimal degrees to DMS format, can be accomplished by multiplying the decimal portion of your coordinates by 60; the minutes are the portion of that result to the left of the decimal point, and the seconds can be calculated by taking the remaining fractional part and multiplying it by 60 again. To convert the parking lot's latitude from decimal degrees to DMS:

```
38.4160° =
Degrees = 38°
Minutes = .4160 * 60 = 24.96'
Seconds = .96   * 60 = 57.60"
        = 38° 24' 57.60" N
```

To get degree/decimal-minute format, just stop when you have the minutes in decimal form (Minutes = .4160 * 60 = 24.96').

## Converting Lat/Long to Lat/Long using PROJ.4

PROJ.4 is the open source cartographic projections library. PROJ.4, which can be obtained from *http://proj.maptools.org/*, includes the Swiss Army Chainsaw of coordinate conversions: a command-line tool called *cs2cs*. Among the many tricks of *cs2cs* is its ability to convert lat/long between different formats. The following example converts from decimal degrees to DMS:

```
$ cs2cs +proj=latlong  +to +proj=latlong
-122.50 38.75
122d30'W     38d45'N 0.00
```

Using the format (-f) parameter, you can change the value from DMS to decimal degrees:

```
$ cs2cs +proj=latlong +to +proj=latlong -f "%.2f" \
122d45'W 35d12'N
-122.75 35.20 0.00
```

You can also use shell redirection to convert a whole file of coordinates at once:

```
$ cs2cs +proj=latlong +to +proj=latlong < coords.txt
125d19'6.6"E    12d6'29.16"N 0.000
90d33'26.64"W   33d25'56.28"N 0.000
15d30'E           39d18'S 0.000
```

See "Work with Different Coordinate Systems" [Hack #26] for other uses of PROJ.4.

> Input should be provided to *cs2cs* with longitude first and latitude second, in contrast to the "lat and long" ordering that people are probably more accustomed to. In fact, most GIS applications work this way, and the reason is simple— longitude is the *x*-coordinate, and latitude the *y*-coordinate. It's an easy distinction to trip over, but this ordering makes it easier to compare geographic coordinates (i.e., long and lat) to other kinds of coordinate systems.

## Converting Lat/Long to Lat/Long in Perl

If you need more fine-grained control over the conversion, you'll probably want to use a program, rather than calculating by hand or using PROJ.4. Walt Mankowski has written the CPAN module Geo::Coordinates:: DecimalDegrees, which takes care of the details. Assuming you have a standard Perl installation, you should be able to install it with this command:

```
perl -MCPAN -e 'install Geo::Coordinates::DecimalDegrees'
```

Here is a bit of Perl to illustrate the use of this module on the same parking lot latitude:

```perl
#!/usr/bin/perl
use Geo::Coordinates::DecimalDegrees;

my ($deg, $min, $sec) = @ARGV;
print "$deg $min' $sec\"\tDMS\n";

my $decimal_degrees = dms2decimal($deg, $min, $sec);
print "$decimal_degrees\tDecimal degrees\n";

($deg, $min, $sec) = decimal2dms($decimal_degrees);
print "$deg $min' $sec\"\tBack to DMS\n";

($deg, $min) = decimal2dm($decimal_degrees);
print "$deg $min'\tDegrees + decimal minutes\n";
```

Put this sample code in a file called *decimal.pl* and execute it to yield the following output:

```
$ perl decimal.pl 38 24 57
38 24' 57"               DMS
38.4158333333333         Decimal degrees
38 24' 56.9999999999941" Back to DMS
38 24.9499999999999'     Degrees-decimal minutes
```

Note that rounding causes some loss of accuracy.

## HACK #26 Work with Different Coordinate Systems

Your GPS gives you latitude and longitude, but the maps in your GIS system use UTM coordinates. Fortunately, you can reconcile the two.

Living on a round planet has its pros and cons. On the pro side, you can't, for example, sail or fly off the edge! This is a pretty big pro, all things considered. The con side, however, is that the task of mapping the planet is riddled with difficulties for would-be cartographers. For example, doing any kind of comparison between locations using latitude and longitude requires deploying heavy-duty spherical trigonometry [Hack #27]. It sure would be nice to be able to conveniently ignore the roundness of our lovely planet as needed, but, to do so, we have to somehow project its surface onto a plane in a way that preserves distance and bearing—or else, why bother?

Enter the *Universal Transverse Mercator*, or UTM, coordinate system. UTM is a rectangular coordinate system that treats Earth as a single flat plane or, rather, as 60 flat planes called *UTM zones*. As you'll probably recall from looking at maps of the world, the Mercator projection preserves land shapes well near the equator but distorts them very badly at the Poles. The Transverse Mercator projection rotates the Mercator by 90 degrees, so that the distortion is pushed out to the sides instead. This makes the Transverse Mercator a popular choice for mapping regions that are longer north-to-south than east-to-west, such as Great Britain, for example.

The *universal* aspect of UTM lies in the way it divides most of the world into rectangles, or zones, oriented north-to-south to minimize distortion, each one 6 degrees of longitude wide by 8 degrees of latitude high. At the equator, each zone is about 414 miles wide by 552 miles high. Each of the north/south columns is numbered from 1 to 60, starting at the international date line, going east. The rows are given letters, starting with C for the row from 72 to 80 degrees South, up to row X for 72 to 84 degrees North. The letters I and O are not used to avoid confusion with 1 and 0. A couple of minor alterations are made to this grid system in the North Sea to keep bits of Norway in the same zone. A nice map of UTM grid zones is at *http://www.dmap. co.uk/utmworld.htm*.

Within each zone, UTM coordinates are expressed in meters as an *easting* offset from the base longitude, and a *northing* offset from the base latitude. To ensure that UTM coordinates are always positive, a *false easting* of 500,000 meters is added to all UTM coordinates, along with a *false northing* of 10,000,000 meters when coordinates lie south of the equator.

The main advantage of UTM is that it is generally easier to think in terms of meters than degrees, minutes, and seconds. Similarly, it is much easier to calculate an imperfect but reasonably accurate distance between two UTM coordinates by ignoring the curvature of the Earth and simply using the Pythagorean Theorem. Distances calculated this way should be multiplied by a *scale factor* of .9996 to average out the effects of distortion across the zone.

Like converting different representations of latitude and longitude [Hack #25], the easiest way to "convert" Lat/Long to UTM is to simply have your GPS receiver display coordinates in your preferred format. On some Garmin units, you can select Menu → Setup → Position and select "UTM/UPS" as your position format.

The next easiest conversion approach is to use an online coordinate converter, such as *http://www.ngs.noaa.gov/TOOLS/utm.html*.

## Converting with the PROJ.4 Toolkit

The PROJ.4 toolkit provides a tool called *proj* for just this sort of task. PROJ.4 is in Debian APT and can also be obtained at *http://proj.maptools. org/*. *proj* accepts coordinate pairs, one per line, separated by whitespace, with longitude given first. Anything after the first two numbers is considered to be a label and is preserved in the output. Suppose we have some data in *places.txt*:

```
123d03'02.97"W 38d21'56.98"N Alice Rock
122d48'13.00"W 38d34'09.01"N Allan Ranch
122d23'57.01"W 38d16'27.01"N Arrowhead Mount
123d02'26.01"W 38d28'44.00"N Austin Gap
```

We can use *proj* to turn these coordinates into UTM as follows:

```
$ proj +proj=utm +zone=10 < places.txt
495559.96      4246406.86 Alice Rock
517108.31      4268986.90 Allan Ranch
552554.55      4236406.09 Arrowhead Mount
496462.37      4258951.69 Austin Gap
```

The only downside of using *proj* this way is that you have to know which longitudinal zone you're in. In this case, we knew we were in zone 10 by looking at the UTM grid zone map at *http://www.dmap.co.uk/utmworld.htm*. Although this example used coordinates in DMS format, you can also use degrees and decimal minutes, or just decimal degrees (see "Work with Multiple Lat/Long Formats" **[Hack #25]** for more details).

You can use the *invproj* program from PROJ.4, with the same command-line arguments and file format, to convert UTM coordinates back into Lat/Long.

## Perl to the Rescue (Again)

The Geo::Coordinates::UTM module by Graham Crookham provides both a readable description of the UTM system, as well as a nice bit of Perl to convert UTM to and from lat/long. Geo::Coordinates::UTM is available from the CPAN. The following code performs the conversion:

```
#!/usr/bin/perl

use Geo::Coordinates::UTM;

my ($longitude, $latitude) = @ARGV;
my $ellipsoid = 23; # WGS-84

($zone,$easting,$northing)=latlon_to_utm($ellipsoid,$latitude,$longitude);
print "easting: $easting northing: $northing zone: $zone\n";

($latitude,$longitude)=utm_to_latlon($ellipsoid,$zone,$easting,$northing);
print "latitude: $latitude longitude: $longitude\n";
```

Running this we get:

```
$ perl utm_example.pl -122.829027 38.402528
easting: 514928.556644582 northing: 4250491.70355821 zone: 10S
latitude: 38.4025280009781 longitude: -122.829026999993
```

For more on lat/long conversions, see "Work with Multiple Lat/Long Formats" [Hack #25]

### HACK #27    Calculate the Distance Between Points on the Earth's Surface

A little spherical trigonometry can go a long way.

The task of calculating the distance between two points on the Earth's surface is not quite as simple as it might seem. At first, we might be inclined to dust off the well-known *Pythagorean Theorem* from high school algebra, which calculates the length of the hypotenuse of a right triangle.

$$a^2 + b^2 = c^2$$

If we have two points $(x1, y1)$ and $(x2, y2)$, then the difference between our two $x$-coordinates and the difference between our two $y$-coordinates are the legs of our right triangle, and the hypotenuse measures the distance between the points:

$$c = sqrt(\ (x2 - x1)^2 + (y2 - y1)^2\ )$$

One hitch to this approach is that the distance between lines of longitude decreases as you head toward the poles, which is a symptom of the fact that, in contrast to our right triangle, the Earth isn't flat. (Damn you, Columbus!) Worse, over distances greater than 20 kilometers or so, the curvature of the Earth turns our straight hypotenuse into an arc, making the Pythagorean Theorem more or less useless for this purpose. This arc, if we were to extend it all the way around the world through both points, describes a figure known as a *great circle*. The distance between two points on the Earth is therefore sometimes referred to as the great-circle distance. We show how to draw great circles in "Plot a Great Circle on a Flat Map" [Hack #30].

> You can still use the Pythagorean Theorem for calculating distances reliably in rectangular coordinate systems like UTM, which is one compelling reason to use these systems instead of latitude and longitude, as discussed in "Work with Different Coordinate Systems" [Hack #26].

In order to determine the great-circle distance between two points, we can apply the *Law of Cosines*, which is itself a generalization of the Pythagorean theorem to triangles that lack a right angle. The Law of Cosines for spherical trigonometry states that:

$$\cos c = \cos a \cos b + \sin a \sin b \cos C$$

In this relation, $C$ is the angle between edges $a$ and $b$ on a "triangle" connecting three points on a spherical surface. If we place the third vertex of our spherical triangle at the North Pole, then the edges $a$ and $b$, which connect our two points to the third vertex, can be measured in units of latitude, and angle $C$ conveniently becomes the difference in longitude between them. Figure 3-15 depicts this relationship, using the great circle between Lagos, Nigeria, and San Francisco, California. We can then apply the inverse cosine function to the Law of Cosines to get the length of edge $c$, which is the distance between our two original points:

$$c = \cos^{-1}(\ \cos(90 - lat_1) \cos(90 - lat_2)$$
$$+ \sin(90 - lat_1) \sin(90 - lat_2) \cos(lon_2 - lon_1)\ )$$

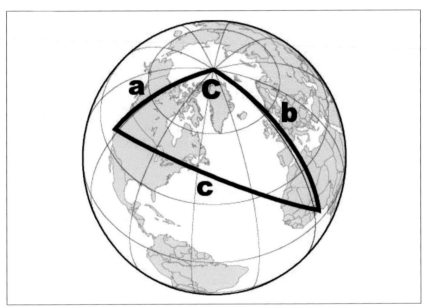

Figure 3-15. The Law of Cosines, exemplified with the great circle connecting San Francisco and Lagos

## The Code

However, our work is not quite done yet. For starters, most computational implementations of trigonometric functions take arguments measured in radians, not degrees. (Degrees can be converted to radians by multiplying by $\pi/180$.) Also, the result $c$ is returned in *radians* (i.e., a proportion of the radius of a unit sphere), which needs to be scaled to a real world measure to be useful. The following Perl code incorporates these extra steps:

```perl
use Math::Trig;

use constant RADIUS => 6367; # kilometers

sub great_circle {
    my ($lat1, $lon1, $lat2, $lon2) = @_;

    my $a = deg2rad( 90 - $lat1 );
    my $b = deg2rad( 90 - $lat2 );
    my $theta = deg2rad( $lon2 - $lon1 );
    my $c = acos( cos($a) * cos($b) +
                  sin($a) * sin($b) * cos($theta) );

    return RADIUS * $c;
}
```

The Math::Trig module, which comes with Perl, supplies the deg2rad( ) and acos( ) functions. Math::Trig also supplies a great_circle_distance( ) function, which can be used to simplify the preceding code as follows:

```perl
use Math::Trig 'great_circle_distance';

use constant RADIUS => 6367; # kilometers

sub great_circle {
    my ($lat1, $lon1, $lat2, $lon2) = map(deg2rad($_), @_);
    return great_circle_distance( $lon1, $lat1, $lon2, $lat2, RADIUS );
}
```

> As usual, latitudes south of the equator and longitudes west of the prime meridian should be given as negative values. Also, as is common with GIS-related tools, great_circle_distance( ) takes its arguments with longitude first, because, after all, longitude is the x-coordinate and latitude the y-coordinate.

The functionality embodied in our great_circle( ) function is also provided by the Geo::Distance module, which can be downloaded from the CPAN. Geo::Distance provides a nice wrapper for this method, allowing us to specify our units in English:

```perl
use Geo::Distance 'distance_calc';

my $dist_in_kilometers =
    distance_calc( kilometer => $lon1, $lat1, $lon2, $lat2 );

my $dist_in_miles =
    distance_calc( mile => $lon1, $lat1, $lon2, $lat2 );
```

Geo::Distance has a few other nice features; see **perldoc Geo::Distance** for more details.

## Other Considerations

Conventional wisdom holds that this approach has one major drawback, in that it relies on the mathematical properties of the inverse cosine function, which suffers badly from rounding errors for distances separated by less than a few degrees of arc. As an alternative, the formula given by the Law of Cosines can be rewritten using various trigonometric identities to yield the *Haversine formula*, which does not rely on the inverse cosine function to calculate great-circle distances.

However, with the number of significant figures used in modern double-precision floating math, the rounding errors expected with the inverse cosine function are actually not typically an issue. In fact, in temperate latitudes, the inverse-cosine formula for great-circle distances appears to be substantially more accurate than the Haversine formula. For distances wholly within the polar latitudes, the Haversine formula may or may not be more accurate.

The attentive reader may have noticed one other potentially serious hitch, which we have heretofore glossed over: although Earth is most certainly not flat, it is not exactly round, either. Rather, Earth is an oblate spheroid, slightly flattened at the poles. The WGS84 geodetic datum gives Earth an equatorial (or *semimajor*) radius of 6,378 kilometers, but a polar (or *semiminor*) radius of only 6,356 kilometers—a difference of about 22 kilometers. The value we used earlier is simply the arithmetic mean of these two values. Does the difference matter? For sake of argument, let's calculate the distance from London (51.52°N, 0.10°W) to Sydney (33.87°S, 151.21°E) using the two extremes:

```
use Geo::Distance ':all';

reg_unit( 'semimajor', 6378 );
reg_unit( 'semiminor', 6356 );

print "$_: ", distance_calc( $_, -0.10, 51.52, 151.21, -33.87 ), "\n"
        for qw( semimajor semiminor );
```

We use the reg_unit( ) function to register our own units for the radius of Earth and then call distance_calc( ) with each of our custom units in order to compare them. The result looks like this:

```
semimajor: 17010.3827750906
semiminor: 16951.7078893816
```

The difference between using the semimajor and semiminor radii of Earth yields a discrepancy of almost 60 kilometers! Looked at one way, this distance equals half a degree of longitude, but, looked at another way, it's only a 0.35% difference in measuring a line that stretches halfway across the world. Using the mean of the semimajor and semiminor radii mitigates the potential for error somewhat, but, obviously, the amount of time you spend considering this issue should bear some relation to the actual degree of accuracy you're after.

### See Also

- "Plot a Great Circle on a Flat Map" **[Hack #30]**
- "Work with Different Coordinate Systems" **[Hack #26]**
- Sinnott, R.W. "Virtues of the Haversine." Sky and Telescope, Vol. 68, No. 2, 1984, p. 159.
- See *http://mappinghacks.com/projects/distance/* for a discussion of different ways to simplify distance calculations.

## H A C K #28 Experiment with Different Cartographic Projections

There are lots of ways to depict a round planet on a flat plane, but, fortunately, there are also versatile tools for exploring the aesthetic compromises embodied in different cartographic projections.

One of the main challenges of mapping our world is how to represent its round surface on the flat plane of a map. Most projections involve some process of *projecting* Earth's spheroid surface directly onto a flat plane, or onto the surface of another figure which can be "unwrapped" into a flat plane without warping or tearing, such as a cylinder or cone. The projection surface may be aligned in a *conventional*, *transverse* (at a right angle), or *oblique* (i.e., at some other angle) fashion.

The projection process necessarily introduces distortions of one kind or another. Different cartographic projections make different choices about the trade-offs inherent in preserving one or more aspects of the planet's surface, at the expense of others. Table 3-1 outlines some of the properties that projections can preserve or distort.

*Table 3-1. Some properties of cartographic projections*

| Property | Map feature | Preserved by... |
| --- | --- | --- |
| Area | Relative areas of landmasses | Peters, Mollweide, Albers Equal-Area Conic |
| Conformality | Shapes of landmasses | Mercator, Stereographic, Lambert's Conformal Conic |

*Table 3-1. Some properties of cartographic projections (continued)*

| Property | Map feature | Preserved by... |
|---|---|---|
| Direction | The relative direction between two points (useful for navigation) | Mercator, Gnomonic |
| Distance | Distances from the center of the map | Azimuthal Equidistant |
| Scale | Ratio of distances on the map versus distances in the world | Many projections, but typically only along meridians or standard parallels |

In general, cartographic distortion tends to increase as one moves away from some "standard" parallels or meridians, which are used as parameters of the projection process. The canonical example of this tendency is Greenland, as depicted on a Mercator projection of the world, looming over North America like Godzilla eyeing downtown Tokyo. This results in part from the Mercator's conventional use of the equator as a standard parallel, which leads it to distort area to terrifyingly swollen proportions near the Poles.

The University of Hawaii's *Generic Mapping Tools*, or GMT, offer a useful way of experimenting with different map projections. GMT was originally intended for generating maps for inclusion in scientific publications, incorporating a series of useful command-line tools for plotting maps in a broad variety of projections. In addition, GMT includes vector data of reasonable quality of coastlines and political boundaries for the whole world, so it makes worthwhile maps right out of the box. Naturally, it's published under the GNU Public License, so the code and data are all "free as in freedom."

You can get GMT from its homepage at *http//gmt.soest.hawaii.edu/*. In general, you can follow the installation directions. Binaries are available for Windows from the FTP site, which can be accessed via the mirrors page. If you're running Debian or OS X, we recommend getting GMT from APT or Fink. If you're running Fedora Core or another RPM-based distribution, you can get binary packages of GMT from the Mapping Hacks RPM repository at *http://mappinghacks.com/rpm*. If you decide to install from source, you can have the web site generate an installation script for you, which, when run, will download and build GMT automatically. If you choose this route, you'll probably want to select shared libraries built with *gcc*.

Whichever way you decide to install GMT, don't forget to install the *netCDF* library as well. Most of the Unix-like installation options will do it for you automatically, but on Windows, you'll want to be sure to grab the precompiled DLL from the GMT FTP site.

Because of its origins in scientific publishing, GMT's primary output format is PostScript, which is great if you plan to make hardcopies of your maps—because, as a vector format, PostScript can be scaled to any size—but a little unwieldy otherwise. *Ghostview* (a.k.a. *gv*) is the ideal way to view Post-Script on Linux, and *GSview* is a solid, free PostScript viewer for Windows and OS X. You can find out more about these viewers at *http://www.cs.wisc.edu/~ghost/*. You should also be able to load and edit PostScript in most modern image editors, including the GIMP, in order to export your maps to other formats, like PNG or JPEG.

> If you want to jump right in and start making these maps on your own, without first installing GMT, try visiting the Online Map Creation site at *http://www.aquarius.geomar.de/omc/*. There, you'll find a very nice, simplified web-based frontend to GMT, which will allow you to experiment with some simple projections, and probably whet your appetite to do more!

### Cylindrical Projections

Frequently used cylindrical projections include Mercator, Transverse Mercator, and Peters projections.

**The Mercator projection.** The one projection that nearly everyone is familiar with, the *Mercator*, is a classic example of a cylindrical projection, which maps the surface of the planet onto that of a cylinder, and then unwraps it into a flat plane. The following GMT command renders a world map as a Mercator projection:

```
$ pscoast -JM18c -R-180/180/-75/85 -Bg30/g15 -G64/255/128 -S64/128/255 > \
mercator.ps
```

We use the *pscoast* command from GMT to generate a map of the world's landmasses. The -JM18c parameter requests a Mercator projection 18 centimeters wide, which should be big enough to fill a page, more or less. The -R command specifies the area we want mapped, west-by-east and south-by-north, with west longitudes and south latitudes given as negative values. -Bg30/g15 tells GMT we want a grid spaced every 30 degrees longitudinally and every 15 degrees latitudinally. Finally, -G and -S specify the fill colors for land and water areas, respectively. The colors are given in red/green/blue components, so the previous command would yield a light green for land areas and a light blue for water.

> Don't forget that, like many mapping applications, GMT typically expects longitude arguments first, followed by latitude. Think *x-y*, not latitude-longitude.

Like any good Unix tool, *pscoast* writes directly to its standard output. We've used shell redirection to dump the map to a file called *mercator.ps*, which is shown in Figure 3-16.

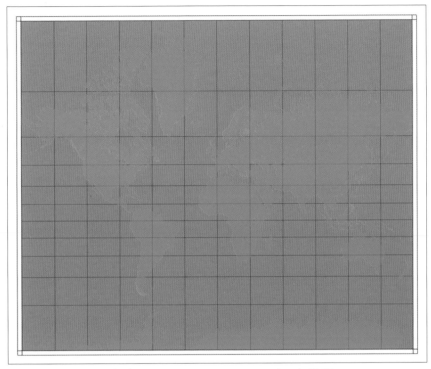

*Figure 3-16. The standard Mercator projection, generated with GMT*

Although the Mercator map distorts land area terribly near the poles, it has one enormously useful property, which is that any straight line on a Mercator projection follows a constant bearing in the real world. You can head off in the exact direction indicated by the map and actually arrive at the intended destination. (This can't be done with most cartographic projections, which ordinarily bend straight lines in the real world.) This direction-preserving property has made the Mercator projection valuable to marine navigators for the last 450 years!

**The Transverse Mercator projection.** In "Work with Different Coordinate Systems" [Hack #26], we discuss the enormous utility of the *Transverse Mercator* projection for mapping small regions of the world with minimal distortion, but they can be used to map larger regions as well. The "transverse" aspect of the Transverse Mercator projection refers to the fact that the cylindrical surface used in the projection gets turned on its side, so that the enormous polar distortion associated with the Mercator projection ends up being pushed out to the sides of the map. This property makes the Transverse Mercator projection useful for mapping regions longer north-by-south than east-by-west, like Chile, Great Britain, or a UTM zone. The following command generates a map as a Transverse Mercator projection similar to one used by the British National Grid system:

```
$ pscoast -JT0/18c -R-11/2/50/59 -G64/255/128 -S64/128/255 -W3 -Di -P > \
british_isles.ps
```

The -JT0/18c parameter requests a Transverse Mercator projection centered at 0 degrees longitude, with a width of 18 centimeters. The -R, -G, and -S parameters are used as explained earlier. The -W parameter asks GMT to outline the landmasses, in this case with a line 3 pixels wide. The -Di parameter requests a map based on intermediate resolution data, rather than the default low-res vectors. Finally, -P requests the map be presented portrait orientation, instead of the default landscape orientation—this is a map of an area longer north-by-south, after all. Figure 3-17 shows the result.

Although GMT offers five levels of vector resolution—crude, low, intermediate, high, and full—only the first three levels are shipped with GMT by default.

Incidentally, you can quite visibly demonstrate the manner in which the Transverse Mercator distorts landmasses away from the central meridian toward the sides, rather than the top and bottom, by mapping the whole world with it, using the following command:

```
$ pscoast -JT0/18c -R-180/180/-85/85 -Bg30/g15 -G64/255/128 -S64/128/255 > \
world_tm.ps
```

You can see the result in Figure 3-18. Note the extreme distortion of Central America, western South America, southern India, Sri Lanka, Indonesia, and so on; these are all regions that lie around 90°E or 90°W, near the equator. Meanwhile, Greenland and Antarctica, two places often given short shrift in cartographic projections, are shown in their proper size and shape, although Antarctica *is* bisected in this projection. Try setting the central meridian of a Transverse Mercator world map to your home longitude and see what you end up with.

The Peters projection. Other compromises can be made with cylindrical projections. One response to concerns that the Mercator projection distorts the perceived size, and hence the perceived importance, of northern countries at the expense of equatorial countries was the promotion of the *Peters* projection. The Peters projection is a special case of the *basic cylindrical*

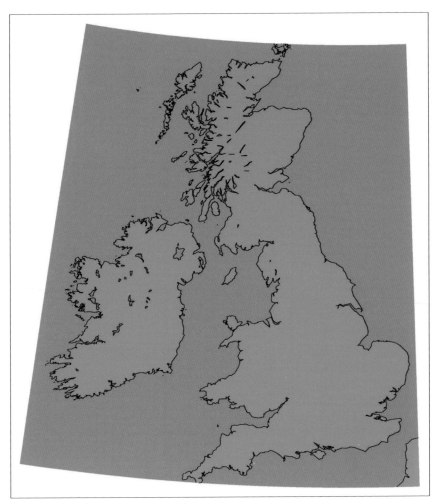

*Figure 3-17. A Transverse Mercator projection of Great Britain and Ireland*

projection, with the standard parallels placed at 45° North and South. Consequently, size and scale are preserved in the Peters projection at those latitudes but distorted elsewhere, in order to preserve relative size overall. Although this makes the shapes of most countries look a bit strange (except for those along the 45th parallel, like Germany or France), the result is a map that at least shows the correct size relationships between countries.

The following *pscoast* command generates a Peters projection map of the world:

```
$ pscoast -JY0/45/18c -R-180/180/-85/85 -Bg30/g15 -G64/255/128 -S64/128/255 \
-N1 -A5000 > peters.ps
```

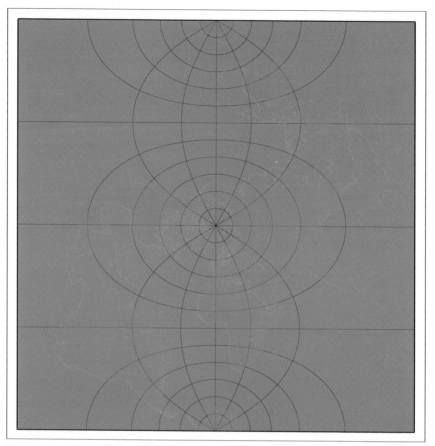

*Figure 3-18. The world in a Transverse Mercator projection, centered on 0° longitude*

Figure 3-19 shows the map itself. We've used the -JY0/45/18c parameter, which requests a map in the basic cylindrical projection, with its central parallels at 45°. To see what other kinds of maps you can make with the cylindrical projection, try playing with the central meridian and parallels. We've also used the -N1 option to display international borders, and the -A option to filter out features such as lakes and islands that have less than 5,000 km² total area, to make the map a little neater.

The Equidistant Cylindrical projection.  The *Equidistant Cylindrical (Plate Carrée)*, projection is a cylindrical projection that treats all lines of latitude as having the same length. Although this results in considerable distortions of scale away from the equator, it makes the calculations needed to plot things on the map trivial, to say the least. *pscoast* generates Equidistant Cylindrical

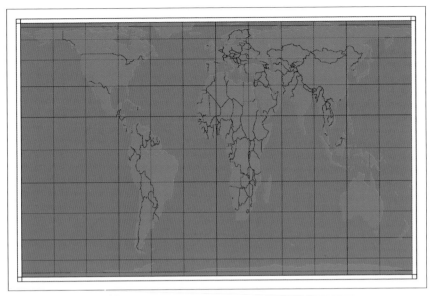

*Figure 3-19. The world in a Peters projection*

maps with the -Jq option. We discuss this projection in great detail in "Plot Arbitrary Points on a World Map" [Hack #29].

## Azimuthal Projections

In contrast to cylindrical projections, *azimuthal* projections are created by projecting, or in some way unwrapping, Earth's surface on to a flat plane. This style of projection lends itself very well to mapping the poles.

Stereographic projections. The following *pscoast* command plots a *stereographic* projection of the North Pole, which can be seen in Figure 3-20:

```
$ pscoast -JG0/90/18c -R-180/180/45/90 -Bg30/g15 -G64/255/128 -S64/128/255 \
-N1 -A5000 > n_pole.ps
```

The -JG0/90/18c parameter gives us a stereographic projection of the upper half of the Northern Hemisphere, oriented to 0° longitude, and centered on 90° North—i.e., the North Pole. The stereographic projection is essentially the image that would result if a light were projected through the planet from the opposite side of the planet onto a flat plane touching the surface at exactly one point. As it happens, the stereographic projection is a conformal projection, which, if you'll recall, means that it preserves the shapes of landmasses. Interesting results can be created if different center points and extents are chosen—try it!

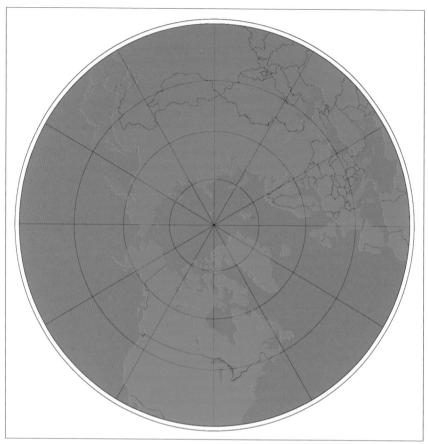

*Figure 3-20. The North Pole, shown in a stereographic projection*

Orthographic projections. The *orthographic* projection shows a single hemisphere in perspective. Although it distorts both area and direction, the orthographic projection is popular because, well, it looks like half a globe. *pscoast* generates orthographic projections with the -JG option. Figure 3-1 from "Digging to China" [Hack #22] features a GMT-generated orthographic map centered on San Francisco.

The Azimuthal Equidistant projection. The *Azimuthal Equidistant* projection is just what it sounds like: an azimuthal projection that preserves distance and direction from the center of the map. The result can look pretty interesting. Figure 3-21 shows an Azimuthal Equidistant projection of the world, centered near New York City at 40°N 75°W, as generated with the following command:

```
$ pscoast -JE-75/40/18c -R-180/180/-90/90 -Bg30 -G64/255/128 -S64/128/255 \
  -A5000 > nyc.ps
```

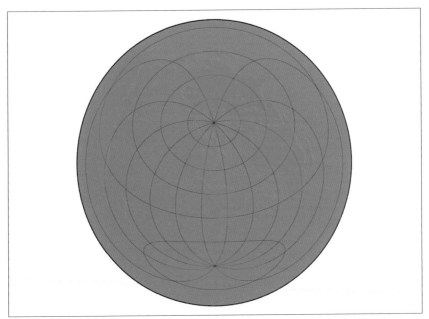

*Figure 3-21. The world shown relative to distance and direction from New York City*

The big blob on the left side is Australia, which is greatly distorted in shape and size due to its extreme distance from New York. In contrast, Figure 3-22 shows the same projection centered in the vicinity of Sydney, at 30°S 150°E.

**The Gnomonic projection.** Other types of azimuthal projection are possible, as well. The *Gnomonic* projection is similar to the stereographic projection, except that the "light" source used to project the planet's surface is placed at the center of the planet, instead of at the side opposite the point that the projection surface touches the planet. The following *pscoast* command generates a Gnomonic projection extending 75 degrees in each direction from 51°N 0°E, near London, as shown in Figure 3-23:

```
$ pscoast -JF0/51/75/18c -R-180/180/-90/90 -Bg30 -G64/255/128 -S64/128/255 \
-A5000 > gnomonic.ps
```

The really nifty thing about the Gnomonic projection is that every straight line on a Gnomonic projection follows a *great circle*, which is the shortest line between two points on the surface of a globe. This makes the Gnomonic projection exceptionally useful for air navigation, in much the same way as the Mercator is useful for marine navigation.

The Gnomonic projection can also be applied to project Earth's surface onto the faces of a polyhedron, such as a cube, instead of a single flat plane. Buckminster Fuller's *Dymaxion* projection is a special example of a Gnomonic projection of Earth's surface onto an icosahedron, a 20-sided

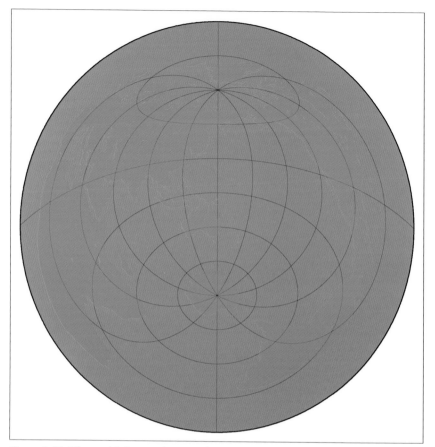

*Figure 3-22. The world shown relative to distance and direction from Sydney*

three-dimensional figure. We discuss how to make use of Fuller's projection in "Plot Dymaxion Maps in Perl" **[Hack #31]**.

## Conic Projections

Yet a third type of projection can be constructed by projecting a globe onto the surface of a cone placed over the top of it. If cylindrical projections are traditionally used to map equatorial regions with a minimum of distortion, and azimuthal projections to map polar regions similarly, then conic projections are traditionally used to map the middle latitudes most effectively.

**Lambert's Conformal Conic projection.** With the following command, we can use *Lambert's Conformal Conic* projection to make a quite reasonable map of Europe, as shown in Figure 3-24:

```
$ pscoast -JL15/50/40/65/18c -R-12/50/34/72 -G64/255/128 -S64/128/255 -N1 \
-A5000 > europe.ps
```

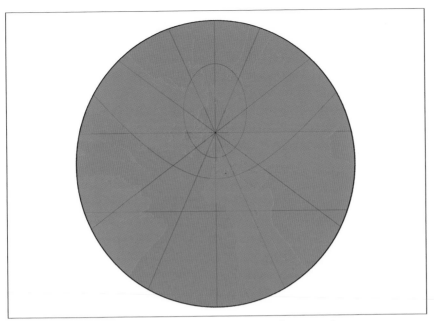

*Figure 3-23. A Gnomonic projection of the world, centered near London*

*pscoast* takes five arguments for its -JL option, which generates a Lambert's Conformal Conic projection. The first two are the longitude and latitude of the center of the projection, the next two are the two standard parallels of the projection—i.e., the lines of minimum distortion—and the last one, of course, is the map size.

Lambert's Conformal Conic projection preserves shapes and is often used to map regions that are broader east-to-west than north-to-south, like the continental United States.

Albers Equal-Area Conic projection. The *Albers Equal-Area Conic* projection is another common conic projection, used for purposes similar to that of Lambert's Conformal Conic. As the name suggests, this projection preserves area at the expense of shapes, but the choice between the two is largely aesthetic. For comparison's sake, Figure 3-25 shows the previous Lambert's Conformal Conic map of Europe in gray, with a matching Albers Equal-Area Conic projection overlaid in black. As you can see, two projections differ significantly from each other only as you move away from the projection center.

The map shown in Figure 3-25 was made with the following two commands and relies on the handy overlay feature in *pscoast*:

```
$ pscoast -JL15/50/40/65/18c -R-12/50/34/72 -W2/64/64/64 -N1/1/64/64/64 \
-A5000 -K > overlay.ps
$ pscoast -JB15/50/40/65/18c -R-12/50/34/72 -W2 -N1 -A5000 -O >> overlay.ps
```

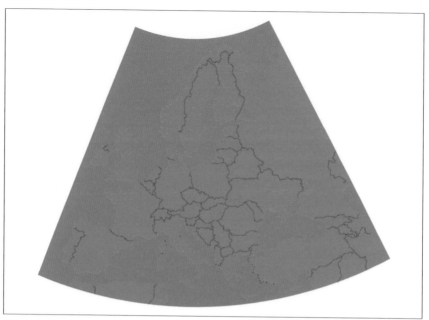

*Figure 3-24. Europe, in Lambert's Conformal Conic projection, with standard parallels of 40° and 65° N*

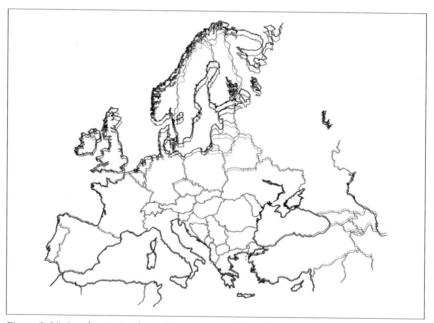

*Figure 3-25. Lambert's Conformal Conic versus Albers Equal-Area*

The first command generates the Lambert's projection in gray, using the -K command to tell *pscoast* to leave out the PostScript footers that indicate that the document is finished. The second command appends an Albers Equal-Area projection to the PostScript file using the -JB option, which utilizes the same projection parameters. The -O command tells *pscoast* to omit the Post-Script headers from the second map, which will cause the second map to simply be drawn on top of the first. The -K and -O commands can be combined to successively overlay three or more layers of output from GMT.

## Pseudocylindrical Projections

Some projections have a mathematical, rather than geometric, origin. The *sinusoidal* projection, for example, plots straight parallels against meridians that are curved relative to the cosine of the longitude. Imagine what you might get if you smoothed the ends of the cylinder to a point before attempting a Mercator projection, and you have the basic idea, which is why the sinusoidal projection is sometimes referred to as a *pseudocylindrical* projection. The result is shown in Figure 3-26, which we generated using the -JI option to *pscoast*.

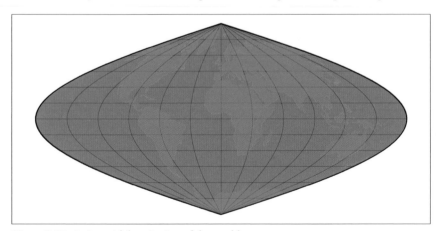

*Figure 3-26. A sinusoidal projection of the world*

Although the sinusoidal projection distorts shapes rather badly away from the equator, it preserves land area, and it has the advantage of being nearly as easy to calculate as the Equidistant Cylindrical projection. Figure 3-27 shows a more aesthetically pleasing sinusoidal map of the world, made by *interrupting* the projection at 160°W, 20°E, and 60°E.

Figure 3-27 was generated with a shell script called *sinusoidal.sh*, containing the following commands:

```
#!/bin/sh
pscoast -Ji-95/0.05c -R-170/-20/-90/90 -Bg30/g15 -G64/255/128 -S64/128/255
-A5000 -K
```

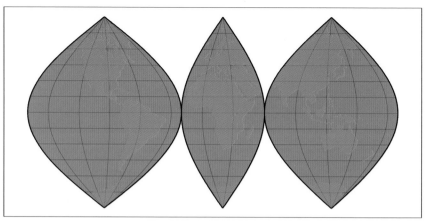

*Figure 3-27. An interrupted sinusoidal projection of the world*

```
pscoast -Ji20/0.05c  -R-20/60/-90/90 -Bg30/g15 -G64/255/128 -S64/128/255
-A5000 -X7.5c -O -K
pscoast -Ji125/0.05c -R60/190/-90/90 -Bg30/g15 -G64/255/128 -S64/128/255
-A5000 -X4c -O
```

The script was then run as follows:

```
$ sh ./sinusoidal.sh > sinusoidal.ps
```

In GMT, if a projection is specified with a lowercase letter (-Ji), rather than an uppercase letter (-JI), then the size measurement is taken to specify the width of a single degree at the equator (or standard parallel), rather than the size of the whole map. A 360-degree map of Earth at 0.05 cm per degree would therefore yield a map 18 cm wide. We used this style of *pscoast* invocation here because it made the value of the -X option, which specifies how far to offset each interrupted segment of the map along the $x$ axis, a little easier to calculate. (*pscoast* also supports a -Y option.) Note the use of both -K and -O to allow overlays as described earlier.

## Plotting Locations with GMT

We've by no means exhausted either the list of possible cartographic projections or the full range of GMT's features. GMT comes with a lot more tools than just *pscoast*, but we'll have to refer you to the documentation at *http://gmt.soest.hawaii.edu/* to learn what else it can do. We'll just finish by highlighting the *psxy* command from GMT, which plots longitude/latitude points in PostScript.

Given a list of the longitudes and latitudes of the world's 50 largest cities, separated by commas, one pair per line, in a file called *cities.txt*, we can use *psxy* to plot them on a Robinson projection of the world. The Robinson projection is a modified cylindrical projection, popular for balancing the trade-offs in size and shape on world maps. In this example, we'll plot the cities with .25 cm wide red stars and center the map at 10°E, in order to avoid splitting Siberia. We'll leave further exploration of the following GMT commands as an exercise for the gentle reader, but you can see the map they produce in Figure 3-28:

```
$ pscoast -JN10/18c -R-170/190/-90/90 -G64/255/128 -S64/128/255 -A5000 -K > \
cities.ps
$ psxy cities.txt -JN10/18c -R-170/190/-90/90 -Bg30/g15 -Sa.25c -G255/0/0 -O \
>> cities.ps
```

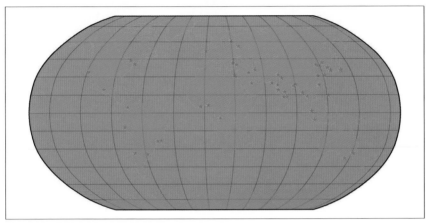

*Figure 3-28. The world's 50 largest cities, plotted on a Robinson projection*

## See Also

- "Work with Different Coordinate Systems" [Hack #26]
- "Plot Arbitrary Points on a World Map" [Hack #29]
- "Digging to China" [Hack #22]
- "Plot Dymaxion Maps in Perl" [Hack #31]
- Generic Mapping Tools home page (*http://gmt.soest.hawaii.edu/*)
- Online Map Creation site (*http://www.aquarius.geomar.de/omc/*)

### HACK #29 Plot Arbitrary Points on a World Map

Of the dozens of common cartographic projections used to depict the entire world, the Equidistant Cylindrical projection—also known as the rectangular projection—is by far the most hackable, making it easy to plot points wherever you want.

Since our lovely world is round but our maps are not, the would-be map hacker has a choice to make when selecting a cartographic projection for a given map. The range of available choices are described in detail in

"Experiment with Different Cartographic Projections" [Hack #28]. Sometimes, the best projection, however, is no projection at all. The *Equidistant Cylindrical* projection is made by treating every degree of latitude and longitude as equal in length, resulting in a perfectly rectangular map with a 2:1 width-to-height ratio. First attributed to Eratosthenes of Cyrene in the third century BC, this projection does not preserve area, shape, direction, distance, or scale (except along meridians), but it has one supreme advantage. It's easy to hack!

Here's why: since meridians and parallels in this projection meet at equally spaced right angles, latitude and longitude can simply be treated as rectangular coordinates, shortcutting the tortuous spherical trigonometry that usually plagues the art of cartographic projection. By consequence, the Equidistant Cylindrical projection is also referred to as *equirectangular*, or simply *rectangular*. (You'll also see it referred to as the *Plate Carrée* projection, which is French for "square plane.") Naturally, some cartographers think it's cheating to simply set $x = R\lambda$ and $y = R\phi$, and so maps of this kind are also referred to as *unprojected*.

## Finding Base Maps on the Web

Because the Equidistant Cylindrical projection is so hackable, lots of interesting mapping apps like *xplanet* [Hack #46] and *worldKit* [Hack #39] rely on it, making good base maps easy to find on the Web. For example, NASA's beautiful *Blue Marble* imagery is provided in this form. You can find free images on NASA's Earth Observatory at *http://earthobservatory.nasa.gov/ Newsroom/BlueMarble/BlueMarble.html*. Another great source of world maps in this projection is the *flatplanet* maps catalog, which can be found at *http://flatplanet.sourceforge.net/maps/*. We couldn't find a rectangular projection base map with political borders that we liked, so we made one of our own, using the Blue Marble imagery, *GMT*, and *the GIMP* [Hack #32]. You can download our Blue Marble, political-borders base map at *http:// mappinghacks.com/maps/*.

## The Code

Here's a sample Perl script called *plot_points.pl* that uses Arnar Hrafnkelsson's excellent Imager module to plot locations on a rectangular-projection world map. You can get Imager from the CPAN at *http://search.cpan.org/ ~addi/Imager/*:

```
#!/usr/bin/perl

use Imager;
use strict;
```

```
my ($in, $out) = @ARGV;
die "Usage: $0 <input.jpg> <output.jpg>\n" unless $in and $out;

my ($top, $left)     = (  90, -180 );
my ($bottom, $right) = ( -90,  180 );

my $map = Imager->new;
$map->open( file => $in ) or die $map->errstr;

my $x_scale = $map->getwidth  / ($right - $left);
my $y_scale = $map->getheight / ($bottom - $top);

while (<STDIN>) {
    my ($lat, $lon) = /(-?\d+\.?\d*)/gos;
    next if $lon > $right or $lon < $left or $lat < $bottom or $lat > $top;

    my $x = ($lon - $left) * $x_scale;
    my $y = ($lat - $top)  * $y_scale;

    $map->circle( color => "white", r => 5, x => $x, y => $y );
    $map->circle( color => "red",   r => 4, x => $x, y => $y );
}

$map->write( file => $out ) or die $map->errstr;
```

*plot_points.pl* takes two arguments on the command line: a filename to read
the world map from, and another filename to write the map plus the points
into. The script hinges on the fact that, in an Equidistant Cylindrical projection, each pixel will take up a fixed number of degrees of both latitude and
longitude, no matter where it lies on the map. (This is not the case with
other projections, of course.) So we start by getting the image width and
height, and then calculate the scale in pixels per degree for both the *x*- and
*y*-axes.

> Although, by definition, the *x*- and *y*-scales should be the
> same, calculating them separately is only a little extra work,
> and it guarantees that our script will still work on rectangu-
> lar maps that have been squashed or stretched consistently
> in one dimension or the other.

*plot_points.pl* then tries to read coordinates from its standard input, one pair
per line, latitude first, in decimal degree notation, and does a little bounds
checking. Then, for each axis, it calculates the distance to the edge of the
map in degrees and converts this value to pixels by multiplying by the scale
values calculated earlier. And that's all the heavy lifting there is! A red circle
is drawn inside a slightly larger white circle to obtain a nice border effect
(though there are actually better ways of doing this in Imager), and then,
after all the points are read, the whole thing is written to disk.

Note that there's nothing particularly Perl-ish about our script. The same technique should be easy to implement in any language. In fact, in "Plot Points on an Interactive Map Using DHTML" **[Hack #41]**, we'll show off the exact same technique in JavaScript, with a few added wrinkles.

## Running the Code

Here's a sample run of *plot_points.pl*, run on the Pathfinder image from the *flatplanet* gallery and fed points for London, New York, and Tokyo. You can hit Ctrl-D after you're done entering points by hand. Figure 3-29 shows the result:

```
$ perl plot_points.pl PathfinderMap.jpg three_cities.jpg
51 0
40 -74
35 140
```

Figure 3-29. *London, New York, and Tokyo, plotted on an Equidistant Cylindrical world map*

Of course, if you have a file full of points, you can just use shell redirection to dump the list right into the script. If the file contains other things, such as labels for each point, that's okay, so long as the first two decimal numbers on each line are the latitude and longitude, respectively. For example, suppose you have a tab-separated file of the world's 7,000 largest cities, sorted by population, in a file called *cities.txt*:

| place name | country | current population | latitude | longitude |
|---|---|---|---|---|
| Mumbai | India | 12383146 | 18.96° | 72.82° |
| Buenos Aires | Argentina | 12116379 | -34.61° | -58.37° |
| "Kar&#257;chi" | Pakistan | 10537226 | 24.86° | 67.01° |

```
Manila          Philippines    10232924       14.62°       120.97°
Dilli           India          10203687       28.67°        77.21°
...
```

If you wanted to plot just the 50 largest cities, you couldn't feed it directly into *plot_points.pl*, because (a) you'd get all 7,000 that way and (b) the population figure appears before the latitude and longitude in each line. But you *could* feed it through the Unix *head(1)* and *cut(1)* commands, and pipe that into *plot_points.pl*:

```
$ head -50 cities.txt | cut -f4,5 | perl plot_points.pl PathfinderMap.jpg
biggest.jpg
```

If you don't have such a file of your own, you can get ours from *http:// mappinghacks.com/data/cities.txt*. The map thus generated looks something like Figure 3-30. Isn't the Unix shell neat?

*Figure 3-30. The world's 50 largest cities, plotted on an Equidistant Cylindrical map*

## Why Use Any Other Projection, if This One Is So Simple?

Well, sadly, even though the Equidistant Cylindrical projection looks fine at a global scale, and would even look all right for places near the equator, where lines of latitude and longitude really are about the same length, all that stuff near the Poles *is* pretty badly distorted. On the maps we've been looking at, that doesn't really matter much, but the Equidistant Cylindrical projection definitely won't make for such great maps of smaller regions farther away from the equator.

The *sinusoidal* projection offers one alternative. Instead of treating latitude and longitude as equal, distances between two lines of longitude are scaled to the cosine of the latitude, as would be depicted on a globe. Instead of using the following code to determine the *x*-coordinate:

```
my $x = ($lon - $left) * $x_scale;
```

we could use this calculation to plot a sinusoidal projection of our data:

```
my $x = ($lon - $left) * $x_scale * cos( $lat );
```

Although this distorts the shapes of large areas, it's easy to calculate, and it preserves the relationship of latitude and longitude better at temperate latitudes. For this reason, the TIGER Map Server makes use of the sinusoidal projection, as discussed in "Make Free Maps of the United States Online" [Hack #14].

We examine still other cartographic projections in "Experiment with Different Cartographic Projections" [Hack #28]. Still, no other projection beats the Equidistant Cylindrical projection for ease of use, and there's absolutely something to be said for that.

### See Also

- "View Your Photo Thumbnails on a Flash Map" [Hack #39]
- "Experiment with Different Cartographic Projections" [Hack #28]
- "Make Free Maps of the United States Online" [Hack #14]
- "Plot Points on an Interactive Map Using DHTML" [Hack #41]
- *http://flatplanet.sourceforge.net/maps/*
- *http://mappinghacks.com/maps/*

### HACK #30   Plot a Great Circle on a Flat Map

Wherein our heroes discover that the shortest distance between two points on a globe is not a straight line, after all.

What's so great about a *great circle*? A great circle, technically speaking, is any circle that goes all the way around a sphere, with its center on the exact center point of the sphere. As it turns out, when a great circle connects two points on a sphere, the arc between them is always the shortest distance between those two points. Naturally, being able to take the shortest possible path is a matter of great financial and practical importance in this modern era of air travel.

Familiar two-dimensional map projections don't give a good impression of great-circle distance. On a Mercator map, the straight line that seems to be the shortest route between San Francisco and London passes through

Boston; but, in fact, due to the curvature of the globe, the *actual* shortest route runs nearer to the North Pole, passing over the south of Greenland.

This hack makes use of *Generic Mapping Tools*, or GMT [Hack #28] to show how to plot segments of a great circle on many different cartographic projections, including those designed for marine and aerial navigation. We'll also show you how you can try this yourself with a quick Perl script.

## Great Circles on a Mercator Projection

The Mercator projection was historically useful because it preserved navigational direction along lines of constant bearing, known as *rhumb lines*. One could draw a straight line to one's destination on the map, set off in the direction indicated by that line, and actually arrive at the intended destination sometime in the future. Navigating by a Mercator map therefore had the great advantage of simplicity, but the disadvantage was that the rhumb line between two points was often not the shortest path.

Instead, the shortest path between two points follows a line of variable bearing, which turns out to be the arc of a great circle. This may seem counterintuitive, because a great-circle arc will usually end up looking curved on a flat map. Figure 3-31 depicts the great-circle arc connecting San Francisco and London on a Mercator projection of the world.

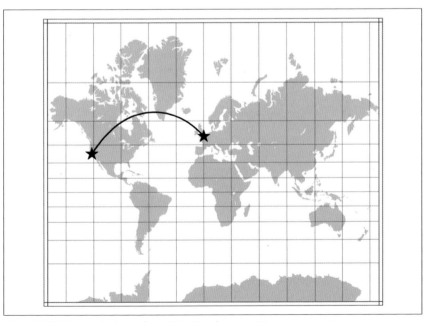

*Figure 3-31. Great-circle arc from SF to London on a Mercator projection*

The following commands, using *pscoast* and *psxy* from GMT, were used to generate Figure 3-31:

```
$ pscoast -JM18c -R-170/190/-75/85 -Bg30/g15 -A5000 -G192/192/192 -K > \
mercator.ps
$ psxy points.txt -JM18c -R-170/190/-75/85 -W8 -O -K >> mercator.ps
$ psxy points.txt -JM18c -R-170/190/-75/85 -Sa.75c -G0/0/0 -O >> mercator.ps
```

The call to *pscoast* draws the graticule (i.e., grid lines) and the base map of the continents. We recommend reviewing [Hack #28] to understand exactly how these particular *pscoast* options do their magic. The first call to *psxy* actually draws the great-circle arc into the same file. We give *psxy* the same projection parameters we did *pscoast*, along with a filename, *points.txt*. The *points.txt* file simply contains the following:

```
-122,38
0,51
```

The geographically savvy reader will recognize these as the longitude and latitude coordinates of San Francisco and London, respectively. The -W8 option to *psxy* tells it to make the great-circle arc 8 pixels thick. Finally, we call *psxy* one more time, with the same projection parameters and filename containing our points, but this time we give the -S option to request that symbols be drawn at each point, instead of a line connecting them. In this case, the -Sa.75c option draws us a star .75 centimeters wide at each end point, coloring each one black via the -G option.

> The shortest line between two points on any geometric figure is referred to as a *geodesic*, of which the great circle along a spherical surface is but an example. For this reason, the GRASS command for drawing great circles is called *r. geodesic*. The word *geodesic*, which comes from the Greek words for "dividing the Earth," is also used to describe Buckminster Fuller's dome structures, in the way that they systematically divide the surface of a sphere (or hemisphere) into triangular faces.

## Great Circles on an Orthographic Projection

The fact that a great circle forms the shortest line between two points doesn't seem quite as odd, however, when you look at a globe. Figure 3-32 depicts the same great-circle arc connecting San Francisco and London on an orthographic projection, which presents a flat perspective view of a globe. From this vantage, it becomes evident that the shortest route from San Francisco to London really does sort of run *over* the curve of the earth, as it were, rather than around it. Consequently, the line that runs between them through Boston—the line one might have *thought* was the shortest, looking at a Mercator map—is actually quite hopelessly roundabout.

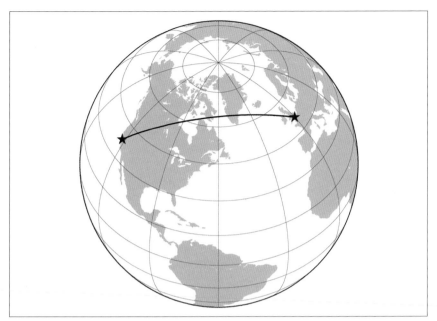

*Figure 3-32. Great-circle arc from San Francisco to London on an orthographic
projection*

Figure 3-32 was made using the same GMT commands as Figure 3-31,
except that the -JM18c parameter for generating a Mercator projection was
replaced with -JG-60/45/18c, which draws an orthographic projection 18
centimeters wide, centered on 60° W and 45° N.

## Great Circles on a Gnomonic Projection

There are other ways to visualize great circles on a flat map, of course. If we
want a map that depicts the shortest distance between two points as a
straight line, we can turn to the Gnomonic projection. Basically, any straight
line on a Gnomonic projection, regardless of origin or bearing, represents a
great-circle arc on Earth's surface. Although the Gnomonic projection distorts the shape and area of landmasses something fierce, the property of
showing any great-circle arc as a straight line makes it quite useful for the
purposes of air navigation. Figure 3-33 shows the great circle connecting
London and San Francisco on a Gnomonic projection of the world.
Figure 3-33 was generated with GMT in the same fashion as Figures 3-31
and 3-32, using the -JF-75/60/60/18c option to plot the Gnomonic projection centered on 75° W and 60° N, with a radius of 60°.

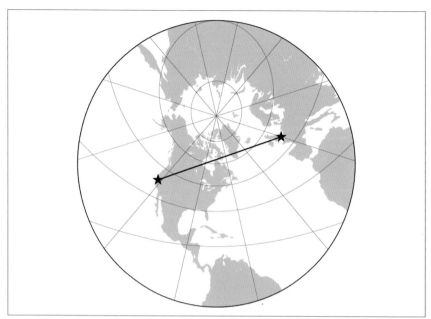

*Figure 3-33. Great-circle arc from San Francisco to London on a Gnomonic projection*

## Great Circles of Perl

In practice, great-circle routes are hard to navigate precisely, because the bearing of a great circle relative to True North changes continually, unlike that of a rhumb line. In fact, the conventional way to navigate a great-circle route is to approximate it with a series of short rhumb lines. We can use this same technique to draw the path of a great-circle arc on a flat map in Perl:

```perl
#!/usr/bin/perl

use Math::Trig qw(great_circle_direction  deg2rad);
use Imager;
use strict;

my ($mapfile, $lon1, $lat1, $lon2, $lat2) = @ARGV;
my @origin = ($lon1, $lat1);
my @dest   = ($lon2, $lat2);
my $step   = .1;

my @position = @origin;
my @points;

until (abs($position[0] - $dest[0]) < $step
    and abs($position[1] - $dest[1]) < $step) {
      my $bearing = great_circle_direction(
          deg2rad( $position[0] ),
```

```
        deg2rad( 90 - $position[1] ),
        deg2rad( $dest[0] ),
        deg2rad( 90 - $dest[1] )
    );

    $position[0] += sin($bearing) * $step / cos(deg2rad($position[1])) ;
    $position[1] += cos($bearing) * $step;

    $position[0] += 360 if $position[0] < -180;
    $position[0] -= 360 if $position[0] > 180;

    push @points, @position;
}
```

In the first part of our script, we do the actual approximation of rhumb lines to a great circle, using the great_circle_direction() function from the Math::Trig module, which ships with Perl. We get the name of an image containing an Equidistant Cylindrical projection, as well as the longitude and latitude of our start and end points from the command line. We set @origin to the longitude and latitude of our starting point, and @dest to that of our destination. $step is chosen to roughly approximate the length of each component rhumb line. The current position is stored in @position, which gets initialized to our origin.

At each step, we call great_circle_direction() to find the bearing from True North at our current position along the great circle to our destination. Since great_circle_direction() expects its arguments in radians, not degrees, and places the zero latitude at the North Pole, rather than the equator, we have to make the proper adjustments before passing those values. We store the result in radians in $bearing, which we then use to update our current position.

Updating the latitude of our current position, as stored in $position[1], is easy: simply add the cosine of our bearing scaled by the length of our rhumb line to find the latitude of our next end point. If you dig deep into the mists of your high school trigonometry education, you'll remember why this is so: If we take $step to be the length of the hypotenuse of a right triangle, then the cosine of the bearing is equal to the length of the adjacent side divided by the length of the hypotenuse.

Multiplying both sides of the equation by $step yields the code shown earlier for updating $position[1].

Updating the longitude, however is a little trickier. We could simply take our current longitude, stored in $position[0], and add the sine of our current bearing, scaled by the length of our rhumb line, but we would be ignoring an important fact about our round world. As you head toward the poles, the distance between two lines of longitude gets shorter in proportion to the cosine of the latitude. At the equator, the distance separating one degree of longitude is *cos(0°)* = 1 degree of latitude. At the North Pole, the distance is *cos(90°)*, which is zero. Thus we divide our longitude increment by the cosine of the current latitude, in order to keep in step with the actual great-circle arc.

 Actually, we fibbed slightly. The distance separating one degree of longitude at the equator isn't *quite* equal to one degree of latitude, because Earth isn't a perfect sphere— it's an oblate spheroid, which means it's slightly flattened at the poles and slightly bulged around the middle, due to rotational and tidal forces. Because the difference is insignificant for our purposes, though, we'll otherwise ignore this fact in our discussion.

Finally, we do some bounds checking, to keep our longitude from running off the edge of the map. Having done so, we add our new current position to @points, and repeat, until we're close enough to our destination that it's not worth continuing.

Now that we have a list of longitude/latitude coordinates in @points, representing the end points of the rhumb line segments that approximate our great-circle arc, we can use any suitable method to plot them on a flat map. For simplicity's sake, we'll use the method outlined in "Plot Arbitrary Points on a World Map" **[Hack #29]** to draw the great-circle arc between San Francisco and London on an Equidistant Cylindrical map of the world. The remainder of our script, then, reads as follows:

```
my ($top, $left)     = (  90, -180 );
my ($bottom, $right) = ( -90,  180 );

my $map = Imager->new;
$map->open( file => $mapfile ) or die $map->errstr;

my $x_scale = $map->getwidth  / ($right - $left);
my $y_scale = $map->getheight / ($bottom - $top);

while (@points) {
    my (@x, @y);
    while (my ($lon, $lat) = splice @points, 0, 2) {
        push @x, ($lon - $left) * $x_scale;
        push @y, ($lat - $top)  * $y_scale;
        last if @points and $lon < -170 and $points[0] > -170;
    }
    $map->polyline( x => \@x, y => \@y, color => "red" );
}

$map->write( fh => \*STDOUT, type => "jpeg" ) or die $map->errstr;
```

Since this method of plotting points on a rectangular map [Hack #29] is explained elsewhere, we'll gloss over the details here. We load the map image stored earlier in $mapfile into an object stored in $map. The crucial bit happens in the while( ) loop, where we shift coordinate pairs off of @points, and convert the longitude and latitude to x- and y-coordinates on the map image. Once we've done this, we send our lists of x and y end points to $map->polyline( ), to draw the actual arc on the map. We have to be sure to test for the case where the arc crosses the international date line, and break the polyline into two parts, if necessary. The last if @points... statement tests for this possibility. Finally, the map is dumped to standard output. The code to run is as follows:

```
$ perl greatcircle.pl PathfinderMap.jpg  -122 38 0 51 > sf_to_london.jpg
```

We give the script the name of our Equidistant Cylindrical map file [Hack #29] for good sources of such maps), as well as the longitude and latitude of San Francisco and London, in that order. The map, which is shown in Figure 3-34, shows the great-circle arc connecting them. Adding embellishments, such as a marker at each end, is left as an exercise for the reader.

*Figure 3-34. Great-circle arc from SF to London, plotted with Perl, on a Equidistant Cylindrical projection*

Of course, having found the shortest route from San Francisco to London, you will probably immediately want to know how long that route is, which is a question tackled in "Calculate the Distance Between Points on the Earth's Surface" [Hack #27].

## See Also

- "Experiment with Different Cartographic Projections" [Hack #28]
- "Plot Arbitrary Points on a World Map" [Hack #29]
- "Calculate the Distance Between Points on the Earth's Surface" [Hack #27]

## HACK #31  Plot Dymaxion Maps in Perl

See Earth's surface as one world in one ocean, just as Bucky Fuller intended.

Any projection of Earth's surface onto a flat plane necessarily introduces distortions of one kind or another. "Experiment with Different Cartographic Projections" [Hack #28] discusses the most common sorts of trade-offs that cartographic projections typically make in trying to preserve the area, shape, or relative locations of Earth's landmasses. However, cartographic projections can emphasize other aspects of the world's surface, as well.

Toward the end of "a precise means for seeing the world from the dynamic, cosmic and comprehensive viewpoint," R. Buckminster Fuller labored for decades to invent the Dymaxion projection, which projects Earth's spheroid onto an icosahedron aligned in such a way that 18 of its 20 triangular faces can be unwrapped onto a flat plane without splitting landmasses. The other two faces artfully split the Yellow Sea and the Indian Ocean. Across each individual face, distortion is relatively slight, so that the world is shown as "one island in one ocean," with the shapes and areas of the landmasses more or less preserved. Fuller's projection, although useless for navigation, can serve to represent other relationships in our world, without introducing the possibility of psychological distortion that some argue is engendered by more conventional cartographic projections.

For example, we might want to see the world's 100 major population centers on a Dymaxion projection, a visualization that can dispense with navigation as a potential requirement. Plotting latitude and longitude on a Dymaxion map, however, involves a bit of spherical trigonometry; the coordinates must first be converted to (x,y,z) coordinates on a spheroid with Earth's center as its origin, and then these points must be rotated and translated through space onto the flat plane that comprises our map. The mathematics is hardly for the faint of heart, which is why we're lucky that there are several sources of code out there that will do the trig for us!

## The Code

One such source is Robert W. Gray's homepage, which offers some code for Dymaxion coordinate transformation at *http://www.rwgrayprojects.com/ rbfnotes/maps/graymap6.html*. Gray's code does all the math, but it's written in C—a little complicated for simple visualization work. To make life a little easier on people who want to experiment with the Dymaxion projection, I used Brian Ingerson's terrific *Inline.pm* module to seamlessly glue Gray's code onto a Perl module called Geo::Dymaxion, which is freely distributed on the CPAN. Geo::Dymaxion requires you to have *Inline* installed, but you can install both automatically using the CPAN shell:

```
$ perl -MCPAN -e 'install Geo::Dymaxion'
```

If you've never used the CPAN shell before, you will be asked a series of silly questions, but you will only need to do it once.

The Geo::Dymaxion API only has two method calls: new( ), which creates a map object and specifies its dimensions in pixels (or other arbitrary measure), and plot( ), which takes a point specified in latitude and longitude and returns its location on the Dymaxion map, using the upper left corner as the origin. The coordinates returned by plot( ) can be used by an image-manipulation library, like *Imager.pm*. You can install *Imager* using the CPAN shell, as above.

The following script, which we'll call *plot_cities.pl*, uses *Imager.pm* and Geo::Dymaxion to plot a list of cities on a Dymaxion map of the world:

```perl
#!/usr/bin/perl
use Imager;
use Geo::Dymaxion;
use strict;

my $map = Imager->new;
$map->open( file => "dymaxion.png" );

my $dymax = Geo::Dymaxion->new( $map->getwidth, $map->getheight );

open CITIES, "<cities.txt" or die "Can't read cities.txt: $!";
scalar <CITIES>; # throw away the header line

for (1 .. 50) {
    my $line = <CITIES>;
    my @field = split /\t/, $line;

    my $lat  = $field[-2];
    $lat  *= -1 if $lat  =~ /S/;
    $lat  =~ y/0-9.-//cd; # throw away non-numeric characters

    my $long = $field[-1];
    $long *= -1 if $long =~ /W/;
    $long =~ y/0-9.-//cd; # throw away non-numeric characters

    my ($x, $y) = $dymax->plot( $lat, $long );
    $map->circle( x => $x, y => $y, r => 3, color => "red" );
}
```

```
$map->write( file => "world_cities.png" )
    or die $map->errstr;
```

The script starts by opening a text file called *cities.txt* and then discards the header line. Next, it reads the next 50 lines, one by one, splitting each line up into tab-separated fields, extracting the latitude and longitude from the second-to-last and last fields on each line, respectively. One important thing to note is that Geo::Dymaxion expects latitudes south of the equator and longitudes west of the prime meridian to be expressed with negative values; this is taken care of by the two regular expression matches in the main loop. The latitude and longitude are fed to Geo::Dymaxion, and the *x*- and *y*-coordinates are used to draw a three-pixel-wide red dot on the map in the appropriate location. Finally, the updated map is written to a PNG image called *world_cities.png*.

## Running the Code

In order to run this code, we'll first need a list of cities. We've compiled just such a list for you, using data from *world-gazetteer.com*, which you can fetch from *http://mappinghacks.com/data/cities.txt*. The file is tab-separated and contains a bunch of other information, about which we won't go into detail here, but that you might find useful for other mapping projects. Next, we'll need a Dymaxion map of the world. Dymaxion maps are astonishingly hard to find on the Internet, so we prepared one—again, using Geo::Dymaxion— that you can download from *http://mappinghacks.com/maps/dymaxion.png*. We put all three files in the same directory, and simply run the Perl script:

```
$ perl plot_cities.pl
```

After running this code, you should have a nice Dymaxion map in *world_cities.png*, as shown in Figure 3-35, with the world's 100 largest cities by population highlighted with three-pixel-wide red dots.

> If you're not interested in going through all of this work, but you still want to bask in the glow of Fuller's genius, you can explore the interactive web-based demo we've set up at *http://mappinghacks.com/projects/dymaxion/*.

That's all there is to using Geo::Dymaxion; a future version may instead rely on the Dymaxion routines from the Virtual Terrain Project (*http://vterrain.org/*), which would allow you to not onlly project lat/long points into the Fuller projection but to do the inverse as well, making it possible to script server-side HTML image maps of the Dymaxion projection. Finally, there is one thing you should be aware of, vis à vis the Dymaxion code that Geo::Dymaxion uses currently: it is distributed under a license that prohibits

*Figure 3-35. The world's 50 largest cities by population, as shown on a Dymaxion projection*

commercial use without Robert W. Gray's explicit permission. Find out more from his web site, if you happen to want to use Geo::Dymaxion in a commercial application. (Changing Geo::Dymaxion to rely on the VTP's BSD-licensed rendition of this code would fix that issue, also.)

Bucky Fuller once wrote, "When I am working on a problem, I never think about beauty. I only think about how to solve the problem. But when I have finished, if the solution is not beautiful, I know it is wrong." With luck, the Dymaxion projection—and Geo::Dymaxion—will help you explore the world's many pressing questions, and find solutions that are both beautiful and right!

### See Also

- "Experiment with Different Cartographic Projections" [Hack #28]
- The Buckminster Fuller Institute (*http://bfi.org/map.htm*)

### HACK #32 Hack on Base Maps in Your Favorite Image Editor

You don't always have to rely on complicated GIS software to make maps that tell your story. In fact, sometimes it's a lot easier not to.

While writing "Plot Arbitrary Points on a World Map" [Hack #29], we had the chance to explore the *flatplanet* catalog of free world maps, which can be found online at *http://flatplanet.sourceforge.net/maps/*. This collection offers world maps based on satellite imagery, topography, temperature, rainfall, land use, demographics, plate tectonics, and more, but not a single map featuring political boundaries. (Actually, the population growth map shows political boundaries, but it also completely omits places for which no data was available—e.g., Greenland, Western Sahara, Eritrea, et al.)

Although we are philosophically opposed to the social and economic inequalities that political borders serve to maintain and foster, there is no denying that the same political borders offer a very immediate source of context to the stories we can tell with maps. From a storytelling context, borders offer a way of breaking up huge landmasses into smaller places that people have heard of, and maybe know something about. Wouldn't it be nice to have some of this lovely Earth imagery show international boundaries, as a way of offering more context to the other things we'd like to display on a world map?

At this point, a professional digital cartographer might reach for his GIS software and start loading vector layers, but we wanted something easier. For starters, where to get a decent vector layer that represents the world's current set of political borders and isn't encumbered by licensing restrictions? One easy answer is the *Generic Mapping Tools*, or *GMT*, which includes a free, reasonably current set of international-boundary vectors at a reasonable resolution. GMT is covered in great detail in "Experiment with Different Cartographic Projections" **[Hack #28]**. For now, we'll simply assume you have it installed.

GMT outputs its maps in PostScript, which makes good sense for a software package whose original purpose in life was to help scientists make maps for publications. However, even though it can be used to draw very precise vector maps, PostScript is not particularly renowned as a common GIS format. Many image editors, on the other hand, can work with Post-Script just fine, including our favorite, *the GIMP*. The same image editors also have no trouble with the JPEG images available from the *flatplanet* project. So why not use them to make new maps? Let's walk through what we did to add political borders to the Blue Marble map of Earth.

## Drawing the Political Boundary Layer

Let's start by generating the political-borders layer in PostScript using the *pscoast* command from GMT, as follows:

```
$ pscoast -JQ0/11i -R-180/180/-90/90 -N1/3 -A4000/0/2 > world.ps
```

The -JQ0/11 option to *pscoast* tells it that we want an Equidistant Cylindrical projection of the world to match the projection used in the *flatplanet* maps, centered on the prime meridian (i.e., 0 degrees longitude), plotted 11 inches wide, which is the largest size page that the GIMP will import. -R-180/180/-90/90 asks *pscoast* for a map of the whole world. The -N option tells it to draw political boundaries. In this case, we want just the international borders, drawn with a three-pixel-wide pen. Note that we're not asking *pscoast* to draw coastlines, or fill any of the shapes, because we will want to see coastlines and landmass details from our underlying JPEG base map instead.

Finally, -A4000/0/2 filters *pscoast*'s vector database in such a way that features less than 4,000 km² in area, or more than two levels down hierarchically (out of a total of four levels), are omitted. You'll want to refer to the GMT documentation for further clarification on how this works, but our particular selection ensures that most nations and large lakes are included, but small islands, smaller lakes, and rivers will be excluded. Without specifying -A, we get everything in the vector database that ships with GMT, which is quite a lot, and really too much detail for the scale of the map we want to draw.

> The pen size and feature filter size that we fed into GMT were chosen mostly through trial and error to fit our example. There's not much science to this; if you need to make a map for a larger or smaller scale, then you may want to play with these values a bit to get the final map to look the way you want. We did say it was a hack!

Figure 3-36 shows the output from *pscoast*. It's kind of interesting to see just how much of the world's political boundaries are formed by the shapes of the planet's coastlines. You might notice, for example, that New Zealand and bits of eastern Siberia are missing from the image; that's because there are no land boundaries in that part of the world!

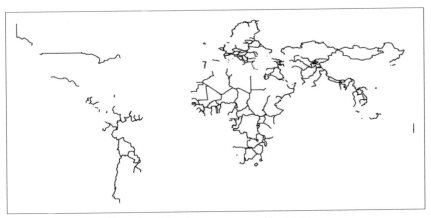

*Figure 3-36. The world's political borders, as generated by GMT*

## Importing the Map Layers

Now, let's switch to our image editor. We like the GIMP, but any advanced image editor—like Photoshop, for example—will have all of the features and tools we describe. First, grab the image you want to overlay the political boundaries on. We chose the 2048x1024 pixel Blue Marble image from *http://flatplanet.sourceforge.net/maps/natural.html*, but any of the images on that page will do. You can also find a copy of this image at *http//mappinghacks.com/maps/land_shallow_topo_2048.jpg*. Save it to your hard drive, and load it up in your image editor. This image will serve as the base layer, over which we'll drape the boundaries layer. Figure 3-37 shows what this image looks like.

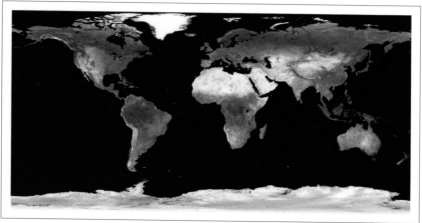

*Figure 3-37. NASA's Blue Marble map of Earth*

Next, we'll import the boundaries layer, which we saved earlier as *world.ps*. Loading a PostScript file will trigger a dialog that provides the image editor with some hints about how to rasterize the vector data. In the GIMP, Post-Script files always load in portrait orientation at 8.5"x11", so the resolution we select influences how many pixels wide and high the imported image will be. We want to select a resolution that will make the two images come out the same size. Since our underlying JPEG image is 2048 pixels wide, we need to divide 2048 pixels by 11 inches to get a resolution of around 186 dots per inch (dpi), which will make the two images more or less match. At this resolution, the boundary layer becomes 2046 pixels wide, which is close enough.

The PostScript import dialog in the GIMP also offers *anti-aliasing* options. Anti-aliasing fuzzes out the curves and corners in the rasterized version of the vector drawing, so we don't end up with jagged-looking edges. We opted for high graphical anti-aliasing for our boundary layer, but you might want to tweak this setting to see what you end up with. You should now have two different images loaded, one of the satellite imagery and another of the political boundaries.

## Combining the Layers to Make a New Map

The first thing you'll notice about the boundary layer—in the GIMP, anyway—is that it's lying on its side! That's because GMT produces landscape-oriented PostScript by default, but the GIMP assumes that all PostScript is portrait-oriented. So the first thing to do is to correct this, by clicking on the boundary layer, and then selecting "Image → Transform → Rotate 90 degrees CW" from the drop-down menu. This should rotate the image such that it's now oriented correctly. Now execute Edit → Selection → Select All to select the entire image, and then Edit → Copy to copy it to the clipboard.

Next, click on the Blue Marble image and run Edit → Paste to paste the boundary image in as a floating layer, which should make the Blue Marble image disappear beneath it. We need to alter the opacity of the boundary layer so that the white parts become transparent, leaving only the black borders. In the GIMP, you can go to Tools → Layer Dialog, which pops up a dialog displaying both layers of the current image. Click on the upper of the two, which should be the floating layer containing our political boundaries. Then click the drop-down menu labeled *Opacity*, and change it from *Normal* to *Multiply*. Suddenly, the white background of the boundary layer disappears, and the topographic map of Earth reappears beneath it!

The last thing we need to fix is that the boundary layer is probably in the wrong place with respect to the Blue Marble image underneath. Select the Move tool from the toolbox (or hit the M key in the GIMP), and you should be able to drag the political boundary layer around over the top of the topographic map. You should be able to drag the boundaries almost into place with the mouse; then zoom in and nudge the image with your arrow keys, until the upper layer falls into place. The last couple of pixels might be a little challenging, so try zooming in on a region that you're really familiar with for this part. We chose the area around Michigan and Ontario as a good place for aligning the two layers, because the border there conforms pretty closely to the shape of the land and lake areas. Finally, hit the Anchor Layer button on the Layer dialog, and you're done! Figure 3-38 shows the two layers, aligned and merged. You can find a copy of this map image online at *http://mappinghacks.com/maps/* for use in your own projects.

Now, a GIS expert might be horrified at this approach, but you're not going to be using this map for oil drilling or disaster relief, are you? When you're telling stories with maps, and precision is not a great concern, there's nothing wrong with using the tools you have at hand.

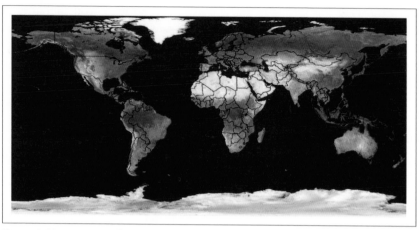

*Figure 3-38. Our new political map of the world, using NASA's Blue Marble imagery and international boundary vectors from GMT*

## See Also

- "Experiment with Different Cartographic Projections" [Hack #28]
- "Plot Arbitrary Points on a World Map" [Hack #29]

### HACK #33  Georeference an Arbitrary Tourist Map

Make any old map tell your story, using a simple JavaScript client to georeference an image so you can later plot your own points, lines, and shapes on it.

Back from a journey or a holiday, you can use the crumpled tourist maps and street atlas pages at the bottom of your handbag or in the back seat of your car to ell the story of your travels. Digital holiday snapshots add accents and highlights to your stories; GPS traces provide a narrative structure for them. To get started, though, you need a base map which is *georeferenced*—one for which you know the geospatial position of the top left corner, the space represented by each pixel in the image, and the rotation or skew of the image away from True North.

How can we georeference a random tourist map? If you know the precise location of several points on the ground and can identify them on the map, you can align them to fit on the map. It's possible to do this by hand, adjusting the projection of the points until they fit, but after we'd done this manually a few times, we were yearning for an automated solution—so we wrote one.

You need at least three points that you have a position for and can definitively identify on the map; these are *ground control points*, or GCPs. The technique we use here uses the known distance between the ground control points in the real world to derive a formula to estimate the scale of the map. For those interested in digging into the math, the Least Squares Approximation is a common method for coming up with a solution to the linear equations used to georeference a map from GCPs. (For the truly mathematically inclined, cartographers sometimes use quadratic and cubic approximation methods as well.) For those just interested in getting it working, we've provided a JavaScript interface that will do the calculation for you.

## The Web Interface

Before starting, you should have at least three waypoints that you've collected "on the ground," with an east and a north coordinate for each point. The waypoints should be well separated from each other on the map you want to georeference. This will provide a more accurate approximation of the map's extents, rotation, and scale.

Next, visit *http://mappinghacks.com/georeference/* to load up the interactive georeferencer. Hit the "Browse" button to view an image from your local hard drive. Now start adding ground control points. The program doesn't care about the kind of values you use for the spatial positions, so they can be in WGS84 latitude and longitude, the default for GPS units, or in UTM, which can be a lot easier for doing spatial calculations and plotting points.

Figure 3-39 shows the work in progress. For each ground control point, click the place on the map where your waypoint was taken. The x- and y-coordinates, in pixels relative to the image, will appear on the lefthand side. Type in your longitude or UTM easting, and latitude or UTM northing. Now click "Add GCP" to add this point as a ground control point. You should see a number appear on the map, indicating your new point. After three or more points have been added, the map is ready to "Rectify."

If successful, you should see a series of six long numbers in the box on the lefthand side. What are they? They represent the coefficients of a *matrix transformation* that can be applied to the digital image, to reproject it into cartographic space. Now what?

If you're a fan of GRASS, you might like to know that GRASS has similar functionality built in, in the form of the *i. points* and *i.rectify* commands. Although the principles are the same, you can find out more about using these commands in the GRASS user manual.

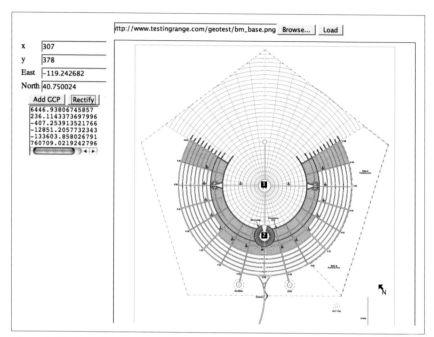

*Figure 3-39. Georeferencing an image with the JavaScript client*

## The World File

The simplest way to make use of this transformation is to put it in a separate file that accompanies the image. The format is just the list of six numbers, separated with line breaks. This is called a *world file*, often seen in the company of TIFFs as a TIFF world file (*.tfw*). A world file can accompany any image format with GIS raster data in it. A common convention is to take the first and last letters of the file extension, followed by a "w," for the world file extension—so a JPEG would travel with a *.jgw*, or an ESRI BIL raster with a *.blw*.

Once you have a world file describing an image, you can load it into your favorite GIS program. QGIS is a good choice for quick-and-easy viewing of GIS data. Also, the GDAL toolkit understands world files and can use them to convert raster data between different formats and different coordinate systems, as described in "Convert Geospatial Data Between Different Formats" [Hack #68].

## The Matrix Transformation

The six numbers (coefficients) in the world file are values from a 3x3 *affine transformation matrix*. The matrix describes a linear transformation between one 2-D coordinate space and another—say, from pixels to latitude and longitude. For each dimension, $x$ and $y$, there's a scale between one coordinate system and the other, the skew between one and the other, and the offset of the image—e.g., where it begins, at its northwestern corner. Figure 3-40 shows the linear algebra used in the affine transform.

Figure 3-40. Transforming coordinates via an affine matrix

**a** is the $x$ scale

**b** is the $y$ rotation/skew

**c** is the $x$ rotation/skew

**d** is the $y$ scale

**e** is the $x$ offset

**f** is the $y$ offset

The last three values are constants there to make the matrix algebra work out, and in an affine transformation, they are always [0 0 1]. So the matrix can be represented as a vector of numbers [$a$ $b$ $c$ $d$ $e$ $f$]. This is the order that the world file lists the coefficients in. If a map is oriented to True North, then the rotational coefficients $b$ and $c$ from its world file will be zero.

This transformation matrix might be used in the following fashion. Suppose that we have a map in a rectangular projection. If a user clicks on the map at $(x, y)$, what is the geographic location corresponding to that point? If we have a world file expressed, for example, in UTM coordinates, then we can calculate the easting and northing as $(x', y')$ with the following formulas:

```
x' = ax + cy + e
y' = bx + dy + f
```

The actual target coordinate system doesn't matter; one can use the same technique to turn $(x, y)$ into latitude and longitude, if the world file uses the same coordinates.

## Projecting Arbitrary Maps in SVG

The affine transformation matrix doesn't have to be stored in a world file. SVG, the Scalable Vector Graphics format, has native support for matrix transformation. To take a raster map and use it directly as a base map in an SVG document, we can apply a transformation to the image like this:

```
<g id="image_group" transform="matrix(3.854  0.00554 -0.00947 -1.9266
2497122 6015150)">
```

```
        <image width="629" height="768" xlink:href="suomenlinna-1024.jpg" />
    </g>
    <!-- nifca -->
    <circle cy="6014319" cx="2498291" r="10" fill="red" />
    <!-- submarine -->
    <circle cy="6014238" cx="2498956" r="10" fill="red" />
    <!-- labour camp -->
    <circle cy="6014484" cx="2499052" r="10" fill="red" />
    <!-- ferry -->
    <circle cy="6014910" cx="2498424" r="10" fill="red" />
```

The content of the *transform* parameter, you'll notice, is a matrix transform in exactly the form as the one in the world file! Now you can plot points in their original geographic coordinates directly onto this map. Unfortunately, the transformation process can produce a lossy effect in the SVG viewer, and the map can look jagged, blurry, or warped—especially at extreme latitudes, if you're using unprojected coordinates. The other downside is that SVG viewers typically only display points with integer accuracy, so you have to multiply latitude and longitude by 100,000 to scale them up to something viewable.

Another approach to the same problem might be to transform the geometry of the points and leave the map alone. We can do this by taking the inverse of the original affine matrix, and applying it to the points, instead of the base map.

## H A C K  Map Other Planets
## #34  Explore the celestial spheres (and spheroids) with standard GIS tools.

> *The universe is a big place, perhaps the biggest.*
> —Kurt Vonnegut

NASA's recent missions to other planets in our solar system have had a substantial mapping component, notably the Venus Magellan and the Mars Pathfinder missions. Mars and Venus, our nearest neighbors, have the best coverage of extraterrestrial imagery and GIS data available on the Web. However, the best Solar System mapping resources on the Web don't come directly from NASA. Many promising links to older data sets now return *404 Not Found* errors, and their mission homepages feature lots of media-friendly space imagery and "For Kids" sections. For the hard work of planetary cartography, NASA collaborates with the astrogeology department at the U.S. Geological Survey, *http://astrogeology.usgs.gov/*.

### Making Flat Maps of Other Planets

Visit the USGS Astrogeology FTP site at *ftp://ftpflag.wr.usgs.gov/dist/pigpen/* for a mother lode of other-planetary GIS data on Mars, Venus, our moon, and Jupiter's moons. The FTP site *ftp://webgis.wr.usgs.gov/mars/usgs/topo/ MOLA_contours_25Mscale/Mars_MOLA_contours_colorimages.zip* contains a great selection of vectors and rasters for making topographical maps of Mars. Many files give instructions for ArcExplorer, but the open source GIS products featured in this book are more than apt for the task. Additionally, you can get lots of nice data from the USGS Map-A-Planet site at *http:// pdsmaps.wr.usgs.gov/*.

Quantum GIS **[Hack #64]**, is a great basic viewer for extraterrestrial GIS data. Figure 3-41 shows an Equirectangular projection map displayed in Quantum GIS, zoomed in to Olympus Mons and Pavonis Mons, with overlaid topographical shapefiles from the same data set.

*Figure 3-41. Raster map of Mars with overlaid topo vectors*

Many extraterrestrial maps available on the Web use the visually familiar technique of *hypsographic tinting*—features shaded in an attractive, earthly scheme showing lowest altitudes in marine blue, and mountain peaks in a burnt-out yellow. This coloring scheme lends Earth maps a pleasing "natural look"; seeing other planets drawn with hypsographic tints reveals the attractive illusion for what it is.

## Rendering 3-D Imagery of Other Planets

Raster maps in cylindrical projections are also suitable for use with *xplanet*, the 3-D planet renderer covered in "Map Global Weather Conditions" **[Hack #46]**. *xplanet* was designed for rendering images of planetary surfaces and is a really good place to get started in this area. You can find code, images, and sample configurations at *http//xplanet.sf.net/*. A good compendium of planetary maps available online in cylindrical projections can be found at *http://www. johnstonsarchive.net/spaceart/planetcylmaps.html*.

The same cylindrical projection maps are perfect for rendering planets in POV-Ray, free raytracing software **[Hack #20]**. Using data from the Viking missions, available at *http://solarviews.com/eng/homepage.htm*, we rendered a 3-D image of Mars with the following *.pov* file:

```
camera {
  location  <0, 0, -2.5>
  look_at   <.01, 0, 0>
}

light_source { <3,0,-5> color <1,1,1> }

sphere {
  <0,0,0>, 1
  pigment {
    image_map {
        jpeg "marscyl1l.jpg"
        map_type 1
    }
  }
  normal {
    bump_map {
        png "marscyl2.png"
        map_type 1
        bump_size 10
    }
  }
  finish {
    ambient 0.1
    diffuse 1
    specular 0.2
    roughness .2
  }
  rotate <0,180,-25>
}
```

The core of this rendering is the sphere section, which provides the shape of the planet. The image_map section specifies the appearance of the surface, with the map_type of 1 causing the JPEG to be wrapped around the sphere. The bump_map section provides the elevation data, with the bump_size parameter emphasizing the terrain for visual effect. (We had to use the *convert* tool from ImageMagick to turn the original TIFF height field into a PNG. For reasons unknown, POV-Ray didn't care for the TIFF.) Finally, the rendering of Mars is rotated around to show the Valles Marineris and the Tharsis volcanos, and is tilted to reflect the planet's actual rotational tilt. The rendering is shown in Figure 3-42.

*Figure 3-42. The Valles Marineris and the Tharsis volcanos of Mars, rendered in POV-Ray*

Finally, if you're a fan of Manifold **[Hack #65]**, an excellent and inexpensive commercial GIS package, you'll be pleased to know that it, too, offers 3-D surfaces for all the planets in the Solar System; Mars and Earth are modeled as spheroids, and the other planetary bodies are modeled as spheres.

## Other Otherworldly Resources

- Ralph Aeschliman's web site (*http://ralphaeschliman.com/*) is a delight for the planetary-mapping enthusiast. Formerly a researcher at the USGS astrogeology department, he has produced a beautiful series of handcrafted art maps of Mars, Venus, and Earth's moon based on GIS data published by the USGS—highly recommended viewing.

- James Hastings-Trew maintains another nice gallery of planetary images and data sets (*http://gw.marketingden.com/planets/planets.html*), with an emphasis more on art than on accuracy.

- "Representing Star Fields" (*http://astronomy.swin.edu.au/~pbourke/povray/ starfield/*) is a good tutorial on rendering star field backgrounds in POV-Ray.

- Celestia (*http://celestia.sourceforge.net/*) is an open source "Universe Simulator" with which you can "travel throughout the solar system, to any of over 100,000 stars, or even beyond the galaxy," with contributions from a large community of enthusiasts.

- The National Space Science Data Center (*http://nssdc.gsfc.nasa.gov/ planetary/*) has a lot of data available on CD-ROM, particularly for Venus.

NASA's Solar System Simulator (*http://maps.jpl.nasa.gov/*) has a fine selection of non-GIS maps for all the bodies in our solar system that have been closely inspected.

# CHAPTER FOUR

# Mapping (on) the Web
## Hacks 35–46

*We're all pilgrims on the same journey—but
some pilgrims have better road maps.*
—Nelson DeMille

*A plague upon it! I have forgot the map.*
—Hotspur, in Shakespeare's *Henry IV Part I, III:1*

It may be a small world, but the Web is a big scary place. Search-engine providers are looking for new ways to provide "relevant" content; weblog writers are looking for new ways to connect with audiences "near" to them.

"Mapping (on) the Web" illustrates simple techniques for spatializing web content and producing interesting geographic visualizations of web-found things, making the most of existing web mapping services.

Commercial web mapping services, while being careful to exercise their perceived intellectual property rights, gain a lot from allowing people to annotate their maps; a model of user-contributed, "added-value content" that has worked out so well for Amazon.com.

Meanwhile, web toolkits made by enthusiastic amateurs, like WorldKit and GPSVisualizer, allow you to make your own maps via the Web. Geourl, a successful early system for adding geotags to web pages, has been succeeded by different schemes for annotating weblog feeds—in any of several flavors of the RSS (Really Simple Syndication or Rich Site Summary) format.

Once your web pages or weblog entries are annotated with geotags, not only can you make interesting visualizations of them, but anyone with the desire and a big enough set of hard drives can crawl the Web and make spatial indexes of what's where. Tagging content with latitiude and longitude is just one option for geo-annotating the Web; Chapter 7 illustrates many things you can do with "best-fit" locations for place names.

Geolocating web content is an especially interesting prospect for search engines, which will be able to provide targeted directory services to the next generation of web-capable mobile devices. The "global village" vision offered by Internet pioneers starts to look like a set of interconnected, tiny hamlets; a Web that looks more like the world looks.

Some mobile telecom companies want to provide "walled gardens," leading the user by the nose through a set of carefully vetted, sponsored Points of Interest. Spatial web search could also lead to balkanization of the Web into islands. MSN's new web search, in beta as of writing, provides a "Find Near Me" option that is only available to users connecting to their site via an Internet address in the United States. Non-U.S. users can't look at or experiment with, the spatial search options. This technique, known as *IP geolocation*, can roughly approximate the location of a user in a country, because "blocks" of addresses are loosely allocated on a country-by-country basis. IP geolocation was notoriously used to stop non-U.S. users from accessing *http://www.georgewbush.com/* in the run-up to the 2004 presidential elections.

Yoking what you can see on the Web to where you're looking at it from leads to no two people ever having quite the same view of the Internet. Perhaps this helps reflect reality; no two people ever have the same worldview. Geo-annotations, along with collaborative recommendation systems, allow people or groups of people to create their own filtered spatial experiences: all the coffee shops and bookshops in London that an anarchist might visit, or the places that might interest a stockbroker. It's important to be able to share worldviews, and try out different people's filters for a day, to have the choice to explore Seattle using maps of Utrecht or visit a virtual Bangalore from your living room in Riga.

We hope this chapter illustrates how, with simple techniques that don't require a massive re-engineering of a geospatial web, you can build interesting sites that will plug into a future world of "locative services," yet still be interesting on today's desktop.

### HACK #35   Search Local, Find Global

Google and Yahoo! are entering the localized-search field with inherent advantages, but there's plenty of room for smaller, deeper spatial search interfaces.

The big search engines were not slow to realize the great potential in the geospatial web: targeted, localized advertising! Geocoded information and spatial metadata, combined with natural-language inference techniques, can massively enrich the relevance and narrative of the search engine offerings.

It's probably better to have information with "local color" covered densely over a small area, rather than broad coverage from afar, so the game changes a bit for the big searches. "Big iron" infrastructure helps a lot with spatial analysis, and the trend towards centralized aggregation of local information is currently strong.

Both the two major search engines, Google and Yahoo!, have local search services in beta, as of this writing. Visit *http://local.yahoo.com/* and *http:// local.google.com/* to compare and contrast. Both sites let you type in a city and state (or U.S. ZIP Code) and a search term or set of terms, find local points of interest, and plot the search results on a map. Figures 4-1 and 4-2 compare the results for the same search—"Maps" in "San Francisco, CA"— on both Google and Yahoo! Local search sites.

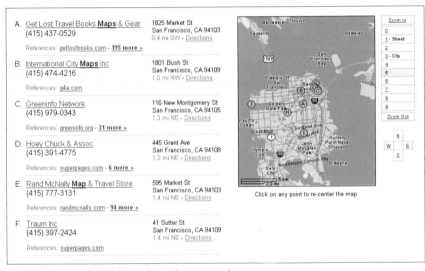

*Figure 4-1. Google local search results, mapped*

The search results are backed by business directory services, and it shows. What these pictures show is 10 search results at a time plotted as colored, lettered icons over a MapQuest-style street map. This is arguably the simplest thing that will work, but lacks a real aesthetic. Google adheres to its familiar look and feel, though it has tried hard to make more out of the spatial arrangement of the map on the web page since its late-2004 relaunch. Spatial search and locative services can and should be about so much more than a business directory with a map on it! Local online authors, public services, campaigns, local history and characters, imagery and media annotation are all things that a local search has the potential to reveal and represent.

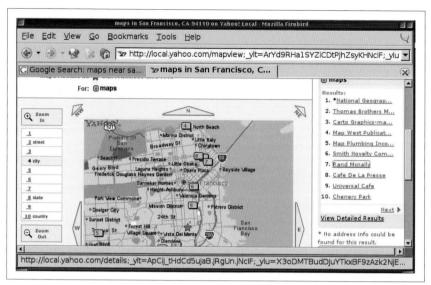

*Figure 4-2. Yahoo! local search results, mapped*

One noteworthy point about Google's local search service: when searching for "Doctor," the sponsored ads at the top of each page have managed to infer or assume that you're looking for a medical doctor's services. The top place search results, however, feature many other services that have the name "doctor" in their title: Bike Doctor, Tofu Doctor, Doctor Bombay's Bar. It's frustrating to see inference, or keyword-purchase, for advertising being done with better taste and efficiency than inference about actual documents on the Web. Yahoo! Local search currently handles this kind of *sense disambiguation* much more smartly, inferring the right context for a word with multiple potential meanings

Both Google and Yahoo! Local search use the NavTeq data set for their maps; as of writing, the map display essentially looks identical.

Yahoo! Local search offers its own rating system, available for use by logged-in site members. Integration with the rest of an online profile seems like the big win for its service; the site uses logged-in member status to its advantage, allowing you to store a number of "Saved Locations" of personal interest. Google, a server-side lightweight, allows you to store only one location in a cookie. However, Google scores points for trying to direct you to other sites offering relevant ratings and reviews for the places in your search results, including a list of other sites that refer to the one you're looking at.

Google displays your results as part of a larger category index, showing you what it thinks are subcategories of what you searched for. Yahoo! doesn't display this information, though Google's category system is probably based on Yahoo!'s directory in the first place! Perhaps the existence of long-established categories of similarity underlies Yahoo!'s superficially better presentation of relevant results.

## Hacking Local Search URLs

The simplest Google local search URL is as follows:

```
http://local.google.com/local?q=maps&near=94110&dm=full
```

The near value is a U.S. ZIP Code. You can also append the start parameter to page through the search results 10 at a time. For example, this URL does the same search but starts at the 20th listing:

```
http://local.google.com/local?q=maps&near=94110&dm=full&start=20
```

The simplest equivalent Yahoo! URL is not quite as human-readable:

```
http://local.yahoo.com/mapview?csz=94110&ip=94110&stx=maps
```

As always with commercial map sites, remember to check your Terms of Service before trying interesting hacks!

## Looking for More

The current mainstream local search interfaces are promising but underwhelming. What stops the big searches from joining the mapping revolution and experimenting with more dynamic, rich GIS-style interfaces to their local search applications? Perhaps it's a fear that, at the lowest common denominator, people won't use them.

Simple extra features like a set of "my saved places," the ability to select individual points (or shapes) to overlay on a map, and the ability to re-set the spatial center of the query by clicking on the map do not raise the bar for web-enabled GIS or involve much skill in implementation.

The picture of local search services changes in a putative near-future world where mobile devices and soft phones are picking up and querying for services in the local area. Collaborative filtering and social history of local information are becoming both practical and necessary.

As of this writing, Google and Yahoo! provide local search and map services for the United States only. There's no European, African or Asian equivalent for the service that we know of; and the pain of making separate licensing negotiations with each different national mapping vendor works against economies of scale.

# HACK  Shorten Online Map URLs
## #36  Slim down the bloated URLs generated by online map services to make life easier when you send travel directions by email.

How many times has someone emailed you a link to some online travel directions to their house or office, only to have the lengthy, gibberish-filled URL break into two or more unusable pieces, which then need to be laboriously scooped back together and manually entered into your web browser location bar? This is typically so treacherous an operation that the slightest mistype will transform your desperately needed directions into so much digital garbage, a solemn po'-faced error page, or worse, directions to a place you do not want to travel to.

Here's a typical *http://mapquest.com* URL for O'Reilly Media's global headquarters in Sebastopol, California:

```
http://www.mapquest.com/maps/map.adp?country=US&countryid=US&addtohistory
=&searchtab=address&searchtype=address&address=1005+Gravenstein+Hwy+N&city=S
ebastopol&state=CA&zipcode=95472&search=++Search++
```

Worse, here's a link to MapQuest for driving directions from O'Reilly to the White House in Washington, DC:

```
http//www.mapquest.com/directions/main.adp?go=1&do=nw&1ex=1&2ex=1&src=maps&
ct=NA&1a=1005%20Gravenstein%20Hwy%20N&1c=Sebastopol&1s=CA&1z=95472%2d2811&1y
=US&1pn=&1l=2YcHLejezMA%3d&1g=4Et9yZWt5s38n17Vi4Ympw%3d%3d&1v=ADDRESS&1pl=&2
a=1600%20Pennsylvania%20Ave&2c=Washington&2s=DC&2z=&2y=
```

The previous URL is so bad that it made MS Word on OS X crash each time it was pasted on *three consecutive attempts* at writing this hack. Clearly, something has to be done about this terrifying state of affairs, and suggesting that one use vi or Emacs does not actually constitute a solution to the problem.

Fortunately for us, that something has already been done, and it's called *URL shortening.* Web sites such as *http://metamark.net, http://makeashorterlink.com,* and *http://notlong.com* allow you to paste a long URL like these MapQuest links one into a web form and, upon clicking Submit, receive a refreshingly short URL in return. When you *or anyone else* visits this abbreviated link, the URL shortening services look up the shortened link in a database and then automatically redirect your web browser to the original, verbosely linked destination.

For example, Metamark turns the first URL into the terse and eminently pasteable *http://xrl.us/cnrw,* which, we are earnestly informed, is 9% of the length of the original URL. Metamark also offers the option of selecting your own nickname for a URL, so that, for example, the second link can be found at *http://xrl.us/ora2dc*, which is only slightly longer than the other one, but arguably a bit easier to remember. Alternatively, *notlong.com* offers the same feature, but as part of the domain name, so that the first link can also be found at *http://ora.notlong.com*. Look, Ma, no broken links in your email!

URL-shortening services have other tricks up their sleeves, too. For example, most of them offer password protection if privacy is a concern. Almost all of them also have a companion *bookmarklet*, which is a little wodge of JavaScript that you can save to your browser's bookmark list or toolbar. If you've saved a bookmarklet for your favorite shortening service, you can simply click it any time you want a shortened URL for the web page you're currently looking at. One click! They can't make it any easier.

The various URL-shortening services offer other elaborations on this basic idea, and pretty much all of them promise to keep your link around for anywhere from five years from the last time it was clicked to more or less forever. We prefer Metamark and MakeAShorterLink, because they were built by various friends of ours, but you can find a comprehensive list to choose from online at *http://notlong.com/links/*.

## HACK #37  Tweak the Look and Feel of Web Maps

Create your own custom maps with this next-generation web mapping service.

An all-too-common experience on web mapping sites is clicking around a postcard-sized map image, zooming in and out while trying to squash a mental model into a field 320x240 pixels in size. In this century of lavish bandwidth and storage, why keep all your users in the 1990s?

Thankfully, one good web mapping site, Maporama (*http://www.maporama. com/*) gives you the chance to customize web map display in many ways. Their "Personalise your map" sidebar allows you to set the size of the map display, up to a screen-hogging 860x684 XXL size. You can also set the units, choosing between miles and kilometers. A printable version lets you export your custom map in a nice clean view.

More excitingly, you can choose from a range of custom styles for your map. Figures 4-3 and 4-4 show the same map, of Altea on the coast of Spain, in two different configurable styles: a "light" style more pastel and pleasing in resolution than the standard map, and an ES style familiar to users of Spanish Geographical Survey Maps.

Maporama is also possibly the only world map service that will still display the latitude and longitude for an address that it has successfully geocoded,

*Figure 4-3. Maporama map in "light" style*

*Figure 4-4. Maporama map in "ES" style*

in both decimal and degrees-minutes-seconds (DMS) formats, making it ideal for use by amateur GPS Orienteers.

Maporama's business-services APIs promise a SOAP/XML interface. Their coverage of places outside of the U.S. and Western Europe can be rather weak, but Maporama holds great promise; it comes the closest we've seen of all the global sites to "getting it" with regard to mapping services on the geospatial web.

# HACK #38 Add Location to Weblogs and RSS Feeds

Here are two easy ways to add location tags to your weblog entries or RSS feed items.

Weblogs and RSS syndication are drastically changing the way people read, write, and experience the Web. As could be predicted, location figures heavily into many of the sort of things people like to blog about: vacations, sporting events, concerts, and so on. We'll examine two simple methods to add location tags to your weblog, using plug-ins for Movable Type and Radio Userland, but the same principles apply to any RSS feed.

First, let's have a closer look at *geotagged RSS*. RSS 1.0, 2.0 (*http://blogs.law. harvard.edu/tech/rss*), and Atom are extendable with XML namespaces. There are two commonly used namespaces to represent location: the RDF Interest Group Geo vocabulary (*http://www.w3.org/2003/01/geo/*) and the ICBM namespace (*http://postneo.com/icbm/*). The examples here will use RSS 2.0 with the RDFIG Geo vocabulary, but other combinations are possible. Here's what RSS2+Geo looks like:

```
<item>
    <title>Taqueria Vallarta</title>
    <link>http://www.taqueria-vallarta.com</link>
    <description>
        This taqueria in Santa Cruz, CA is an excellent value. Get the
        Super Vegetarian with extra guacamole.
    </description>
    <geo:lat> 36.9716 </geo:lat>
    <geo:lon> -122.0253 </geo:lon>
</item>
```

That's all there is to it. Now, mapping applications that know how to speak RDFIG Geo will able to make use of this information when reading your blog feeds, while RSS readers and aggregators that don't will simply read the item as normal.

You'll note that the longitude given for Taqueria Vallarta is negative, because Santa Cruz, California, is west of the prime meridian. In general, most cartographic applications expect west longitude and south latitude to be given with negative values, unless otherwise specified.

## Adding Location Tags to Movable Type

To publish RSS2+Geo with Movable Type, we'll build on Timothy App-nel's Meta plug-in (*http://mt-plugins.org/archives/entry/meta.php*). It's described as "a simple lightweight Movable Type plugin for displaying embedded meta data in either keywords or text_more fields represented in a basic XML format." The plug-in uses an XML format with a meta root element and a single layer of XML elements and values, which are then available as key-value pairs to any Movable Type template.

Install the plug-in on your Movable Type server, and choose either the keywords or text_more field for entering geographic metadata. (We'll assume keywords from here on.) Make sure that field is visible on the Edit Entry screen, via the "Customize the display of this page" link. When writing an entry, you can specify the location of the entry with a small bit of markup, indicating its latitude and longitude:

```
<meta>
    <lat>36.9716</lat>
    <lon>-122.0253</lon>
</meta>
```

In order for this meta markup to show up in your RSS feed, you'll next need to edit the RSS 2.0 template on the Edit Templates screen, adding the following code. There are several Movable Type tags implemented by the Meta plug-in. Used as follows within an RSS item, a latitude and longitude will be added to the RSS feed whenever they are present:

```
<MTMeta field="keywords">
    <MTMetaValueExists name="lat">
        <geo:lat><$MTMetaValue name="lat"$></geo:lat>
    </MTMetaValueExists>
    <MTMetaValueExists name="lon">
        <geo:lon><$MTMetaValue name="lon"$></geo:lon>
    </MTMetaValueExists>
</MTMeta>
```

Finally, don't forget to declare the geo namespace, by adding the following attribute to the <rss> root element:

```
<rss version="2.0"
    xmlns:geo="http://www.w3.org/2003/01/geo/wgs84_pos#">
```

 This technique can also be used to add location tags to your RSS 1.0 feed, by applying the same changes to your RSS 1.0 Index template. In RSS 1.0, the root element is rdf:RDF instead of rss, but other than that, the details are identical.

## Adding Location Tags to Radio Userland

For Radio Userland, it's a bit of an easier ride to get to RSS2+Geo. The Location tool (*http://radio.weblogs.com/0100875/location/*) uses Radio's callback mechanisms to add latitude and longitude inputs to the post form and includes those entries in the RSS file. Simply download and install the tool, and you're all set.

The Location tool also defines a `<%locationlink%>` tag, which displays a small globe linking to a map of the location specified. You can add it to your *itemTemplate.txt* like so:

```
<%locationlink(<%itemNum%>)%>
```

Congratulations, your weblog posts are now location-enabled and ready to be mapped, for example, with RDFMapper **[Hack #21]**! See *http://www.mapbureau.com/rdfmapper/* for more on this, or the next hack "View Your Photo Thumbnails on a Flash Map" **[Hack #39]** for a related hack.

*—Mikel Maron*

H A C K

## #39  View Your Photo Thumbnails on a Flash Map

Showing the original locations of your photos on a map is a neat trick, but worldKit lets you go one further, by showing the image thumbnails right on the map itself.

*worldKit* is a web mapping toolkit that runs in Macromedia's ubiquitous Flash Player. With a little bit of XML, you can configure worldKit to plot a geotagged RSS feed on a map of your choice. We'll look at using your favorite blogging tool to record the places where your photos were taken, and then having worldKit show a thumbnail of each photo in the right place on the map. As an example, check out El Oso's photo map at *http://www.el-oso.net/travels/*. You can download worldKit and find documentation and examples at *http://brainoff.com/worldkit/*.

We're going to presume you've already set up your RSS feed to include latitude and longitude. If not, start with "Add Location to Weblogs and RSS Feeds" **[Hack #38]**. Once that's done, we'll configure the RSS 2.0 feed in both Movable Type and Radio Userland to include a pointer to the thumbnail of the photo you want to map. If you don't use either of these blogging tools, read on anyway; the same principles can be applied to any blogging system that lets you fine-tune its RSS output. Finally, we'll set up worldKit, and point it at your geotagged RSS feed.

## Adding Thumbnail Links to Your RSS Feed

For Movable Type, you can specify the URL of the image thumbnail as follows, in either the keywords or text_more fields:

```
<meta>
    <lat>36.9716 </lat>
    <lon>-122.0253</lon>
    <imgurl>/images/powerkite.jpg</imgurl>
</meta>
```

In order for MT to turn this into RSS, you'll need to add following to your RSS 2.0 template, inside the MTMeta tag:

```
<MTMetaValueExists name="imgurl">
    <photo:thumbnail><$MTMetaValue name="imgurl"$></photo:thumbnail>
</MTMetaValueExists>
```

Notice that we use a photo:thumbnail element to specify the location of the thumbnail in the RSS feed. This means we'll also have to declare the photo namespace in the RSS root node in the same template, as follows:

```
<rss version="2.0"
    xmlns:geo="http://www.w3.org/2003/01/geo/wgs84_pos#"
    xmlns:photo="http://pheed.com/photo/">
```

For Radio Userland, the Location tool also provides this facility. Below the post form, there's an input field for the thumbnail URL. When you provide a URL, it's automatically added to the RSS feed.

## Configuring worldKit to Display the Thumbnails

With the data feed in place, all that's left to do is to install and configure worldKit. worldKit relies on a file called *config.xml* for its configuration details. Here's an example:

```
<worldkitconf>
    <width>500</width>
    <height>250</height>
    <displaytype>daynight</displaytype>
    <dayimg>day.jpg</dayimg>
    <nightimg>night.jpg</nightimg>
    <dataurl>rss.xml</dataurl>
    <update>60</update>
    <showonlynew>false</showonlynew>
</worldkitconf>
```

In order to get worldKit to display your photoblog thumbnails, change the values in the dataurl element to match the URL of your photoblog's RSS feed. For the dayimg element, you can use the default Blue Marble world map included with worldKit, or perhaps try MapProxy (*http://brainoff.com/worldkit/mapproxy/*) to find some aerial photo imagery of your neighborhood.

If possible, you should store your thumbnails on the same server as the map and RSS feed. This will prevent Flash from issuing unnecessary security warnings.

To install worldKit, upload the files from the distribution into a directory on your web site. Next, drop your modified *config.xml* file in the same directory. Finally, as described in the worldKit documentation, enter the following bit of HTML to embed worldKit in a web page on your site:

```
<object classid="clsid:D27CDB6E-AE6D-11cf-96B8-444553540000"
    codebase="http://download.macromedia.com/pub/shockwave/cabs/flash/
swflash.cab#version=6,0,0,0"    width="1000" height="500" id="worldkit">
    <param name="movie" value="worldkit.swf">
    <param name="quality" value="high">
    <param name="bgcolor" value="#000000">

    <embed src="worldkit.swf" quality=high bgcolor=#000000
        width="1000" height="500" name="worldkit" align=""
        type="application/x-shockwave-flash"
        pluginspage="http://www.macromedia.com/go/getflashplayer">
    </embed>
</object>
```

When a visitor to your web site loads the page containing the embedded worldKit map, they'll see each of the thumbnails displayed in turn, next to a colored dot marking its location. Figure 4-5 shows a close-up of a worldKit thumbnail map in action. The user can then roll her mouse over the dot to see the thumbnail again, or click on it to be taken to the relevant weblog entry.

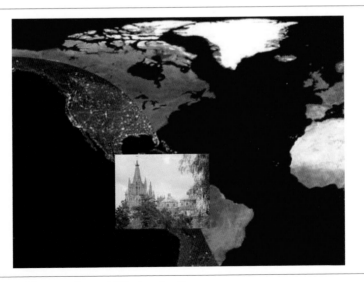

*Figure 4-5. Close-up of a worldKit thumbnail map*

And that's all there is to it. Now, every image with a latitude and longitude that you add to your photoblog will automatically show up as a thumbnail on your Flash map. See "Publish Maps of Your Photos on the Web" [Hack #8] for another method to add photos to a map.

—*Mikel Maron*

## Plot Points on a Spinning Globe Applet

An interactive, spinning globe easily adds the "oh, wow" factor to your geocoded web pages.

Looking for a compelling way to display globally dispersed data that can be tagged with latitude and longitude coordinates, such as travel photos or events? Or perhaps you have a web form or JavaScript-enabled program that needs latitude/longitude input and you'd like to provide your users with a quick way to pinpoint the desired location.

Geosphere is an open source, versatile Java applet that does these things and more, by providing an interactive globe you can embed in your web page. The user can spin the globe, zoom in and out, and select pinpoints you have specified or input their own coordinates. If you choose to display pinpoints, they are hotlinked to URLs that will load in the browser when the user selects them. The pinpoints can be separated into groups that the user can opt to display or hide at will. Geosphere is highly customizable, so it is simple to fit it into your web site design. Best of all, if you know how to edit a web page, you know almost everything you need to know to use Geosphere.

You can download the latest version from *http://hm-geosphere.sourceforge.net/*. After unzipping, you will find two *.jar* files, *GlobeApplet.jar* and *sjg_xml.jar*. Place these in a publicly accessible directory underneath your web server's document root directory. (If you have FTP-only access to your web server, this will usually be your default home directory.) Next create an HTML page in which to embed the applet. Put the HTML file in the same directory as the *.jar* files.

In the HTML, add the following code:

```
<applet name="Globe"
        codebase="."
        archive="GlobeApplet.jar,sjg_xml.jar"
        code="org.akuaku.geosphere.globe.GlobeApplet.class"
        width=200 height=300 MAYSCRIPT>
<param name="size" value="200">
<param name="bgcolor" value="FFFFFF">
You need Java to see Globe Applet.
</applet><br/>
```

Load the web page, and you should see a shiny blue marble with white coastlines on a white background. You can drag with your mouse to spin it about.

Pretty, but not interesting for very long. To make it more interesting, you can do one (or both) of two things:

- Tack some pinpoints on it that are tied to URLs.
- Use it for coordinate input: for example, to input latitude/longitude coordinates into a web form.

## Display and Interact with Points on the Geosphere

To tack on some pinpoints, you need to define them in an XML file and then tell the applet to load them from the file.

Create an XML file in this format:

```
<geosphere>
 <group name="" title="" color="" on=""/>
 <site group="" latitude="" longitude="" href="">name</site>
</geosphere>
```

The XML file has following specifications:

- The `<site>` tag specifies a pinpoint that may belong to a group, which is specified by a `<group>` tag. The site tag is associated with its corresponding group by using the same name specified in the `<group name="">` as the value for the `<site group="">` attribute.
- You can have zero or more `<group>` tags. If you have zero, then you can of course omit the group="" attribute in the `<site>` tag.
- The `<group on="">` attribute determines whether this group of locations is initially displayed on the globe.
- The `<site href="">` attribute is the URL that the pinpoint is linked to. When the user double-clicks on this point, the browser will load this URL.
- The text specified between the `<site></site>` tags is the name displayed when the user hovers the mouse pointer over the pinpoint.
- Make sure that the `<site>` tag is defined all on one line (as in the following example) because *sjg_xml* is weird about multiline attribute lists.

Example:

```
<geosphere>
 <group name="group1" title="first group" color="ff0000" on="true"/>
 <group name="group2" title="second group" color="00ff00" on="false"/>
 <group name="group3" title="third group" color="00ffff" on="false"/>
 <site group="group1" latitude="52.22" longitude="4.53"
```

```
href="http://mysite.com/amsterdam/">amsterdam</site>
  <site group="group1" latitude="51.32" longitude="0.5"
href="http://mysite.com/london/">london</site>
  <site group="group2" latitude="8.58" longitude="-79.32"
href="http://mysite.com/panama/">panama city</site>
  <site group="group2" latitude="9.4833" longitude="-82.6667"
href="http://mysite.com/panama/">isla grande</site>
  <site group="group2" latitude="7.5333" longitude="-80.0333"
href="http://mysite.com/panama/">pedasi</site>
  <site group="group3" latitude="3.08" longitude="101.42"
href="http://mysite.com/malaysia/">kuala lumpur</site>
  <site group="group3" latitude="1.18" longitude="103.50"
href="http://mysite.com/singapore/">singapore</site>
  <site group="group3" latitude="31.47" longitude="35.13"
href="http://mysite.com/palestine/">jerusalem</site>
  <site group="group3" latitude="32.0667" longitude="34.7667"
href="http://mysite.com/palestine/">tel aviv</site>
</geosphere>
```

Now place this XML file in the same directory on your server as the HTML file
with the embedded applet. Add the following tag inside the `<applet></applet>`
section in the HTML file, where *geosphere.xml* is the name of your XML file:

```
<param name="coordinatesXML" value="geosphere.xml">
```

Reload the applet page in your browser, and you should now see your points
(as illustrated in Figure 4-6) and be able to double-click on them. When you
double-click on a pinpoint, the associated URL loads in the browser. If you
want to load the URL in a different browser window or frame, use this
parameter:

```
<param name="browsertarget" value="new">
```

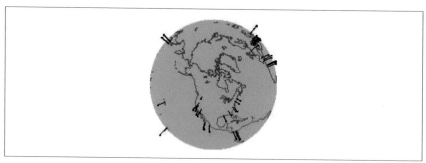

*Figure 4-6. Geosphere with pinpoints*

You will notice that if you double-click in a region that has two or more
points close together, the applet will zoom in on them. This allows you to
see the distinct points more clearly and decide which one to select. You can
also drag with the right mouse button to zoom. To allow the user to
unzoom fully in one easy click, you need to do one of two things.

You can either display the applet's internal Unzoom button by adding this param to the applet tag in the HTML file:

```
<param name="showzoomoutbutton" value="true">
```

which adds a not very attractive but perfectly functional Unzoom button to the applet.

Or you can use JavaScript to call the applet's zoomFullOut( ) method. This allows you to use a button or image of your choice on the web page, outside of the applet's area, to Unzoom, giving you better control of the look of your page. For example:

```
<img src="unzoom.png" onClick="document.Globe.zoomFullOut( )"/>
```

If you use the previous sample XML, when you load the applet page you'll see only London and Amsterdam pinpoints. This is because they belong to group1, which was the only group with the attribute on="true".

How do you allow the user to choose whether or not to display specific groups? Use JavaScript to call the applet's displayGroup(groupName,boolean) method. For example:

```
<form name="groupdisplay">
<!--Display Group 1:-->
<input type="checkbox" name="group1" CHECKED onClick="document.Globe.
displayGroup('group1',document.groupdisplay.group1.checked)"/><br/>

<!--Display Group 2:-->
<input type="checkbox" name="group2" onClick="document.Globe.
displayGroup('group2',document.groupdisplay.group2.checked)"/><br/>

<!--Display Group 3:-->
<input type="checkbox" name="group3"
onClick="document.Globe.displayGroup('group3',document.groupdisplay.group3.
checked)"/><br/>
</form>
```

You can change many things about the applet, including most of the colors used and which features are displayed on the globe. The *INSTALL.txt* file in the distribution has a complete list of available parameters you can specify.

## Use the Geosphere to Plot Your Own Coordinates

Figure 4-7 shows the geosphere centered on a custom coordinate latitude/ longitude pair. There are two ways to use the geosphere to allow a user to specify coordinates.

**Add coordinates with HTML.** First add this <param> tag inside the applet tag:

```
<param name="showinputbutton" value="true">
```

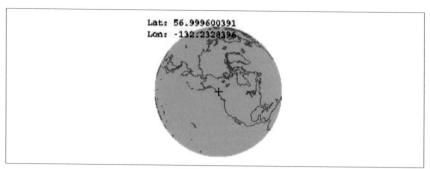

Figure 4-7. Geosphere centered on user-defined coordinates

This draws crosshairs in the middle of the globe and adds a "Use Target" button to the applet. When the user pushes the button, the coordinates under the crosshairs are sent to the web page's JavaScript setCoordinates( ) function, which must be defined in the HTML. For example:

```
<SCRIPT>
  function setCoordinates(lat, lon) {
    alert('lat='+lat+' and lon='+lon);
  }
</SCRIPT>
```

**Add coordinates with JavaScript.** Next, use JavaScript to call the applet's getLatitude( ) and getLongitude( ) methods. You'll probably want to turn on the crosshair target and perhaps the coordinates display using these <param> tags:

```
<param name="showtarget" value="true">
<param name="showcoords" value="true">
```

Example javascript:

```
<SCRIPT>
  function displayCoordinates( ) {
    lat = document.Globe.getLatitude( );
    lon = document.Globe.getLongitude( );
    alert('lat='+lat+' and lon='+lon);
  }
</SCRIPT>
```

```
<img src="SelectCoords.png" onClick="displayCoordinates( )"/>
```

Since you can define how to use the coordinates in JavaScript, you can do anything JavaScript allows, including using them as input to a web form, or even as input to an embedded Flash movie or another applet!

# HACK #41  Plot Points on an Interactive Map Using DHTML

Adding JavaScript to interactive maps on the Web can make them more responsive by eliminating the need to hit the network for updates.

Suppose we want to make a little web application that puts a star on a map of the world, at a given latitude and longitude. We might imagine building a simple form interface with some HTML that looks like this:

```
<html>
<body>
<div>
    <form name="location">
        Latitude:  <input name="lat" type="text" size="11" />
        Longitude: <input name="lon" type="text" size="11" />
        <input type="submit" value="Go" />
    </form>
</div>
<div>
    <img id="basemap" src="PathfinderMap.jpg" />
</div>
</body>
</html>
```

In a web browser, the page might look something like Figure 4-8. We have two text input boxes, one called lat and the other lon, and a Go button. The map shown is the 1024x512 pixel AVHRR Pathfinder map from Dave Pape's *Earth Images* collection (*http://www.evl.uic.edu/pape/data/Earth/*), scaled down to 800 pixels wide.

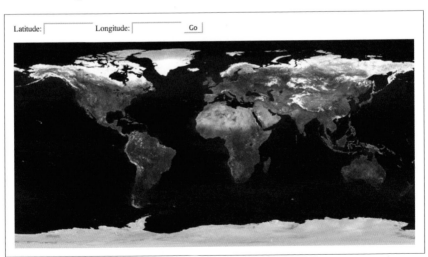

*Figure 4-8. A simple web-based map interface*

Obviously, one way to turn this interface into an application would be to point the form action at a CGI script, do all of the work on the web server, and return a dynamically generated version of the world map. The main reason not to do this is, quite frankly, that it's *slow*. The time that a user spends waiting for their web browser to go out over the network, request the page, have the image rendered server-side, download everything, and then render the web page itself is time that they're not spending getting information out of our map. If we can do all of our calculations in the browser itself, and overlay the star on top of the map dynamically, then the usability of our map goes way up.

Fortunately, if the map projection is simple enough, we can do this by hacking together a bit of JavaScript with some Cascading Style Sheet (CSS) properties. (When JavaScript is used to push bits of HTML and CSS around, the result is called *Dynamic HTML*, or DHTML.) As it happens, the Pathfinder map is a *Plate Carrée*, or an Equidistant Cylindrical, projection, so the math required to turn a latitude and longitude into a point on the map image is quite simple, as discussed in [Hack #29], and well within the means of JavaScript. We'll step through the process of building this form so that a user can enter points and have them displayed on the map, without having to hit the server each time.

## Adding the Star to the Interface

First, we'll need to add the star to the HTML layout. We want the star to be rendered within the same container as the base map, but we don't want it to be visible until the user enters a set of coordinates. To accomplish this, we set its CSS visibility property to hidden.

```
<div>
    <img id="basemap" src="PathfinderMap.jpg" />
    <img id="star" src="star.gif" style="visibility: hidden;" />
</div>
```

Now we're ready to add some JavaScript code to make the star appear in the right place and time.

## The Code

The following block of JavaScript code makes the star appear on the map image. The code goes in the same file as our HTML interface.

```
1   <script language="JavaScript">
2   var top    = 90,
3       left   = -180,
4       bottom = -90,
5       right  = 180;
```

```
6
7    function moveStar (form) {
8        var form = document.forms["location"];
9        var lon = form["lon"].value,
10           lat = form["lat"].value;
11
12       if (lat > top || lat < bottom || lon > right || lon < left) {
13           alert("Latitude must between -90 and 90, " +
14                   "and longitude between -180 and 180!");
15           return;
16       }
17
18       var basemap = document.getElementById("basemap");
19       var x_scale = basemap.width / (right - left);
20       var y_scale = basemap.height / (bottom - top);
21
22       var x = (lon - left) * x_scale;
23       var y = (lat - top)  * y_scale;
24
25       for (parent = basemap; parent; parent = parent.offsetParent) {
26           x += parent.offsetLeft;
27           y += parent.offsetTop;
28       }
29
30       var star = document.getElementById("star");
31       x -= star.width / 2;
32       y -= star.height / 2;
33
34       star.setAttribute("style", "position: absolute; "  +
35                                   "visibility: visible; " +
36                                   "top: " + y + "; "          +
37                                   "left: " + x + "; ");
38   }
39   </script>
```

We start by defining the boundaries, in degrees, of our world map, which will be used shortly. Next, we introduce a function, moveStar( ), which will be called when the user clicks Go. The object representing our input form is passed as an argument to the function. In lines 9–16, we extract the latitude and longitude values from the form, check to see if they're within the boundaries of our map, and kick out an error pop-up if they're not.

Then we come to the heart of the matter. In line 18, we call the Document Object Model API to find the image element containing our base map, in order to query its width and height. These figures are used on lines 19 and 20 to calculate the scale of the map, or the number of pixels per degree, in the fashion described in "Plot Arbitrary Points on a World Map" [Hack #29]. Calculating the scale on the fly means that the map can change and our code will still do the right thing.

In similar fashion to "Plot Arbitrary Points on a World Map" [Hack #29], we calculate the number of degrees from our point to the left edge of the map on line 22, and then multiply that by our scale value to get the number of pixels. Then we do the same for the vertical axis on line 23.

Now, here's an added wrinkle: absolute positioning in CSS is reckoned from the edge of the browser window, *not* the edge of the enclosing HTML element. However, our base map image might not be rendered at the exact top or left edges of the document. What's worse, the DOM API will only tell us how far the map image rests from the edge of its immediate parent element, rather than from the edge of the window. So, in lines 25–28, we walk upward through the chain of nested HTML elements, and add up each horizontal and vertical offset, until we get to the very top of the document.

Next, we deal with one final hitch in lines 30–32, which is that we really want the star centered over the point in question, not placed on its corner. To achieve this result, we have to find the width and height of the star and subtract half of each from our *x*- and *y*-coordinates, so that the star appears centered over our point. Again, we could hardcode the width and height of the star, but doing it this way allows us to use any image in place of our little star without having to touch the code.

At last, we're ready to plot the star on top of the map, which we do in lines 34 through 37, by setting the style attribute of the star to make it visible at the calculated location.

## Running the Code

Now that we can plot the star on the map, we need to trigger the star's placement when the user presses Go. There are a number of ways to accomplish this, but we'll settle for setting a JavaScript action on our original form element, which triggers the JavaScript function moveStar(this) as its only argument:

```
<div>
    <form name="location" action="javascript:moveStar(this)">
        Latitude:   <input name="lat" type="text" size="11" />
</div>
```

Now we can load our web page into a browser, enter some coordinates, and have the star plotted in the right place. You can try out this example for yourself at *http://mappinghacks.com/code/dhtml/*. Figure 4-9 shows our working interface, with the star positioned more or less over New York City.

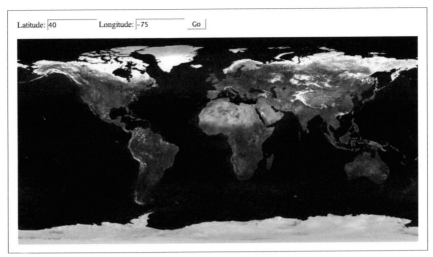

Latitude: 40    Longitude: -75    Go

*Figure 4-9. The same web-based map interface, powered by JavaScript*

## Hacking the Hack

Now, in and of itself, this demo application isn't very interesting, because people don't usually think of places in terms of latitude and longitude, per se. If we wanted to use this application to show the world's 50 largest cities, we might have something a little more interesting, but we'd still have to hit the network to look up the location of a selected city in a database somewhere—unless we happened to put that list in JavaScript somewhere, as well. The following is an excerpt from *cities.js*, which just happens to be such a list:

```
var cities = [
    [ "Mumbai, India [12.4M]", 18.96, 72.82 ],
    [ "Buenos Aires, Argentina [12.1M]", -34.61, -58.37 ],
    [ "Kar\u0101chi, Pakistan [10.5M]", 24.86, 67.01 ],
    [ "Manila, Philippines [10.2M]", 14.62, 120.97 ],
    // ... and so on, for 46 more lines ...
];
```

This data structure is just a list of lists, in which each inner list contains the name and population of the city, as well as its latitude and longitude. You can find a copy of the full *cities.js* in *http://mappinghacks.com/code/dhtml/*, which was generated using the list of cities found at *http://mappinghacks.com/data/cities.txt*. We can pull it into our HTML interface, by adding an external script reference to it, like so:

```
<script language="JavaScript" src="cities.js" ></script>
```

You may be wondering about the \u0101 in Kar\u0101chi. It's called a Unicode escape sequence. Your web browser's Java-Script engine is supposed to interpret this as "the Unicode character with hexadecimal code 0101" (or decimal 257), which is the letter *a* with a bar on top of it.

We'll need to add a drop-down menu to our HTML interface, to allow the user to select a city to display. We'll also need to add an onLoad event to dynamically populate the drop-down box from the list of cities in *cities.js*. Here are the changes to the HTML:

```
<body onLoad="populateCityList()">
<div>
<form name="location" action="javascript:moveStar()">
    Latitude: <input name="lat" type="text" size="11" />
    Longitude: <input name="lon" type="text" size="11" />
    <input type="submit" value="Go" />
    <select name="city" onChange="selectCity(this)"></select>
</form>
</div>
```

You'll notice that the drop-down menu is initially empty. That's all right; as soon as the document loads, the browser calls populateCityList(), which creates the drop-down options by iterating through the list of cities. Also, the drop-down box has an onChange event that is called when a user selects a city to display. This event calls selectCity(), which updates the latitude and longitude fields in the form and refreshes the map. Here's the code for that:

```
function populateCityList () {
    for (i = 0; i < cities.length; i++)
        document.forms["location"].city.options[i] = new
Option(cities[i][0], i);
}

function selectCity (item) {
    item.form["lat"].value  = cities[item.selectedIndex][1];
    item.form["lon"].value = cities[item.selectedIndex][2];
    item.form.submit();
}
```

So, with only a little extra work, we're now using JavaScript data structures and UI events to power an application that maps the world's largest cities. You can see a working demo of this at *http://mappinghacks.com/code/dhtml/cities.html*. It may not sound like much, but try it! Odds are, unless you're all but the very biggest geography buff, you will run across at least one enormous metropolis that you've never heard of, or never knew the actual location of. For such a simple web application, this quickly turns into a fascinating geographic exploration! Figure 4-10 shows the enhanced interface, with Buenos Aires selected.

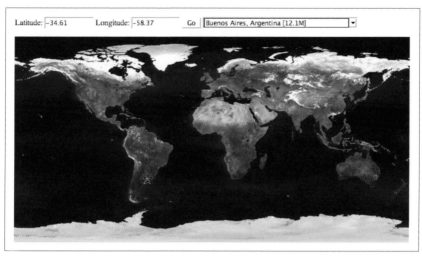

Figure 4-10. An interactive world city browser, in JavaScript

## Hacking Other Projections

"This is all well and good," you may be thinking, "but what if I want to plot points in JavaScript on maps that aren't in a rectangular projection?" Well, that's a little bit more of a challenge. For some projections, like the sinusoidal projection, the math still isn't *that* hard, and JavaScript can pull it off. For others, even seemingly simple projections like the Mercator, the amount of time you'll spend writing the conversion, or the amount of time the client-side will spend performing it, may outweigh the benefits of doing such a calculation in the web browser.

Consider this, however: if your server-side scripts permit you to populate a JavaScript data structure with the latitude and longitudes of a constrained list of places you're interested in, why not precalculate the projected coordinates on the server-side, and get the best of both worlds, as it were?

For another way to plot points on a world map, see "Plot Arbitrary Points on a World Map" [Hack #29]

### HACK #42 Map Your Tracklogs on the Web

GPS Visualizer makes zoomable SVG vector maps of your tracks via a web site.

SVG is a perfect vector format for web mapping. It's in XML, which allows you to look at the source code, see how it works, and borrow bits you like. The SVG Viewer from Adobe is a popular plug-in: your web browser will probably attempt to install or find it for you the first time you look at a bit of SVG on the Web.

GPS Visualizer is a neat service on the Web, to which you can upload your tracklogs in many different formats and get back interesting SVG maps of your travels. As usual, coverage is biased toward the U.S. because of the many good sources of free geospatial data available there. You can overlay your tracks on top of vector street maps, aerial photographs, or topographical maps.

## Making Tracklog Maps on the Web

To get started, visit *http://www.gpsvisualizer.com/map/* where you'll be presented with a form that looks like Figure 4-11. Append ?form=simple to this URL to see a refreshingly simplified version of the form. You can upload from your hard drive as many as 12 separate tracks to put on the same map; currently there is a volume limit of 2 MB of tracks at once.

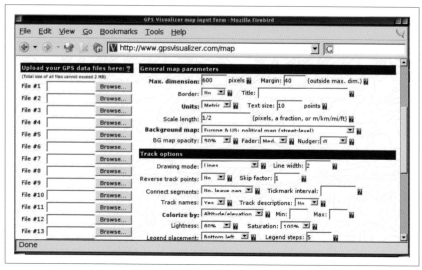

*Figure 4-11. Uploading tracks to GPS Visualizer*

GPS Visualizer will read many popular tracklog formats including Garmin, some XML formats, and regular comma-separated values. You can upload *.csv* files in the format of your choice, as long as the first row consists of "headers" indicating the name of that field—particularly latitude and longitude—so GPS Visualizer knows what to do with it. So the simplest possible tracklog format is:

```
latitude,longitude
24.9699926,121.5500093
25.0620890,121.6402817
25.0620890,121.6402602
```

These are the points recorded when our GPS device was turned on for testing in Taiwan!

**General map parameters.** You can set size and presentation for your map, and give an optional label and scale. GPS Visualizer uses a range of different web mapping services to overlay your tracks on a map. For the U.S. and Canada, there are a lot of options, including better resolution aerial photographs and topographical outlines. For these maps, which are from free sources, GPS Visualizer also offers a "localize" service that allows you to copy a map for online use at *http://www.gpsvisualize.com/localize*. You can also create a "fader" control that allows you to tune the appearance of your SVG map dynamically.

**Track options.** Sometimes you don't care about the sequence implied by the spatial display of your points. There are options to view tracks simply as points, as lines, or as a continuous shape. You also have the option of displaying waypoints and their labels. You are able to move labels around in the final SVG map. Tracks can also be colored according to altitude, distance, and other factors.

**Waypoint options.** You can display waypoints, and optionally their descriptions, over a map. Append `?form=waypoints` to the map-page address to get a text box where you can paste or type in a collection of points with their descriptions.

Figure 4-12 shows GPS Visualizer's basic output: in this case, a tracklog of part of a journey from San Francisco to San Diego, overlaid on a colorized USGS topo map. GPS Visualizer will also accept georeferenced logs from Netstumbler, so you can make maps of the wireless access points you pick up while walking or driving around [Hack #17].

GPS Visualizer has yet another trick; once you create a map, you can download your SVG file to your local drive. This is shown in Figure 4-13. Once you have the SVG file on your own machine, you can do whatever you'd like with it. GPS Visualizer is an amazingly easy and flexible tool, so get online and start mapping your tracks!

## HACK #43  Map Earthquakes in (Nearly) Real Time

With an RSS feed and a bit of Flash, you can map earthquakes around the world, as they happen.

Originally, this hack was going to cover some pretty straightforward HTML screen scraping from the USGS Earthquake web site, but, lucky for us, times have changed. The happiest end for any screen-scraping application is when

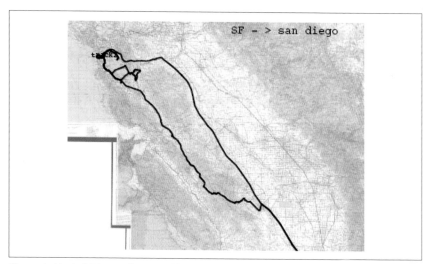

*Figure 4-12. A GPS Visualizer tracklog map*

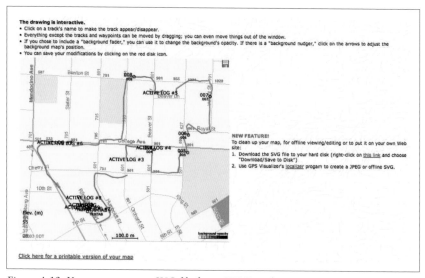

*Figure 4-13. You can save your SVG file from GPS Visualizer*

the screen scraper is no longer needed because the scrapee has made the data available in a machine-readable format. Yesss! In just such a case, the USGS has recently started publishing earthquake alerts in RSS 2.0, which makes mapping recent earthquakes in worldKit a snap.

The USGS's recent earthquake RSS feeds are listed at *http://earthquake.usgs. gov/recenteqsww/rss.html*, along with directions on how to subscribe to them with several popular RSS newsreaders. Several feeds are available, arranged by magnitude and age. For mapping applications, these RSS files make use of a couple RSS namespaces to include metadata on each quake. The latitude and longitude of each quake epicenter is included via the ICBM namespace (*http://postneo.com/icbm/*), and the integer value of the Richter Scale magnitude is included in the Dublin Core dc:subject element (*http://dublincore.org/*).

Here's an example of the format of an RSS item about an earthquake.

```
<item>
    <title>Loma Prieta Earthquake October 17, 1989 5:04 pm</title>
    <link>http://wrgis.wr.usgs.gov/dds/dds-29/</link>
    <icbm:lat>37.04</icbm:lat>
    <icbm:lon>-121.88</icbm:lon>
    <dc:subject>7</dc:subject>
</item>
```

Mapping an RSS feed like this is easy with *worldKit* [Hack #39]. You can find the download, documentation, and examples at *http://brainoff.com/worldkit/*.

After worldKit is downloaded and installed, the next step is to configure the data feed and images in *config.xml*. The data feed is specified in the dataurl element, as one of two choices: you can either point the data feed directly to the USGS feed of your choice, or the RSS feed can be periodically downloaded to your server. The difference is primarily in their respective disadvantages. The first option will generate a security warning in the Flash plug-in, since, by default, the player can only make connections to the site where the SWF file is hosted. Keeping a local copy of the feed requires setting up a small cron job to download the file to your server. The entry in your crontab would look something like:

```
17 * * * * wget -O $HOME/public_html/quakemap/quake.rss http://earthquake.
usgs.gov/recenteqsww/eqs1day-M2.5.xml
```

The above command should be on one line in your crontab file. You would then point the dataurl element of config.xml at the file on your web server. The other downside of this, of course, is that your local copy of the feed will only be up to date once an hour (or however frequently you set the cron job to run).

As for imagery, the Blue Marble image packaged with worldKit will work just fine out of the box. If you're feeling inspired, you can find other Earth imagery at NASA's Earth Observatory site located at *http://earthobservatory. nasa.gov/*, and decent world topographic maps can be found at *http://flatplanet.sourceforge.net/maps/topo.html*. For that matter, any cylindrical-projection (e.g., Mercator) world map will suffice. Save the image on your server, and point worldKit to it in your *config.xml* file with the dayimg element; you should see something like Figure 4-14.

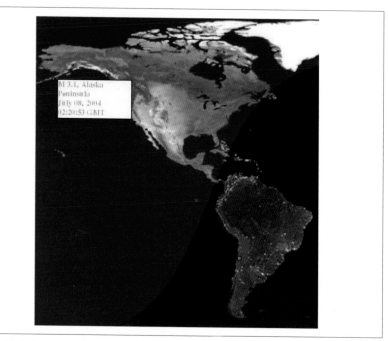

*Figure 4-14. An excerpt from a worldKit earthquake map, showing the Western Hemisphere*

Given that the USGS includes the magnitude of each quake in the dc: subject element, you can also configure worldKit to plot the location of each quake with a different size marker relative to its rating on the Richter Scale. Figure 4-14 shows part of a worldKit map made this way. All that's needed is an additional plotsize element in *config.xml*, which accepts subtags with names corresponding to dc:subject values. The values of the subtags establish the corresponding marker sizes. For earthquake feeds, you can expect Richter magnitudes ranging from 1 to 10, so that's what we'll feed into worldKit:

```
<plotsize>6
    <1>2</1><2>4</2><3>6</3><4>8</4><5>10</5>
    <6>12</6><7>14</7><8>16</8><9>18</9><10>20</10>
</plotsize>
```

The default plotsize is given by the first value (in this case, 6), to be used when an item's dc:subject is missing or otherwise unusable.

worldKit's use of purely numeric names for XML tags is not exactly legal XML—but worldKit handles them without complaint.

## Hacking the Hack

What if you're primarily interested in quakes in your immediate neighborhood? In that case, you can specify a bounding box for your map in terms of latitude and longitude in your *config.xml* file. Here's an example that covers the San Francisco Bay Area:

```
<north>38.20</north>
<south>37.30</south>
<west>-121.87</west>
<east>-123.00</east>
```

If a bounding box is specified, worldKit will only display items in the feed within the bounding box. You only need to provide an image that corresponds to your location. If you don't have a map of your area handy, we can offer a couple of suggestions on how to obtain one easily.

First, you might try *MapProxy* (*http://brainoff.com/worldkit/mapproxy/*), a simple web interface to TerraServer, which can fetch U.S. topo maps or aerial photos, given a ZIP Code and distance. MapProxy generates the corresponding worldKit bounding box configuration for you, as well.

Failing that, you can take one of the world maps, and extract the area corresponding to your bounding box with Photoshop or ImageMagick. To convert the bounding box in latitude and longitude to *x*- and *y*-coordinates in the image, use the following formulas from Table 4-1.

*Table 4-1. Formulas for converting a bounding box into image coordinates*

| Side | Conversion formula |
| --- | --- |
| Top | (90 - north) * height / 180 |
| Bottom | (90 - south) * height / 180 |
| Left | (180 + west) * width / 360 |
| Right | (180 + east) * width / 360 |

*—Mikel Maron*

## H A C K #44 Plot Statistics Against Shapes

Easily render demographic maps in SVG from shapes and CSV or Excel files.

In late 2003, we helped a bit with tech support on the Matt Gonzalez mayoral election campaign in San Francisco. Among the many different groups of volunteers were a couple of academic GIS specialists. Adorning the walls of the Decision Support Room were fascinating maps, showing statistics plotted against voting precincts: voter turnout, voter registration rates, first and second choice votes in the previous round of the election and in previous elections. These maps were used to identify and target wards where "Get Out the Vote" and other canvassing initiatives would have the best effect on our candidate's chances.

The maps were produced by the high priesthood of GIS: crafted in ArcInfo and Illustrator, and exported to PDF for view on the Web, making real-time analysis of exit-poll data difficult. Well, we thought, the data is in the public domain, and we can make analysis maps with free software for ourselves. Now so can you, using the Perl module SVG::Shapefile, available from CPAN (*http://search.cpan.org/*).

The demo that accompanies this module and shows the uses of it is available at *http://locative.us/indymapper/*.

## The Web Interface

Indymapper allows you to take your own shapefiles and spreadsheets—in CSV or Excel format, or the *.dbf* format that comes with shapefiles—and make maps out of your data via a simple web interface.

> Shapefiles (*.shp*) are a format created by ESRI for storing map data. They're one of the most common kinds of map file you'll find.

We built a web service at *http://locative.us/indymapper/* where you can upload your own data and generate SVG maps with PNG screenshots. Indymapper was designed to become a part of Indyvoter, the political-social networking software at *http://indyvoter.org/*. Figure 4-15 shows the core of the Indymapper map-making interface.

You can upload your own datafiles or select from a few sample *mapkits*, which consist of a shape, a data table, and various views on that table. Once you've selected or created a mapkit, the program looks at the columns in the shapefile's *.dbf* metadata and the column names from the spreadsheet. It presents you with several lists, with which you can match up the ID of each shape to a key column in your spreadsheet and plot the values of a second column against them. You can plot a range of values—e.g., a continuous numeric sequence that will be shaded between two colors—or a group of values, where you choose a different color for each distinct value in your data.

A *choropleth map* is a map that has appropriate shadings (value, texture, intensity) assigned to each area defined on the map. Choropleth shading works best for numbers with a consistent scale: the values should be ratios (e.g., "Number of Voters per 100,000 Inhabitants"), not absolute values

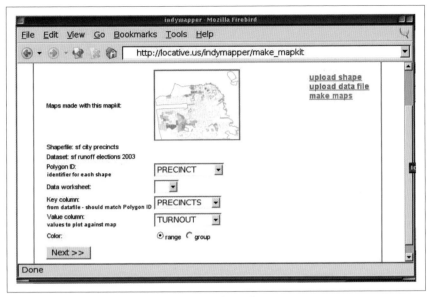

*Figure 4-15. Plotting stats against shapes on the Web*

(e.g., "Number of Voters"). Look carefully at choropleth maps you see in the press; what they represent can easily be illusory! Not all data should be uploaded to Indymapper; if you can normalize it, for example, by turning "Polling place incidents" into "Polling place incidents per 1,000 registered voters," then do so. Absolute values are best represented on a proportional symbol map, showing an icon shrink or grow according to the mapped value.

The rest of this hack should give you a clearer idea of what SVG::Shapefile and Indymapper can do, and illustrate how to "roll your own" map with code available from the Perl CPAN repository.

## Rolling Your Own

Installing modules from CPAN is easy. As your system's root user, type:

```
#> perl -MCPAN -e shell
cpan> install SVG::Shapefile
cpan> install DBD::Excel
```

For more in-depth instructions on installing modules from CPAN, see "Set Up an OpenGuide for Your Hometown" [Hack #97].

You can use SVG::Shapefile to plot a range of colors: one representing a low value, the other a high value, with a blend to and from white between them.

You can also use it to plot specific values using a color palette that you supply. The first technique is the more useful here.

For this hack, we've provided a sample shapefile, voting precincts in San Francisco as of 2003, and an Excel file that has data that maps to it. You should be able to use any freely available political shape you find, if you can find or create statistics that share a key column with it. SVG::Shapefile reads *.csv* and *.xls* files using the Perl DBI interface, so you can hook it up directly to an SQL database if you want.

## The Code

This script assumes you have the zipped-up shapefile and the Excel file in the same directory you run it from. Get them from *http://mappinghacks.com/data/PRECINCTS.zip* and *http://mappinghacks.com/data/SF_runoff.xls*. Type **unzip PRECINCTS.zip** to extract the contents of the shapefile, and then run this script:

```perl
#!/usr/bin/perl

use strict;
use lib qw(/home/jo/indymapper);
use SVG::Shapefile;

my $svg = SVG::Shapefile->new(ShapeFile => 'PRECINCTS.shp',
                    PolygonID => 'PRECINCT',
                        DataFile => 'SF_runoff.xls',
                        KeyColumn => 'PRECINCTS',
                        ValueColumn => 'TURNOUT',
                    Colors => [[0,255,0],[255,0,0]]
                        );
$svg->render('map.svg');
```

Reading large shapefiles and converting them to SVG geometry can take some time, so don't worry if the script waits for quite a few seconds before returning.

The PolygonID option specifies the identifier in the shapefile to use as the ID for each shape in the SVG. If it's not supplied, the default OBJECTID from the shapefile will be used. The values for the PolygonID column must match the values in the KeyColumn from the Excel or CSV file.

> If you're making maps from your own shapes and aren't sure which values they identify, **ogrinfo -a** *shapefile.shp* is a quick way to see all their metadata.

The KeyColumn and DataColumn options allow you to choose a key that corresponds to each shape and a value that you want to color the shapes with.

The Colors option allows you to specify two colors as RGB values: the first color is the lowest in the range, and the second color is the highest. The two colors are both shaded to white.

The results of running this script are illustrated in Figure 4-16.

Figure 4-16. Map showing voter turnout in San Francisco (note the central "progressive crescent" of political engagement)

You don't have to be a GIS geek to make your own political maps (though you probably still have to be a spreadsheet geek). Hopefully, once you're done with this book, it'll be a no-brainer.

### HACK #45 Extract a Spatial Model from Wikipedia

The Wiki encyclopedia covers the world; mine its data structure for use in mapping applications.

Wikipedia is the fantastic publicly editable online world encyclopedia. Maintained by casual online volunteers, many who are experts in their fields, it aims for a "neutral point of view" in recounting world knowledge, history, places, and political systems. This hack discusses the English Wikipedia (*http://en.wikipedia.org/*), but the principle will work with any of their many language editions, featuring mostly original articles.

"Wiki nature" allows anyone on the Web to edit each page; it also allows anyone to create links between pages using a simple markup, which encloses the page name in square brackets [[Like This]]. In Wikipedia, there's a special URL syntax to get a list of which Wikipedia sites link to each Wikipedia page. For example, *http://en.wikipedia.org/wiki/Argentina* is the country page for Argentina, and *http://en.wikipedia.org/w/wiki.phtml?title=Special: WhatlinkshereGtarget=Argentina* is the page showing all the *backlinks* to every page that refers to Argentina, shown in Figure 4-17.

*Figure 4-17. Pages linking to a country in Wikipedia*

## Modeling Wikipedia

Implicit in the structure of Wikipedia is kind of spatial index to events and people and ideas! Some of these links will be to places we can identify and geocode in their own right: country, cities, towns, regions.

For each country page in Wikipedia, we can build a set of related pages through backlinks. Some of them are lists in which every country appears; others are "History of..." and "Politics Of..." pages, sites about towns and cities, and pages about important dates and people. Each of these pages links to one or many countries and cities in turn.

Wikipedia has a lot of spatial data in it, including the available reference data from the CIA World Factbook for each country. Many country pages have beautifully drawn flat maps. Wikipedia is rich with information about the government and administration structures of many countries, but it doesn't have structured metadata that is machine-intelligible. We'll have to do good guesswork to geolocate pages.

Countries. First we need a list of things that Wikipedia identifies as countries. There is a Wikipedia page on countries with ISO codes, which is a great place to start. With a quick regular expression, we can extract the list:

```perl
#!/usr/bin/perl

use strict;
use LWP::UserAgent;

# download the page from wikipedia

my $ua = new LWP::UserAgent;
$ua->agent("WikiMap/1.0 " . $ua->agent);
my $page = $ua->get('http://en.wikipedia.org/wiki/ISO_3166-1_alpha-2')->
content;

my @lines = split("\n",$page);
my %countries;

foreach (@lines) {
        # match a 2-uppercase-letter code, and a title
        my ($code,$name) = $_ =~ /\<tt\>([A-Z]{2}).+title\=\"([^"]+)/;
        $countries{$code} = $name if $name;
}
```

This gives us a list of everything Wikipedia thinks is a country, with its two-letter ISO code. We can use this list to collect the country page backlinks from Wikipedia. To be reasonably polite to the site, we sleep for a few seconds between each page request.

This script uses a simple Perl RDF store, Class::RDF, to store the model of Wikipedia. The model is a graph, each node is a page, and there are arcs of connections between them. Web links don't differentiate between different kinds of connections, so we'll just define one relationship, "connects," that describes how one page links to another:

```perl
foreach my $c (keys %countries) {
        my $code = $iso_base.uc($c);
        my $url = $wiki_base .'wiki/'. $countries{$c};
        my $country = Class::RDF::Object->new(
        rdf->type => wm->Country,
        iso->code => $code,
        iso->name => $countries{$c},
        wm->wiki_page => $url);

        my $links = $wiki_base . 'w/wiki.phtml?title=Special:
            Whatlinkshere&target='.$countries{$c};

        my $doc = $ua->get($links)->content;

        my @lines = split("\n",$doc);
        foreach (@lines) {
```

```
my ($link,$name) = $doc =~ /\<li\>\<a href\=\"\/([^"])\"\>
    ([\w| ])\<\/a/;
if ($link and $name) {
    $link = $wiki_base.$link;
    my ($object) = Class::RDF->search(wm->wiki_page =>
        $link);
    $object = Class::RDF::Object->create(wm->wiki_page
        => $link, wm->name => $name) if not $object;
    $object->wm::connects($country);
}
    }
}
```

Watching this script run is like watching a potted conceptual history of the world. Now, we've built a graph of all the countries in the world, according to Wikipedia, with links to famous people, places, and events. But we don't know which are which, nor can we distinguish casual from important mentions.

**Cities and other spatial things.**  We can deepen this spatial index by using a gazetteer service. "Build a Free World Gazetteer" [Hack #84] was written with this purpose in mind. We go through the list of each country's backlinks and, for page names that look likely to be places, try to find them in the gazetteer. We use a simple set of rules of thumb, partially borrowed from Maciej Ceglowski (*http://www.idlewords.com*), to identify things worth trying to geocode:

- Things beginning with numbers are not cities.
- If the name is three or more words long, it's probably not a city name.
- If this is a city name, all the words will be capitalized.

To request the information about the city from the gazetteer, we issue this GET request (you can try this out in a web browser):

```
http://mappinghacks.com/cgi-bin/gazetteer.cgi?query=Placename&country=ISO&
format=rdf
```

We might get multiple results back for the same place name, in which case we'll lazily attach them all to the Wikipedia page. They may be different types of features: an administrative area, a populated place, and also a natural or landmark feature sharing its name.

## Graphing Wikipedia

To graph Wikipedia, we'll draw something that we could call a *cartogram*. A cartogram represents spatial relations, but without conforming to a particular geometry or projection—a more abstract way of drawing pictures of geospatial data than cartographic maps. As our model of Wikipedia is a graph of connections, it's ideal for GraphViz, the excellent free graph layout program. GraphViz is available at *http://www.graphviz.org/*, and RPMs are available for Linux distributions (you can get it in Debian by running apt-get install graphviz as root). The GraphViz Perl module allows us to easily get at it programmatically.

Figure 4-18 shows the graph of a small section of Wikipedia's spatial relations, centered on the UK. The graph of all spatial interconnections in Wikipedia is too big for GraphViz to easily handle!

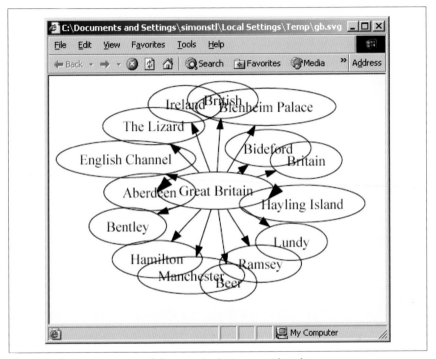

*Figure 4-18. Graphing some of the spatial relations in Wikipedia*

## Hacking the Hack

You can use these techniques with any corpus of text that you have on a disk somewhere, over which it might be useful to have a spatial index. A collection of news articles or RSS feeds that you want to display on a map, or old email archives to map project activity.

We chose to ignore pages whose titles were numbers. Collecting all pages whose titles are four digits and/or that match the expression /As of ^\d{4}$/, you could build a pretty nice temporal index of Wikipedia. Imagine a map where you adjust a knob and see local content and political boundaries change through time. "As of" is a recent naming convention for dating pages, sometimes used in different ways, and the temporal index probably won't reveal much depth yet, but Wikipedia is always growing and refining itself.

# Map Global Weather Conditions

Make your own animated weather maps, just like the ones they show on the evening news.

Lucky for the weather enthusiasts among us—and who isn't a weather enthusiast, when it comes right down to it?—there are loads of free weather images from geostationary satellites available on the Web. In particular, the University of Dundee provides an interface to frequently updated imagery from several satellites covering the entire globe (*http://www.sat.dundee.ac.uk/ pdus.html*). The good people from the *Xplanet* project have stitched together these images into a single picture of global cloud cover, available for download to use in Xplanet or other applications. We'll fetch a sequence of these images and make an animated GIF of global weather conditions to amaze and astound your friends and family.

Information on the Xplanet cloud map is at *http://xplanet.sourceforge.net/ clouds.php*. The cloud map is free to use, with the restriction that the image is not downloaded more often than once every three hours. The image is rather large, and excessive downloads have caused bandwidth problems previously, so this restriction is pretty rigorously enforced. That's okay by us, since the image is only updated every three hours anyway.

Xplanet can take this cloud map and overlay it on world map imagery from Blue Marble or elsewhere. Xplanet has lots of other cool features, so it's definitely worth some exploration. Download and install Xplanet from *http:// xplanet.sourceforge.net/*. While Xplanet runs on both Windows and most Unix-like operating systems, we'll need the power of Unix-like shell scripting and cron-job scheduling to accomplish the task at hand. The default configuration for cloud maps on such systems is stored in the file */etc/ xplanet/config/overlay_clouds* (or wherever Xplanet installed it), and it uses *clouds.jpg* from the current directory for the weather imagery, and *earth.jpg* and *night.jpg* from */usr/share/xplanet/images* for the base images.

To build our animated GIF, first make a directory on your system to hold the images. Then fetch the *download_clouds.py* script from the Xplanet cloud map page and put it in the same directory. Next, write the following shell commands to a file called *render_clouds.sh*, and then chmod +x the file:

```
#!/bin/sh
cd /home/foobar/xplanet                      # or wherever you put the files
python download_clouds.py clouds.jpg
xplanet -config overlay_clouds -make_cloud_maps
```

This script fetches the latest cloud overlay and then calls Xplanet to create the final images. Run it once with *./render_clouds.sh* to see it in action.

Xplanet should generate two files in the current directory, one called *day_clouds.jpg* and the other *night_clouds.jpg*. Have a look at them in your favorite image viewer: one should contain the world's cloud cover over the daytime map, as depicted in Figure 4-19, and the other the same over a nighttime map. Pretty cool, huh? But we're not done yet!

*Figure 4-19. Sample day_clouds.jpg from Xplanet, showing current cloud cover*

Now we can collect a sequence of these images and then animate them. Let's start by adding the following line to *render_clouds.sh*:

```
cp day_clouds.jpg clouds_`date +%Y%m%d_%H%M`.jpg
```

This additional step copies the daytime cloud-cover map to a file with a timestamped name. We can build up a set of these files by having the cron daemon run *render_clouds.sh* every three hours, at some point during the hour. Add the following to your crontab, adjusting for local directory structure, and let it run overnight:

```
40 */3 * * *        /home/foobar/xplanet/render_clouds.sh 2>/dev/null
```

It doesn't matter if this runs a little less than three hours since the last time you ran it; *download_clouds.py* will check the last-modification timestamp of *clouds.jpg* and bail if it ran too recently. The redirection to */dev/null* is just to keep cron from spamming your inbox with the output of *render_clouds.sh* every three hours.

Within a day or so, you should have a directory with some of these files accumulated:

```
$ ls clouds_*.jpg
clouds_20040707_1940.jpg    clouds_20040707_2240.jpg    clouds_20040708_
0140.jpg    clouds_20040708_0440.jpg    clouds_20040708_0740.jpg    clouds_
20040708_1040.jpg    clouds_20040708_1340.jpg    clouds_20040708_1640.jpg
```

Now we can use the ImageMagick utility convert to create an animated gif. While many Linux distributions ship with ImageMagick, if it isn't already installed on your machine, you can find it at *http://www.imagemagick.org/*.

```
$ convert -resize 800x400 -loop 0 -delay 30 clouds_*.jpg clouds_animated.gif
```

You should get back a nice animated map of the world's weather in *clouds_ animated.gif*, which you can use to do the aforementioned amazing and astounding. Turning this process into a cron job to automate the creation of the animated GIF is left as an exercise for the reader. One final note: you may find that the cloud cover renderings will start to fill up in that directory, making a rendering of recent weather phenomena increasingly difficult. In that case, the following crontab entry, which (at least on GNU-based systems) removes any cloud imagery two days old, might be handy:

```
* 0 * * *    rm /home/foobar/xplanet/clouds_`date +%Y%m%d -d "2 days ago"`.jpg
```

—*Mikel Maron*

# CHAPTER FIVE

# Mapping with Gadgets
## Hacks 47–63

*You got to be careful if you don't know where you're going, because you might not get there.*
—Yogi Berra

We like to know where we are! We're fascinated with location and what location says about narratives and journeys. One of the earliest written works in the Western tradition is *The Odyssey*, recounting brave Odysseus's journey home from Troy, and his problems with (the wrong!) location. The rise of affordable personal GPS units has given a huge boost to our interest in place, in maps, and in narratives of place. GPS units allow us to document the journey of our own lives with specific times and locations.

## How GPS Works

The Global Positioning System, or GPS for short, is a marvel of modern technology. The 24 NAVSTAR satellites that make up the orbital component of the Global Positioning System were launched by the U.S. Air Force, starting in 1978. The satellites orbit Earth about 650 kilometers above its surface and are staggered in such a way that three or four should be overhead, anywhere on Earth, at any time. Each satellite carries an atomic clock on board, which it uses to transmit the precise time over a microwave signal back to receivers on Earth, along with a set of 3-D position data, called an *ephemeris*, which describes the satellite's location in the sky.

According to Einstein's Special Theory of Relativity, a radio signal should travel at a constant speed in a vacuum. Therefore, in principle, if you know what time a radio signal was transmitted and where it was transmitted from, then you can deduce how far away the transmitter is from how long it took the signal to arrive. However, just because you know how far a radio signal traveled doesn't mean you know which direction it came from. This means that, given a signal from a single satellite, we can only estimate our position to be within the radius of a circle of that distance around the satellite in question.

If we attempt to listen to more than one satellite at a time, we can build up a series of overlapping circles, as shown in Figure 5-1. Each circle progressively narrows the portion of Earth's surface that we can be in, based on the radio signals we're receiving. In principle, three circles are sufficient to establish a two-dimensional fix on our own position, and four are enough to establish a three-dimensional fix. Ultimately, with enough satellite signals, we can narrow down the estimate of our position on Earth's surface to within as little as five meters—which is one-eightieth of one percent of the planet's circumference! Not bad at all.

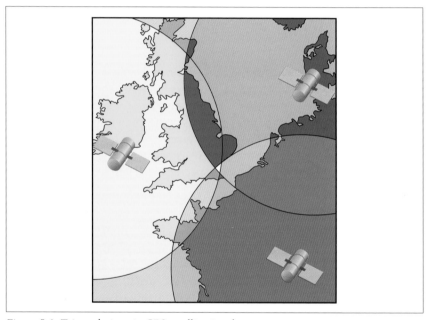

*Figure 5-1. Triangulation via GPS satellite signals*

In practice, though, GPS reception varies widely with the time of day, the state of Earth's ionosphere, and particularly with nearby terrain. Hills, buildings, and trees can all cut GPS reception to nothing, so your results may vary. GPS reception doesn't work at all indoors (except sometimes near windows) or underwater.

Other global positioning systems are in use as well. The U.S. maintains a ground-based maritime navigation system called LORAN-C, which operates along similar principles. Russia still maintains its own satellite-based GPS, known as GLONASS. More recently, other nations, including the European Union and China, are working together to field their own satellite-based global positioning system, called Galileo, which they hope to have online by 2007.

 One curious side note about satellite-based GPS stems from a prediction of Einstein's General Theory of Relativity that time should travel more slowly as one gets closer to a large gravitational source, such as a planet. In fact, the atomic clocks in orbit on board GPS satellites actually do run faster than their Earth-bound counterparts, to the tune of 12 microseconds a year. While you can blink and miss a duration that brief, it turns out that this discrepancy causes a noticeable error in GPS triangulation, and the satellite clocks must be corrected for the difference. This strange fact makes for an interesting and oddly practical verification of Einstein's well-known theory!

**Leave your own breadcrumbs: tracklogs and waypoints.** Most handheld GPS units provide an easy way to save a marker to your current position. These are called *waypoints*, and they are great at allowing you to capture your own experiences. If you press and hold the "mark" button, the GPS will display a screen allowing you to name the waypoint. A *tracklog* is a series of position points that shows where you were. A tracklog may also contain the time and the elevation at that point. In contrast to waypoints, which must be set manually, GPS receivers will typically record tracklogs automatically as you move about.

You can read waypoints and tracklogs into your computer with Garnix [Hack #49], GPSBabel [Hack #51], or many other programs. There are too many formats for storing waypoint and tracklog data! Fortunately GPSBabel can convert just about any of them to any other. We strongly recommend the use of GPX for storing tracklogs and waypoints. GPX is an XML format that is designed to facilitate the exchange of GPS data between applications and on the Web. It's supported by lots of applications, including many of those described in this book. You can find out more about GPX at *http:// topografix.com/gpx*.

Since a tracklog is just a list of points, you can create or re-create a tracklog from a paper map or other record of a trip. See "Give Your Great-Great-Grandfather a GPS" [Hack #98] for an example of creating a tracklog from the diary of an Oregon Trail emigrant.

Once you have a tracklog, you can display it over an aerial photo with Wissenbach 3D, 3Dem, or Terra Browser. You can also create an animation of your journey [Hack #56]. These are tools that treat the tracklog as a line.

The tool provided at http://www.mappinghacks.com/projects/linkmedia/ [Hack #59] will take a tracklog and a list of timestamps, perhaps representing the times at which you took pictures, and tell you where you were at those times. It will also tell you how fast you were going, and what direction you were going (your heading) based on that tracklog.

**Understanding tracklog options.** Different GPS units store different numbers of track points. The basic Garmin Etrex stores 1,536 points, while the Etrex legend can hold 10,000. The Earthmate BlueLogger has "over 50,000." How many points is enough? When I bought my Garmin IIIplus, I was sure that its 1.44 MB of RAM and 1,900 track points would be enough for me!

I was wrong. See "Don't Lose Your Tracklogs!" [Hack #58] for a discussion of tracklog loggers that can effectively allow you to store an unlimited number of track points.

Tracklogs are like electronic breadcrumbs. You can usually select how often you want to drop a crumb. Because the bag is a fixed size, you will run out of crumbs more quickly if you drop crumbs more frequently. If you have a basic GPS with 1,500 or so track points, then saving a track point every second will fill your memory in less then 30 minutes. And even 10,000 points would last less than three hours! The default GPS settings are a reasonable compromise, but if you are planning to do interesting things with your tracklogs, you should experiment before you set out on a trip. As the owner of a camera store once told me, "You 'going on a trip' guys scare me."

**What about precision?** You often see coordinates displayed with more precision than is strictly relevant, and GPS units can display position with more precision than their accuracy. *Precision* measures how many digits your GPS receiver can approximate its results to, and *accuracy* measures how close this approximation comes to the true results. Thus, a value of 38.432212 is more precise than 38.43. But that doesn't mean it is more accurate.

O'Reilly Media's headquarters is located at latitude = 38.411269, longitude = –122.841256. What does that mean? If we go back to our knowledge of the meter, we can develop a rule of thumb about digits of precision in terms of geographical position. The original definition of a meter was 1/10,000,000th (one ten-millionth) of the distance from the equator to the North Pole by way of Paris. So 1 meter is equal to 90 degrees divided by 10,000,000—or 0.000009 degrees. A one-digit difference in the 6th decimal place is the distance from 0.000000 to 0. 000001 degrees, which is equal to 1/9th of a meter. This is equal to about 11 centimeters, or 4.4 inches. Your GPS receiver is not accurate to 4 inches!

Specifying coordinates to four decimal places gives you approximately 10-meter precision. That is close enough for normal automobile navigation, and your GPS receiver isn't really that accurate either. I like to store six digits, because those last digits obscure any rounding errors that might creep in. Here is a table of approximate distances by decimal place:

| Degrees north or south | Equivalent metric/English distances |
| --- | --- |
| 1 degree | 111 km (69 mi) |
| 1/10 of a degree | 11.1 km (6.9 mi) |
| 1/100 of a degree | 1.11 km (0.69 mi) |
| 1/1,000 of a degree | 111 m (364 ft) |
| 1/10,000 of a degree | 11.1 m (36.4 ft) |
| 1/100,000 of a degree | 1.11 m (3.64 ft) |
| 1/1,000,000 of a degree | 11 cm (4.4 in) |

The normal practice is to match your precision and your accuracy, but you can play games with that convention. The U.S. Census Bureau publishes their TIGER/Line data with six degrees of precision. When you get out in the field, the data is often several hundred feet off, implying that at best it is accurate to about four decimal places. But the TIGER data uses that false precision to indicate the relative positions of things.

For example, when you give road directions based on your odometer, you are limited to a precision of 1/10th of a mile, which is the limit of your measuring tool. But if you see three houses within the same tenth of a mile, say 2.1 miles from a landmark, you could indicate their relative positions by adding a false decimal of accuracy and say that the first house was at 2.1 miles, the second at 2.13, and the third at 2.16.

You want to find a balance among precision, accuracy, and usefulness!

### HACK #47 Get Maps on Your Mobile Phone

Simplify your life by putting maps on a device that many of us carry anyway.

If you're strolling through a city, a laptop is kind of bulky to lug around and a GPS device is pretty specialized. Fortunately, many people carry another device that makes an easy container for maps: their cell phones. Cell phones of a recent vintage have clear enough screens, enough memory, and a good enough interface to give you convenient access to the data.

There are a lot of different map solutions available for specific operating systems and environments. To demonstrate the possibilities, we'll show Tom-Tom City Maps London, one of a variety of map software programs available for the Nokia 60 series—including the Nokia 7650, 3650, 3660, 3620, 6600, or N-Gage. TomTom City Maps works with or without a separate GPS unit, connected via Bluetooth.

TomTom City Maps (and a lot of other mapping software for mobile devices) is available from *http://handango.com/*. City Maps London, shown here, costs U.S. $4.99. Similar maps are available for many European cities, as well as a few American ones.

When you start out looking at London, there's a lot to it, as shown in Figure 5-2.

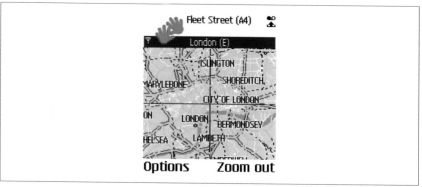

*Figure 5-2. An overview of London, seen in a Nokia cell phone*

You can zoom in for a much closer view at street level, complete with information about which streets are one-way, as shown in Figure 5-3.

City Maps can also give directions from a location to a location, using your preferences for road types. If you have a Bluetooth GPS device, City Maps can show you where you are on the map and adjust your planning accordingly. Without GPS, you can still use the directions, but you'll have to manually tell the software when you've reached an endpoint.

City Maps installation requires Windows XP, but the distribution is simple enough that Mac users can also put the information on their phone. Both Mac and Linux users can unzip the downloaded ZIP archive (one of mine was *s60_cm_london.zip*), navigate to the *CityMaps/N9210* directory (the bit after the *N* may differ, depending on your map), and send the *.sis* files to the

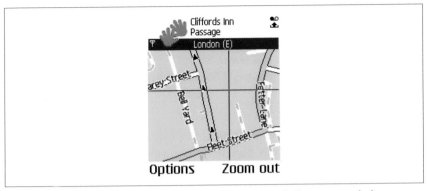

*Figure 5-3. Zooming in on Fleet Street to get a better idea of where you might be*

handset via Bluetooth. Open each incoming file (using the Messaging app) and install them in turn (order doesn't seem to matter).

The Handango web site can also download applications directly to many models of mobile devices.

—*Rael Dornfest and Simon St.Laurent*

## HACK #48 Accessorize Your GPS

Get more enjoyment out of your GPS by making and buying simple accessories.

The heart of a GPS receiver is pretty simple: a small box of electronics that does magic. In the introduction to this chapter, we learned a bit about the features of a GPS receiver that contribute to buying decisions. Now let's go wild and discuss accessories!

### Waterproof Floating Cases

Typical GPS units are rated as waterproof to one foot. While I'm sure this is true for the new, just-off-the-shelf unit, I know for a fact that this is less true if the GPS receiver is three years old and subject to a harsh Channel Islands crossing on an open boat. In addition, your GPS receiver is certainly not waterproof at the depths to which it will surely plunge when it manages to escape the bounds of your boat. On a recent dive trip, I came upon a small pile of gear that had obviously fallen off the back of a boat: a single fin, dive knife, and a watch. I stashed the loot in my lobster bag, but first looked at the watch. "Darn," I thought. "Is that really the time? There is no way I'm going to be able to get another dive in before the night dive."

I was able to make use of the knife and the watch, but if there had been a GPS in the pile, I would have cried over the waste of now-ruined technology. Fortunately there is a simple answer: a floating waterproof bag. See *http://www.waterproofcases.net* for a line of waterproof cases that start at $24.99. Or do a Google search for "GPS case" and scan the 9,140 results.

## Mounting the GPS

Handheld GPSes are nice in your hand but leave a bit to be desired when you try to add them to your bicycle, motorcycle, automobile, or Burning Man art car. In these cases, you need a GPS mount. Fortunately there are a lot of options.

For years, I have had a strip of Velcro on the bottom of my GPS and Velcro pads on each side of the front of my cars. Driver or passenger, I'm never far from my personal digital carrier pigeon.

A less useful technique with the Garmin Rino is to string a strip of Velcro through the small hole between the antennas, wrap that around your steering wheel, and Velcro it shut. This appears to work for long periods, but when the Velcro loosens, as it will when you turn a corner, the GPS will flop down into your lap, causing you to experience great driving difficulty and almost run into a parked car.

Trust me on this one. Velcroing the GPS to your steering wheel seems like a good idea, since it keeps the GPS handy right at a spot where you can easily look. But this turns out to be a bad idea. Fortunately the GPS industry has responded to the crowds of folks with electronics flopping in their laps with a wealth of GPS mounting options.

RAM Mounts at *http://www.cycoactive.com/gps/gps_mounts.html* has the coolest-looking mounts for motorcycles and bicycles. They are made from stainless steel and come with shock mounts and places to route the power cable. I have to agree with their site: "beautiful construction, looks like it was made in a robotics laboratory."

The folks at RAM Mounts also have a great page discussing the problems of operating a GPS under extreme vibration (*http://www.cycoactive.com/gps/ gps_batteries.html*).

## Batteries?

Rechargeable Nickel Metal Hybrid batteries are the best choice for digital cameras, but they don't seem to match the power curve of GPS units as well. Still, if you don't mind swapping batteries during a trip, NiMH batteries are great. I've done battery-life comparisons with three different units that used

2, 3, and 4 AA batteries. In all cases, I get around 18 hours on Alkaline batteries and closer to 12 hours on NiMH cells.

## External Antennas

Some GPS units will let you attach an external antenna. This can boost your reception substantially, especially if you're working with the device inside a vehicle or another signal-reducing area. Even if you have an antenna permanently mounted, if you started with a handheld GPS, you'll be able to occasionally remove the GPS to walk around: just free the GPS, disconnect the antenna, and you're off. Antennas seem to start around $30 and go up from there, depending on the application. (If you're feeling adventurous and want to build your own antenna, see *http://www.arrl.org/tis/info/pdf/0210036.pdf* for one set of plans.)

## Power and Data Cables

GPS units go through batteries quickly. If you are using your GPS in your car, you can use a car cigarette-lighter adapter. Perhaps you want to track your location to a GPS tracklog logger or a laptop at the same time you want to power the GPS from the car. You can do so with a combined PC interface and cigarette-lighter adapter.

The GPS vendors are happy to sell cables. A PC interface cable or cigarette-lighter adapter for the Garmin Rino is just under $40. The combined cable? $50 even.

## Make Your Own Garmin Data Cable

Larry Berg bought a Garmin GPS-45 and wanted to connect it to his computer. For some odd reason, the Garmin used a proprietary cable, and Larry didn't want to pay $30 for a connector and a bit of wire. (The full story is at *http://pfranc.com/projects/g45contr/g45story.htm.*) In 1996, he made his own mold and ended up with extra connectors, which he offered for free. The power of the Net took off, and now he is the head of a worldwide network of "pfrancs." You can offer a pledge to your local pfranc, and they will send you two connectors for free.

If you like the connectors, you honor your pledge, and the worldwide network of good feeling continues. They also have a serial-to-USB adapter, essential for getting your tracklogs when all you have are USB ports [Hack #50].

Get inspired, get involved, and check out *http://pfranc.com* for your GPS accessory needs.

## Maps

Many GPS units allow you to upload maps. Garmin has its MapSource product line, with CDs of detailed maps covering everything from marine charts to topo maps. Check out the Garmin Cartography page: *http://www. garmin.com/cartography*. And if you don't see a map for the area you want, see "Create Your Own Maps for a Garmin GPS" [Hack #54] to learn how to hack your own maps for Garmin GPS devices. There are also lots of vendors in this space worth exploring.

Bottom line? There is always another gadget or accessory to add to your hobby!

### HACK #49    Get Your Tracklogs in Windows or Linux

Get your tracklogs and waypoints with command-line tools to enjoy the power of scripting.

Tracklogs and waypoints are the raw material for your stories. You want to pull those out of your GPS receiver and onto your computer. There are a number of utilities to do this. Browse the Free GIS project site (*http://freegis. org*) for many examples of graphical and command-line tools.

Garnix is a free software program for downloading tracklogs, waypoints, and routes. It was written by Anton Helm and is available at *http://homepage.ntlworld.com/anton.helm/garnix.html*. I've used Garnix for more than four years, and until recently, I found its elegance of interface and features to be compelling. Lately I've also been using GPSBabel [Hack #51].

Command-line tools give you the power to chain together functions and automate tasks. For example, I have a script that will import my tracklogs, clean up the format, create an animation of the tracklog [Hack #56], and then upload that animation to my home server.

It was hard for me to learn the command-line tools and string them together in a script, but now my post-trip workflow is accomplished more quickly than trying to do the same thing with individual GUI tools. This is an example of a productivity paradox. Ease of use and ease of learning don't always go together; learning often carries the price of short-term inefficiency.

A word on post-trip workflow: I've been known to crawl into a hotel at 1:00 A.M., only to open two laptops in order to import photos, download tracklogs and waypoints, burn CD copies of my notes and pictures, import my voice-recorder annotations, and upload the whole mess to a web site. I'm not saying that this is the only, best, or right way to live one's life. But it is how I live mine, and since it is how I live my life, I am interested in ways to speed up my processing.

## Garnix for Linux, Windows, or DOS

The installation of Garnix is basically the same for Linux or Windows/DOS. Download the appropriate binary file and uncompress it into a new directory. For the Linux version, you need to make the program executable with chmod +x garnix. Source code is also available, as well as an interesting document that reverse-engineers the Garmin protocol.

To check that it is working, make sure you have the GPS set in Garmin protocol mode and connect the GPS to your serial port. Under Linux, you may need to be root, or run *sudo*, to have access to your serial port.

```
[rich@testingrange garnix]$ sudo ./garnix
Password:
Device ID:    GPS III+ Software Version  2.03
Device Info 1: VERBMAP Americas Highway Land Data 1.00
Device Time:   12:32:28-2004/08/11

Current Position (WGS84):
Latitude    38deg 40min 47.98sec
Longitude -123deg 17min  3.59sec
```

If you can't remember an option, type garnix -h for a terse help screen.

Garnix has three different display formats: degrees-minutes-seconds (DMS) with symbols, DMS with abbreviations, or Waypoint Plus format.

Here's how to apply the three formats to waypoints.

Waypoints in DMS with abbreviations ("text" mode):

```
$ garnix -w -x -f myway.txt
```

Example:

```
38deg 24min 12.32sec -122deg 49min  6.76sec 0.0 WGS84 OREILY "CRTD 19:34
31-AUG-00" [wpt_dot N];
```

Waypoints in DMS with symbols:

```
$ garnix -w -s -f myway.txt
```

Example:

```
38° 24' 12.32" -122° 49'  6.76" 0.0 WGS84 OREILY "CRTD 19:34 31-AUG-00"
[wpt_dot N];
```

Waypoints in Waypoint Plus format:

```
$ garnix -w -y -f myway.txt
```

Example:

```
WP,D,OREILY, 38.40342,-122.81854,12/31/1969,16:00:00,CRTD 19:34 31-AUG-00
```

Garnix configuration is set in the file *garnix.cfg*. This is where you set your
serial port (under Linux, */dev/ttyS0* is the first serial port), and if you add deg_
min_sec; then imports will use the DMS format by default. The big win for
the Waypoint Plus format is that Lat, Long is displayed in decimal degrees.

Garnix Waypoint DMS format looks like this (from the file *garnix.txt*):

```
<lat> <lon> <height> <datum> <name> <comment> [<map symbol> <display mode>];
```

The important fields are <lat>, <lon>, <height> (not available in older units),
the waypoint name (<name>), and the waypoint comment (<comment>). If you
don't enter another comment in the GPS unit, then <comment> will be the
date and time the waypoint was created. In the previous example, I created,
or updated, that waypoint at 7:34 P.M. on August 31, 2000.

Garnix tracklogs follow the same general pattern as waypoints.

Tracklogs in DMS with abbreviations ("text" mode):

```
$ garnix -t -x -f mytrack.txt
```

Example:

```
42deg 11min 47.75sec -122deg 42min 57.36sec 0.0 WGS84 00:00:00-1970/01/01 [1];
42deg 10min  5.79sec -122deg 39min 30.57sec 0.0 WGS84 00:00:00-1970/01/01 [0];
...
38deg 27min 51.70sec -122deg 39min 53.47sec 0.0 WGS84 07:38:45-2004/08/07 [1];
38deg 27min 51.84sec -122deg 39min 53.84sec 0.0 WGS84 07:38:47-2004/08/07 [0];
```

Tracklogs in DMS with symbols:

```
$ garnix -t -s -f mytrack.txt
```

Example:

```
42° 11' 47.75" -122° 42' 57.36" 0.0 WGS84 00:00:00-1970/01/01 [1];
42° 10'  5.79" -122° 39' 30.57" 0.0 WGS84 00:00:00-1970/01/01 [0];
..
38° 27' 51.70" -122° 39' 53.47" 0.0 WGS84 07:38:45-2004/08/07 [1];
38° 27' 51.84" -122° 39' 53.84" 0.0 WGS84 07:38:47-2004/08/07 [0];
```

Garnix Tracklog DMS format (from the file *garnix.txt*):

```
<lat> <lon> <height> <datum> <date/time> <segment flag>;
```

> Garmin GPS units allow you to save 10 tracks. This seems
> like a great and useful feature, and in "Use Your Track Mem-
> ory as a GPS Base Map" [Hack #55] we'll see a use for this fea-
> ture, but most of the time you DO NOT want to "save" your
> tracklogs. When you save your tracklogs, you lose track-
> point resolution, and more importantly, you lose all of the
> timestamps!

These [1] and [0] values at the end of each line are interesting. Unlike some of the free programs, Garnix includes the *track segment* flag. What if you are on a trip and the GPS runs out of batteries, powers down, and stops saving the tracklog? Ten minutes later, you put new batteries in and you are good to go. But now you have a gap in your tracklog. The GPS is capable of determining that this has happened, so when you power back up, the first track point is marked with the *start of segment* flag, shown as [1], so you can decide what you want to do with the data. Sometimes it is better to have no data, rather than bad data.

## An Important Lesson

We get into ruts in the ways in which we use tools. Sometimes it takes the non-maskable interrupt of life to jar us from our ruts. I have used Garnix for over four years and have always been annoyed by the "feature" of loading coordinates in DMS, instead of decimal degrees. I have written way too many little Perl scripts to munge the data into my preferred format, and even had to do the same in "How Far? How Fast? Geo-Enabling Your Spreadsheet" [Hack #11]. And, now, in the process of actually *looking* at the Garnix documentation and trying all of the options, I realize that the Waypoint Plus format appears to have everything I need, without the annoyance of the more-difficult-to-parse DMS format.

The lesson is that we are all neophytes in the world, and periodically glancing at the documentation for our core tools, rather than obsessively reading Slashdot, offers great rewards.

## See Also

*GPSTrans (http://gpstrans.sourceforge.net/)*
   Another command-line GPS interface.

*GPSBabel (http://gpsbabel.sourceforge.net)*
   Described in "Speak in Geotongues: GPSBabel to the Rescue" [Hack #51].

*Pygarmin (http://pygarmin.sourceforge.net)*
   A Python module to connect to a Garmin GPS.

*Freegis.org (http://freegis.org/browse.en.html?category=app&app=gps)*
   Freegis.org has a category for GPS software.

# The Serial Port to USB Conundrum
#### #50
The march of progress brings much, but where's my serial port?

Your GPS receiver has a serial port, but your computer has a USB port. How are you going to transfer your tracklogs and waypoints? It is true that more GPS units are arriving with Bluetooth and USB interfaces, but most still use the old RS232 serial interface. We can get a serial-to-USB converter that will allow us to use our GPS with Windows, Linux, and Mac USB ports.

Converting USB to serial turns out to be complex, due to the way that USB devices work. Basically the serial-to-USB converter includes a small computer (well, a microcontroller) that translates USB to RS232 and back. Not all serial-to-USB converters properly implement the whole RS232 specification.

Even with this complexity, we can find devices that work. One choice is the BF-810 from BAFO (*http://bafo.com*). BAFO has drivers for Mac OS X, Windows, and Linux. Another option is to visit our friends at *http://pfranc.com*. How can you resist people who have this question on their FAQ?

> Q6: Are most people cool? (AKA Good?)
>
> A: YES --- like maybe a million or more to one!

You can read about the good and the *bad things* about their adapters at *http://pfranc.com/usb/usb.mhtml*. They have drivers for Windows, OS X, and Linux. They also provide the custom Gamin connectors **[Hack #48]**, which allow you to build your own data cables.

The following instructions refer to the BAFO BF-810. However, the same general principles will apply to other devices. You need to install the proper driver software and then determine the name that your operating system gives to that *port* or *device*.

## Configuring and Using the Serial-to-USB Adapter Under OS X

Download the latest driver from the BAFO driver's page (*http://bafo.com/bafo/prodrivers.asp*). Decompress the file and install it by double-clicking on *ProlificUSBSerial105.pkg*.

This should create the serial-to-USB device. You can check that this created the device in a Terminal window:

```
$ ls -al /dev/cu*
crw-rw-rw-  1 root  wheel   8,  1 24 Sep 11:24 /dev/cu.modem
crw-rw-rw-  1 root  wheel   8,  3 24 Sep 11:28 /dev/cu.usbserial0
```

You want to use the *cu.usbserial0* device.

Here is how to read GPS waypoints from a Garmin GPS using GPSBabel on a Mac. The device or file is specified with the -f parameter. In this case, it is -f /dev/cu.usbserial0:

```
sudo gpsbabel -D9 -i garmin -f /dev/cu.usbserial0 -o gpx -F foo.gpx
```

This includes the debugging flag -D9, so we will get lots of extra information to help confirm that the transfer is operating correctly.

See "Speak in Geotongues: GPSBabel to the Rescue" **[Hack #51]** for more examples.

## Configuring and Using the Serial-to-USB Adapter Under Windows

Download the latest driver for your version of Windows from the BAFO driver's page (*http://bafo.com/bafo/prodrivers.asp*). Unzip it and then connect the serial-to-USB adapter. The "Add New Hardware" wizard will likely see the new device. Give the wizard the location of the file that you downloaded and follow the instructions.

Once it is finished, you can also test the GPS connection under Windows by setting your GPS to NMEA mode, and then starting HyperTerminal (Start → Accessories → Communications → HyperTerminal). Create a new connection using *com3*, and set the speed to 4800 bits per second. You should then start seeing NMEA sentences.

GPSBabel works the same way across the three platforms, with the exception of the operating-system-dependent way that you refer to serial ports. Under Windows, the serial-to-USB adapter maps the USB to a regular COM port: *com3* in our example. To fetch waypoints from a Garmin GPS using the serial-to-USB adapter under Windows:

```
C:\> gpsbabel -D9 -i garmin -f com3 -o gpx -F waypoint.gpx
```

## Configuring and Using the Serial-to-USB Adapter Under Linux

The BAFO-810 uses the Prolific PL230 driver. Connect the serial-to-USB adapter while watching the system log in */var/log/messages*. It should display "PL-2303 converter detected" and create the device node */udev/ttyUSB0*. You should then be able to connect with GPSBabel.

Both of these commands worked in fetching waypoints from a Garmin GPS:

```
$ sudo gpsbabel -D9 -i garmin -f /dev/ttyUSB0 -o gpx -F foobar.gpx
```

and:

```
$ sudo gpsbabel -D9 -i garmin -f /udev/ttyUSB0 -o gpx -F foobar.gpx
```

## Troubleshooting

With older Garmin GPS units, under all three platforms GPSBabel will sometimes have trouble connecting. This is true even when it is directly connected to the serial port, rather than to a USB adapter. The common error is:

```
GPS_Packet_Read: No DLE
GARMIN:Can't init com3
```

The port specified will vary with operating system. Under Windows USB it will be *com3*. A Linux serial port is */dev/ttyS0* (or */dev/ttyUSB0* for USB). */dev/cu.USBserial0* is for a Mac OS X USB port.

If you retry, sometimes four to five times, it seems to finally "get it" and start transferring data.

The -D9 switch to GPSBabel enables the display of debugging information. If you have trouble, try turning your GPS off and back on. Some GPS units will show you the progress of their data downloads and uploads. On the Garmin III Plus, this is displayed under Menu → Setup → Interface. The Garmin Rino does not show the status of the data transfer.

## HACK #51 Speak in Geotongues: GPSBabel to the Rescue

Too many formats! Use the Swiss Army Chainsaw of tracklog and waypoint tools to convert between different formats and to read and write to your GPS.

Your tracklog and waypoint data is available in too many darn formats. GPSBabel allows you to convert data to different formats and transfer it between different GPS units and your computer. You can also merge multiple files, while checking for duplicates, and filter waypoints based on their distance from a point or a route.

You can set up a route that you plan to travel and then have GPSBabel load your GPS with all of the geocaches that were near your planned route. A big use is to read waypoints and tracklogs from your GPS unit and save them in the GPX format that can be used by many of the hacks in this book.

GPSBabel is available for Macintosh, Windows, and *NIX at *http://gpsbabel. sourceforge.net*. There are binary packages available for Windows and Mac OS X. For Windows and OS X, download the package and decompress the files.

Under Linux, download the source package, decompress it, and run **make**.

### Using the Graphical User Interface

There are GUI wrappers for GPSBabel for each platform.

- Under Windows, run **gpsbabelfront**.
- Under Mac OS X, run **MacGPSBabel**.
- Under Linux, run **guibabel**. You must ensure that the *gpsbabel* program is in your path before starting *guibabel*.

Figure 5-4 shows the Windows version of GPSBabel, set up to read waypoints from a Garmin GPS via the serial port, *com1*, and save them to the GPX format file named *waypoint.gpx*.

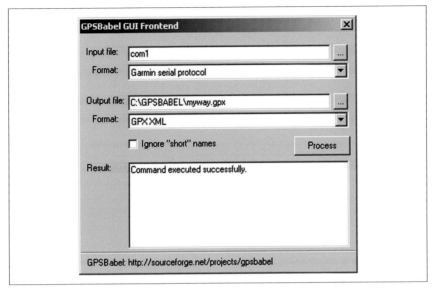

Figure 5-4. GUI wrapper for GPSBabel, gpsbabelfront, under Microsoft Windows

Much of the power of GPSBabel is masked by the graphical user interfaces, however. As an example, only the Mac OS X GUI allows access to the Filter commands, and even it does not support the newer filter options.

## Using GPSBabel from the Command Line

As with many powerful tools, the command line is where the interesting functionality lives. The trade-off is a small learning curve. The basic GPSBabel command looks like this:

```
gpsbabel [options] -i INTYPE -f INFILE -o OUTTYPE -F OUTFILE
```

INTYPE and OUTTYPE are formats that GPSBabel understands, and INFILE and OUTFILE are the locations of that data. That location can be either a file or the name of a physical device, such as *com1* under Windows or */dev/ttyS0* under Linux.

Let's say you have latitude, longitude, and waypoint name in the file *way.csv*:

```
40.70175, -103.68998, First Waypoint
39.28553, -123.79357, Another point
42.49638, -108.72995, And a third
```

Use this command to convert this file to the GPX-format file *way.gpx*:

```
$ gpsbabel -i csv -f way.csv -o gpx -F way.gpx
```

Deconstructing the command line, -i csv indicates that the input file uses comma-separated values; -f way.csv (note that this is lowercase) specifies

the name of the input file (or the name of the input serial port); -o gpx specifies the output is a GPX file; and -F way.gpx (uppercase "F") provides the
name of the output file (or output serial port).

You can then convert that GPX file to an HTML file that provides a summary list of the waypoints, with references to extended descriptions of each
point:

```
$ gpsbabel -i gpx -f way.gpx -o html -F way.html
```

## Exchanging Waypoints and Tracklogs with a GPS

GPSBabel directly supports Garmin and Magellan GPS units. Connect your
GPS to your serial cable, or see "The Serial Port to USB Conundrum" [Hack
#50] if you lack a serial port. A Garmin serial GPS is specified with -i garmin,
while a Magellan is indicated with -i magellan. Use the -f and -F parameters to specify the serial port for your GPS: use -f when you read from the
GPS and -F to write to the GPS.

You can get more information by running **gpsbabel -?** and by reading the
*README* file. Here is an example of a command that reads waypoints from
a Garmin GPS and writes them to a GPX-formatted file named *waypoint.
gpx*. Under Windows, assume the GPS is attached to the first serial port:

```
C:\> gpsbabel -i garmin -f com1 -o gpx -F waypoint.gpx
```

Under Linux, assume the GPS is attached to the first serial port (you will
need to run as a user who has rights to read the serial port, so you should
probably run as root or with *sudo*).

```
$ gpsbabel -i garmin -f /dev/ttyS0 -o gpx -F waypoint.gpx
```

Under OS X, assume the GPS is attached to a serial-to-USB adapter:

```
$ gpsbabel -i garmin -f /dev/cu.usbserial0 -o gpx -F waypoint.gpx
```

To read tracklogs, just add a -t in front of the input (-i) specifier. So, to
input tracklogs under Windows:

```
C:\> gpsbabel -t -i garmin -f com1 -o gpx -F tracklog.gpx
```

In the same way, you can read or write routes with the -r parameter:

```
C:\> gpsbabel -r -i garmin -f com1 -o gpx -F route.gpx
```

You can also write tracklogs, waypoints, and routes back to your GPS by
swapping the input and output parameters. To write waypoints from *way-
point.gpx* to a Garmin unit under Windows:

```
C:\> gpsbabel -i gpx -f waypoint.gpx -o garmin -F com1
```

GPSBabel uses the same command format for Windows, Linux, and OS X,
but the name of the serial device varies with each of these platforms.

## Using GPSBabel to Merge Files

You can specify more than one input file and more than one output file, so you can use GPSBabel to merge multiple files. This command will merge the GPX-format waypoint files *way1.gpx* and *way2.gpx* and put them into both the GPX file *merge.gpx and* the Geocaching *loc* file *cache.loc*:

```
$ gpsbabel -i gpx -f way1.gpx -f way2.gpx -o gpx -F merge.gpx -o geo -F
cache.loc
```

This is useful when you have multiple files full of waypoints and you want to create one canonical list. This is especially useful when combined with the -x duplicate filter (discussed in "Using Filters") to remove waypoints that mark the same place.

## Using Filters

GPSBabel also lets you filter your results. This command takes two GPX files as inputs and then outputs those waypoints within five miles of 40.75°N, 119.25°W into the GPX file *merge.gpx*:

```
$ gpsbabel -i gpx -f way_iii.gpx -f way_rino.gpx \
-x  radius,distance=5M,lat=40.75,lon=-119.25 -o gpx -F merge.gpx
```

You can also filter waypoints by different criteria. This command searches two GPX files, *way_iii.gpx* and *way_rino.gpx*; outputs all the waypoints that are within 10 miles of the toll plaza of the Golden Gate Bridge; and then sorts that list by waypoint name. Since there is no output type (-o), GPSBabel sends the output to the terminal:

```
$ gpsbabel -i gpx -f way_iii.gpx -f way_rino.gpx \
-x radius,distance=10M,lat=37.81,lon=-122.47 -x  sort

37.768593N 122.470796W BRDTRE/CRTD 13:42 06-JAN-01
37.781870N 122.404310W CAACADSCNC/CAACADSCNC 19.000000
37.760660N 122.419305W CANCUN/CANCUN 11.000000
```

So you could load your GPS with San Francisco waypoints with this command:

```
C:\> gpsbabel -i gpx -f way_iii.gpx -f way_rino.gpx  \
-x radius,distance=10M,lat=37.81,lon=-122.47 -x sort    -o garmin -f com1
```

You can also use GPSBabel to remove duplicates and nearby points. We can guarantee that we have duplicates to test by merging two copies of the same file:

```
C:\> gpsbabel -i gpx -f way_iii.gpx -f way_iii.gpx   \
-x radius,distance=10M,lat=37.81,lon=-122.47 -x sort -o gpx -F dupes.gpx
```

The file *dupes.gpx* now contains two copies of each of our waypoints that is within 10 miles of 37.81°N, 122.47°W.

We can verify that we now have duplicate waypoints:

```
C:\> gpsbabel -i gpx -f dupes.gpx
37.768593N 122.470796W BRDTRE/CRTD 13:42 06-JAN-01
37.768593N 122.470796W BRDTRE/CRTD 13:42 06-JAN-01
```

We can remove the dupes with the duplicate filter and show them to the screen by leaving off the -o output specification:

```
C:\> gpsbabel -i gpx -f dupes.gpx -x duplicate,shortname,location
37.768593N 122.470796W BRDTRE/CRTD 13:42 06-JAN-01
```

We can use -x duplicate,shortname to remove duplicates based on name, use -x duplicate,location to remove duplicates based on location, and use -x duplicate,shortname,location to remove only those waypoints that share the same name and location.

There are certain problems with floating-point precision when transferring data to and from Garmin GPS units. For this reason, you may want to couple a duplicate removal with the -x position filter. This filter removes all waypoints that are too close to each other.

So assume that we have two waypoints that are just slightly different from each other:

```
37.7685N 122.470796W BRDTRE/CRTD 13:42 06-JAN-01
37.7686N 122.470796W BRDTRE/CRTD 13:42 06-JAN-01
```

Look closely at the latitudes: 37.7685 versus 37.7686. In this case, these two points are within about 35 feet of each other. Let's remove the duplicates and then chain the results to the next filter to remove close points:

```
C:\> gpsbabel -i gpx -f dupes.gpx -x duplicate,shortname,location \
-x position,distance=36f

37.768600N 122.470796W BRDTRE/CRTD 13:42 06-JAN-01
37.803703N 122.450373W EXPLRE/CRTD 16:54 04-MAR-01
37.807512N 122.476037W GGATE /CRTD 11:33 27-AUG-00
```

Note how we can chain together the -x filters. In this case, we first get rid of the duplicates and then we remove every waypoint that is within 36 feet of another one. The program walks through waypoints in order and rejects those that are within 36 feet of a point that has already been loaded.

As befits a Swiss Army Chainsaw, GPSBabel has a dozen other powerful features, but one final interesting feature is the -x arc filter. You can convert a tracklog to a GPSBabel arc file and then filter waypoints based on their proximity to that "arc," or route.

Let's look at our *allwaypoints.gpx* file using the Unix word-count filter:

```
$ gpsbabel -i gpx -f allwaypoints.gpx | wc
486    2563   23669
There are 486 waypoints in the file.
```

Then we create a GPSBabel arc filter file from a tracklog:

```
$ gpsbabel -i gpx -f track.gpx -o arc -F arcfile.txt
```

Then we apply the arc filter to include only those waypoints that are within one mile of that track:

```
$ gpsbabel -i gpx -f allwaypoints.gpx  -x arc,file=arcfile.txt,distance=1M | wc
```

```
    61      322     3022
```

So 61 of our waypoints were within one mile of the path described in *track.gpx*.

This is interesting because as you fill your waypoint memory with points, it is easy to forget where those points are. When I ran this arc filter test, I was surprised when my waypoint "PEACE" appeared. I was sure that was the Peace Dive boat in Ventura, California. So I explored:

```
$ gpsbabel -i gpx -f allwaypoints.gpx | grep -i PEA
```

```
38.403327N 122.847930W PEACE /CRTD 15:52 15-SEP-00
34.241402N 119.263898W PEACEB/CRTD 17:25 16-OCT-01
```

Ah! Now I remember! "PEACE" is the Peace Park near my house. It was certainly within one mile of the track in the filter example. The Peace Dive boat was "PEACEB," for "Peace Boat." This sort of name collision is inevitable when you start seriously hoarding waypoints in a device with a six-character limit on names! Tools such as GPSBabel filters can help make some sense out of the whole mess.

## HACK #52 Show Your Waypoints on Aerial Photos with Terrabrowser

Show your waypoints over aerial photos and topographic maps on your Mac.

Terrabrowser is a Mac OS X program that lets you browse satellite photos and topo maps. It can show your current position on the map, as well as allow you to load and display waypoints in the GPX format. And like most fun tools, it has a few surprises to share. You can do some of the same things under Windows with Wissenbach Map3D **[Hack #53]**.

You can read more about Terrabrowser and download the program on their web page (*http://www.chimoosoft.com/terrabrowser.html*). The new alpha version uses Cocoa and supports tracklogs. But the old version is more stable and has better GPS support. Since both versions have interesting features, this hack will be clear about which version is being discussed.

Download the *Terrabrowser 1.1.0.sit* file and decompress it. Like most Mac OS X apps, you can run the program from that location or copy it into your *Applications* folder.

### Live Tracking in Terrabrowser Version 1.1.0

Under Version 1.1.0, you can connect a Garmin GPS to your computer and have live tracking of your position over an aerial photo.

You may need to allow the program access to your serial ports:

```
$ sudo chmod 777 /dev/cu*
```

and then set your GPS to output data in NMEA format. Then in Terrabrowser, select the following menu options, as shown in Figure 5-5:

```
GPS->Protocol->NMEA,
GPS->Serial Port->usbserial0
GPS->Connect (figure 1)
GPS->Enable Live Tracking
```

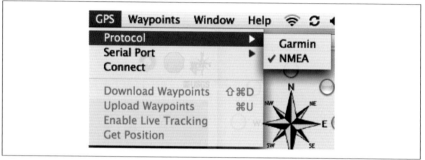

Figure 5-5. The Terrabrowser GPS Connection menu

An aerial photo should pop up with your current location shown. If you happen to be visiting me in Sebastopol, California, it will look identical to Figure 5-6; otherwise, you will see a photo of your location.

The new version provides additional information on the GPS status, but live tracking is not yet bug-free.

### Using Terrabrowser to View and Edit Waypoints

In addition to live position tracking, Terrabrowser implements a very nice multifile GPX waypoint editor and viewer, shown in Figure 5-7. You can open multiple GPX files, edit waypoints, and copy and paste between waypoint files with a nice tabular interface. The waypoint editor also allows you full access to all the waypoint features, including a nice drop-down of waypoint symbols.

Another great feature is the ability to search by ZIP Code. Select Navigate → Find City (or press ⌘-F) and you can enter a ZIP Code. Terrabrowser then fetches the appropriate image, centered vaguely on that ZIP Code. This is an

*Figure 5-6. Terrabrowser live tracking*

imprecise process for two reasons. First, Terraserver returns images in "tiles," so when you request the image for a lat/long, you get the tile that contains that point, but it is not centered. Also ZIP Codes are not points, so converting a ZIP Code to a single point is a tad imprecise.

You can open a GPX-format waypoint file, and then select Waypoints → Center on Waypoint to fetch the Terraserver image, or USGS topo, for that point. In Figure 5-8, we centered on the waypoint "Box1."

Terrabrowser is shareware and well worth the $15 registration fee.

### HACK #53 Visualize Your Tracks in Three Dimensions

With free Windows software and a little tweaking, you can make nice 3-D models of your outdoor perambulations.

Wouldn't it be nice if you could get a better feeling for the terrain you just crossed or the magnificent view you saw earlier? Wouldn't you like to be able to do something with all of those tracklog files you've been collecting?

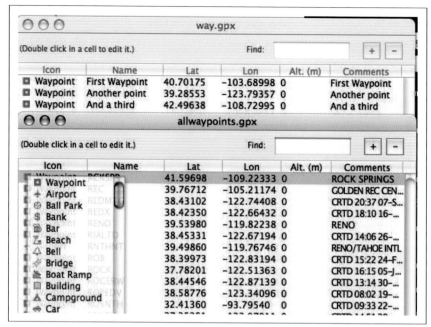

Figure 5-7. Terrabrowser waypoint display and editing

Wissenbach Map3D is a GPL-licensed Windows application that reads track-logs in GPX format and then plots them over aerial photos and three-dimensional terrain models. 3DEM is a Windows program that allows you to quickly explore elevation models in many different formats and to overlay images on these terrain models. You can also export views and terrain models, and create fly-by animations. One of the best parts about it is that it "just works" to open and display digital elevation model (DEM) files.

## Loading the Example

Wissenbach Map3D is available at *http://www.gpstrailmaps.com/map3d/*. Download *http://www.gpstrailmaps.com/map3d/SetupYosemite3D.exe* to get a copy of the program with sample data from Yosemite National Park in California.

Following the instructions in the *Readme* file, you can open the sample GPX file by going to the File menu and selecting *Yosemite.gpx*. A Map Description dialog will load; you can just click OK. Wissenbach Map3D will then attempt to fetch the aerial photography for Yosemite from Microsoft's *Terraserver* service —so you'll need to be connected to the Internet. When it's done, you should see tracklogs and waypoints from that GPX file displayed over the aerial photography. Neat, huh? You ain't seen nothing yet!

*Figure 5-8. Terrabrowser centered on waypoint "Box1"*

Now, click the *3DMap* option from the menu bar at the top, which loads the Scene Properties dialog. Although we recommend experimenting with this on your own, for now just click OK. The program will take a minute or so to render the scene, and then it will display a 3-D model of Yosemite Valley! You can then "fly through" the Yosemite Valley by selecting Camera Mode → Slide. Navigate through the valley by dragging the mouse. Figure 5-9 shows one view of the sample track snaking up the side of the valley. Speaking as one who has spent time navigating that valley on foot, using the mouse is much quicker!

## Loading Your Own Data

Once you tire of exploring Yosemite you can load *Digital Raster Graphics* (DRGs) and *Digital Elevation Models* (DEMs) for your own area. Since sources of data vary, you'll want to follow the instructions provided by the source's web site.

*Figure 5-9. The Yosemite Falls trail shown in Wissenbach Map3D*

Once you start the program, you need to set an "area of interest." You can do this in one of three ways. Select View → Pick Center to manually enter a point to be the center of your map. Alternatively, you can connect a GPS to your system and read points directly, or you can load a waypoint from a GPX file.

If you open a GPX file, the program will fetch aerial photos or topo maps from Terraserver and plot your tracklog over the image, once you're zoomed in close enough. You can select a USGS topographic base map (i.e., a DRG) with File → JPG Topo Basemap, or an aerial photo base map with File → JPG Photo Basemap. Figure 5-10 shows a GPX tracklog from Black Rock City, Nevada laid over an aerial photo automatically downloaded from Terraserver.

## Loading New Elevation Models

Wissenbach Map3D uses USGS DEM files, each of which covers a seven-minute named quadrangle (about 8 miles by 6.5 miles) at a resolution of one arc second (~30m) or one-third arc second (~10m). The 30-meter DEMs are plenty good enough to experiment with at first, and they involve downloading a lot less data than the 10-meter DEMs. Later, if you really get into playing with digital elevation models, you can go back and get the 10-meter DEMs.

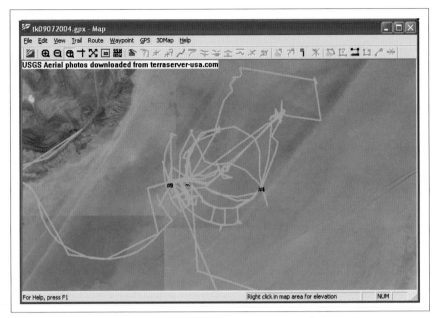

*Figure 5-10. A tracklog from Burning Man shown over an aerial photo*

The GeoCommunity's GIS Data Depot hosts free DEM data sets for the USGS at *http://data.geocomm.com/dem/demdownload.html*. The DEM files are organized by state and county. To figure out exactly which quadrangles you'll need, though, you can search the USGS Geographic Names Information System (GNIS) by place name at *http://geonames.usgs.gov/*. Alternatively, you can search for quad names on an interactive map by visiting the USGS Geospatial Data Availability site at *http://statgraph.cr.usgs.gov/*. Once you find the quads you want in the GIS Data Depot download listing, you'll notice a seven-character unit code like 38122f7 in parentheses next to the quadrangle name; make a note of this, because you'll need it later.

The seven character USGS quadrangle unit code—e.g., 38122d7—identifies the location of the quadrangle. The letter d implies that the upper left corner of the DEM will be approximately 7½ minutes x 4 units = 30', or 0.5° north of 38° N. Likewise, the number 7 means that the same corner will be 7½ minutes x 7 units = 52.5', or 0.875° west of 122° W.

At this point, you should be able to download one or more compressed DEM files from the GIS Data Depot. Unfortunately, these datafiles are in the much-reviled *Spatial Data Transfer Standard* (SDTS) format, so we'll have to convert them back to the USGS's native DEM format for Wissenbach

Map3D to make use of them. Start by extracting the DEM from the *TAR.GZ* archive using WinZip, or any archive utility of your choosing. The names of the *.DDF* files inside will start with a four-digit number, like 8505. Make a note of this as well.

Next, fetch the *sdts2dem* utility from *http://www.cs.arizona.edu/topovista/ sdts2dem/* and simply run it from the DOS command line. You'll see a series of prompts as follows:

```
Enter first 4 charcters of the base SDTS file name: 8505
Enter base output file name (exclude any extension): o38122f7
```

Enter in the four-digit SDTS filename prefix, followed by the USGS quadrangle unit code prefixed by the letter o. You should be able to copy this into your Wissenbach DEM directory, which is defined under File → DRG, DEM Directories. Wissenbach Map3D should now be able to make use of your new elevation models.

> If you happen to have GDAL handy, the following gdal_translate command might work for you instead of having to use *sdts2dem*:
>
> ```
> gdal_translate -of USGSDEM 8505CATD.DDF x38122f7.dem
> ```
>
> See "Convert Geospatial Data Between Different Formats" **[Hack #68]** for more details.

Wissenbach has stated plans to extend the program to use elevation data loaded from "Seamless Data Download from the USGS" **[Hack #67]**, which would make this process a whole lot easier, so stay tuned.

## Adding Elevation to a Tracklog

In addition to providing nice visualizations, Wissenbach Map3D solves the tricky problem of adding elevation data to a tracklog. While many modern GPS units log elevation as you go, others do not. You can get the elevation of your track points *ex post facto* by using Perl, Python, or perhaps a bit of GRASS to look up the elevation of each point in a slew of DEMs, SRTM data, or GTOPO30, etc. This involves enough scripting and tedium that it almost isn't worth documenting—at least now it isn't, since Wissenbach Map3D solves the problem with a nice GUI!

The program allows you to load tracklogs from GPX files, and it also allows you to create GPX files by drawing over the map in the display window. You can then add altitude to the new or loaded tracklog.

Select a "Trail" (e.g., a tracklog) with Edit → Select Trail, and then click on the tracklog. Then select Trail → Trail Properties. Click on the checkbox labeled "Ground Trail to DEM Elevation," and then click OK. That is all you need to do. Assuming you have loaded the proper DEMs, the program will add elevation to your tracklog. You can now select File → Save to save this tracklog with elevation data included and use that tracklog in other programs that use elevation.

## Hacking the Maps

Since DRGs are images in TIFF or JPEG format, you can edit the images and create your own views of the data. Download a DRG that covers your area, make a copy of it, and then load it into an image editor, such as Photoshop or the GIMP. If you save your customized image in a PNG file, you can retain the original DRG as the TIFF image. Alternatively, create a new layer, set the opacity to 50%, and use the base layer as a guide to your own creation!

## Three-Dimensional Terrain Models in 3DEM

While Wissenbach Map3D is great at combining tracklogs and elevation models, it can be a bit of a challenge to work with if all you want to do is render 3-D scenery. For that, try *3DEM*, a fantastic piece of free software for Windows.

3DEM has some features in common with Wissenbach Map3D, but Wissenbach assumes that you know where you want to explore and that you have already downloaded the relevant elevation data. This makes Wissenbach more "transparent" at letting you follow a tracklog, while 3DEM is much easier to use to explore the DEMs that you have downloaded.

3DEM can be found on the Web at *http://www.visualizationsoftware.com/3dem.html*. The download page includes links to digital elevation models (including DEMs of Mars!) and a helpful tutorial on finding additional DEMs on the Web.

3DEM has other features, including the ability to save virtual-reality markup language (VRML), save worlds, create fly-by animations, and it can even be used to orthorectify ground images.

Like Wissenbach Map3D, you can load tracklogs into 3DEM for display on the map. A nice feature is that if you do not have the altitude for your track points, it will be automatically added when you save the file. The downside is that 3DEM is a tad particular about the tracklog format it will accept. The 3DEM tracklog format is simple:

```
lat    long    elevation
```

But if you don't have an elevation you *must* include a 0 for your elevation field. This makes it a bit harder to load your own tracklogs. If you have *gpsbabel* [Hack #51], you can convert your GPX format tracklogs to 3DEM format using this *gpsbabel* stylesheet. Save this as *3dem.style*:

```
FIELD_DELIMITER     WHITESPACE
RECORD_DELIMITER    NEWLINE

OFIELD LAT_DECIMAL, "", "%08.5f"
OFIELD LON_DECIMAL, "", "%08.5f"
OFIELD ALT_FEET,"","%.0f"
```

You can then convert your GPX-format tracklogs to 3DEM format with this command, and then you can see your tracklog over an elevation model, as shown in Figure 5-11.

```
$ gpsbabel -t -i gpx -f yourfile.gpx -o xcsv,style=3demstyle \
-F your3demfile.txt
```

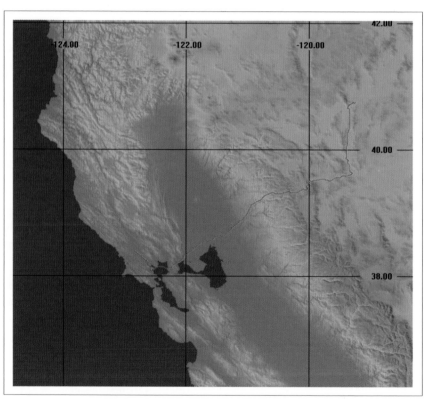

*Figure 5-11. Tracklog over an elevation model from 3Dem*

While it is a basic principle of geography that terrain shapes human behavior, it was still a surprise to me to see the image in Figure 5-11 and to again get the lesson! Transportation geography is a fascinating subject. I've spent a bit of time studying the Transport Geography page at *http://www.geog. umontreal.ca/Geotrans/.*

## Create Your Own Maps for a Garmin GPS

**#54** The base maps and purchasable maps for a Garmin GPS are nice, but sometimes you really want your own maps.

When you buy a map-capable Garmin GPS, it comes with a base map that's helpful for long-distance navigation but doesn't have much detail. Garmin and others are happy to sell maps—at least for some parts of the world—that have more detail, but that's not always a perfect solution either. If you fall into any of these categories, you may have a good reason to make your own maps for the GPS:

- You're visiting a temporary location, which has its own geography for a brief period of time. The Burning Man festival and military encampments are two wildly divergent examples. Even a large permanent camp may not be on many maps if it's on private property.

- You need data that just isn't available through commercial GPS map providers. You might want to know where known toxic waste dumps are, which areas in a forest are inhabited by particular birds, boundary lines for tax parcels in your neighborhood, the crops in particular fields, or where the bars and restaurants are that a particular reviewer found good.

- You want to personalize your map data and possibly share it.

There are a number of tools available for creating maps on these devices and uploading the maps to your GPS. Many of the tools for creating maps have free versions and commercial versions, while uploading is generally done with either sendMap, described here, or Garmin's commercial MapSource tool, which comes with their map products. Sadly for Macintosh and Linux users, many of these tools are Windows-only.

There are a number of different applications available for creating Garmin GPS maps, but this hack uses GPSMapEdit, available from *http://www. geopainting.com/.* GPSMapEdit is shareware; you can try it out and use it for free, but the author requests 44 Euros or $54. Source code is also available if you want to tinker, though it isn't under an open source license. GPSMapEdit lets you import data from a number of sources, create your own map objects, and save the maps in a standard text format. With the installation of another free program, cGpsMapper (*http://cgpsmapper.com/*), GPSMapEdit can produce maps in the IMG format used by Garmin GPS devices. The creator of cGpsMapper also provides a program called send-Map, which will let you put your maps on the GPS device. I recommend Version 2.0.

For my first map, I started by importing a shapefile derived from TIGER census data. While it's just roads, it gives me much more detail than the base map in the receiver. I got the file from the same repository that was used for "Extract Data from Maps with Manifold" [Hack #65]. To bring a county's worth of roads into GPS format, I went to File → Import → ESRI Shape (*.shp*) in the GPSMapEdit program. After the file dialog box to select the shapefile, the program asked me what kind of objects I was importing, as shown in Figure 5-12.

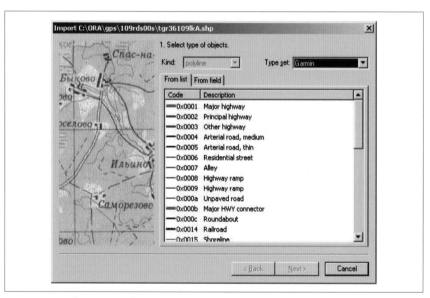

*Figure 5-12. Choosing an object type*

There are two ways to select objects here. The blunt way, shown on the first tab, is to pick a type of GPS map object for everything in the file. (If there are different kinds of objects in the file—polylines, polygons, etc.—you can pick one type of GPS map object for each type of object in the shapefile.) The smart way, on the second tab, lets you pick a field in the data underlying the shapefile, though that field has to specify the type for each object using the Garmin numbering. For my purposes, calling everything an "Arterial road, thin" street is okay, if not ideal. When I have time, I'll go back and get it right.

The next step, shown in Figure 5-13, is to choose a source for label information, again from the data included in the shapefile. It only lets you pick one column, which is frustrating. Again, you could create a shapefile that includes the road name as one column rather than as parts split across three columns.

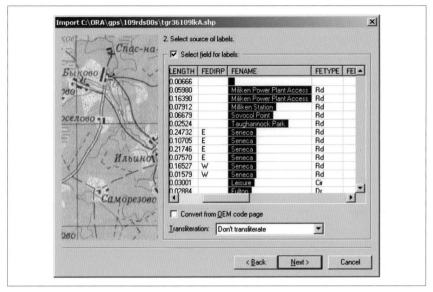

Figure 5-13. Choosing a label source

After you've chosen a label source, GPSMapEdit shows you some basic geographic information derived from the file, as shown in Figure 5-14. You can't change much of the information here, but it's definitely an opportunity to sanity-check. Do the latitude and longitude boundaries look right? If you have a map that wasn't projected right, these numbers will likely be very wrong. The changes you can make on this page are limited by the coordinate system of the underlying data. Make sure the datum is set correctly. The first time I imported a WGS84 map, I left the datum set to Zaperij, and my map was consistently wrong by a few hundred yards. That was no big deal when I was on the highway, but horribly confusing in a residential neighborhood.

When in doubt, stick with the WGS84 datum, which is what the GPS satellites themselves use.

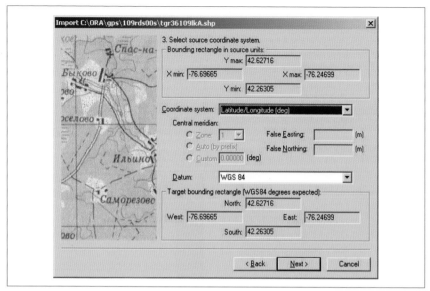

*Figure 5-14. Setting the source coordinate system*

The last option, shown in Figure 5-15, lets you choose which zoom levels to import. You can add additional zoom levels later if you need, through the Levels tab of File → Map Properties.

When you click Finish, you'll see something like Figure 5-16, displaying the data just imported from a very high-level view.

Zooming in on the map will show you the road system, complete with road-name labels imported from the shapefile (see Figure 5-17).

You can make changes to the map with GPSMapEdit's tools, which will let you add objects as you deem appropriate. When the map is ready, you'll need to save a copy at this point in the Polish format (*.mp*), which is GPS-MapEdit's native format and the base that the *cgpsmapper* program uses to generate the binary files that go into the GPS.

> Polish format is a text-based format, so if you want to generate these files directly from other tools, you can do that. Documentation is available at *http://plrecgps.pp.org.pl/bin/ view/GPS/PFMsyntaxDescr*.

Before you can turn this data into a map, you need to assign it a name and an ID, using the Header tab at File → Map Properties, as shown in Figure 5-18.

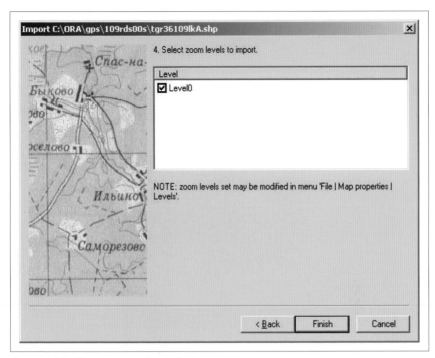

*Figure 5-15. Choosing zoom levels for import*

The ID value should be unique, at least among the maps you'll be upload-ing to the device, and a meaningful name will help users later. Once you've done this, you can safely export the map to Garmin's binary IMG format. To save the map in the Garmin IMG format, you'll need to select File → Export → Garmin IMG / cgpsmapper.exe. When you choose this option, GPSMapEdit will ask you where cgpsmapper is located and will then present you with a dialog box for overseeing the export. After you click the Run but-ton, GPSMapEdit will call cgpsmapper, which will process the file for a while and produce a report like that shown in Figure 5-19.

Now that you have an IMG file, connect your Garmin GPS to the computer. You can drop the file on the sendmap20 program icon or run *sendmap20* from the command line as shown here:

```
C:\ORA\gps\sendmap20>sendmap20 tompkins3.img
Sendmap2.0 by gps_mapper, kozicki@cgpsmapper.com
Trying: usb
Trying: com1
Detected          : eTrex Vista Software Version 3.40
Available memory  : 25149440
Max number of maps: 525
Map uploaded!
```

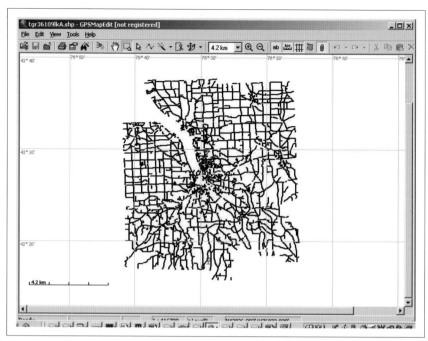

Figure 5-16. Freshly imported map

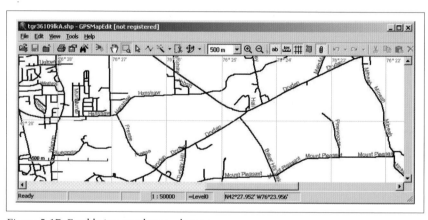

Figure 5-17. Freshly imported map, close up

 Uploading sometimes takes a few attempts. I regularly get a "Couldn't change speed" error, but it always goes away after a while. Remember to set the interface on your Garmin receiver to Garmin mode. NMEA mode will *not* work!

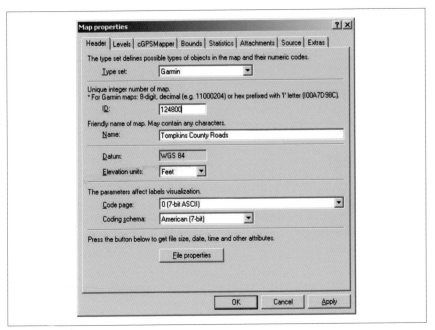

*Figure 5-18. Setting the name and ID for a map*

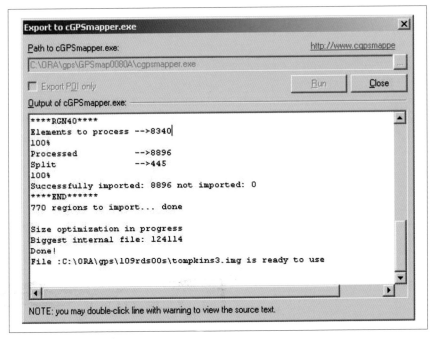

*Figure 5-19. Report on export*

You may have to tell the device to use the map you've added, but as Figure 5-20 shows, the map is now installed and ready for use.

> If you want to use Garmin's MapSource program to upload maps you created yourself, visit *http://www.keenpeople.com/ index.php?option=articles&task=viewarticle&artid=4&Itemid =3* for a description of a registry hack that will let Map-Source work with your maps.

## Hacking the Hack

Using other people's data to create maps is great, but sometimes you'll need to use your own. To put a map of a small trail into my GPS, I hiked the trail, pulled my tracklog out with MapSource, saved it to a file, and then opened that file in GPSMapEdit. The tracklog looked like Figure 5-21.

To turn this into a trail, I shift-clicked on both parts of the log (the GPS lost satellite at one point), then right-clicked to bring up a menu. I chose Convert To → Polyline. I picked "0x0016 Trail" from the list of possible types, shown in Figure 5-22, and GPSMapEdit created a trail on top of the track-log.

The tracklog is still there, though; I had to cut the trail to reach the tracklog and delete it. After doing that, and selecting Modify → Label from the right-click context menu to change the name, I had the trail map shown in Figure 5-23.

Putting this map onto a GPS requires a few more steps, all of them under Map → Properties. First, set an ID and a name as described earlier and shown in Figure 5-18. Then, go to the Levels tab to identify at which zoom levels this map should be shown. Clicking the "Insert Before" button will add two default zooms, though it's probably a good idea to change them (with the Change button) to something more like those shown in Figure 5-24.

Once this is set, save the file, export it to an IMG, and upload it to the device just like you did before. As shown in Figure 5-25, the new map will integrate itself with the earlier map just perfectly in the device.

You can take this to much greater lengths, of course, and there are a variety of software packages, many of them free or shareware, available to help. For a partial list, see *http://www.keenpeople.com/index.php?option=com_ downloads&Itemid=50&func=selectcat&cat=2.*

—*Simon St.Laurent*

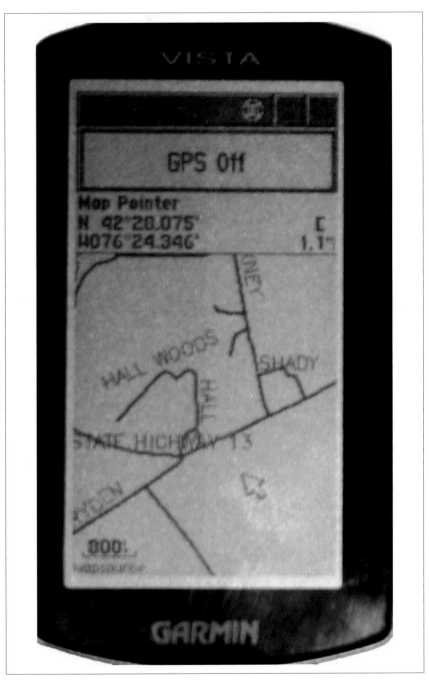

*Figure 5-20. The created map, seen in a Garmin eTrex Vista*

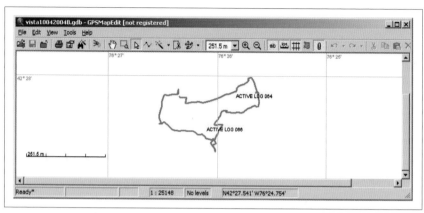

Figure 5-21. A tracklog, as viewed in GPSMapEdit

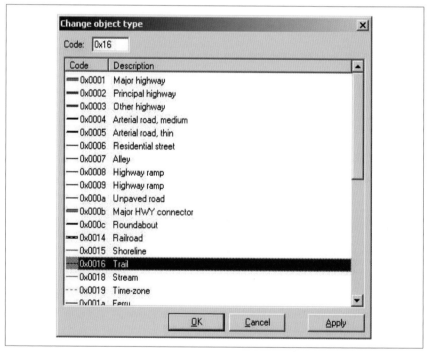

Figure 5-22. Choosing an object type for the polyline representing a trail

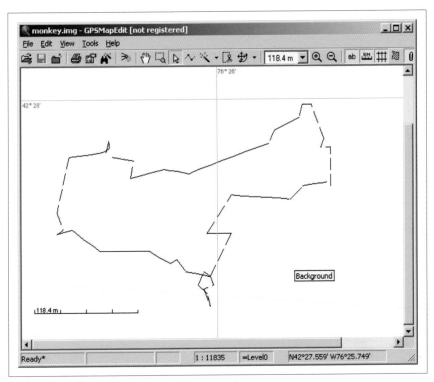

Figure 5-23. *The tracklog in its new life as a trail*

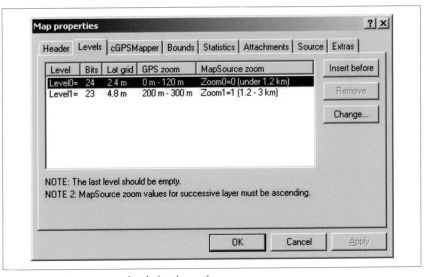

Figure 5-24. *Setting zoom levels for the trail*

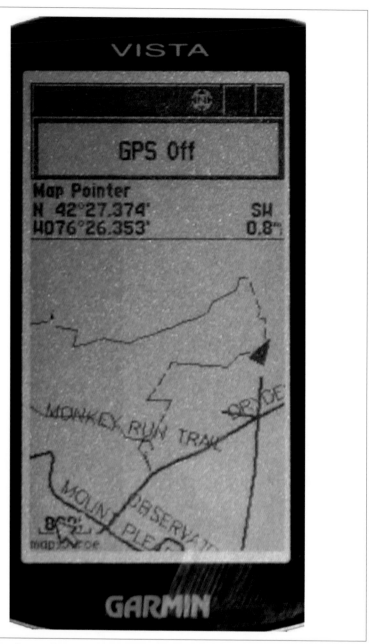

Figure 5-25. The Monkey Run Trail and Tompkins County Roads maps shown at the same time in the GPS

## Use Your Track Memory as a GPS Base Map

Use your own past traces to provide you with context for street navigation and low-rent GPS maps.

Newer GPS devices come with many megabytes of memory to store base maps. Companies like Garmin and MAPSource (*http://mapsource.com/*) sell CDs compiled from public domain data and some proprietary data to load onto your Garmin device, providing you with context for where you are: roads, names, places, and often small recommendation databases for local services.

These GPS base maps provide context and help you to navigate, but sometimes they interfere with your own story. And other times, for various reasons, there are no maps for where you are going. You can use your GPS to create your own base map out of your tracklogs and waypoints.

### Turn Off Your Base Map to Turn On Your Own Story

Maps tell stories, and the stories that maps tell both reflect and create reality. Our experience of a place is created, or altered, through our interactions with maps. We sit surrounded by our wealth of cartographic data, and we forget ourselves and our own stories in favor of the authority of an external mapmaker.

The base map in your GPS reflects (someone's) reality, but it isn't your story. You build your own story over the course of your travels. Storing tracklogs and setting waypoints provides an amazing amount of context for a mapping display. Try turning off your base maps, or setting the level of detail to the lowest setting. You are then able to fill in a huge amount of detail about the places you have been, based on your experiences and the reminders provided by your waypoints and tracklogs, as shown in Figure 5-26.

We live in a phenomenal universe. This means we experience reality strictly through our senses. We don't "see" a river; rather, photons of light bounce off of the river and strike our eyes. We experience the energy of those photons, and our brains construct a reality of the river. In the same way, our experience of a place is limited to the physical phenomena that we experience: the atoms that we inhale and interpret as smells, the waves of energy we interpret as sound, the photons bouncing off of everything around us.

Since we live in a phenomenal universe, then what happens when we see a map? If that map is our first experience of a place, then our personal reality of the place is limited to what we experience from that map, plus whatever inferences we are able to make based on other contexts. For example, if you

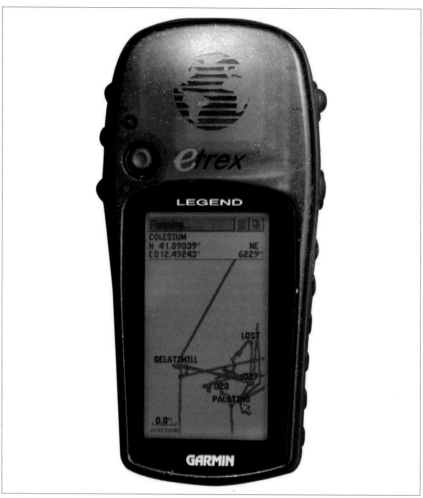

*Figure 5-26. Using tracklogs as a GPS base map*

showed me a map of an "as yet unexplored by me" bit of Mexico that was near to a place I had been, I would automatically and unconsciously create an internal model of that place that included the information from the map and what I know about that part of the country from personal experience, as well as the hearsay of other travelers.

You are your own cartographer!

You might not wish to shell out for MapSource for base maps, or you might be in an area without much digital map coverage: most places outside of North America, Western Europe, and Japan. You might just enjoy the experience of trace-based map autoconstruction. This approach can be particularly fun in the places that you visit often but that are outside of your normal routine.

In the 1950s, the French Situationists realized that we tend to live our lives in ruts. In one study, they tracked the movements of a young lady in Paris over the course of a month. Her Paris was a triangle defined by her apartment, her job, and the studio of her piano teacher. In part out of reaction to this intolerable closing of mental frontiers, they created the idea of the *derive* as a sort of forced wandering.

Over the course of three visits to conferences in Amsterdam, I built up a comprehensive base map of street coverage of the Eastern side of Amsterdam. The experience led to serendipitous spatial exploration, too; I would decide to traverse smaller streets and take small detours so I could extend my tracklog map further in detail. In Oxford, I managed to create such a map for the center of town in a couple of afternoons. This act of forcing ourselves to engage in a task allows us to engage our goal-seeking instincts while not allowing those goal-seeking behaviors to dominate the experience. We are put into the state of forced wandering, of the *derive*.

On a GPS track map, especially one taken at walking or cycling pace, you find a context that is at the same level of detail as your life. Waypoints, too, provide landmarks and navigation hints, and a reassuring sense of relative distance. However, it's unusual for GPS units to store and emit timestamps with waypoints; if the temporal aspect of your travels is important to you, then you'll need to correlate your waypoints with your tracklogs after the event.

We have a friend who's collecting a "life track" for his small child, a GPS on the buggy reconstructing a narrative of where the child has been. Another friend publishes his daily life track as a geo-annotated RSS feed.

Be careful with track memory, though, if you subsequently want to download your tracks and use them to animate your journey or to geo-annotate pictures you took at the same time. When a Garmin GPS saves your track, it forgets the timestamp for each point. See "Don't Lose Your Tracklogs!" **[Hack #58]** for the lowdown on how Garmin GPS devices store tracks, a "gotcha" that catches every GPS carrier once!

## See Also

How can you make use of your track map outside of your own GPS? In "Create Your Own Maps for a Garmin GPS" **[Hack #54]**, we suggest how you could make your own simple base map to load onto other Garmin devices. "Speak in Geotongues: GPSBabel to the Rescue" **[Hack #51]** uses the flexible

GPSBabel to convert between different, custom GPS data output formats into one that different applications can work with.

## Animate Your Tracklogs

Get more from your tracklogs by making them move.

Maps are static things. We dump our tracklogs on a map, and there they sit like old Popsicle sticks, marking the carcass of something that was good at the time but now is done. Tracklogs represent movement, so what if we could animate our tracklogs to keep alive that sense of motion? Well we can. If you have a tracklog in a GPX file, you can animate it at *http://www. mappinghacks.com/projects/animate*. If you have a tracklog that is not in GPX format, then review "Speak in Geotongues: GPSBabel to the Rescue" [Hack #51].

Click the link "Simple Animation of a Track Log," Select a tracklog from your system in GPX format and click on "Make Animation," as shown in Figure 5-27. You can also upload a waypoint file in GPX format.

## Animate A GPX File

This is animate.cgi, a sample from the Perl module Geo::Track::Animate.

Track log in GPX Format: [        ]    Browse...

Waypoint in GPX Format: [        ]    Browse...

[ Make Animation ]   [ Show source code ]

*Figure 5-27. The simplest way to animate a tracklog: animate.cgi*

You'll get a simple animation like that shown in Figure 5-28. But do you see the problem? Exactly! The printed version shows all the animation of a Tupperware party on the moon. Fortunately the web version is a tad more active.

### Hacking the Hack: Do More with Geo::Track::Animate

This animate script uses the Perl module `Geo::Track::Animate` to create a Scalable Vector Graphics (SVG) image. With a bit of programming, you can do even more! First install the module from CPAN:

```
$ perl -MCPAN -e "install Geo::Track::Animate"
```

As usual with CPAN modules, a look at the documentation is a good first step:

```
$ perldoc Geo::Track::Animate
```

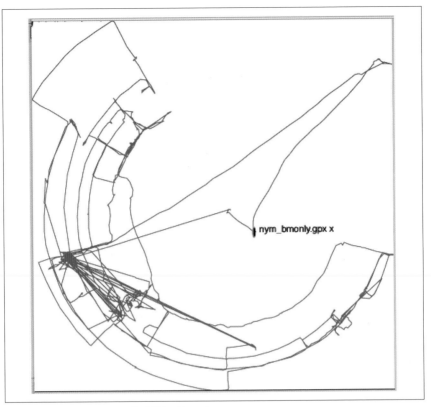

*Figure 5-28. Trust me: on the Web, this swings*

The animation at *http://www.mappinghacks.com/projects/animate* uses the sample script *animate.cgi*, which comes with the Geo::Track::Animate module, in the *eg* directory. This serves as a good example of how to use the module.

The *animate.cgi* script accepts a single GPX file, but Geo::Track::Animate accepts multiple tracklogs and can animate all of them. See the example in the script *eg/animate_tracks.pl*, which allows you to animate multiple GPX track files, with an optional file of waypoints:

```
$ ./animate_tracks.pl -wayfile mywaypoints.gpx tk*.gpx
```

This command will animate the tracklogs in all of the GPX files that start out with the letters tk and overlay the waypoints contained in *mywaypoints.gpx*. The output file will be stored in *testfile.svg*.

## See Also

The "Geo::Track::Animate" page at *http://www.mappinghacks.com/projects/animate* for more examples and sample code.

# #57  Connect to Your GPS from Multiple Applications

In Linux, BSD, and OS X, you can get live GPS data across different processes—and even different computers—simultaneously.

While almost miraculous in their basic operation, your average GPS receiver lacks much in the way of wits all on its own. Even the fanciest of them can do little more than plot your location on a map, and maybe give directions to a destination. Once combined with a computer, though, that same GPS receiver can power a wide range of new and different applications, from auto navigation systems like gpsdrive [Hack #63] to network sensing tools like Kismet and Macstumbler [Hack #17]. However, the very nature of the serial connection linking the two—be it RS-232, USB, or Bluetooth—limits the GPS to talking to one application at a time. As soon as you want to do more than one thing at a time with the data you're getting from that GPS receiver, you will find yourself in a world of sadness and regret.

Fortunately, there is a way around this tragic outcome! For salvation, you can turn to *gpsd*, a GPS data multiplexer, which runs as a daemon on *NIX operating systems, including OS X. *gpsd* handles the nitty-gritty details of listening to the GPS receiver and then rebroadcasts the information it receives to other applications over a TCP/IP socket, using a simple text-based protocol. This arrangement allows applications that know how to talk to *gpsd* to avoid the hassle of needing permissions to set up the serial port or dealing with the specific details of different GPS receivers. Furthermore, since *gpsd* uses TCP to relay GPS data, a client application can talk to it across a network—or even across the Internet!

## Installing gpsd

You can get the source code to *gpsd* from *http://www.pygps.org/gpsd/downloads/*. The source code unpacks and builds in the usual way. Use the following commands, in which *x.xx* is the latest revision of gpsd:

```
$ tar xvfz gpsd-x.xx.tar.gz
$ cd gpsd-x.xx
$ ./configure
$ make
$ make install
```

You may get an error something like the following when you run **make**:

```
In file included from netlib.c:12:
…/include/varargs.h:4:2: #error "GCC no longer implements <varargs.h>."
…/include/varargs.h:5:2: #error "Revise your code to use <stdarg.h>."
```

If this happens, it's because *gpsd* was written against gcc headers that your particular system no longer supports. Fortunately, this is easy to fix. Run the following bit of perl, and then run *make* again. Everything should build just fine:

```
$ perl -pi -e 's/varargs.h/stdarg.h/g' *.c
$ make
```

## Running gpsd

First, you'll need to make sure your GPS receiver is on and properly connected to your computer (see "The Serial Port to USB Conundrum" **[Hack #50]** if your computer doesn't have a serial port). Next, you'll want to be sure your GPS receiver is configured to output NMEA-0183. Chances are good that the GPS receiver has an option for this in a setup menu, but check your owner's manual to be sure. Several new models of Garmin GPS units no longer speak NMEA. There is discussion of extending *gpsd* to support the proprietary Garmin protocol, but if you are in the market for a new GPS, you may want to add standards compliance to your list of purchase requirements!

> *NMEA-0183* is an industry-standard protocol, published by the National Marine Electronics Association, for transmitting position data over a serial line. The protocol consists of a continuous stream of ASCII text "sentences," sent at 4800 baud, that convey not just position information but potentially also accuracy, speed, bearing, time, satellite visibility, and more. Although implementations of NMEA-0183 vary from one manufacturer to the next, *gpsd* understands a basic subset spoken by nearly all GPS receivers. You can find an excellent FAQ on NMEA-0183 at *http://vancouver-webpages. com/peter/nmeafaq.txt.*

Starting *gpsd* is pretty straightforward. If you've already symlinked */dev/gps* to the serial device to which your GPS receiver is typically connected, just enter:

```
$ /usr/local/sbin/gpsd
```

However, if you need to explicitly set the serial port or baud rate, you can do that as well:

```
$ /usr/local/sbin/gpsd -p /dev/ttyS1 -s 4800
```

Users with a DeLorme EarthMate USB GPS receiver will need to set special options for the EarthMate:

```
$ /usr/local/sbin/gpsd -Te -s 9600
```

Once running, *gpsd* listens on TCP port 2947 for incoming connections. You can test it out by using *telnet* to type commands directly to *gpsd*:

```
$ telnet localhost 2947
Trying 127.0.0.1...
Connected to localhost.
Escape character is '^]'.
s
GPSD,S=0
s
GPSD,S=1
p
GPSD,P=37.739000 -122.419000
```

Commands to *gpsd* take the form of one or more letters, followed by a new line. Each letter is a single command. The s command, for example, requests the status of the GPS connection, returning a 1 if the GPS is connected, and a 0 if it's not. This can be useful for testing purposes, but, as you can see, *gpsd* doesn't always return a successful status on the first try, so give it a couple tries before deciding that you need to troubleshoot the connection. As you can see, the p command requests the current position. Another useful command for debugging is r, which requests a raw dump of the NMEA data:

```
r
GPSD,R=1
$GPRMC,085400,A,3744.0000,N,12225.0000,W,0.0,359.6,060804,15.1,E,A*39
$GPRMB,A,9.99,R,,Exit 192,4402.6514,N,12302.9773,W,379.131,355.9,,V,A*42
$GPGGA,085400,3744.3751,N,12225.1963,W,1,05,2.5,81.1,M,-28.1,M,,*4A
r
GPSD,R=0
```

Pretty ugly, huh? A second r command terminates the raw dump. Control-] followed by quit gets you out of *telnet*. Table 5-1 lists some other *gpsd* commands.

*Table 5-1. gpsd commands*

| Command | Description |
| --- | --- |
| p | Latitude/longitude, in decimal degrees. |
| d | Date/time, in MM/DD/YYYY HH:MM:SS format. |
| a | Altitude, in meters. |
| v | Current speed, in knots. |
| s | GPS status (0 = Disconnected; 1 = No GPS Fix; 2 = 2-D Fix; 3 = 3-D Fix) |
| m | Operating mode (0 = Disconnected; 1 = GPS; 2 = DGPS / WAAS) |

## Visualizing the Output of gpsd

Another useful tool that ships with *gpsd* is called, simply, *gps*, and it's an X11 program for visualizing *gpsd* output. You start it by running */usr/local/ bin/gps*. Figure 5-29 shows a typical *gps* display, including the nifty satellite visibility chart.

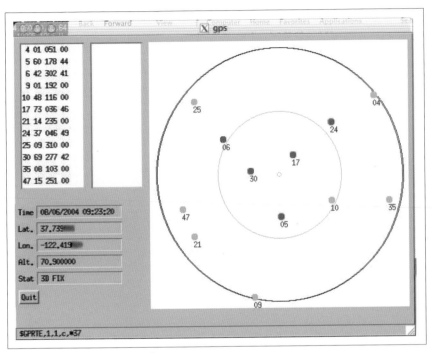

*Figure 5-29. A typical gps display*

What's particularly cool about this screenshot is that it was taken on a different machine than the one the GPS was connected to; the two computers were connected via a wireless network, with *gpsd* running on the one with the serial link to the GPS. We then ran gps -p *x.x.x.x*:2947 on the other laptop, where *x.x.x.x* was the IP address of the gpsd machine, and voilà!

## Hacking the Hack

At this point, you should be ready to run *kismet* [Hack #17] or *gpsdrive* [Hack #63], or *kismet* and *gpsdrive* together, or, indeed, your choice of GPS-using *NIX applications. The nice thing about *gpsd* is that once you've got it running, you can kind of forget about it. So we'd like to share with you just one more

thing you can do with *gpsd*, which is to set up a little CGI application on the
Web that shows your current location in real time:

```perl
#!/usr/bin/perl

use CGI;
use CGI::Carp 'fatalsToBrowser';
use IO::Socket::INET;
use strict;

my $GPSD_Server = "yourhostname.here:2947";
my $Map_Width   = 0.25; # degrees
my $Map_Pixels  = 320;

######

my $gpsd = IO::Socket::INET->new( $GPSD_Server )
    or die "Couldn't connect to GPS server.\n";

my $data = <$gpsd>;
my ($lat, $lon) = ($data =~ /(-?\d+\.\d+) (-?\d+\.\d+)/gos);

my $map = "http://tiger.census.gov/cgi-bin/mapgen?" .
          "lon=$lon&lat=$lat&wid=$Map_Width&ht=$Map_Width" .
          "&iht=$Map_Pixels&iwd=$Map_Pixels" .
          "&mark=$lon,$lat,redpin";

print CGI->header, <<End;
<html>
<head><title>Where am I?</title></head>
<body>
<h1>Where am I?</h1>
<img src="$map" width="$Map_Pixels" height="$Map_Pixels" border="1" />
<div><small>($lat, $lon)</small></div>
</body>
</html>
End
```

This CGI script connects to a *gpsd* running on the server specified by $GPSD_
Server, fetches the current latitude and longitude, and shows the location on
a TIGER Map Server map [Hack #14]. If you have a *NIX laptop running *gpsd*,
and a Net connection with some kind of dynamic DNS alias, this script
could live on a web server on the Internet and connect to your laptop on
demand to give others a general idea of your whereabouts. Assuming you
were somewhere in the U.S. at the time, interested parties would see something like Figure 5-30.

Although this example is a bit contrived (and does almost no error checking
to speak of), it demonstrates the simplicity and power of *gpsd*. You can find
out more about *gpsd* at *http://gpsd.berlios.de*.

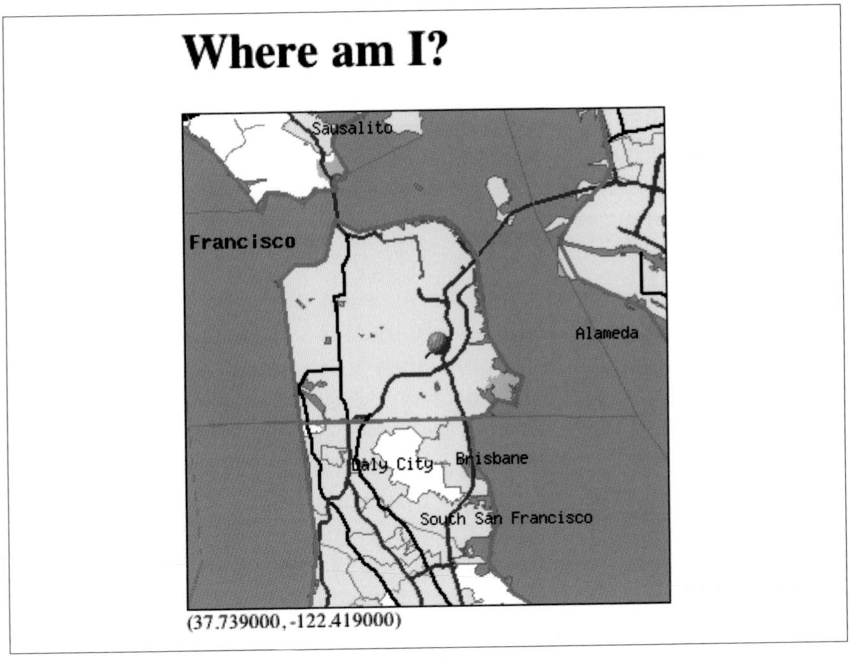

# Where am I?

(37.739000, -122.419000)

*Figure 5-30. Where am I? Live, thanks to gpsd*

## See Also

- "The Serial Port to USB Conundrum" **[Hack #50]**
- "Don't Lose Your Tracklogs!" **[Hack #58]**
- "Make Free Maps of the United States Online" **[Hack #14]**
- "Map Nearby Wi-Fi Hotspots" **[Hack #17]**
- "Build Your Own Car Navigation System with GpsDrive" **[Hack #63]**

---

HACK
**#58**

## Don't Lose Your Tracklogs!

Tracklogs are the stuff of your stories. Here are simple ways to preserve them for future use, and a harder but more satisfying way to annotate your tracks.

GPS tracklog memories are great, until you run out of space. On one trip, I had to decide whether I'd prefer to have some data for the whole trip, but lose date and timestamps, or just lose the data for the end of the trip. That choice continues to haunt me. Once you get started collecting tracklogs and you explore their possibilities, you may become fanatically obsessed about preserving these stories from your travels!

There are two risks associated with saving your tracklogs. The obvious risk is running out of space. A typical GPS unit may store approximately 1,500 track points, or 25 minutes of points if you store points at the admittedly extreme rate of one point per second. Higher-end units, like the Garmin Legend and Vista hold 10,000 points, or almost three hours at one point a second. It would be more common to store points less frequently, so those 1,500 points are quite useful, and 10,000 is almost an acceptable number for those tracklog freaks. (Some recent GPS devices are offering 50,000 and more, though 10,000 is still common.)

Sometimes a shortage of track memory leads to odd predicaments. On several trips, I've brought an old laptop solely to download tracklogs because I didn't have a USB cable to connect my serial-only GPS to my USB-only iBook. I also didn't have a way to get my tracklogs off my old laptop and onto the iBook. I didn't have a way, that is, until I remembered that I had a PCMCIA–to–Compact Flash adapter that worked great on the old laptop. I copied the tracklogs to the CF card and then put the card into my digital camera, which I connected to the iBook with a USB cable. The camera happily reported itself to the iBook as a mass storage device, allowing me to copy off the tracklogs.

The more insidious risk of tracklog preservation is thinking that you have space that you actually don't. Garmin GPS units have an active tracklog, plus a number of "saved" tracklogs. It would be reasonable to think you could save your active log in one of the saved logs. Sadly, this doesn't work. When you save a tracklog, the software compresses the points, getting rid of duplicates and discarding the date and timestamps. This makes sense if you are using the saved tracks for your own base maps [Hack #55], or as the data for the Track Back feature, where the GPS will guide you to retrace your steps to take you home. But if you care about the temporality of your track points, you don't want to save your tracklogs in your GPS.

## GPS Data Loggers

What if 10,000 track points aren't enough for you? You need a Tracklog Logger. These devices connect to your GPS and continually log the GPS output. They understand the National Marine Electronics Association (NMEA) standard and will thus work with almost any GPS that has a serial port.

Prairie Geomatics (*http://www.prairie.mb.ca/*) sells a line of GPS data loggers. The "basic" DGPS-XM4 can store position, date, and time for 393,000 points. At one sample per second, that is about four and a half days of tracklogs. The SRVY-XM4-ALT costs the same amount, also tracks altitude, and stores 308,800 points. Prairie Geomatics also offers the DGPS-XM4-ME, shown in Figure 5-31.

*Figure 5-31. Prairie Geomatics DGPS-XM4-ME*

This device will store position, date, and time, plus it has five "event" buttons on the front. Each time a button is pushed, it stores a timestamped position with a label identifying which button you pushed. This allows you to quickly mark positions. For example, you could do population surveys while in a moving vehicle, or you could use it to mark noteworthy items while traveling.

## Hacking the Hack: Build Your Own Data Logger

Being a geek, you probably read that section and thought "Ah, I could make one of those." Well of course you can! You can get the same effect by connecting your GPS unit to a laptop and logging everything that comes through. If you have a budget and an assigned project that requires a solid "solution," then the GPS data loggers are smaller, consume less power, and are less complicated. But it is more fun to make your own!

You could write a small program to directly open the serial port and log the GPS output, but that means that only one program at a time can get position information. The answer? Run *gpsd* **[Hack #57]** and then run a program to catch and log the position information that it reports.

Here is a program called *gpslogger.pl* that connects to the *gpsd* process and logs position, and a little bit more:

```perl
#!/usr/bin/perl

use 5.6.1;
use IO::Socket;
use Term::ReadKey;
use strict;

BEGIN { $|++ }; # autoflush STDOUT.

# Set parameters based on command line options, with defaults.
my $Rate        = 1;
my $extended    = shift( @ARGV ) || 0;
warn "extended: $extended\n";
my $GPSD        = shift( @ARGV ) || "localhost:2947";
# Connect to gpsd.
my $gps = IO::Socket::INET->new($GPSD)
    or die "Can't connect to gpsd at $GPSD: $!\n";

while (1) {
    my $key;
    if ($extended) {
        warn "Enter an annotation, followed by <enter> \n";
        $key = <>;
        chomp $key;
    } else {
        ReadMode 'cbreak';
        $key = ReadKey(-1);
    }
    # Tell gpsd we want position, altitude, date, and status.
    $gps->print("pads\n");

    # Parse out the response. If the date is blank, gpsd needs
    # a second to catch up.
    my $location = <$gps>;
    my ($lat, $long, $alt, $date, $status) =
        ($location =~ /P=(.+?) (.+?),A=(.+?),D=(.+?),S=(.+?)/gos);

    next unless $status or $key;

    # Print a line of data to both STDOUT and STDERR, and wait.
    print $_ join("|", $lat, $long, $alt, $date, $key || "" ), "\n"
        for ( \*STDOUT, \*STDERR );

    sleep( $Rate );
}
```

Start the program:

```
$ ./gpslogger.pl   > annotation.txt

38.414367|-122.790083|87.100000|2004-10-23T23:25:33Z|A
```

```
38.414467|-122.789900|87.100000|2004-10-23T23:25:34Z|
38.414617|-122.789650|87.100000|2004-10-23T23:25:35Z|D
```

The output is pretty obvious: lat, long, elevation, and a timestamp, all delimited with the pipe symbol (|). But what is that character at the end of the line? That is the homebrew answer to the DGPS-XM4-ME's "event" buttons. When *log_position.pl* is running in the foreground and you press a key, it logs that key, the date and time, and your current location. Later, you can map the points with color codes for the different keys.

We can use the *shapelib* utilities **[Hack #92]** to create a script to convert this output to a shapefile that contains the tracklog, timestamp, and the buttons that you pushed:

```
#!/bin/sh
shpcreate events point
dbfcreate events -n  elevation  5 0, -s timestamp 19, -s event 5
grep -v "^#" $1 | \
awk -F\| '{print "shpadd events " $1 " " $2 "; dbfadd events \""  $3  "\" \
"" $4 "\" \"" $5 "\""}' | \
sh
```

To run the script, use this command:

```
$ ./evt2shp.sh data.txt
```

This will create a shapefile named *events*. This really refers to three files: *events.shp*, *events.shx*, and *events.dbf*. The file *events.dbf* is a dBase-format file that can be read in many different programs. The elevation, timestamp, and event fields are shown in Excel in Figure 5-32.

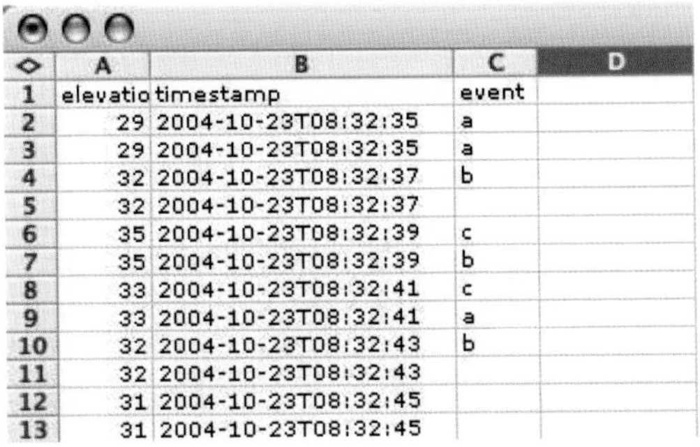

| | A | B | C | D |
|---|---|---|---|---|
| 1 | elevatio | timestamp | event | |
| 2 | 29 | 2004-10-23T08:32:35 | a | |
| 3 | 29 | 2004-10-23T08:32:35 | a | |
| 4 | 32 | 2004-10-23T08:32:37 | b | |
| 5 | 32 | 2004-10-23T08:32:37 | | |
| 6 | 35 | 2004-10-23T08:32:39 | c | |
| 7 | 35 | 2004-10-23T08:32:39 | b | |
| 8 | 33 | 2004-10-23T08:32:41 | c | |
| 9 | 33 | 2004-10-23T08:32:41 | a | |
| 10 | 32 | 2004-10-23T08:32:43 | b | |
| 11 | 32 | 2004-10-23T08:32:43 | | |
| 12 | 31 | 2004-10-23T08:32:45 | | |
| 13 | 31 | 2004-10-23T08:32:45 | | |

*Figure 5-32. The dbf file from a shapefile*

To see the contents of the *dbf* file from the command line, use the *dbfdump* utility from the *shapelib* utilities: **dbfdump events.dbf**. The latitude and longitude are stored in the *shp* and *shx* files and can be viewed by running the *shpdump* utility from *shapelib*: **shpdump events.shp**.

Our program logs "key presses," but if we salvage the keyboard encoder from a surplus keyboard, we can push the meaning of a "keyboard" well past the breaking point. There is a whole culture of people creating arcade game emulators using the Multiple Arcade Machine Emulator (MAME) software. These folks have created a full literature on using the electronics from old keyboards in new and entertaining ways as general data-input devices. Do a Google search on "hacking keyboard encoders" for more information.

We can put this all together to create a compact and efficient portable tracklog-logging and event-logging system. In Figure 5-33, we see one such system. The computer is a Fujitsu Stylistic obtained at a surplus price. This is a 486-based tablet machine running the Pebble distribution of Linux. (Note: Pebble defaults to running *getty* on the serial port, so in order to get *gpsd* to work, you must comment out all lines in your */etc/inittab* that refer to your serial port: */dev/ttyS0* on the Stylistic.) A Garmin GPS is connected via a serial cable. The Stylistic has an external keyboard connector, so we are using the "little man" keyboard. Pressing the buttons that make up his face generates keystrokes. (We could also use the Happy Hacker keyboard on the steering wheel if we wanted to be a tad less photogenic.)

*Figure 5-33. A homebrewed geo-annotation device with custom "little man" keyboard*

Using this setup, we can input GPS data and then map our results in terms of button pushes of the "left eye," "right eye," "nose," and "mouth parts 1 to 4." These work the same as the Track log Logger event buttons.

The *gpslogger.pl* program has one other trick: it can do extended annotations. If you start it with a command-line parameter, it will pause and wait for you to create an annotation that ends with the <enter> key:

```
$./gpslogger.pl yes > extended.txt

Enter an annotation, followed by <enter>
Fireman with dog
38.403367|-122.829733|55.100000|2004-10-26T01:13:24Z|Fireman with dog
```

The extended annotations can be converted to shapefiles with (almost) the same script as the previous one. The one change is to increase the size of the event field. In the line:

```
dbfcreate events -n  elevation  5 0, -s timestamp 19, -s event 5
```

change -s event 5 to -s event 1024. This number (1024) needs to be larger than your longest annotation. In Figure 5-34, we see part of the results of extended geo-annotation. Note how the dots that mark annotations are slightly offset from the street.

*Figure 5-34. Florence Avenue in downtown Sebastopol*

This package, along with the saw blade at the base of the "keyboard," makes a perfect data-logging and geo-annotating solution, except for the possible difficulty in getting through airport security and the always possible risk of personal injury. What if we could use an ultra small computer? The Gumstix Waysmall computers (*http://gumstix.com/*) are tiny!

They are full Linux computers running on the Intel XScale PXA255 processor. They have two serial ports, one that you normally reserve to connect to the console in order to control the unit, and the second free and waiting to connect to your GPS unit. Add a 128 MB SDRAM card, and you should be able to store tracklogs at one-second intervals for over two weeks.

I have my Waysmall Computer and a GPS waiting in my workshop, ready to sacrifice all in support of my dreams of a capture device to support "Quantitative Psychogeography" as well as "Geospatially-aware narrative." As the unofficial motto of the Locative Media Lab runs, "Location: It's everywhere!"

## HACK #59 Geocode Your Voice Recordings and Other Media

One way to make a chunk o'media better is to know where it was created!

We talk about geocoding photographs elsewhere (see "View Your Photo Thumbnails on a Flash Map" [Hack #39]), but what about other media? How about that digital voice recorder? A recording athletic heart-rate monitor? Even SMS messages have timestamps. If you have GPS tracklogs, then you can use a simple web site to geocode anything! The trick is to use timestamps and tracklogs to determine where you were when you created a file.

You can geocode any media that has a timestamp using the linkmedia tool at *http://mappinghacks.com/projects/linkmedia/*. This hack uses the *linkmedia.cgi* script that is included with the Perl module `Geo::Track::Log`. Select the link to "linkmedia," and you get the web page shown in Figure 5-35.

This program lets you upload a text file that I call a "media description file," along with a GPX-format tracklog file. A media description file contains one line for each item to be geocoded. The first field is a filename, followed by the pipe symbol (|), and a date and timestamp, followed by another pipe. Anything else can appear after the date and timestamp. Here is a sample line from a media description file:

```
random.txt|2004-04-03 19:23|
```

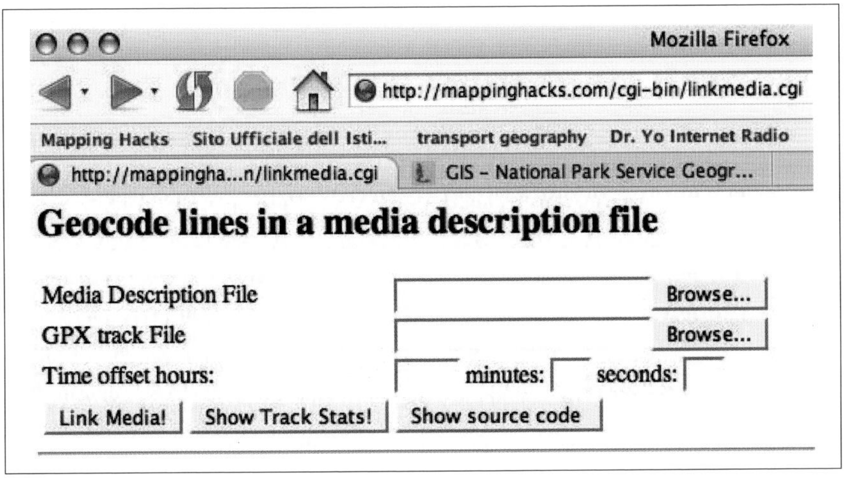

*Figure 5-35. linkmedia.cgi file selection page*

You can create the media description file in any text editor for any media that you have. For example, you can create a media description file for a list of photographs. As it happens, I created this module so that I could geocode audio files and create audio travelogues. I have an Olympus DS-330 Digital Voice Recorder that allows me to record sound clips and download them to my computer in individual DSS format files. Each file contains a header with the date and time that the clip was started, and some other information. I created the Perl module Audio::DSS to extract this metadata and output it in the media description file format.

Audio::DSS is available on CPAN. It includes the script *dumpdss.pl* that extracts DSS-file metadata. The script is in the *eg/* directory. Copy *dumpdss. pl* to somewhere in your path, and then change directories to your audio file directory.

```
$ dumpdss.pl FolderB/*.dss
```

Here is a partial list of these files, along with their metadata. The first field is the filename; the second is the date the sound clip was started, when it was completed, the time in seconds, and a comment. The DSS Recorder software lets you add a comment of up to 100 characters. The first time I tried to do this I was reminded of the importance of synchronizing the time on my voice recorder with my GPS:

```
FolderB/DS330271.dss|2004-09-06 21:22:55|2004-09-06 21:23:06|000010|Start
Segment|
FolderB/DS330278.dss|2004-09-06 21:24:32|2004-09-06 21:24:52|000020|Why is
it that color?|
```

```
FolderB/DS330279.dss|2004-09-06 21:29:21|2004-09-06 21:29:28|000007|News on
the radio|
FolderB/DS330343.dss|2004-09-06 21:38:53|2004-09-06 21:39:45|000052|Rock'M
Sock'M robot action!|
```

You can geocode the media description file and output a media description file with latitude and longitude added to it by clicking on "link media."

```
39.589177|-119.441896|FolderB/DS330271.dss|2004-09-06 21:22:55|2004-09-06
21:23:06|000010|Start Segment|
39.582250|-119.469884|FolderB/DS330278.dss|2004-09-06 21:24:32|2004-09-06
21:24:52|000020|Why is it that color?|
39.555830|-119.561804|FolderB/DS330279.dss|2004-09-06 21:29:21|2004-09-06
21:29:28|000007|News on the radio|
39.529747|-119.728585|FolderB/DS330343.dss|2004-09-06 21:38:53|2004-09-06
21:39:45|000052|Rock'M Sock'M robot action!|
```

But wait, there's more! If you click on "show track stats," you will get statistics about your GPX file, as shown in Figure 5-36.

| Time | Lat/Long | Distance feet | Elapsed Time seconds | Speed MPH | Cumulative Track Distance (miles) | Cumulative Total Distance (miles) |
|---|---|---|---|---|---|---|
| 2004-09-06 21:22:53 | (39.589149,-119.441317) | | | | New track or track segment | |
| 2004-09-06 21:22:57 | (39.589206,-119.442476) | 326 | 4 | 55.57 | 0.06 | 0.06 |
| 2004-09-06 21:22:58 | (39.589206,-119.442779) | 85 | 1 | 57.95 | 0.08 | 0.08 |
| 2004-09-06 21:23:19 | (39.589833,-119.449270) | 1838 | 21 | 59.68 | 0.43 | 0.43 |
| 2004-09-06 21:23:42 | (39.590493,-119.457027) | 2193 | 23 | 65.01 | 0.84 | 0.84 |
| 2004-09-06 21:23:43 | (39.590445,-119.457376) | 99 | 1 | 67.50 | 0.86 | 0.86 |
| 2004-09-06 21:23:52 | (39.589472,-119.460355) | 909 | 9 | 68.86 | 1.03 | 1.03 |
| 2004-09-06 21:24:04 | (39.587530,-119.463469) | 1126 | 12 | 63.98 | 1.25 | 1.25 |
| 2004-09-06 21:24:15 | (39.586028,-119.466642) | 1046 | 11 | 64.83 | 1.44 | 1.44 |
| 2004-09-06 21:24:24 | (39.584300,-119.468807) | 876 | 9 | 66.36 | 1.61 | 1.61 |
| 2004-09-06 21:24:33 | (39.581994,-119.470019) | 907 | 9 | 68.71 | 1.78 | 1.78 |

*Figure 5-36. GPX Tracklog statistics*

I've long been interested in the geospatial component of what people do, since everything that people do has a geospatial component. After all, we are somewhere whenever we do anything. This tool does not actually require a GPS unit or a real tracklog. As shown in "Give Your Great-Great-Grandfather a GPS" [Hack #98], you can geocode historic documents and events, and then use tools like these to extend the narrative and add additional context.

See *http://mappinghacks.com/projects/linkmedia/* for more on geocoding, mapping arbitrary media, and creating online voice-annotated travelogues.

# Improve the Accuracy of Your GPS with Differential GPS

### The GPS system is amazing, but here is a way to make it even better.

Why does your GPS receiver give you an error reading, and why are the values it gives you often in tens of meters? The accuracy of your signal depends not only on how many satellites you can see, but also the atmospheric interference between them in low earth orbit and you with your feet on the ground.

Satellite-based global positioning systems rely on the basic property of our universe that radio signals travel at a constant speed through a vacuum. If we can estimate how long a GPS signal has taken to travel to our receiver from a satellite in orbit, we can multiply our time estimate by that constant speed to arrive at an estimate of how far away the satellite is. If we combine enough of these estimates, we can arrive at a pretty good idea of where we are on the planet's surface. So far, so accurate!

But this simple physics solution doesn't work so well in the real universe. GPS signals don't travel through a vacuum to reach us; they travel through Earth's atmosphere, and, in much the same way that sound waves travel at different speeds through air or water or other mediums, the radio signals from GPS satellites end up traveling at different speeds to reach Earth's surface. While certain parts of the atmosphere have a predictably constant density that can be accounted for easily, others do not.

Our atmosphere, starting at about 60 km above sea level, interacts with solar and cosmic radiation to produce a layer of ionized particles that surrounds the planet, known as the *ionosphere*. The electrically charged particles that make up the ionosphere are the cause of the Northern Lights, the beautiful aurorae that can be sometimes seen at extreme latitudes, but their charge and their widely variable density affects how easily high-frequency radio waves, such as GPS signals, can pass through them. This "ionospheric delay" can cause GPS errors of 10 meters or more. And changing conditions on Earth's surface can add another one or two meters of error to your GPS reading.

## How Does GPS Error Correction Work?

There are a couple of ways of detecting and canceling out the effects of atmospheric delay. One solution is to use a receiver that listens for GPS signals on two different frequencies. Since ionospheric delay is roughly inversely proportional to signal frequency, a dual-frequency receiver can work out the relative delay for the same signal transmitted over the two different frequencies and then estimate the total delay.

This is the solution employed by military-grade receivers, but it comes at a price: each dual-frequency GPS receiver needs to have two antennas, two GPS radios, and so on, effectively doubling the cost of the receiver. Furthermore, the U.S. military, for obvious reasons, keeps the second NAVSTAR GPS signal encrypted. As a result, this option is basically out for ordinary civilian GPS users.

A second way of correcting atmospheric delay error is to place a second, stationary GPS receiver at an already well-surveyed location. Since we already know the exact longitude and latitude of this stationary receiver, we can calculate the effects of atmospheric delay and other errors on local GPS reception quite accurately. If we broadcast this information over ground-based radio, nearby GPS receivers can listen for our estimates of local GPS error and correct their readings accordingly. In fact, this is exactly what the U.S. Coast Guard does—and their GPS correction broadcasts can be pulled in with a suitable radio receiver listening in the 200–300 kHz range and fed to an ordinary consumer GPS unit.

This method of correcting atmospheric error is referred to as *differential GPS*, or DGPS, and it can bring GPS accuracy to within five meters or less! DGPS can even overcome the deliberate errors caused by *Selective Availability*, the U.S. government's term for the "fuzzing" of the civilian NAVSTAR GPS signals, which were formerly used to degrade GPS accuracy to hundreds, rather than dozens, of meters. Selective Availability was finally turned off in May 2000, but the U.S. government nominally reserves the right to turn it back on at will.

There are still two main issues with using differential GPS, of course. The first is the relatively local nature of ionospheric conditions, which means that DGPS information is only really useful for navigation within about 500 km of the DGPS base station, and there's not really any way around that. The other issue is, again, cost. In order to pick up the free DGPS corrections broadcast by the U.S. Coast Guard, we need an expensive radio, tunable to the appropriate frequencies and equipped to provide correction data over a serial line to a GPS receiver.

Naturally, we can get around this second obstacle to using differential GPS if we opt for an alternate medium for disseminating the data. This is the approach taken by DGPS-over-IP, a protocol for relaying DGPS corrections over the Internet. The dgpsip server, written by Wolfgang S. Rupprecht, accepts incoming TCP connections and then simply takes the serial data output by his Garmin DBR-21 DGPS receiver near San Francisco, stuffs it into a TCP/IP packet, and sends it back out. The correction data is in RTCM SC-104 format, a protocol published by an industry group called the Radio Technical Commission for Maritime Services. Most consumer GPS equipment can be configured to accept RTCM DGPS corrections, so all a DGPS-over-IP client needs to do is assemble the SC-104 data on the receiving end and pipe it out to the GPS receiver over a serial port. The net effect of DGPS-over-IP is, in essence, to treat the Internet as an indefinitely long RS-232 extension cable!

## Setting Up DGPS-over-IP on Linux

In order to use DGPS-over-IP, you'll need to get a suitable client. If you're running Debian Linux, you can simply run apt-get install dgpsip. If you're running a different *NIX, you can get the latest source code tarball from *http://www.wsrcc.com/wolfgang/ftp/*. The file should be called *dgpsip-x.xx. tar.gz*, where *x.xx* is the latest version (1.33, as of this writing). You can build and install it as follows:

```
$ tar xvfz dgpsip-x.xx.tar.gz
$ cd dgpsip-x.xx
$ ./configure
$ make
```

Then, as root, run:

```
$ make install
```

Next, you may want to symlink your serial port (usually, */dev/ttyS0* for the first serial port, but it might be */dev/ttyS1*) to */dev/gps*, so that dgpsip knows by default where to look:

```
$ ln -s ttyS0 /dev/gps
```

Finally, check your */etc/services* file to make sure that port 2101 is registered for rtcm-sc104:

```
$ grep rtcm-sc104 /etc/services
rtcm-sc104      2101/tcp            # RTCM SC-104 IANA 1/29/99
rtcm-sc104      2101/udp
```

If the output of this command doesn't print anything out, you'll want to add the two rtcm lines to your */etc/services* file, so that the dgpsip client knows which port to use to talk with the server. (You can leave out the part of the line following the hash mark, #—it's just a comment).

## Setting up DGPS-over-IP on Windows

You can also get a DGPS-over-IP client for Windows from *http://www.wsrcc. com/wolfgang/ftp/*. Look for a file called *Jdgpsip1.01.exe* in that same directory and download and execute it. The file is a self-extracting ZIP archive that will install the Jdgpsip application on your system. You'll then need to configure your GPS receiver to accept RTCM data at 4800 baud, and, ideally, output NMEA data. This setting should be available in the setup menu on your receiver, but check your owner's manual for details. Then connect your GPS to your computer via the serial cable provided by your manufacturer. Make sure you know which serial port you've connected it to—often COM1 or COM2.

You'll want to try getting DGPS corrections somewhere where you can get a reasonably clear view of the sky. Indoor GPS reception tends to be weak, at best, due to the extremely low power of the satellite transmissions, so you may want to go outside. A laptop with Wi-Fi makes this enormously easier.

Make sure your computer is connected to the Internet and your GPS receiver is connected and powered on. Wait until your GPS gets a satellite lock. If it doesn't get a lock, you may need to find another location with a better view of the sky. Note the accuracy that your GPS reports.

## Getting Better Differentials

Now, start up dgpsip (or Jdgpsip). The dgpsip client should connect to *dgps.wsrcc.com* on port 2101 by default. If you're running the *NIX version of dgpsip, you can start it as `dgpsip -v2` to get periodic position and accuracy updates printed to your terminal. Regardless of which client you're using, if you're in Europe, you should try connecting to *gnssip.ing.uniroma1.it* instead, which is located in Rome.

Let the DGPS client run for a few minutes and check the accuracy reported by your GPS. If you're more than a couple thousand kilometers away from San Francisco or Rome, you may not see much of an improvement. However, when we tried it from our home in San Francisco, our accuracy jumped from 12 meters to 4 meters in a matter of minutes!

Be aware that both the Windows and the *NIX versions will attempt to send your position data back to the dgpsip server. The clients do this in order to allow the dgpsip server to collect statistics about how well it offers corrections in various locales. This may cause some privacy concerns, but the data is sent with an accuracy of about three or four kilometers. Obviously, at that level of granularity, it would be next to impossible to identify any individual DGPS-over-IP user, but we mention it for completeness's sake.

For many general purposes, the accuracy offered by uncorrected GPS receivers is sufficient. Still, as you can see, differential GPS can offer a significant improvement in positioning accuracy, especially if the United States government ever decides to turn Selective Availability back on. One potential use for this technology, for example, might be to hook it into a car navigation system and use a cellular uplink or opportunistic Wi-Fi connections to obtain DGPS corrections. Of course, it would work a lot better if more DGPS-over-IP servers were available in a wider variety of locations—a part of the vision articulated by Wolfgang Rupprecht on his DGPS-over-IP homepage. You can read more about it at *http://www.wsrcc.com/wolfgang/gps/dgps-ip.html* and at his GPS Hacks page at *http://www.wsrcc.com/wolfgang/gps*. Maybe you'll be inspired to provide your own DGPS-over-IP server or build your own DGPS backpack.

## HACK #61 Build a Map of Local GSM Cells

Use GPS to make maps of cell-tower locations and start building cheap location-based services.

Ever wanted to figure out where you are from the signals received by your mobile phone? The telecommunications companies, the emergency service providers, and, by extension, many "authorities" have access to this map of where mobile phone users are, where they have been, and where they are likely to be heading. Now you can build such a map for yourself and your friends!

From most Nokia phones, including older models, you can get the *cell ID* of the base tower you are connected to. Earlier models had a "monitor" mode that could scan for all available cell towers and their respective signal strengths; on later models, this has been locked down.

Fortunately, we can still get the current cell tower ID and signal strength from the phone, via Bluetooth or a serial cable, using an extended version of plain old AT modem commands! We used a Perl script to connect to the phone at intervals—every seven seconds, though we were bicycling and could have set the interval as short as once per second—and ask it for its cell ID metadata, which includes a *Location Area Code* (LAC), and a *Cell ID* (CID). Taken together, the LAC and CID form a unique identifier for any cell in a wireless provider's national network.

The script, which we'll call *cellstumbler.pl*, uses an interface to the *gpsd* daemon to correlate mobile phone cell IDs with GPS coordinates. By running *gpsd* instead of connecting to the GPS directly from our script, we were able to use Kismet to talk to *gpsd* as well, to correlate Wi-Fi traces with GPS coordinates at the same time. See "Connect to Your GPS from Multiple Applications" [Hack #57] for detailed instructions on running *gpsd*.

Also, you'll need the Device::Modem module from the CPAN to run this code. You can obtain it by running **perl -MCPAN -e 'install Device::Modem'** as root on your Linux system.

## The Code

Here is the code contained in *cellstumbler.pl*:

```perl
#!/usr/bin/perl

use 5.6.1;
use IO::Socket;
use Device::Modem;
use Getopt::Std;
use strict;
use warnings;

BEGIN { $|++ }; # autoflush STDOUT.

# Read command line options.
my %opt;
getopt('gpr', \%opt);

# Set parameters based on command line options, with defaults.
my $GPSD     = $opt{g} || "localhost:2947";
my $GSM_Port = $opt{p} || "/dev/ttyS0";
my $GSM_Baud = $opt{b} || 115_200;
my $Rate     = $opt{r} || 1;

# Connect to gpsd.
my $gps = IO::Socket::INET->new($GPSD)
    or die "Can't connect to gpsd at $GPSD: $!\n";

# Connect to the cell phone.
my $gsm = Device::Modem->new( port => $GSM_Port );
$gsm->connect( baudrate => $GSM_Baud )
    or die "Can't connect to modem on $GSM_Port: $!\n";

# Tell the cell phone we want all the network registration data it has.
$gsm->reset;
$gsm->atsend( "AT+CREG=2\r" );
die "AT+CREG not recognized by modem on $GSM_Port"
    unless $gsm->answer eq "OK";

while (1) {
    # Tell gpsd we want position, date, and status.
    $gps->print("pds\n");

    # Parse out the response. If the date is blank, gpsd needs a second to
catch up.
    my $location = <$gps>;
    my ($lat, $long, $date, $status) =
```

```
($location =~ /P=(.+?) (.+?),D=(.+?),S=(.+?)/gos);
next unless $date;

# Turn the date into an RFC 2445 ICal date string.
my ($mo, $d, $y, $h, $m, $s) = split /[ \/:]/o, $date;
$date = "${y}${mo}${d}T${h}${m}${s}Z";

# Query cell ID and location area code.
$gsm->atsend( "AT+CREG?\r" );
my ($cid, $lac) = ($gsm->answer =~ /"([\dA-F]{4})"/gios);

# Query signal strength.
$gsm->atsend( "AT+CSQ\r" );
my ($signal) = ($gsm->answer =~ /(\d+)/gos);
$signal = -113 + $signal * 2;

# Print a line of data and wait.
print join(",", $date, $status, $lat, $long,
         hex($cid), hex($lac), $signal), "\n";
sleep( $Rate );
}
```

## Running the Code

As mentioned earlier, you need to have *gpsd* running before starting *cell-stumbler.pl*. We used a Bluetooth RFCOMM serial connection to talk to a Nokia 3650, so we had to bind an RFCOMM port first, using the six-part Bluetooth ID of the phone. You can use **hcitool scan** in Linux to search for the Bluetooth ID of your phone. If your phone doesn't have Bluetooth, then you'll need a serial cable, but you can skip the whole RFCOMM bit. You may need to use a terminal program like *minicom* to poke around your system's serial ports to figure out which the phone is accessible on. You'll know it's working when you type **AT<enter>** into the terminal program, and get an OK from the phone in response.

Finally, assuming *cellstumbler.pl* is in the current directory and marked as executable, you can start it like this, where *xx:xx* etc is the Bluetooth ID of your phone:

```
$ rfcomm bind /dev/rfcomm0 xx:xx:xx:xx:xx:xx
$ ./cellstumbler.pl -p /dev/rfcomm0 -r 5 > cell_data.txt
```

In this particular case, we're telling *cellstumbler.pl* to talk to the phone on the /dev/rfcomm0 serial port with the -p option and to collect a sample every five seconds with the -r option. There's a -b option available in case you need to explicitly set the baud rate on the serial line to the phone, and a -g option, just in case you're running *gpsd* on a different port (or different machine!) than the default.

If you want to see the cell ID data go by as you collect it, you can use the very handy tee shell command:

```
$ ./cellstumbler.pl -p /dev/rfcomm0 | tee cell_data.txt
```

The standard output of *cellstumbler.pl* contains one sample per line, with seven comma-separated fields. In order, they are:

> timestamp (in iCal format)
> GPS status
> latitude
> longitude
> CID (in hexadecimal)
> LAC (in hexadecimal)
> signal strength (measured in dBm)

The value in the GPS status field is returned directly from *gpsd*, which will be 0 if the GPS has no satellite lock, 1 if it has a satellite lock, and 2 if the location reading is differentially corrected (e,g,, via a WAAS signal).

## Evaluating the Data

Given a set of readings of the ID of some radio frequency beacon and its signal strength, and the latitude and longitude and time at which the measurement was taken, how can we figure out where the radio antennas are? We could start with a naive interpolation technique that doesn't even make use of the signal strength data.

First, we convert the latitude and longitude from the GPS readings into UTM, to make Cartesian calculations easier. (See "Work with Different Coordinate Systems" [Hack #26] for more details on this process.) We take the numerical average of all the GPS points collected for the same cell-ID reading, and call this the "center" of the cell. We take the distance from the center of the cell to the matching point farthest away and make that the radius of the circle. It's a quick-and-dirty technique, but it will give approximate "good-enough" measurements for many kinds of spatial navigation in urban areas: a map of a surrounding 500m radius, or interesting places less than half a mile's walk away.

We can get better results based on signal strength and by using more interesting algorithms, such as inverse distance weighting and particle filters. We also have to be aware of problems or flaws in different radio technologies. Buildings and trees block lines of sight and dampen or divert radio waves; our perfect circles are more likely to be distended blobs. Intel's PlaceLab project implements some of these more advanced techniques; you can find PlaceLab's source code at *http://placelab.org*.

These same techniques are equally viable for making RF frequency maps for other channels and protocols, particularly 802.11 wireless. As mentioned previously, while cellstumbling for mobile phone base stations, we also used Kismet to talk to *gpsd* and collect readings for 802.11 access points, including information about whether they provide open service and offer DHCP addresses.

Now that we've gathered all this data, we might want to submit it to a repository, to make it useful for other applications or to visualize it. Figure 5-37 shows part of a simple map we made with the support of RIXC, a Latvian cultural organization (*http://rixc.lv*), showing cellular reception in central Riga. The map, made in SVG, depicts a circle representing each centroid, with a label for each cell ID. An obvious next step for this "bubble diagram" would be to plot it over a base map of the area to provide context.

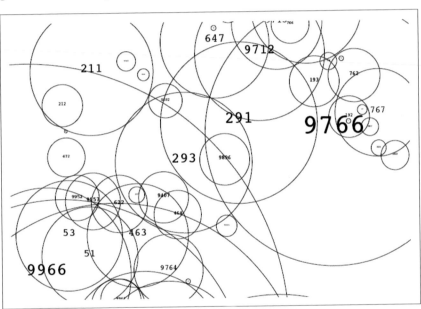

*Figure 5-37. Part of an SVG bubble diagram of Riga's cellular network*

Envision the possibilities that can blossom when individuals go out, collect cell ID samples, and compile them together in a collaborative database. Suddenly, applications can be written for smart phones, like those running the Symbian OS, which can look up a user's location in a database simply by examining the current cell ID, with no need for a GPS on the phone. You can explore this idea further at *http://mappinghacks.com/cell/*, where we provide a demo of a small web service that allows people to upload files full of points or post individual points in real time. The full sources of the various scripts described here—for calculating centroids, generating SVG bubble diagrams, and so on—are available on the site as well.

### See Also:

- Intel Research's free placelab product has GSM spotting capacities—see *http://placelab.org/*
- Cellspotting is another collaborative cellstumbling resource—see *http://cellspotting.org/*

### HACK #62    Build a Car Computer

A project that will consume all your time and money, but make you the envy of your nerd friends.

If you have not experienced driving with GPS navigation, you are missing out on a great experience. It does not make much difference for your daily commute, but when you are lost or just exploring a new area, a GPS navigation system can make a world of difference.

Right now, there are a number of ways to get GPS navigation in your car. On the cheap end of the scale, you can buy a handheld outdoor GPS like those made by Garmin or Magellan. For a little more money, there are units that sit on your dashboard and have a larger screen and more storage space for street data. If you have a laptop or PDA already, you can connect an external GPS to it and run mapping software that will track your position and provide driving directions. Finally, top-of-the-line navigation systems come as an option in some new cars and sometimes can be purchased in the form of aftermarket parts.

Of all these options, only two are easily hackable: the PDA and the laptop. A PDA is a convenient size but is difficult to see while driving. The laptop approach has a few drawbacks in the car, namely the difficulty of finding a good location for the laptop, cables getting tangled, potential for theft, and poor visibility in direct sunlight. On the positive side, a laptop has an enormous amount of power and storage and is highly configurable for navigation purposes. See Figure 5-38 for an example of navigation software running on a laptop.

In order to overcome the shortcomings of a laptop, people have learned to build small PCs into their cars. This impressive hack generally involves a small, low-power motherboard along with a small daylight-viewable LCD (6 or 7 inches) running one of the many navigation software packages available. For extra credit, you can mount the screen into your dashboard. Figure 5-39 shows a typical system diagram of a car computer.

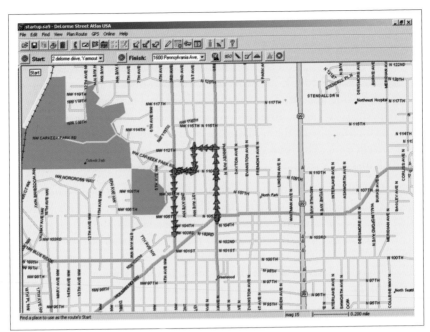

Figure 5-38. Delorme Atlas USA running on a laptop with a GPS

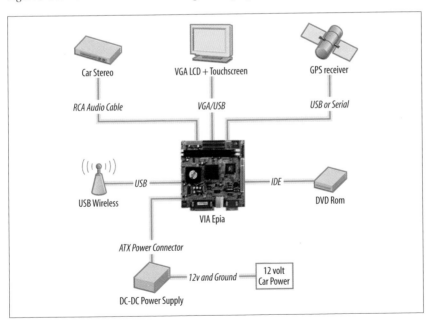

Figure 5-39. A typical system diagram for a car computer

Running a computer in your car opens up a world of possibilities that extend beyond basic navigation. One popular application involves creating a mobile multimedia system. A connection to the car stereo allows for MP3 playback, and an LCD on the dashboard can display live television, DVDs, or any other supported video formats. Wireless cards are also common and allow wardriving [Hack #17], Internet surfing, and easy media changes when an access point is in range. Another use of a car computer involves a custom cable to interface with the OBDII (On Board Diagnostics System) port on more recent cars. This link allows the car computer to access operational and diagnostic information collected by the car's internal electronics.

One interesting concept discussed on a car-computer message board shows how customizable these systems are. The project involved a GPS, various video cameras, and engine-monitoring software, all set up inside a racing car. During a race, the driver is able to record all aspects of the car's position, the surrounding track, and the status of various vehicle systems. This information can later be analyzed in order to improve driving style or tweak aspects of the car.

The process of building a car computer can easily consume a large amount of time and money. Common pitfalls include accidental damage to hardware, accessories that end up not working well, and the ultimate bad luck: theft. Fortunately, during the process you are bound to expand your knowledge in several technical areas that will be invaluable in the future. You will also gain respect from your techie friends.

A key component of any car computer is the motherboard. In the early days of hobby car computers, the only option was full-sized ATX machines that consumed lots of power and required a good deal of space. Today, life is easier, thanks to a new breed of tiny low-power and low-heat motherboards. The company that has done the most in this area is VIA, with their line of Mini-ITX EPIA motherboards. This line's boards all measure 170x170 mm and commonly contain a fan-less CPU with onboard VGA, TV-out, sound, and LAN. Other accessories can be connected to a single PCI slot, or by using USB, serial, or parallel ports. Figure 5-40 shows a VIA EPIA ME 6000 motherboard alongside an Opus DC-DC power supply designed for automotive applications.

Probably the second most important part of any car computer is the display. In the last few years, online retailers and eBay sellers have started offering inexpensive seven-inch LCD screens that accept VGA and include a touch screen input (see Figure 5-41). These screens are brighter than laptop and desktop screens and often fit in the dashboard, simply by removing the

*Figure 5-40. EPIA ME600 motherboard and Opus power supply (Courtesy of Nico Voss, http://www.mini-itx.com/projects/bmwpc/)*

*Figure 5-41. Seven-inch Lilliput LCD mounted in a Volvo*

factory stereo. Although these screens are getting better, many of today's models suffer from less-than-perfect reliability and quality control problems.

Once you nail down a hardware blueprint, you can start thinking about software. The easiest route is to run Windows with an off-the-shelf navigation package. Popular titles include Delorme Street Atlas, Microsoft Streets & Trips, and CoPilot by ALK Technologies. For the more adventurous, Linux makes for a stable and easily hackable platform. The major drawback of Linux is the lack of mapping software that comes with high-quality maps. This will likely change in the future, so keep an eye out for emerging projects.

Regardless of what operating system you choose, you can always have fun writing custom code to integrate with your mobile computer. When starting on a project like this, some of the newer high-level languages can make for a rapid and painless development experience. Python is a perfect example of this and, as you will see in the following examples, can be used to build a visual GPS plotter with only a few pages of code.

### Connecting a GPS to Your Car Computer

If you have access to a GPS with a serial interface, it is quite easy to extract latitude and longitude into your computer. Just about all GPS devices support a protocol called NMEA-0183 (National Marine Electronics Association), which is streamed over the serial port at 4800 baud. The NMEA-0183 protocol is text-based and quite easy to parse. You can use the following Python code to connect with a GPS or explore *gpsd*, which provides a server interface to the GPS. *gpsd* is described in "Connect to Your GPS from Multiple Applications" [Hack #57]. NMEA consists of various sentences with data fields separated by commas. Each line of a NMEA sentence starts with a $ and a sentence type. Each sentence type provides different information in the fields that follow the sentence-type designator. Here is what a typical stream looks like:

```
$GPVTG,269.6,T,250.8,M,019.9,N,0036.8,K*76
$GPRMC,011106,A,4742.1321,N,12221.2108,W,021.0,270.5,240804,018.9,E*67
$GPGGA,011106,4742.1321,N,12221.2108,W,1,10,1.3,115.5,M,-18.4,M,,*79
$GPGSA,A,3,07,08,10,11,,19,26,27,28,29,31,,1.8,1.3,1.3*3F
$GPGSV,3,1,11,07,19,190,41,08,73,092,47,10,09,252,46,11,12,101,37*75
$GPGSV,3,2,11,13,01,161,,19,26,047,43,26,34,308,44,27,47,113,44*78
$GPGSV,3,3,11,28,69,254,49,29,42,299,45,31,32,180,35,,,,*40
```

Contained in these sentences is information including latitude, longitude, altitude, speed, heading, time, signal strength, satellite positions, positional error, and tons of other information. For a complete list, check out "The NMEA FAQ" written by Peter Bennett and available online at *http://vancouver-webpages.com/pub/peter/nmeafaq.txt*.

For our first example, we want to find the current position in latitude and longitude. This information is present in the $GPGGA sentences. We are interested in the second through fourth fields, which contain the information 4742.1321,N,12221.2108,W. This tells us that our position is 47 degrees and 42.1321 minutes north, and 122 degrees and 21.2108 minutes west. Unfortunately, providing separate values for degrees, minutes, and direction is not the preferred format. The following Python code takes a position in NMEA format as its input and then returns a decimal position, such as (47.702201, −122.3535):

```
def NMEA_to_DecDeg(nmea_coord, direction):
    """Convert a NMEA style coordinate into decimal degrees

    Keyword arguments:
    nmea_coord -- numeric part of a NMEA coordinate
    direction -- a character indicating [N]orth, [S]outh, [E]ast, [W]est

    """
    sign = 1.0
    # if we are west or south, the answer should be negative
    if (direction in ["S", "W"]):
        sign = -1.0
    nmea_coord = abs(nmea_coord)      # strip the input sign
    deg = math.floor(nmea_coord/100)      # extract the degrees
    minutes = nmea_coord - (deg*100)      # extract the minutes
    ret_value = deg + (minutes/60.0)       # re-combine degrees and minutes
    return ret_value * sign            # re-apply the sign
```

With a little more code, we can capture NMEA sentences from a serial port
and display our latitude and longitude in real time:

```
def parse_NMEA_GPGGA(input_sentence):
    """Extract latitude and longitude from a NMEA $GPGGA string

    Keyword arguments:
    input_sentence -- string containing entire NMEA $GPGGA sentence
    """
    lat_value, lat_dir, lon_value, lon_dir = string.split(input_sentence,
        ",")[2:6]
    lat = NMEA_to_DecDeg(float(lat_value), lat_dir)
    lon = NMEA_to_DecDeg(float(lon_value), lon_dir)
    return (lat, lon)

def parse_NMEA_file(fp):
    """Parse a file containing NMEA sentences and extract positions
        Input is an open file handle"""
    #fp = open(source_name)
    position_list = []
    while 1:
        line = fp.readline()
        if not line:
            break
        # check to see if this is a GGA sentence, which
        # contains a Lat/Lon position
        if(line[0:6] == "$GPGGA"):
            # display the latitude / longitude
            position = parse_NMEA_GPGGA(line)
            print "Position: ", position[0] , ",", position[1]
            position_list.append(position)
    return position_list

import serial
fp = serial.Serial("COM3", baudrate=4800)
parse_NMEA_file(fp)
```

This code requires a Python module called *pySerial*. This module is available at *http://pyserial.sourceforge.net/*.

## Displaying GPS Data in a GUI Application

Text-based mapping software is not very exciting. A more useful approach is to render map data onto a 2-D window. In the following example, we will see how to build a cross-platform Python application that uses the Tkinter GUI library to display GPS data, with the ability to zoom and pan. Figure 5-42 shows this application displaying a captured GPS session along with Wi-Fi locations located using NetStumbler (a free wireless-network sniffer for Windows). You can also use this program to display waypoints captured on a hike, general points of interest, geocaches, and so on.

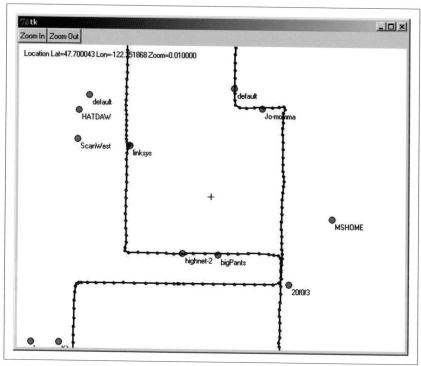

*Figure 5-42. Our sample application displaying a GPS log and Wi-Fi hotspots in the area*

It is easy to be intimidated by mapping software, but it is really quite simple after you master coordinate conversions. There are two coordinate planes involved in our application: the latitude/longitude plane and the $x/y$ pixel plane on our GUI drawing surface. Real-world coordinates are bounded by $(-90,-180)$ and $(90,180)$, whereas GUI surfaces are bounded by $(0,0)$ and (width,height). Translating between these is just a matter of scaling and shifting coordinate values. Since we need the ability to zoom and pan in our application, we must introduce an intermediate step to crop our world plane to fit a smaller viewing area. The complete coordinate conversion process is demonstrated in Figure 5-43.

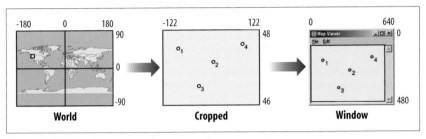

Figure 5-43. Visual representation of coordinate conversion

The following Python class encapsulates all the work necessary to reproject coordinates in our application. The class needs to know the width and height of the output window upon creation. Internally, the class stores the latitude and longitude at the center of its real-world map along with a zoom variable that describes how large of a section to display. The zoom value is actually the distance from the center of the map to the left or right edge. Because of this, a large zoom value will display the entire world, and a small value will show a close-up map:

```python
class MapCoords:
    """Translate between Lat/Lon coordinates and screen x,y positions"""
    def __init__(self, in_width, in_height):
        self.width  = in_width;
        self.height = in_height;
        self.zoom = 0.02
        self.ratio = float(self.height) / float(self.width)
        # place your starting position here:
        self.set_center(47.7000427246 , -122.351867676)
    def set_center(self, new_lat, new_lon):
        self.lat = new_lat
        self.lon = new_lon
    def zoom_in(self):
        self.zoom /= 2.0
    def zoom_out(self):
        self.zoom *= 2.0
    def latlon_to_pixels(self, (in_lat, in_lon)):
        x = math.floor( ( in_lon - (self.lon - (self.zoom / 2.0) ) ) /
            ( self.zoom ) * self.width )
        y = math.floor( ( in_lat - (self.lat - (self.zoom * self.ratio / 2.0)
            ) ) / ( self.zoom * self.ratio ) * self.height )
        return (x, y)
    def pixels_to_latlon(self, (in_x, in_y)):
```

```
       lon = (float(in_x)/self.width) * self.zoom + (self.lon - self.zoom/2.0)
       lat = (float(in_y)/self.height) * self.zoom * self.ratio + (self.lat
           - self.zoom * self.ratio / 2.0)
       return (lat, lon)
```

Once this class is instantiated, we can pan or zoom the map, as well as convert back and forth between lat/lon and screen pixels.

The next step is to create a few classes to store and draw our map data. The Waypoint class allows us to parse a CSV file and display waypoints with a red dot and a text label. The GpsTrack class parses and displays a file containing NMEA sentences. The GPS log is rendered as a multisegment line with blue dots on the intersections. The result is a smooth path showing our route history. Both of these classes have a draw( ) method that converts each data point into a pixel *x,y* location and then renders the object onto a Tkinter canvas object. For more information about the Tkinter library, see the Python documentation at *http://docs.python.org*.

```
class Waypoints:
    """Load and draw waypoints in a file with this format:
    47.2543,-121.5324,Linksys
    47.2534,-121.4634,Default
    """

    def __init__(self, filename):
        fp = open(filename)
        self.waypoints = [ ]
        while(1):
            line = fp.readline( )
            if not line:
                break
            lat, lon, name = string.split(line, ",")
            # store lat, lon, and waypoint name
            self.waypoints.append( (float(lat), float(lon), name) )
    def draw(self, map, canvas):
        """Draw waypoints by translating coordinates and drawing onto a Tk
        canvas

        Keyword arguments:
        mapc -- an object of type MapCoords
        canvas -- a Tk canvas object
        """

        for (lat, lon, name) in self.waypoints:
            # translate real-world coordinates to x,y locations
            x, y = map.latlon_to_pixels( (lat, lon) )
            # draw a red circle and a text label
            canvas.create_oval((x-5, y-5, x+5, y+5), fill="red")
            canvas.create_text(x+5, y+5, text=name, anchor="nw")

class GpsTrack:
    """Load and draw a GPS track file in NMEA format"""
    def __init__(self, filename):
```

```
        fp = open(filename)
        self.track = parse_NMEA_file(fp)
    def draw(self, map, canvas):
        old_x = 0
        for position in self.track:
            # convert real-world to x,y pixel locations
            new_x, new_y = map.latlon_to_pixels(position)
            if old_x:
                # connect last position to this one with a black line
                canvas.create_line(old_x, old_y, new_x, new_y, width=2)
            # draw a blue circle at each intersection
            canvas.create_oval((new_x-2, new_y-2, new_x+2, new_y+2),
                fill="blue", outline="black")
            # store last coordinates
            old_x, old_y = new_x, new_y
```

Now that we have code to draw our map data, it is time to build a GUI interface. The following code creates a window with the ability to zoom and recenter by clicking a button or the map:

```
class App:
    """Created a TK GUI that allows viewing of a map containing
    a gps track and waypoints.  Zooming and panning are supported."""
    def __init__(self, master):
        """This ctor requires a Tk object to be passed in master"""
        self.width, self.height = 640, 480
        self.map = MapCoords(self.width, self.height)
        # create the buttons at the top
        toolbar = Frame(master)
        toolbar.pack(side=TOP, fill=X)
        Button(toolbar, text="Zoom In", command=self.zoom_in).pack(side=LEFT)
        Button(toolbar, text="Zoom Out", command=self.zoom_out).pack(side=LEFT)
        # create the canvas we will use for drawing a map
        self.canvas = Canvas(root, height=self.height, width=self.width,
            background="white")
        # capture mouse click events on the map
        self.canvas.bind("<Button-1>", self.click)
        self.wpt = Waypoints("wifi.txt")
        self.track = GpsTrack("nmea.txt")
        self.draw_map()
    def click(self, event):
        """This is the callback for clicks in the canvas area.  Clicks are
            translated into lat, lon and used to re-position the map"""
        # translate the on-screen x,y coordinates into real-world lat, lon
        lat, lon = self.map.pixels_to_latlon((event.x, event.y))
        # re-center map and re-draw
        print lat, ",", lon
        self.map.set_center(lat, lon)
        self.draw_map()
    def zoom_out(self):
        self.map.zoom_out()
        self.draw_map()
    def zoom_in(self):
```

```
            self.map.zoom_in( )
            self.draw_map( )
      def draw_map(self):
          """Remove all drawing objects from the Tk canvas, and re-draw them
              with new coordinates"""
          # delete old drawing items
          self.canvas.delete("all")
          # show the current viewing position and zoom
          self.canvas.create_text(10,10,text="Location Lat=%f Lon=%f Zoom=%f"
              % (self.map.lat, self.map.lon, self.map.zoom), anchor="nw")
          self.wpt.draw(self.map, self.canvas)
          self.track.draw(self.map, self.canvas)
          # place a crosshair in the middle of the screen
          self.canvas.create_line(self.width/2-5, self.height/2, self.width
              /2+5, self.height/2)
          self.canvas.create_line(self.width/2, self.height/2-5, self.width/2,
              self.height/2+5)
          self.canvas.pack( )

  from Tkinter import *
  root = Tk( )
  app = App(root)
  root.mainloop( )
```

Since this application only displays data stored in a file, it does not take advantage of a mobile computer with a live GPS feed. In order to display live updates, the previous code would need an additional thread to populate new data into the GUI. If you are interested in adding this functionality, see *http://www.mappinghacks.com/projects/carcomputer* and the next hack, "Build Your Own Car Navigation System with GpsDrive" [Hack #63].

—*Thomas Hargrove*

# HACK #63  Build Your Own Car Navigation System with GpsDrive

Watch your position on a map move as you move. What a novel concept!

Thomas Hargrove is right in "Build a Car Computer" [Hack #62] that having an in-car (or on-bike) navigation system makes you the envy of all your (geek) friends. GpsDrive is an open source Linux, FreeBSD, and Mac OS X program that connects to a GPS and displays your current position and your track on a map. GpsDrive also has an interface to aid you in downloading maps from Expedia, or you can make your own maps.

One night I tested the program's map-download function on a drive down to a hosting center in Fremont. I needed to add another hard drive to the server that hosts *http://geocoder.us* and *http://mappinghacks.com*. As I headed south, I left the area of the GpsDrive map that I had prepared in advance. If you drive off of the current map, GpsDrive stops showing your current position. So when I pulled up at a stoplight in San Francisco, I connected to a random open wireless network and downloaded a map. I repeated this pattern through most of the city: stop at a light, try to connect, download one or two maps, and then pull away.

There is something strangely compelling about seeing your track as it picks its way across a map that you just downloaded while stopped at a light.

## Installing and Using GpsDrive

GpsDrive is available at: *http://www.gpsdrive.de*. Under Linux, download the appropriate RPM and then type:

```
$ rpm -ivh gpsdrive-2.09.i386.rpm.
```

Of course, you can also compile from source code. Under FreeBSD, use the ports collection:

```
$ cd /usr/ports/astro/gpsdrive
$ sudo make install; make clean
$ rehash
```

And then start GpsDrive:

```
$ gpsdrive
```

GpsDrive supports various GPS options. I connected a Garmin III plus to the serial port on a machine running Fedora Core 2. In GpsDrive, click on Preferences → Settings 2. I set my GPS to communicate in NMEA mode, and so I selected "Use serial conn" to directly talk to the serial port. I set the serial port to */dev/ttyS1*, and then used *chmod* to set the permissions on */dev/ttyS1*. NMEA talks at 4800 by default, so leave that alone.

Clicking "Download map" brings up the dialog shown in Figure 5-44. You can select the source of your map and the scale. The filename is automatically incremented, so you can download as many maps as you want. The maps are stored as GIF images in the directory specified under Preferences → Settings 2 → Maps directory. GpsDrive uses the file *map_koord.txt* (can you tell it was written by Germans?) as a simple georeferencing system.

A sample *map_koord.txt* file:

```
map_file0000.gif 38.44337 -122.71536 3950
map_file0001.gif 38.44346 -122.71544 98750
```

In this example, *map_file0001.gif* is centered at 38.44346, −122.71544 and will be shown when you zoom out at a scale of about 1:100,000 (Figure 5-45).

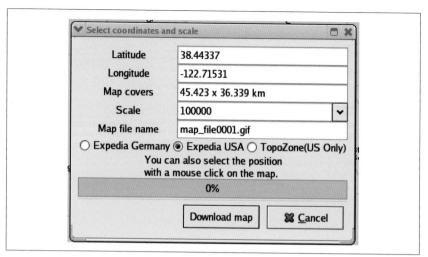

Figure 5-44. GpsDrive map download window

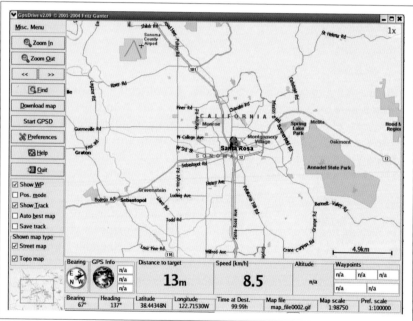

Figure 5-45. Downloaded map in GpsDrive

When you zoom in too far, you can see the effects of wandering GPS accuracy. In Figure 5-46, you can see a "track" I gathered while standing still.

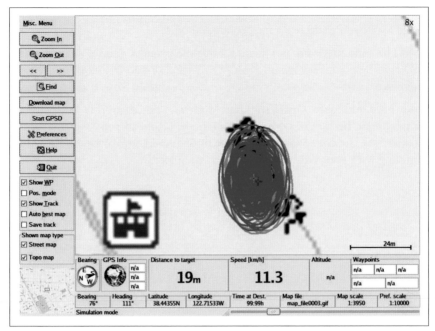

*Figure 5-46. Zooming in while sitting still shows the effects of GPS "drift"*

## Adding Your Own Maps

Since GpsDrive maps are regular images, you can create your own maps. A GpsDrive map is a 1280×1024 pixel GIF image. You can use the Misc Menu → Maps → Import map tool to import a map, or you can directly edit the *map_koord.txt* file.

Any image named *map_filennnn* (where *nnnn* is replaced with a number) can be used as a GpsDrive map. You can also edit the maps that GpsDrive downloads from Expedia. Maps are stored in your home directory in *./gpsdrive*.

Each line contains a filename, the latitude at the center of the map, and a scale. So you can customize a map by taking an existing map and adding your own annotations. If you select "Auto Best Map" from the checkboxes on the left side of the screen, GpsDrive will automatically pick the best scale for the map. You can then set the largest-scale maps to be regular photographs. It's fun to pull up at your destination and have your navigation system show you a picture.

## Playing Nice with Others

Since GpsDrive can use *gpsd* [Hack #57], you can run other GPS-aware applications in conjunction with your navigation system. For example, you can run

Kismet to do network wardriving [Hack #17], and the *gpslogger.pl* script [Hack #58] to allow you to do real time geo-annotaion.

If you like the program as much as I do, then send Friedrich Ganter a few dollars to help with his hosting fees. The PayPal donation link is on the Gps-Drive site.

Now have fun with GpsDrive, but (and you can hear this one coming, right?) please be careful while driving (and yes, I mean *you*, with the laptop balanced on the console, cup of coffee in one hand, cell phone in the other, fumbling with your GPS, trying to get a signal lock!).

# Mapping on Your Desktop
## Hack 64–77

> As geographers... crowd into the edges of their
> maps parts of the world which they do not know
> about, adding notes in the margin to the effect
> that beyond this lies nothing but sandy deserts
> full of wild beasts, and unapproachable bogs.
> —Plutarch, *The Life of Theseus*

At the far frontier of the world of maps, we find the province of Geographic Information Systems. Geographic Information Systems, better known as GIS, come in a number of shapes and sizes, but they all focus on the acquisition, management, analysis, and presentation of data with a spatial component. GIS tools are used by local and national governments around the world to collect and analyze the demographic patterns of their citizens and to plan roads, parks, and other civic infrastructure; by public utilities to record and plan telephone, power, water, gas, and sewer-line deployment and maintenance; by scientists to gather and interpret experimental data about our planet and the multitude of creatures that live on it; and by commercial enterprises for sales analysis and to plan the manufacture, warehousing, and shipping of goods all around the world.

It used to be the case that GIS tools were only available to academics and professionals at great expense, but the explosion of personal computing on commodity hardware and the revolution of open source software have combined to make Geographic Information Systems accessible to anyone with the patience to download a GIS tool and learn how it works. Not, mind you, that this is a trivial task to accomplish, but, if you're at all like us, we bet you'll be hooked from the instant you render your first map in GRASS or Quantum GIS and get that first glimpse of the possibilities inherent in GIS-based locative storytelling.

GIS is more than mere cartography, of course. The concept of Geographic Information Systems implies the ability to perform analysis on spatially connected data sets, to ask—and answer—questions with a geographic component. What is the median income of the residents of this area? How many earthquakes occurred in this region in the last decade? Which parts of the river will flood when it rains? Where is the best place to put a park, a gas station, a day care, a stadium, an airport? What endangered species or fragile ecosystems will be affected if we do so? All these questions, and many more like them, are approachable with a GIS and the right data sets.

Before we dive into the realm of GIS and desktop mapping, let's take a moment to consider what kinds of data are useful in Geographic Information Systems. Broadly, the two basic types of GIS data you'll find are raster data and vector data.

*Raster data* typically consists of a layer of cells laid out in a grid, just like a bitmap image, except that the raster layer corresponds to some explicit region of Earth's surface. Each cell is rather like the pixels of a bitmap, in that a numeric value is associated with each cell, representing something about the corresponding place. If the raster layer represents elevation, then the cell values might be meters above sea level. If the raster layer depicts ecosystems, then the cell values might correspond to ecosystem types. Alternatively, if the raster layer contains a scanned hand-drawn map or an aerial photo, then the cell might actually be a bitmap pixel!

In contrast, *vector data* is used to represent the geometry of place. Individual locations, such as archaeological sites and wireless network nodes, are often described as a point, with a single coordinate pair. Linear features, such as roads and rivers, are often depicted as a connected series of points, forming a line. Finally, sequences of connected line segments can form polygons, which are used to represent things that have physical boundaries, such as parks, municipal boundaries, national borders, and coastlines. With these three geometric primitives—points, lines, and polygons—nearly every aspect of our world can be cataloged and depicted at any scale.

Geography students are often taught that "raster is faster, but vector is correcter." With that in mind, let's get started!

A word to Linux users about obtaining GRASS and other bits of open source GIS software: if you're running Debian GNU/Linux, you should add the *DebianGis* repository to your */etc/apt/sources.list*. You can find out more about *DebianGis* at *http://pkg-grass.alioth.debian.org/cgi-bin/wiki.pl*. If you're running Fedora Core or any other RPM-based distribution (Mandrake, SuSE, etc.), check out the Mapping Hacks repository of GIS packages at *http://mappinghacks.com/rpm*.

## HACK #64 Mapping Local Areas of Interest with Quantum GIS

When you need to explore a new area but don't have a quick way to get a "bird's-eye" view of the land, a GIS browser can come in handy.

Sometimes you find yourself interested in an area, perhaps for recreation, relocation, or just out of an overwhelming sense of curiosity. There are many sources of free GIS data and imagery available on the Internet—maybe you've gotten a hold of a piece of geospatial data and just want to see what it contains. In this hack, we are going to explore a new area by downloading an aerial photograph and the corresponding topographic map. We will use *Quantum GIS*, or *QGIS* to its friends, to display the data. QGIS runs under Linux and various flavors of Unix.

First you need to download and install QGIS. QGIS source code, RPMs, and installation instructions are available from *http://qgis.org/*. Debian Linux users will find the apt repository at *http://bullhorn.org/debian/* useful.

### Selecting Our Area of Interest

The first task is to find the spot we are interested in and download some data. Suppose we want to make a trip to the Grand Canyon and are interested in taking a look at some of its features prior to traveling. For the purposes of this hack, we will choose an area around Burro Canyon. The next task is to find the image(s) and topographic map from a free source. Since we don't know exactly where Burro Canyon is (we've only heard about it in line at the espresso stand), we will use the USGS Geographic Names Information System search tool.

### Finding Our Spot

The GNIS tool can be found at *http://geonames.usgs.gov/gnishome.html*. GNIS contains information on about two million geographic features in the U.S. The other good thing about GNIS is that it is integrated with Terraserver **[Hack #4]**. Once we find the right Burro Canyon, we can jump right to the data we want. The GNIS search page allows searching by feature name, state, county, elevation, feature type, and some other parameters. Figure 6-1 shows the GNIS search page with our Burro Canyon search parameters already entered.

After running the query, we are presented with a list of eight candidates that match our search criteria. A little clicking around reveals that the Burro Canyon in the Havasupai Point 7.5-minute quadrangle is the one we want. By

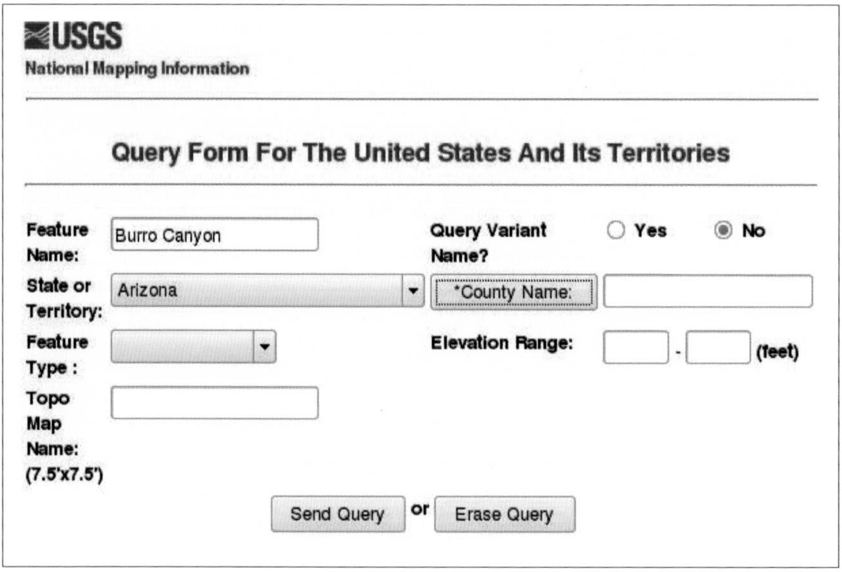

*Figure 6-1. Searching the GNIS*

clicking on the hyperlink shown in Figure 6-2, we can get to the page that has links to both the USGS *Digital Orthophoto Quadrangle* (DOQ) aerial photograph and the *Digital Raster Graphic* (DRG), which is the digitized USGS topographic map. Microsoft's Terraserver [Hack #4] hosts both of these items.

## Getting the Data

Using the DRG and DOQ links on the GNIS search result page, we can navigate Terraserver and download the images.

To fetch the DRG:

1. Click on the View USGS Digital Raster Graphic (DRG) link on the GNIS results page. The Terraserver web site loads the selected area of interest.

2. In the left panel, change the map size to Large.

3. At the top of the page, click on Download.

4. Follow the instructions to the left of the image to save it. When saving the image, give it a reasonable name (e.g., *burro_canyon_topo.jpg*).

5. To display the image in the proper coordinate system, we also need the world file. Click on the "GIS World Coordinates" link in the left panel and save the coordinate file as *burro_canyon_topo.jgw*. This file is known as a world file and is used to place the image in a real-world coordinate system.

National Mapping Information

| Feature Name: | Burro Canyon |
|---|---|
| Feature Type: | valley |
| State: | Arizona |
| County: | Coconino |
| Latitude / Longitude (nn°nn'nn" / nnn°nn'nn") | USGS 7.5' x 7.5' Map |
| 361440N 1122103W | Havasupai Point |
| 361605N 1122111W | King Arthur Castle |

TopoZone.com Display feature in TopoZone.

Display FIPS55 Place Code Note: Not all place codes are available through this site. To search the FIPS55 database or download FIPS55 files, go to the FIPS55 site

View USGS Digital Raster Graphic (DRG) covering this feature from TerraServer. A DRG is a digitized version of a USGS topographic map. Visit the USGS Digital Backyard for more information.

View USGS Digital Orthophoto Quadrangle (DOQ) covering this feature from TerraServer. A DOQ is a black-and-white, aerial photographic image map. Note that images are not available for all locations. Visit the USGS Digital Backyard for more information.

*Figure 6-2. Search results from the GNIS*

Now we have the georeferenced DRG saved as a JPEG image.

Next we will get the DOQ for the same area. Click on the "Back to Terraserver" link below the DRG image to go back to the map display. To download the DOQ:

1. Find the "Other Imagery" section in the left panel. For Burro Canyon there is a link to an aerial photo taken September 21, 1992.

2. Click on the link to display the image.

3. Download and save both the image and the world file using the same process used for the DRG (Steps 4–6). Name the image *burro_canyon_doq.jpg* and the world file *burro_canyon_doq.jgw*.

## Displaying the Data

Now we can look at the data layers we have downloaded. The advantage to using a GIS is that we can view the layers along with other data we might

have. QGIS allows you to overlay multiple layers, including data imported
from a GPS using the QGIS GPS-importer plug-in.

To display the Burro Canyon data, start QGIS and follow these steps:

1. Click on the "Add a Raster Layer" toolbar button or choose "Add a Raster Layer" from the View menu.

2. Change the "File type" to "All other files" (*.*).

3. Navigate to the directory where you saved the data.

4. Hold down the Ctrl key and click on both the DOQ and the DRQ JPEG files.

5. Click Open to load the layers.

QGIS should now look similar to Figure 6-3. Your view may look different if
the DRG was loaded on top of the DOQ.

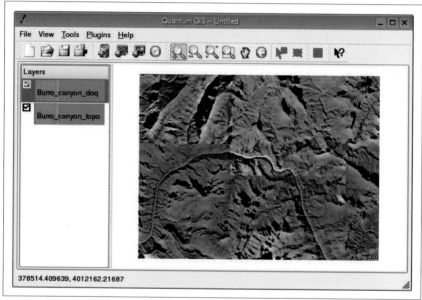

*Figure 6-3. QGIS, with the Burro Canyon DOQ and DRG loaded*

It's not very useful to have one image covered up by the other, so QGIS
allows you to set transparency on an image. With the topographic map and
aerial photograph, we can get an interesting, almost 3-D appearance by setting the top layer to about 55 percent transparency. To set transparency for
the DOQ (our top layer), double-click on the *burro_canyon_doq* name in the
legend. This will bring up the "Raster Layer Properties" dialog shown in
Figure 6-4.

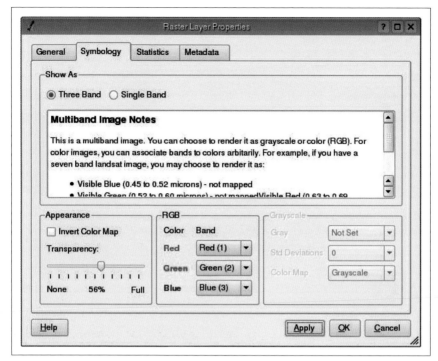

*Figure 6-4. QGIS's Raster Layer Properties dialog*

Click on the Symbology tab, move the transparency slider to the desired level, and click the Apply button. There are a number of other settings that can be adjusted. You can modify the colors, invert the color map, and change the pseudocolor. On the General tab, you can set the display name for the layer. Right now the display name is set to the filename. You can change it to something more aesthetically pleasing if you like.

After adjusting the transparency and any other setting you would like to change, click OK. Now we get a pseudo-3-D effect with the aerial photo and the topographic layer working together, as shown in Figure 6-5. Notice that we have changed the display name for the two layers. We also zoomed in a bit to better display the Burro Canyon area.

## Adding Vector Data

The pseudo 3-D image is nice to look at, but we could add more data to the map that would give us even more information. Some examples might be GPS tracks or waypoints, cultural features, or other boundaries. There are numerous sources of free data on the Internet. Since the Grand Canyon is a National Park, data is available from the National Park Service

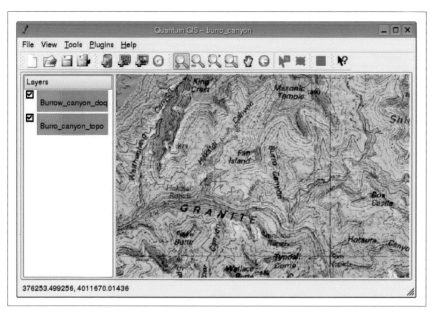

*Figure 6-5. QGIS, showing Burro Canyon, with the DOQ layer at 56% transparency*

clearinghouse at *http://nps.gov/gis/data_info/clearinghouse.html*. Using the clearinghouse web site, you can download data by selecting a state and viewing what's available. Following the links to Grand Canyon National Park, we can download additional data for our area of interest. To give this a try, download the hydrology data from *http://www.nps.gov/gis/park_gisdata/ arizona/grca.htm*, unzip it, and add the *hydro_main* (rivers/streams) layer to the map.

Projection problems.  The first thing you will notice is that, as Figure 6-6 illustrates, the newly added hydro layer does not line up properly with the topographic or DOQ layer. The hydro layer is offset to the southeast of the topographic layer, which is a sure sign that something is amiss with the cartographic projections used in our two data sets.

In this case, we have a classic example of datum mismatch. The Terraserver images are based on the North American Datum of 1983 (NAD83). If we look at the metadata—a really useful thing to do when using GIS data—for the hydro layer, we see that the spatial reference section indicates that it uses the North American Datum of 1927 (NAD27). The difference between these two geodetic datums, or coordinate origins, can be off by as much as a kilometer, depending on the latitude and longitude.

Dealing with it.  We could do a datum transformation using the NadCon standard (*http://www.ngs.noaa.gov/TOOLS/Nadcon/Nadcon.html*), provided that

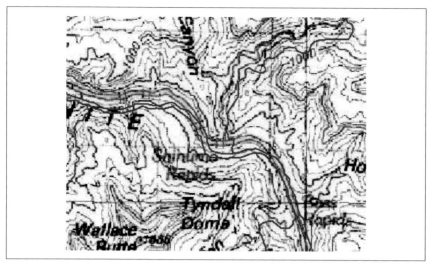

*Figure 6-6. Datum problem*

we had appropriate tools at our disposal. Alternatively, we could try using the *ogr2ogr* tool to transform the hydro layer into the NAD83 datum, as described in detail in "Convert Geospatial Data Between Different Formats" [Hack #68]. Or, we can just do a quick hack to line up the data, realizing that:

- The transformation should not be used for any sort of analysis.
- The transformation won't be perfect over all areas of our map.

**Making it line up.** Remember the world files we downloaded for each of the images? We can modify them to get a better alignment between our images and the hydro layer. A world file consists of map units per pixel, rotation information, and, most importantly for our purposes, the coordinates of the upper left corner of the image. By modifying the *x*- and *y*-coordinates of the upper left corner, we can "move" the image. The world file for the topographic layer contains:

```
16.000000
0.000000
0.000000
-16.000000
371200.000000
4016000.00000
```

These last two lines represent the upper left corner of our image, in meters from the projection origin.

First we must determine the offset. Zoom into an area with an identifying feature, such as a stream intersection or sharp bend. QGIS displays the (*x*, *y*) coordinate of the cursor in the status bar. This information can be used to get the coordinates of our stream intersection on the hydro layer and on the topographic layer. By calculating the difference, we can adjust the world file to line up the image with the hydro layer.

The *x* and *y* offsets are approximately 112 meters and 197 meters, respectively. Edit the world file stored in *burro_canyon_topo.jgw* and change the (*x*, *y*) coordinates in the last two lines of the file accordingly:

```
16.000000
0.000000
0.000000
-16.000000
371312.000000
4015803.000000
```

We can now remove the topo layer from QGIS and add it back in to see the changes. Figure 6-7 shows the same view with the adjusted topo layer. Note that the hydro layer now lines up much better. Remember this is a hack—not the recommended way to transform rasters to match other data. But for display/cartographic purposes, it is one quick-and-dirty way to line up the data.

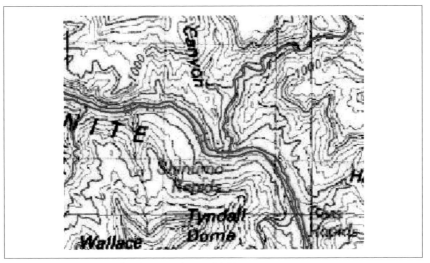

*Figure 6-7. After manually adjusting the world file*

## In Conclusion

With a large amount of free data available on the Internet, we can fairly quickly display an area of interest. QGIS, in conjunction with the other web sites and tools available, makes it easy to visualize the data. Sometimes the data are in differing projections and/or datums, but with a little clever manipulation, you can always torture it into submission.

If Python and wxWidgets are more to your liking than C++ and Qt, you might have a look at *Thuban*, which has many features similar to QGIS, as well as a similar license. We don't have the space to cover Thuban as well, so we'll just point you to its web site, *http://thuban.intevation.net/*.

—*Gary Sherman*

# Extract Data from Maps with Manifold

**#65**  Just getting map data isn't enough to give you all the information the map might contain. If you're working with complex data, a GUI interface that lets you select the areas you consider relevant and then calculate the results can be extremely convenient—if you can do it cheaply!

Manifold (*http://manifold.net*), a Windows-based GIS application, costs $245 but offers much of the same functionality as its "traditional" but much more expensive GIS counterparts. It can read a wide variety of map formats and provides a user interface that's deliberately familiar to people who work in Windows. You can open a map, select the bits in which you're interested, and do quick calculations on the data associated with your selected areas. Manifold also lets you create maps and perform sophisticated analysis, though this hack doesn't have the space to go into that.

For a recent project, I needed to know the population and number of houses in a specific area. While I've usually been able to get that kind of information from the American Fact Finder web site (*http://factfinder.census.gov/ home/saff/main.html?_lang=en*), making effective use of that prepackaged data means that the areas you're interested in have to match up with the places defined by the Census Bureau. In my case, since I was trying to calculate the population of the hamlet of Varna, New York, a place with no municipal government, the prepackaged data wasn't much help. Instead, I turned to census block data available through maps at the Cornell University Geospatial Repository (CUGIR, at *http://cugir.mannlib.cornell.edu/*) and created a cluster of blocks that roughly corresponded to the boundaries of the hamlet.

The first step was getting the information I needed. In my case, that meant visiting *http://new-gis.mannlib.cornell.edu/CUGIR_Data/cens2000/109blk00s. zip* (a file that contains census block maps and data for Tompkins County, where Varna is) and extracting its contents. There are several files in there, but the primary ones I needed to work with were *tgr109blk00s.shp* (the shapefile) and *tgr109blk00s.dbf* (the underlying datafile).

To try this project yourself, download and extract the census block maps and open Manifold. Create a new project (through File → New) and go to

File → Import → Drawing to open the shapefile. When you choose the shapefile, Manifold also imports the data from the database file. It asks which pieces you want, as shown in Figure 6-8.

*Figure 6-8. Importing data with a shapefile in Manifold*

You can then open the drawing and double-click on "Tgr109blks00s Drawing" in the Project pane at right, displaying the census blocks of Tompkins County, as shown in Figure 6-9.

To zoom in, click the magnifying glass with the plus sign in it and then click on the map where you'd like to see more detail. Figure 6-10 shows a closer view of Varna, which is centered roughly on –76.4363, 42.4561.

After turning off the magnification cursor (by clicking on the magnifying glass with the plus sign in it again), you can select a parcel and then examine its field. Click on a parcel to select it (it will turn red) and then right-click it and select "Fields..." If you scroll down the dialog box that appears, you'll see the data for that particular census block, as shown in Figure 6-11.

> While this general approach will work for any map you import into Manifold, the metadata information describing this map at *http://cugir2.mannlib.cornell.edu/Isite/CUGIR_METADATA/blk00s.html* indicates that this map was created for New York State, and you may or may not be able to find similarly convenient maps for census blocks for other places.

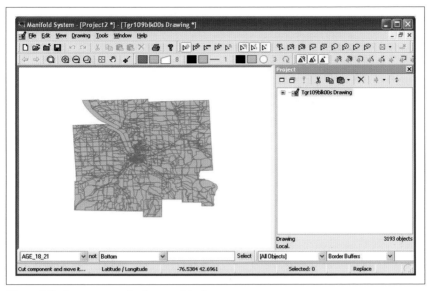

Figure 6-9. A county worth of census blocks

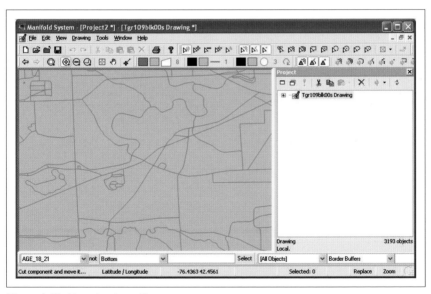

Figure 6-10. Zooming in on Varna

The next step was to select census blocks that correspond to Varna. In the Comprehensive Plan I was working with, the "hamlet area" of Varna was defined as the set of parcels shown in Figure 6-12.

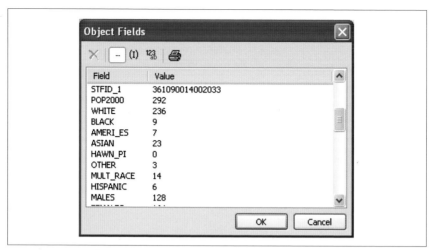

Figure 6-11. Data for one census block in Varna

Figure 6-12. Varna, defined as tax parcels

Those parcels don't precisely map to census blocks, unfortunately, but the problem is manageable because the parts of the blocks that extend beyond the parcels are largely uninhabited. (It's much easier to do reliable map processing when you can check out the area physically on occasion.) Selecting all the parcels that contain the Varna hamlet area by Control-clicking produces the selection shown in Figure 6-13.

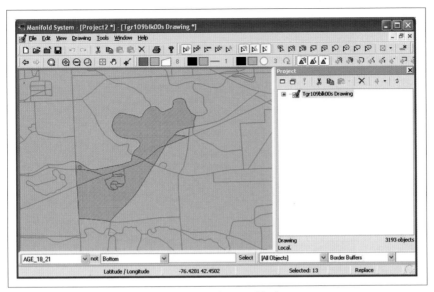

*Figure 6-13. Varna, defined as a collection of census blocks*

The easiest way to calculate the total population for this area is combine all of these blocks into a single selection. Rather than making the change to the original map, copy the blocks. Then, go to File → Create → Drawing and create a drawing named *VarnaCoreBlocks* or something similar. You'll need to double-click it in the Project pane at right to open it, and then paste in your blocks. Manifold will show you that it's adding data to the table with a dialog box like that shown in Figure 6-14, and the result will look like Figure 6-15.

The easiest way to get totals for the information in these blocks is to dissolve them into a single large piece. The Drawing menu's "Dissolve..." option does just this. When you select it, you'll see a dialog box like that shown in Figure 6-16.

In this case, the point is simply to dissolve all of the boundaries, but Manifold expects that people will be somewhat more selective. You can choose between [All Objects] and [Selected Objects], letting you dissolve across an entire drawing or just selected parts. You can also choose a field to match on for combining objects. To dissolve all the boundaries, choose a field in which all the values for the field are identical. In this case, STATE will work fine, since all of the pieces are in New York State. Clicking OK produces the result shown in Figure 6-17, and showing the fields for that one area produces the result shown in Figure 6-18.

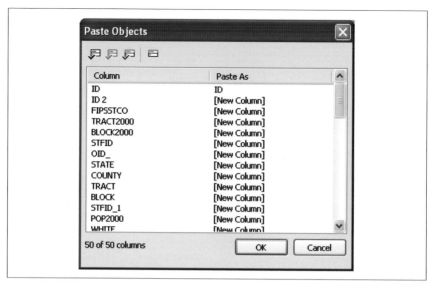

Figure 6-14. Data being pasted

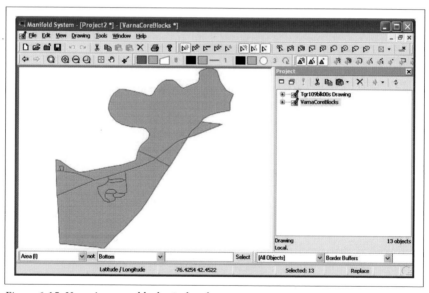

Figure 6-15. Varna's census blocks, isolated

The population of Varna, as defined by the plan noted earlier, is 679 people, according to the 2000 census. (Because Manifold adds all the values, the
averages included in the data don't come out so well and need to be recalcu-
lated.) One final nice touch is that you can combine the new drawing with

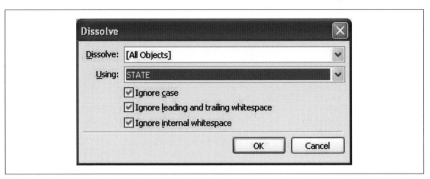

Figure 6-16. *Choosing a field for dissolving boundaries*

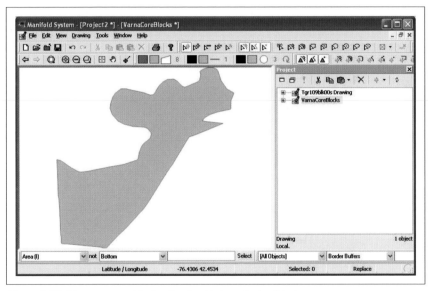

Figure 6-17. *Varna census blocks dissolved into a single object*

the old one to create a map that highlights the area chosen for calculation. In Manifold, go to File → Create → Map..., and select the two drawings, as shown in Figure 6-19.

Open the map you've created and then right-click on the tab for "Tgr109blk00s Drawing." Choose "Opacity..." from the menu that appears, and set it to 30%. If you then zoom in a little, you'll see the darker Varna area standing out against the surrounding blocks, and the divisions for the blocks it contains are still visible, as shown in Figure 6-20.

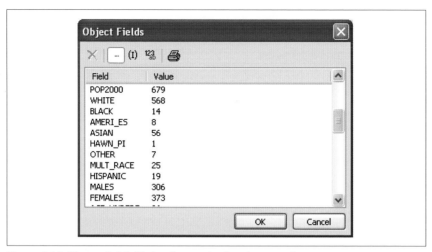

*Figure 6-18. The totaled fields for that single object's census data*

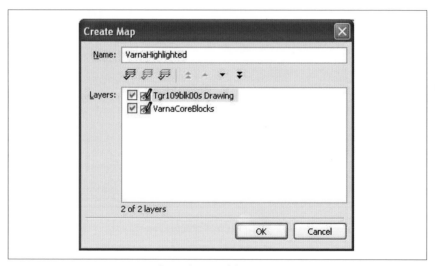

*Figure 6-19. Creating a map with two layers of drawings*

This is barely scratching the surface of the kinds of things you can do with Manifold, which lets you create, edit, and analyze maps in ways this hack can't begin to explain.

—*Simon St.Laurent*

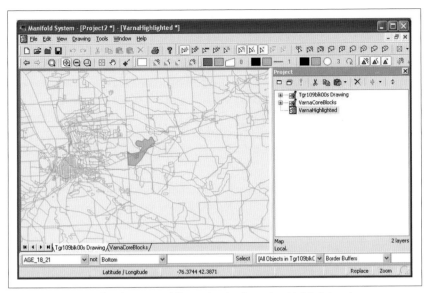

*Figure 6-20. Two related maps at different levels of opacity, highlighting the area on which calculations were made*

## Java-Based Desktop Mapping with Openmap

**#66** Make personalized maps on your desktop using a free Java program.

While its history goes back farther than written language, serious cartography has always been a pursuit of governments or wealthy, esoteric intellectuals—until now. For the past decade or so, we have had the computational power to run mapping software on desktop PCs, and a number of companies have provided us with digital atlases with extensive street maps. In the mid-1990s, MapQuest exploded onto the scene, forever changing the way people send out party directions. None of this software, however, really allowed people to *personalize* their maps. That continued to be a feature of software that cost thousands, if not tens of thousands, of dollars. Only recently has lower-priced, consumer-grade *mapmaking* software become commonplace, and it still isn't as easy to use as your average Microsoft or Adobe product. However, for über-hackers like us, it's ready for prime time!

### Preparation

This hack gets us started with mapmaking in Java by installing an open source application called Openmap and making a custom map of the United States with it. First we'll need to install Java. Openmap requires only a Java

Runtime Environment (JRE), but since we're hackers, we'll install a Java Software Development Kit (JSDK), so that we can compile Java code in addition to executing others' programs. Download and install a JSDK from *java.sun.com*, making sure you get Version 1.4 or higher. Then download Openmap from *openmap.bbn.com*. While Openmap is open source, it is not licensed under the GPL, so if this concerns you, be sure to carefully read the license before downloading. Just make sure to copy the file *openmap.properties* from the program's installation directory into your home directory. This will be important later, as the primary way to customize the application is by editing this file.

Make sure everything is going well by running Openmap. If you get something that looks like Figure 6-21, congratulations on making your first map!

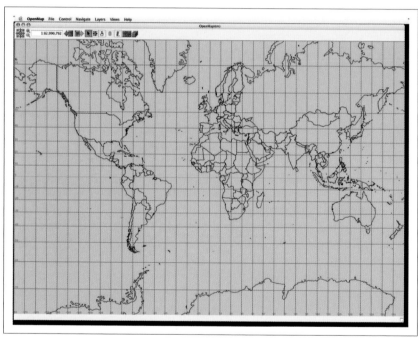

*Figure 6-21. Starting Openmap*

## Take a Spin Around Openmap

Unlike a graphics program like Photoshop or Flash, Openmap knows the real-world location of every pixel on the map. Pass your mouse over the world and see the geographic (*Lat, Lon*) and screen (*x, y*) coordinates displayed underneath Antarctica. The first thing you probably want to do is zoom in on interesting places. Openmap provides a few different ways to navigate, but we'll use the simplest to get started. Notice the navigation compass in the top left corner of the window. Click on the magnifying glass with the + in the middle to zoom in, and the one with the - to zoom out. Click on the arrows to move laterally in a given direction. You can also zoom to "bookmarked" places on the map that appear in the Layer menu. Right now, there is only one item, "World." We're going to add a new one so that our map opens to the United States.

Quit the program and open a copy of *openmap.properties* in your home directory using your favorite text editor. Search for gotoMenu.views=. There should be a number of commented-out lines that define three bookmarks for Argentina, India, and the United States. Uncomment these now. This will reveal the bookmarks in Openmap, so save your work, start the program again, and use these new menu items to quickly zoom in on the United States.

The next feature we'll reveal is the wealth of data that comes with the program. From the Layers menu, select "World Cities." The map should now look like it has the measles, covered with little red dots. We can do better than this, though. Choose "Edit Layers..." from the Layers menu. In the dialog box that appears, scroll down to find "World Cities" and click on the legend icon, which sits between the light bulb and the layer name. In the new dialog box, check "Show Location Names" and "Declutter Names." Close the "World Cities" and the Layers dialogs. Now you're well on your way to building your own personal atlas.

 If the map draws too slowly on your computer, try unchecking "Declutter Names."

## Add Data from the Web

One great thing about being in the United States is that the government provides crazy amounts of geographic data for free or very little cost. We're going to get state boundaries from the U.S. Geological Survey to add a little more detail to our U.S. maps. There are a number of other places to download data, such as *www.geo-one-stop.gov* and *nationalmap.usgs.gov*, but for our simple purposes, the National Atlas, found at *nationalatlas.gov*, is the best place to start. Go to *http://nationalatlas.gov/mapit.html*, read the system requirements, and select "Go straight to the Map Maker." Later you can explore this pretty cool site for hours, but we're just going to grab a file and go. Click on the Download button in the top right corner of the page. In the page that pops up, search for "States." You'll encounter a number of interesting pieces of data that you could download and add to your personal atlas, including crime and employment statistics, but for now keep searching until you find the data set entitled "States." Click on the link to download *statesp020.tar.gz*, and unpack this file when you're done. You should end up with a directory called *statesp020* containing these files:

- *statesp020.dbf*
- *statesp020.shp*
- *statesp020.shx*
- *statesp020.txt*

Put this folder somewhere convenient. I like to keep all my geographic data in one place, organized by country and province or state. For example, I put these files in */geodata/us/countrywide/*.

If it's not already running, fire up Openmap. From the Layers menu, choose "Add Layers..." Select "Shape Layer with Attributes" from the drop-down menu, and replace "Layer Name" with something more useful, like "U.S. States." Now we need to tell Openmap where to find the actual data. To do this, hit the Configure button. This presents the intimidating dialog box, shown in Figure 6-22.

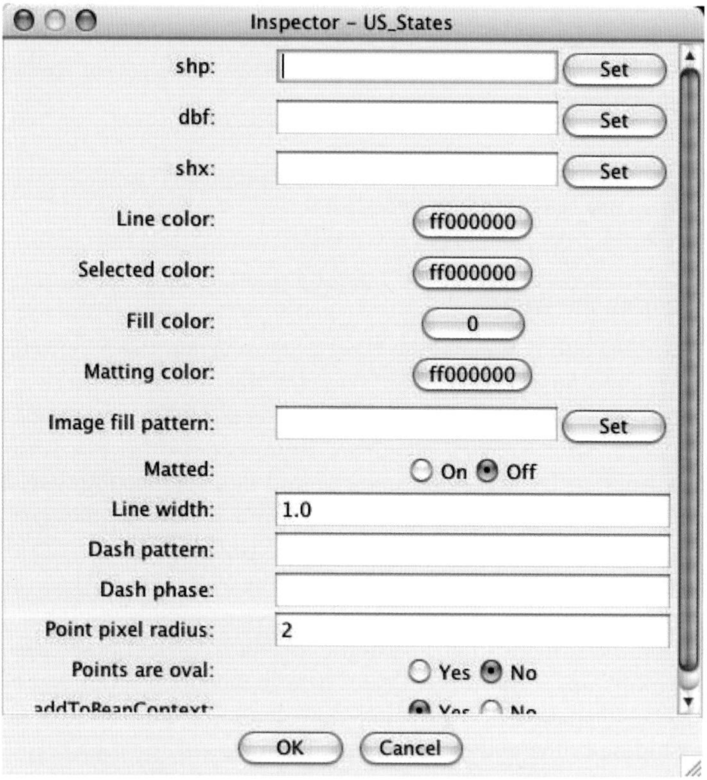

Figure 6-22. Configuring a layer in Openmap

After the first three lines, this dialog is all about cartographic symboliza-tion—picking the colors your data will draw in. The important thing to know is that default values are filled in for everything, so you just need to fill in the locations of the data set components. If you saved the data using the directory structure I used, your *.shp* file path will be */geodata/us/country-wide/states/statesp020.shp*. Similarly, your *.dbf* path will be */geodata/us/coun-trywide/states/statesp020.dbf*, and *.shx* will be */geodata/us/countrywide/states/statesp020.shx*. Enter these values and press OK. After a few seconds, the U.S. states should draw on your map in (almost) exactly the right places, as illustrated in Figure 6-23.

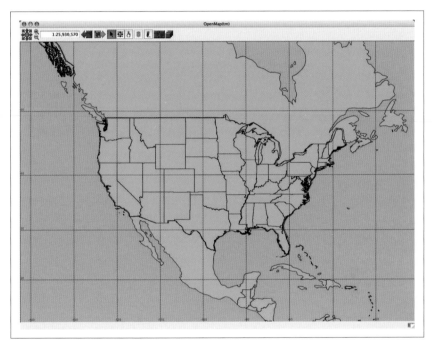

*Figure 6-23. U.S. state borders, shown in Openmap*

## Hacking the Hack: Preserve Your Settings

That was exciting, but as soon as you quit Openmap, the U.S. States layer is gone. You'll probably want to add this layer to the basic ones that are always available in the program (if you live in the U.S.). The program doesn't have a save function, but you can program this layer into Openmap's startup file. Open your *openmap.properties* file again. This time, search for openmap.layers=. This is where you specify what data should show up on your map. The rest of the file consists entirely of prop-erties that describe the location of datafiles and how they should be carto-graphically symbolized, but they won't show up at all if they aren't listed in openmap.layers. Put the word usstates at the beginning of your list, which should now look something like this:

```
openmap.layers=usstates date dtlayer distlayer quake daynight cities test
graticule demo shapePolitical
```

You may also want to add usstates to openmap.startUpLayers, so that it's visible when the program starts.

The next step is to specify what we mean by usstates. We'll enter the same information we used when specifying our "Shape Layer with Attributes" from within the program, but here we use a different syntax. Go to the end of the file and type in the following lines:

```
# My US States layer
usstates.class=com.bbn.openmap.layer.shape.ShapeLayer
usstates.prettyName=US State Boundaries
usstates.shapeFile=/ geodata/us/nationwide/states/statesp020.shp
usstates.lineColor=ff000000
usstates.fillColor=ffffffcc
```

This tells the program where to find the data. It also specifies that the outlines of all polygons should be drawn in black and the insides should be a light yellow, as shown in Figure 6-24.

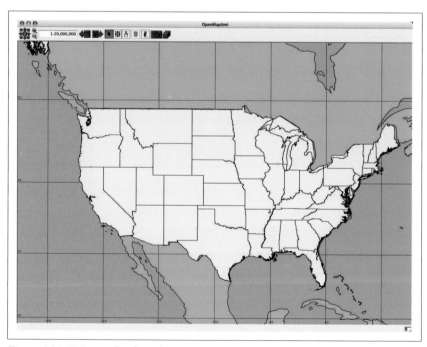

*Figure 6-24. U.S. state borders, shown in Openmap*

## The Results

I'm sure you've had that eureka moment by now, realizing you have the basic skills needed to be the best mapmaker on your block. In addition to the sites mentioned earlier, government resources like EPA's Enviromapper (*http://www.epa.gov/enviro/wme/* and *http://www.epa.gov/enviro/html/multisystem_query_java.html*) can tell you all about pollution in your community, and the Census Bureau (*http://www.census.gov/*) gives you the scoop on demographic statistics like race, income, and employment. Just think of the killer maps you can help your children produce for their next class paper!

—*Raj Singh*

## HACK #67  Seamless Data Download from the USGS

Finding geospatial data for your area becomes (almost) seamless with help from the USGS.

Need digital map data for some region of the United States, but don't know your FIPS codes from your NADs? Help is at hand in the *USGS Seamless Data Distribution System*, or SDDS. The SDDS is a web-based, DHTML interface that allows you to zoom in on a map of the U.S., select an area visually, and download the data layers of your choice, corresponding to your visual selection. This sure beats the traditional method of fetching GIS data from random FTP servers by USGS topo quadrangle name or, worse yet, some obscurely coded filename!

Start by firing up *http://seamless.usgs.gov/* in your web browser. At the time of writing, the service is still in beta, and new data sources are being added regularly. Follow the links to the SDDS service.

At a minimum, you should be able to get elevation models from the Shuttle Radar Topography Mission (SRTM) data sets, at 30 m or 90 m resolution, as well as feature data including road and hydrography (i.e., water) features. A full list of what's available now is available on the right of the display, under the Download tab. Presently, it's possible to view a lot more on the display than is actually available for download.

When the SDDS browser loads, you're presented with a map of the whole U.S., zoomed all the way out. The navigation options on the top left let you zoom in and out, and also let you select an area to zoom in on: click and hold, then drag the mouse to show the area you've outlined expanded in red or green.

Figure 6-25 shows a sample region selection in the SDDS, outlined in green. Whether the outline is red or green depends on whether it's possible to download data for that area directly from the SDDS, or whether you'll have to order hardcopy media. This in turn depends on how much data you want. If you select the 30 m SRTM data over a large area, which has high data density, you won't be able to download the whole set through Seamless. The SDDS also lets you zoom in directly to a state or a major city. Some local areas may have extra data available; for example, Sacramento, California, has a separate set of local orthophotos in addition to the U.S.-wide imagery.

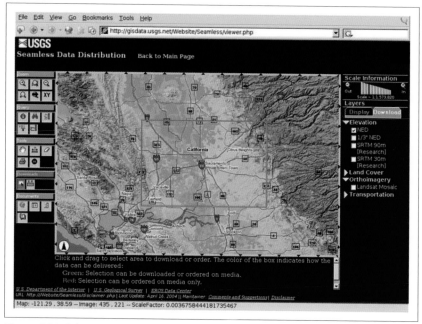

*Figure 6-25. Selecting a region to download via the SDDS*

The SDDS "rubber band" selector has one funny quirk. If you get a red outline immediately after clicking on the map, the outline won't subsequently turn green, because you've started out by including an area that Seamless doesn't cover. If this happens, try clicking a little closer in to the city or geographic feature you're trying to get data for, until your outline starts out green with your first click. You'll get a lot better results in terms of the kind of data you can download this way.

Once you've zoomed in to the extent you want to download data for, click the "Select Extent" icon on the lower left. Select a region as described earlier, and a Request Summary page will open, showing you the data sets available for that region, including data format and file size. Each data set is delivered as a ZIP file with an eight-digit filename, which contains all the relevant data and metadata. Download and unzip this file, and you should be able to load up the data set in a GIS browser like QGIS or GRASS right away.

The SDDS toolbar has a host of other nifty features. You can enter a lat/long pair in decimal format to zoom directly to that location. Or you can click on the map to get a lat/long coordinate for that point; unfortunately, this comes in degrees, minutes, and seconds! You can also measure distances between points and along a line that you describe by adding points. You can see elevation data for a point by clicking on the map, or you can create an elevation profile, a 2-D plot of the ground topography between the points, useful for line-of-sight evaluation for radio transmission.

The USGS Seamless Data Distribution System is an impressive example of how much can be done to alleviate data-access pain in a relatively low-tech, cross-browser fashion, with little more than JavaScript and flat images!

## HACK #68 Convert Geospatial Data Between Different Formats

The wide range of arcane GIS data formats can be confusing and difficult to manage, but with the right tools, you can make quick work of them.

So you found some GIS data about an area of interest: now what do you do with it? In many cases, the next step is to try to import it into a GIS application, such as GRASS or Quantum GIS. But what if you want to convert it into a more useful format first? Or what if you just want to find out what format the data is already in, what coordinate system it uses, or what region it covers?

Before we address these questions, it might help to quickly review the basics of geospatial data formats. There are two kinds of geospatial data: vector and raster. Much like a digital photo, *raster data* takes the form of a matrix of rows and columns of rectangular pixels, or *cells*. In the same way that each pixel of a digital photo has some value describing its color, each cell of a raster layer has some value associated with it that represents some detail about the world—perhaps elevation, population, land-use patterns, rainfall, or ecological criteria, like rainfall or biodiversity. Raster layers are specified with *extents*, which are the spatial coordinates the layer represents, and *spatial resolution*, which indicates how much of the surface of the planet each cell corresponds to. Each layer of raster data in a given data set is referred to as a *band*, and a single data set can contain multiple bands.

GIS gurus like to say that "raster is faster, but vector is corrector." *Vector data* is made up of points, lines, and polygons. It's typically used to represent individual locations, such as water, rail and road networks, political boundaries, park areas, municipal districts, military reservations, and so on.

Of course, be it raster or vector, most geospatial data comes with a bit of *metadata*, which describes everything we need to know to use the data, including the extents, resolution or scale, data type (e.g., integer or floating point), coordinate system and datum, and more. Sometimes the metadata is stored in the same file or files as the data itself; more often it is stored in a separate set of files, which are sometimes referred to as world files or projection files.

> Different GIS formats abound, many of them legacy or proprietary formats—such as ESRI's Ungenerate, or E00, format—which have incomplete or nonexistent free/open source implementations. We'd suggest that the canonical forms for open geodata are *GeoTIFF* for raster data and *ESRI Shapefile* for vector data, with the latter remaining the standard until GML stabilizes and is popularized.

For most of our open source geodata conversion desires, we need look no further than Frank Warmerdam's amazing Geospatial Data Abstraction Library, or *GDAL*. The GDAL library and utilities deal exclusively with raster data formats. The *OGR* library and utilities, which are shipped as part of the GDAL package, are useful for managing vector data. (The acronym OGR doesn't actually stand for anything.) Together, GDAL and OGR form a sort of Swiss Army Knife for GIS data. The GDAL package is available in source and binary forms at *http://remotesensing.org/gdal/*. You can also find it in Debian APT under *gdal-bin*.

### Converting Raster Data Between Different Formats

To illustrate use of GDAL, we'll convert a digital elevation model that we got from the U.S. Geological Survey's Seamless Data Distribution System [Hack #67] to GeoTIFF format. We selected a region of San Francisco and then opted to download the 1/3" National Elevation Data for the city. The data comes in ArcGrid format, in a ZIP file with an eight-digit filename. If we unzip this file and look inside, there's quite a lot of stuff there:

```
$ unzip 79314780.zip
$ cd 79314780
$ ls -R
79314780    METADATA.dbf METADATA.shp info
79314780.aux METADATA.prj METADATA.shx meta1.html
```

```
./79314780:
dblbnd.adf   hdr.adf      prj.adf      sta.adf      w001001.adf  w001001x.
adf

./info:
arc.dir      arc0000.dat  arc0000.nit  arc0001.dat  arc0001.nit
```

We can use the *gdalinfo* utility distributed with GDAL to examine the metadata properties of this data set. Ordinarily, *gdalinfo* is only run on a single file, but the important part of this complex arrangement of files is the directory named *79314780*, so we'll run it on that:

```
$ gdalinfo 79314780
Driver: AIG/Arc/Info Binary Grid
Size is 570, 416
Coordinate System is:
GEOGCS["NAD83",
    DATUM["North_American_Datum_1983",
    ...
    AUTHORITY["EPSG","4269"]]
Origin = (-122.517015,37.812947)
Pixel Size = (0.00027777,-0.00027777)
Corner Coordinates:
Upper Left  (-122.5170148,  37.8129466)
Lower Left  (-122.5170148,  37.6973942)
Upper Right (-122.3586859,  37.8129466)
Lower Right (-122.3586859,  37.6973942)
Center      (-122.4378504,  37.7551704)
Band 1 Block=285x4 Type=Float32, ColorInterp=Undefined
    Min=-2.201 Max=284.040
```

There's a ton of metadata here, which we excerpted earlier. The key things to note are that the data is in Arc/Info Binary Grid format, 570 pixels wide and 416 high, referenced to geographic coordinates (i.e., latitude and longitude) against the NAD 1983 datum. The origin and resolution (i.e., pixel size) are given, and from these figures the coordinates of the corners are collected. This data set consists of one band— representing elevation above sea level, presumably—in 32-bit floating-point representation, ranging from about −2 (meters, as it happens) to 284.

Now that we know a little bit about this data set, we can use another GDAL utility, *gdal_translate*, to convert our elevation to GeoTIFF, possibly in order to import it into another application:

```
$ gdal_translate -of GTiff 79314780 sf_dem.tif
Input file size is 570, 416
0...10...20...30...40...50...60...70...80...90...100 - done.
```

If you run *gdalinfo* on the resulting GeoTIFF, you'll see that the essential details are preserved. The single output file contains all of the data, and most of the metadata, of the original zipped ArcGrid file. *gdal_translate* can read and write a variety of formats; run it without any options to see which ones your version supports.

## Clipping and Warping Raster Data

*gdal_translate* has some other tricks up its sleeve. For example, if we want to extract just the portion of the digital elevation model that covers the Presidio, a national park in the northwest corner of San Francisco, we can use the "projection window" parameter of *gdal_translate* to clip out that bit and save it to a separate file. (Note that, as usual, longitude comes before latitude because it's the *x*-coordinate.)

```
$ gdal_translate -projwin -122.4862 37.8116 -122.4462 37.7860 sf_dem.tif
presidio.tif
Input file size is 570, 416
Computed -srcwin 111 4 144 92 from projected window.
0...10...20...30...40...50...60...70...80...90...100 - done.
```

If you don't specify an output format with -of, *gdal_translate* assumes you want a GeoTIFF by default.

Another common problem you find when working with geodata is that you're using one coordinate system or projection in your GIS—say, Universal Transverse Mercator—while the data you have is in another projection or coordinate system, such as latitude and longitude. Unfortunately, the situation is a bit like apples and oranges, so the new data needs to be converted to your existing projection. This process is referred to as reprojecting or *warping* the raster data, and, quite logically, the tool for the task is called *gdalwarp*. If we want to warp our DEM of the Presidio into a UTM projection in order to, say, combine it with a UTM topo layer, we might use *gdalwarp* as follows:

```
$ gdalwarp -t_srs "+proj=utm +zone=10" presidio.tif  presidio_utm.tif
0...10...20...30...40...50...60...70...80...90...100 - done.
```

The -t_srs parameter stands for "target spatial reference system," which is quite a mouthful, but it just refers to the projection you want your data warped into. *gdalwarp* also supports a -s_srs option, short for "source spatial reference system," which allows you to specify the projection and/or coordinate system that your data originates in. You usually won't need to bother specifying a source projection, but it's handy to have when dealing with raster data that doesn't have projection metadata directly attached. The projection parameters for *gdalwarp* use the same format as the PROJ.4 toolkit **[Hack #26]** and are documented more thoroughly on the PROJ.4 homepage (*http://remotesensing.org/proj/*).

*gdal_translate* and *gdalwarp* have plenty of other options, so don't hesitate
to read their manpages!

## Once More from the Top, with Vectors

That's all well and good for raster data, but what about vector data? Fortunately, the OGR half of the GDAL toolkit features a counterpart to *gdalinfo*
called *ogrinfo*. We can use *ogrinfo* to determine the features of a given vector data set as follows:

```
$ unzip tgr06075.zip
$ ls TGR*
TGR06075.MET TGR06075.RT4 TGR06075.RT7 TGR06075.RTC TGR06075.RTI TGR06075.
RTS
TGR06075.RT1 TGR06075.RT5 TGR06075.RT8 TGR06075.RTE TGR06075.RTP TGR06075.
RTT
TGR06075.RT2 TGR06075.RT6 TGR06075.RTA TGR06075.RTH TGR06075.RTR TGR06075.
RTZ
$ ogrinfo TGR06075.RT1
ERROR 4: Tiger Driver doesn't support update.
Had to open data source read-only.
INFO: Open of `TGR06075.RT1'
using driver `TIGER' successful.
1: CompleteChain (Line String)
2: AltName (None)
3: FeatureIds (None)
4: ZipCodes (None)
5: Landmarks (Point)
...
```

Here, we take the ZIP file from the Census Bureau's download site containing the TIGER/Line data for San Francisco and unpack it into the current
directory. As you can see, the 2003 TIGER/Line data set contains 17 different record types, plus a metadata file. *ogrinfo* shows the name of each layer,
along with the geometry type. If we give *ogrinfo* a specific layer name, it
returns the metadata about that particular layer:

```
$ ogrinfo -ro -so TGR06075.RT1 CompleteChain
Layer name: CompleteChain
Geometry: Line String
Feature Count: 16355
Extent: (-123.173825, 37.639830) - (-122.281780, 37.929824)
Layer SRS WKT:
GEOGCS["NAD83",
    DATUM["North_American_Datum_1983",
        SPHEROID["GRS 1980",6378137,298.257222101]]]
MODULE: String (8.0)
TLID: Integer (10.0)
SIDE1: Integer (1.0)
SOURCE: String (1.0)
FEDIRP: String (2.0)
```

```
FENAME: String (30.0)
FETYPE: String (4.0)
FEDIRS: String (2.0)
CFCC: String (3.0)
...
```

The -ro option in *ogrinfo* stands for "read-only" and is there mostly just to spare the warning about TIGER/Line being read-only. More importantly, the -so option stands for "summary only"; try running *ogrinfo* on the TIGER/Line CompleteChain layer without it! The layer metadata more or less speaks for itself. The layer consists of line strings—as opposed to polygons or points—and the GEOGCS["NAD83", ...] bit tells us that the coordinate system is latitude and longitude, using the NAD 1983 datum. After the metadata properties, we get a list of data attributes associated with each geometric feature in the layer. So far, so good.

You might be wondering what a geometry type of "None" signifies. In this case, it represents data in TIGER/Line that isn't attributable to any particular geometric feature. OGR can extract the values to a DBase-type *.dbf* file, but that's about it.

Now, let's extract the CompleteChain layer—which is, in this case, all the line segments of various kinds in San Francisco—into a more portable ESRI Shapefile, possibly for import into another GIS application.

```
$ ogr2ogr -f "ESRI Shapefile" san_fran.shp TGR06075.RT1 CompleteChain
$ ls san_fran.*
san_fran.dbf san_fran.prj san_fran.shp san_fran.shx
```

Here, we've used OGR's vector-wielding counterpart to *gdal_translate*, a utility called *ogr2ogr*. The -f option tells *ogr2ogr* in what format we expect the output; otherwise, the order of arguments is reversed from *gdal_translate*, in that the target file is put first and the data source second. This is primarily so that a list of layers to be converted can be given afterward. (We only specified one layer, but *ogr2ogr* permits multiple layers to be converted at once.) The output is an ESRI Shapefile—actually, a collection of files—which together can be imported into another application. As you might expect, you can run *ogrinfo* on the resulting shapefile to see that the data is indeed converted. You can run *ogr2ogr* without any arguments to see which formats your build supports.

## Points and Lines and Polygons, Oh My

Naturally, *ogr2ogr* also offers spatial clipping of vector data, which can be accessed via the -spat parameter. Somewhat more interesting is the option to filter based on attribute values, using an SQL-like syntax, with the -where parameter. For example, the following generates a shapefile of interstate freeways in San Francisco, by filtering the "feature name" attribute for routes beginning with the prefix I-:

```
$ ogr2ogr -where 'fename like "I-%"' sf_freeways.shp TGR06075.RT1
CompleteChain
```

The following example, perhaps slightly more useful, extracts just the street features from all the other gobbledygook in TIGER/Line, by matching features with Census Feature Classification Codes beginning with the letter A:

```
$ ogr2ogr -where 'cfcc like "A%"' sf_streets.shp TGR06075.RT1 CompleteChain
```

As you might have guessed, if the -f option to *ogr2ogr* is omitted, output to ESRI Shapefile is assumed.

Most basic SQL comparison and logical operators (e.g., =, <>, and, or, etc.) are supported in the -where clause. Finally, should you ever find it necessary, *ogr2ogr* will happily reproject your vector data sets, using the same good old -t_srs and -s_srs options supported by *gdalwarp*. Of course, *ogr2ogr* has a lot of other options, so be sure to peruse the manpage if you need to munge some vector data and you're not sure if OGR can do it.

One of the most frequent causes of the failure of two geospatial data sets in the same projection to properly line up with each other is a difference in *geodetic datum*, which is the definition of the precise origin of the spatial coordinate system. There are hundreds of standard geodetic datums, with NAD27, NAD83, and WGS84 being the most common you'll encounter.

GDAL can fix datum mismatches. For example, the following bit of code translates the NAD27-referenced hydrographic data from "Mapping Local Areas of Interest with Quantum GIS" [Hack #64] to NAD83, to make it match up with the underlying raster layer:

```
$ ogr2ogr -s_srs "+proj=UTM +zone=12 +datum=NAD27" \
-t_srs "+proj=UTM +zone=12 +datum=NAD83" \
hydro_nad83.shp hydro_main.shp
```

Similarly, the following command, which uses the *gdalwarp* utility, converts a raster in GeoTIFF format from NAD83 to NAD27:

```
$ gdalwarp -s_srs "+proj=UTM +zone=12 \
+datum=NAD83"  -t_srs "+proj=UTM +zone=12 \
+datum=NAD27" doq_nad83.tif doq_nad27.tif
```

As a side note, WGS84 and NAD83 are identical to the eighth decimal place, so you usually don't need to convert between them.

The GDAL and OGR utilities can take a little getting used to, but they make a lot of things possible and even easy that would have been difficult or impossible otherwise. What's more, many an open source GIS application depends on the GDAL and OGR libraries for GIS data handling.

## H A C K    Find Your Way Around GRASS
## #69    The full power of GIS can be a little overwhelming at first, but a little patience and a little practice is all it takes to make GRASS do your bidding.

GRASS is a powerful and free set of tools for analyzing and presenting geographic data. For details on how to install GRASS, see *http://mappinghacks. com/GRASS/*. Once you've done that, it's time to download the global sample data set and try out some basic tasks to get a feel for how GRASS works.

First, make a directory somewhere on your system in which to store your GRASS data, which can be anywhere convenient that you have write access to (I put mine in */home/sderle/gis/grass*). Then download the sample global data set from *http://grass.itc.it/sampledata/global_grass5data.tar.gz*. Unpack the tar file inside your GRASS data directory:

```
$ cd ~/grass       # or wherever you put it
$ tar xvfz ~/global_grass5data.tar.gz
```

You should see a bunch of files unpack into that directory. Now, start up the GRASS 5 shell by executing **grass5** at your shell prompt. You'll be taken to an introductory menu screen that looks like the following:

```
LOCATION:   <UNKNOWN>_____    (enter list for a list of locations)
MAPSET:     <UNKNOWN>_____    (or mapsets within a location)

DATABASE:   /home/sderle/gis/grass_____


     AFTER COMPLETING ALL ANSWERS, HIT <ESC><ENTER> TO CONTINUE
               (OR <Ctrl-C> TO CANCEL)
```

A bit of explanation is in order before we proceed. In GRASS, a *location* is just that—the place we are doing geographic analysis on. As such, the current GRASS location will include relevant bits of information about the area we're interested in, such as the geographic rectangle (or *extents*) that covers it, the coordinate system and geodetic datum in use, and the default grid resolution. Similarly, the current *region*, which we'll get into later, is the geographic subset of the current location.

A GRASS *mapset* is just a convenient way of grouping pieces of geographic data under a given location. GRASS mapsets allow multiple users to work on the same location without interfering with each other. GRASS supports a special mapset, called *PERMANENT*, which is used to store map layers that are available across any mapset in that location.

Finally, the GRASS *database* is just GRASS's name for the directory you set aside to store your GRASS data. Start by using the arrow keys to move down to the DATABASE: prompt, and fill in the path to that directory. Then use the arrow keys to move back up to the LOCATION: prompt, type in **list**, and hit the spacebar a few times to erase whatever might have been there previously. Then hit the Escape key, followed by the Enter key. You should now see something like the following:

```
Available locations:
----------------------
global
----------------------

Hit RETURN -->
```

This global location was created in GRASS when you unpacked the sample data set in your GRASS directory. Hit Return to go back to the intro menu, and enter the word **global** as your location. Since we'll be creating a new mapset to experiment in, invent a convenient name for the MAPSET: prompt (your username isn't a bad choice) and use the spacebar to remove whatever else was there previously. Your startup screen will now look something like this:

```
LOCATION:   global_____    (enter list for a list of locations)
MAPSET:     sderle_____    (or mapsets within a location)

DATABASE:   /home/sderle/gis/grass_____

     AFTER COMPLETING ALL ANSWERS, HIT <ESC><ENTER> TO CONTINUE
              (OR <Ctrl-C> TO CANCEL)
```

Hit the Escape key, followed by the Enter key. You should see some introductory text, followed by the GRASS prompt:

```
This version running thru the Bash Shell (/bin/bash)
Help is available with the command:        g.help
See the licence terms with:                g.version -c
Start the graphical user interface with:   tcltkgrass&
When ready to quit enter:                  exit

GRASS:~/gis >
```

Congratulations, you're working in GRASS! One interesting thing to note is that the GRASS shell is just a thin layer of environment variables laid on top of your ordinary Unix shell. To demonstrate this, try running **g.version -c**, which prints out license and version info for GRASS. It scrolls by too

quickly to read, right? So pipe the output through your favorite pager—e.g.,
**g.version -c | less**.

As you can see from this trivial example, GRASS extends the Unix tools philosophy—small programs that each do one thing well—into the world of
Geographic Information Systems. This means, very simply, that everything
that you're accustomed to doing in your Unix shell—command-line history, enviroment variables, command auto-completion, pipelines, scripting,
etc.—can also be done within GRASS. Pretty neat, huh? Now let's make
some maps.

Run the command **d.mon start=x0**, which should cause a blank window to
pop up. This blank window is a GRASS *monitor*, which is the virtual device
that GRASS uses to display graphics. Next, run **g.list type=rast**. This
shows us a list of the raster layers available in our current mapset. Let's view
the eco raster layer in our monitor, by running **d.rast eco**. A map of the
world in a strange mosaic of colors should appear in your monitor.

Let's take a closer look, by zooming in on Western Europe. Run **d.zoom**. You
should be presented with this somewhat cryptic menu:

```
Buttons:
Left:   1. corner
Middle: Unzoom
Right:  Quit
```

GRASS's *d.zoom* tool takes a little getting used to, so bear with it. Start by
left-clicking in the North Atlantic near Iceland. Now we have a rectangle
that we can move about. When we select the second corner of this rectangle
by middle-clicking—*not* left-clicking again, as you might expect—GRASS
attempts to fill the monitor with the selected region. So middle-click somewhere to the right of Italy in the Mediterranean to select the second corner,
and GRASS should zoom in on Western Europe. Now you can left-click to
begin selecting an area to zoom in on further, middle-click to zoom out and
try again, or right-click to exit *d.zoom*. Hitting Ctrl-C in your GRASS shell
will also exit *d.zoom*.

So what do the strange colors represent, exactly? To find out, use the com-
mmand **d.what.rast**, and then left-click on a colored point on the monitor.
Clicking near London yields the following in our shell:

```
0:01:19.425E 51:13:37.875N
eco in PERMANENT  (31)Non Woods-Warm/Hot Farms/Towns
```

By the same method, we discover that salmon is "Heath & Moorland,"
magenta is "Interrupted Woods," light cyan is "Major Woods," and so on.
But suppose we don't really care for this color scheme? Right-click on the

monitor or hit Ctrl-C in the shell to get out of *d.what.rast*. Run **r.colors** to alter the color table in the eco raster layer. When prompted for the name of a raster file, enter **eco**, and then enter **ryg** (which stands for "red-yellow-green") as the color table. Hit Enter to accept the defaults for all the other options, and finally *r.colors* will report:

```
Color table for [eco] set to ryg
```

Now run **d.redraw** to refresh the monitor. Figure 6-26 shows the eco raster layer with the ryg color map applied. If you don't like the resulting color scheme, run **r.colors** to try out some of the other preset color tables. The random color choice is a particularly interesting option. You can also set the color table from the command line with **r.colors map=eco color=random**.

*Figure 6-26. The eco raster layer with the ryg color map applied*

In general, most GRASS commands have two operating modes: interactive and command-line-option based. If you run a GRASS command with no options, expect the interactive mode. If you want to see which command-line options a GRASS command supports, run the command with a -? option (e.g., **r.colors -?**). If you want specific details on what a command does, well, this *is* Unix—try reading the manpage!

Now, let's add some context to this ecology map by overlaying national boundaries. Run **g.list type=vect** to get a list of the vector layers available in this mapset:

```
------------------------------------------------
vector files available in mapset PERMANENT:
coastlines
------------------------------------------------
```

Fancy that! The sample global data set doesn't even include a vector layer consisting of national borders. Well, we'll just have to make our own. Note that our earlier listing of raster layers included a nations layer. Let's view that one in our display now, with **d.rast nations**. You can use **d.what.rast** to ensure that GRASS knows which country is which, if you're curious. Now let's use *r.to.vect* to turn the outlines of each raster area into a polygon on a new vector layer.

```
GRASS:~/gis > r.to.vect in=nations out=borders feature=area
```

In versions of GRASS prior to 5.7, the tool for converting raster areas to vector polygons was called *r.poly*, and you had to run *v.support* afterwards on the new vector layer to generate the layer's support files. In GRASS 5.7, *v.support* is called *v.build*, and *r.to.vect* runs it for you automatically.

Now, let's see the new borders layer on its own. It should appear as white lines on a black background.

```
GRASS:~/gis > d.erase
GRASS:~/gis > d.vect borders type=boundary
```

Figure 6-27 shows our new borders layer. Sure enough, that's Western Europe, more or less. However, you may see weird lines cutting through some of the countries that hang off the edge of our current view—what's going on there? Let's start by saving our current view, using **g.region -s Western_Europe**, which tells GRASS to save a *region* under the name Western_ Europe. This way, we can poke around and still come back to this exact view later. Now use *d.zoom* to zoom out.

*Figure 6-27. Our new borders vector layer*

What's this? Our vector layer of national boundaries got cut off at the edges of our former region! This is, of course, an interesting lesson in the ways of GRASS. As it happens, most operations that act on individual layers only do so within the currently selected region. Sometimes, this is what you want; many operations in GRASS take a long time to run, and restricting them to run only within a constrained region of your whole location will make them run faster, if that's all you're interested in. But you should be aware of this "feature," as it may cause behavior you're not expecting when you're zoomed in on a small portion of your current location.

So let's try making that vector map again, but let's reset our region to the whole world first:

```
GRASS:~/gis > g.region rast=nations
GRASS:~/gis > r.to.vect in=nations out=borders feature=area
GRASS:~/gis > d.erase
GRASS:~/gis > d.vect borders type=boundary
```

Okay, that's more like it. Now let's zoom back in on Western Europe and redraw our ecology map with the national borders on top:

```
GRASS:~/gis > d.erase
GRASS:~/gis > g.region Western_Europe
GRASS:~/gis > d.rast eco
GRASS:~/gis > d.vect borders type=boundary color=black
```

 By now, you've probably noticed that there's a scheme behind the naming of GRASS commands. Commands that start with g. are general-purpose, d. commands are display related, r. commands work on rasters, v. commands work on vectors, and so on.

Figure 6-28 shows our revised borders layer drawn in black on top of the eco layer. You'll note that the political boundaries and the ecology map don't quite match up around the coastlines. Unfortunately, this is simply a side effect of using very low-resolution sample data—not much we can do about it here. (Also, you'll probably notice that these boundaries date to before 1990, but that's beside the point).

Now that we've made this informative and attractive map, what if we want to get back to it later? Fortunately, GRASS provides the *d.save* command, which generates a shell script of the commands used to generate the current view in our monitor. Run **d.save -c > europe.sh** and examine the contents of *europe.sh*:

```
# Shell Script created by d.save Sun Jun 27 18:16:20 2004

d.erase
g.region n=60:04:48N s=36:43:12N e=18:48E w=13:07:12W nsres=0:04:48 ewres=0:
04:48

d.rast map=eco                                                    # 2
d.vect map=borders type=boundary color=black                      # 1

d.frame -s frame=full_screen
```

We cover this topic in further detail in "Share Your GRASS Maps with the World" [Hack #75].

## See Also

- "Share Your GRASS Maps with the World" [Hack #75]
- GRASS 5.7 reference manual (*http://grass.itc.it/grass57/manuals/html57_user/*)
- GRASS 5.7 online tutorial (*http://grass.itc.it/grass57/tutorial/*)

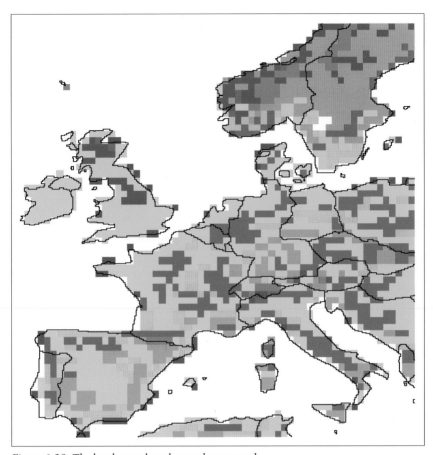

*Figure 6-28. The borders and eco layers shown together*

## HACK #70 Import Your GPS Waypoints and Tracklogs into GRASS

Use GRASS to tell the story of *your* travels on a customized map.

GRASS has a reputation as a complicated program that can do anything, but at the cost of hair-pulling pain. Here is a (relatively) simple guide to getting GRASS to do interesting things with your own GPS data. Along the way, we'll also convince GRASS to show us some interesting base-map layers as a way of providing context for our own story. By this point, you've probably loaded some waypoints and tracklogs from your GPS receiver onto your computer: now, let's import them into GRASS!

Before Version 5.7, GRASS referred to point data as "site" data, and there were *s.* commands to manipulate site data. As of Version 5.7, points are included in the much improved "Vector" format. A point is just the simplest vector. Some of the old *s.* sites commands now work with point data but store the points in the new vector format.

The *s.in.ascii* command imports text data into a vector file. You can specify a comma as your input field separator and import data that looks like this:

```
easting,northing,[attribute]
```

Data fields provided to *s.in.ascii* can also be separated by tabs, spaces, or an arbitrary separator of your choice. Meanwhile, here's an example of what we're starting with, a few lines of tracklog data downloaded via *gpstrans*.

```
Format: DDD  UTC Offset:  -8.00 hrs  Datum[100]: WGS 84
T       03/03/2004 16:53:01     38.4018946      -122.8440571
T       03/03/2004 16:53:02     38.4018946      -122.8440785
```

After the header line, each line of data consists of four tab-separated fields: a data type (T, for tracklog), a timestamp, and a latitude/longitude pair. Use this quick Perl script to convert *gpstrans* output into a form that can be handled by *s.in.ascii*.

```perl
#!/usr/bin/perl

while (my $point = <>) {
    chomp $point;
    my ($type, $date, $lat, $long) = split /\t/, $point;
    next unless $lat and $long;
    print "$long,$lat,$date\n";
}
```

Note that latitude and longitude are reversed in the output, because "easting" here is measured in degrees of longitude. Here is an extract from a tracklog that has been cleaned up to import into GRASS.

```
-122.8440571,38.4018946,03/03/2004 16:53:01
-122.8440785,38.4018946,03/03/2004 16:53:02
```

Now we import the tracklog into GRASS. First start GRASS and load the global data set with the U.S. state boundaries that we assembled in "Find Your Way Around GRASS" [Hack #69].

```
GRASS:~/wa/gps > perl ./fix_track.pl tk_2004-03-03-rino.txt > temp.txt
GRASS:~/wa/gps > s.in.ascii output=tracklog input=temp.txt fs=,
```

Let's see what's there:

```
GRASS:~/wa/gps > d.mon start=x0
GRASS:~/wa/gps > d.vect map=tracklog color=green size=2
```

I've used the *d.zoom* command to center the map over my area of interest, producing Figure 6-29.

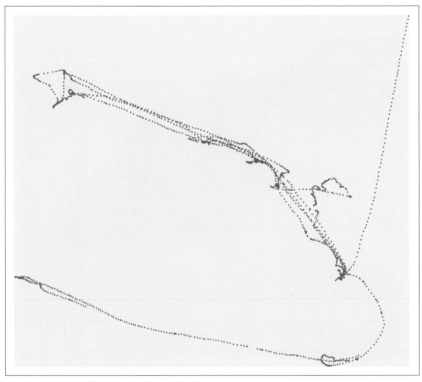

*Figure 6-29. Tracklog on Catalina Island*

That is a record of a weeklong dive trip around Catalina Island off the coast of Southern California. Now let's add some context.

Here is a bit of a waypoint file.

```
-121.970944444444  37.3223055555556  HITHAI
-122.829027777778  38.4025277777778  HOME
```

Note that now it is delimited with spaces, so the *field separator* (fs) is now set to space. We can import this into GRASS and display the waypoints, along with our states layer, with the commands:

```
GRASS:~/wa/gps > s.in.ascii output=waypoint input=wy102103.asc fs=space
GRASS:~/wa/gps > d.vect map=states color=grey
GRASS:~/wa/gps > d.vect map=tracklog color=green size=2
GRASS:~/wa/gps > d.vect map=waypoint icon=basic/diamond size=8 \
                 color=grey fcolor=red
```

Figure 6-30 shows all the components of our map together: the tracklog, the nearby waypoints, and the state borders underneath provide context.

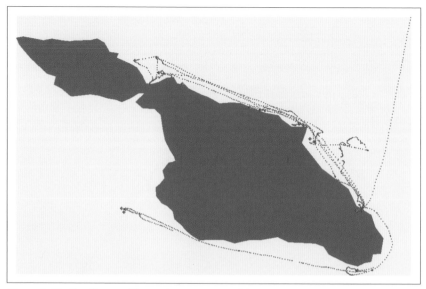

*Figure 6-30. Catalina tracklog with waypoints and base map*

This map has one problem: tracks are displayed as discrete points. This gives the resulting maps a faint fairy-tracing appearance. I find the effect soothing, as it hints of an ambiguity in time and place. The GPS seems to speak to me, telling me, "Sure, I knew where you were at this moment, and then at this moment, and on through the day, but between those times, I don't know where you were." It is as though I traveled through a series of quantum jumps, disregarding intervening space (a trick that those driving the Nebraska panhandle will find themselves wanting to add to their travel kits).

See the next hack, "Turn Your Tracklogs into ESRI Shapefiles" **[Hack #71]** for a way to convert the discrete points to lines.

# #71    Turn Your Tracklogs into ESRI Shapefiles

Converting your GPS tracklogs into a standard vector format allows you to import them into any GIS or mapping application automatically.

Once you've gotten your GPS tracklogs into GRASS as site data [Hack #70], something you'll notice almost right away is that, when you zoom in close, your tracklog points appear as, well, individual points, and not as the tracks you might expect. The reason for this hardly needs explanation. Your GPS receiver's tracklog is really just a sample of your location over time, rather than a continuous stream. When you import that data into GRASS as point data, you are telling GRASS that you want to see it as a set of points, rather than as the connected arc that (approximately) describes your path through time and space. What's more, as site data in GRASS, it's relatively difficult to get that data back out and display it in a GIS browser, such as Quantum GIS or Mapserver.

One neat answer to this whole set of problems is ESRI's Shapefile format, an openly published vector data format that has become a sort of lingua franca for GIS vector data. Shapefiles offer a way of portably grouping and storing points, sets of points, arcs, and polygons. Frank Warmerdam's shapelib project offers a good, free C API for reading and writing shapefiles, so most GIS and mapping applications that speak vector data will speak ESRI's shapefile format. We'll hack up a quick fifty-line Perl script to turn your *gpstrans* tracklogs into shapefiles, so that they can be exported to other applications as line data, rather than as point data.

> As it happens, the term *shapefile* itself is a bit of a misno-mer: a shapefile actually consists of three or four separate files, usually distributed together in a ZIP archive or tarball. The *.shp* file contains the actual vector data. Typically, you will find a *.shx* file that contains index data about the shape-file. Sometimes there's a *.prj* file that describes the projec-tion of the vector data. Finally, you'll often also see a *.dbf* file, which is—no lie!—a DBase/FoxPro database that con-tains quantitative data about the features described in the shapefile, such as population or land area. You can actually browse this *.dbf* file in Excel or Gnumeric!

We'll use Geo::Shapelib, which is a thin layer of Perl wrapped around *shapelib*, to generate all three of these files from your tracklog.

You can get Geo::Shapelib from the CPAN using the following command as the superuser from a *NIX shell:

```
# perl -MCPAN -e 'install Geo::Shapelib'
```

In this script, which we'll call *track2shp.pl*, we'll also use the very handy Time::Piece module to parse the dates of the tracklog entries and do calcula-tions with them. You can get Time::Piece from the CPAN.

Here's a sample bit of tracklog as output by **gpstrans -dt**:

```
Format: DDD  UTC Offset:  -8.00 hrs  Datum[100]: WGS 84
T      02/07/2004 11:40:07    37.7396250    -122.4198818
T      02/07/2004 11:41:20    37.7395391    -122.4198604
T      02/07/2004 11:47:56    37.7394533    -122.4197745
T      02/07/2004 11:48:13    37.7394962    -122.4199033
T      02/07/2004 12:00:50    37.7393031    -122.4196029
T      02/07/2004 12:06:54    37.7394533    -122.4198604
```

As you can see, the *gpstrans* output format is very simple. There's a header line with some metadata, followed by several lines of data, each containing four tab-separated fields: the data type (i.e., T for tracklog), the timestamp, and a latitude/longitude pair. Obviously, the output from other GPS data download programs will look different, but the principle is the same. Extending the following code to work with the output of GARNIX and other programs is left as an exercise for the reader.

On the Mapping Hacks web site, you'll find a GPX-based version of *track2shp.pl* under *http://mappinghacks.com/code/*.

## The Code

```perl
#!/usr/bin/perl

use Geo::Shapelib;
use Time::Piece;
use constant TIME_THRESHOLD  => 10;      # minutes
use constant TIME_FORMAT     => "%m/%d/%Y %H:%M:%S";
use strict;
use warnings;

my ($in, $out) = @ARGV;
die "Usage: $0  \n" unless $in and $out;

my $shp = new Geo::Shapelib;
$shp->{Name}       = $out;
$shp->{Shapetype}  = 3; # PolyLine, according to Geo::Shapelib source
$shp->{FieldNames} = ['ID', 'Date'];
$shp->{FieldTypes} = ['Integer', 'String:16'];

open TRACK, "<", $in or die "Can't open $in: $!";

my $id = 0;
my (@vertices, $previous);

sub add_shape {
    return unless @vertices > 2;
    push @{$shp->{Shapes}}, {
        SHPType => 3, # PolyLine
        ShapeId => $id,
        NVertices => scalar @vertices,
        Vertices  => [@vertices]
    };
    push @{$shp->{ShapeRecords}}, [$id++, $previous->ymd];
    @vertices = ();
}

while () {
```

```
chomp;
my ($type, $date, $lat, $long) = split /\t/, $_, 4;
my $now = eval { Time::Piece->strptime($date, TIME_FORMAT) };
next unless $now;

if (@vertices) {
    add_shape() if $now - $previous > TIME_THRESHOLD * 60;
}

push @vertices, [$long, $lat]; # note, long before lat!
$previous = $now;
}

add_shape();
$shp->save($out);
```

In its broadest outline, *track2shp.pl* reads each line from the given tracklog, splitting the line up into its component fields and throwing away the lines it can't parse. The script builds up a set of vertices from the tracklog points, storing them together as needed in a single PolyLine shape. (*PolyLine* is just ESRI's term for a series of connected line segments.) Finally, all of the accumulated PolyLines are dumped to the shapefile(s).

## Running the Code

Assuming the script is marked as executable and is in your current directory, you can run it as follows:

```
$ gpstrans -dt > tracklog.txt
$ ./track2shp.pl tracklog.txt tracklog.shp
$ ls
track2shp.pl  tracklog.dbf  tracklog.shp  tracklog.shx  tracklog.txt
```

As you can see, you should have three new files in the same directory: the *.shp* file containing the shapes, the *.shx* index file, and the *.dbf* datafile.

Figure 6-31 shows a sample map of a trip we made through Los Angeles, stopping off in Hollywood to pick up friends and then visiting Venice Beach, before dropping our friends off and continuing north on Interstate 5. This map was made with about five minutes of work in Quantum GIS, using the U.S. state borders and major roads layers from *http://nationalatlas.gov* and, of course, a GPS track processed with *gpstrans* and *track2shp.pl*.

## Understanding the Code

We have glossed over some of the details of this script. For example, what's this TIME_THRESHOLD business? Well, at first blush, we might consider it easiest to simply whack the whole tracklog together into a single PolyLine and call it done. The problem with this is that GPS reception frequently suffers

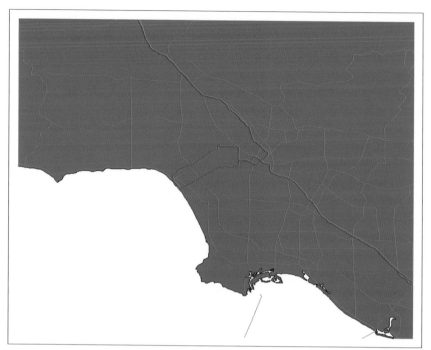

*Figure 6-31. A Shapefile made from a trip through Los Angeles*

dropouts of varying kinds, leading to missing data points. Sometimes dropouts are momentary, perhaps the result of your receiver simply losing its satellite lock for a minute or two as you drove past an inopportunely placed hill or building. In this case, we can probably just draw a straight line between the two known-good points on either side, and call it close enough.

But what if you lose reception for more than a few minutes, as can easily happen in urban areas? What if you shut your GPS receiver off and don't turn it back on until many days or many kilometers later? In these circumstances, it would be downright inaccurate and even misleading to simply interpolate a straight line between the two otherwise correct points on either side. This is where the TIME_THRESHOLD value comes in: *track2shp.pl* keeps track of how much time has elapsed between successive log entries. If the elapsed time is more than 10 minutes, then *track2shp.pl* assumes that a dropout (accidental or otherwise) has occurred and treats it as a signal to start a new PolyLine. In this fashion, we can tweak the TIME_THRESHOLD setting to group tracklogs of different trips together in a single shapefile, while treating them as individual features for the sake of mapping or GIS use.

There are a few other things worth mentioning about this script. First, note the TIME_FORMAT constant defined at the top. This string is passed to

`Time::Piece` to tell it how to parse the timestamp in each tracklog entry. If you need to alter it for any reason, refer to the manual page for *strptime(3)* on your system for the syntax. One could make this "Do What I Mean" in more and different circumstances by replacing `Time::Piece` with `Date::Parse` from the CPAN, which would be more flexible but far less efficient.

Finally, note the use of the `$shp->{ShapeRecords}` array, which allows us to associate other data values with each feature in the shapefile. The data fields are defined by `$shp->{FieldNames}` and `$shp->{FieldTypes}`, about which you can read more in **perldoc Geo::Shapelib**. The important thing is that `Geo::Shapelib` stores the values from `$shp->{ShapeRecords}` in the resulting .*dbf* file, which you can read with most modern spreadsheet programs, such as Gnumeric or Excel. Load the .*dbf* file produced by *track2shp.pl* in one of these programs, and you should see two columns. The first is an arbitrary numeric identifier for each feature that *track2shp.pl* found in the tracklog, and the second is the date on which that feature was finally recorded, which is returned from the call to `$previous->ymd`. Obviously, with a little experimentation, you can add more fields and put all kinds of other stuff in here, such as the start and stop times of each individual track, the time elapsed, distance traveled, average speed, and more.

You can now import and visualize your tracklog in a plethora of mapping and GIS applications, including GRASS, Quantum GIS, Thuban, Mapserver, Manifold, and even ArcView.

## Hacking the Hack

There is one other weak point remaining in this hack, which is the possibility of spurious data in the GPS tracklog. In one real-life example, a drive from San Francisco to Oakland on the lower deck of the Bay Bridge caused the GPS reception to cut out completely, with the exception of a single reading placed off the coast of Baja California. If we treat this point as valid, then it appears as if the automobile suddenly teleported from one end of the bridge out to the Tropic of Cancer over the Pacific Ocean and then back to the other end of the bridge, all in a matter of minutes! This effect is shown in Figure 6-32 by the two red lines shooting off to the south of the map.

Presumably, the GPS signals bouncing around inside the steel infrastructure of the bridge resulted in an accumulation of multipath error in the receiver, causing the sudden and obviously false data point. How can we detect and eliminate these errors from our shapefiles? One way might be to calculate the mean velocity between successive tracklog points. If the calculated velocity is in excess of any speed a human being is likely to be traveling near the surface of the earth—say, the 800 km/h cruising speed of your average jet

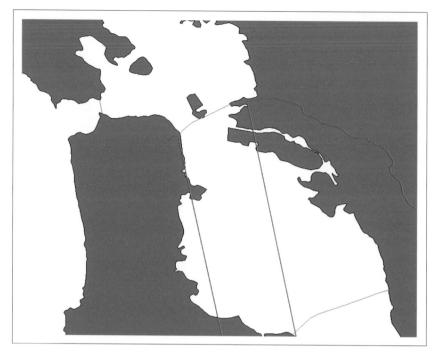

*Figure 6-32. A sudden, unexplained jaunt to Baja California*

airliner—then we can safely assume that the next data point is spurious and ought to be ignored.

In order to calculate velocity, we need measures of time, which are already in the tracklog, and distance, which for reasons described in "Calculate the Distance Between Points on the Earth's Surface" **[Hack #27]** can be a bit tricky for short hops. For the sake of expediency—this is a hack, after all—we will rely on Geo::Distance, which will suffice insofar as we are not after exact distances so much as a rule of thumb with which to judge the validity of our collected position data. Geo::Distance can be obtained from the CPAN.

First, make the following additions near the top of *track2shp.pl*:

```
use Geo::Shapelib;
use Geo::Distance ':all'
use Time::Piece;
use constant SPEED_THRESHOLD => 1000;    # km/h
use constant TIME_THRESHOLD  => 10;      # minutes
use constant TIME_FORMAT     => "%m/%d/%Y %H:%M:%S";
use strict;
```

Next, in the main loop, add the distance calculation:

```
if (@vertices) {
    my $d = distance_calc( kilometer => $vertices[-1], [$long, $lat] );
```

```
  next if $d / ($now - $previous) > SPEED_THRESHOLD / 3600;
  add_shape() if $now - $previous > TIME_THRESHOLD * 60;
}
```

For the call to distance_calc(), we pass the units we want back, the previous point in the vertex list, and the current point we want to test. If the result divided by the time difference is greater than our threshold speed (scaled here to km/s for calculation purposes), then the next data point is assumed to be spurious and is skipped. With four extra lines of code, we have extended *track2shp.pl* to filter out bad data caused by intermittent GPS reception. Figure 6-33 shows the resulting shapefile.

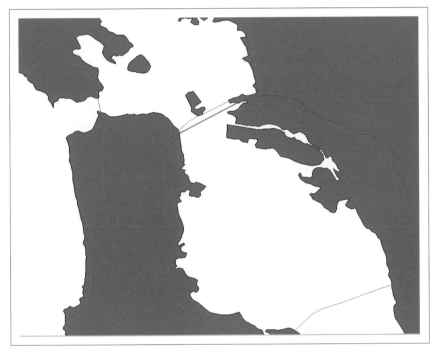

*Figure 6-33. The same shapefile, corrected*

Although the line interpolated across the Bay in place of actual data doesn't quite overlap perfectly with the vector feature matching the bridge, it certainly comes a lot closer than our previous version did!

This filtering method has other potential drawbacks. Should the first data point collected be spurious and the rest valid, the script will make the mistake of assuming the subsequent points are wrong. Also, as mentioned earlier, the results returned from Geo::Distance might be inaccurate for very small distances, which could conceivably trigger false positives in exceptional circumstances. Meanwhile, *track2shp.pl* is starting to accumulate a few configurable settings that good software design dictates should be turned into command-line options, rather than source code constants. Of course, if we solved all of these remaining issues, we might find ourselves with something a lot closer to a software product than a simple hack!

## HACK #72    Add Relief to Your Topographic Maps

Using GRASS and some digital elevation models, you can give existing topo maps a more expressive "3-D" look.

Topographic maps can be a useful tool for getting a sense of the lay of the land, but the contour lines used to express topographic variation can be a little hard to get one's head around at a glance. Does that path lead uphill or downhill? By adding shadows to the map that correspond to the contours of the land (as if the sun were overhead), we can create the impression of relief on our topo maps, making it easier for the eye to pick out hills and valleys. This technique is called *hill shading*, and GRASS offers several tools for adding hill shading to a topographic map.

### Getting the Data

For simplicity—and because there is a wealth of freely available data for the region—we'll try our hand at adding hill shading to a topographic map of San Francisco. Hill shading involves not only a nice topo map, but also elevation data to plot the relief with. Fortunately, the USGS Bay Area Regional Database at *http://bard.wr.usgs.gov/* offers both (and more!) for the San Francisco Bay Area. We'll start by downloading the data to make our relief map. Visit *http://bard.wr.usgs.gov/htmldir/sf_100k.html* and download the *digital raster graphic* (DRG) and the DRG *world file* for the San Francisco quadrangle. Then go to *http://bard.wr.usgs.gov/htmldir/dem_html/dem10_mtr_sf.html* and get the *gzip*-compressed *digital elevation model* (DEM) files for Point Bonita, San Francisco North, San Francisco South, San Francisco South West, Oakland West, and Hunter's Point. All told, you'll be downloading a bit less than 9 MB of compressed data.

Now we'll uncompress the data we just downloaded. If you put all of these files into a new directory, you can just run:

```
$ gunzip *.gz
```

This may take a few moments. Now we have 71 MB of uncompressed data. Let's run *gdalinfo* [Hack #68], which is part of the GDAL package, on one of the DEM files, to see what projection they're in. If you don't already have GDAL installed, you can get it from Debian apt or download source code or binaries from *http://gdal.maptools.org/*. The output from *gdalinfo* looks like this:

```
$ gdalinfo sf_north.dem
Driver: USGSDEM/USGS Optional ASCII DEM
Size is 1109, 1395
Coordinate System is:
PROJCS["UTM Zone 10, Northern Hemisphere",
    GEOGCS["NAD27",
        DATUM["North_American_Datum_1927",
            SPHEROID["Clarke 1866",6378206.4,294.978698213898,
                AUTHORITY["EPSG","7008"]],
            TOWGS84[-3,142,183,0,0,0,0],
            AUTHORITY["EPSG","6267"]],
        PRIMEM["Greenwich",0,
            AUTHORITY["EPSG","8901"]],
        UNIT["degree",0.0174532925199433,
            AUTHORITY["EPSG","9108"]],
    PROJECTION["Transverse_Mercator"],
    PARAMETER["latitude_of_origin",0],
    PARAMETER["central_meridian",-123],
```

That's quite a bit of metadata, but it tells us a few things we need to know in order to create a new location in GRASS. As usual, a lot of the USGS's freely available topographic data is stored in UTM coordinates, referenced to the NAD27 geodetic datum. (NAD27 has since been superseded by NAD83, but the USGS still has most of its data kicking about in NAD27.)

> If you're outside the Bay Area, you might try getting *National Elevation Data* (NED) and other base maps from the USGS Seamless Data Distribution System **[Hack #67]**. Obviously, the smaller the resolution you can get, the better. For areas outside the U.S., you might try NASA's *Shuttle Radar Topography Mission* (SRTM) data, available from the Global Land Cover Facility at *http://landcover.org/data/srtm/*. In either event, you may need to "Convert Geospatial Data Between Different Formats" **[Hack #68]** first.

## Creating a New Location in GRASS

Start up GRASS, and create a new location using the UTM coordinate system. The NAD27 datum is based on the Clarke 1866 ellipsoid model, so select clark66 for your ellipsoid and nad27 for your map datum. San Francisco is in the Northern Hemisphere, in UTM zone 10. You can leave the extents at their defaults. Once you're back at the opening menu, load your new location. You should now be at the GRASS prompt.

Let's start by importing the digital raster graphic containing the topo map. Remember that DRG world file you downloaded? Sometimes GeoTIFF files

keep their projection metadata stored in a separate world file. GRASS's raster import utility, *r.in.gdal* (so named for the GDAL raster data library it's
based on) needs this file to figure out how your DRG is georeferenced, but,
for whatever reason, it expects a different file extension, so we'll have to
rename the world file before feeding the DRG to *r.in.gdal*. Then we'll import
the topo map into a raster layer called sf_topo and view it on a graphics
monitor. Since the DRG doesn't have any projection metadata attached,
we'll have to tell *r.in.glad* that we know that the image is correct, by giving it
the -o option to override the current GRASS projection:

```
GRASS:~/shade > mv sanfrancisco_ca.tiffw  sanfrancisco_ca.tfw
GRASS:~/shade > r.in.gdal -o in=sanfrancisco_ca.tiff  out=sf_topo
GRASS:~/shade > g.region raster=sf_topo
GRASS:~/shade > d.mon start=x0
using default visual which is TrueColor
ncolors: 16777216
Graphics driver [x0] started
GRASS:~/shade > d.rast sf_topo
  100%
```

Voilà! Figure 6-34 shows a rather nice looking topo map of San Francisco
and its surroundings, albeit from a distance. Use *d.zoom* to zoom in and get
a feel for the contents of the topo map. If you zoom in all the way, you can
see curved brown lines that represent the topographic contours. It's a bit
hard to tell just from looking where the hills begin and end, isn't it?

> In binary distributions of older versions of GRASS, *r.in.gdal*
> had an unfortunate tendency to segfault. If you're running
> one of these versions, try one of the other *r.in* functions, like
> *r.in.tiff*. If your data isn't already in GeoTIFF format, you
> can always "Convert Geospatial Data Between Different For-
> mats" **[Hack #68]** first outside of GRASS—as we do with the
> DEM files later on in this hack—and then import it.

Now zoom back out, and try to frame the city of San Francisco in your monitor. Save this region to your current mapset, in case you want to get back to
it later:

```
GRASS:~/shade > d.zoom

Buttons:
Left:   1. corner
Middle: Unzoom
Right:  Quit

4182926.07100085(N)  545891.94510076(E)

GRASS:~/shade > g.region save=San_Francisco
```

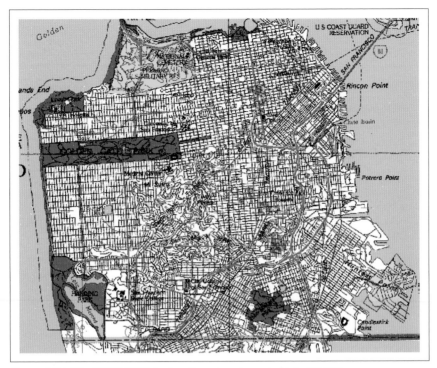

*Figure 6-34. The USGS DRG for San Francisco, imported into GRASS*

Now you can zoom in and out as you like and return to this view of San Francisco by typing **g.region San_Francisco**, followed by **d.redraw**.

> If you got a single DEM from the USGS Seamless Data Distribution System or the Global Land Cover Facility, you can skip over this next part.

## Making a Composite Elevation Model

Next, let's get the DEMs we downloaded imported into GRASS as raster layers. Ordinarily, *r.in.gdal* can be used to read DEM files directly into GRASS, but, for reasons unclear, this causes segmentation faults in the version of GRASS we used. However, the GDAL package offers a tool called *gdal_translate*, which will let us turn the DEMs into GeoTIFFs, and then *r.in.gdal* can import those GeoTIFFs into GRASS as usual. Because there are a few DEM files we want to convert, we wrote a quick *bash* script called *import_dem.sh* to do the job:

```
#!/bin/bash
for dem in $@; do
```

```
      out=${dem%.dem}
      gdal_translate $dem $out.tiff
      r.in.gdal -o in=$out.tiff out=${out}_dem
      rm $out.tiff
done
```

This makes importing the DEMs a piece of cake:

```
GRASS:~/shade > chmod +x import_dem.sh
GRASS:~/shade > ./import_dem.sh *.dem
```

The script will take a few moments to run, and then we will have a whole
new set of raster layers in our GRASS mapset:

```
GRASS:~/shade > g.list type=rast
----------------------------------------------
raster files available in mapset sderle:
hunters_pt_dem    pt_bonita_dem  sf_south_dem     sf_topo
oakland_west_dem  sf_north_dem   sf_south_oe_dem

----------------------------------------------
```

Next, we need to stitch these DEM layers together into a single unified layer,
so that we can do shading with it. The *r.patch* tool does this job admirably.
Note that GRASS only does raster processing within the current region, so
the resulting layer, which we'll call sf_elevation, will be clipped to the box
we drew around San Francisco earlier. Make sure you list all the DEM files
on a single line, with no spaces between the commas; GRASS commands are
sensitive to whitespace. Finally, use *r.colors* to colorize the elevation file and
then display it on the monitor using *d.rast*:

```
GRASS:~/shade > r.patch in=pt_bonita_dem,sf_north_dem,sf_south_dem,sf_south_
oe_dem,hunters_pt_dem,oakland_west_dem out=sf_elevation
r.patch: percent complete:   100%
CREATING SUPPORT FILES FOR sf_elevation
GRASS:~/shade > r.colors sf_elevation color=grey
Color table for [sf_elevation] set to grey
GRASS:~/shade > d.rast sf_elevation
   100%
```

Figure 6-35 shows the elevation contours of San Francisco laid out in a
ghostly grayscale, with Twin Peaks and Mt. Sutro standing out as a complex of white in the middle. Now that we have all our data imported into
GRASS, we can begin the process of hill shading our topo map in earnest.

## Applying the Hill Shading

We'll begin this step by using the *r.shaded.relief* script that comes with
GRASS to generate a separate shading layer from our patched DEMs. The
*r.shaded.relief* script uses *r.mapcalc* internally to calculate the shadows cast
by the sun, given its azimuth (or direction) and its height above the hori-

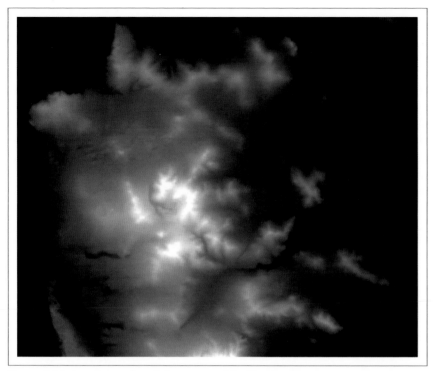

*Figure 6-35. A composite digital elevation model of San Francisco*

zon. Both the azimuth and the altitude of the sun are measured in degrees. For sake of argument, we'll place the sun due west at 30 degrees high:

```
GRASS:~/shade > r.shaded.relief azimuth=270 altitude=30 \
map=sf_elevation

Please provide the altitude of the sun in degrees above the
horizon and the azimuth of the sun in degrees to the east of
north (N:0 E:90 S:180 W:270)

Using altitude:30 azimuth:270 elevation:sf_elevation@sderle

Running r.mapcalc, please stand by.
Your new map will be named sf_elevation_relshade. Please consider renaming.
 100%
Color table for [sf_elevation_relshade] set to grey

Shaded relief map created and named sf_elevation_relshade. Consider
renaming.
```

Our new relief map is stored in a raster layer called sf_elevation_relshade. You can use *g.rename* to rename it, but we won't bother. If you're curious to know what it looks like, try **d.rast sf_elevation_relshade**.

In older versions of GRASS, *r.shaded.relief* was called *shade. rel.sh*, but the basic details were the same.

Now we want to combine this shading layer with our original topo map to overlay this nifty relief effect. For that, we turn to *d.his*, which combines hue, intensity, and saturation values (hence *his*) from two or three raster layers for visual effect. To shade our topo map, we want the hues from the topo map and the intensity from our shading map, which will darken the parts of the topo map that fall into shadow, creating the illusion of relief. The *d.his* tool is simple to run, and it displays its output immediately, as shown in Figure 6-36:

```
GRASS:~/shade > d.erase
GRASS:~/shade > d.his h=sf_topo i=sf_elevation_relshade
  100%
```

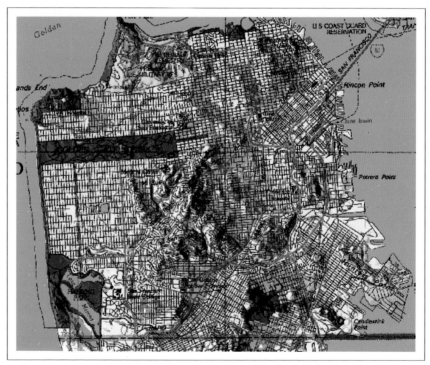

*Figure 6-36. A shaded relief map of San Francisco*

Suddenly, the topographic layout of San Francisco makes sense! You can make out the curved roads that run up and down the sides of the hills and the places where hilltops have been turned into squares or parks. Zooming in reveals the logic of the contour lines in a way that wasn't immediately apparent before. Start another graphics monitor with **d.mon start=x1** and use **d.rast sf_topo** to display the original and the shaded topo maps side by side.

You should play with the azimuth and altitude values provided to *r.shaded. relief* to get a sense for the hill shading that's most visually appealing to you. Some will definitely look better than others. Read the *r.shaded.relief* and *d. his* manpages for more details. Also, you might want to try using the PNG driver to output your map to a graphic that you can share with the world [Hack #75]. Then you should track down the topo maps and elevation data for your own neighborhood and make your own shaded relief maps!

## Hacking the Hack

Of course, picking the azimuth and altitude values out of a hat isn't good enough for some people. For the hard-bitten realists among us, there is another option: you can always input the actual height and direction of the sun as it's shining out your window right now (or, at least, where it would be if it were daytime and not sleeting outside, etc.). Although the *r.sun* and *r.sunmask* tools provided with GRASS will do some of this math for you, their usage is a little bit complex, and it might be easier to simply get the angle values from another source.

One option is the NOAA Solar Position Calculator at *http://www.srrb.noaa. gov/highlights/sunrise/azel.html*. You can select your location from a drop-down box of cities, or provide your own latitude and longitude, as well as select the date and time that you want a solar position estimate for. A JavaScript-powered calculator then provides estimates of solar altitude and azimuth, plus a bunch of other figures, for the given place and time. We chose San Francisco at 2:00 pm (GMT –8) on March 18, 2004, approximately the time of this writing, and got values of 219 degrees azimuth and 44 degrees altitude. Figure 6-37 shows the resulting relief map, which, frankly, looks a bit nicer than the one made with the values we invented earlier!

### HACK #73 Make Your Own Contour Maps

Why buy expensive contour maps when you can make your own, using free elevation data?

Anyone who's done a bit of hiking or other outdoor activity is probably familiar with the idea of a contour map. Contour lines offer a convenient way of visualizing the lay of the land on a flat map by showing successive increments of ground elevation as nested lines or figures. When the lines are

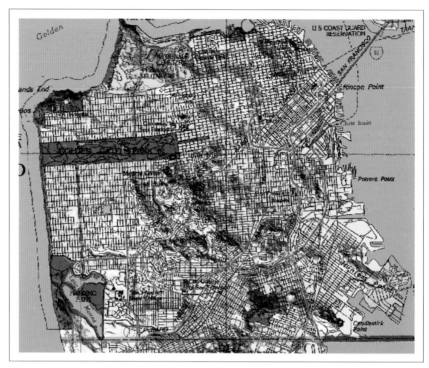

*Figure 6-37. A shaded relief map of San Francisco, calculated from actual solar angles*

spaced far apart, elevation change is gradual, and when they are closer together, steeper terrain is indicated. A good contour map can cost a pretty chunk of change, but it's easy to use GRASS to make one of your own.

All you need to get started is a working version of GRASS and some elevation data for the area you're interested in mapping. Any elevation data will do, from the kilometer-resolution GTOPO30 data available from NASA for the whole world, all the way down to the really nice 10-meter resolution digital elevation models available for parts of the U.S. from the U.S. Geological Survey. For simplicity's sake, we'll make a contour map of San Francisco, using the data we imported in "Add Relief to Your Topographic Maps" [Hack #72].

Start GRASS in the San_Francisco location used earlier [Hack #72]. Start a new monitor with *d.mon* and use *g.region* to center the display on San Francisco with the region we saved previously, without actually displaying anything in particular yet:

```
GRASS:~/contour > d.mon start=x0
GRASS:~/contour > g.region San_Francisco
```

Next, we'll use the *r.contour* tool that ships with GRASS to create a vector layer containing our contour lines. This program just samples the elevation model, noting where the terrain crosses a particular threshold and generating an outline of the contour at each of these points. We'll start our contour lines at sea level and show a new line for every 50-meter rise in elevation. You will be prompted with the minimum and maximum contour values found—go ahead and accept them. Finally, use *d.vect* to display the new vector layer on the monitor:

```
GRASS:~/contour > r.contour in=sf_elevation out=sf_contour min=0 step=50
GRASS:~/contour > d.vect sf_contour color=blue
```

Figure 6-38 shows the contours of San Francisco, shown in blue, with 50-meter steps between contour lines. The result looks pretty good, but the map is a bit busy.

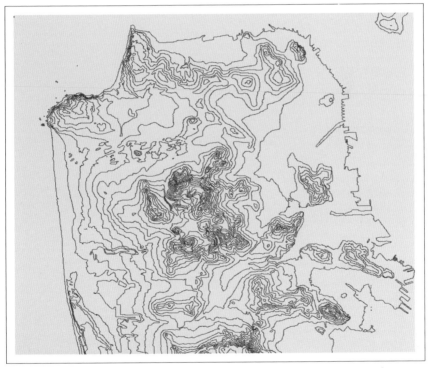

*Figure 6-38. A contour map of San Francisco, with 50 m steps between contour lines*

We can use the cut parameter for *r.contour* to clean up the more spurious bits, by discarding contour lines with fewer than a certain number of points. We'll use a value of 200 to demonstrate the effect:

```
GRASS:~/contour > r.contour in=sf_elevation out=sf_contour \
min=0 step=50 cut=200
GRASS:~/contour > d.redraw
```

If we place the two maps side by side (perhaps by writing to a different layer and starting another X11 monitor), we can see that our new map sacrifices detail for the sake of clarity. Such is always the prime trade-off inherent in the art of cartography! Another approach we can take, if the contour map still looks too busy, is to raise the step parameter to a higher increment, say, 100 meters:

```
GRASS:~/contour > r.contour in=sf_elevation out=sf_contour min=0 step=100
cut=50
GRASS:~/contour > d.redraw
```

Figure 6-39 shows the resulting map, which is enormously simpler, but with the basic information still conveyed. Obviously, you should play with the options for *r.contour* when mapping your own data and see which set of trade-offs looks best to you.

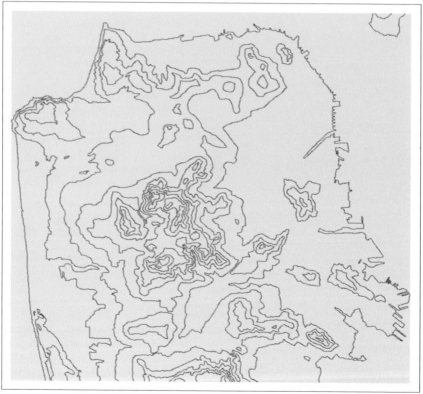

*Figure 6-39. A contour map of San Francisco, with 100 m steps between contour lines.*

Finally, just to prove to ourselves that this is indeed the elevation data we think we're looking at, let's plot our 100-meter contour map on top of the original elevation data:

```
GRASS:~/contour > r.colors sf_elevation color=aspect
GRASS:~/contour > d.erase
GRASS:~/contour > d.rast sf_elevation
GRASS:~/contour > d.vect sf_contour color=blue
```

Sure enough, all the terrain features are still shown in Figure 6-40, now outlined in blue by our contour layer. That's all there is to it!

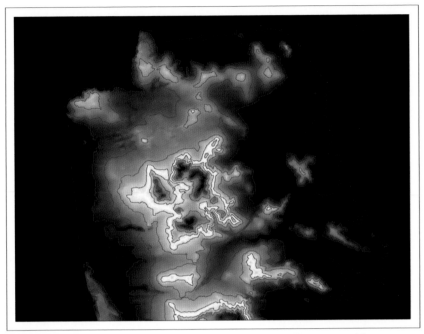

*Figure 6-40. The same contour map, draped over the original elevation model*

Now you can use this layer to make new maps or augment other maps in GRASS. You can generate a PostScript rendition of your new contour map for printing to hardcopy **[Hack #75]**. You can even work with your new contour layer in other mapping applications by exporting it to an ESRI Shapefile:

```
GRASS:~/contour > v.out.ogr in=sf_contour dsn=. layer=sf_contour type=line
GRASS:~/contour > ls sf_contour*
sf_contour.dbf  sf_contour.shp  sf_contour.shx
```

> In versions of GRASS prior to 5.7, you would use **v.out.**
> **shape map=sf_contour type=line**, instead of *v.out.ogr*. In
> more recent versions of GRASS, *v.out.ogr* has subsumed
> many of the *v.out* commands.

# HACK #74  Plot Wireless Network Viewsheds with GRASS

With a little GRASS scripting, you can build sophisticated models of radio-frequency reception for wireless network planning—and find out where the black holes are.

If your local terrain is hilly, planning wireless community networks can be a big hassle, as 802.11 depends on line-of-sight between nodes. "Planning" is somewhat of a misnomer; networks grow organically according to movements of people. When you move to a new town, the question "Can I get on your free network?" is most often answered with "We don't know!" Before we start hanging out of the window waving an antenna about, we can start answering this question with *viewshed* maps, which display the area visible from a given point on an elevation model. Knowing where you *can't* get directly connected from is a good start.

In "Why You Can't Watch Broadcast TV" [Hack #18], we used a tool called *SPLAT!* for mapping radio viewsheds. Although SPLAT! is easy to use, it also has several shortcomings. In this hack, we'll look at doing much more sophisticated modeling with GRASS. Using GRASS, we can map wireless viewsheds over any arbitrary base map, taking terrain effects and antenna height, angle, and beam width into account.

Being geeks, when we moved to San Francisco, the first thing we wanted to do was get connected to SFLan, the wireless community network spearheaded by the wonderful Internet Archive. SFLan's home on the Web is at *http://archive.org/sflan/*. We'll use GRASS to plot a viewshed for SFLan node #11, which is situated on a tower at the peak of San Francisco's Mount Olympus, to a couple of locations in the friendly Potrero Hill and Bernal Heights neighborhoods, and see if we might have line-of-sight to SFLan11.

## Loading the Terrain into GRASS

For this hack, we'll use the digital elevation model and digital raster graphic that we imported into GRASS for "Add Relief to Your Topographic Maps" [Hack #72]. Load GRASS with the San_Francisco location we created in that hack. Then load the stored region we created for San Francisco and call up the USGS digital raster graphic stored in the sf_topo raster layer:

```
GRASS:~/hacks/viewshed > d.mon start=x0
GRASS:~/hacks/viewshed > g.region san_francisco
GRASS:~/hacks/viewshed > d.rast sf_topo
100%
```

Next, let's import our three locations into GRASS as a site layer. We'll put the locations into a tab-delimited text file called *sites.txt* as follows:

```
-122.4444    37.7631 SFLan11
-122.4008    37.7576 Potrero
-122.4197    37.7394 Bernal
```

Our three fields are longitude and latitude in the WGS84 datum, and a site label. Of course, longitude comes first, as it's the *x*-coordinate in our pair, and the longitude values are negative, as they are all west of the prime meridian. Our GRASS location is projected into UTM zone 10 against the NAD27 datum, as we can see from the output of *g.proj*, excerpted here:

```
GRASS:~/hacks/viewshed > g.proj -p
----------------------------------------------------------
PROJ_INFO file:
name:    UTM
datum:   nad27
dx:      -22.000000
dy:      157.000000
dz:      176.000000
proj:    utm
ellps:   clark66
```

> In earlier versions of GRASS, the *g.projinfo* tool was the primary means of querying the current GRASS location's projection.

We need to convert our data to UTM and NAD27 before importing it into GRASS, so that the two different projections match up. We can use the *proj* utility, which isn't part of GRASS, but is a utility from the *PROJ.4* cartographic projection library. If you don't have PROJ.4, you can get it from Debian APT with **apt-get install proj**, or from its homepage at *http://www.remotesensing.org/proj/* in a variety of forms. The *proj* utility accepts coordinates, one pair per line, in a source projection, and outputs the same coordinates in the specified target projection. We'll use *proj* to convert our *sites.txt* file from lat/long against WGS84 to UTM zone 10 against NAD27:

```
GRASS:~/hacks/viewshed > proj +proj=utm +zone=10 +datum=NAD27 sites.txt >
sites_utm.txt
GRASS:~/hacks/viewshed > cat sites_utm.txt
548938.11    4179471.21    SFLan11
552782.41    4178884.71    Potrero
551130.05    4176854.99    Bernal
```

Now we can import *sites_utm.txt* directly into a vector layer called nodes in GRASS, by feeding the file into the standard input of the *v.in.ascii* utility. However, *v.in.ascii* expects the data to be separated by pipe (|) characters, so we'll have to use the standard Unix *tr* command to change the delimiter for us:

```
GRASS:~/hacks/viewshed > tr '\t' '|' < sites_utm.txt | v.in.ascii out=nodes
```

Next, we can display these points, and then label them, with the following commands:

```
GRASS:~/hacks/viewshed > d.vect nodes display=shape \
icon=basic/box color=blue
GRASS:~/hacks/viewshed > d.vect nodes display=attr attrcol=str_1 \
lcolor=blue bgcolor=white xref=left yref=bottom
```

The display=attr option to *d.vect* instructs it to display shape attributes, rather than the shapes themselves. In GRASS 5.7, every shape in a vector layer is potentially associated with a row of *attributes*—labels, statistics, and so on—stored in data tables inside GRASS. We don't really have the space to get into why *v.in.ascii* put the labels into an attribute column with the unimaginative title of str_1, but if you're interested, try running **v.info -c nodes**, and possibly **echo "select * from nodes" | db.select** (really!) to see how this sort of thing works under the hood.

> In versions prior to GRASS 5.7, point data was stored in separate *site* layers, rather than as vector layers containing points. If you're running an older version of GRASS, you'll need to use the following commands instead:
>
> ```
> GRASS:~/hacks/viewshed > s.in.ascii sites=nodes \
> in=sites_utm.txt
> ```
> ```
> GRASS:~/hacks/viewshed > d.sites nodes color=blue \
> type=box
> ```
> ```
> GRASS:~/hacks/viewshed > d.site.labels nodes \
> color=blue back=white xref=left yref=bottom
> ```
> Consult the manpages for each of these commands for further details.

At this point, you should see all three locations appear over the map of San Francisco on the graphics monitor. Now, use the *d.zoom* tool to constrain our viewing region to an area that just includes our three nodes. We ended up with a region extending from *(4176114, 548712)* to *(4179786, 553358)*. You can set this region manually in GRASS by typing **g.region s=4176114 w=548712 n=4179786 e=553358** and then save the region with **g.region save=sflan**. You can then recall it at any time with **g.region sflan**. After doing this, run **d.redraw** to refresh your display. Figure 6-41 shows the zoomed-in map with all three sites displayed.

## Making the Radio Viewshed Layer

Now that we have our locations set in GRASS, we could go ahead and run the *r.los* tool, which plots a *viewshed* from a given location (i.e., the total area to which that location has line of sight) against an elevation layer.

*Figure 6-41. Map showing potential SFLan sites*

However, *r.los* plots the viewshed in all directions, which we decidedly don't want; the SFLan11 node probably has a directional antenna on its tower, with approximately a 60-degree beam width. Any receiver falling outside that 60-degree arc originating from SFLan11 is going to have a hard time getting a signal, even if it might otherwise have line of sight.

Fortunately, *r.los* has a patt_map, or pattern map, option, which lets us limit the area to which *r.los* plots line of sight by supplying a raster layer containing a value of 1 in every cell we want line of sight for, and a 0 in every cell we don't. We're going to have to generate this pattern-map layer from scratch, unfortunately, because GRASS doesn't offer a built-in way of plotting arcs in a given direction from an arbitrary location.

Fortunately, GRASS does offer the extremely powerful and complex *r.map-calc* tool, which allows us to feed it equations, perhaps based on values from existing map layers, and output the results of those equations to a new raster layer. Among *r.mapcalc*'s supported functions is the conventional two-argument atan( ) function. We give it the difference along the *x*- and *y*-axes between our origin and our destination, and get back the bearing in degrees between the two points. If the bearing to any arbitrary point falls within the arc direction and beam width, then we include that point in our pattern map; otherwise, we leave it out. (Note that *r.mapcalc* does loads more than this; take a look at its manpage to get a sense of its scope.)

## Generating the Line-of-Sight Layer

The following is the entirety of a GRASS script we concocted called *r.slice.sh*, a shell script that wraps *r.mapcalc* to generate *r.los* pattern-map layers:

```
#!/bin/bash

for i
do
    case $i in
        arc=*)
            arc=${i#arc=} ;;
        azi*=*)
            azimuth=${i#azi*=} ;;
        map=*)
            map=${i#map=} ;;
        coord*=*)
            coord=${i#coord*=}; x=${coord%,*}; y=${coord#*,} ;;
    esac
done

if [ ! "$arc" -o ! "$azimuth" -o ! "$map" -o ! "$x" -o ! "$y" ];
then
    echo "Usage: $(basename $0)"
    echo "    map=raster coordinates=x,y arc=value azimuth=value"
    exit -1
fi

r.mapcalc <<EOF
$map = eval( \\
    min   = $azimuth - ($arc / 2), \\
    max   = $azimuth + ($arc / 2), \\
    theta = atan( y() - $y, x() - $x ), \\
    if( \\
        ((theta >= min) && (theta <= max)) || \\
        ((theta - 360 >= min) && (theta - 360 <= max)), \\
        1, 0 ) \\
)
EOF

r.colors map=$map color=rules <<EOF
0 black
1 white
EOF
```

Once we have all the parameters we need, we feed them into *r.mapcalc* using shell substitution in a *here document*. The extra clause in the *r.mapcalc* code involving the theta - 360 calculation handles the edge case where the antenna arc crosses the 0-degree line. Finally, the script assigns a simple black and white color map to our new antenna-arc layer, to make it easy to view.

Now, assuming that SFLan11 has a 60-degree panel pointed to the southeast at 115 degrees true, we can use *r.slice.sh* to generate our antenna-arc layer like so:

```
GRASS:~/hacks/viewshed > ./r.slice.sh map=antenna_arc coord=548938.
11,4179471.21 azi=115 arc=60
100%
Color table for [antenna_arc] set to rules
```

The coordinates for SFLan11 have simply been taken from *sites_utm.txt*. Use **d.rast antenna_arc** to view the resulting raster layer, shown in Figure 6-42.

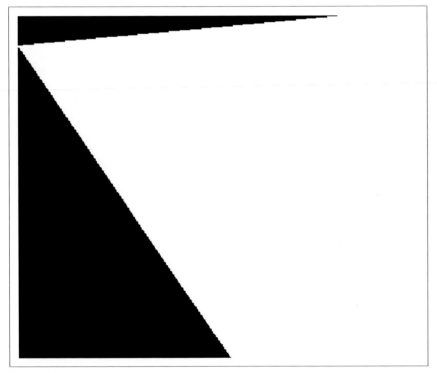

*Figure 6-42. Map showing antenna arc*

With our new pattern-map layer, we can make realistic models of our wireless viewshed. Feed it to *r.los*, along with the elevation model loaded from "Add Relief to Your Topographic Maps" [Hack #72] in the raster layer called sf_elevation. Typically, *r.los* takes a *very* long time to run—especially on large regions, where the time to run seems to grow exponentially with the size of the region, which is one of the reasons we zoomed in on our area of interest earlier. Here's the call to *r.los*:

```
GRASS:~/hacks/viewshed > r.los in=sf_elevation out=los coord=548938.
11,4179471.21 patt_map=antenna_arc obs_elev=25 max_dist=5000
   100%
```

The obs_elev parameter to *r.los* tells it that the observer (really, the transmitter in this case) is 25 meters above ground level, and the max_dist parameter specifies line-of-sight calculations out to 5 kilometers from the viewing point. The viewshed is written to a raster layer we called los. This command took seven and a half minutes to run on a 1 GHz laptop running Debian Linux! The progress indicator for *r.los* appears to advance inconsistently, so don't take that as an absolute measure of its actual progress, either. Let's view the new layer in our display using **d.rast los**, as shown in Figure 6-43.

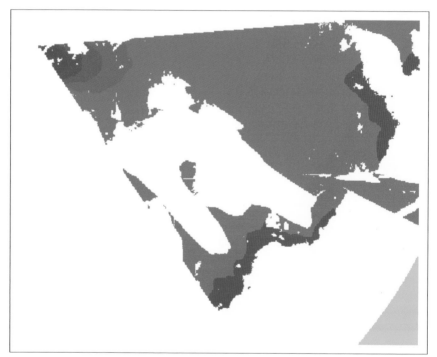

*Figure 6-43. Line-of-sight plot*

The new line-of-sight layer is colored according to the vertical angle between the transmitter and each point in the viewshed. The yellow arc you see at the bottom right of the layer is where *r.los* wrote values of zero into the layer because those points were beyond the 5000-meter limit specified by max_dist. Really, those values should be null (i.e., no data) instead of zero, so that they don't interfere with the display of underlying layers when we put everything together, so let's use the *r.null* tool to reset them:

```
GRASS:~/hacks/viewshed > r.null los setnull=0
Writing new data for [los]... 100%
GRASS:~/hacks/viewshed > d.redraw
  100%
```

## Superimposing Line-of-Sight and Base Map Layers

Now we can put everything together on one map:

```
GRASS:~/hacks/viewshed > d.erase
GRASS:~/hacks/viewshed > d.rast sf_topo
  100%
GRASS:~/hacks/viewshed > d.rast -o los
  100%
GRASS:~/hacks/viewshed > d.vect nodes display=shape,attr attrcol=str_1
icon=basic/box color=orange lcolor=orange bgcolor=white xref=left
yref=bottom
```

The -o option to *d.rast* tells it to overlay the los layer on top of the sf_topo layer, rather than overwriting it, leaving the underlying layer present wherever there are null values in the top layer. Note that we changed the site colors to orange from blue, just to make them a little easier to see over the line-of-sight plot. Figure 6-44 shows the result.

Not bad, eh? In Potrero Hill and Bernal Heights, we should think about buying wireless equipment, but maybe our friends on the eastern side of both hills should wait until someone closer or more advantageously located gets connected before obtaining their own setup.

The underlying elevation model is still a little hard to visualize, though. If you went through all the steps involved in "Add Relief to Your Topographic Maps" [Hack #72], you should still have a layer called sf_elevation_relshade in your mapset. You can determine this for sure by running **g.list type=rast**. If so, we can use the method described in that hack to display a topo relief layer as our base map:

```
GRASS:~/hacks/viewshed > d.his h_map=sf_topo i_map=sf_elevation_relshade
  100%
GRASS:~/hacks/viewshed > d.rast -o los
  100%
```

You can then plot the sites and site labels as before. The result looks something like Figure 6-45.

*Figure 6-44. Shaded line of sight*

In reality, of course, you can use any base map you like. If we want to dump this map to a graphic file, so that we can share the good news with our friends, we can export this set of layers to a PNG file [Hack #75].

## Caveats

Using GRASS to analyze line of sight for wireless networks still comes with a few caveats. First, you may have noticed that we didn't specify a receiver height; that's because *r.los* doesn't allow us to do so, so we're stuck with a map that shows us line of sight to a receiver at ground level. In this particular case, it won't make much difference, but one can imagine circumstances where it might. Second, *r.los* is abysmally slow for anything but the shortest distance plots, and even passing it a pattern map doesn't really speed things up much. One alternative that purports to solve these issues is *r.cva*, a "cumulative viewshed analysis" tool that ships separately from GRASS and must be built against a compiled GRASS source tree. The *r.cva* tool runs faster and allows you to specify receiver height, but the calling conventions to *r.cva* are a bit more complicated, so we'll leave its use as an exercise for the reader. You can get the source for *r.cva* from *http://www.ucl.ac.uk/ ~tcrnmar/GIS/r.cva.html*.

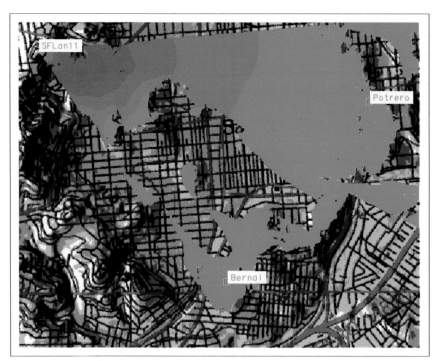

*Figure 6-45. Relief map with site labels*

Again, we have to emphasize that analysis from elevation models is only the beginning for building wireless networks. Even if the line-of-sight plot says the network is marginal or it only barely can't be done, you might want to try to set up the link anyway; digital elevation models have been known to be erroneous, or at least inaccurate. Further, no terrain model can properly account for ground clutter, such as buildings and trees. In the end, all this sort of analysis can do is help you prioritize your options to help to figure out which ones are more or less likely to work—but, sometimes, that's all you need to get started.

### See Also

- "Why You Can't Watch Broadcast TV" **[Hack #18]**
- "Add Relief to Your Topographic Maps" **[Hack #72]**
- "Share Your GRASS Maps with the World" **[Hack #75]**
- "Analyze Elevation Profiles for Wireless Community Networks" **[Hack #19]**

# Share Your GRASS Maps with the World

Export your carefully crafted GIS layers into human-compatible formats.

If you've worked through the GRASS hacks in this book, you might have noticed a standard finale: "Now see "Share Your GRASS Maps with the World" [Hack #75] to export your maps to an image file." Having got this far, congratulations! Now the world can know of your triumphant ascent of the GRASS learning curve.

The *r.out* set of GRASS functions provides many ways to export your raster layers into different GIS-compatible formats, such as ESRI's ArcInfo, binary vector format, etc. However, the most useful formats to share map data in— *PNG* for viewing on the Web, or *PostScript* for print publication—both involve some fiddling.

## Publish Raster Maps as PNG Images

In the simplest case, you might just have a raster layer in GRASS that you want to export as a PNG image. *r.out.png* is ideal for these purposes:

```
GRASS:~ > r.out.png in=nations out=nations.png
rows = 2250, cols = 4500
Converting nations...  96%
Done.
```

You should note that *r.out.png*, like most GRASS raster functions, only operates on the current region. Be sure to run **g.region rast=...** first if you want to export the whole raster layer.

## Publish PNG Images via the Display Monitor

If you have a whole set of different layers you want to export together, it's better to use the PNG display driver that comes with GRASS. This works just like writing to an X monitor with *d.mon*, except that it's writing directly to a *.png* file.

```
GRASS:~ > d.mon start=PNG
PNG: GRASS_TRUECOLOR status: FALSE
PNG: collecting to file: map.png,
     GRASS_WIDTH=640, GRASS_HEIGHT=480
Graphics driver [PNG] started
GRASS:~ > d.rast eco
  100%
GRASS:~ > d.vect borders type=boundary color=black
GRASS:~ > d.mon stop=PNG
Monitor 'PNG' terminated
```

The disadvantage of this approach is that you can't see the image while you're creating it, and it can be annoying to have to repeat a long sequence of command-line actions if you make a small mistake. This is where *d.save* will save you.

As discussed in "Find Your Way Around GRASS" [Hack #69], d.save -c prints the list of commands that were used to generate the current contents of the display monitor to its standard output. You can use shell redirection to pipe this list to a file and then manually add the d.mon start=png line to the beginning and the d.mon stop=png line to the end. The result is a shell script that will generate your PNG. You can run it directly from the GRASS shell and tweak the lines until you're quite happy with the results.

By default, the PNG monitor generates a 256-color image 640 pixels wide and 480 pixels high and stores it in a file called *map.png*, but we can alter that outcome with a variety of environment variables. The following commands export the map described in "Find Your Way Around GRASS" [Hack #69] with a black background to an 800×600 pixel True Color PNG file called *western_europe.png*:

```
GRASS:~ > export GRASS_WIDTH=800
GRASS:~ > export GRASS_HEIGHT=600
GRASS:~ > export GRASS_TRUECOLOR=TRUE
GRASS:~ > export GRASS_BACKGROUNDCOLOR=000000
GRASS:~ > export GRASS_PNGFILE=western_europe.png
GRASS:~ > d.mon start=PNG
PNG: GRASS_TRUECOLOR status: TRUE
PNG: collecting to file: western_europe.png,
     GRASS_WIDTH=800, GRASS_HEIGHT=600
     Graphics driver [PNG] started
GRASS:~ > sh ./europe.sh
 100%
GRASS:~ > d.mon stop=PNG
Monitor 'PNG' terminated
GRASS:~ > d.mon select=x0
```

The last *d.mon* command reselects our original X11 monitor, so that any further display commands are sent there, rather than to the now-closed PNG monitor. You can now view the PNG file in an ordinary image viewer or upload it to the Web to share with your friends and colleagues.

> You will probably find that, on the whole, the images output by the GRASS PNG monitor look a lot better with GRASS_TRUECOLOR set to TRUE.

## Publish GRASS Maps as PostScript Files

Generating PostScript images from GRASS isn't quite as straightforward as generating PNGs, but the results will often look a lot nicer. The *ps.map* utility provided for this purpose is classic GRASS: it's flexible, powerful, and utterly arcane. *ps.map* is driven by a "little language" for display scripting that, when fed to GRASS, will generate PostScript code. With *ps.map*, you can add color tables, legends, custom fonts, and scale indicators, all the visual trappings of professional looking print cartography.

Figure 6-46 shows a PostScript map of selected nodes from SFLan, a community wireless network based in San Francisco. The map was made with TIGER/Line street data, National Elevation Data obtained from the USGS SDDS, and, of course, *ps.map*. The contour lines were generated in the fashion described in "Make Your Own Contour Maps" **[Hack #73]**.

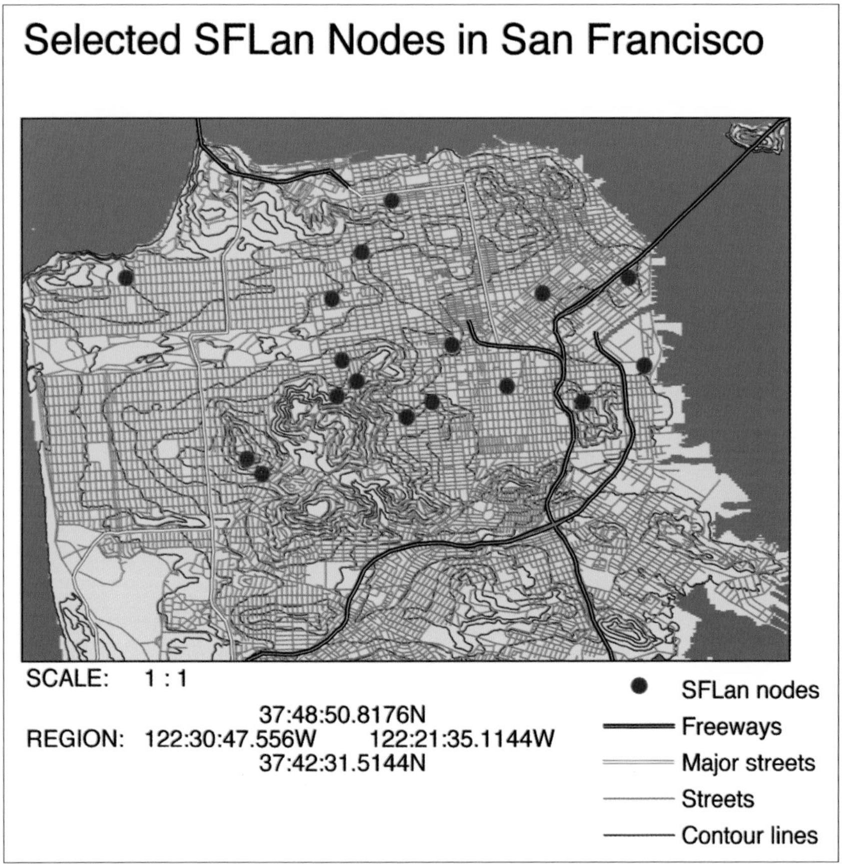

*Figure 6-46. A map of San Francisco generated with ps.map*

Example 6-1 shows the set of *ps.map* commands used to tell GRASS to generate Figure 6-46.

*Example 6-1. sf_tiger.txt: ps.map commands used to generate Figure 6-46*

```
 1   raster dem
 2
 3   vpoints sflan
 4      label SFLan nodes
 5      color blue
 6      fcolor 64 64 128
 7      symbol basic/circle
 8      size 10
 9   end
10
11   vlines tiger
12      where CFCC ~ 'A1'
13      label Freeways
14      color red
15      width 1
16      hcolor black
17      hwidth 1
18   end
19
20   vlines tiger
21      where CFCC ~ 'A3' OR CFCC ~ 'A2'
22      label Major streets
23      color white
24      width 1
25      hcolor red
26      hwidth 1
27   end
28
29   vlines tiger
30      where CFCC ~ 'A5' or CFCC ~ 'A4'
31      label Streets
32      color grey
33      width 1
34   end
35
36   vlines sfcontour
37      label Contour lines
38      color 64 64 0
39   end
40
41   vlegend
42      where 6 0
43      fontsize 16
44   end
45
46   mapinfo
47      where 0 0
```

*Example 6-1. sf_tiger.txt: ps.map commands used to generate Figure 6-46 (continued)*

```
48      fontsize 16
49    end
50
51    header
52       file sf_tiger_hdr.txt
53       fontsize 28
54    end
```

The raster command in line 1 of *sf_tiger.txt* draws the digital elevation
model of San Francisco as a raster base layer, which had been previously colored to distinguish land and water areas. Lines 3–9 draw the location of
SFLan nodes from the sflan vector layer, with circles drawn in blue and
filled with a darker shade of blue. Lines 11–18 introduce a vlines block,
which draws a portion of a layer called tiger. The where command in line 12
filters the vectors to draw only those that have a Census Feature Class Code
(CFCC) attribute matching A1, which corresponds to limited-access highways. (The CFCC attribute is just a property of the particular data set used
to draw the map.) These features are given the label "Freeways" and drawn
in a red line 1 pixel wide, with a black highlight 1 pixel wide on either side.
Major streets and ordinary streets are given corresponding treatment in lines
20–34. In lines 36–39, the contour lines from the sfcontour vector layer are
drawn in brown. The legend and map information are placed in lines 41–49,
and lines 51–54 display the contents of a text file called *sf_tiger_hdr.txt*
across the header of the map, in 28-point type.

> Interestingly, *ps.map* draws vector layers in the *reverse* order
> that they are listed in the map file.

*ps.map* is run in the following fashion:

```
GRASS:~ > ps.map input=sf_tiger.txt output=sf_tiger.ps
```

If you don't have a PostScript viewer, some free alternatives are available in
"Experiment with Different Cartographic Projections" [Hack #28]. If, for whatever reason, you prefer Encapsulated PostScript, *ps.map* will generate that
instead, with the -e option. From there, you can use a tool like the *epstopdf*
program that ships with GhostScript to convert PostScript or EPS to PDF,
for example.

One drawback with *ps.map* is that it can only read one raster layer into a
PostScript image, unless you're using three rasters to make RGB color com-
posites. If you want to display the results of layering more than one raster
image together—for example, the topographical height field as a transpar-

---

ent layer over a DRG street map **[Hack #72]**—you have to first combine them into one raster layer, perhaps by using *r.patch* or *r.composite*.

As PostScript is a vector format, vector display is where it really shines, and you can layer as many vectors into your PostScript document as you like. *ps. map* has different vector options for importing shapes, lines, and points. However, the parameters are more or less the same for each vector option.

Obviously, with a tool as powerful as *ps.map*, we can only offer the outlines of its general functionality, and we strongly recommend perusing the documentation if you're interested in publishing your maps to the world this way.

## Explore the Effects of Global Warming
**See what sea-level change means for the world's coastlines and the people who live near them.**

If present trends in greenhouse gas production, deforestation, and average surface temperature continue, it seems likely that Earth's ice caps will continue to melt, dumping untold quantities of water back into the oceans from whence they came and causing sea levels to rise all around the world. Of course, the consequences of such an event would be dramatic, but what exactly would be the result? Where would Earth's new coastlines lie? How many people might be affected? Questions like these can reveal the full power of GIS, which allows us to pose—and hopefully answer—"what if?" queries that have a geospatial component.

### Importing the Elevation Data

The first part of this question—where will the new coastlines be—depends on where the current coastlines are. We can start by getting a one-kilometer resolution digital elevation model (DEM) from the GLOBE Project and importing it into GRASS. The GLOBE project's site is *http://www.ngdc.noaa. gov/seg/topo/globe.shtml*, but you can get the data directly from *http://www. ngdc.noaa.gov/seg/topo/globeget.shtml*. Click the link to "Select Your Own Area," and you'll be taken to a form where you can specify the details of the DEM you want. Select the Custom... region from the drop-down box on the left and then enter the bounding box for the DEM. We selected -12 degrees for the western edge, 30 degrees for the eastern edge, 65 degrees for the northern edge, and 34 for the southern edge. Beneath the extent selection area, you'll see a whole raft of datafile formatting options. Select ESRI ArcView as your "Export type," a "Data type" of int16, Compressed TAR file as the "Compression option," and FTP as the "Transfer option." Give the data set a custom filename like *europe_dem*. Finally, click "Get Data." You'll be taken to a download page that will update periodically with the progress of the data set assembly on the server side, which takes about a minute. (Note the cute stick figure juggling 10 balls!) Finally, your browser will download the tarball, which should weigh in at about 13 MB.

The DEM will be in ESRI Binary Interleaved, or *BIL format*, which can fortuitously be read by GRASS's *r.in.gdal* tool. Make a new directory, and unpack the tarball inside it:

```
GRASS 5.7.0:~ > mkdir climate
GRASS 5.7.0:~ > cd climate
GRASS 5.7.0:~/climate > tar xvfz ~/Desktop/europe_dem.tgz
europe_dem.bil
europe_dem.hdr
europe_dem.clr
GRASS 5.7.0:~/climate > r.in.gdal -o in=europe_dem.bil out=dem
 100%
CREATING SUPPORT FILES FOR dem
```

The tarball contains three files: a *.bil* file that contains the actual elevation data, a *.hdr* file that contains the metadata, and a *.clr* file that contains a default color map. We use *r.in.gdal* to parse the BIL file into a raster layer called dem. The -o option of *r.in.gdal* tells it to ignore the fact that the BIL file has no associated projection information. This isn't problematic, as the DEM data is referenced with geographic coordinates (i.e., latitude and longitude) and isn't in a particular projection.

 *r.in.gdal* only recently acquired the ability to automatically load BIL files into the right extents. If your installed version of the GDAL library is older than 1.2.1, you may have to use *r.in.bin*, which has a significantly more complex syntax. This might be a good excuse to get newer versions of GDAL and GRASS, or maybe trying rebuilding them from source!

We can assign a simple green-yellow-red color map to the dem layer, set the current region to that of the raster layer, and then display it on an X monitor:

```
GRASS 5.7.0:~/climate > r.colors dem color=gyr
Color table for [dem] set to gyr
GRASS 5.7.0:~/climate > g.region rast=dem
GRASS 5.7.0:~/climate > d.mon start=x0
using default visual which is TrueColor
ncolors: 16777216
Graphics driver [x0] started
GRASS 5.7.0:~/climate > d.rast dem bg=blue
 100%
```

Since the DEM layer import sets existing ocean cell values to *null* (i.e., no value), we use the bg parameter of *d.rast* to display these background cells as blue, instead of white. Figure 6-47 shows the result. Now we can start to examine what the coastlines will look like if the sea levels rise.

*Figure 6-47. A colorized elevation model of Western Europe*

## Method 1: Hacking the Color Table

Let us suppose the effect of global warming is to cause sea levels to rise by 10 meters, or about 32 feet. This is hopefully a very pessimistic prediction, but it will serve to highlight the effects in question. There are two ways of approaching our visualization of the resulting coastline. The really hackish approach, which we will look at first, is to leave the data itself alone but hack the DEM layer's color table, so that the submerged bits appear to be underwater.

First, let's assign a custom color map to the DEM, using the rules option of *r.colors*, which lets us specify a set of values (in this case, elevation in meters) and a color to assign to each one. GRASS will then shade each cell in the DEM relative to the values we specify in our color map:

```
GRASS 5.7.0:~/climate > r.colors dem color=rules
Enter rules, "end" when done, "help" if you need it.
```

```
Data range is -103 to 4570
> -103 blue
> 0 green
> 1000 yellow
> 4570 red
> end
Color table for [dem] set to rules
GRASS 5.7.0:~/climate > d.redraw
  100%
```

In essence, this color map says, "Color all the cells below sea level in blue shades, land near sea level in green, land from there up to 1000 meters in increasingly yellow shades, land higher than 1000 meters in increasingly red shades up to 4570 meters, our maximum value." Figure 6-48 shows the result, in which the topography of Western Europe stands out a little more strongly than in the previous figure.

*Figure 6-48. Western Europe, sporting a custom color map*

> User-supplied color maps in GRASS don't have to completely cover the range of values in the raster layer, but *r.colors* will complain if they don't. You can also use *r.info* to find out what the range is before creating a new color map.

Now, if we want to visualize which parts of Western Europe will be underwater if the sea level rises 10 meters, the easiest way to do so is to just adjust the color map so we see blue all the way up to 10 meters. To make the color map easier to tweak, we can dump the following rules into in a text file called *dem.rules*:

```
-103 blue
10 blue
11 green
1000 yellow
4570 red
```

The new set of color map rules says "Turn everything up to 10 meters blue and make the rest green, yellow, and red as before." We feed *dem.rules* into *r.colors* via redirection—this is a Unix shell, after all! Figure 6-49 shows the result of raising the apparent sea level to 10 meters by hacking the color map:

```
GRASS 5.7.0:~/climate > r.colors dem color=rules <dem.rules
Color table for [dem] set to rules
GRASS 5.7.0:~/climate > d.redraw
    100%
```

*Figure 6-49. Western Europe, with apparent sea level raised to 10 meters*

The first thing we notice is that the Netherlands almost disappear completely! Additionally, major cities like London, Copenhagen, and Venice fare rather poorly. This visualization practically begs our other question: if the sea level were to rise by 10 meters, how many people might be displaced? To address this question, we'll have to redo our analysis to specifically identify which cells in our DEM raster will be submerged.

## Method 2: Applying Raster Algebra

Our second approach will use *raster algebra* to identify which parts of our elevation model lie below 10 meters, and hence are at risk of being submerged. Raster algebra is simply any process that derives each cell of a new output layer by applying a user-specified equation to each corresponding cell in a set of input layers. The *r.mapcalc* tool performs this function in GRASS:

```
GRASS 5.7.0:~/climate > r.mapcalc 'submerged = if(dem <= 10, 1, null())'
  100%
GRASS 5.7.0:~/climate > r.colors submerged color=rules
Enter rules, "end" when done, "help" if you need it.
Data range is 1 to 1
> 1 blue
> end
Color table for [submerged] set to rules
```

Our call to *r.mapcalc* creates a new layer called submerged, which contains a value of 1 everywhere dem contains a value less than or equal to 10, and a null value everywhere else. This gives us a raster layer that consists solely of the land areas that would be submerged, which we then color blue. If we reset the colors of our dem layer, we can display the original coastlines subsequently overlaid with the new coastline, giving us a map that looks schematically similar to the map we made in Figure 6-49:

```
GRASS 5.7.0:~/climate > r.colors dem color=gyr
Color table for [dem] set to gyr
GRASS 5.7.0:~/climate > d.erase
GRASS 5.7.0:~/climate > d.rast dem bg=blue
  100%
GRASS 5.7.0:~/climate > d.rast -o submerged
  100%
```

The -o option to *d.rast* causes it to filter out the null values in submerged, rather than erasing the dem layer underneath, resulting in an overlay effect. If we want to highlight, rather than blend in, the submerged areas, we can assign a different color to that layer and redraw. Figure 6-50 shows the highlighted areas overlaid on the original map.

```
GRASS 5.7.0:~/climate > r.colors submerged color=rules
Enter rules, "end" when done, "help" if you need it.
Data range is 1 to 1
```

```
> 1 red
> end
Color table for [submerged] set to rules
GRASS 5.7.0:~/climate > d.redraw
  100%
```

*Figure 6-50. Western Europe, with potentially submerged areas highlighted*

All of the potential elaborations of this idea, such as using *r.mapcalc* to combine the original and submerged land areas into a single layer or using *v.in.ascii* (or *s.in.ascii* in GRASS 5.3 and earlier) to import and overlay a map of major European cities, are left as exercises for the reader, so that we can get back to our second question.

> You may have noticed a fallacy in our consideration of rising sea levels, which is the assumption that all land areas below our new, hypothetical sea level will be automatically submerged, whether or not the areas are anywhere near an ocean. After all, even in contemporary Europe, significant land areas lie below sea level, sometimes as a result of human intervention. A proper GIS treatment of the subject would take hydrology models, geodetic models, meteorological patterns, and other factors into account, and so our naïve analysis, is at best, a first approximation. We did say it was a hack!

## Adding Population Data into the Mix

At last, we return to our second question: how many people in Western Europe might be affected by a 10-meter rise in global sea level? To answer this, we will need to import a layer containing population data, which we can combine with our elevation layers to begin making estimates. The "Gridded Population Map of the World," offered by Colombia University's Center for International Earth Information Science Network at *http://sedac. ciesin.org/plue/gpw/*, is an excellent source of global population data. Download the binary version of their most recent adjusted population data for Europe (from 1995, as of this writing) from *ftp://ftp.ciesin.org/pub/gpw/ europe/v2eup95agi.zip* and unpack it into your working directory. Inside you'll find another BIL data set, which, in principle, should be imported into GRASS in the same fashion as the elevation data we imported earlier:

```
GRASS 5.7.0:~/climate > unzip v2eup95agi.zip
Archive:  v2eup95agi.zip
  inflating: eup95agi.bil
  inflating: eup95agi.blw
  inflating: eup95agi.hdr
 extracting: eup95agi.stx
  inflating: readme.txt
```

However, in practice, the GDAL driver has no way to distinguish between 32-bit floating point values and the 32-bit integers actually stored in the BIL file, due to a bug in the BIL format specification. There are two ways around this. One is to use *r.in.bin*, but that means calculating the extents of the file by hand. The other way is to use GDAL's "virtual raster" driver to explicitly specify the file structure of the BIL file by means of a separate XML file. We'll take the latter approach. If you run *gdalinfo* on the data set, you can get the extents and spatial resolution (i.e., degrees per pixel) of the raster layer. We'll use the -mm option to have GDAL count the minimum and maximum values, just to verify that it has trouble with this data set:

```
GRASS 5.7.0:~/gis/europe > gdalinfo -mm eup95agi.bil
Driver: EHdr/ESRI .hdr Labelled
Size is 1680, 1320
Coordinate System is `'
Origin = (-25.000000,85.000000)
Pixel Size = (0.04166667,-0.04166667)
Corner Coordinates:
Upper Left  (  -25.0000000,  85.0000000)
Lower Left  (  -25.0000000,  30.0000000)
Upper Right (   45.0000000,  85.0000000)
Lower Right (   45.0000000,  30.0000000)
Center      (   10.0000000,  57.5000000)
Band 1 Block=1680x1 Type=Float32, ColorInterp=Undefined
    Computed Min/Max=0.000,0.000
```

As you can see, GDAL gets the minimum and maximum values wrong, as well as the data type (Float32 instead of Int32). Using the geographic origin, and the layer height, width, and pixel size indicated by *gdalinfo*, we can create a GDAL virtual-raster description that explicitly sets the cell data type to 32-bit integer. Fire up a text editor and dump the following to a file called *eup95agi.vrt*:

```
<VRTDataset rasterXSize="1680" rasterYSize="1320">
  <GeoTransform>-25,0.0416666667,0,85,0,-0.0416666667</GeoTransform>
  <VRTRasterBand dataType="Int32" band="1" subClass="VRTRawRasterBand">
    <SourceFilename relativetoVRT="1">eup95agi.bil</SourceFilename>
    <ByteOrder>MSB</ByteOrder>
  </VRTRasterBand>
</VRTDataset>
```

As you can see, we've copied in the raster filename, as well as its height and width. The format of the GeoTransform element is (*X origin, X resolution, X rotation, Y origin, Y rotation, Y resolution*), where the origin is the geographic coordinates of the upper lefthand corner of the layer, as given by GDAL. We copied in the origin and resolution values from *gdalinfo* and left the rotation values at zero, since we presume that the image is oriented north-up. Finally, we set the byte order to most significant byte first, or MSB (which you can derive yourself by examining the *eup95agi.hdr* file).

> The other option for ByteOrder is least significant byte first, or LSB. The difference is the same as the little-endian/big-endian byte ordering that distinguishes different computing architectures. When dealing with raw GIS data (e.g., BIL format data), your best bet is usually to pick one, and if that gives you really bizarre values, then try the other. In general, bizarre values in GIS data sets are often a sign of data-type or byte-order issues. The GDAL virtual driver, which is documented at *http://gdal.org/gdal_vrttut.html*, can really come in handy when dealing with these circumstances.

Now you can treat this XML file as if it were an ordinary GDAL layer, by running the following in GRASS:

```
GRASS 5.7.0:~/climate > r.in.gdal -o in=eup95agi.vrt out=population
100%
CREATING SUPPORT FILES FOR population
```

In our new population layer, each cell has a value equal to the estimated number of people that lived in the area represented by that cell in 1995. Unlike the elevation data, the population data doesn't differentiate between water areas and places that are simply uninhabited, which would appear as an undifferentiated mess if you ran **d.rast population** at this point. (Try it and see, if you like. *d.what.rast* can be used to query individual raster cells with your mouse.)

To address this, we'll employ *r.null* to set unpopulated areas in our population data set to "No Value." For good measure, we will replace the original population layer with the new one and assign it a custom color map, since none of the built-in color maps look very good with it:

```
GRASS 5.7.0:~/gis/europe > r.null population setnull=0
Writing new data for [population]...  100%
GRASS 5.7.0:~/climate > r.colors population color=rules
Enter rules, "end" when done, "help" if you need it.
Data range is 0 to 626281
> 0 green
> 1000 yellow
> 10000 red
> 700000 purple
> end
Color table for [population] set to rules
GRASS 5.7.0:~/climate > d.erase
GRASS 5.7.0:~/climate > d.rast population bg=blue
  100%
```

Once the custom color map is applied, we get a very nice looking population map of Europe, as shown in Figure 6-51.

## Estimating Population Displacement

Now, back to our second question, which was, "How many people in Western Europe will be displaced from their homes by a 10-meter rise in sea level?" We are finally at the point where we can estimate this number, by tallying up the values of all the cells in our population layer that match the non-null cells in our submerged layer. Fortunately, GRASS provides a function for summing all the values of a given raster layer, and, if you already guessed that this function was called *r.sum*, give yourself a gold star.

As a check, let's run *r.sum* on our population layer and see if it produces a reasonable value. In order to make this work, we'll need to make sure that the resolution of the current GRASS region matches that of the population layer, or some values might end up being counted multiple times, which will throw the sum off. Running *r.info* on the population layer yields the following metadata:

```
GRASS 5.7.0:~/climate > r.info population
...
 |        N:    85N    S: 30N   Res: 0:02:30             |
 |        E:    45E    W: 25W   Res: 0:02:30
...
```

*Figure 6-51. A population map of Western Europe*

This tells us that the spatial resolution of the image is 2.5 minutes per pixel. We can feed this value directly into *g.region* and then run *r.sum* on the population layer:

```
GRASS 5.7.0:~/gis/europe > g.region res=0:02:30
GRASS 5.7.0:~/gis/europe > r.sum population
Reading pop... 100%
SUM = 604283674.000000
```

The value we get back, around 604 million, seems about right for the area depicted on our graphics monitor. Now let's create a displaced layer that contains the population values for all the areas in the submerged layer. In order to do this, the submerged layer and the population layer have to have the same resolution, or we'll be comparing apples to oranges. We can use *r.resample* to down-sample our submerged layer to the resolution of the population layer, and then use *r.mapcalc* to synthesize the displaced layer:

```
GRASS 5.7.0:~/gis/europe > r.resample in=submerged out=submerged2
percent complete:  100%
Creating support files for submerged2
creating new cats file...
GRASS 5.7.0:~/gis/europe > r.mapcalc 'displaced = if(isnull(submerged),
null( ), population)'
  100%
```

Finally, we can use *r.sum* to estimate how many people live in the potentially submerged areas:

```
GRASS 5.7.0:~/gis/europe > r.sum displaced
Reading displaced... 100%
SUM = 41109241.000000
```

Our answer is that about 41 million people will be displaced from their homes in Western and Central Europe, should the current sea levels rise by 10 meters. That's more than one in every 15 people! If we perform the same analysis for the East Coast of the United States, we find that as many as 25 million people there may be displaced, and, mind you, all this is based on population data that is already 10 years old. We haven't performed this analysis for, say, Bangladesh or Southeast Asia, but you can do the math yourself.

## Conclusion

As you can see, GIS is more than just about making maps; it offers us the chance to explore and explicate the state of our world not only in the past and present, but our future as well. The conclusion that we'd like you to draw is not that chaos and disaster are the eventual lot of humanity, although that may turn out to be the case. Instead, we hope that this exercise presents a cautionary tale about one possible future and that, through education and communication, our fate as one species among many on this precious planet may yet turn out bright.

### Become a GRASS Ninja
H A C K   Or, Zen and the Art of open source GIS.
#77

As children playing Make Believe, my friends and I would sometimes imagine ourselves to be a gang of ninja warriors, entrusted with some fiendishly difficult mission of infiltration and surprise. For whatever reason, ninja-hood, at least as we envisioned it, was the epitome of competence, resourcefulness, and daring. Ninjas could go anywhere, do anything, and, above all, they were unstoppable. Perhaps it's just the crowd I circulate in, but I still hear the word *ninja* used from time to time, to signify the presence of those qualities in one context or another. If one could say of a person that she was, for example, a culinary ninja, then, without a doubt, she was the person you wanted to have catering your son's Bar Mitzvah party.

In this hack, we'll talk about the kind of thinking it takes to become that most formidable of open source GIS users, a *GRASS ninja*. Mind you, I don't claim to be one by any stretch of the imagination, but in the preparation of this book, I've seen just enough of GRASS to want to gesticulate in the direction in which GRASS ninjahood might lie. In the process, I want to show why open source GIS in the Unix environment is at least as good, if not better—for values of "better" that might be important to hackers—than any flashy, GUI-laden, commercial GIS application you can imagine.

## Objective #1: Secure the World's Borders

The objective for this GRASS ninja-training mission is to obtain a high-quality vector map of the world's contemporary international borders,[*] with attribute values identifying which country each polygon belongs to. Ideally, the map should have no restrictions on its use and redistribution and be suitable for creating derivations, such as SVG base maps and so on. That's all. Nothing fancy. Right?

Well, you might think so, and if you weren't me, you might be right. But my coauthors and I searched high and low on the Web for a decent vector map of the world's international borders, and we didn't find one straight off the bat. We found a bunch of old data, like *VMAP0*, formerly known as the *Digital Chart of the World*, which is also a bit large and unwieldy to work with. We found out how to get the polygons out of the *Generic Mapping Tools* (see "Experiment with Different Cartographic Projections" **[Hack #28]**), only to discover that the countries weren't identified. We found different services, such as ESRI's world base map, or Pennsylvania State University's online DCW server, that only allow you to download a bit of the world at a time. We found some vector data of dubious provenance in ESRI's undocumented *Ungenerate*, or *E00*, format, which GRASS apparently decided it didn't like at all.

We found the United Nations Environmental Programme's GEO Data Portal (*http://geodata.grid.unep.ch/*), which offered a map of the world's first-level administrative divisions circa 1998 from ESRI in shapefile format. At first, we shied away from downloading it, because we were concerned about redistribution rights, but over on ESRI's site, we found some verbiage to the effect the data was all drawn from public domain sources—CIAWorld Data Bank II and so on—and that they claimed no intellectual property rights in the data set, beyond the shapefile format itself. So we downloaded the 5 MB ZIP file from *http://geodata.grid.unep.ch/download/admin98_po_shp.zip* and unpacked it, yielding about 13 MB of ESRI Shapefile:

```
GRASS:~/hacks/world > ls -la admin98*
-rw-rw-rw-  1 schuyler  staff    635858 Aug  4  1999 admin98.dbf
```

---

[*] We will ignore, for the moment, the fact that people often have quite heated differences of opinion on precisely whose international borders lie where.

```
-rw-rw-rw-  1 schuyler  staff    26733 Jul 23  2003 admin98.html
-rw-rw-rw-  1 schuyler  staff 12439792 Aug  4  1999 admin98.shp
-rw-rw-rw-  1 schuyler  staff    20932 Aug  4  1999 admin98.shx
-rw-r--r--  1 schuyler  staff  4877493 Sep 23 14:54 admin98_po_shp.zip
GRASS:~/hacks/world > v.in.ogr -o dsn=. layer=admin98 out=admin
```

The next thing we did was to try to get the data into GRASS so that we could have a look at it, play with it, and see what was in it. *v.in.ogr* was our tool of choice, with the -o option to tell GRASS to ignore the fact that the shapefile came without machine-readable projection metadata. This was safe to do, as the human-readable metadata in the HTML file assured us that the data was given in geographic coordinates (i.e., latitude and longitude) and therefore matched our current GRASS location.

> If we'd needed to create a new GRASS location for this, the thing to do would have been to create a latitude-longitude location, decline to set a geodetic datum, set the ellipsoid to something sensible like wgs84, and leave the default region alone (or set it to 90° N / −90° S / −180° W / 180° E).

Well, *v.in.ogr* chewed and puffed over the data for quite some time, importing it into GRASS's internal vector format, cleaning up the polygons, snapping vertices, eliminating redundant edges, and generally making sure that the topology of the vector data was correct and so forth. Finally, once it had finished and the dust had settled a bit, we found ourselves in possession of a new high-resolution vector layer of the world! Figure 6-52 shows a portion of Western Europe from the admin layer.

The attribute data was even demonstrably all there. GRASS 5.7 has a terrific vector-attribute model, in which each vector layer can be associated with a table of attributes, and then each feature in the layer can be associated with a row of data in the table, by means of a numeric *category ID*. GRASS offers a set of commands prefixed with *db*, which permit SQL-like interactions with a vector layer's attribute table. You can use *v.info* to get a list of attribute columns for a given table, and *db.select* to view the actual contents of those columns:

```
GRASS:~ > v.info -c admin
Displaying column type for database connection of field 1:
INTEGER|cat
CHARACTER|FIPS_ADMIN
CHARACTER|GMI_ADMIN
CHARACTER|ADMIN_NAME
CHARACTER|FIPS_CNTRY
CHARACTER|GMI_CNTRY
CHARACTER|CNTRY_NAME
...
```

*Figure 6-52. Part of a first attempt to get a vector map of the world into GRASS*

```
GRASS:~ > echo "select CAT,FIPS_CNTRY,CNTRY_NAME,ADMIN_NAME from admin" |
db.select | less
cat|FIPS_CNTRY|CNTRY_NAME|ADMIN_NAME
1|AA|Aruba|Aruba
2|AC|Antigua and Barbuda|Antigua and Barbuda
3|AF|Afghanistan|Badakhshan
4|AF|Afghanistan|Badghis
5|AF|Afghanistan|Baghlan
6|AF|Afghanistan|Bamian
...
```

We say "SQL-like" because, by default, the actual table is stored on disk in a
DBase IV *.dbf* file, but a vector layer can (at least in theory) be associated
with a table from an actual relational database, like MySQL or PostgreSQL.
The interested reader can refer to the GRASS documentation for further
details.

So far, so good. However, a single glance at Figure 6-52 immediately reveals that it depicts rather a few more boundaries than one is accustomed to seeing on a map of Europe. The international boundaries are there, to be sure, but so is every other first-level administrative boundary in the world, making individual countries a bit hard to pick out. This is well and good, but it also means we're not done yet.

> As it turns out, ESRI distributes a *cntry98.shp* data set that avoids some of these data-creation issues. However, we've never been able to find a copy of this data set available for download on the Web.

## Objective #2: Reunite the World's Nations

The would-be GRASS ninja is not daunted at this juncture. Surely, the ninja trainee must concur, GRASS must have some facility for merging polygons. We simply tell GRASS to merge all of the adjacent shapes belonging to the same country in a new vector layer, and we are done.

If a ninja-in-training may be permitted one flaw, perhaps that flaw is over-confidence. After a bit of poking in the GRASS documentation, we were forced to conclude that GRASS had no such tool, per se. GRASS has a tool, *v.extract*—which extracts vector features into a new layer, possibly based on an SQL WHERE query against the attribute table—and even has an option to "dissolve" the borders of adjacent polygons in the process. GRASS also has a tool called *v.patch*, which will patch multiple vector layers into a single one. The problem is that *v.extract* must be run separately for each of the 251 countries or country-like territories in the admin layer and then *v.patch* must patch each country into a new international borders layer. Worse, the attribute data that identifies each country by name and FIPS code must somehow be preserved in the process. To attempt the task by hand would be tedious even to contemplate.

However, you may have gathered that the ninja is second only to MacGyver in sheer resourcefulness. If there is a means at hand, the ninja must find some way to exploit it. First, we need a list of the countries and assorted territories involved. The FIPS code will suffice for this purpose:

```
GRASS:~/hacks/world > echo "select fips_cntry from admin" | db.select | sort
| uniq >fips.list
```

We're obliged to use the hoary Unix *sort* and *uniq* commands to extract the list of unique countries, because GRASS's rudimentary SQL parser doesn't support DISTINCT. Now, for each country in *fips.list*, we must *v.extract* it out of admin, and *v.patch* it into our new layer, which we will call borders. We could feed the list of countries to a bit of Perl and have the Perl script generate the necessary GRASS commands for us. That bit of Perl might look as follows:

```
while (<>) {
    chomp;
    print qq/v.extract -d in=admin out=tmp new=$. where="FIPS_CNTRY = '$_'"\n/;
    print qq/v.patch -a in=tmp out=borders\n/;
}
```

The -d option to *v.extract* instructs it to dissolve internal borders between shapes. *v.extract* then writes the shapes for each country to a layer called tmp. In the process, the shapes are assigned a new category value equal to $., which is Perl for "the current line number of the input file." Recall that *fips. list* is alphabetized. As a result, all the shapes from the first country from our *fips.list* file (Aruba) will receive the category #1 in the new layer, the second country (Antigua and Barbuda) #2, the third (Afghanistan) #3, and so on. This will turn out to be important later.

Next, the -a option to *v.patch* tells it to append the input layer to the output layer rather than overwriting the output layer, which is the default. So each call to *v.patch* will successively add each country to the borders layer, until they're all in there. We use this wodge of Perl as follows, and then run the script it generates:

```
GRASS:~/hacks/world > perl gen_extract.pl <fips.list >extract.sh
GRASS:~/hacks/world > less extract.sh
v.extract -d in=admin out=tmp new=1 where="FIPS_CNTRY = 'AA'"
v.patch -a in=tmp out=borders
v.extract -d in=admin out=tmp new=2 where="FIPS_CNTRY = 'AC'"
v.patch -a in=tmp out=borders
v.extract -d in=admin out=tmp new=3 where="FIPS_CNTRY = 'AF'"
v.patch -a in=tmp out=borders
v.extract -d in=admin out=tmp new=4 where="FIPS_CNTRY = 'AG'"
v.patch -a in=tmp out=borders
...
GRASS:~/hacks/world > sh ./extract.sh
```

And then we sit back and wait, while GRASS extracts, merges, and patches every polygon belonging to each of the world's 251 countries or country-like territories. Fortunately, waiting comes easy to the would-be ninja. The would-be ninja is not even fazed by the irritating console beep emitted by *v. extract* each time it runs, warning that the tmp layer is being overwritten. (The true would-be ninja would have thought to silence his handiwork by adding a print qq/g.remove vect=tmp\n/ to the top of the loop in *gen_extract. pl*, but never mind that.)

Some minutes later, GRASS completes its labors without complaint; however d.vect borders type=area fails to reveal the goods. Any landmass completely within a single country—such as the British Isle—shows up, but any landmass spanning more than one country—like, say, mainland North America—has simply disappeared. However, d.vect borders type=boundary shows that the vectors are all there. What gives?

It turns out that, had the ninja trainee paid close attention, as every ninja must, he would have noted the following warning emitted by each execution of *v.patch*:

```
Patch complete. 1 files patched.
Intersections at borders will have to be snapped.
Lines common between files will have to be edited.
The header information also may have to be edited.
```

A message like this from GRASS is a sure sign that the vector layer in question needs a run through *v.clean* to fix what ails it and reassure GRASS that the polygons contained therein really are polygons. The following does the trick:

```
GRASS:~/hacks/world > v.clean in=borders out=borders2 tool=rmdupl,snap,bpol
```

*v.clean* needs a few minutes to work its magic (this is 13 megs of vector data, after all) and it won't overwrite the original layer, so we have to create a new layer called borders2. A quick call to *d.vect* reveals, as shown in Figure 6-53, that the borders2 layer does indeed contain a vector map of the world's international boundaries.

Having verified for ourselves that this is indeed the case, we can engage in a bit of cleanup work, as a proper ninja always covers her tracks:

```
GRASS:~/hacks/world > g.remove vect=borders
GRASS:~/hacks/world > g.copy vect=borders2,borders
GRASS:~/hacks/world > g.remove vect=borders2,tmp
```

However, if we now run *v.info* on the new borders layer, to see what sort of attribute data made it through the extraction process, we are brought up a bit short:

```
GRASS:~/hacks/world > v.info -c borders
Database connection for map <borders> is not defined in DB file
```

The answer is that no attribute data made it through. In fact, GRASS is saying that the borders layer doesn't even have an attribute table. It is as though the ninjas have successfully infiltrated the tower, only to find that the villain has absconded with the princess. Honor demands that we give chase!

## Objective #3: Recover the Missing Plans

Fortunately, if you'll recall, in our current set up, the vector-layer attribute tables are just DBase *.dbf* files stored in the filesystem. It would be awful

*Figure 6-53. Part of a vector map of national boundaries successfully extracted from the first-level administrative boundaries layer*

nice if we could just pipe a CREATE TABLE command to *db.execute* to create the data table for the borders layer, but GRASS's DBF driver isn't nearly that cooperative. So we have to resort to some other means of creating a *.dbf* file.

The admin layer already has all the data we need, and, if you'll recall, we took care to assign category numbers to each country that correspond to its place in an alphabetized list of FIPS country codes. We can generate a pipe character (|) delimited text file containing all the attribute data we need for our borders layer with a single line of shell, as follows:

```
GRASS:~/hacks/world > echo "select fips_cntry, cntry_name from admin" | db.
select | sort | uniq | perl -ne 'print "$.|$_"' > borders.txt
```

Now, that's one heck of a shell command, but let's parse it bit by bit. The *db.select* command will dump the FIPS country code and the country name of each feature, separated by a pipe, in the admin layer. When the list goes through *sort* and then *uniq*, we will get a list of unique country codes and names, sorted alphabetically by code. You may recognize our old friend $. in the subsequent *perl* command, which simply prints out each line of input with the current line number plus a pipe character added to the front of the line. The *borders.txt* file ends up looking like this:

```
1|AA|Aruba
2|AC|Antigua and Barbuda
3|AF|Afghanistan
4|AG|Algeria
...
```

All it needs is a header line, which we can add by loading it up in our favorite text editor, and making it look like this:

```
CAT|FIPS|NAME
1|AA|Aruba
2|AC|Antigua and Barbuda
3|AF|Afghanistan
4|AG|Algeria
...
```

The upshot is that the category numbers that we gave each country's features in the extraction step are now matched up to that country's name and FIPS code in the current step. GRASS likes the column containing the category numbers to be called CAT, but that's not a problem at all. The only step that remains is to get this attribute data into an actual *.dbf* file and then tell GRASS about it.

There are a bunch of options out there, but—remember what we said about ninjas and resourcefulness—the easiest one turned out to be a bloody spreadsheet program, because a spreadsheet is all a *.dbf* file is, really, and all modern spreadsheet programs know how to read and write them. You could very easily rely on OpenOffice for this, but we just used Microsoft Excel because it happened to be on the machine we were using at the time. Load *borders.txt*, set the delimiter to the pipe character, import all columns, and then save in DBase IV format to *borders.dbf*. We had to do this twice, because DBF is a fixed-width format, and MS Excel decided to chop each column at the width that it defaulted to on import (i.e., the width of the column name), which truncated some of the country names. The fix was to select each column in Excel in turn, go to Format → Column → AutoFit Selection, and then save the whole thing in *.dbf* again. No problem. No doubt if we had used more suitable tools for dealing with DBF—such as, say, Perl's DBD::XBase—this wouldn't have been an issue.

Next, we need to put the file where GRASS can find it, which is usually *$GISDBASE/$LOCATION_NAME/$MAPSET/dbf/*. Our database directory is */home/sderle/grass*, our current location is called global, and our current mapset sderle, so, by default, GRASS looks for the DBF file in */home/sderle/ grass/global/sderle/dbf/*, although we could put it somewhere else if we really wanted to. We choose to go with the default, copy *borders.dbf* into that directory, and then inform GRASS using *v.db.connect*:

```
GRASS:~/hacks/world > v.db.connect borders driver=dbf table=borders
WARNING: The table <borders> is now part of vector map <borders> and may be
         deleted or overwritten by GRASS modules.
```

Our work here is done. v.info -c borders gives us the output we expect:

```
GRASS:~/hacks/world > v.info -c borders
Displaying column type for database connection of field 1:
INTEGER|CAT
CHARACTER|FIPS
CHARACTER|NAME
```

Ordinarily, we might verify that the attribute data was correctly assigned by running *d.what.vect* and clicking around on the X display monitor. Another, somewhat more roundabout, way of testing this would be to pick any country (say, Spain), zoom in on that country, use *d.vect* to display only that country, and see what comes out:

```
GRASS:~/hacks/world > d.erase
GRASS:~/hacks/world > d.vect borders type=area where="NAME = 'Spain'"
```

If all of Spain, and only Spain, is what shows up, then we can be more or less confident that the attribute data has come through correctly. Figure 6-54 suggests that this is indeed the case. The princess is saved, the villain in ruins—in other words, success!

*Figure 6-54. Spain, by way of testing the attribute data from our vector map of the world*

## The Path to Ninjahood

The path to becoming a true ninja of any kind is fraught with danger and pitfalls. Following that path demands flexibility, ingenuity, and clarity of mind. When it comes to mastering GRASS, one must always bear in mind the Unix tools philosophy: the idea that an operating system, or a GIS, is best made up of a myriad of small, interconnectable tools, each of which should do one thing very well. GRASS's integration with the Unix shell environment—and all of the tools that come with it—means that, in the hands of a capable ninja, GRASS is the hacker's GIS, and easily the equal of any fancy, flashy, graphical GIS environment you could care to stack it up against. Remember the example of the ninja, and you too will in short order be using GRASS to make neat work of your cartographic and geographic problems.

# CHAPTER SEVEN

# Names and Places
## Hacks 78–86

*It is not down in any map; true places never are.*
—Herman Melville, *Moby Dick*

Apparently, human beings are pretty bad at naming things; sometimes we can't even agree how to agree that we're talking about the same object. However, we're quite good at filtering differences and recognizing identities: "Avenue," "Av," "Ave," and "Ave." are all apparently the same street suffix.

There are strategies for naming places to help humans and machines compensate for each others' weaknesses and provide practical assistance to one another. There are many standard code systems in the world, which unambiguously map a place to a location identified by the code. In the United States, the ZIP and ZIP+4 postal codes allow us to do good-enough, near-enough geolocation. Most countries have a postal code that identifies specific areas at some level of resolution.

For identifying countries and connecting regions and towns to them, there are the U.S. FIPS codes and the two- and three-letter ISO codes, which allow us to take different spellings, or different versions of country names, and unambiguously identify the same "place" being talked about.

Sadly, not many countries have the open geographic data policy maintained by the U.S. Census Bureau and Geological Survey, so a lot of world-mapping resources described in this chapter are dependent on data provided by the U.S. government. Local names for places may be "overwritten" by their U.S. English variants on world maps. Databases of postal codes and of street addresses are only available at a handsome price for an annual license—out of the hands of the keen, amateur, free-GIS hacker.

# What to Do if Your Government Is Hoarding Geographic Data

*Geospatial data is a priceless public resource, but few national governments see it that way. How can you get free and fair use of it?*

If you're not based in North America, you're probably flipping through this book thinking, "Almost all these hacks are based on U.S. data! How can I make my own maps of London/Karachi/Accra/Quito"?

This isn't regrettable cultural arrogance on the part of the authors; it is a reflection on the lack of geographic data available in the public domain. Even the world maps and gazetteers built in this book are mostly derived from data published by U.S. intelligence agencies, not from local sources.

National mapping agencies are in a difficult position. They provide an essential public service and are arguably part of the core machinery of government, along with roads, street lamps, and schools: the kinds of services that would not be adequately provided by market forces alone. But mapping agencies are squeezed by commercial pressures; because they have a clear potential revenue model, they are liable to be privatized. Citizens who paid handsomely in taxes for the initial data collection now pay to have it sold back to them piecemeal, without access to or means to contribute to the raw data from which the maps are generated.

Long-established national mapping agencies tend to have a military origin, like Britain's Ordnance Survey and *nima.mil*, formerly the Defense Mapping Agency. They bring to mind visions of action-men bent over a strategic map spread out over a table, moving tiny flags on a wall-mounted territorial display as the frontline advances and retreats. Maps essentially have their origin as military instruments: a hundred-meter calculation error in the bend of a river or the slope of a hillside could mean death for many thousands, the fall of a city. Without the map to demarcate the territory, how can it be defended? But geographic data is also key to many other more peaceable government functions: road building, public transport planning, pollution monitoring, political boundary (re)drawing, refuse collection, school and hospital catchment-area sizing, just-in-time route planning for emergency services. Location: it's everywhere!

Across the world, centralized, national mapping agencies collect and maintain spatial data as government sub-departments. They are under pressure to realize their commercial potential as a geodata-licensing monopoly, and are having budgets cut or statuses changed as a result. Meanwhile local government departments and community groups are obliged to buy back the maps and processed data from the national agency. They pay millions for proprietary software and consultancy and create their own data in undocumented formats. They can't share the data with each other because they don't have clear legal rights to redistribute it; they can't connect it to their other logistics systems over the Web because the interfaces are closed. The raw geodata underlying the map is not for use by ordinary citizens at all. Academic and nonprofit institutions get a discount.

The European Union faces a particularly challenging set of problems, with 10 new countries and 9 new official languages recently added to the standing 15. It now must deal with 25 "territories," each with different naming conventions for regions, districts, postal codes, and political systems, which need to be accounted for.

There is an exciting prospect, were the underlying map data opened up to free use by these nations, that academics and enthusiasts would solve many of these problems while "scratching their itches." Environmental scientists could predict floods in areas that cross borders, determined linguists could translate metadata models into Welsh from Polish, and hackers could write geocoders for street addresses in different forms to support locative services.

One common argument against freeing national geodata is that national mapping agencies, *NMAs*, would lose a lot of their revenue model; anyone from a small to medium business, to a local councillor with a copy of Manifold, to an inspired reader of this book could make and maintain his own maps. The mapping agency would be merely left with the task of geodata collection and maintenance. Some of this data needs to stay in the public domain: remote and rural areas, for example, which a purely commercial market (such as cell-tower telephony) would not have an economic incentive to cover. This is surely an argument for keeping geodata collection in the hands of elected authorities, an important source of trust for data distribution.

There are drawbacks to the U.S. model of local free geodata. The mapping agencies, not making commercial offerings, are dependent on federal or state funding, which can fluctuate between administrations. Meanwhile huge companies like Navteq, who can afford to rent time on aerial photography satellites and send fleets of scouts out "ground truthing" with GPS units, are augmenting the free TIGER/Line data with more accurate data and up-to-date feature sets, with no obligation to enrich the public domain with new data.

In truth, these huge companies already have accurate thematic maps and feature databases, and they aren't going into the public domain whether or not state-owned geodata is publicly released. And for the first time since the descrambling of the U.S. GPS signals, with the international offering

GALILEO on the way, ordinary citizens have the affordable technology and the free tools outlined in this book to actively contribute to the maps that describe their world. Open geodata would be a millions-saving boon to small businesses and local government departments. The latter would have the means to collect and make sense of metadata about their communities at a local level.

A principled idealist might argue that national mapping data should be released under a GPL or ShareAlike license; *http://www.ollivier.co.nz/atlas/ freeworldmaps.html* makes this case convincingly. But this might prove unacceptable to large businesses and detrimental to some smaller ones focused on mapping. It might also widen the gap between public domain geodata and commercial offerings, in both coverage and intent. That person who controls the map controls how people perceive the world. If you would like to own your map, and the government where you live has a restrictive policy on geodata:

- Formulate a project, a "cool hack," ideally with an educational and civic aspect. Write to named members of your national mapping agency, making the exact scope of what you need clear. If they seem unreceptive, ask if you can come in for a meeting and chat anyway, offering to share your specialist knowledge.

- Get together with other geohackers on the Web working on related projects or ideas. Hold a show-and-tell workshop about your projects and invite some mapping agency representatives.

- If your national mapping agency is still unreceptive, try going upstream: write to the government department that nominally runs or funds your national mapping agency. Stress the fact that data withholding is throttling innovation in the mobile market and masking the true nature of local statistics.

- Look for possible legal recourse; many countries, including Canada, have a Freedom of Information Act that guarantees access to government-held data that is in the national interest, at a reasonable cost. The European Union's Public Sector Information Directive is enforced from July 2005.

- Do it yourself! Focus on a small area around you and start making your own shapefiles from GPS traces, annotating local sites of interest in an Open Guide, map the local community wireless network.

**If you're in the U.S.** You have nothing to worry about! Under U.S. law, all information published by the federal government must be copyright-free and must be made available at the nominal cost of copying it. In 1997, Bruce

Perens purchased the U.S. Census Bureau's TIGER data set on CD-ROM and made the data freely available on his FTP site. This prompted the Census Bureau to publish all its data for free download over the Web. Now the U.S. government is running a "one-stop shop" initiative that includes free data from the National Imagery and Mapping Agency and the U.S. Geological Survey (*http://www.geodata.gov/*). The latter provides the excellent "seamless" system featured in "Seamless Data Download from the USGS" [Hack #67].

**If you're in Canada.** Your luck is improving! Partly as a result of grassroots lobbying by GIS industry experts, a government policy study recommended that "Digital geospatial data that are collected or created by any level of government should be made as readily available electronically to the public as possible." Canada now publishes increasing amounts of free data through its "geoconnections" web site, *http://cgdi.gc.ca/english/index.html*.

**If you're in Australia or New Zealand.** You have ANZLIC (*http://www.anzlic.org.au/*), the Spatial Information Council that covers Australia and New Zealand and publishes metadata standards based on ISO 19115, which in turn is converging with the OGC standards. Geoscience Australia is at *http://www.ga.gov.au/*, and its Australian Spatial Data Directory (ASDD) is a one-stop data-directory service for Australia. There are free topographic and digital elevation models available, as well as a selection of feature and geoscience data sets that are deemed "fundamental." There's not much in the way of demographic data

The Australian government geodata policy states that "Fundamental spatial data will be provided free of charge over the Internet, and at no more than the marginal cost of transfer for packaged products" (see *http://www.osdm.gov.au/osdm/policy.html*).

**If you are in Denmark.** You are lucky! The Danish government has the most liberal data policy in the EU. *http://www.geodata-info.dk/* is a central portal service. *http://dk.space.frot.org/* is an interesting semantic web service based on the complete, public-domain set of Danish addresses.

**If you're elsewhere in the EU.** You need deep pockets. Most EU National Mapping Agencies operate on a partial cost-recovery-by-user payment model. At the time of writing, there is a European Commission–proposed directive aiming to establish a common European Spatial Data Infrastructure that covers intellectual property and licensing policy.

At *http://www.ec-gis.org/inspire/* are a series of enlightening documents assessing the "state of play" in GIS infrastructure in the then 15 EU and 10 accession countries. Included are URLs and contact details for the individual national mapping agencies. Most are part-government, part-privately funded and are under pressure to "pay for" the costs of their activities, even though many of the licensing fees are "false profits," coming from other branches of publicly funded activity, such as local government, environmental monitoring, and city planning.

**If you're in India.** The Geological Survey of India (*http://www.gsi.gov.in/aboutgsi.htm*) was founded in 1851. They publish hardcopy maps, carry out geological surveys, and have digitization of their databases at hand. Their Web presence is a bit scattershot, but there must be an amazing amount of potential data and depth in there. There is currently no available geodata or digital mapping provided by the Indian national mapping agency. It seems ironic that the UK's Ordnance Survey now outsources its digital map drawing to Delhi.

**If you're in Japan.** Oddly for a country so renowned for its obsession with mobile devices, their mapping agency (*http://www.gsi.go.jp/*) seems very old-fashioned. However, the Japanese mapping agency is working hard to organize data-sharing efforts throughout Asia and indeed the rest of the world. But at the time of writing, no raw geodata is available for Japan itself.

**If you are in the Asia/Pacific area.** Check out the Permanent Committee on GIS Infrastructure for Asia and the Pacific (*http://www.pcgiap.org*). This inter-mapping-agency institution, hosted on the Web by the Japanese national mapping agency, seems more concerned with the social and organizational aspects of mapping than the very technical. It encompasses almost all of central and eastern Asia and the Pacific. Their problem set is even more complicated than Europe; many countries use obscure or outdated ellipsoid projections and have different character sets.

**If you are in South America.** The Mexico-hosted Instituto Panamericano de Geografía E Historia has existed in some form since 1928 and has a dense organizational structure. On its list of activities you can find conferences on remote sensing alongside "Estudios de Filosofia Practica e Historia de las Ideas."

Interestingly, many South American national mapping agencies are still overtly military concerns. Others integrate national mapping with national statistics. Brazil's national mapping agency has a lot of arbitrary census data and maps files free for download at *http://www.ibge.gov.br/*.

Otherwise, map offerings are mostly conventional, paper-based cartographic products. Chile and Argentina both offer proprietary digital GIS packages at high cost.

UNESCO maintains an excellent current index of world mapping agencies, with web sites and contact email addresses where available, and phone and street address in most cases (see *http://whc.unesco.org/map-agencies.htm*).

If you're in Africa. National mapping coverage of Africa is patchy. Though most countries have a geological survey or government cartographical body, many in Sub-Saharan Africa don't have an online presence at all. Most data is to be found in the hands of uncoordinated relief agencies and NGOs. South Africa runs a modern, commercial national mapping agency with DEM, with topographic data for sale, and looks best positioned to lead intracontinental efforts. Try the UNESCO list (*http://whc.unesco.org/map-agencies.htm*) to obtain national mapping agency contact information.

Another tantalizing possibility has arisen with the availability of one-meter resolution commercial satellite imagery, such as those available from the IKONOS satellite. Although the images themselves cannot be redistributed, the license that comes with their purchase usually explicitly permits the redistribution of new derivative works, such as vector layers of road and rail networks extracted from the imagery (either by hand or through some automated process). With such imagery typically costing less than $1,000 for a minimum purchase of 50 km², hackers and other interested parties in urban areas outside the U.S. can in theory take up a collection for the price of the imagery, use it to build a vector data set of their home cities, and then release the resulting street data under an open licence (e.g., Creative Commons), thereby completely sidestepping the NMAs. An example of one such ongoing effort is the London Free Map (*http://uo.space.frot.org/*), which hopes not only to produce a comprehensive, free vector map of London but also to develop Open Source tools to help repeat the process elsewhere.

## Geocode a U.S. Street Address
You know the address, but where is that in GPS terms?

You know your friend's address, but that won't help you program your GPS or aim your ICBM. For that, you need her latitude and longitude: you want to "geocode" her address! Geocoding is the process of adding geographic coordinates, such as latitude/longitude, to other information. You can geocode street addresses, or any other information that has a geographic component.

One Saturday we were sitting around thinking that we really ought to go
see the Power Tool Drag Races. We knew that they were put on by Qbox
(*http://www.qbox.org/*), and we even knew their address, but where exactly
*is* that? Sure, we could use a commercial mapping service and have it tell us
to turn left here, and in circles there, but what I wanted was to program my
GPS and have it just sort of point the way. At one level, this is much harder
to follow than turn-by-turn directions, except that directions only work as
long as you follow them. Since I have little confidence in my ability to follow directions in San Francisco, I am very happy to have the safety net of
the GPS pointer.

To cut to the chase, just enter this URL (Figure 7-1 shows what it should
return):

```
http://geocoder.us/demo.cgi?address=950+Hudson+Street%2C+san+francisco%2C+ca
```

*Figure 7-1. The Power Tool Drag Races at Qbox.com*

We plugged (37.734085, −122.377589) into our GPS unit, and off we went
for a day of power-tool debauchery.

There are commercial services that provide geocoding for U.S. addresses and
for other parts of the world. Do a Google search for "Geocode Addresses"
for commercial services.

A geocoder is also at the heart of all the online map services. When you
enter a street address into MapQuest, it is geocoded and the map you get is
generated from the returned coordinates. In the good old days of the Web,
pretty much all of the online map services returned the lat/long for addresses

as a "freebie." And then they decided that geocoding had added value, and one by one they pulled the plug.

There is a strong movement of people who believe in open data and open data formats. Mapping sites' removal of free geocoding led directly to the creation of the free *geocoder.us* site. As William Gibson famously noted, "the street finds its own uses for things," and that use can transcend and exceed the original vision of the tool.

## The Birth of geocoder.us

Strangely enough, the removal of useful features from online map services seemed to occur right before a surge of interest in free sources of geodata occurred among the free and open source software community.

Collecting this data and keeping it up to date with "ground truth squads" who go around and verify that streets are where they are supposed to be and that houses haven't up and run off, is quite expensive.

An alternative to the full expense of this data lies in the U.S. Census Bureau. They have compiled TIGER (Topologically Integrated Geographic Encoding and Referencing system) data. TIGER data is used as part of the normal fulfillment of their duties to do an actual enumeration of the people every 10 years. This data is imperfect, but the regular tasks of census workers are similar to our own needs. They wish to identify the location of a residence based on a street address, just as we do when we geocode.

Again, it is important to stress that TIGER data is imperfect, but "imperfect but free" has its own charm! TIGER data is also used as the basis for the free TIGER Map Server offered by the Census Bureau at *http://tiger.census.gov/cgi-bin/mapsurfer*.

There is a lot of interesting information about geography and the challenges of capturing complex and inconsistent information to be found in the TIGER documentation. But for simple geocoding, all you really need to know is that the TIGER data endeavors to include information on every street segment in the U.S. For each block, the TIGER data includes the street name, the latitude and longitude at each end of the block, and the range of address numbers for the left and the right side of the street.

Here is the entry that includes 1005 Gravenstein Hwy N, Sebastopol, CA 95472 (O'Reilly Media's headquarters):

```
11003   67518936 A  Gravenstein              Hwy    A31       1001
1019      1000     101801009547295472       06060970979298092980
70770707701534031534032012400 9-122816102+38390313-122815686+38389814
```

This street segment goes from (38.390313, −122.816102) to (38.389814, −122.81515686); one side of the street includes addresses from 1001 through 1019, and the other covers addresses from 1000 to 1018. We can interpolate that "1005" is about a fifth of the way from 1001 to 1019 and, assuming the street is straight, that it will be about a fifth of the way between the ends of the blocks.

There is a lot of other information in this line, and in the other files that make up the data set for a county. TIGER/Line comprises some 24 gigabytes of data for the whole country. Including information on curves in the road that are not the ends of street segments, but in the interests of compressing that 24 GB into something searchable, we will simplify away that extra information.

Fortunately for us, Schuyler Erle has stripped away all of that complexity at *http://geocoder.us/*, a free geocoding web site and web service for U.S. addresses based on the U.S. Census TIGER/Line data.

You may use the web site to geocode individual addresses or use one of three web-service interfaces to geocode via code, as illustrated in "Automatically Geocode U.S. Addresses" [Hack #80]. You can even download the source code from CPAN, the Perl code repository at *http://cpan.org*, and the TIGER/Line data from the census and create your own geocoding service.

The site provides a text box for entry of an address or an intersection. So entering "1005 Gravenstein Highway North, Sebastopol, CA" will return the location of O'Reilly Media. You can also enter an intersection, like "Hollywood and Vine, Hollywood, CA" or "Florence Ave and Wilton, Sebastopol, CA 95472."

If your address is one of the majority of those that *geocoder.us* successfully geocodes, it will return the latitude and longitude. As a bonus, it will display a map, created dynamically by the TIGER/Line Map Server, with your address marked and centered.

The results with lat/long appear quickly, but it can take longer for the map to be fetched from the TIGER/Line Map Server. The map will be blank and the little circle on the right will be red until the map is loaded.

In Seattle, Washington, you can indirectly use the geocoder at *http://seattle. wifimug.org/nearby.cgi* to get "Caffeinated and Unstrung" by finding the nearest location that offers coffee and free wireless access, as illustrated in Figure 7-2

## See Also

The U.S. Census Bureau and Geography page provides lots of great information (*http://www.census.gov/geo/www/index.html*)

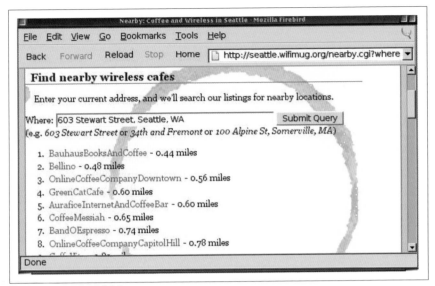

*Figure 7-2. Caffeinated and Unstrung: building on Geocoder.us*

## Automatically Geocode U.S. Addresses

**HACK #80**

Use the geocoder.us web services to geocode batches of address

In "Geocode a U.S. Street Address" [Hack #79], you saw how easy it is to geocode an individual address. But what about a whole database of addresses? What about geocoding addresses as people enter them into a web form? You don't need to webscrape *http://geocoder.us/*! There are three different web-service interfaces. *geocoder.us* supports XML-RPC and a lightweight REST-ful interface. There is also an embryonic SOAP interface (for more information and a code sample, consult the *geocoder.us* web site).

A *web service* is a way for a program to communicate with another program over the Web. In this case, it is as though you had a magical assistant entering addresses into the *geocoder.us* site and returning the resulting coordinates in your program.

Except this assistant is itself a program, and it is optimized to get just the information that you need and return that information to your program. An example is "Caffeinated and Unstrung: A Guide to Seattle's Free Wireless Coffee Shops" (*http://seattle.wifimug.org*), created by Kellan Elliot-McCrea. You can go to the site, select the "Search Nearby" option, enter your address, and find a spot that provides both coffee and a wireless connection. At first glance, this may seem like overkill, but given the coffee habit of the Seattle wireless community, a place to get connected is a fine thing!

*geocoder.us* can be queried via the XML-RPC and REST-ful interfaces, which are available to any reasonable programming language. The basic steps are:

1. Get an address from a web form, database, or file.
2. Format that address and create a web-service request.
3. Call the geocoder.
4. Do something interesting with the result.

## Geocoding with XML-RPC

XML-RPC is a way of making a request of a remote system (a Remote Procedure Call, or RPC) and receiving the results in XML. The XML response from *geocoder.us* is easy to script in Perl by using the XMLRPC::Lite module. Most modern languages have a library that will parse XML-RPC and return results in an easy-to-manage form:

```perl
#!/usr/bin/perl

use XMLRPC::Lite;
use Data::Dumper;
use strict;
use warnings;

my $where = shift @ARGV
    or die "Usage: $0 \"111 Main St, Anytown, KS\"\n";

my $result = XMLRPC::Lite
  -> proxy( 'http://rpc.geocoder.us/service/xmlrpc' )
  -> geocode( $where )
  -> result;

print Dumper $result;
```

Before running the code, you need to install the XMLRPC::Lite Perl module. This can be done via CPAN from the shell by typing **sudo perl -MCPAN -e "XMLRPC::Lite"**.

## Running the Hack

Write the previous script to a file called *simplest_xmlrpc.pl* and run it like this:

```
./simplest_xmlrpc.pl "1005 Gravenstein Highway North, Sebastopol, CA 95472"
```

It should show you the following data structure:

```
$VAR1 = [
        {
          'lat' => '38.411908',
          'state' => 'CA',
```

```
          'zip' => '95472',
          'prefix' => '',
          'long' => '-122.842232',
          'suffix' => 'N',
          'number' => '1005',
          'type' => 'Hwy',
          'city' => 'Sebastopol',
          'street' => 'Gravenstein'
      }
    ];
```

In this example, the geocoder found one and only one possible match, but in the case of ambiguous addresses, you can come up with multiple possible matches. For example, try geocoding this address:

```
./simplest_xmlrpc.pl "800 oxford Ave, Los Angeles, CA"
```

The geocoder finds three possible addresses in different parts of the city: an Oxford Avenue North, South, and unknown. This often occurs when you try to identify a location from incomplete information, and it is also a potential trouble spot if you are geocoding a full database where you don't have additional context. Fortunately each of the Oxford Avenues is in a different ZIP Code, and they can be further disambiguated by including the full address, including the directional. The important point is to remember that you can get multiple results, so plan accordingly. In the sample batch geocoding script in the section "Geocoding a List of Addresses," (later in this hack), multiple addresses will be marked and specifically not geocoded, following the theory that bad data is worse than no data.

The XMLRPC::Lite method returns an array of hash refs, one array element for each address that is geocoded. Processing the returned value is trivial in Perl. The last line of the sample is:

```
print Dumper $result;
```

This uses the built-in Perl Data::Dumper module to print complex data structures. Replacing that line with the following code will walk through all the returned addresses and print out the city, state, ZIP, latitude, and longitude:

```
foreach my $row (@$result) {
        print $row->{city} . ',' . $row->{state} . ',';
        print $row->{zip} .  $row->{lat} . ',' . $row->{long} . "\n";
}
```

The geocoder also returns the address that you passed to it in a cleaned-up form, split back into fields. So you can use the XML-RPC interface as a poor man's address parser.

Casey West is working on a Perl module to extract the address-splitting functionality of the geocoder and put it into its own module. As always, keep an eye on CPAN!

## Geocoding with the RDF/REST Interface

REST stands for "Representational State Transfer" and is a way to treat web-services requests as parameters to standard GET and POST requests. This means that you enter a normal human-readable URL. To make a RESTful request to the geocoder, you need to create a URI-safe version of the address. The address needs to be converted to a form that can appear on the address line of your browser (which means replacing spaces with + signs and using special escape sequences). Here is an example of a RESTful call. The advantage over the XML-RPC version is that you can paste this directly into your browser, so there is no need for XML parsing libraries:

```
http://rpc.geocoder.us/service/rest?address=1005+Gravenstein+Hwy+N+
sebastopol+ca
```

This returns an RDF/XML document that includes the results of your request, which will be displayed in different ways depending on your browser. Apple's Safari browser displays the full RDF/XML document, as shown in Figure 7-3.

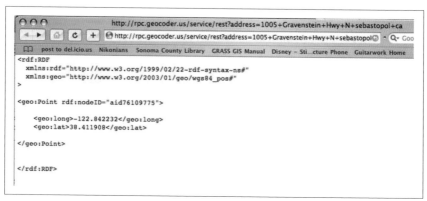

*Figure 7-3. The results of a REST-ful RDF request shown in Safari*

Older or non-RDF-aware browsers will ignore the tags that they don't recognize (such as <geo:Point>), leaving just the coordinates. Opera reveals the bare coordinates:

```
-122.842232 38.411908
```

Here's an example of a simple program to script the REST interface with Perl:

```
#!/usr/bin/perl

use LWP::Simple;
use URI::Escape;
```

```
my $where = shift @ARGV
    or die "Usage: $0 \"111 Main St, Anytown, KS\"\n";

my $addr = uri_escape($where);
print get "http://rpc.geocoder.us/service/rest?address=$addr";
```

Call the program by putting an address on the command line:

```
./simplest_rest.pl "1005 Gravenstein Hwy N, Sebastopol, CA"
```

You can also substitute + for spaces and skip the quotes:

```
./simplest_rest.pl 1005+Gravenstein+Hwy+N+Sebastopol+CA
```

The full RDF document as shown in Figure 7-3 is returned. This can be parsed with the Perl module RDF::Simple::Parser.

## Geocoding a List of Addresses

The Monterey Express is a dive boat in Monterey, California. A list of dive-related resources for the boat is maintained at *http://www.montereyexpress.com/DiveLinks.htm*. A real-world application would be to geocode these addresses in order to create a "find your closest dive resource" application. This sample Perl code fetches the list, does a simplistic (and demonstrably wrong in some cases) parse to get the addresses, geocodes the addresses, and returns the results:

```
#!/usr/bin/perl

# divecode.pl - Geocode the Monterey Express dive resources list

use LWP::Simple;
use XMLRPC::Lite;

my $lines;
#$lines = get "http://www.montereyexpress.com/DiveLinks.htm";

#or use STDIN
{local $/; undef $/; $lines = <>;}

my ($shop_name, $shop_address);
while ($lines =~ s/(.+)<br>//m) {
        $st = $1;
        chomp $st;
        # is this the address?
        ($shop_address)  = ($st =~ /^\s*Address:(.+)/);
        if ($shop_address) {
                $shop_address =~ s/<br>//;
                print "$shop_name\n";
                print "$shop_address\n";
                my $result = XMLRPC::Lite
                   -> proxy( 'http://rpc.geocoder.us/service/xmlrpc' )
                   -> geocode( $shop_address )
```

```
                     -> result;
              # assume we only get one address
              print $result->[0]->{lat} . ',' . $result->[0]->{long};
              print "\n\n";
          }
          # just assume that the shop name is the line before the address
          $shop_name = $st;
      }
```

To run this hack, just execute the script, which produces the following results:

```
Rich-Gibson-iBook:~/wa/geohacks/geocode_web_service rich$ ./divecode.pl
Aquatic Dreams Scuba Center,1212 Kansas Avenue, Modesto, CA 95351,37.
647585,-121.028297
Bamboo Reef (Monterey),614 Lighthouse Avenue, Monterey, CA 93940,36.613716,-
121.901494
Bamboo Reef,584 4th Street, San Francisco, CA 94107,37.778529,-122.396631
...
```

Out of 26 "legitimate" addresses, all but four were successfully geocoded. The remaining four didn't work because the addresses were broken across extra lines in the original document, and I didn't write a very good parser. Better results could be obtained by using the HTML::Parser module and spending a bit more time studying this particular data set, but the goal was to illustrate how easy it can be to get 85% success with such a simplistic approach (and 37 lines of Perl).

Happy geocoding!

## Setting up your own Geocoding server

Do you have too many addresses to geocode, or want the control of running your own server? You can set up your own geocoder with the Geocoder code.

You need to install the Perl Module Geo::Coder::US from CPAN, follow the instructions to download the relevant TIGER data for the areas you wish to cover, and then refer to the Geo::Coder::US documentation on how to load the database.

## See Also

*http://www.xmlrpc.com*
    For the world of XML-RPC.

*http://www.xmlrpc.com/directory/1568/implementations*
    A whole list of XML-RPC implementations to support almost any language.

## Clean Up U.S. Addresses

**HACK #81** As all election officials know, identifying the same address when it is formatted differently can be a tricky problem.

Many of the hacks in this book are meant to help us work with large volumes of geographical information. Most of the data sets described in this book are systematically gathered and organized by mapping, surveying, and databasing professionals. This results in well-defined and well-formatted data, ideal for programmatic processing (and hacking). However, other interesting data sets are populated by humans running around in the world at large who love to make typos, misspell words, enter data in the wrong fields, and mangle information in every (un)imaginable way.

"Who Are the Neighbors Voting For?" **[Hack #16]** was powered by just such a messy database that is distributed, conveniently, by the United States Federal Election Commission. The FEC provides software for campaigns and political committees to file their contribution records electronically, but this software is fed by people contributing over the Web or by staffers entering data from contributions collected at fundraising events or via paper mail. These filings are archived and posted by the FEC on the Web at *http://herndon2.sdrdc.com/dcdev/*. They contain the amount and date of each contribution, as well as the name, street address, city, state, ZIP Code, occupation, and employer of the contributor.

The data was not entirely useless in its original format. U.S. ZIP Codes, for example, are relatively clean because they are simply five numeric digits that are hard to screw up when typed into a computer and easy to validate as input. They allowed for cross-referencing with U.S. census data and for making national maps aggregated by county, ZIP Code, and state. The resulting maps were interesting, but hardly the kind of hack that was going to attract millions of visitors to the site.

Only after the contribution records were geocoded, allowing for street-by-street "money maps" and geocentric "neighbor search" did Fundrace shine in its full glory. However, some fraction of the addresses in the database did not pass muster. There was little to be done about individual or unique mistakes such as blatant misspellings of actual street names, but there should have been a method implemented to clean up more predictable mistakes.

Generally speaking, a good geohack combines a number of different types of information, all with some kind of geospatial significance, in a new, fun, interesting way. But what to do when one of those data sources is too much of a mess to be cross-referenced against the others with an acceptable success rate, as was the case with the FEC contribution records? Go nuts with regular expressions of course! They are ideal for such clean-up operations as normalizing street types/prefixes/suffixes, dropping extraneous intra-building indicators, and excising the general detritus of human input.

## The Code

The following Perl code was used by Fundrace to clean up each street address so that it could be successfully geocoded [Hack #79]. This allowed us to use the spatial data in thousands and thousands of additional records to make political money maps. Mostly composed of a series of regular expressions that expand odd abbreviations, it was written with New York City street-naming idiosyncrasies in mind, but a selection from it should work anywhere in the U.S:

```perl
#!/usr/bin/perl
use strict;
my $addr = shift;
print cleanAddr($addr);

#for turning numerical spellings into digits
our $spelled_nums = {
    first => '1st',
    second => '2nd',
    third => '3rd',
    fourth => '4th',
    fifth => '5th',
    sixth => '6th',
    seventh => '7th',
    eigth => '8th',
    nineth => '9th',
    tenth => '10th',
    eleventh => '11th',
    twelfth => '12th',
    thiteenth => '13th',
    fourteenth => '14th',
    fifteenth => '15th',
    sixteenth => '16th',
    seventeenth => '17th',
    eighteenth => '18th',
    nineteenth => '19th',
    one => 1,
    two => 2,
    three => 3,
    four => 4,
    five => 5,
    six => 6,
    seven => 7,
    eight => 8,
    nine => 9,
    ten => 10,
};
```

```
#for adding the correct suffixes to numerically named streets
our $num_suffixes = {
    1 => 'st',
    2 => 'nd',
    3 => 'rd',
    4 => 'th',
    5 => 'th',
    6 => 'th',
    7 => 'th',
    8 => 'th',
    9 => 'th',
};

sub cleanAddr {
    my $addr = shift;
    my $orig = $addr;


    # dropping off all intra-building identifiers
    $addr =~ s/\#.*$//i;
    $addr =~ s/\,.*$//i;
    $addr =~ s/\bApt\b.*$//i;
    $addr =~ s/\bApartment.*$//i;
    $addr =~ s/\bLoft\b.*$//i;

    $addr =~ s/\d+[a-z]*\s*Fl\b.*$//i;
    $addr =~ s/\d+[a-z]*\s*Floor.*$//i;

    $addr =~ s/\bFl\b.*$//i;
    $addr =~ s/\bFloor.*$//i;

    $addr =~ s/\bRm\b.*$//i;
    $addr =~ s/\bRoom\b.*$//i;

    $addr =~ s/\bPMB\b.*$//i;
    $addr =~ s/\bBsmt\b.*$//i;
    $addr =~ s/\bBasement.*$//i;

    $addr =~ s/\bPH\b.*$//i;
    $addr =~ s/\bPenthouse\b.*$//i;

    $addr =~ s/\bSte\b.*$//i;
    $addr =~ s/\bSuite\b.*$//i;

    # Real numeric suffixes ('st', 'nd', 'rd' as in 1st, 2nd, 3rd)
    # are all more than 1 character.  Thus, we assume that a number
    # followed by only one letter is an apartment indicator, if it has
    # been preceeded by some text.
    $addr =~ s/(.*[a-z]+.*)\b\d+[a-z]\b/$1/i;

    # In NYC, people sometimes write E12 for E 12th street
    $addr =~ s/(E|W|East|West)(\d)/$1 $2/i;
```

```
$addr =~ s/\bEast\b/E/i;
$addr =~ s/\bWest\b/W/i;

# There is a "West St" in NYC
$addr =~ s/\bW St/West St/i;

# got me?!?!?
$addr =~ s/^(\d+)[a-z]+(\s)/$1$2/i;

# Broadway often abbreviated as B'way
$addr =~ s/B.way/Broadway/;

# Normalize the most common street types, and some common misspellings
$addr =~ s/\bAvenue\b/Ave/i;
$addr =~ s/\bAvfenue\b/Ave/i;
$addr =~ s/\bStreet\b/St/i;
$addr =~ s/\bRoad\b/Rd/i;
$addr =~ s/\bBoulevard\b/Blvd/i;
$addr =~ s/\bPlaza\b/Plz/i;
$addr =~ s/\bStret\b/St/i;
$addr =~ s/\bTreet\b/St/i;
$addr =~ s/\bPlace\b/Pl/i;


# Turn spelled numbers into digits
while( my ($k, $v) = each(%$spelled_nums)) {
$addr =~ s/(\b)$k(\b)/$1$v$2/is;
}

# They do weird things with bipartite addresses in Queens, NY
$addr =~ s/[^\s\d\w\-]/ /ig;


# fixing numerical suffixes
while(my ($num, $suf) = each(%$num_suffixes)) {
$_ = $addr;

my ($digits, $currNum, $currSuff) = /[^\d](\d*)($num)([a-z]+)\b/is;

if(defined($currNum) && defined($currSuff) && lc($currSuff) ne $suf) {
    my $oldAddr = $addr;

    # if it's a teen, then suffix is always 'th'
    if(defined($digits) && length($digits) > 0 && $digits =~ /1$/) {
    $suf = "th";
    }

    if($currSuff =~ /\w+st$/i) {
    $suf .= " St";
    }

    $addr =~
    s/([^\d])$digits($num[a-z]+)(\b)/$1$digits$currNum$suf$3/is;
```

```
        last;
    }
}

# no extra whitespace
$addr =~ s/\s+/ /igs;

return $addr;
}
```

—*Michael Frumin*

## Find Nearby Things Using U.S. ZIP Codes

ZIP Codes are everywhere, and ideal for taking advantage of "What's near me?" services.

Everywhere on the Web are forms asking for your ZIP Code and promising to get you in touch with your nearest latte, sandwich, or golf course. Now you can join the in-crowd and provide your own Location Based Services (LBS) based on ZIP Codes.

If you know your ZIP Code, then you can figure out where you are...sort of. United States ZIP Codes were established to help deliver the mail. They were not optimized to ease the burden of 21st century geowankers, which is a pity, since they provide a ubiquitous and useful label for most people in the United States. There is a method to the madness of U.S. ZIP Codes, but sadly for those of us with a locative bent, that method has nothing to do with topography and everything to do with efficient mail delivery.

ZIP Codes describe arbitrary, irregular shapes and sizes. Similar ZIP Codes tend to be close to each other, but there are places where successive ZIP Codes are spread across metropolitan areas. Because the boundaries are irregular, it is quite possible to be in one ZIP Code on the border of a second ZIP Code, and to actually be closer to a third ZIP Code than to the center of the second.

In spite of these obstacles to perfection, we can do a lot with ZIP Codes! The first step is to acquire a geocoded ZIP Code database. This is a database of ZIP Codes to which has been added the ZIP Code of the centroid of each ZIP Code. Imagine that you could slice a ZIP Code off the ground's surface and hold it suspended in air, sitting only on a pencil (a very, very strong pencil).

The *centroid* is the point where the ZIP Code would balance, that is, the center of mass of the area covered by the ZIP Code. This usually works well in helping to geocode ZIP Codes—except when it doesn't. For example, depending on how you calculate it, the centroid of ZIP Code 94123 in San

Francisco is roughly 15 miles out to sea. Why? Because that ZIP Code also includes the Farallon islands, which are 27 miles straight out from the Golden Gate. So the "mass" we are interested in is not always the mass we get!

The easiest way to get a current clean geocoded database is to buy it from a company like Melissa Data Corp (*http://www.melissadata.com*). Their ZIP*Data product is a high-quality geocoded ZIP Code database. You can get more information about the product, as well as download the manual for free, at *http://www.melissadata.com/zd.html*. I recommend reading the manual even if you don't decide to buy the database. It includes lots of examples of distance and bearing calculations.

The only bad thing about ZIP*Data is the price: $150 per quarter, or $395 for four quarterly updates. Note: The data doesn't "expire" or get locked in some fashion; it just gets more and more out of date. This is actually a good price for quality geocoded ZIP Code data, but it is quite a hurdle for casual experiments or for use by nonprofits.

Fortunately the U.S. government again comes to the rescue of the itinerant hacker. The U.S. Census Bureau maintains a geocoded ZIP Code database. It is not subject to regular updates, so the data can be "stale." But for many applications, "free" is more important than "perfect."

Schuyler Erle has compiled a completely free ZIP Code database from 100% public domain sources. It is available at *http://civicspacelabs.org/zipcodedb*. The database comes in two forms: a MySQL dump file that can be used to directly create and load a ZIP Code table within MySQL, and a comma-separated-values version that is useful for simple scripts.

If you download the CSV version and uncompress it, you can use this script to query the data. (You can also use the Unix *grep* utility. The idea is to show that dealing with ZIP Code need not be complicated):

```perl
#!/usr/bin/perl

my ($search_zip, $zipcodefile) = @ARGV;
open ZIP, $zipcodefile or die "can't open zip code file $!\n";

# find the lat long for this zip code
my ($zip, $city, $state, $zip_lat, $zip_long);
while (my $st = <ZIP>) {
    $st =~ s/"//g;
    ($zip, $city, $state, $zip_lat, $zip_long) = split(/,/, $st);
    last if $zip =~ $search_zip;
}
close ZIP;
print "$zip_lat, $zip_long, $city, $state, $zip\n";
```

Then, you can run the script as follows:

```
ziplookup.pl  95472 zipcodes.csv
```

```
38.393314, -122.83666, Sebastopol, CA, 95472
```

We can then use *nearest.pl* to return all the points from a datafile that are within a specified distance of a point. The datafile looks like this:

```
40.70175, -103.68998, 100 MILES
39.22394, -123.76648, ALBION
```

And here is the code for *./nearest.pl*:

```perl
#!/usr/bin/perl
use Geo::Distance;

# This is a linear sort of the zipcode file.
my ($search_lat, $search_long, $datafile, $distance) = @ARGV;
print "distance: $distance\n";

# now look for the nearest $lat, $long within the file DATA
my $geo = new Geo::Distance;
my $points;
open DATA, $datafile or die "can't open datafile $!\n";
while (my $st = <DATA>) {
    chomp $st;
    my ($lat, $long, @rest) = split(/,/,$st);
    my $rest = join " ", @rest;
    $points->{$rest}->{lat} = $lat;
    $points->{$rest}->{long} = $long;
    my $dist = $geo->distance(unit=>'mile', lat1=>$lat, lon1=>$long, lat2=>
        $search_lat, lon2=>$search_long);
    $points->{$rest}->{dist} = sprintf("%5.2f", $dist);
}
# print points with dist < the passed distance

foreach my $p (sort { $points->{$a}->{dist} <=> $points->{$b}->{dist}} keys
%$points) {
    print "$points->{$p}->{dist}\t$p\n";
    last if ($points->{$p}->{dist} > $distance);
}
```

We can run the script as follows, specifying the latitude, longitude, datafile name, and distance in miles:

```
nearest.pl 38.393314  -122.83666 datafile.txt 10
 0.69    SEBASTOPOL
 0.93    HWY 116
 3.06    HOPYARD
 5.79    STONYPOINT RD
10.72    WINDSOR
```

## Who Is Nearby?

The president of a former employer of mine gave presentations for our customers a few times a year. Each time, I was asked to produce a list of our customers whom we should invite to the event, based on their proximity to the speaking location. I did this in the old days using FoxPro for DOS, but we can bring this method up to date with MySQL.

First download the MySQL dump version of the Civic Space ZIP Code database (*http://civicspacelabs.org/zipcodedb*) and uncompress it. Then, create a MySQL database (or you can simply add the ZIP Codes table to an existing database):

```
mysqladmin create zipcodes
```

Load it up:

```
mysql zipcodes < zipcodes-mysql-10-Aug-2004/zipcodes.mysql
```

You can now start MySQL:

```
mysql zipcodes
```

And start looking at ZIP Codes:

```
select * from zipcodes where zip="95472"
+-------+------------+-------+-----------+-------------+-----------+-----+
| zip   | city       | state | latitude  | longitude   | time zone | dst |
+-------+------------+-------+-----------+-------------+-----------+-----+
| 95472 | Sebastopol | CA    | 38.393314 | -122.836660 |        -8 |  1|
+-------+------------+-------+-----------+-------------+-----------+-----+
1 row in set (0.00 sec)
```

The simplest way to select the nearby items is to define a *bounding box*: a rectangular area specified by the corners of a rectangle that you know is larger than your area of interest. We know that at the equator, one degree of latitude and longitude are both equal to about 69 miles. The distance of a degree of longitude decreases as you move toward the Poles, but if the cost of including extra records is low, then we can comfortably ignore that fact. (If the difference really matters to you, then it may help to know that the distance between any two lines of longitude decreases away from the equator specifically in proportion to the cosine of the latitude.)

A bounding box 25 miles wide around the ZIP Code 95472 is approximated with:

```
Maximum latitude   38.393 + 25/69
Minimum latitude   38.393 - 25/69
Maximum Longitude  -122.834 + 25/69
Minimum Longitude  -122.834 - 25/69
```

And the SQL for this bounding box is:

```
select * from zipcodes
where latitude between 38.393 - 25/69 and 38.393 + 25/69
and longitude between -122.834 - 25/69 and -122.834 + 25/69
```

Again, this is not totally correct because the width of the bounding box is overstated, but it is sufficient to be useful. This method also has the advantage of being very, very fast. If you need the answer to be more precise, then you should make this a two-step process. First, select the records within your bounding box (as previously stated) and then calculate the distance for each record within the box, discard those ZIP Codes that are outside of your range, and sort the survivors by distance.

A sample script to do this is available at *http://mappinghacks.com/cgi-bin/ziprange.cgi.*

You call the script with a ZIP Code and a distance, and it returns a list of ZIP Codes less than the specified distance from your target ZIP Code. It excludes all ZIP Codes where the distance to the centroid exceeds your limit. We could change the ZIP Code table to have it refer to our own geocoded data, say a list of our customers, or suppliers. Then we would be able to find our nearest customers based on ZIP Code.

### HACK #83    Map Numerical Data the Easy Way

Hacking the color palette of a GIF image offers a cheap and simple route to mapping all sorts of quantitative data.

Geographical maps are often used to represent some quantifiable property of each country or region depicted, such as population, GDP, health, and so on. Making similar maps of your own involves finding a base map and then coloring each country or region based on the value in question. A number of commercial applications are able to do something along these lines, but for a price. And, of course, it ain't much of a hack if you let your MS Excel plug-in do the work.

This hack is based on the fact that pixels in a GIF are internally just indexes in a palette and is therefore somewhat similar to the old palette animation trick. A simple GIF image starts with 13 bytes of header data, followed by the palette, which is then followed by the actual image data. Modifying the image data on the fly is hard, since it is compressed. However, modifying the palette information is not difficult. The palette is basically just a list of byte triplets, each describing the RGB color of one pixel, holding a maximum of 256 entries.

Note that hacking the GIF palette works for mapping countries of the world or, say, states of the U.S., because there are fewer than 256 of each. If you were interested in mapping voter turnout across San Francisco's more than 400 voting precincts, you'd need to use a different technique, such as the one described in "Plot Statistics Against Shapes" **[Hack #44]**.

## Hacking the GIF Palette

Let's work our way up from a simple example. Say we want to convert a color GIF into grayscale. Using Python and some image library, this can perhaps be done more elegantly, but if we don't care too much about image size, the following little script will do. If we assume that f is a file-like object containing a GIF and o is a file-like object able to receive a GIF, then this bit of Python will recolor the image in grayscale and dump it to o:

```
1  header = f.read(13)
2  o.write( header )
3  for i in range(1 << ( (ord(header[10]) & 7) +1 )):
4      gray = (ord(f.read(1)) + ord(f.read(1)) + ord(f.read(1)))/3
5      o.write(3*chr(gray))
6  o.write( f.read() )
```

Not bad for six lines of code! In the third line, we calculate the size of the palette by left-shifting the lowest 4 bits of the tenth byte of the header. Then we loop through the palette and average each RGB triple and write that to the output. We finish by writing what's left in the buffer back to the output.

In order to make this work for a map, obviously we're going to need a map where each distinct region/country is color-coded in a special way. If we had a list of regions numbered 0 through $n$, and we could palette-index $i$ for country $i$, then this would be easy. Unfortunately, most imaging tools work with colors and not with palette indexes. Furthermore, these imaging tools tend to reshuffle the palette as they see fit, which makes this setup rather risky. Instead, we can use the RGB color scheme, using a unique color for each country, which we can later replace on the fly with the color needed.

## Getting the Data

Let's say we want to create maps showing the population growth in different shades of red for all countries. The CIA Factbook supplies this information in a nice parseable HTML format at *http://www.cia.gov/cia/publications/factbook/fields/2002.html*. In addition to population growth, other interesting CIA-gathered facts can be used for mapping. (You can find a list of some possibilities at *http://www.cia.gov/cia/publications/factbook/docs/notesanddefs.html*.)

The following Python code harvests the population data by downloading the page and scraping the HTML. The output is, interestingly, another Python script, which contains the population growth values and can be imported into yet another Python script to generate the imagery. A more advanced version of this hack might save the data in a database somewhere for later use, but...this is a hack, after all:

```
import urllib

res = [ ]
html = urllib.urlopen('http://www.cia.gov/cia/publications/factbook/fields/
2002.html').read( )
for tag in html.split('class="CountryLink">')[1:]:
    country, tag = tag.split('</a',1)
    growth = tag.split('class="Normal">',1)[1].split('%')[0].strip( )
    if growth[0]=='N': growth = None
    else: growth = float(growth)
    res.append( [country,growth] )
print "countryList = %s" % `res`
```

Note the use of the backticks in the last line, which causes Python to produce the representation of the associated list in Python code. We save the Python code generated by this script as *countryList.py*:

```
$ python getCountryList.py > countryList.py
```

## Tying It All Together

Now, fire up your favorite image editor, load a world map with countries on it, and give country *i* in the produced list RGB color (*i*, 255 - *i*, 238). Yes, it might take some time, and each country needs to be done in the exact order it's listed in your data set, but the task will be quite good for your sense of geography! Alternatively, if you're feeling lazy, you can download such a map from *http://mappinghacks.com/maps/worldmap.gif*. Save the map as *worldmap.gif*. Figure 7-4 shows what the "pristine" version of this file looks like, with one shade per country.

Our main code is going to do something very similar to the "grayer" in the first code fragment we looked at. However, instead of replacing all palette entries with averages of red, green, and blue, it checks whether blue is 238 and red equals 255 minus green. If so, then we'll replace the entry by the target color of the country—in this case, the result of an equation converting the growth of the country to RGB:

```
for i in range(1 << ( (ord(header[10]) & 7) +1 )):
    r,g,b = [ord(c) for c in f.read(3)]
    if r==255-g and b==238:
        growth = countryList[r][1]
        if growth!=None:
```

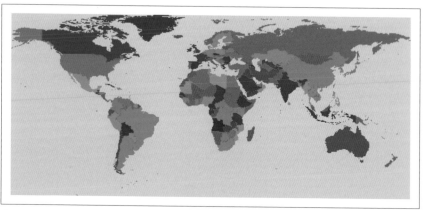

*Figure 7-4. worldmap.gif, with its original color palette*

```
        r = int(30*max(0,growth+2))+64
        g = b = 92
    else:
        r = g = b = 64
o.write( chr(r)+chr(g)+chr(b) )
```

Variations of this code can be used to generate all kinds of dynamic maps. It is probably most useful as a CGI script on a web site, where one could use it to generate dynamic maps: for example, a map showing where your web site visitors are coming from. The following code is an implementation of the population growth map as a CGI script.

```
#!/usr/bin/python

print "Content-Type: image/gif\n\n"

from countryList import countryList

f = open( 'worldmap.gif', 'rb' )
output = f.read(13)
for i in range(1 << ( (ord(output[10]) & 7) +1 )):
    r,g,b = [ord(c) for c in f.read(3)]
    if r==255-g and b==238:
        growth = countryList[r][1]
        if growth!=None:
            r = int(30*max(0,growth+2))+64
            g = b = 92
        else:
            r = g = b = 64
    output += chr(r)+chr(g)+chr(b)

print output + f.read( )
```

As it happens, the exact same technique is used to make the maps explored in "Map the Places You've Visited" [Hack #3]. The result is shown in Figure 7-5.

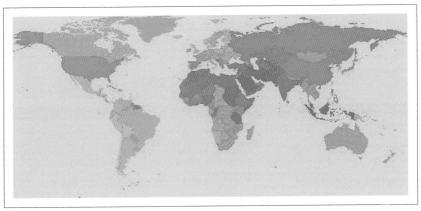

Figure 7-5. worldmap.gif recolored to show population growth by country

## See Also

- "Search Local, Find Global" [Hack #35]
- "Map the Places You've Visited" [Hack #3]
- "Land Geist" (*http://douweosinga.com/projects/landgeist*) shows Google shares for different word-country combinations using the techniques in this hack.

—*Douwe Osinga*

### HACK
### #84
# Build a Free World Gazetteer

Build on the free GEONet data set about millions of world cities and landmarks.

A *gazetteer* is "a geographical dictionary; a book giving the names and descriptions, etc., of many places" (Webster's). Many commercial gazetteer services exist online. They provide an index of "interesting places" with geospatial coordinates: an index for a world atlas.

A gazetteer service is useful in helping to extract spatial information from text. It helps you decide where your own interesting places are near.

## The Web Interface

You can try out this simple gazetteer at *http://mappinghacks.com/cgi-bin/gazetteer.cgi*. Try typing a place name into the search box. Figure 7-6 shows the results of a sample search. You can search for an exact match, or you can match from the start or the end of the name. An option to filter results by country is available. You should see any matches for your place name, along with the country it's in, the *feature type* of the place, and an approximate GPS reference for it.

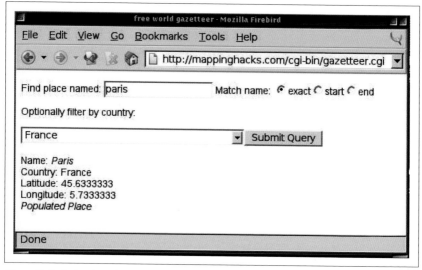

*Figure 7-6. A simple web gazetteer service*

The gazetteer responds to simple GET requests. You can add query=*place* to look for a place name, and filter by asking for country=*ISO code*. This will only return exact matches for the name; optionally, you can try a fuzzy match from the start or the end of your query by appending match=start or match=end to the URL. This gazetteer also has a simple machine-readable output. The following URL, with format=rdf appended to the end, will return the same data in easy-to-parse XML:

```
http://mappinghacks.com/cgi-bin/index.cgi?query=London&country=UK&format=rdf
```

How does this gazetteer work? It is built from a source of free data known as GEOnet, published by the U.S. government's National Geospatial Intelligence Agency, formerly the National Imagery and Mapping Agency. It provides coverage of interesting places—not just populated places, but hydro features, landmarks, and some transport infrastructure information. GEOnet offers feature indexes with locations for the whole world for free download. They are in some areas inaccurate and outdated, but they are a good start for building your own free world gazetteer.

## The Data

At *http://earth-info.nga.mil/gns/html/index.html* is the GEOnet nameserver. Here you'll find the raw data and a web browsing interface for all the GEOnet data. All the GEOnet datafiles are available via FTP as well as HTTP. Grab them all using the *ncftpget* client, part of the *ncftp* package standard on *NIX machines:

```
> ncftpget ftp://ftp.nga.mil/pub/gns_data/*.zip
```

This will download all the GNS files in ZIP format into the current directory. Zipped, the data is a little under 200 MB in size! Each file consists of a tab-separated list of values in a common format. The format is explained in more detail at *http://earth-info.nga.mil/gns/html/gis_countryfiles.html*.

The fields we are particularly interested in are:

*LAT and LONG*
> WGS84 latitude in decimal format

*UFI*
> A unique feature identifier, which we'll keep for future proofing purposes

*DSG*
> A "Feature Designation Code," which identifies the different types of features

*FULL_NAME*
> The full name of the place

The GEOnet data has "Feature Classification" info for all kinds of metadata, including Vegetation and Undersea features, but for the most part, it consists of information about populated places. This can be tremendously useful for asking "Show me all GP's surgeries near Birmingham," for example. We created a list of GEOnet feature types found on the Web and used them to populate our gazetteer.

Each of the GEOnet country files has a two-letter code. These aren't the familiar ISO two-letter codes, though; they are FIPS codes used by the U.S. Census. Most of the rest of the world uses ISO codes, as well as other applications that might use a gazetteer service, so we'll convert from FIPS to ISO while building our database. However, be aware that the ISO may contain some copyrights on ISO country codes!

To store our world model, we'll use a simple SQL schema. This could be any SQL database, such as MySQL. We used sqlite, an SQL interface to *dbm* files, to build this example. To get you started, we've provided a SQL file with the model of countries and their codes, and the various feature types, which you can download from *http://mappinghacks.com/gazetteer/*, along with the original files and short scripts from which it was built:

```
create table country(
    id integer primary key not null,
    name varchar(255),
    iso varchar(2),
    fips varchar(2)
);
create table feature (
    id integer primary key not null,
    name varchar(64),
    code varchar(4),
    fc varchar(2)
);

CREATE TABLE place (
    id integer primary key not null,
    name varchar(255),
    country integer,
    ufi integer,
    feature_type integer,
    lat double,
    lon double,
    alt double
);
create index name_index on place (name);
```

## The Code

We wrote a quick script to go through the GEOnet.*zip* files one by one, unpacking them and looking up their country and feature codes:

```perl
#!/usr/bin/perl

use strict;
use Archive::Zip;
use Data::Dumper;
use DBI;
my $dbh = DBI->connect('dbi:SQLite:gaz.db','','',{AutoCommit => 0});

my $dir = shift;
opendir( DIR, $dir) or die "Couldnt read $dir : $!";
my @files = grep {/zip/} readdir(DIR);
my (%countries,%types);
```

```perl
my $sth = $dbh->prepare("select id, fips from country");
$sth->execute;
while (my $row = $sth->fetchrow_hashref) {
    $countries{lc($row->{fips})} = $row->{id};
}

my $sth = $dbh->prepare("select id, code from feature");
$sth->execute;
while (my $row = $sth->fetchrow_hashref) {
        $types{$row->{code}} = $row->{id};
}

my $count = 0;
foreach my $f (@files) {
    my $zip = Archive::Zip->new;
    chdir($dir);
    print $zip->read( $dir.$f );
    my $code = $f;
    $code =~ s/\.zip//;
    my @members = $zip->members;
    my $txt;
    foreach (@members) {
        $txt = $zip->extractMember($_);
    }

    open(FILE,$dir.$code.'.txt');
    while (<FILE>) {
        my @fields = split("\t",$_);
        my ($RC,$UFI,$LAT,$LONG,$FC,$DSG,$ADM1,$ADM2,$GENERIC,$FULL_NAME) =
            @fields[0,1,3,4,9,10,13,14,20,22];
        my $sql = "INSERT INTO place (name,country,ufi,feature_type,lat,lon)
            values (".$dbh->quote($FULL_NAME).",'$countries{$code}','$UFI',
            '$types{$DSG}','$LAT','$LONG')";
        $dbh->do($sql);
        $count++;
        if ($count > 5000) {
            $dbh->commit;
            $count = 0;
        }
    }
    close FILE;
}
```

How do we read our new dictionary of places? Before we've built in an interface to it, we can write simple queries to it in SQL. The next statement looks for all place names matching "Abu" and returns the place and country:

```sql
> SELECT place.name, country.iso from place, country
WHERE place.name like '%Abu%'
AND country.id = place.country;
```

Once we've found the place we're looking for—e.g., Abu Dhabi—we can look for geospatial information about it:

```
> SELECT place.name, place.lat,place.lon,feature.name from place, feature
WHERE place.name = 'Abu Dhabi'
AND feature.id = place.feature_type;
```

We might want a list of all populated places, or all rivers, in a country. This will be especially useful when we have a list of things and want to figure out which ones are cities, such as in trying to extract spatial proper nouns from news items, or extracting spatial references **[Hack #45]**.

### Hacking the Hack

If you have access to a PostGIS database, you can make the gazetteer more interesting by storing the latitude and longitude as POINT geometry types, rather than just character strings. With polygons representing country borders or political administrative areas, you can make much more sophisticated spatial queries; distance between points and "is this place in this area" are just the start. A further hack that pursues these ideas can be found online at *http://mappinghacks.com/projects/gutenmap/*, where the GNS is used as the basis for a (rough) interactive map of the Peloponnesian War. See "Build a Spatially Indexed Data Store" **[Hack #87]**, which covers PostGIS geometry functions in much more detail.

## Geocode U.S. Locations with the GNIS
#### HACK #85    Make ordinary place names mappable.

As you become a mapping fanatic, you'll want to put all kinds of things on a map. The problem is that most things, although they obviously represent a place on Earth, don't come with geographic coordinates. This is why it's handy to have a toolkit of geocoding resources at your disposal whenever you're creating a new database.

This isn't a difficult thing to do, but it can be a very time-consuming and monotonous process. We'll make use of a terrific government resource, the USGS Geographic Names Information System (GNIS) at *http://geonames.usgs.gov/gnishome.html*. This site is a nice gateway into the wealth of geographic information available from the federal government about your neighborhood. More important for our purposes is its ability to give us geographic coordinates for any of "2 million physical and cultural geographic features in the United States."

Unfortunately, the GNIS doesn't have an API, so in order to automate the lookup of place names, we'll have to do some HTML form emulation and screen-scraping. Here's a Java program that does exactly this. First, we have a class called GNISCoords.java, shown in Example 7-1. Given a state and place name, it knows how to look up the geographic coordinates in the GNIS.

*Example 7-1. GNISCoords.java*

```java
package org.rajsingh.maphacks;

import java.io.*;
import java.net.*;
import java.util.*;

/**
 * Get the latitude and longitude for a place name from the USGS
 * Geographic Names Information Service (USGS GNIS)
 */
public class GNISCoords {
    public String gnisQueryService = "http://geonames.usgs.gov/pls/gnis/";

    /**
     * Make a request to the USGS GNIS. Parse the table that is returned
     * and return the coordinates in a 2-member String[]. The first element
     * will be the longitude (a negative number in the continental US), and
     * the second will be the latitude.
     * @param gnisRequest call to the USGS GNIS
     * @return longitude and latitude
     */
    private String[] requestCoords(URL gnisRequest) {
        String[] coords = new String[2];

        try {
            BufferedReader in = new BufferedReader(new InputStreamReader
                (gnisRequest.openStream()));
            String l = "";
            Vector webPage = new Vector();
            while ( (l=in.readLine()) != null ) webPage.add(l);

            if ( getNumCols(webPage) > 2 ) {
                // find the URL for requesting the 1st matching place
                URL newRequest = getFirstOption(webPage);
                // try again to make the request
                coords = requestCoords(newRequest);
            } else { // the table has the coordinates we want
                coords = findCoords(webPage);
            }
        } catch (IOException ioe) {
            ioe.printStackTrace();
        }

        return coords;
    }
```

*Example 7-1. GNISCoords.java (continued)*

```java
/**
 * Make a request to the USGS GNIS to get the geographic coordinates
 * of a place in the US and return the coordinates in a 2-member String[].
 * The first element will be the longitude (a negative number in the
 * continental US), and the second will be the latitude.
 * @param townName town name, e.g. Cambridge
 * @param stateName full state name, e.g. Massachusetts
 * @return longitude and latitude
 */
public String[] requestCoords(String townName, String stateName) {
    try {
        String req = gnisQueryService;
        req += "web_query.gnisprod?f_name="+URLEncoder.encode(townName,
            "UTF-8");
        req += "&f_state="+URLEncoder.encode(stateName,"UTF-8");
        // these don't change (for our purposes)
        req += "&f_ty=populated+place";
        req += "&variant=N";
        req += "&f_cnty=&f_ty=&elev1=&elev2=&cell=&my_function=Send+Query";
        req += "&last_name=&last_state=&last_cnty=&page_cnt=&record_
            cnt=&tab=Y";

        URL gnis = new URL(req);
        return requestCoords(gnis);
    } catch (MalformedURLException mue) {
        mue.printStackTrace();
    } catch (IOException ioe) {
        ioe.printStackTrace();
    }
    return null;
}

/**
 * Use the coordinates from the link called,
 * "View USGS Digital Raster Graphic (DRG)"
 * @param webPageTable
 * @return longitude and latitude
 */
private String[] findCoords(Vector webPage) {
    String[] coords = new String[2];
    for (Iterator iter = webPage.iterator(); iter.hasNext();) {
        String line = iter.next().toString().toLowerCase();
        if ( line.indexOf("view usgs digital raster graphic") > 0 ) {
            int begin = line.indexOf("lon=")+4;
            int end = line.indexOf("\"", begin);
            coords[0] = line.substring(begin, end);
            begin = line.indexOf("lat=")+4;
            end = line.indexOf("&lon=", begin);
            coords[1] = line.substring(begin, end);
            return coords;
```

*Example 7-1. GNISCoords.java (continued)*

```java
            }
        }
        return null;
    }

    /**
     * Parse a table listing matches for a town lookup.
     * The first URL on the page will be the one we want
     * @param webPageTable
     * @return
     */
    private URL getFirstOption(Vector webPage) {
        String req = null;
        for (Iterator iter = webPage.iterator(); iter.hasNext();) {
            String line = iter.next().toString();
            if ( line.indexOf("web_query.GetDetail?") > 0 ) {
                int begin = line.indexOf("web_query.GetDetail");
                int end = line.indexOf("\"", begin);
                req = line.substring(begin, end);
                break;
            }
        }

        if ( req != null ) {
            try {
                URL ru = new URL(gnisQueryService + req);
                return ru;
            } catch (MalformedURLException e) {
                e.printStackTrace();
            }
        }
        return null;
    }

    private int getNumCols(Vector webPage) {
        int colcount = 0;
        boolean inrow = false;
        for (Iterator iter = webPage.iterator(); iter.hasNext();) {
            String line = iter.next().toString().toLowerCase();
            if ( line.startsWith("<tr") ) {
                inrow = true;
                continue;
            }
            if ( line.startsWith("</tr") ) break;
            if ( inrow ) colcount++;
        }
        return colcount;
    }
}
```

### Running the Hack

Compile the Java file like this.

```
% javac org/rajsingh/maphacks /GNISCoords.java
```

Now you can run the program.

*—Raj Singh*

H A C K
#86

## Track a Package Across the U.S.

Use free data sources to map your package's progress across the U.S.

Being able to see where a package is on its way to your door was developed as a business process-management tool. But it has turned out to be really popular with customers, too. What if you could take the next step, not only seeing a list of towns your new cell phone is visiting, but seeing them on a map! This hack presents one way of doing this.

### Preparation

If you didn't do "Java-Based Desktop Mapping with Openmap" [Hack #66], take a quick look at it, because Openmap will be used to map our package shipment stops. In essence, you need to install a Version 1.4 or later Java Development Kit and Openmap 4.6. Make sure to copy the file *openmap. properties* from the program's installation directory into your home directory. After Java and Openmap are set up, you need to make a small modification to the *openmap.properties* file. Open *openmap.properties* in a text editor. Search for openmap.layers=. The second occurrence should look something like this:

```
openmap.layers=date dtlayer distlayer quake daynight cities test graticule
demo shapePolitical
```

We will be creating a new layer that we want to show up on the map, so add the word "shipment" at the front of the list, which should give you this:

```
openmap.layers=shipment date dtlayer distlayer quake daynight cities test
graticule demo shapePolitical
```

### Getting Location Information

The first thing we have to do, obviously, is find out where the package has been. There are a variety of ways to do this, depending on the shipping company. Most, such as UPS and FedEx, have APIs for accessing the information you can get from their web site. Unfortunately, these are more difficult to get going with than, for example, the Amazon, eBay, or Google API.

Working with them quickly transforms your project from a hack into a full-scale software development effort.

Instead of making use of the programming APIs of the major shippers, we'll use a much older hacking technique: copy and paste. Look up your package's tracking information in the usual way. Then create a text file listing the city and state of each location in chronological order, and save it in a file named *places.txt*. Your file should look something like this:

```
Seattle, WA
Austin, Texas
Chicago, Illinois
Boston, Massachusetts
Medford, Massachusetts
```

Now we're ready to map these locations. To do this, we'll need to translate our list of place names into a list of geographic coordinates, which is a job we already tackled in "Geocode U.S. Locations with the GNIS" [Hack #85], which leverages a U.S. Geological Survey database of places for this purpose.

## The Code

*PackageTracker.java* is a Java program that can be run from the command line. It knows how to read the little place-name text file we created and use the GNISCoords class [Hack #85] for geocoding the entries. It can write the new information to disk, or simply to *stdout*, which can be piped into other applications on Unix-ish operating systems like Mac OS X, Linux, and Solaris. For our purposes, write it to disk so that our mapping program can find it.

The program is too long to print here in full, so we've made it available online at *http://mappinghacks.com/code/PackageTracker.java*.

## Running the Hack

Compile the Java file like this.

```
$ javac org/rajsingh/maphacks/shipment/PackageTracker.java
```

If you did the GNIS hack in another place, move the file *GNISCoords.class* to the same directory as *PackageTracker.class* and *PackageTracker.java*.

Now you can run the program. You'll have to provide three items of information on the command line:

- The full path to the file containing the place names, which we called *places.txt*.
- The full path for the file in which you want the geocoded information saved.

- A value of yes to signal the program to modify Openmap's properties. If you're curious about the Openmap properties file, there's plenty of information about it at *http://openmap.bbn.com/cgi-bin/faqw. py?req=show&file=faq06.004.htp.*

```
$ java -cp . org.rajsingh.maphacks.shipment.PackageTracker \
    <path to places.txt> <path to a new file name> yes
```

## The Results

Remember that we started this hack wanting to put our package "on the map"? Well, we're finally there. Since we automatically added our data to Openmap's properties file, all we need to do is run the program. Your final result should look something like Figure 7-7.

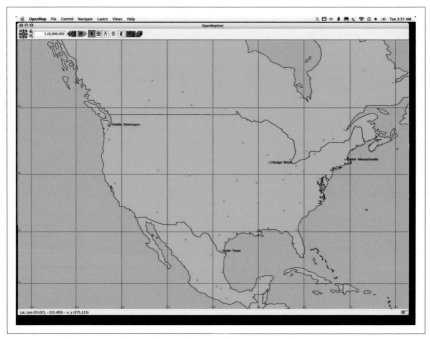

*Figure 7-7. The resting places of a random package, as it makes its way across the U.S.*

See "Java-Based Desktop Mapping with Openmap" [Hack #66] to learn how to get state boundaries on your map as well.

—*Raj Singh*

# Building the Geospatial Web
## Hacks 87–92

Many of the hacks we've looked at create maps of new, previously unmapped data, such as Wi-Fi usage, your GPS tracklogs, or the news. Most of these hacks are built on top of other maps that give them context. Usually they have a step like "Go to *http://example.com/data/download* to fetch a certain file." The web sites with the map data are all over the place, and the maps are often in different formats. GIS professionals are used to spending a large amount of time simply finding the data they need to do their actual work.

The notion of a *geospatial web* seeks to address this problem. Already we have seen the shift the Internet has brought toward textual information, with unheard of quantities of documents a search engine away. The vision for geospatial information has been referred to as a "digital Earth," where you could simply input a point on the globe and have instant access to all mapping data available at that point—not just what the U.S. census gathered five years ago as TIGER street data, but also the city's zoning information, the current weather map, Rich's favorite bike routes, Jo's corrections on the TIGER street data, public Wi-Fi nodes, and Anselm's social network. Every map created with the help of this book could be available to users online, searchable by coordinates and/or information about the map, and instantly available.

The most immediate effect of this would be more customizable maps; users would be able to select which layers they wanted to display. A map of Wi-Fi nodes could be overlaid on street data, along with the coastline and a common route to work. But the geospatial web could go much further. The Internet has the potential to serve as the transport mechanism for the next leap in mapmaking. GIS as a discipline has essentially passed by most of the potential of computers in favor of traditional mapmaking. The maps currently available on the Internet are essentially paper maps with a nice zoom button. Much more can be done, but only if it is much easier to find and actually use the vast quantities of real spatial information.

The problem with current Internet maps is that you can't really do anything exciting with them because they do not let you have the data behind the maps they provide. You cannot plot your own information on top, combine one map with others, or do any analysis on it. This is because it is a mere picture of the geospatial data. All of the major Internet mapping sites pay large companies like NavTeq for their data. If they gave you real information about the location, then that data would be available to all, since you could systematically step through the U.S. and download a map database. And NavTeq would no longer be able to make money. The geospatial web seeks to make the real data about our world available, which would provide a base for the next leap in mapmaking. It is the canvas upon which new ways of mapping and seeing the world can be painted.

With the advent of the geospatial web, users could customize their display, showing only Wi-Fi nodes that are public or on a particular provider's network. They could get a map layer with all the restaurants in the city and customize that layer to only display the ones that serve Mexican food that someone in their social network has given a five-star rating to, which are within walking distance of their current location. With advances in mobile devices, users could simply ask their PDA for the walking directions to the restaurant selected.

Mapmaking has traditionally been used as a measure of control. Philip II of Spain thought his maps sufficiently subversive to keep them under lock and key as a state secret. To this day, many governments hoard their geospatial data, treating it not as a public utility but as a source of profit. And even in countries like the U.S. that have a general policy of opening their data, it is not always easy to find all the information. A geospatial web would render the commons of information about our world truly useful, making the power of that information accessible in seconds to anyone with an Internet connection. "If a picture or map is a worth a thousand words, then power in the realms of representation may end up being as important as power over the materiality of spatial organization itself." (David Harvey, *The Condition of Postmodernity*) The geospatial web would put that power in the hands of everyone.

Making all mapping data available to anyone with an Internet connection sounds great, but wouldn't it be a lot of work to actually make that happen? Thankfully a number of smart people have been thinking very hard about this problem for a number of years and have been working together to evolve standards to enable a spatial web. The Internet was around for 20 years before the explosion of the World Wide Web, and arguably the key that allowed that to happen was standards. The disparate programs that operated on the network agreed to operate in a standard way. HTML, HTTP, and TCP/IP are all openly specified for anyone to implement. In the geo world, the OpenGIS Consortium (now the Open Geospatial Consortium, or OGC) has emerged to write specifications for the geospatial web.

The OGC is "a non-profit, international, voluntary consensus standards organization that is leading the development of standards for geospatial and location based services" (from *http://opengis.org/*). It was founded in 1994, with its roots in the Open GRASS Foundation (OGF), which was created by the GRASS user community to drive a process for the management of GRASS affairs. The OGC emerged to define standards to allow geoprocessing systems to communicate on the Internet through a set of open interfaces. Since 1994, the OGC has grown from 20 member organizations to over 250 from all over the world in commercial, academic, nonprofit, and government sectors.

All standards that the OGC adopts are freely available and directly downloadable from their web site. The process of creation, revision, and adoption is open to any participating company, agency, or organization. Unfortunately membership does cost money, and thus the process is a bit more closed than some other standards organizations, but the OGC is the best hope the geospatial world has, and it does a good job of being as open and inclusive as possible, encouraging participation from varied organizations.

The two most useful OGC specifications, from an end user's perspective, are the Web Map Service (WMS) and Web Feature Service (WFS). Both are web services; instead of returning a web page, they directly return the information the user requests. Both operate over HTTP, so all web browsers, and indeed all clients that use HTTP, can issue requests. Web Map Service is the more established specification; a large number of vendors offer WMS interfaces to their products. The interfaces for WMS and WFS are similar; the main difference is what they return. A WMS returns an image, as a JPEG, a GeoTIFF file, a bitmap, SVG, and so on. It operates like most mapping sites on the Internet, but the key is that it is an interoperable interface, meaning a single client can request maps from all sorts of different servers on the Internet.

The WFS spec does not return images, but raw data in GML (Geographic Markup Language), an XML data format. This allows clients to do far more, as they have the *real* geographic data, not just a picture of it. A WFS also supports complex filtering operations—e.g., "Give me all street names that start with S and are more than two miles long." There are extensions to WMS that allow it to do similar things, but in WFS, you can just request the information directly. The WFS specification also supports *Transactions*, which facilitate user-supplied changes to GML data, making WFS a generic interface for keeping data up to date. Transactions also allow users to update the maps themselves. Figure 8-1 shows a world map of users of Geo-Server, the popular free WFS server. It's viewable online at *http://www. moximedia.com:8080/imf-ows/imf.jsp?site=gs_users.*

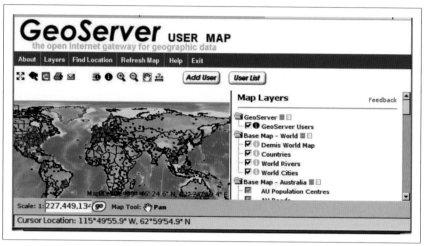

*Figure 8-1. GeoServer users shown via a Web Map Service*

The display is done with a MapServer WMS; when you query it by clicking the "i" button, a WFS command is issued, which gives more detailed information than a WMS can provide. The site also allows you to add yourself to the user map, which issues a WFS Insert request, putting your record in the backend database that the WMS also makes use of. Unfortunately the IMF client site used in this example is not open source, but the backend servers all are.

AskTheSpider (*http://www.askthespider.com/*) is a geospatial data-discovery service that allows you to search through a registry of different services, using the WFS and WMS protocols to publish on the Web and find different catalogs of geodata.

Right now, WMS and WFS are for early adopters. Why not join them?

—*Chris Holmes*

## Build a Spatially Indexed Data Store

Spatial extensions to the PostgreSQL database are useful in many applications.

A spatial database allows you to make lots of interesting statistical and geometrical queries. Find things within a bounding box, or within a distance; calculate the areas of shapes, and have data types for points, lines, and shapes in your database tables.

PostgreSQL, the popular free SQL database, has spatial extensions called "Geographic Objects For PostgreSQL." PostGIS, an open source project by Refractions Research, includes data types to handle geometrical "simple features"—such as points, lines, and shapes—many kinds of spatial queries, and different geographical datums. PostGIS can be used as a backend for GRASS, Mapserver, GeoServer, and QGIS, among other open source GIS projects.

PostGIS is available from *http://postgis.refractions.net/*. Debian packages, RPMs, and SRPMS for Fedora and Mandrake Linux are provided at this site. You will probably find it safer to build the RPMs on your own system from the SRPMS using `rpmbuild --rebuild`; we had to do this to avoid library loading problems. (You can download our RPMs from *http://mappinghacks.com/rpm*.) For Windows users, there is a CygWin binary available for Post-GIS. The rest of these instructions in this hack assume a POSIX-like shell environment.

Alternatively, you can build PostGIS from source. It requires a PostgreSQL source tree against which it must be built. There are good instructions for this process at *http://postgis.refractions.net/*.

### Set Up the Database

If this is a new PostgreSQL installation, you will need to set up a directory under which PostgreSQL stores its databases. This may be supplied by default as */var/lib/pgsql*, also the home directory of your system's postgres user:

```
#> initdb -D /var/pgsql
```

Now create a database for your spatial data. As the postgres user on your system, enter:

```
#> createdb tiger
```

where *tiger* is the name you give to your database. This next step is key for PostGIS to work properly, because it needs the PL/SQL language extensions:

```
#> createlang plpgsql tiger
```

This step loads the PostGIS schema and functions into your new database:

```
#> psql -d tiger -f postgis.sql
```

You may need to provide the full path to wherever *postgis.sql* was installed on your system. One final step is needed to add data to the spatial_ref_sys table, which contains metadata about the different spatial projections that the geometry can be in:

```
#> psql -d tiger -f spatial_ref_sys.sql
```

If everything's working, you should see the last line COMMIT (see also *http://postgis.refractions.net/docs/x83.htm*).

## Getting Data into PostGIS

A spatial database is no fun without spatially meaningful data. There are several techniques for getting your information into PostGIS.

**Import a shapefile into PostGIS with shp2pgsql.** You can use *shp2pgsql* to import geospatial data in shapefile format into PostGIS. For example, you might have a shapefile that contains a set of political boundaries for which you want to ask, "Which voting area contains this address? Where is the nearest polling station? What was the voter turnout rate in the last election?"

The *shp2pgsql* script comes with PostGIS and will convert a shapefile into a set of insert statements suitable for loading into a PostGIS database. To import a shapefile, try the following command:

```
shp2pgsql -c shapefile [database_name.]table_name
```

The database name is optional. To see the other options of this simple conversion program, just type shp2pgsql into your shell.

**Import many formats into PostGIS with ogr2ogr.** The *ogr2ogr* program comes with Frank Warmerdam's wonderful OGR/GDAL utilities [Hack #68].

Packages containing GDAL are also available at the PostGIS download area. The *ogr2ogr* format conversion utility will export directly to a PostGIS data store.

TIGER, the Topologically Integrated Geographic Encoding and Referencing system, is a topological model of the United States compiled by the U.S. Census Bureau, released on the Web (*http://www.census.gov/geo/www/tiger/*) and on CD-ROM for free. The database "defines the location and relationship of streets, rivers, railroads, and other features to each other and to the numerous geographic entities for which the Census Bureau tabulates data from its censuses."

The full TIGER/Line data set is nearly 4 GB compressed. You can download some or all of it at your preference (At the time of writing, the 2003 data set has been released.) These options ask *wget* to traverse directories recursively downward, but not upward:

```
#> wget -Azip -np -r http://www2.census.gov/geo/tiger/tiger2003/
```

Now to import the TIGER model into PostGIS:

```
#> ogr2ogr | less
```

Called without options, *ogr2ogr* shows you whether your version of GDAL has support for PostgreSQL built in. If not, you will have to rebuild GDAL at this stage. Source RPMs for GDAL are also available at the PostGIS address given earlier.

This quick shell script traverses the directory tree and uses the GDAL utility *ogr2ogr* to import the TIGER data straight into PostGIS:

```
#!/bin/bash

DATABASE=tiger

while read zip; do
    rm *.RT? *.MET
    unzip $zip
    ogr2ogr $APPEND -f PostgreSQL \
        PG:dbname=$DATABASE *.RT1 \
        -lco LAUNDER=yes -nln complete_chain CompleteChain
    APPEND=-append
done
```

CompleteChain is the layer containing the complete line data in TIGER; the -nln option instructs it to translate its name to one PostgreSQL is happier with. Since PostgreSQL treats table and column names case-sensitively, converting all the names to lowercase here ensures that we won't have trouble later on with other applications that talk to PostgreSQL, such as MapServer.

Head to the base directory of the census data you downloaded, and use the following line to find all ZIP files and unpack the line layer from them with the shell script:

```
#> cd www2.census.gov
#> find -name *.zip |time import_tiger_data.sh
```

You don't need the *time* command, but it's interesting to find out how long this takes to run! The TIGER data for all 50 states of the U.S., uncompressed, is over 24 GB in size. Whether you imported all or merely some of TIGER/Line's complete chains, you can now visualize the layer of polylines in applications that can connect to PostGIS databases, including Map

Server, Quantum GIS, and GRASS. For further hacking the hack, visit *http://mappinghacks.com/projects/tiger2pqsql/* to see how we got the TIGER/Line polygons imported into PostGIS, as well.

## HACK #88 Load Your Waypoints into a Spatial Database

The powerful PostGIS database lets you make complex spatial queries about where you've been.

Spreadsheets provide power and flexibility in numerical analysis, but once you've used them for a while, you run into limitations and you start looking for a tool on the next rung of the ladder of power. Database systems have been the desktop power user's tool of choice for nearly 20 years.

In "How Far? How Fast? Geo-Enabling Your Spreadsheet" **[Hack #11]**, we learned how to use a spreadsheet for geospatial analysis. And in "Build a Spatially Indexed Data Store" **[Hack #87]**, we learned how to set up a PostGIS spatial database and import existing spatial data sets. In this hack, we explore the world of "what if" with a database using GPS waypoints.

In this hack, we'll create a database schema to support waypoints and provide a small script to load waypoints into the database. We'll finish up by exploring some examples that illustrate the power of using a database for geospatial analysis.

### Consider Your Database Design

If you ask three database developers about a database design, or schema, you'll get between zero and MAXINT opinions. For the purposes of this hack, let's just assume that you want the simplest useful schema: a table to store waypoints. To be even more simplistic, let's create a table for waypoints that were originally in GPX format. As discussed in "Speak in Geotongues: GPS-Babel to the Rescue" **[Hack #51]**, GPX is a simple XML format to store tracklog and waypoint information. Within a GPX file, a waypoint looks like this:

```
<wpt lat="38.403423" lon="-122.818544">
  <name>OREILY</name>
  <cmt>Old O'Reilly offices</cmt>
  <desc>CRTD 19:34 31-AUG-00</desc>
  <sym>Waypoint</sym>
</wpt>
```

### Create Database and Tables

We need to write some SQL code that will create a waypoint table to match the attribute names used by the GPX format. The one hitch is that GPX uses <desc> for a description field, which is an SQL-reserved word, so we'll use descr instead. The GPX format defines additional elements that can exist in the format, but since my Garmin GPS doesn't support those elements, we can ignore them for now.

You can create a new table in an existing database, or create a new database. Recapping from "Build a Spatially Indexed Data Store" [Hack #87], you can create a new database and add the spatial extensions in PostGIS with these commands:

```
$ createdb gpswork
$ createlang plpgsql gpswork
$ psql -d gpswork -f /usr/share/pgsql/postgis.sql
$ psql -d gpswork -f /usr/share/pgsql/spatial_ref_sys.sql
```

Your copies of *postgis.sql* and *spatial_ref_sys.sql* might be in another directory.

These SQL statements will create the table to match the GPX format:

```
create table waypoint (
 waypoint_id serial NOT NULL,
 name varchar(32),
 cmt varchar(255),
 descr varchar(255),
 sym varchar(255));

select AddGeometryColumn('gpswork', 'waypoint', 'location', 4326, 'POINT', 2);
```

The AddGeometryColumn function also inserts our column into the table geometry_columns. This is crucial to the workings of PostGIS.

If you put these statements into the file *create_waypoint.sql*, you can create the table from the command line:

```
$ psql -d gpswork -f create_waypoint.sql
```

The -d parameter specifies the database, and -f indicates the file containing SQL commands to execute.

## Importing Waypoints

We need to create a series of SQL insert statements for our waypoints and tracklogs. I use GPSBabel [Hack #51] to read waypoints from my GPS and write them in GPX format.

The following Perl code will read a GPX file of waypoints and write out a set of SQL insert statements. This code uses the XML::Simple module. Install it from CPAN by typing **perl -MCPAN -e "install XML::Simple"** from a shell:

```
#!/usr/bin/perl
use XML::Simple;
my $gpx = XMLin($ARGV[0] , NormalizeSpace=>1 );
```

```
foreach my $wpt (keys %{$gpx->{wpt}}) {
    $p = $gpx->{wpt}->{$wpt};
    print qq(
        insert into waypoint (name, cmt, descr, sym, location)
        values
        (
            '$wpt',
            '$p->{cmt}',
            '$p->{desc}',
            '$p->{sym}',
            GeometryFromText('POINT($p->{lon} $p->{lat})', 4326)
        );
    );
}
```

Note to the XML purists: the GPX protocol is defined at
*http://www.topografix.com/gpx.asp*. This import code is very
naive, ignoring important aspects of the GPX format. But
this script has the advantage of doing most of what you
might need and being very simple.

Save this code into a file (for example, *parse_gpx_way.pl*) and run it like this:

```
$ ./parse_gpx_way.pl gpx_waypoint_file.gpx > import.sql
```

The output of the script, directed into the file *import.sql*, will now contain a
series of SQL insert statements that look like this.

```
INSERT INTO waypoint (name, cmt, descr, sym, location)
        VALUES
        (
                'OREILY',
                'CRTD 19:34 31-AUG-00',
                'CRTD 19:34 31-AUG-00',
                'Waypoint',
                GeometryFromText('POINT(-122.818544 38.403423)', 4326)
        );
```

This is mostly straight SQL. The interesting bit is the location field:
GeometryFromText('POINT(-122.818544 38.403423)', 4326). PostGIS stores
spatial information in a special "geometry" type.

The 4326 is an OGC Spatial Reference System ID, or SRID, and refers to a
record in the spatial_ref_sys table that includes the information about the
datum, spheroid, and projection that PostGIS will use when working with
this record. "Map Imaginary Places" **[Hack #100]** explains the inner workings of
the SRID in more detail.

OGC SRS is utterly arcane. You want 4326 because it means
EPSG 4326, which means geographic coordinates referenced
to the WGS 1984 ellipsoid and datum. We know that 4326
is the WGS 1984 ellipsoid because it is defined in the
spatial_ref_sys table. Run **select * from spatial_ref_sys
where srid = 4326;** inside the *psql* shell to see how PostGIS
defines this SRID. Take note of the column devoted to
PROJ.4 parameters: this is how PostGIS knows what to do
with this particular spatial reference ID. You need to understand the spatial reference options if you want to master
PostGIS, but for now, sit back, relax, and trust the hack.

We can combine the conversion of waypoints with loading the database
using the Unix tool chain:

```
./parse_gpx_way.pl gpx_waypoints_file.gpx | psql -d gpswork
```

Congratulations! You now have waypoints loaded into a spatial database.
Let's start PostGIS with the command psql gpswork and take a look at what
we can do:

```
gpswork=# select name, cmt, descr from waypoint order by name;
   name  |          cmt          |        descr
---------+-----------------------+----------------------
  100    | 100 MILES             | 100 MILES
  588    | CRTD 14:58 06-SEP-04  | CRTD 14:58 06-SEP-04
  ABSPOT | CRTD 10:15 08-SEP-01  | CRTD 10:15 08-SEP-01
  AC1    | CRTD 15:04 16-AUG-00  | CRTD 15:04 16-AUG-00
  ...
```

## Calculating Distances in PostGIS

Let's say we want to calculate the distance from O'Reilly to the toll plaza of
the Golden Gate Bridge. This query does it:

```
select distance_spheroid(
    GeometryFromText('POINT(-122.8412 38.4112)', 4326),
    GeometryFromText('POINT(-122.4750 37.8073)', 4326),
    'SPHEROID["WGS_1984",6378137,298.257223563]'
    )    / 1609.344
```

It returns the absurdly overprecise answer: 46.1856112886502 miles.

PostGIS is incredibly powerful and flexible. Sometimes that means it is
harder to do the easy things. In this case, calculating lat/long distances is a
tad cumbersome. The distance_spheroid( ) function returns the distance
between two points over an ellipsoidal model of Earth. You need to give the
function two points as well as a description in "Well Known Text" format of
the shape of the earth, shown here:

```
SPHEROID["WGS_1984",6378137,298.257223563]
```

This says that we want to use the spheroid called WGS_1984, which assumes an Earth radius of 6,378,137 meters (3,963 miles) and a flattening factor of about 298 meters.

Here is a query to return the distance between any two waypoints. ORA2 is the waypoint of the new O'Reilly campus, and TOLPLZ is the toll plaza for the Golden Gate Bridge. The query returns the distance in meters, so we divide the answer by 1609.344, which is the number of meters in a mile, to return the result in miles:

```
gpswork-# select distance_spheroid(
w1.location,
w2.location,
'SPHEROID["WGS_1984",6378137,298.257223563]'
)       / 1609.344

from waypoint w1, waypoint w2
where w1.name = 'ORA2'
and w2.name = 'TOLPLZ';
      ?column?
------------------
 46.1867561160993
(1 row)
```

Here's a brief taste of what we can do with waypoints in PostGIS. This query calculates the distance from my house to all of my waypoints:

```
select distinct w1.name, w2.name, round(distance_spheroid(
      w1.location,
      w2.location,
      'SPHEROID["WGS_1984",6378137,298.257223563]'
      ) / 1609.344) as my_dist
from waypoint w1, waypoint w2
where w1.name = 'HOME'
order by w2.name
```

The results should look like this (with 496 waypoints you probably don't care about omitted):

```
name |  name  | my_dist
------+--------+---------
HOME | 100    |    1032
HOME | 588    |     178
HOME | ABSPOT |      80
```

## Not Quite a Cross Tab Query

Here are two queries that together calculate the distances between multiple waypoints. In this case, they calculate the distance from the first three waypoints to the last two waypoints. These are determined by the limit clauses within the sub-select queries:

```
create temporary table foo as
    select w1.name, w2.name as name2,
        w1.location as l1, w2.location as l2
        from waypoint w1, waypoint w2
        where w1.name in (select name from waypoint order by name limit 3 )
        and w2.name in (select name from waypoint order by name desc limit 2);

select name as from , name2 as to,
    distance_spheroid(l1, l2,
        'SPHEROID["WGS_1984",6378137,298.257223563]' )/1607 as dist_miles
    from foo;

  from  |  to   |   dist_miles
--------+-------+------------------
 ABSPOT | ZOOSF | 127.989654055968
 ABSPOT | ZOO   | 1007.02197434096
 100    | ZOOSF | 1029.38780724023
 100    | ZOO   | 93.6502054006563
 AC1    | ZOOSF | 799.97009495917
 AC1    | ZOO   | 273.898428769347
(6 rows)
```

This is not quite the same as the distance grid created in "Create a Distance Grid in Excel" [Hack #12], but it is the same idea.

You could also replace the sub-selects to specify particular queries. This example extracts the distances between three named waypoints and the last two waypoints by name in the table:

```
create temporary table foo as
    select w1.name, w2.name as name2, w1.location as l1, w2.location as l2
    from waypoint w1, waypoint w2
    where w1.name in (
        select name from waypoint
        where name in ('HOME', 'TOLPLZ', 'MOM')
        order by name)
    and w2.name in (select name from waypoint order by name desc limit 2);

select name as from, name2 as to,
    round(distance_spheroid(l1, l2,
        'SPHEROID["WGS_1984",6378137,298.257223563]' )/1607) as dist_miles
    from foo;

  from  |  to   | dist_miles
--------+-------+------------
 MOM    | ZOOSF |         19
 MOM    | ZOO   |        952
 HOME   | ZOOSF |         49
 HOME   | ZOO   |        966
 TOLPLZ | ZOOSF |          5
 TOLPLZ | ZOO   |        956
```

The idea behind these samples is to provide a hint of the power of doing spatial analysis with PostGIS. Many open source GIS viewing and publishing applications support PostGIS as a backend, so it's also an ideal vehicle for sharing your data on the geospatial web; we'll show how to do this with GeoServer and MapServer in the rest of this chapter.

## H A C K #89 Publish Your Geodata to the Web with GeoServer

If the OGC web standards meet your needs, GeoServer is a great way to get started.

At the beginning of this chapter, we introduced the OpenGIS Consortium's vision for accessible GIS with their Geography Markup Language, Web Feature Service, and Web Map Service standards. If you decide that WFS, WMS, and GML fit your needs, GeoServer is a great place to start.

GeoServer is a Java-servlet-based toolkit that aspires to be the Apache of the geospatial web, designed to make it easy for new users to install and publish their existing geodata. GeoServer is GPL and is available from Sourceforge at *http://geoserver.sf.net/*. The project's main supporter is a nonprofit called The Open Planning Project, which believes that more accessible data about our environment will help to give citizens a greater say about the planning decisions that affect their lives.

GeoServer is a J2EE application built as a thin layer on top of the excellent GeoTools Java GIS toolkit. This allows it to support a wide variety of data formats, as GeoTools strives to make adding new data formats as easy as possible. In this hack, we'll get a GeoServer instance up and running.

### Setting up GeoServer

You will need Java installed on your computer. GeoServer requires at least Version 1.4, which can be downloaded from Sun's web site or from *http:// blackdown.org/* for many Linux distributions. You will also need a Java Servlet Container. There are a variety of open source and commercial Servlet Container implementations; two good ones are Tomcat (by Apache's Jakarta project, freely available to all) and Resin (by Caucho, a commercial company, free for development purposes and hobbyists, and very fast). Both are easy to set up and have built-in web servers, so Apache need not also be installed. To use GeoServer's web-based administration tool, Tomcat 5 is required, as it supports Version 2.0 of the Servlet specification.

You can get the latest version of GeoServer from the download area at *http:// geoserver.sf.net/*. At the time of writing, this is Version 1.2.0. The quickest way to get started is to grab the WAR file: the latest version is always *geoserver.war*. This can be dropped right into the Servlet Container's *webapps* directory, without requiring more Java expertise. To build it from scratch requires the ant build tool.

## Starting up GeoServer

The *.war* contains all the code, libraries, and configuration files to run GeoServer. Both Tomcat and Resin have a directory named *webapps/* where the *.war* file should be placed. If the container is already running, it may need to be restarted, but as soon as it is, the *.war* will expand and GeoServer will load up. The best way to check to see if GeoServer is working is to issue a GetCapabilities request through any web browser. If the container is running on your local machine on the default port, the capabilities request will look like this:

```
http://localhost:8080/geoserver/wfs?request=GetCapabilities
```

This should return a WFS *Capabilities.xsd* document with sample values. You should also see a couple of *FeatureTypes*, samples in the default GeoServer installation. These can be queried with GetFeature and DescribeFeatureType requests. GeoServer also has an integrated Web Map Server; its *Capabilities* document is queried in a similar way:

```
http://localhost:8080/geoserver/wms?request=GetCapabilities
```

Configuring GeoServer. Now that GeoServer is up and running, it is time to configure it with your own information and data. GeoServer has a web-based user interface to make this as easy as possible. It is accessed at:

```
http://localhost:8080/geoserver/
```

This will show a welcome page, with links to the Capabilities page. It also has a link to the TestWfsPost servlet, which is quite useful for playing with the XML-post portions of the Web Feature Service. WFS requests can be written directly into the text box and issued to GeoServer. A few other pages can also be accessed, such as contact information and basic statistics. But to actually configure GeoServer, you must log in. Attempting to do any administrative-type action or hitting the log in button will take you to the page to log in. To log in, the default username is "admin" and the password is "geoserver."

The admin page shows various stats and allows the releasing of locks. The relevant page for now is Config, shown in Figure 8-2.

GeoServer configuration is divided into four basic sections: Server, which contains global application settings and contact information; WFS and

Publish Your Geodata to the Web with GeoServer

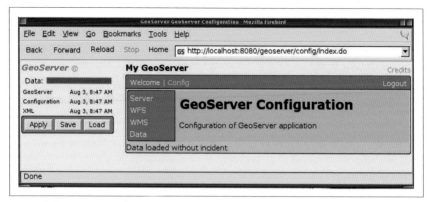

*Figure 8-2. GeoServer administration*

WMS, which configure their specific settings; and Data, where different data formats are loaded and configured to serve as layers (in WMS) and Feature-Types (in WFS).

Setting global settings and contact information. The first thing to configure is the global settings and contact information in Server, shown in Figure 8-3. Maximum Features allows you to specify a limit on the number of Features that can be returned. GeoServer can now return 15 MB of geographic data operating on a Java Virtual Machine (JVM) with a maximum of 10 or less MB of memory. It has also been tested to handle over 10,000 simultaneous GetCapabilities requests. But the Maximum Features value is still useful for extremely large data sets that clients do not necessarily want to receive all at once.

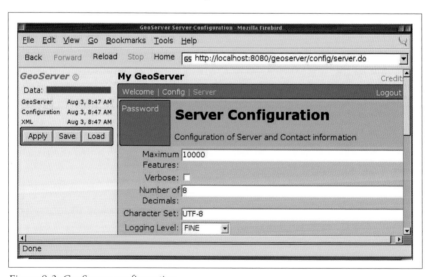

*Figure 8-3. GeoServer configuration*

The Verbose field can be set to indicate whether the returned XML documents should have pretty printing, that is, nice indents and spacing for human readability. This can be useful when getting started, but when actually in production, most clients will likely be computer programs that do not care at all about pretty printing; indeed the spaces and carriage returns will just slow down processing slightly. Note that most browsers now will put XML into human-readable form on their own, so you will likely still be able to easily read GeoServer's output if you set Verbose to false.

Other fields can limit the number of decimals returned in GetFeature responses, which can help cut down bandwidth (but also accuracy). The Character Set can be changed to specific encodings, but UTF-8 is recommended. And the Logging Level determines how much information goes to the logs.

The contact information section is pretty self-explanatory; it will show up in the WMS-capabilities contact information section (the WFS 1.0 specification does not have a matching section, but we anticipate that a future version of the specification will).

**Applying and saving your changes.** To get your new contact information and configurations to show up in GeoServer, you must first hit the Submit button. You can preview the changes by hitting the Apply button on the left-hand side of the screen. The first place this should show up is in the contact link in the upper left corner of the screen, which should be replaced with your name. Clicking on it should take you to a page of the contact information you just submitted. The changes will also be reflected in the WMS Capabilities document; just issue a request like:

```
http://localhost:8080/geoserver/wms?request=GetCapabilities
```

The second section should have your updated information.

After previewing the changes with the Apply button, the changes can be persisted to the configuration files with the Save button. Then your changes will be there when GeoServer is next started. If you don't want to submit the changes made after hitting Apply, then hit Load to roll GeoServer back to the state it was in the last time a save was made.

## Publishing Your Own Data

After setting up the new contact information, the next step is to make your own data available. The Data page (Figure 8-4) is the place to do this. It is divided into four sections: Stores, which defines the connection parameters to various data formats; Namespace, which configures the XML namespaces available for FeatureTypes; Style, where WMS styles can be added; and

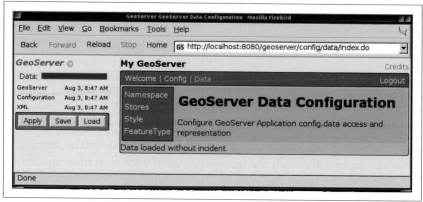

Figure 8-4. GeoServer data management

FeatureType, which defines the specific FeatureTypes from the available DataStores.

A DataStore is the GeoTools abstraction for the location of geographic data. It can be a file, such as a shapefile, or a database, such as PostGIS, Oracle Spatial, or ArcSDE. A DataStore will contain one or more FeatureTypes. For databases, a FeatureType is generally a specific table; each row in the table is a feature. The current shapefile implementation contains only one Feature-Type per DataStore, but one could imagine other file types where a DataStore is a directory that contains a number of different files. To create a new DataStore, click on the Stores link and then the New button. This will take you to a page like that shown in Figure 8-5.

Figure 8-5. Add a GeoServer DataStore

We'll add a PostGIS data store. "Build a Spatially Indexed Data Store" [Hack #87] shows you how to get started, and "Load Your Waypoints into a Spatial Database" [Hack #88] explains how to convert your tracklogs into an indexed PostGIS database.

In the GeoServer DataStore screen, select "PostGIS Spatial Database" from the drop-down menu and enter a DataStore ID. The ID can be almost anything, but it's good to pick something fairly descriptive. After clicking New, you will get a screen like Figure 8-6. Putting the mouse over the text will pop up help notes describing what the fields are. Enabled should be set to True; choose a namespace from the list (you can add your own namespaces with the Namespace menu) and write a brief description of the DataStore. The next fields are the connection parameters for your PostGIS database. If it is running on the same machine, then Host should be "localhost"; otherwise, it should be the IP address of the computer where PostGIS is running. The default PostGIS port is 5432, and Database will be the name of the database that you set up. After filling in your values, hit Submit. Then apply the changes so that the FeatureTypes will be available.

When running PostgreSQL, be sure to start it up with the -i option, which allows it to accept outside connections, such as from GeoServer.

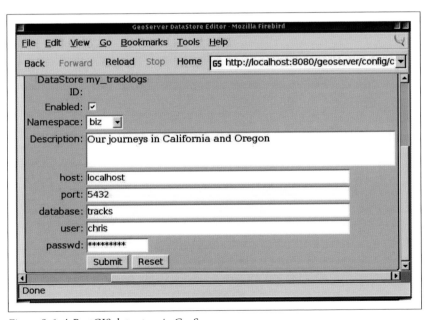

Figure 8-6. A PostGIS data store in GeoServer

Next go to the FeatureType page and hit New. The tables of your PostGIS database should show up appended to the DataStore ID that you gave your newly created Store. Select one that you would like to make available to the geospatial web.

After hitting New, you will be taken to the FeatureTypeEditor screen. This information is primarily for the Capabilities document; it is the meta-information about the FeatureType. The SRS is probably the most important field; it should be an EPSG number—a serial number allocated by the European Petroleum Survey Group—for the projection of your data. You can also edit the schema information to hide certain attributes and to make others mandatory. GeoServer generates the DescribeFeatureType responses automatically, depending on how you configure these attributes. After editing your feature, submit it and click Apply. Your feature should then show up in the Capabilities documents for WMS and WFS, and you can even query it.

> If in doubt, you can use an SRS of EPSG:4326, which corresponds to geographic coordinates (i.e. lat/long) referenced to the WGS84 spheroid and datum. If you need to use a different spatial reference system, try looking through the contents of the spatial_ref_sys table in your PostGIS database to see what other EPSG codes are standard.

### Viewing Your Data with GeoServer's WMS

Though GeoServer started by focusing on the WFS specification, it soon became obvious that an integrated WMS would be a very useful feature to have. Users can simply set up their FeatureTypes in one place and have them available for WMS and WFS. After you've set up your FeatureType, you can issue a WMS GetMap request like the following:

```
http://localhost:8080/geoserver/wms?request=GetMap
&layers=topp:bc_roads
&bbox=489153,5433000,529000,5460816
&width=800&height=400
&srs=EPSG:27354
&styles=normal
&format=image/png
```

The bbox parameter specifies a bounding box that specifies the area of the data to be viewed. To figure out the size of the bbox to issue, the easiest thing to do is to issue a WFS request on the same FeatureType. So if you

named your FeatureType nas:blorg, then you would perform the following
GetFeature request:

```
http://localhost:8080/geoserver/wfs?request=GetFeature
&typename=nas:blorg
```

This will return a GML document of a FeatureCollection containing all your
features. Every FeatureCollection must have a boundedBy element, and from
the gml:Box contained therein, it is easy to figure out the bbox parameter.
The top of the response will look something like:

```
<gml:boundedBy>
    <gml:Box srsName="http://www.opengis.net/gml/srs/epsg.xml#27354">
     <gml:coordinates decimal="." cs="," ts=" ">
    -73.933217,40.78587 -73.933217,40.914404 -73.768722,40.914404 -73.768722,40.
78587
        </gml:coordinates>
     </gml:Box>
</gml:boundedBy>
```

The first coordinate (the lower lefthand corner of the box) and the third
coordinate (the upper righthand corner of the box) make up the appropriate WMS bbox parameter. So for the previous request, the WMS request will
look like:

```
http://localhost:8080/geoserver/wms?request=GetMap
&layers=nas:blorg
&bbox=-73.933217,40.78587,-73.768722,40.914404
&width=800&height=400
&srs=EPSG:4326
&styles=normal
&format=image/png
```

This should return a rendered map of your data. You can experiment with
different image formats, which are advertised in the WMS Capabilities document. There is much more that you can do with GeoServer, including
Transactions and Locking, advanced Filter queries, styling with SLD, and
more. The GeoServer homepage has much more information, and the developer community is generally quite responsive. The easiest point of entry is
the *geotools-devel@lists.sourceforge.net* email list.

If you're interested in hosting WMS or WFS layers, but Java
is not to your taste, you might take a look at UMN's
MapServer [Hack #91], which also supports serving WMS and
WFS layers. See the documentation at *http://mapserver.gis.
umn.edu/* for more info.

—*Chris Holmes*

## Crawl the Geospatial Web with RedSpider

#### HACK #90

RedSpider provides a web-based client to view Web Map Service and Web Feature Service layers—good for testing and instant gratification!

Perhaps, after reading this far, you've decided to take the plunge into the Open Geospatial Consortium web mapping standards to share your map data and let others build on your applications. "Publish Your Geodata to the Web with GeoServer" [Hack #89] shows how to set up GeoServer, the OGC equivalent of the Apache web server, to publish from your existing geographic data sources, such as a PostGIS spatial database or an existing ArcInfo resource.

Now that you've published your spatial data, you want instant gratification. This is where RedSpider comes in. RedSpider (*http://redspider.us/viewer/*) is a *Web Map Service* and *Web Feature Service* client that works in a web browser. It's not open source, but it's free to use and is the nicest closed-source viewer available on the Web.

RedSpider comes preloaded with a large set of layers that represent mostly U.S.-derived global maps. There are weather reports, city names, and country outlines among the default features. However, if you just want to use RedSpider to view your own WFS/WMS published data, you probably want to turn most of these layers off. Figure 8-7 shows the U.S. feature map you see when RedSpider loads up.

The layer-manipulation commands on the toolbar are indicated by a stack of papers. "Manage Layers," the plain stack of paper, will allow you to inspect the vast amount of free U.S. data that RedSpider has access to.

The stack with a plus sign over it indicates "Add Layers to your Context." This is where we can add our newly published WMS or WFS data as a layer in RedSpider. Click on the "Add Layers" icon, and it will present you with an input box, where you can select a WFS or WMS to add to your view (your Context) and enter a URL.

For example, we set up a simple WFS at *http://mappinghacks.com:8080/wfs/geoserver* that publishes a snapshot of the community wireless network in the UK, *http://wirelesslondon.info*. Figure 8-8 shows the list of WFS layers available from our server when we enter it into RedSpider.

After adding a selected layer to RedSpider, hit Submit and your new data will be available in the interface. You probably won't be able to see it, though; if your data encompasses a small part of the world, the client won't be centered on it, and it may be hidden by other layers.

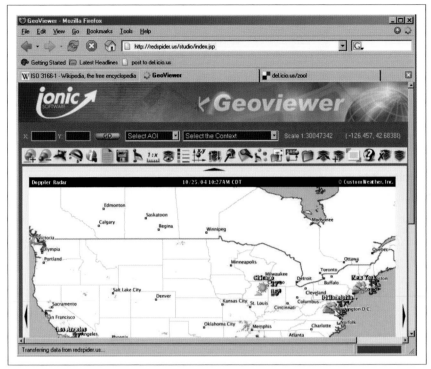

*Figure 8-7. A default view of RedSpider*

To recenter the view so that the *bounding box*, the area of space shown in the image, is the same as the bounding box of your data set, select the stack icon with two arrows protruding from it: the "Fit to Layer" option. This will recenter RedSpider's view of your data. Any new layers you've added should appear at the top of the list. Select them, and hit Submit to zoom in on your data.

The stack with an eye icon over it, "Layer Visibility," allows you to toggle on and off the layers that you want displayed on your web map. Ctrl-click to select a range of them; unselected layers will stay invisible. Again, your new layers will be at the top of the list. At the bottom of the list are layers for world countries and major cities, dating to 1998; these are always useful as a base reference.

This should induce instant gratification! Figure 8-9 shows a map we were able to produce very simply with RedSpider, showing nodes on the UK community wireless network.

WFS holds great promise in terms of being able to chain geographic data services together with no programming effort. *Styled Layer Descriptor* is a

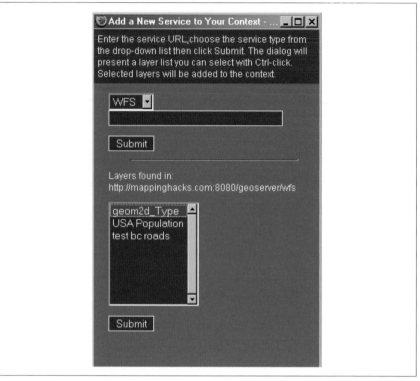

*Figure 8-8. RedSpider Add Layer interface*

developing effort that will allow you to provide custom styles and symbols for map clients to display your layers with. The future is promising!

# H A C K    Build Interactive Web-Based Map
# #91    Applications

MapServer offers a powerful way to publish interactive maps on the World Wide Web.

Bringing interactive maps to the Web may seem like a daunting task. I initially set out to display a map of my home area and plot additional points on top. When I first went on this quest, I was afraid I would have to write kilobytes of code by myself. Fortunately, there are packages out there that do the hard parts, allowing us to focus on making maps.

MapServer, which lives at *http://mapserver.gis.umn.edu/*, is a great package for making interactive maps. It is a CGI program written in C that creates interactive maps from your spatial data. (You can also use MapServer with Perl, Python, and PHP using the provided MapScript modules). MapServer

*Figure 8-9. A map of community wireless nodes in the UK, as shown by RedSpider*

supports a wide range of spatial data formats, databases, and display formats; it makes publishing maps on the Web not only easier, but also extensible.

## Getting and Installing MapServer

MapServer source code is available at *http://mapserver.gis.umn.edu/dload. html*. There is also a precompiled binary for Windows machines. Binary RPMs for various platforms can be found as part of the PostGIS distribution at *http://postgis.refractions.net/rpms/*, or from the Mapping Hacks RPM archive at *http://mappinghacks.com/rpm*. Debian packages are also available, from *http://pkg-grass.alioth.debian.org/debian-gis*.

MapServer supports a stunning variety of options, from numerous data sources (e.g., PostGIS database) and map output formats (e.g., PDF, SVG, Flash, images). Any binary package must assume some set of pre-installed libraries. Getting these dependencies sorted out adds a lot of complexity to the installation process, which interferes with what is, at heart, a rather simple program. Ironically, the easiest way to get started may be to compile from source:

```
$ ./configure
$ make
```

This is not the "right" way to configure MapServer, but there is a good chance that this will work (especially if you already have the GD image libraries installed). The document "HOWTO for Getting Started with MapServer" (*http://mapserver.gis.umn.edu/doc/getstarted-howto.html*) contains links to detailed instructions for building MapServer under other platforms, and with more options.

Once you've compiled MapServer, you can test its capabilities:

```
$ ./mapserv -v

MapServer version 4.2.4 OUTPUT=PNG OUTPUT=JPEG OUTPUT=WBMP SUPPORTS=FREETYPE
INPUT=TIFF INPUT=EPPL7 INPUT=JPEG INPUT=SHAPEFILE
```

This means that MapServer can read ESRI Shapefiles and write JPEG and PNG images. This is just a taste of what MapServer can do, but "tall trees from little acorns grow."

Copy the program *mapserv* to a directory that can execute CGI programs. On a default Fedora or Debian system, that is likely to be */var/www/cgi-bin* (on a SuSE system, it is probably */srv/www/cgi-bin*). Test that the web server is correctly configured by going to *http://localhost/cgi-bin/mapserv*, or use the server's Internet domain name if you are testing a remote machine (e.g., *http://yourserver.com/cgi-bin/mapserv*). You should get the message:

```
No query information to decode.  QUERY_STRING is set, but empty.
```

This means that the program is running but you have not given it anything to do. So how do you give it something to do?

Well, first you need some data. Since our copy of *mapserv* can display ESRI Shapefiles, let's get the outline of the United States. *NationalAtlas.gov* contains large amounts of free data about the United States. Go to the "Map Layers Warehouse" page at *http://nationalatlas.gov/atlasftp.html*. Download the *States Information* file from *http://edcftp.cr.usgs.gov/pub/data/ nationalatlas/statesp020.tar.gz*. Decompress the files and put them in your data directory, which can be anywhere as long as your web server has permission to read files there.

## Directories

You will need to have some other web-server-readable directories in your filesystem for storing the various components of your MapServer installation. I tend to use Fedora-flavored systems, so modify this to suit your preferences:

*/var/www/cgi-bin*

> A directory that your web server uses for CGI programs. Copy the *mapserv* CGI program here.

*/var/www/html*

> Your document root. This is where the initialization HTML file and the map file (*.map*) should go.

*/var/www/html/data*

> This will be the repository for your geodata files.

*/var/www/html/temp*

> Temporary directory for images. Your web server must have write permission for this directory.

## The Map File

The map file is where you specify what MapServer should do. Here is possibly the simplest map file that will display a shapefile:

```
MAP
        SIZE            400 400
        EXTENT          -125 50 -65 24
        LAYER
                TYPE            LINE
                STATUS          DEFAULT
                DATA            "/var/www/html/data/statesp020.shp"
                CLASS
                        COLOR   0 0 0
                END
        END
END
```

Each section of the map file starts with the name of that section and ends with the word END. Some sections can be nested. This map file says to create an image 400 pixels wide by 400 pixels high that covers the Continental United States, from 65° W to 125° W and from 24° N to 50° N.

One map layer will be shown, and it is the shapefile of the state boundaries. It will be presented in the color black; the colors are RGB triples, so 250 0 0 is all red, 0 255 0 is green, 0 0 255 is blue, and there are $2^{24}$ more shades of color available.

Name this file *mini.map* and make sure that the *statesp020.shp*, *.shx*, and *.dbf* files are in the *data* directory. Figure 8-10 shows the map of the U.S. that you can now generate by going to *http://yourserver.com/cgi-bin/mapserv?map=/var/www/html/mini.map&mode=map*.

*Figure 8-10. The United States, as presented by MapServer*

You can also include that URL in your web pages as an image:

```
<img src="/cgi-bin/mapserv?map=/var/www/html/mini.map&mode=map">
```

The `map=/var/www/html/mini.map` parameter points to the map file that describes how the map will be generated. The second parameter, `mode=map`, causes MapServer to return an image file directly.

> Arguably, allowing the user to set the full path to the map file in the URL might constitute a security breach on some systems. One way around having to allow this is to create a shell script that hardcodes the map file in the shell environment before executing *mapserv*:
>
> ```
> #!/bin/sh
> export MS_MAPFILE=/var/www/html/mini.map
> exec /var/www/cgi-bin/mapserv
> ```
>
> Having done this, you can place that shell script in your *cgi-bin* directory, and use it instead of using mapserv directly, in which case you will no longer need to provide a `map=` option through the MapServer URL.

## Adding Interactivity

Generating an image from passed parameters is just the tip of the map. You can also create a full layer-based interactive map viewer with just a bit more effort.

For this example, we'll use a shapefile of local roads in Allegheny County, available from *http://www.pasda.psu.edu*. The specific URL of the file is *ftp://pasda.cac.psu.edu/pub/pasda/padot/local/padot-locroads-allegheny_2001.zip*.

Unzip this file, and put it in your *data* directory. Be sure that the user permissions for the unzipped files are readable by the web server, or you will get errors telling you: *Failed to draw layer*!

We now want a more elaborate map file. Save the following text as *mapserver.map* and put it into your document root (e.g., */var/www/html*):

```
map
        size            400 400
        extent          -80.475 39.96 -79.475 40.96

        web
                template        mapserver.html
                imagepath       "/var/www/html/temp/"
                imageurl        "/temp/"
        end

        layer
                name            allegheny
                type            line
                status          default
                data            "data/allegheny.shp"
                class
                        color   0 0 0
                end
        end
end
```

In this file we have zoomed in to the area from 39.96°N, 80.475°W to 40.96°N, 79.475°W. This map file also includes a web section. The template parameter specifies the name of an HTML file that provides the formatting for the web display of our map. In this case, the directory is shown relative to the location of our map file. When we use a template file, *mapserv* creates an image of the map and writes it to a temporary file in the directory specified by the imagepath parameter. The imageurl parameter specifies the location of that directory relative to our document root, so that the web browser can access those images:

```
<html>
<body bgcolor=#FFFFFF>
<form method=GET>
<INPUT NAME="img" TYPE="image" SRC="[img]" width=400 height=400 bord
er=1> <BR>
<input type="submit" value="Refresh/Query"><BR>
[ Zoom In <input type=radio name=zoomdir value=1 [zoomdir_1_check]>]
[ Pan <input type=radio name=zoomdir value=0 [zoomdir_0_check]>]
[ Zoom Out <input type=radio name=zoomdir value=-1 [zoomdir_-1_check
]>]
Zoom Size <input type=text name=zoomsize size=4 value=2>
<input type="hidden" name="imgext" value="[mapext]">
<input type="hidden" name="map" value="[map]">
</form>
</body></html>
```

When you invoke MapServer with the previous map file, it will read this HTML template, replacing the appropriate keywords in square brackets, such as [img] and [mapext], with their intended values. There are extensive ways to flesh out the HTML, including JavaScript, Perl, and PHP through MapScript. This is only a brief example, so it includes only the basics needed to display the map and provide minimal navigation. Save this file as *mapserver.html* in your document root directory.

MapServer is stateless, which means that the program running on the server does not store information about your session. Each request to MapServer includes all of the parameters of your current session. For example, if you zoom in on a map, your current extent (the area that is displayed) is sent with your HTTP request.

We need a way to initialize our MapServer session. There are many possible parameters that we can provide, but the only mandatory parameter is the name of a map file. We can pass this by including it on the command line, or by putting it into a hidden form variable in an HTML file:

```
<html>
<body bgcolor="#FFFFFF">
This will initialize Mapserver.<BR>
<form method=GET action="/cgi-bin/mapserv">
<input type="hidden" name="map" value="/var/www/html/mapserver.map">
<input type="submit" value="Initialize">
</form>
</body></html>
```

Save this file to *index.html* (or whatever you want), and then load it in your web browser. This displays the message "This will initialize MapServer" and a button labeled Initialize. Click the button, and you will get a map. Alternatively, you can construct a URL with a query string directly in your browser—e.g., *http://yourserver.com/cgi-bin/mapserv?map=/var/www/html/mapserver.map*. In either case, you must provide the full path to your map file relative to the root directory of your filesystem.

Both the URI method and the file method do the same job of passing the location of our map file to MapServer. MapServer then reads the rest the map file and creates a map. The initial output should be a black gob of roads. You should also see the path of the Ohio, Monongahela, and Allegheny rivers as cutouts against the local roadways.

By clicking on the resulting image, it should recenter the image to where you have clicked. The radio buttons at the bottom allow you to zoom in, zoom out, or pan the image. You can select the "zoom in" radio button and then click on the image. The map in Figure 8-11 shows the result of zooming in a bit on our initial squiggle of roads.

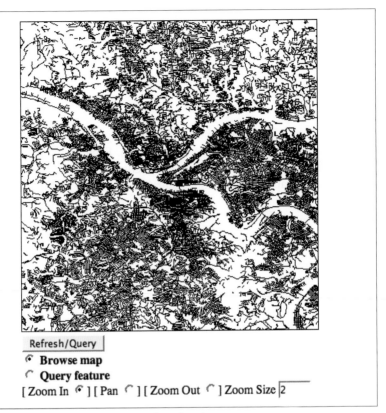

*Figure 8-11. MapServer and the streets of Pittsburgh*

## Adding a Point

You can add a point directly in the map file to indicate anything you wish. You can even specify points via URLs, through a database, or from another file. Here, we will specify just one point, for my favorite local coffee shop with free Wi-Fi. First, let's define the symbol that will mark our point. Add this section before the final end tag in your map file:

```
symbol
    name "coffee_wifi"
    type ellipse
    filled true
    points 2 1 end
end
```

This creates a symbol named `coffee_wifi` as an ellipse that is twice as wide as it is tall. This does not control the absolute size at which the symbol will be displayed; that will be determined by the size parameter in the layer that uses the symbol.

Now we can add another layer for our coffee shop, after the `coffee_wifi` symbol and before our final end tag:

```
layer
        name           beehive
        type           point
        status         default
        class
            color    0 0 255
            symbol   "coffee_wifi"
            size     15
            label
                position ur
                size medium
                color 0 0 255
                outlinecolor 255 255 255
            end
        end

        feature
            points -79.98403 40.42775 end
            text    "Beehive"
        end
    end
```

Note how we use the `coffee_wifi` symbol that we defined earlier, but we set the size and color here. We also set the position of the label to ur, or upper right of the symbol.

The feature section defines an individual point. We can add multiple feature blocks, each with the points (longitude first, as usual) and text (name or label). You should now see a blue dot labeled "Beehive" on the South Side of Pittsburgh, as shown in Figure 8-12.

MapServer does a heck of a lot more than this: raster layers, on-the-fly reprojection, automatic labeling, TrueType fonts, layer queries, attribute filtering, database lookups, and more. Obviously, the next step is to tailor the images to your liking by tweaking your map file and the corresponding HTML. We'll look a little more into this in "Map Wardriving (and other!) Data with MapServer" [Hack #92].

## See Also

*http://terrasip.gis.umn.edu/projects/tutorial/*
    MapServer tutorial

*http://mapserver.gis.umn.edu/doc/getstarted-howto.html*
    Getting started with MapServer

*http://omsug.ca/dl/osgis2004/MsTutorialGuide.doc*
    How to use (almost) every vector data format with MapServer

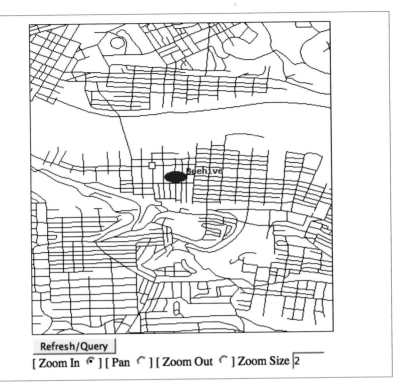

*Figure 8-12. The Beehive Coffee Shop with free Wi-Fi*

*http://omsug.ca/osgis2004/proceedings.html*
> From the proceedings of the 2004 North American Open Source GIS Conference

*http://maptools.org/ms4w/*
> MapServer for Windows (MS4W): includes Apache and everything to get started (and more, perhaps too much!)

> —*Drew from Zhrodague*

### HACK #92 Map Wardriving (and other!) Data with MapServer

Use shapelib and a little script to convert wardriving data to shapefiles, and then map them!

I collect a lot of wardriving data from just about every commute, cruise, and highway adventure I take. Naturally, I want to plot my findings and publish them on the Web. MapServer provides a great way to do this, but the wardriving data first needs to be converted to something that MapServer can display. We can do this with a quick script.

## The Shapefile of Things to Come

*Shapelib* is a library for handling ESRI Shapefiles, written by Frank Warmerdam. It includes utility programs that allow us to create and dump the contents of shapefiles and their matching database files from the command line. The program is available at *http://shapelib.maptools.org/*. There is a binary version for Windows and an RPM for Shapelib available at *http://freegis.org/*, which also features other neat GIS-related software and links.

If you decide to build from source, the instructions suggest editing the *Makefile* to suit your environment, but I was able to decompress the file and successfully compile the library without manual configuration under FreeBSD, Mac OS X, and Fedora Core 2. Type **make** to compile the library and the associated binaries. This will create the utility programs *shpcreate*, *shpadd*, *dbfcreate*, *dbfadd*, *shpdump*, and *dbfdump*.

To create a shapefile, you need to generate *.shp*, *.shx*, and *.dbf* files. For each item in your input data, you need to add the latitude and longitude to the *.shp* and *.shx* files, and add any associated attribute data to the *.dbf* file. For wardriving data, attributes might take the form of the ESSID, or name, of the networks that you find, or the time that you recorded the network's location. It's very important to line up the data properly, as the order of the entries is what links a single record across the *.dbf* and *.shp/.shx* files.

In practice, you can accomplish this by using the *shpcreate* command to specify the filename to create (without extension) and the type of shapefile to create. Use *dbfcreate* to create the *.dbf* file and specify the attribute(s) that you want to associate with this shapefile:

```
$ shpcreate myshape  point
$ dbfcreate myshape -s name 24
```

This example creates the files *myshape.shp*, *myshape.shx*, and *myshape.dbf*. The *.dbf* file contains one attribute, a string field called name that is 24 characters wide.

Then walk through your wardriving datafile and add points to the shapefile and attributes to the *.dbf* for each network you found:

```
$ shpadd myshape -122.09089 37.45894
$ dbfadd myshape "NoCat"
$ shpadd myshape -122.15489 37.49283
$ dbfadd myshape "QueenFleeWee"
```

You can check the shapefile with the *shpdump* and *dbfdump* commands that come with Shapelib:

```
$ shpdump myshape
Shapefile Type: Point   # of Shapes: 2
```

```
File Bounds: (    -122.155,    37.459,0,0)
         to (    -122.091,    37.493,0,0)

Shape:0 (Point)  nVertices=1, nParts=0
  Bounds:(    -122.091,    37.459, 0, 0)
      to (    -122.091,    37.459, 0, 0)
      (    -122.091,    37.459, 0, 0)

Shape:1 (Point)  nVertices=1, nParts=0
  Bounds:(    -122.155,    37.493, 0, 0)
      to (    -122.155,    37.493, 0, 0)
      (    -122.155,    37.493, 0, 0)

$ dbfdump myshape
name
NoCat
QueenFleeWee
```

 Note that *shpadd* expects longitude first, not latitude!
Remember that the *x*-coordinate comes before the *y*-coordinate, where longitude is measured along the *x*-axis. As usual,
coordinates west of Greenwich and south of the equator are
given negative values.

MapServer more or less requires you to provide the geographic extents of
the area you want to map. If you were creating a map file from the previous
example, you would take your extents from the File Bounds section, and
your extent line would look like this:

```
EXTENT -122.155 37.493 -122.091 37.459
```

You can also check a shapefile's extents with ogrinfo, a utility included with
the GDAL library. The command ogrinfo -al -summary myshape will show
the metadata from all layers in a shapefile. See "Convert Geospatial Data
Between Different Formats" **[Hack #68]** for more on the OGR and GDAL
utilities.

## From Wardriving to Shapefiles

Netstumbler, the network scanning software I use, supports a logging format called *WiScan*. WiScan is a tab-delimited ASCII text format with a simple header, which our script will ignore. You can experiment on your own
with handling the other parameters in the file:

```
# $Format: wi-scan summary with extensions
# Latitude  Longitude    ( SSID )    Type    ( BSSID )   Time (GMT)  [ SNR
Sig Noise ]   # ( Name )  Flags   Channelbits BcnIntvl
# $DateGMT: 2004-09-29
N 37.418873  W 121.064453  W    ( belkin54g ) BSS ( 00:11:50:0a:91:85 ) 22:
10:23 (GMT)  [ 22 22 0 ] # (  ) 0011    0040    0
```

```
N 37.371231 W 122.044531    ( NETGEAR ) BSS ( 00:09:5b:e9:5d:54 )   22:10:03
(GMT)  [ 25 25 0 ] # (   ) 0001   0040   0
```

Here is an extremely simplistic script to create a shapefile from a WiScan file. The *shpadd* program uses negative numbers for West longitude and South latitude. Unfortunately, the WiScan format specifies GPS coordinates with N and W, instead of + and -. This script ignores the directional letters completely and assumes northern latitude, and western longitude—so it will only work in my part of the world:

```
#!/bin/sh
shpcreate wiscan point
dbfcreate wiscan -s name 24
grep -v "^#" $1 | \
        awk '{print "-" $4 " " $2 " " ; dbfadd \"" $6 $7 $8 $9}' | \
        awk -F\) '{print "shpadd wiscan " $1 "\""}' | \
        sh
```

**$ wiscan my_wiscan.txt**

The script creates the *.shp*, *.shx*, and *.dbf* files and then it uses grep and awk to create a series of shell commands that it then pipes to the shell, which executes the commands to add the location of each wireless node to the shapefile *wiscan*.

You can see what the script is doing by copying this fragment into the file demo:

```
grep -v "^#" $1 | \
        awk '{print "-" $4 " " $2 " " ; dbfadd wiscan \"" $6 $7 $8 $9}' | \
        awk -F\) '{print "shpadd wiscan " $1 "\""}'
```

**$ demo my_wiscan.txt**

The first line runs *grep* against the file you enter on the command line and removes all the comments from the file (comments are lines that start with #). It then sends the cleaned-up file to the *awk* command:

```
awk '{print "-" $4 " " $2 " " ; dbfadd  wiscan \"" $6 $7 $8 $9}'
```

*awk* treats the text within single quotes as a command. The braces { } tell *awk* to apply the rest of the command to each line in the file. *awk* then prints a minus sign followed by the fourth field in the file, which is the longitude. This is where the longitude is hardcoded as West longitude. It then prints a space and then the second parameter, the latitude. Then it prints the string: ; dbfadd wiscan, followed by fields 6–9:

```
-122.15488 37.49284  ; ./dbfadd wiscan "QueenFleeWee)BSS(
```

That is getting close to what we want, but we're not quite there:

```
awk -F\) '{print "shpadd  wiscan " $1 "\""}'
```

This line takes the output of the previous line from the script and creates our final command:

```
./shpadd wiscan -122.15488 37.49284  ; ./dbfadd wiscan "QueenFleeWee"
```

It does this by printing the *shpadd* WiScan, followed by the rest of the first "field" that was passed in. The default field separator is whitespace, but you can use -F to set the field separator. In this case, we set it to ), so we get everything up to the )BSS(.

## Map This Shapefile!

Throw the shapefiles into your data directory [Hack #91], and then add a layer to an existing map file:

```
layer
    name          wiscan
    type          point
    status        default
    data          "wiscan.shp"
    labelitem     "name"
    class
        label
            size      tiny
            color     255 0 0
        end
            color    0 0 255
    end
end
```

This layer contains only simple parameters, enough to get the layer to display. Note the labelitem entry, and the label class. These control the label display. In our case, we are using the SSID name, which is extracted from the *.dbf* file and stored in the name field. The label will be red (R = 255, G = 0, B = 0), and the dot marking the station will be blue (R = 0, G = 0, B = 255).

A thorough reference to map-file syntax can be found in the MapServer documentation (*http://mapserver.gis.umn.edu*).

## Hacking the Hack: Adding Aerial Photographs

Once you've set up MapServer and have a few shapefiles going, you might want to use aerial photographs in your maps. There is an easy way to do this, but there are a couple of pitfalls. Once you have the right things in place, however, it just works.

The U.S. government produces aerial and satellite Earth imagery as *Digital Orthographic Quads* (*DOQ*) for various purposes. To make these images, either photos are taken from satellite or airplanes are sent with cameras over a given area. These images are homogenized and rectified so that each of them is georeferenced correctly. Some states, counties, and universities distribute this data, usually in the GeoTIFF format.

## GeoTIFF

Aerial photographs usually come as *GeoTIFFs*, which are simply standard TIFF bitmap images with an additional file called a *world file*, which has a *.wld* or *.tfw* file extension. This world file is a text file that contains the georeferencing information used to align and position the image properly. "Georeference an Arbitrary Tourist Map" [Hack #33] explains how world files work and how they can be generated.

For this hack, we'll use the aerial photographs from Pittsburgh, Pennsylvania, where I live. I'll also build upon the existing map file from "Build Interactive Web-Based Map Applications" [Hack #91]. All of the spatial data comes from the same place, PASDA (*ftp://pasda.cac.psu.edu*). The specific aerial photographs are located in *ftp://pasda.cac.psu.edu/pub/pasda/doq*, and we'll use *wget* to fetch them. Make sure your current working directory is your data directory, and unzip them there:

```
#> wget ftp://pasda.cac.psu.edu/pub/pasda/doq/pittsburgh*
```

Be warned, each of the eight files is 40 MB in size and extracts to a 45 MB TIFF. It might be useful to convert the images into JPEGs or another high-compression format. You can do this with *gdal_translate*. ("Convert Geospatial Data Between Different Formats" [Hack #68] should get you started, and for more information, check GDAL's documentation, which is available at *http://www.gdal.org*.)

## Create a Tile Index

Initially, you could add each of these GeoTIFFs as its own unique layer. To make things easier and treat all of the aerial photographs as one layer, we can use gdaltindex to create a *tile index*—a shapefile containing the file locations of the images and the spatial locations where each of the images lays. Run as follows; *gdaltindex* will create the shapefile called *aerial* and add all of the images.

```
gdaltindex aerial *.tif
```

## Create a Map File

Now that you have created this tile index, you can reference it in your *map file* through tileindex and tileitem. tileindex points to the shapefiles we created, while `tileitem` specifies the column containing the file locations. Again, MapServer's web site explains all of this in more detail.

Throw this in your map file as the first layer. This will place the aerial photographs on the bottom and draw the shapefiles on top:

```
layer
        name            aerial_photos
        type            raster
        status          default
        tileindex       "aerial"
        tileitem        "location"
end
```

## Projection Issues

In a sense-making world, our shapefiles and GeoTIFFs would be using the same coordinate system, and we would be done at this stage. Unfortunately, even though our data comes from the same place, our images are being plotted thousands of miles apart (or more).

Fortunately, MapServer has the enormously powerful ability to reproject both raster and vector layers for us on the fly. If we define a `projection` section at the top level of our map file as follows:

```
projection "+proj=utm" "+zone=17" end
```

Then we can add a similar `projection` section within each of our latitude/longitude layers, like so:

```
projection "+proj=latlong" end
```

The combination of the two will prompt MapServer to dynamically reproject those layers into UTM Zone 17, as needed. Meanwhile, the DOQs, which were already in a UTM projection, will remain unchanged, and everything should magically line up. Of course, before that happens, we will first have to adjust the default extents of our map file, since our coordinate system has changed from degrees to easting and northing in meters. In this endeavor, the *proj* utility from the PROJ.4 toolkit is invaluable for converting lat/long extents to UTM and back. The token effort required to reproject the map extents by hand is more than handsomely repaid by the utter ease with which we can subsequently drop in new data sets from any source projection and have them *just work.*

Hacking MapServer map files is an art, but this is a good start!

*—Drew from Zhrodague*

# CHAPTER NINE

# Mapping with Other People
Hacks 93–100

*In thy face I see the map of honor, truth,*
*and loyalty.*
—William Shakespeare, *Henry VI Part II, III:1,*
  the King to his uncle, the Duke of Gloucester

Hopefully you're now as convinced as we are that a new wave in geographic tools and techniques is revolutionizing the way we produce and consume maps. Commodified consumer GPS, Wi-Fi location sensing, open source GIS tools, and web publishing of spatial data—the kind of work that previously could only be carried out by large military, governmental and transnational agencies—can now be used by home users or community groups.

We can all see a little bit of the years to come; we can draw pictures of a shared future with the practice of "collaborative mapping." This doesn't have to be a serious-minded, socially conscious activity. Buckminster Fuller's original vision of the "geoscope," via which "All the world would be dynamically viewable and picturable and radioable to all the world," suggested a "World Game," in which we could playfully work out the consequences of our future plans.

With this in mind, we've looked for playful and unusual ways in which to use and generate spatial information. We've looked for simple applications that you can set up, allowing your friends and neighbors to describe your world in ways that are meaningful to you and re-usable by others.

Those in hyper-networked parts of the world are starting to see "geo games," which locate where you are on your wireless voice device, or freakishly accurate models of cities on their home-gaming consoles, networked up to reflect real-world changes in routes and new features in the built environment. The rules worked out in these play spaces present an interesting counterpoint to the "God's-eye" military simulations that inform and fund immersive virtual world environments such as There.com.

Parts of this chapter are forward-looking, to a future of pervasive computing in which you're tapping out your latest photomoblog to your freak-clique with your data glove on the low-slung table in your favorite recaf-vending geoloc. But we'd also like to look backward, to document civic history and the changing use of space, and tell the stories of our wagon-riding great-grandparents in a medium that our electrolobed gargoyle great-grandchildren will be able to connect with.

The semantic web—a network of machine-understandable, interconnected information sources that complements the existing web of human-readable pages—is our current best hope for creating media annotated with location and time. Many of these hacks use the Resource Description Framework (RDF) graph model and XML format to attempt to bridge between the Web as we know it and the all-singing, all-dancing geospatial web of the hopeful future.

The possibilities inherent in open source GIS, and freely available data with a spatial component, are as endless as all our collective imaginations. The software and the data standards described here allow us to describe our neighborhood, exchange models of our environment and how we might willfully or unwillingly change it, and stitch these models together in a "geoscope." Geofiction blurs with geofact, in ways that we can't yet predict.

### HACK #93 Node Runner

Locative games don't have to involve the latest high-tech phone and hosted service.

Yury Gitman, a "wireless artist" formerly based at NYU, created the game Node Runner: a race to connect to and photograph the most wireless nodes between two points. The original Node Runner was a two-team race to collect as many wireless nodes as possible between the Eyebeam studios and Bryant Park in New York City in two and a half hours. Node Runner is also a great way for hackers to get outside and get some exercise. Participate as a laptop-bearing tribe of gargoyles, rushing about the city to find free net access, and take pictures to prove you were there.

At the start of the game, each team gets a laptop with a digital camera and *net stumbling* software that scans for wireless network nodes. The teams get one point for every five nodes in their scanner logs, and five points for each set of two pictures that they upload via an open access point—a picture of a landmark near the access point, and a picture of a team member standing there. Note to the wireless cognoscenti: the picture requirement eliminated the otherwise winning strategy of playing from a tall building using a large grid antenna.

Figure 9-1 shows the latest web interface for watching noderunners upload pictures in real time. The game was recently played again in Paris with PDAs and local base map data, and it is starting to look very sophisticated. *http:// www.noderunner.com* is a redeveloped version of the site, containing the full rules.

*Figure 9-1. Web interface to Node Runner*

A few months later, at the Cartographic Congress in London, we played our own local version of Node Runner. *http://downlode.org/noderunner/* shows the rules and results for our modified version. We bent the rules a bit to fit our local situation; as Wi-Fi coverage is not as good in London, we awarded a point for each scanned node. And in a free-for-all spirit, we allowed more than two teams to compete. We also required GPS coordinates for each access point the teams logged on to. One team cheated slightly by photographing themselves by three access points within 15 meters of each other! The winner optimized his strategy by charging around a downtown business district that wasn't really on the way from the start to the finish. Used to sedentary wireless access in coffee shops, you may have more difficulty negotiating on city streets with a digital camera and a laptop with attached GPS. Gadgets galore!

**Rich person's location finding.** You can use your GPS unit to take latitude and longitude while you're taking photographs. Better yet, connect your GPS unit to your laptop and get a continuous stream of geo-annotated Wi-Fi stumbles from a program like *kismet* for *NIX, kismac or MacStumbler for the Macintosh, or netstumbler for the PC. See "Map Nearby Wi-Fi Hotspots" [Hack #17] and "Map Wardriving (and other!) Data with MapServer" [Hack #92] for more details on stumbling your own maps of wireless access points.

**Poor person's location finding.** You don't have a GPS. But you have the Internet! A local mapping or geocoding service can help you figure out where you are. In "Geocode a U.S. Street Address" [Hack #79], we show how to use *http://geocoder.us* to provide latitude and longitude for most U.S. addresses, as well as intersections. In the UK, you can get this information from *http://www.streetmap.co.uk/*. Sadly the big online mapping services like MapQuest and Multimap no longer give latitudes and longitudes for free. At the time of writing, Maporama still does, as detailed in "Tweak the Look and Feel of Web Maps" [Hack #37]. One of the authors of this book used the Maporama geocoding service to look up the locations of his hotels for a trip to Italy and then enter them into his GPS.

Instead of recording places with latitude and longitude, you could just record the URL of a mapping site pointing to that location. "Put a Map on It: Mapping Arbitrary Locations with Online Services" [Hack #1] contains tips and tricks for forming and reusing URLs on several popular web map sites.

## Other Wireless Games

We hope Node Runner will give some people ideas for other, more complex, free wireless/locative games. For example, you could design a game to collect virtual objects, "simjects," that are only accessible if you're near a particular place. Node Running is also a fun way of collecting geospatial data about access points to use as a base map for Wi-Fi location-finding software programs, such as PlaceLab. Some of the 3G mobile-service providers now provide simple role-playing games that rely on physical exploration of space. Using the techniques outlined in "Build a Map of Local GSM Cells" [Hack #61], you can make spatial games over phone networks very cheaply.

# Geo-Warchalking with 2-D Barcodes

**HACK #94**

Tagging physical spaces with readable messages for humans has many physical and digital manifestations. What about geotagging for machines?

Geo-warchalking was originally a simple idea of people marking postcodes and latitude/longitude pairs around the urban environment in chalk, similar to the Wi-Fi markings based on symbols chalked by traveling hobos, making the invisible visible.

Written symbols in the world are still hard to get in and out of an electronic location system. You don't really want to be typing in numbers to eight decimal places, or triple-tapping postcodes. Human-understandable is not necessarily machine-readable.

So how can we make reading and writing spatial annotations from handheld devices easy and automatic? Until RFID tags become available in spray cans, anyone can sticker the city...with barcodes.

## Big in Japan

Especially in Japan, many modern mobile phones read 2-D barcodes, in a standard format, using the on-phone camera. These barcodes include a phone number and a URL or email address. These barcodes have infiltrated the business world. People print them on their paper business cards, and advertisements often have a barcode link.

But we want to store other data. We want latitude and longitude. We want places. We want lots of things: we want to barcode tables, chairs, everything! How can we create all these specifications to describe all these things?

Many of them exist already, in the form of RDF schemas. "Model Interactive Spaces" **[Hack #95]** outlines some of the basic options for describing spaces, and things that relate to them, in RDF. There are schemas, or ontologies, to describe positioning (*geo*), places (*spacenamespace, locative*) and even people and homepages (*FOAF*). If you want to describe something else, it's not that hard to make and publish your own special-purpose schema.

Geo-warchalkers propose to use the same standard for barcode encoding as used in Japan: QR Code. It's scalable (up to about 4 KB), it's in the public domain, it handles odd characters (such as Japanese scripts), and it copes pretty well with being readable when the barcode is damaged.

## Making 2-D Geobarcodes

There's a selection of software for generating QR barcodes online, most of it Windows payware. The free web service at *http://nfg.2y.net/system/ qrcodegen.php* allows you to type into a text area, and then generates a barcode from your input. Figure 9-2 shows a chunk of geospatial RDF (the example from the geo workspace at *http://www.w3.org/2003/01/geo/*) encoded as a QR code:

```
<rdf:RDF xmlns:rdf="http://www.w3.org/1999/02/22-rdf-syntax-ns#"
         xmlns:geo="http://www.w3.org/2003/01/geo/wgs84_pos#">
```

*Figure 9-2. An RDF geo-annotation rendered as a 2-D barcode.*

```
<geo:Point>
  <geo:lat>55.701</geo:lat>
  <geo:long>12.552</geo:long>
</geo:Point>
</rdf:RDF>
```

Now, it might be worth being a bit pragmatic and not including the RDF blurb at the beginning (i.e., just encoding the actual geo packet). This is the most compressed representation of a WGS84 latitude and longitude in RDF, and its barcode is shown in Figure 9-3:

```
<geo:Point geo:lat="55.701" geo:long="12.552"/>
```

*Figure 9-3. A minimal geobarcode*

The other thing to add is a human-readable indication of what you're encoding—i.e., the namespace: geo, locative, or FOAF. This makes it possible for you to work out what kind of thing you're scanning or looking for.

And just to prove how crazy this can get, Figure 9-4 shows the description section of my FOAF file.

If you include all my email aliases, it gets to a point where I don't think camera phones can cope.

So, let's annotate the planet! What do we need next?

- A simple standard proposal
- Free open reader and writer software, both for PCs and phones
- Crazy geo-pirate graffiti gangs

*Figure 9-4. A FOAF file encoded with a geobarcode*

## Why-Not Questions

**Why not use RFID?** It's too expensive, and not generally available. All you need with barcodes is a printer.

**Why not just use a pointer or a URI?** This isn't just for connected devices such as camera phones. Your digital camera might use a geobarcode to geoposition your photo. Your GPS could learn more about places and things via barcodes. Encoding the information within the barcode makes the system more open-ended and hackable.

**Why not use n3 triples?** I thought more software and hardware would understand some form of XML, rather than n3. (I have never seen an n3-reading app outside of RDF testbeds.)

**Why not zip/gzip the data first?** This is a pretty good point, which should be investigated. I'm worried that this causes more complexity, and things to go wrong. I want to see if doing this makes the barcodes less fault-tolerant.

## See Also

- "Map Your Friend-of-a-Friend Network" **[Hack #99]**
- "Model Interactive Spaces" **[Hack #95]**
- "Set Up an OpenGuide for Your Hometown" **[Hack #97]**

—*Chris Heathcote*

## Model Interactive Spaces

**HACK #95**

Make a Multi User Dungeon out of the real world.

Once upon a time, there was a globe in a "room" in a MUD, now lost in the misty dawn of the Internet. This globe contained a gazetteer, and as you spun the globe and peered into it, you could examine the detail of the real world. MUDs, Multi User Dimensions (or Dungeons), are built out of complexes of linked rooms and spaces, described with text and navigable by compass directions. In some MUDs, players can build their own quarters, extend the common world, and script objects within the game world, which have interesting behaviors.

The map is the key to the MUD, and popular ones have satellite web sites featuring maps created by players. MUD maps are more *cartogrammatic* than cartographic, conveying some features of space diagramatically, that is, approximately but not "spatially accurate" in a literal sense.

Figure 9-5 shows a classic MUD map, from an online world based on the *Discworld* novel series. A beautiful collection of these MUD maps has been compiled at *http://maps.discworld.nu/*.

In a MUD, each room or open space is a node, linked by lines that represent the connections between nodes. We can give each node in this space metadata properties that affect how it can be used in the online world: who created the room, who is allowed to alter it, what objects it contains, which rooms or streets or other kinds of space you can reach from it. In theory, the kinds of properties we can give each node are unlimited, so why not also tag each space with GPS coordinates and make models of parallel virtual worlds that mirror our own?

We can use geodata on the Web to build a local "world as a MUD," to build simple interactive models that correspond to real spatial coordinates. With RSS feeds and other web content that can be positioned or geo-annotated, we can bring a lot of the "real" virtual world into the "imaginary" one. While lacking the visual impact of Augmented Reality Quake, text-based MUD-style environments provide an interesting way to traverse and make sense of real-world spatial data.

To build a model of the world, we need a simple framework of common terms of reference, a taxonomy or "ontology" of physical spaces that world-builders can share. Many different spatial ontologies exist, from the heavily complex and descriptive, to the domain-specific. One interesting challenge over the next few years of GIS development will be to provide "translation services" between different ontologies—not only translating from one language to another and trying to encapsulate the subtly different usage

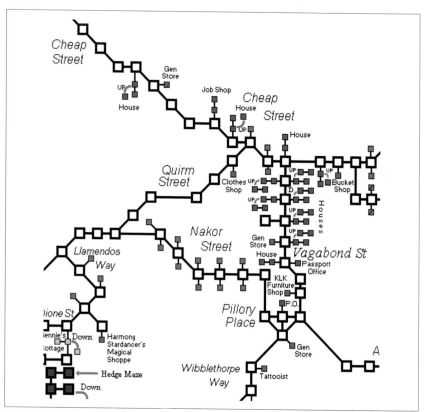

Figure 9-5. Map of a small portion of the Discworld MUD (http://maps.discworld.nu/ maps/aam.gif)

patterns between, say English *factory* and French *usine*, but also to align different spatial ontologies where their contents represent similar but quite different things: a French canton, an English borough, a U.S. county.

## Naming Spaces

The *RDF* model, shorthand for the unevocative *Resource Description Framework*, is an ideal candidate for storing interactive models of space. Like the route-oriented or connection-oriented model of space, it represents a graph of nodes with lines or arcs connecting them. RDF's companion standard, OWL—the *Web Ontology Language*—allows you to describe a taxonomy and publish it on the Web for others to use.

In the RDF model, as shown in Figure 9-6, each node and arc is labeled with an HTTP URL, just like an ordinary web address, except there doesn't have to be anything on the other end of the address: it just has to be unique and always refer to the same thing.

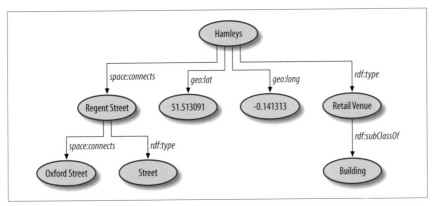

*Figure 9-6. A simple RDF graph describing a physical space*

*Spacenamespace* is an evolving spatial ontology, initially based on the classifications extracted from GEONet data **[Hack #84]**. It was written as part of a spatial annotation project, *mudlondon*; the ontology was expanded by some of the MUD users:

```
<owl:Class rdf:about="http://frot.org/space/0.1/Building">
  <rdfs:label>a Building</rdfs:label>
  <rdfs:subClassOf rdf:resource="http://frot.org/space/0.1/Hypsographic"/>
</owl:Class>
<owl:Class rdf:about="http://frot.org/space/0.1/Public_Building">
  <rdfs:label>a Public Building</rdfs:label>
  <rdfs:subClassOf rdf:resource="http://frot.org/space/0.1/Building"/>
</owl:Class>
<owl:Class rdf:about="http://frot.org/space/0.1/Recreational_Venue">
  <rdfs:label>a kind of Public Building intended for recreational purposes,
like a cinema or club.</rdfs:label>
  <rdfs:subClassOf rdf:resource="http://frot.org/space/0.1/Public_Building"/
>
</owl:Class>
```

This formidable-looking bit of RDF says, "A Building is a kind of Hypsographic Feature." *Hypsographic* is a top-level classification from GEONet and just means something that's found on land. It goes on: "A Public Building is a kind of Building, and a Recreational Venue is a kind of Public Building." Each unique kind of space in a MUD can be labeled with one or more URLs, helping to indicate to people or bots the kind of things that can happen there. There is a growing selection of spatial ontologies on the Web, a short selection of which is available at *http://space.frot.org/ontology.html*.

## Making Models Without Maps

*mudlondon* is a London model, built collaboratively by people who used it from different sources of geo-encoded data on the Web. A geocoded model of London's subway system, the Tube, was scraped from a web site. Many sites of interest were imported from the Open Guide to London; see "Set Up an OpenGuide for Your Hometown" [Hack #97] for details on how to simply export and reuse the geodata in any Open Guide.

*mudlondon* has an Instant Message interface, using the Jabber protocol (see *http://jabber.org*) to connect to different IM systems like AOL Instant Messenger. To explore it, a person just talks to it; wandering around it is like exploring a text adventure game: "You are on Charing Cross Road. You see a Tube Station. You can walk to: Shaftesbury Avenue or Trafalgar Square."

The rules for wandering around *mudlondon* are simple. To build a new space, or connect to an old one, the user types "connect Placename." If a place named Placename is found in the model, it's connected from the user's current location; if not, it is created, and the user is asked "What type of place is this?" (e.g., Building, Park). The bot takes a decent stab at fitting the new type into the spatial ontology and puts new types of places into a pool for later examination by its human friends.

*mudlondon* was written partly as an answer to the "collaborative mapping" problem; with no free sources of geo-encoded data, how can we build maps for ourselves? How can we share our mental models of the world in a way that is useful and can be built upon by others? Publishing RSS feeds of spatial data is a simple way to promote reuse.

## Making Models with Maps

In the U.S., no such problem exists; geodata is available with staggering density from the Geological Survey, the Census Bureau, and other government agencies. By federal law, all data created by the government must be free of copyright and made available for no more than the actual cost of redistribution. Most of the public agencies have interpreted the "cost of redistribution" for web-based data to be "zero," pleasantly ignoring details of server maintenance and bandwidth costs.

To "bootstrap" an interactive RDF model of San Francisco, it was possible to use the TIGER/Line data set to extract a listing of all the streets in San Francisco and calculate the points at which they intersect with other streets. The Geo::TigerLine Perl module available on CPAN provides a detailed, low-level interface to the TIGER database. The code to extract an RDF model from TIGER, along with other spatial RDF goodies, is online at *http://space.frot.org/metasf/*.

So now we have the basis of a spatially accurate interactive environment. What use is it? *mudlondon* was written as an evocative prototype, to demonstrate the power of sharing geospatial data in RDF and the simplicity of tying together distributed sources of data into microlocal, spatially referenced content. Mostly, though, it was a game-like environment; build and explore, augment each other's mental maps, slowly create our own free common map.

In our interactive RDF model of San Francisco, *metasf*, we start out with an "authoritative" map—that contained within the TIGER/Line model of San Francisco. From TIGER we can get a (mostly) complete list of all the streets in San Francisco (or any other U.S. city) and for each segment of a street, the coordinates where it begins and ends. If two different street segments both have an endpoint at the same latitude and longitude, we can infer that they intersect there.

So the more refined "world as a MUD" model treats each line connecting nodes—an exit, an intersection—as if it were a node in itself. From Cortland Street, you can reach the intersection of Cortland and Mission, which is annotated with coordinates, as shown in Figure 9-7.

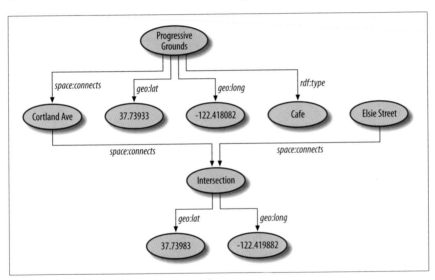

*Figure 9-7. A refined RDF model of spatial connections*

With a geo-annotated model of how streets connect, we can build a lot of interesting things. For example, the city's public transport providers publish route information on their web sites that can be scraped; bus stops tend to be identified by intersections, and subway stations come with addresses. The web services described in "Automatically Geocode U.S. Addresses" **[Hack #80]** make geocoding from addresses or street intersections in the United States trivial. One of the *geocoder.us* web service interfaces directly outputs RDF that can be imported into a spatial model.

A file containing the physical locations of wireless access points, either published by a community network group or by an organization like Intel's PlaceLab, allows you to do approximate location sensing. An RSS feed containing definite addresses for local events—fundraisers in bars, yard sales, political meetups—can be geocoded and added to the model.

Route finding and public transport planning is harder. Sadly, TIGER/Line, being a product of the U.S. Census Bureau, which is more concerned with identifying places than finding places, doesn't contain any information about one-way streets, so you can't make route plans with it—at least not safe ones.

## Interactive Interfaces

Given a set of spatial graphs, either contained in a flat file or available via a web-service interface, a bot or agent can present a "conversational" view of the world model. Source code and advice for RDF bots that will allow you to wander around a spatial graph model are also available from *http://space. frot.org/*.

## Share Geo-Photos on the Web

HACK #96

Share your geo-referenced images with the web-wide world in various forms.

Once, with some help from "Georeference Digital Photos" [Hack #10], you've gotten the hang of producing georeferenced photos, you'll want to take the next step by publishing them to your web site or to other collaborative photo services. As the geo-photo community has grown, so has the list of ways to publish your photos for others to see.

GeoSnapper (*http://geosnapper.com/*) and WWMX (*http://wwmx.org/*) are both services that try to ease the GPS-linking problem by providing tools to process your raw tracklog and photos. WWMX is a Microsoft product and works really well, but is based on the .NET framework, so it will only run on modern Windows operating systems. GeoSnapper works as a web service, and it will work for you as long as you have your tracklogs downloaded to your computer as Garmin MapSource or MacGPS Pro formats. "Speak in Geotongues: GPSBabel to the Rescue" [Hack #51] discusses GPSBabel, an excellent free cross-platform program that will simplify downloading tracks from your GPS and converting them between different common formats. It comes highly recommended!

*http://locative.us/photomap/* holds the two Perl scripts that we wrote to produce photo maps and publish spatial metadata about photographs on the Web. The process happens in two parts. First, we create an RDF feed of metadata that describes the images and tags them with place and timestamps. Second, we use the RDF feed to plot the photographs over a base-map layer. Visit *http://locative.us/photomap/* to download the two scripts, one named *geoloc_media.pl* and the other *plot_rdf.pl*. To run them, you need to have several Perl modules installed from the CPAN code archive: `Geo::Track::Log`, `SVG`, `Image::EXIF`, `XML::Simple` and `RDF::Simple`. "Set Up an OpenGuide for Your Hometown" **[Hack #97]** offers detailed instructions on the easy process of downloading and installing Perl code from CPAN. If you've been working through the hacks in this book, you'll have most of these modules installed already.

## Create an RDF Feed of Photo Metadata

The first Perl script, *geoloc_media.pl*, takes a set of images and a GPS track in GPX format and spits out an RDF description of the images, annotated with time and place stamps and the creator's details.

This script assumes that you have a directory full of images that were taken while recording a tracklog with your GPS. You need to provide an address where that directory is available on the Web; this helps to uniquely identify different pictures and allows others to make descriptions of them.

The script needs to be run with several parameters:

```
perl geoloc_media.pl <offset> <base href> <track.gpx> <maker\@email.com>
<files.jpg> ...
```

- An offset: the difference between the time on the camera and the time on the GPS. Ideally, you'll have synchronized them first; otherwise you can figure out the offset by looking at what they both claim the current time is.

> Take a picture of your GPS showing the current time when you start a trip. This will allow you to check that your camera and GPS are synchronized, and to calculate the offset later if they are not.

- The name of the directory on the Web in which the photos can be found.
- The name of your GPS tracklog file in GPX format. This is a simple XML format for GPS traces. GPSBabel will convert most common formats into GPX.

- The email address of the person who took the photos.
- The names of the files. If they are in a directory, it's easy to enter these with a wildcard: *my_photos/**

Here's a sample run of the *geoloc_media.pl* script:

```
perl geoloc_media.pl 2.5 http://frot.org/20041020/ 20041020.gpx zool@frot.org
/www/frot.org/20041020/* > photos.rdf
```

The end of this sequence, > photos.rdf, sends the output of the script to a file. What the script spits out is a set of locative packets that describes the photographs: where they were taken, when they were taken, and who took them. See "Model Interactive Spaces" **[Hack #95]** for advice on modeling spatial information in RDF. Here's a short sample of an RDF description of photographs taken in Utrecht, September 2004:

```
<locative:Packet rdf:nodeID="aid12326419">
    <geo:long>5.125718</geo:long>
    <geo:lat>52.084616</geo:lat>
    <locative:media rdf:resource="http://iconocla.st/photo/2004/09/06-utreg/
img_1216-1.jpg"/>
</locative:Packet>

<rdf:Description rdf:about="http://iconocla.st/photo/2004/09/06-utreg/img_
1166-1.jpg">
    <ical:datetime>20040906T134632</ical:datetime>
    <foaf:thumbnail rdf:resource="http://iconocla.st/photo/2004/09/06-utreg/
img_1166-s.jpg"/>
    <foaf:maker rdf:nodeID="aid18499619"/>
</rdf:Description>

<foaf:Person rdf:nodeID="aid18499619">
    <foaf:mbox rdf:resource="mailto:zool@frot.org"/>
</foaf:Person>
```

In English, this description says, "Here is some context about a point in space at latitude 5.1257 and longitude 52.0846. There is a piece of media attached to it. The piece of media was created at this time, and the person who created it has the email address *zool@frot.org*."

## Create a Dynamic SVG Map with Pop-Up Photographs

Now that we have all that nice photo metadata, what can we do with it other than share it? One quick way to see your photos in relation to a map is to plot them on it using the *Scalable Vector Graphics* (SVG) format.

The second script, *plot_rdf.pl* takes the RDF/XML file output by the first script and another file describing a base map with its orientation, and overlays the photos on the map.

This is a slightly more complex task, as first we have to acquire a base map and know how it is *georeferenced*. That is, we need to know the coordinates of the top left corner, what the extents of the image represent in terms of geographical space, and how the map is skewed or rotated with respect to True North. What a mouthful!

Luckily, we've already thought of this, and "Georeference an Arbitrary Tourist Map" [Hack #33] demonstrates the appropriate technique. The JavaScript-based client provided for the hack, available at *http:// mappinghacks.com/georeference/*, allows you to figure out the spatial extent of an image, provided that you have three known points that you can identify on it. The client spits out a series of six numbers known as an *affine transformation*, which shows how your map is projected in relation to geographical space.

Use the six numbers to create an XML file that looks like the following example, providing a simple description of your map image: its name, its size, and the transformation that the map went through in relation to geographical space. This is the XML file that was used to create a photo map for the GPS/photo info mentioned earlier:

```
<image>
<name>utreg.gif</name>
<width>890</width>
<height>684</height>
<scale>10000</scale>
<affine>
 0.549457004709508 -0.0298986308382459 0.0250666506000045 -0.52601105571061
 -2699.47952280242 2028.02835472852
</affine>
</image>
```

Finally, you're ready to create a SVG photo-overlaid map. Take the second script, *plot_rdf.pl*, and run it with the XML image file as the first parameter, and the RDF description of your photographs as the second. It will spit out an SVG file that uses your map as a base layer and has an icon for each photograph, which expands to show a photo thumbnail when you move your mouse over it, as shown in Figure 9-8:

```
perl plot_rdf.pl utreg.xml utreg.rdf > map.svg
```

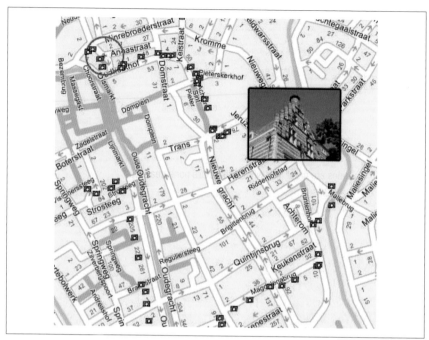

*Figure 9-8. A dynamic map with photos appearing as tooltips*

The art of georeferencing hypermedia and publishing it to the Web continues to be a fast-changing and complex field of activity. In addition to the experimental scripts described in this hack, we have begun work on a project known as the Locative Media Toolkit that will bring together the tasks of downloading GPS traces, rectifying base maps, georeferencing digital media against GPS tracks using timestamps, annotating locations with text and other information, and then finally publishing to the Internet in various human-interactive and machine-readable formats, all under one neat Open Source GUI application designed to run interchangeably on Windows, Mac OS X, and Linux. Can it be done? Find out more about the Locative Media Toolkit at *http://mappinghacks.com/projects/lmt*.

## See Also

*http://www.akuaku.org/archives/2004/10/bluetooth_gps_m.shtml*
　　Dav Coleman's write-up of taking geo-annotated photos in real time using a camera phone and a Bluetooth GPS

*http://flickr.org/*
　　Flickr, a photo-sharing site

*http://geolicious.com/*
> Geolicious, a spatial-media-annotating site.

*http://www.akuaku.org/archives/2003/05/gps_tagged_jpeg.shtml*
> GPS EXIF metadata

*http://mappr.com*
> Mappr, a tool for georeferencing Flickr photos by looking up tags in a gazetteer of world place names

## Set Up an OpenGuide for Your Hometown

### #97    OpenGuides are great, but what if there are none near you?

A *wiki* is a form of web site that is growing massively in popularity. Readers are allowed, even encouraged, to edit and add to the pages on a wiki site. Wikis are a great way to implement a collaboratively written web site. The wiki encyclopedia, Wikipedia [Hack #45] (at *http://www.wikipedia.org/*) is an impressive and addictive example.

A guide to your hometown is very well suited to the wiki format, too; real people on the ground can add and annotate their favorite places. Locals can share knowledge that goes deeper than "find me my nearest branch of Starbucks or WHSmith," and it will make for a more interesting read for travelers than guides to tourist hotspots and pricey eateries published by hotel consortiums.

OpenGuides is a wiki software package enhanced with geospatial attributes. Each node or page can be given a postal code, spatial grid coordinates, venue opening times, and addresses. OpenGuides was originally written to provide a spatial-wiki backend for the Open Guide to London, once known as Grubstreet, which was started so that real geeks could tell each other where to find real ale. Figure 9-9 shows the front page of the Open Guide to London.

### Installing OpenGuides from CPAN

OpenGuides is a Perl/CGI-based application and needs a web server to run it. OpenGuides is available from Perl's archive site, CPAN (*http://cpan.org/*). It's based on an extensible wiki framework that allows you to add any kind of structured metadata to your wiki pages. You can install modules and applications from CPAN automatically, using the CPAN shell; this comes with your installation of *perl* by default.

First let's install `CGI::Wiki` using the CPAN shell. As the superuser, type:

```
# perl -MCPAN -e shell

cpan shell -- CPAN exploration and modules installation (v1.7601)
```

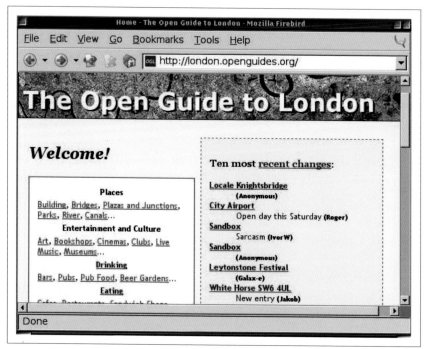

*Figure 9-9. The Open Guide to London*

```
ReadLine support enabled
```

```
cpan> install CGI::Wiki
```

OpenGuides needs the Config::Tiny module in order to be able to configure itself while it installs. Also, we'll be using the lightweight SQLite backend to store the wiki pages, so let's install that, too:

```
cpan> install Config::Tiny
cpan> install DBD::SQLite
cpan> install OpenGuides
```

## Configuring Your OpenGuide

Once the OpenGuides code is downloaded onto your system, the configuration process begins: a simple walkthrough, answering questions with sensible defaults. If everything succeeds, you should see the following prompts:

```
Continue with install? [y] y
Skip OpenGuides configuration? [n] n
```

As this is the first time we've installed OpenGuides on this system, we need
to create a configuration file, so don't stop here! The first task is to choose a

backend database to use to store the pages; there is support for MySQL, PostgreSQL, and SQLite:

```
What type of database do you want the site to run on? SQLite
```

For this database, we're going to use SQLite, a tiny SQL store that uses a single binary file for the backend and doesn't require a database username and password. You need to make sure that the web server has permissions to write to the SQLite database and has write permissions on the directory that contains it.

Once you've set up the database, the configurer will ask you a range of questions about where you want the OpenGuides scripts to be installed, what address they map to on the Web, and various meta-information about your new wiki—its name, city, country, and language. You can change these options afterward by editing the file *wiki.conf*, which installs into the same directory as the CGI scripts.

You need to make sure that the user or group your web server runs as has permission to write to files in the directory where you store the indexes. If you're running the Apache HTTP server, this is likely to be *apache*, *httpd*, *www-data*; check your process table by looking for the httpd process:

```
$ ps -ef | grep apache
apache  5031  5019  0 19:42 pts/4    00:00:00 /usr/sbin/apache-perl
$ groups apache
apache : apache
```

Then set the permissions so that the web server can write to the directory, first adding its group and then making the directory group writable:

```
$ cd ~openguides/indexes
$ chgrp apache .
$ chmod g+w .
```

## Configuring Your Web Server

Now you need to tell your web server where you've installed OpenGuides. If it's in a regular *cgi-bin* (i.e., a directory from which the web server already allows execution of programs called from the Web), you shouldn't need to do anything. Otherwise you have to tell your web server where the executable OpenGuides scripts can be found. The following lines are a sample Apache web server configuration for OpenGuides, which you would typically add inside a <VirtualHost> section:

```
ScriptAlias /openguides/ /home/www/openguides/
<Directory /home/www/openguides>
    AllowOverride None
    Options ExecCGI -MultiViews +SymLinksIfOwnerMatch
    Order allow,deny
    Allow from all
</Directory>
```

Now you should be able to view your OpenGuide on the Web! Open a web browser and visit the URL that maps to your *cgi-bin*, or wherever you just configured your OpenGuide to live.

## Customizing Your OpenGuide

You should now see the front page of your new site; it looks very bare. Click the "Edit this page" link to edit the front page, or select the "Create a new page" link. Then start documenting your favorite interesting pages!

When you edit or create a new page in OpenGuides, you'll see an edit form that will be familiar to you if you've ever used a wiki. The top box in the form is for a description, review, or commentary about the place in question.

There are extra options for place metadata, which make OpenGuides quite different from an ordinary wiki. Figure 9-10 shows some of these options. Each page can go in one or several Categories, and also in one or more Locales. A Locale is a neighborhood or other local area. OpenGuides allows people to define what they think belongs in particular "areas" on a freeform basis.

Figure 9-10. Editing page metadata in OpenGuides

There's also a lot of optional metadata for each page: contact details, opening hours, web links, etc. There's also space for interesting spatial metadata: a street address and postal code, a link to a map, and coordinates.

OpenGuides comes from the UK. It was originally developed to power the flagship London guide, *http://london.openguides.org/*. If you're based in the UK, there are options to add an Ordnance Survey grid reference as *os_x* and *os_y* coordinate fields. The British National Grid is a Transverse Mercator projection of the UK, with the first digit of the coordinates omitted, because it is invariant within the coverage area.

Adding latitude and longitude—available, for example, from the efficient *http://www.streetmap.co.uk/*—allows OpenGuides to provide a "search for nearby places" option on each page, which shows geocoded pages of nearby places. OpenGuides also makes a decent attempt to geocode postcodes. Some international sites do this differently; the Open Guide to San Francisco (*http://sf.openguides.org*) has been adapted to look up street addresses using the free geocoder service at *http://geocoder.us/*. [Hack #79] has more information on how this is done.

Think about what kinds of categories of things, and what kind of neighborhoods, you want your OpenGuide to talk about. Inevitably people will create all manner of weird ad hoc categories on their own (this is a wiki after all), but a bit of "wiki gardening" will give people some direction.

OpenGuides has an active and helpful developer community. You can find their contact details on *http://openguides.org/*. They are prepared to host individual OpenGuides for people who don't have access to a web server and will also delegate DNS subdomains under *openguides.org* to new Open-Guides upon request.

## Make Maps of Your OpenGuide

As your OpenGuide expands, you'll probably want to see a map illustrating the scope of your virtual terrain. Luckily, the OpenGuides software gives you a good place to start; each page in the Guide has an RDF/XML feed that covers its spatial metadata in machine-comprehensible form. "Model Interactive Spaces" [Hack #95] outlines the basics of using the Resource Description Framework to annotate space. Right now, we can jump straight in with the help, as usual, of a quick Perl script.

The original and finest site based on the OpenGuides software is the Open Guide to London (*http://london.openguides.org/*). Each Open Guide has an RDF/XML index of all its pages, which you can read by appending `index.cgi?action=index;format=rdf` to the main site URL. This index page gives us pointers to all the different pages in any Open Guide: Categories, Locales (a Unix-ish term for a neighborhood or area), and each place listed in the Guide itself. The index doesn't show the latitude and longitude of each place, though; for that, you have to look at the RDF version of each page.

For example, if the HTML version of a wiki page is at *http://london.openguides.org/index.cgi?Devonshire_Arms,_NW1_8NL*, then there will be an RDF representation of it at *http://london.openguides.org/index.cgi?id=Devonshire_Arms,_NW1_8NL&format=rdf*. The metadata looks something like this:

```
<geo:SpatialThing rdf:ID="obj" dc:title="Devonshire Arms, NW1 8NL">
  <!-- categories -->
```

```
<dc:subject>Camden</dc:subject>
<dc:subject>Goth</dc:subject>
<dc:subject>Pubs</dc:subject>
<!-- address and geospatial data -->
<city>London</city>    <postalCode>NW1 8NL</postalCode>
<country>United Kingdom</country>
<wn:Neighborhood>Camden</wn:Neighborhood>
<geo:lat>51.539948</geo:lat>
<geo:long>-0.140826</geo:long>
<!-- other attributes -->
</geo:SpatialThing>
```

The following chunk of Perl illustrates how to collect and parse spatial data from an OpenGuide. We use the RDF::Simple module to parse the index page and extract everything in it that is a geo:SpatialThing and therefore likely to have coordinates. For each space we find, we download the RDF version of its page. If there are RDF "triples" for latitude and longitude in that page, we store the lat/long pair, along with the URL pointing to the place, in a list of points.

As usual, there are caveats—that's why this is a "hacks" book and not a "perfect solutions" book. The index page has a couple of XML-toxic characters in it, probably created by a Windows user cutting and pasting a new page name into the wiki; we can get rid of these with a regular expression before passing the document to the RDF parser. There are also a few points that have a latitude and longitude of 0,0, coordinates that are far outside London, a result of people typing coordinates in by hand and making little mistakes.

> The original *http://geourl.org* service had a lot of user-input problems, resulting in the fabled "Ghost Blogs of Tibet." We strongly advise that if you're developing a mapping application where people have to type in coordinates, the application should show those coordinates plotted on a map right away, providing visual feedback. See "Plot Arbitrary Points on a World Map" [Hack #29] for a simple way to do this.

Finally, some of the points are in old-fashioned degrees-minutes-seconds format, rather than newfangled decimal format. Catch these with a regular expression, and it's simple to convert between the two:

```
#!/usr/bin/perl

use strict;
use RDF::Simple::Parser;
use LWP::Simple;

my $parser = RDF::Simple::Parser->new;
```

```
my $rdf = get('http://london.openguides.org/index.
cgi?action=index&format=rdf');
$rdf =~ tr/\240/\040/; # XML-toxic characters
my @triples = $parser->parse_rdf($rdf);

# find all triples where the subject is of rdf:type geo:SpatialThing
my @spaces = grep {$_->[2] =~ /SpatialThing/} @triples;
my @points; # an empty list to hold our points

foreach my $s (@spaces) {
    my $url = $s->[0]; # get the subject url of the triple
    warn("reading $url");
    my @t = $parser->parse_uri($url);
    my ($lat) = grep {$_->[1] =~ /wgs84_pos\#lat/} @t;
    next unless $lat; # don't bother if we can't find a latitude
    next if $lat =~ m/0d/ or $lat !~ m/51/; # we know these are wrong

    my ($lon) = grep {$_->[1] =~ /wgs84_pos\#long/} @t;

    if ($lat =~ m/\d+d \d+m/) {
        # this point is in DMS, not decimal, format
        foreach ($lat,$lon) {
            my ($direction,$d,$m,$s) = $_ =~ /(-?)([\d]+)d (\d+)m ([\d\.]+)s/;
            $_ = $d + $m/60 + $s/3600;
            $_ = 0-$_ if $direction;
        }
    }
    push @points, { lat => $lat, long => $lon, url => $url};
}
```

## Plotting Places over Open Space

Now that we have a list of points, we're ready to roll! What we can do with them, though, depends on where in the world we are. In London, bereft of copyright-free, public domain base maps, the first visualization of Open-Guides was just a plot of points on a blank white background.

The SVG::Plot module, available from CPAN, was written to do this. The module accepts a set of points, each one with an optional URL to turn into a hyperlink, and generates a plot of the points in SVG. Optionally, you can split the points into groups and style each set of points differently—for example, color pubs red and restaurants green, or color the points in each locale differently.

SVG::Plot is indifferent to spatial projections; it will quite cheerfully plot any set of *(x, y)* coordinates to the best of its ability, and work out a height and width for the image, if you don't specify one, from the extents implied by the top left and bottom right points.

If you just hand SVG::Plot a list of latitude-longitude points, you'll quickly run into problems. First, the points will be *unprojected*. As you head further north on Spaceship Earth, the distortion of longitude against latitude becomes greater. At 60 degrees north, degrees of longitude are half the width in meters than they are at the equator, so you'll wind up with a very long, thin, wrong-looking map. Second, SVG only displays at a resolution of one pixel and rounds up or down all decimal fractions of a point. If you try to plot latitude and longitude values over the relatively small area of a city, you'll wind up with one big blob of points layered on top of each other!

For countries that are much taller than they are wide, such as the main landmass of the UK, UTM is often the best-looking projection. (The UK Ordnance Survey's grid system is based on a Transverse Mercator projection.) To convert coordinates to UTM, you have to know which of 60 zones you're in; with the map at *http://www.dmap.co.uk/utmworld.htm*, you can find this out in seconds. For more on UTM conversion, see "Work with Different Coordinate Systems" [Hack #26]

A quick and sophisticated solution is to use the magical *PROJ.4* library to convert your set of lat/long points into an *(x, y)* Cartesian projection. Geo::Proj4 is another of the Perl libraries created during the writing of this book to accomplish this task. The following scrap of Perl continues on from the previous script; we already have the list of points available:

```perl
use Geo::Proj4;
use SVG::Plot;

my @plot;
my $proj = Geo::Proj4->new( proj => "utm", zone => 30 );
foreach (@points) {
    my ($x, $y) = $proj->forward($_->{lat},$_->{long});

    push @plot, [$x,$y,$_->{url}];
}
my $plot = SVG::Plot->new(points => \@plot,scale => 0.01);
print $plot->plot;
```

The result is shown in Figure 9-11.

## Plotting Places over Online Map Services

In the United States, due to the excellent free data provided by the Census Bureau and Geological Survey, there are many better options for do-it-yourself mapmaking. The Tiger Map Server [Hack #14], provided and maintained for free by the USGS, allows you to attach the URL of a file listing points in a simple "lat,long,name" format and get back a flat map with your points on

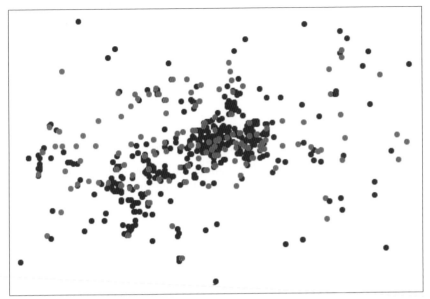

*Figure 9-11. SVG point plot of London Open Guide*

it. To do this, just add the following set of lines to the point-collection Perl script shown earlier:

```
open(FILE, ">points.txt") or die  $!;  # write  to this file, if we're
allowed
foreach  my $p (@points) {
    print FILE $p->{lat}.' ,'.$p->{long}.','.$p->{url}."\n";
}
close FILE;
```

TIGER Map Server will produce a nice static visualization of your point plot, allowing you to use different markers as point symbols, but without much flexibility or interactivity. For a more dynamic map, the services provided free for nonprofit use at *http://mapbureau.com/* are a good way to get started quickly. Map Bureau provides beautiful base maps, created by Donalda Speight, for large U.S. coastal cities. We used the San Francisco base map at Map Bureau, shown in Figure 9-12, to visualize the experimental Open Guide to San Francisco.

You can POST it a URL of a document containing RDF/XML and use one of its base maps to plot the referenced points. (See "Map Health Code Violations with RDFMapper" [Hack #21].) You can also supply your own base map, provided you know the projection the map is in, its origin (i.e., the coordinates for its north-west-most corner), and its extent (i.e., the geographical distance represented by its height and width). To point RDFMapper to your

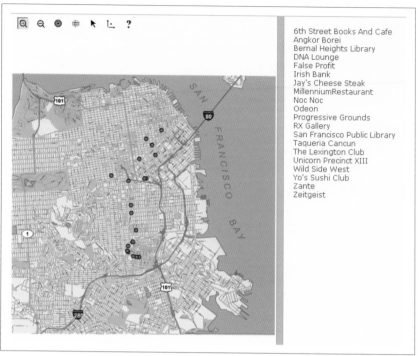

6th Street Books And Cafe
Angkor Borei
Bernal Heights Library
DNA Lounge
False Profit
Irish Bank
Jay's Cheese Steak
MillenniumRestaurant
Noc Noc
Odeon
Progressive Grounds
RX Gallery
San Francisco Public Library
Taqueria Cancun
The Lexington Club
Unicorn Precinct XIII
Wild Side West
Yo's Sushi Club
Zante
Zeitgeist

*Figure 9-12. Map Bureau map of San Francisco Open Guide*

own custom base map, you need to create a file resembling, for example, *http://mapbureau.com/basemaps/sanfrancisco.0.xml.* See *http://mapbureau. com/rdfmapper/* for comprehensive documentation on creating base map files.

## HACK #98   Give Your Great-Great-Grandfather a GPS

Learn how to geocode historic documents.

Tracklogs are simply a series of points. We don't need a GPS to create a series of points. In this hack, we'll take an Oregon Trail diary and geocode it to create a series of waypoints. You can thus create tracklogs of events that predate the creation of the GPS system.

Alfred Korzybski wrote, "The map is not the territory." And nowhere is this more clear than when following the traces of your ancestors. Taking a drive along the Oregon Trail, spending a long weekend eating convenience store food and camping in the car, clambering over fences in order to stand exactly where your great-great-grandfather stood or, more likely, simply passed by with a tired sigh, is an experience of assembling an internal reality, an experience of connecting with the past. As must be the case, these connections are one-way. But does that matter? Does it matter that those particular Missouri farmers had less in common with me today (aside from a bit of genetic material) than I have with today's members of the Locative Media Lab spread around the world?

I don't think that it matters. I spent an awestruck evening on top of Independence Rock in Wyoming, feeling the rock as though it were a reliquary, whispering thanks to my great-great-grandfather for having taken the journey that he did and, by so doing, giving me a context for my own existence. Well, maybe I was giving thanks to the myth of a great-great-grandfather that I had constructed. The evening twilight winds of Wyoming have their own power.

I look upon the extract of the Park Service Oregon Trail map in Figure 9-13, and I can read what it says about Register Cliff: "Of the thousands of names carved by emigrants into the soft sandstone, several hundred are still legible. Some trail ruts, as deep as five feet, are three miles west."

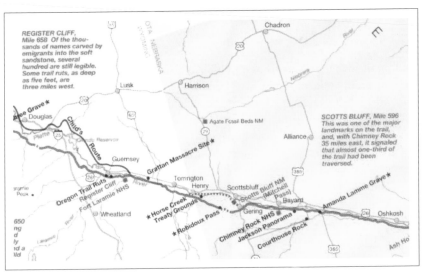

*Figure 9-13. Part of the Oregon Trail in Nebraska and Wyoming*

To my great-great-grandfather, Register Cliff might have been an evening's campsite and the lark of carving his family's names in the soft stone. But it is more likely that he rolled on past, driven by the endless whisper of the coming winter snows. And that map is not the territory that I traveled; yet, it is precisely the territory that I traveled. But my territory looked more like Figure 9-14 and included strange creaking sounds at night, a mix of the modern and the historic, the whispering from remote trail graves reachable only by traveling past new oil and gas pipelines, and always the wind and the sunsets.

*Figure 9-14. Register Cliff in Wyoming*

And all of that brings us to one particular diary of a typical journey on the Oregon Trail. Some of the entries are relatively precise, such as the entry for May 5th, 1852: "Encamped in the Missouri Bottom near Kansville." A web search of the Geographic Names Information System (GNIS) Gazetteer [Hack #85] at *http://geonames.usgs.gov/gnishome.html* comes up empty. A quick search on Google reveals the alternate spelling "Kanesville." The GNIS lists "Kanesville Center," and "Kanesville Tabernacle and Visitor Center," among other entries. These are all near Council Bluffs, Iowa. So geocoding this location is a simple matter of picking one at random as being "close enough."

Other entries are less clear, such as "Camped three miles east of Chimney Rock." Chimney Rock is a well-known Oregon Trail landmark. But if you didn't know that, searching for "Chimney Rock Oregon Trail" brings up many links and reveals that it is located in Nebraska. A return to the GNIS reveals "Chimney Rock National Historic Site," along with a latitude and longitude.

A good set of maps of the trail will help puzzle out where these sites are. But what is one to do with two weeks worth of entries of the form, "Made 18 miles, camped near the river" and "Made 20 miles and camped near a snow bank"?

One approach is to use maps of the trail and follow along, measuring distances. An alternative is to do the same thing within a GIS program like

GRASS or QGIS. Doing a Google search for "Oregon Trail shapefiles" returns some promising links.

Another technique is to interpolate position. In [Hack #11], we learned how to add spatial extensions to Excel. You can download the sample worksheet from that hack from *http://www.mappinghacks.com/geospreadsheet/geodata_sample.xls*. The sheet *myer_diary* contains sample work on geocoding the 1853 Oregon Trail diary of Nathanial Myer.

If we simplistically assume that they traveled in a straight line for the points that we have trouble geocoding (I looked for "snow bank" in the GNIS without great success), then we can use the Bearing, newPosLat, and newPosLong functions to calculate a position based on their reported progress each day:

```
=Bearing(lat1, lon1, lat2, long2)
=newPostLat(la1, lon1, bearing, distance)
=newPostLon(la1, lon1, bearing, distance)
```

I was initially skeptical of the mileage claims in the diary, so I used the posDist(*lat1, lon1, lat2, lon2*) function to compare the diary-reported distances with the straight-line distance between my best guess of the positions that I was able to pin down with some confidence. Most of the mileage claims are reasonably close to the straight-line distances. I get numbers like 138 miles, when the straight-line distance is 134 miles. The distances Nathanial reported seem close enough to be usable.

A helpful hint is to see the trail points over aerial photos. If we export our points from Excel into a tab-delimited file, we can read them into Terrabrowser [Hack #52]. Terrabrowser can then save our work in GPX-format files that can be read in a wide variety of other tools.

In Figure 9-15, we see a series of waypoints marking a portion of the Oregon Trail through Mitchell Pass. These came from a GPS-enabled ramble over this section of the trail, and so show a much higher level of detail than we can get from our historic documents. But even in this detailed image, we can see areas that are "obviously" part of the trail but are not marked. In Terrabrowser, we can Ctrl-click to bring up a context menu that allows us to mark or copy the location under the click. We can use this to clean up our rough geocoded and interpolated locations.

The Terrabrowser context menu also includes the "measure distance" tool. Bring up the context menu, select "measure distance," then move to another point, bring up the context menu, and select "measure distance," and the distance will be displayed in the side pane.

The possibilities are as deep as the past when geocoding historic documents. Sailing ship logs? Where you've lived in the past? Historic trails? It

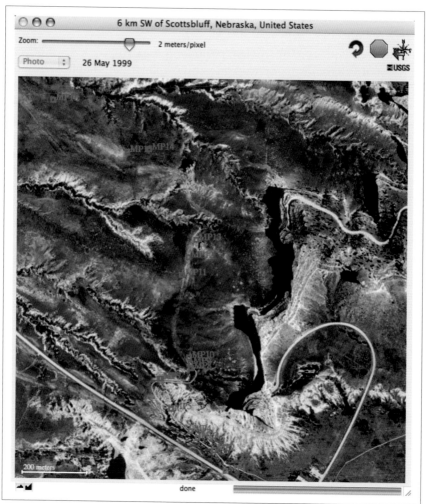

*Figure 9-15. Detail of Mitchell Pass (Scott's Bluff) on the Oregon Trail*

doesn't cost anything (except for your free time), so give a GPS to your great-great-grandfather!

## See Also

*Maps of the Oregon Trail*, Gregory M. Franzwa, The Patrice Press

*The Oregon Trail Revisited*, Gregory M. Franswa, The Patrice Press

*The Magic Mountain*, Thomas Mann

## Map Your Friend-of-a-Friend Network
Spider and map your social network on the Web in easy steps.

What's a Friend of a Friend (FOAF)? Is it the RDF vocabulary for making statements about people; the shadowy originator of urban myths; or the myriad of friend-of-a-friend social networking sites, a few of which support inclusion of FOAF and XFN in XML? For our purposes, we'll concentrate on just the first definition

Before this gets too acronym-heavy, let's explain a few basic principles of FOAF networks. FOAF is the vocabulary that I use for making statements about myself, my "digital identity," and about my social network. In *my* FOAF file, I give my name, nicknames, web site addresses, and encrypted versions of my email addresses. I also publish a list of people I know, using the FOAF knows property. This doesn't distinguish how well I know different people or imply any reciprocity about the relationship.

Both the group-blogging services Typepad and LiveJournal export FOAF information for their users, and there is increasing take-up of it by social networking sites such as tribe.net. Not only can you describe and share data about and via a social network with this information, but for free you get the benefits of many other semantic web vocabularies to describe events, spatial locations, and bits of associated media.

### A Simple FOAF File

```
<rdf:RDF xmlns:foaf="http://xmlns.com/foaf/0.1/"
        xmlns:rdf="http://www.w3.org/1999/02/22-rdf-syntax-ns#"
        xmlns:geo="http://www.w3.org/2003/01/geo/wgs84_pos#">
<foaf:Person rdf:ID="a">
        <foaf:name>A. Person</foaf:name>
        <foaf:nick>ap</foaf:nick>
        <foaf:mbox rdf:resource="mailto:ap@example.com"/>
        <foaf:based_near>
                <geo:SpatialThing geo:lat="37.7422" geo:long="-122.4197"/>
        </foaf:based_near>
        <foaf:knows>
                <foaf:Person rdf:ID="z">
                        <foaf:nick>zool</foaf:nick>
                        <foaf:mbox rdf:resource="mailto:zool@frot.org"/>
                </foaf:Person>
        </foaf:knows>
</foaf:Person>
</rdf:RDF>
```

This file describes *A. Person* and tells you a little about his geospatial location and contact details, as well as providing a small snippet of his social network. It can live on a web server, and it's usual to use the *.rdf* extension and text/rdf+xml MIME type for it.

The FOAF specification, detailed at *http://xmlns.com/foaf/0.1/*, provides some simple ways to indicate your approximate location. You can say you are foaf:based_near a location. The semantics of "near" are intentionally vague. What foaf:based_near points to is a geo:SpatialThing, something that generally has a latitude and longitude property in WGS84.

Alternatively, one can convey approximate location in FOAF using the contact:nearestAirport property. This comes from the "Contact" personal information management vocabulary published by the w3 (*http://www.w3.org/2000/10/swap/pim/contact#*). Airports are referred to by their three-letter international airport code (LHR, SFO, LAX, etc.). The nearestAirport property was designed to allow people to indicate where they are, in an international context, without revealing too much personal contact information.

Each airport has a URL associated with it in RDF, which is defined in an airport schema:

```
<contact:nearestAirport>
        <airport:Airport rdf:about="http://www.daml.org/cgi-bin/
airport?SFO"/>
</contact:nearestAirport>
```

I can also create a link to another FOAF file by attaching:

```
<rdfs:seeAlso rdf:resource="http://example.com/foaf.rdf"/>
```

## Crawling the FOAF Web

The following quick Perl script is a semantic web "scutter" or spider; it accepts a list of files and builds a list of pages to index as it traverses the rdfs:seeAlso list. It uses Class::RDF, a module that is available from CPAN:

```
#!/usr/bin/perl

use strict;
use Class::RDF;
Class::RDF->set_db('dbi:SQLite:foaf.db');
Class::RDF->define('rdfs' => 'http://www.w3.org/2000/01/rdf-schema#',
                'foaf' => 'http://xmlns.com/foaf/0.1/',
                'airport' => 'http://www.daml.org/2001/10/html/airport-
ont#',
                'contact' => 'http://www.w3.org/2000/10/swap/pim/
contact#',   );
Class::RDF::NS->export('rdfs','foaf','airport','contact');

my $air_base = 'http://jibbering.com/rdf/airports.1?';
```

```
my @seen = ();
my @files = (shift);

while (my $traverse = shift @files) {
        print "reading $traverse\n";
        my @objects;
        eval {
                @objects = Class::RDF->parse( uri => $traverse );
        };
        my @follow = grep {$_->rdfs::seeAlso} @objects;
        foreach my $url (map {$_->rdfs::seeAlso->uri->value } @follow) {
                my ($seen) = grep {$_ eq $url} @seen;
                if (not $seen) {
                        push @files, $url;
                        push @seen, $url;
                }
        }
        my @air = grep {$_->contact::nearestAirport} @objects;
        foreach my $airport (@air) {
                eval {
                        Class::RDF->parse( uri => $air_base.$airport->
                                airport::iataCode );
                };
        }
}
```

While it's collecting files from the semantic web, this script is looking for airports in the graphs it gets back. When it finds an IATA code property, it looks it up at the service (e.g., *http://jibbering.com/rdf/airports.1?BRS*). This returns a bigger RDF graph with the airport's location, time zone, name, and other features.

Jim Ley used a crawl of the FOAF web and an SVG world base map to draw the "FOAF people map" shown in Figure 9-16; you can see the SVG version along with other interesting FOAF experiments at *http://www.jibbering.com/*.

## Making Your Own FOAF World Map

Featured in this book are a couple of different web services that will accept a feed of points in RDF/XML or RSS and return an interactive map showing the points plotted over a world map; one is *worldKit* [Hack #39], another is RDFMapper [Hack #21].

The RDFMapper service at Map Bureau takes an RDF file with georeferenced entries, parses key information on it, and presents a set of annotated points on an interactive map. You can also post to it the URLs of functions that you want to use to extract and display information from the RDF model. The functions are written in Fabl, a simple special-purpose RDF-processing language.

*Figure 9-16. Jim Ley's FOAF people map*

The following short Fabl function reads geo-annotated FOAF and looks for the latitude and longitude of things that are foaf:based_near or contact: nearestAirport to something else. This code lives in a file on a web server, just like a regular HTML page, and you send the RDFMapper web service its address:

```
install(namespace('foaf'));
namespace('contact','http://www.w3.org/2000/10/swap/pim/contact#');
install(namespace('contact'));

geom2d:Point function extractFoafLocation(Resource itm)
{

    var Resource geom2d:Point;
    if (count(itm,foaf:based_near)>0)
            return extractGeoLatLong(itm.foaf:based_near);
    if (count(itm,contact:nearestAirport)>0)
            return extractGeoLatLong(itm.contact:nearestAirport);
    return nil ~ geom2d:Point;
}
```

Now we need to make some RDF for RDFMapper to eat. This scrap of Perl finds all the geolocated things in the data model that our scutter built from the semantic web, and all the things that the geolocs are a property of:

```
# same Class::RDF headers as before

my @near = Class::RDF::Object->search(geo->lat);

push @out, @near;

foreach (@near) {
        my @n = Class::RDF::Statement->search(object => $_->uri->value);
```

```
        push @out, map { Class::RDF::Object->new($_->subject->value) } @n;
    }
    print Class::RDF->serialise(@out);
```

We drop this file on a web server somewhere and point the RDFMapper web service at it. The full instructions, including details on customizing the display and page layout, are at *http://www.mapbureau.com/rdfmapper/*.

All the scripts accompanying this hack, and a demo showing the current state of geo-annotated FOAF world, are at *http://mappinghacks.com/foafworld/*.

## Identifying People with FOAF

If you have an eye for RDF/XML, you'll notice that the two *Persons* in our first example are not identified by URL, but by temporary nodes that have temporary IDs relative only to that document—what's known as a *bnode* in RDF terms. In the FOAF world, it can be considered impolite to refer to people by URLs. I am not a number, nor do I want to be assigned a barcode from birth (although the FOAF spec does describe a dna_checksum property). Because we can't, or don't want to, assign a unique global identifier to each person, we use a technique called *smushing* to connect all the information we spidered from the FOAF web into one big graph and figure out which people are actually the same people, mentioned several times.

At *http://xmlns.com/foaf/0.1/*, the FOAF vocabulary lists the classes and properties of people (and other "Agents," such as organizations) that you can talk about in FOAF terms. If you *View Source* on that URL, you'll see a machine-readable RDF version of the document, which applies a few logical constraints to these properties. These are described in OWL, the W3C's Ontology Web Language.

The FOAF schema states that both foaf:mbox and foaf:homepage are of type owl:InverseFunctionalProperty. This implies that given the pairs of statements X foaf:mbox 'mailto:foo@example.com and Y foaf:mbox 'mailto:foo@example.com, we can infer that X and Y refer to the same thing.

I describe my friends' locations in my FOAF file, and they describe them in theirs; we thus end up with two people on the map who are in fact the same person. To give our scutter a bit more integrity, we need to provide it with a *smusher*, an algorithm that will go through our model and join the graphs we found in different files together at their Inverse Functional Properties. A smushing extension to our simple Perl scutter is available with the rest of this hack's background material at *http://www.mappinghacks.com/foafworld/*.

**Map Imaginary Places**

GIS techniques can help actualize your, and others', imagination.

From the shifting shape of Thomas More's *Utopia*, to New World maps losing whole continents between editions, to the introductory maps of J.R.R. Tolkien's *Lord of the Rings*, maps and the imaginary have been intertwined. Early cartography covered unknown continents with speculative features, but in these days of satellite photography, everything on the surface of the earth that can be mapped is.

Where is the unknown to be found? The world of your imagination could fill a dozen atlases: imaginary landscapes, cities, routes. Mapping them is a practice known to some as *geofiction*, defined at *http://geofiction.wikiverse. org/*. With the many tools and techniques covered in this book, you can translate the stuff of your stories beyond paper maps into full-on GIS data models.

### Generate an Ellipsoid and Datum for an Imaginary World

A fictional planet has a size and a shape. Packages such as PostGIS and Manifold will allow you to define your own ellipsoid or spheroid and will support novel or obscure reference datums. Manifold already comes with ellipsoidal or spheroidal definitions for all the planets and some moons in the solar system, useful when you decide to "Map Other Planets" [Hack #34]

Some fictional worlds have clearly defined and imagined topologies, which should be simple to reproduce in a GIS. A Game World in Iain M Banks's *The Player of Games* is a flattened ellipsoid that has one strip of land running around the equator, a forest fire perpetually circling round it each year. We amateur GIS hackers had possibly best avoid weird extraplanetary shapes, such as Banks's artificial torus-shaped Rings or Terry Pratchett's DiscWorld, an upturned saucer with a mountain at the center.

A perfect spheroid is basically defined by one value: the radius of its axis. Figure 9-17 illustrates the slightly more complex definition of an ellipsoid. An ellipsoid is a flattened spheroid, so it has two axes: a *major* and *minor* axis, the former wider than the latter. In GIS, we conventionally define an ellipsoid using two values: the radius of its major axis, known as the *semi-major* axis, and the *inverse flattening*. The *flattening* is the ratio of the difference between the two semi-axes, major and minor, to the major axis ($f = (a-b)/a$). The inverse flattening is just the inverse of the flattening, $1/f$, which probably became a standard because large numbers are easier to deal with programmatically than very small floating-point ones.

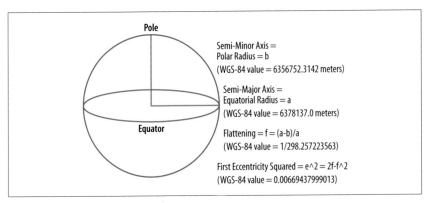

*Figure 9-17. Defining an ellipsoid*

Once you've decided on a size and shape for your imaginary world, you can add this ellipsoid to your favorite GIS program. Here we show how to add an new ellipsoid to a PostGIS database. See "Build a Spatially Indexed Data Store" [Hack #87] to get started with PostGIS.

The PostGIS set of extensions allows you to store spatial information in different projections and do spatial calculations on it. PostGIS stores its reference list of ellipsoids and projections in a table called spatial_ref_sys, which must be included in every spatially enhanced database. Each column in the spatial_ref_sys table has an *SRID*, a commonly known spatial-reference identifier, and a reference to a standards body that manages that SRID and owns the definition of the ellipsoid. Bizarrely enough, this is in many cases the EPSG, the European Petroleum Standards Group. Now you get to impersonate your own standards body—the Intergalactic Astrospatial Consortium, let's say. The IAC, our new self-organization, allocates a serial number to each spatial reference system, so let's pick one at random that hasn't already been bagged by the EPSG.

The following SQL statement is a template for adding an imaginary surface to your PostGIS database. It uses a representation of the geometry called *Well Known Text* (WKT):

```
insert into spatial_ref_sys (srid,auth_name,auth_srid,srtext,proj4text)
            VALUES (9999, 'IAC',9999,
                GEOGCS["GCS_IAC_A2484",
                    DATUM["D_IAC_A2484",
                    SPHEROID["IAC_A2484",3487375,254.5]],
                    PRIMEM["New New Albemuth",0],
                    UNIT["Degree",0.017453292519943295]]',
                '+proj=longlat+ellps=WGS84 +datum=WGS84')
```

The GEOGCS[ entry is where we define our coordinate system, known as A2484, with a prime meridian of New New Albemuth. For future spatial analysis, the important part of this is the SPHEROID definition inside the WKT: SPHEROID("*made_up_name*",*<semi-major axis>*,*<inverse flattening>*). The UNIT is 2π/360, the number of degrees per radian; degree-based coordinate systems are (relatively) simple and familiar, so don't change it. The semi-major axis and inverse flattening tell PostGIS how to calculate distance and area from points based on a latitude/longitude coordinate system. Ours is an unprojected, geographical coordinate system. "Work with Different Coordinate Systems" **[Hack #26]** explains how different projections work in more depth. Try **SELECT SRID,SRTEXT FROM SPATIAL_REF_SYS** from your database shell to see all the different projections normally available in PostGIS.

The last value, PROJ4TEXT, tells *proj4* how to perform coordinate transformations and isn't really necessary for our purposes, so we just borrow the definition for WGS84 for the sake of completeness. For in-depth information about the PostGIS spatial tables, check out the online documentation at *http://postgis.refractions.net/docs/ch04.html*.

Now when you insert and retrieve points or other bits of geometry into Post-GIS, use your new SRID and you can perform realistic spatial querying and indexing on your imaginary world. So far, this may have seemed abstract, but now we have the cornerstone of all manner of geospatial services and interfaces to render your imagination a virtual reality.

## Generate Imaginary Topography

If you can run GNOME, then Terraform (*http://terraform.sf.net/*) comes recommended as a great integrated GNOME application that generates *height fields* for terrain models. It has a selection of beautiful plug-ins to scatter your terrain with craters, volcanoes, and more, and it will also import *DEMs*, digital elevation models, of real places.

For lucky Debian users, Terraform is available from apt; just type **apt-get install terraform**. At the time of writing, packages for OS X are slated for imminent release. Building the application from source should be easy as long as you have the *libgnome-dev* and *libgnomeprint* libraries installed. Run **./configure; make; make test; make install**.

Terraform will also let you import DEMs of real places in *.png*, *.tif*, or *.tga* format and creatively adapt or destroy them. (Ever wondered what your city would look like threaded with a network of canals, or with downtown replaced by a mountain?) Figure 9-18 shows an imaginary place in Terraform.

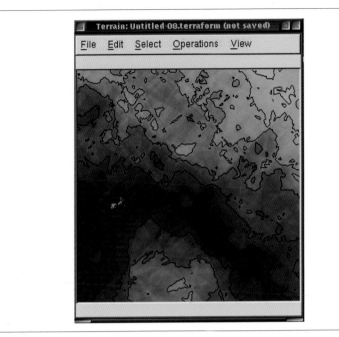

*Figure 9-18. Terraform DEM of imaginary topography*

Consider using Terraform to generate a series of "georeferenced" tiles that represent the height field for your imaginary world at some arbitrary resolution (LANDSAT is available at 30-meters-per-pixel resolution for the U.S., and 90 meters for the rest of the world, which seems like an adequate start. Each tile can come accompanied with a *world file* [Hack #33], which describes its extents in space.

As you may have expected, GRASS also has tools to generate random terrain. GRASS provides the *r.surf.fractal* command that creates a fractal surface. Assuming you've started GRASS, try:

```
GRASS 5.7.0:~ > r.surf.fractal out=fractal_surface d=2.05
GRASS 5.7.0:~ > d.mon start=x1
GRASS 5.7.0:~ > d.rast fractal_surface
```

Every time you run *r.surf.fractal* you get a new output, and I got the image in Figure 9-19.

Another bite at the fractal apple gave me a passable rendition of Two Harbors on Catalina Island in Southern California (Figure 9-20).

*Figure 9-19. A fractal world*

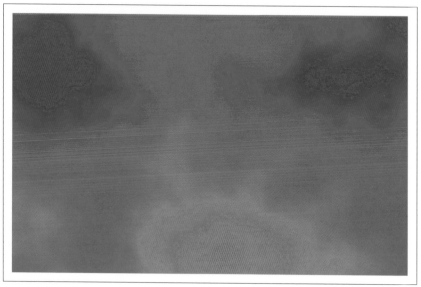

*Figure 9-20. A known place seems to emerge from a "random" fractal*

## Gazetteer for Imaginary Places

With our new imaginary coordinate system, we can geocode fictional places. In "Build a Free World Gazetteer" [Hack #84], we suggested that the "next steps" involve a PostGIS database to store points with proper geometry, rather than separate database columns for latitude and longitude. Here's how you go about adding a geometry column to a Postgres database with PostGIS installed:

```
SELECT AddGeometryColumn ('database_name','table_name','column_name',<SRID>
,'GEOMETRY',2);
```

This statement adds a GEOMETRY field (which can contain points, lines, or shapes) to a table of our choosing. The fourth item in this statement, the SRID, is replaced with our new ellipsoid identifier, 9999, as approved by the Intergalactic Astronavigation Consortium. The last item is dimensionality, indicating that this piece of geometry has two dimensions. The latest release of PostGIS supports four-dimensional geometry, which is, frankly, worrisome.

"Build a Spatially Indexed Data Store" [Hack #87] provides more detail on how to create and query spatial tables in your database. To get started, add new columns describing points into your PostGIS database as shown here, where the last value is the SRID of your imaginary reference system:

```
INSERT INTO table_name (column_name) VALUES
(GeometryFromText('POINT("<latitude> <longitude>")',9999))
```

Now each city, town, and other landmark in your imaginary world can have geometry that can be queried associated with it. Cities might be scattered round an equatorial strip of land near latitude 0, or huddle near the cold poles on a terraformed world uncomfortably near its sun.

## Spatial Index of Imaginary Places

PostGIS allows points, lines, and shapes to be combined in one geometry column in the same table. Now you can think about creating shapefiles for towns and countries, and political and economic districts in your fantasy world. Use Illustrator or another vector drawing environment to create vector shapes that can be converted into ESRI Shapefile format or SVG. If you tire of urban planning by hand, send a fleet of tiny agents to create lowest-shortest-path solutions using a routing algorithm [Hack #2]. Create ambitious public transport networks to carry your citizen-consumers between imaginary continents.

## Web Services about Imaginary Places

Once you have a spatial database representing your imaginary world, consider setting up a Web Feature Service to publish your annotations on the geospatial web. "Publish Your Geodata to the Web with GeoServer" [Hack #89] works by connecting a PostGIS database to a WFS and WMS server. Soon enough, a semantic web autodiscovery agent will be trying to book plane flights to the capital city of your imagination. This could happen sooner than you think! The idiosyncratic Knowhere guide to the UK (*http://www.knowhere.co.uk*), a site that's been around for over 10 years, features the friendly town of Chuffing Hell, somewhere in Yorkshire, with a small but flourishing online community. Other sites—mostly big directories that assemble massive link collections ostensibly related to towns and cities—crawled Knowhere and used its knowledge base to seed an online directory; now a web search for "Knowhere" abounds with listings for Chuffing Hell's local florists, computer retailers, and other exciting services.

Now that you've seen the first hundred mapping hacks, it's time for you to go make your own. There are literally thousands of potential mapping hacks out there, one for every story someone's got to tell. Find selections of our next hundred at *http://mappinghacks.com/*!

# Index

## Numbers

2-D barcodes, 476
3-D raytracing software (see POV-Ray)
3DEM, 230
    terrain models, rendering in three
        dimensions, 235
93 Photo Street, 28–32

## A

aerial photographs
    DOQ images, 469
    GeoTIFF, 470
    specific locations, finding on
        Terraserver, 14–16
affine transformations, 487
    matrix, 158
airline flight tracking, 32
Albers Equal-Area Conic
        projection, 131
annealing, 25
antipodes, mapping of, 98–99
AskTheSpider, xxvii, 436
Azimuthal Equidistant projection, 128
azimuthal projections, 127–130

## B

ballistic navigation, 62
barcodes, using for
        warchalking, 475–478
    2-D barcodes, 476
    generating barcodes, 476

BIL format, 372
bnodes, 507
boomzoom.cgi, 62
bounding boxes, 416, 455
broadcast transmitters, locating, 75

## C

campaign contributions,
        mapping, 65–68
campaign finance web sites, 65, 66
car computers, 279
    building, 278–289
    displays, 281
    GPS units, connecting to, 282
        GUI displays, 284–289
        NMEA protocol, 282
    uses, 280
    VIA motherboards, 281
car navigation systems, building (see
        GpsDrive)
car sickness and route planning, 25–28
cartographic distortion, 120
cartographic generalization, 22
cartographic projections, 120–135
    azimuthal projections, 127–130
    conic projections, 130–133
    cylindrical projections, 122–127
    Dymaxion projection, 148–151
    Equidistant Cylindrical (Plate Carrée)
        projection, 126, 136
    Generic Mapping Tools (see GMT)
    Mercator projection, 122–123

We'd like to hear your suggestions for improving our indexes. Send email to *index@oreilly.com*.

## H

Helm, Anton, 216
historic documents, geocoding
of, 498–502
location searches with google, 500
"How Far Is It" service, 26
hypsographic features, 161, 481

## I

ICBM namespace, 173
ImageMagick, 64
Imager, 136
imaginary places, mapping, 508–514
ellipsoids, generating, 508
gazetteers, 512
spatial indices, 513
Terraform, 510
web services, 513
Indymapper, 196
Indyvoter, 196
InfoUSA, xxvii
Ingerson, Brian, 149
Inline.pm, 149
interactive maps, plotting points using
DHTML, 183–189
Internet services walled gardens, xxvii
ionospheric delay, 270

## J

Java
installing, 311
Openmap (see Openmap)
Jdgpsip, 272

## K

Kindred, Darrell, 28
KisMAC, 71
Kismet, 71

## L

Laake, Jeff, 37
LAC (Location Area Code), 274
Lambert's Conformal Conic
Projection, 130
latitude and longitude, 98, 110
formats, conversion of, 110–113
manual conversion, 111

Perl converters, 113
PROJ.4, 112
other coordinate systems, conversion
to, 113–116
UTM, conversion to, 115
LineDrive, 22–25
Location Area Code (LAC), 274
location sensing technologies, xxiv
locative literacy, impact of, xxx
Longley-Rice Irregular Terrain
Model, 75
LORAN-C, 208

## M

Mac OS X Terrabrowser (see
Terrabrowser)
MacStumbler, 71
MakeAShorterLink, 171
Manifold, 303–310
dissolving boundaries, 307
opening shapefiles, 304
projects, creating, 303
Mankowski, Walt, 113
map URLs, shortening, 170
map_koord.txt, 290
Maporama, 171
mapping
global weather conditions, 204–206
imaginary places, 508–514
ellipsoids, generating, 508
gazetteers, 512
spatial indices, 513
web services, 513
imaginary placesTerraform, 510
online mapping services (see online
mapping services)
technologies, impact of, xxii
visited locations, 12–14
Mapquest
Mapquest Distance, 28
routes, comparing, 16–22
maps, xxii
cartographic projections (see
cartographic projections)
contour maps, making, 351–355
customizing web display of, 171
georeferencing tourist
maps, 156–160
GRASS, publication using, 366–371

## Colophon

Our look is the result of reader comments, our own experimentation, and feedback from distribution channels. Distinctive covers complement our distinctive approach to technical topics, breathing personality and life into potentially dry subjects.

The tool on the cover of *Mapping Hacks* is a compass. Used since the eleventh century as a navigation device, the compass consists of a magnetized needle stabilized on a friction-free pivot point. The lightweight needle acts as a detector for Earth's magnetic field, which attracts the needle such that its north end points toward the North Pole. Contemporary mariners often deploy the more sophisticated gyrocompass for navigation, which uses a spinning wheel constrained by the forces of friction to orient itself toward the North Pole. The gyrocompass is considered superior to its magnetic counterpart because it relies solely on Earth's rotation for its readings and thus always locates True North, as opposed to Magnetic North.

Sanders Kleinfeld was the production editor and copyeditor for *Mapping Hacks*. Linley Dolby was the proofreader. Adam Witwer and Claire Cloutier provided quality control. John Bickelhaupt wrote the index.

Hanna Dyer designed the cover of this book, based on a series design by Edie Freedman. The cover image is from photos.com. Emma Colby produced the cover layout with Adobe InDesign CS using Adobe's Helvetica Neue and ITC Garamond fonts.

David Futato designed the interior layout. This book was converted by Joe Wizda to FrameMaker 5.5.6 with a format conversion tool created by Erik Ray, Jason McIntosh, Neil Walls, and Mike Sierra that uses Perl and XML technologies. The text font is Linotype Birka; the heading font is Adobe Helvetica Neue Condensed; and the code font is LucasFont's TheSans Mono Condensed. The illustrations that appear in the book were produced by Robert Romano and Jessamyn Read using Macromedia FreeHand MX and Adobe Photoshop CS. This colophon was written by Sanders Kleinfeld.

# Keep in touch with O'Reilly

## 1. Download examples from our books

To find example files for a book, go to:
*www.oreilly.com/catalog*
select the book, and follow the "Examples" link.

## 2. Register your O'Reilly books

Register your book at *register.oreilly.com*

Why register your books? Once you've registered your O'Reilly books you can:

- Win O'Reilly books, T-shirts or discount coupons in our monthly drawing.
- Get special offers available only to registered O'Reilly customers.
- Get catalogs announcing new books (US and UK only).
- Get email notification of new editions of the O'Reilly books you own.

## 3. Join our email lists

Sign up to get topic-specific email announcements of new books and conferences, special offers, and O'Reilly Network technology newsletters at:

*elists.oreilly.com*

It's easy to customize your free elists subscription so you'll get exactly the O'Reilly news you want.

## 4. Get the latest news, tips, and tools

*http://www.oreilly.com*

- "Top 100 Sites on the Web"—PC Magazine
- CIO Magazine's Web Business 50 Awards

Our web site contains a library of comprehensive product information (including book excerpts and tables of contents), downloadable software, background articles, interviews with technology leaders, links to relevant sites, book cover art, and more.

## 5. Work for O'Reilly

Check out our web site for current employment opportunities:

*jobs.oreilly.com*

## 6. Contact us

O'Reilly & Associates
1005 Gravenstein Hwy North
Sebastopol, CA 95472 USA

TEL: 707-827-7000 or 800-998-9938
(6am to 5pm PST)

FAX: 707-829-0104

**order@oreilly.com**
For answers to problems regarding your order or our products.
To place a book order online, visit:
*www.oreilly.com/order_new*

**catalog@oreilly.com**
To request a copy of our latest catalog.

**booktech@oreilly.com**
For book content technical questions or corrections.

**corporate@oreilly.com**
For educational, library, government, and corporate sales.

**proposals@oreilly.com**
To submit new book proposals to our editors and product managers.

**international@oreilly.com**
For information about our international distributors or translation queries. For a list of our distributors outside of North America check out:
*international.oreilly.com/distributors.html*

**adoption@oreilly.com**
For information about academic use of O'Reilly books, visit:
*academic.oreilly.com*

---

# O'REILLY®

Our books are available at most retail and online bookstores.
To order direct: 1-800-998-9938 • *order@oreilly.com* • *www.oreilly.com*
Online editions of most O'Reilly titles are available by subscription at *safari.oreilly.com*

# Related Titles Available from O'Reilly

**Hacks**

Amazon Hacks

BSD Hacks

Digital Photography Hacks

eBay Hacks

Excel hacks

Flash Hacks

Gaming Hacks

Google Hacks

Harware Hacking Projects for Geeks

Home Theater Hacks

iPod & iTunes Hacks

Knoppix Hacks

Linux Desktop Hacks

Linux Server Hacks

Mac OS X Hacks

Mac OS X Panther Hacks

Network Security Hacks

PayPal Hacks

PDF Hacks

PC Hacks

Smart Home Hacks

Spidering Hacks

TiVo Hacks

Windows Server Hacks

Windows XP Hacks

Wireless Hacks

Word Hacks